UNITING IN MEASURES OF COMMON GOOD

Uniting in Measures of Common Good

The Construction of Liberal Identities in Central Canada, 1830–1900

DARREN FERRY

McGill-Queen's University Press
Montreal & Kingston • London • Ithaca

© McGill-Queen's University Press 2008

ISBN 978-0-7735-3423-0

Legal deposit fourth quarter 2008
Bibliothèque nationale du Québec

Printed in Canada on acid-free paper that is 100% ancient forest free (100% post-consumer recycled), processed chlorine free

This book has been published with the help of a grant from the Canadian Federation for the Humanities and Social Sciences, through the Aid to Scholarly Publications Programme, using funds provided by the Social Sciences and Humanities Research Council of Canada.

McGill-Queen's University Press acknowledges the support of the Canada Council for the Arts for our publishing program. We also acknowledge the financial support of the Government of Canada through the Book Publishing Industry Development Program (BPIDP) for our publishing activities.

Library and Archives Canada Cataloguing in Publication

Ferry, Darren, 1969–
    Uniting in measures of common good : the construction of collective liberal identities in central Canada, 1830-1900 / Darren Ferry.

Includes bibliographical references and index.
ISBN 978-0-7735-3423-0

  1. Associations, institutions, etc. – Canada, Central – History – 19th century. 2. Liberalism – Canada, Central – History – 19th century. 3. Community organization – Canada, Central – History – 19th century. 4. Social change – Canada, Central – History – 19th century. 5. Canada, Central – Social conditions – 19th century. 6. Common good – Case studies. I. Title.

HN103.F47 2008   366.009713   C2008-903607-7

Typeset by Jay Tee Graphics Ltd. in 10/13 New Baskerville

Contents

Acknowledgments vii

Introduction 3

1 For a More Enlightened Citizenry 20

2 Small-Town Mechanics' Institutes 62

3 Continuity and Change in Temperance Societies 95

4 "A Spirit of Candour, Moderation and Open Generosity" 136

5 Elevating the Cultivators of the Soil 170

6 The Dominion Grange and Patrons of Industry 215

7 A Feast of Popularized Science and Literature 243

Conclusion 282

Notes 291

Bibliography 381

Index 423

Acknowledgments

This monograph has undertaken a very interesting three-year journey from thesis to book, and I would like to express my appreciation to numerous individuals and institutions for their efforts in ensuring that *Uniting in Measures of Common Good* finally saw the light of day.

Not only did my thesis supervisor, Michael Gauvreau, assist with the development of the original dissertation but he also read and reread every reworked chapter with his astute and critical eye, offering careful suggestions and thoughtful analysis of each draft. My debt to him is enormous, particularly for helping me get through a time when I was quite willing to cast the entire manuscript aside to pursue other, non-academic projects. I hope that Michael's insistence that there was a worthwhile story to be told has been justified in the final product. I would also like to express my thanks to the members of my original examining committee, Ken Cruikshank, Wayne Thorpe, Stephen Heathorn, and Bryan Palmer, for their meticulous suggestions, which led me to reformulate some of my original arguments. Nancy Christie constantly offered advice and encouragement during our simultaneous trips to various archives, and she has patiently read much of this work with an eye solely to helping a not-so-young scholar through the pitfalls of publication. Last but not least, I very much appreciate the careful reading given the manuscript by three anonymous readers of the Aid to Scholarly Publications Program, and I am grateful for their suggestions, which ultimately sharpened the final argument of the book. None are responsible, of course, for the errors that remain.

During the research phase of the book, many archivists gave of their time to help with my rather unusual requests. Although they are too numerous to mention by name, I would like to thank the staff of the Archives Nationales in Montreal, Library and Archives Canada in Ottawa, the Archives of Ontario in Toronto, and the staff in the Baldwin Room of the Toronto Reference Library. On a personal level, I would like to express my appreciation for the thoughtfulness of Eleanor McLean of the Blacker-Wood Library at McGill University in Montreal; Jim Leonard of the Centennial Museum and Archives in Peterborough; Steve Brown of the Dufferin County Museum and Archives; Karen Wagner of the Wellington County Museum and Archives; Ellen Millar of the Simcoe County Museum and Archives; as well as John Lutman and Theresa Regnier of the J.J. Talman Regional Collection at the University of Western Ontario in London. My thanks also to the underutilized and underfunded staffs at the London, Guelph, and Kincardine public libraries, and to the staff at the Perth County and Peel County archives. What treasures of the past are housed in these county archives! More should be done to fund their work.

For their generous financial assistance during the research phase, I would like to express my thanks to the Social Sciences and Humanities Research Council of Canada, the Government of Ontario, and McMaster University. This book has been published with the help of a grant from the Canadian Federation for the Humanities and Social Sciences, through the Aid to Scholarly Publications Program, using funds provided by the Social Sciences and Humanities Research Council of Canada. An abbreviated version of chapter 3 appeared as "'To The Interests and Conscience of the Great Mass of the Community': The Evolution of Temperance Societies in Nineteenth-Century Central Canada," *Journal of the Canadian Historical Association*, new series, vol. 14, (2003), 137–63. Similarly, many of the arguments in chapter 6 appeared as "Severing the Connections in a Complex Community: The Grange, Patrons of Industry and the Construction/Contestation of a Late Nineteenth-Century Agrarian Identity in Ontario," *Labour/Le Travail* 53, (fall 2004), 9–47. I would like to thank both publications for their kind permission to include this material in the book.

I cannot give enough praise to the editorial department at McGill-Queen's University Press for the assistance they have rendered to make sure this project got off the ground. Kyla Madden has been an exemplary editor, and I am grateful for all her hard work in getting the project started and ensuring its completion. I would also like to express my appreciation for the difficult task that befell Jane McWhinney, who rendered my prose more readable; many thanks, Jane, for unravelling the knots. Lastly, my thanks and appreciation go to Joan McGilvray for her dedication in making it all come together.

Family members and friends have been encouraging to me over the years I have lived with this project, and I would especially like to thank my mother, Sharon, and my sister, Darlene, for their support. I would like to thank my father, Brian, who provided me with much-needed employment and a gas card for my research trips; without his financial assistance I never would have made it this far. It is my only regret that he did not live long enough to see the finished work. I also keenly feel the loss of fellow historian and friend, Myra Baillie; she, too, offered much support and encouragement during my graduate years. Once again, I am very hopeful that this book will have met her high standards of excellence.

Finally, I would like to thank my own little "community," Caitlin, Rachel, Elena, and Amelia, for helping me to construct my own identity as a typical harried father. While my commitment to the values of inclusion, tolerance, and honest industry might at times be questioned by all of them, I am grateful that we have spent many "liberal" hours of leisure and amusement together, and for that, I thank them profusely. I would like to dedicate this book to my wife, Nathalie. While she has never understood my obsession with something that has paid me so little in monetary terms, I am grateful for the freedom she gave me to pursue it to completion nonetheless. For her support, encouragement and love, and above all her patience, my gratitude will be forever etched in print.

UNITING IN MEASURES OF COMMON GOOD

Introduction

In the late nineteenth century, the exploits of a voluntary organization known as the Lime Juice Club appeared in the pages of a Peterborough, Ontario, weekly newspaper. In a rather satirical look at voluntary societies, the published reports of the Lime Juice Club's activities parodied the most salient features of the voluntary association movement. Meeting in the "Hall of Wisdom," the club lampooned learned scientific and literary societies by advertising lectures from the "Honourable" Darkness Watson – a crackpot inventor of medicines who was soon kicked out of the club for selling his ineffectual wares – on subjects such as "Is Water Wet?" and "Has the World Advanced Enough?" The Lime Juice Club also poked fun at temperance societies, expelling any member who partook of temperance beverages or favoured the prohibition of alcohol. Many of the club's barbs took aim at mutual benefit or charitable societies, exposing several "applicants" for the benefits of the Lime Juice Club as being either fakers or incompetents: "Jamfeld Jones," for example, was refused compensation from the club's directors when he fell, drunk, off a mule.[1]

The creators of the Lime Juice Club also ridiculed sacred philosophies of voluntary associations such as the importance of respectable sociability, as some of the more memorable excursions of the club took place on freight trains with liberal doses of alcohol and featured dog fights and bareknuckle prizefighting as the main attractions. Club members similarly mocked the tenets of industry and production, and the hardy Protestant work ethic, offering lectures on "The Evil of Wealth" and "Is it a Crime to be Poor?," as well as overturning a constitutional amendment on honesty, as honest industry was the "highway to the poorhouse." Club meetings even caricatured strictures of morality, soliciting new members on the premise that the president had run away with a strange woman, the treasurer had skipped town with members' funds, and the secretary was in the county jail. Lauding hypocrisy and deception as the cardinal virtues of membership, one club announcement stated: "In case a circus comes to town, and a member of the Lime Juice Club in good standing cannot raise the necessary wealth to buy a ticket, it is not derogatory to his character to crawl under the canvas."[2]

Despite the satirical stance of the Lime Juice Club, the members' supposed exploits illustrate Canadians' fascination and enthusiasm for voluntary associations. The Canadian experience with voluntarism mirrored that of the United States, which Alexis de Tocqueville described as a "nation of joiners" in reference to the proliferation of voluntary organizations he discovered on his voyage to America. Voluntary societies can serve as useful analytical tools, as they reflect tendencies of the larger society, particularly in the context of North America, with its with burgeoning ideas of participatory democracy. They offer a glimpse of society in microcosm with their complicated rituals, established constitutions, and inclusive membership, and voluntary societies in the North Atlantic triangle are a microcosm of the significant social, political, and cultural changes of the eighteenth and nineteenth centuries.[3] The study of voluntary organizations also makes an intriguing approach to evaluating various social, cultural, and economic processes and problems of class, state, and gender formation. In British and American historiography, the emerging voluntary association movement represents working-class efforts at self-help and the augmentation of associational and occupational ties, as well as the development of a working-class consciousness. Whether speaking of burial societies or friendly societies, mutual aid associations or insurance schemes, historians describe voluntary associations as measures designed for the working classes to acquire habits of industry and thrift, while simultaneously constructing opportunities for sociability and fraternal feelings.[4]

In the process of middle-class formation, voluntary associations were established in both the United States and Great Britain as conduits for the cultural, social, and economic suppression of the working classes by the agents of emerging industrial capitalism. Voluntary organizations in America and Great Britain are prevailingly depicted as conscious instruments of middle-class hegemony – an approach taken by the professional, mercantile, and commercial elites to dictate the pace of state formation and the standards of respectability for all classes in the larger community. The voluntary principle in these organizations is best described as a wish to exert social control and authority while fostering principles of morality and upward mobility.[5] While the proliferation of middle-class participants in voluntary associations in Great Britain and the United States is well documented, more recent scholarly work on voluntary associations has revealed that individuals of other classes joined these societies as well, as a form of civic engagement. Although differing political, occupational, and cultural interests could use voluntary organizations to advance often-incompatible pursuits and aims, voluntary associations also exemplified the search for "social capital," the ordinary citizen's pursuit of the individualistic democratic ideal and collective mutual aid.[6]

The influence of the United States as a continental neighbour and Great Britain as an imperial centre appreciably affects the history of voluntary associations in central Canada. Many voluntary organizations were either American or British transplants that became acclimatized to the colonial experience in a relatively short period of time. Initial studies of voluntary societies demonstrate a strong working-class composition, as skilled workers established associational ties with fellow workers. And yet the cultural and social implications of voluntary associations were co-opted by historians examining the process of middle-class formation, who have contended that the middle classes used voluntary societies as a means to assert power and influence in Canadian society.[7] Canadian voluntary associations have also shown a tendency to assume a larger role in state formation, as successive governing powers were both unwilling and unable to provide the multitudinous civic services supplied by voluntary organizations. As a result, voluntary associations actively participated in liberal state formation, and in the larger project of "nation building" undertaken by the commercial, mercantile, and professional middle classes. More recent historiography suggests that the development of voluntary associations would also account for the increasing influence of public opinion and participatory democracy in colonial society.[8]

What is so highly significant about voluntary associations in the Canadian context is their adaptability and flexibility in adjusting to sociocultural circumstances, as they reproduced the representative values, identities, and ideologies inherent in the colony. However, while voluntary associations could passively reinforce cultural cohesion, they could also become active vehicles in questioning and challenging the governing social, political, and cultural administrations. Individuals who felt marginalized in colonial society could use voluntary organizations as a means of confronting both the material inequalities inherent in the governing social order and the symbols and representations of that authority.[9] In many respects, the present study reflects recent trends in cultural history, in which analysis of various classes and interests illustrates their navigation through material *and* representative structures of power. *Uniting in Measures of Common Good* concentrates far more on the aspects of cultural arbitration and negotiation within the voluntary association movement and is therefore highly influenced by the cultural interpretation of meaning and discourse in its attempt to extract societal beliefs, morals, and expressions from the processes and dynamics of popular culture.[10] Given the interaction of various classes and occupations in voluntary associations, interpretations of the inherent meaning of class identities and cultural forms often became a matter of perception and representation rather than statements of the "reality" of the strict imposition of a governing social order. Despite the cultural negotiations intrinsic to its discourse, the success or failure of a social identity comes through collective representation, a social reality that remains without a fixed meaning but is not entirely open to a completely objective reconstruction.[11] The acclimatization of voluntary organizations both to the representative culture of various classes and interests in society *and* to material class and state formation is a testament to their enduring legacy in nineteenth-century central Canada.

And yet the exposure of a conflictual/consensual paradigm in the Canadian voluntary association movement also suggests that a larger cultural and social project was under construction. At mid-century, this socio-cultural "project" entailed the creation of an inclusive, progressive social order to stabilize a post-Rebellion society in a state of flux. Given the politico-religious turmoil and the increasingly complex occupational structures, previously accepted binary models of the community – based on Old World traditional socio-economic gradations such as the ranking of "high" and "low," or patrician and plebeian – simply became unworkable. By employing the discourse of liberalism, an ideology emphasizing individual liberty, freedom, equality, and socio-cultural inclusion, directors of voluntary societies attempted to engineer consent to a "liberal" social order and also to limit discord in a colonial society teeming with social, ethnic, political, and religious unrest. The ideologies, functions, and services provided by voluntary associations therefore produced a commonsense worldview of how Canadian society was ordered representatively in a cultural and social sense, as well as materially in the economic and political spheres. While voluntary organizations attempted to reflect a liberally inclusive membership that crossed class, ethnic, and gender lines, in many respects these societies and organizations symbolized the governing power of the increasingly visible "middling sorts" in Canadian society.[12]

The formation of the liberal social order in the Canadian context accentuated the primacy of the category of "individual" in ideological and cultural assumptions, as well as in socio-political and economic practices. The works of Fernande Roy and Ian McKay both emphasize the totalizing ideology of the individualist liberal order, as its adherents used the "natural right" philosophies of liberty, equality, and the individual right to hold property in the structuring of both public and private life. This individualistic vision held by leading members of society in the years between 1830 and 1870 was in fact a Canadian "Liberal Revolution" inspired by resilient ideologies of progress, rationality, and individualism.[13] And yet, more recent work on the liberal social order during this period illustrates that while liberalism was an individualist ideology, its doctrines could also connect the category of "individual" with cultural processes and institutions. Jean-Marie Fecteau claims that the Canadian approach to liberalism was not simply one ideology among many others; rather, it was a way of life and a behavioural ethos that confirmed the individual as the basis of society. However, Fecteau also states that this liberalism refused to compartmentalize the public and private spheres, and that cultural institutions such as the state and other organizations therefore became bulwarks of liberal doctrine. As a result of this liberal organizing process, Fecteau argues, collective concepts such as mutualism and humanism were not at all incompatible with Canadian liberalism, as cultural institutions simply merged individualist *and* mutualist modes of liberal thought.[14] In this study, I therefore suggest that while voluntary associations could support the category of "individual" in their promotion of liberal doctrines, these organizations simultaneously buttressed the formation of collective liberal identities in central Canada.

And yet, the inclusive nature of the voluntary association movement itself was simply an illusion, as association activities, ideologies, and functions barely camouflaged the political, religious, and social conflicts simmering just under the surface. Although voluntary societies managed to foster some measure of cultural consensus among intersecting occupational, gender, and ethnic identities, they also generated a great deal of *dis*harmony and tension among these various interests. In attempting to include all elements of central Canadian society, these same voluntary associations often marginalized and disempowered those outside the perceived boundaries and ideological standards of "liberal" society. As McKay argues, liberalism could also silence and eliminate opposition to its ideology, as women, workers, ethnic minorities, and Amerindians were marked as the "other," unworthy to take up the burdens and responsibilities of full individuality.[15] As a result, voluntary organizations were often a battleground of competing politico-religious, ethnic, gendered, and even class identities as their directors endeavoured to regulate socio-cultural disputes. The fluidity and subjectivity of occupational structures, political and religious identities, and ethnicity and gender, tended to produce as much dissension and discord in voluntary associations as liberal ideology would be prone to disguise. Evidently, the doctrines of liberalism were not a categorically unifying set of principles in voluntary associations, as ongoing social and cultural negotiation frequently occurred between directors and members, and between members and non-members alike.[16]

The "limits of liberalism" in Canadian society manifested even more noticeably in the last three decades of the nineteenth century, as the demarcations of nation, gender, and particularly socio-economic gradations between classes, became increasingly intricate and complex. With the development of industrial capitalism and the rather belated arrival of an Industrial Revolution in Canada, the boundaries of class became much more rigid and intractable. The late nineteenth century can therefore be characterized as a period of intense class formation, as a conscious, urbanized industrial working class, a politically aware agricultural class, and a commercially robust middle class staked out their various positions across an enhanced socio-economic landscape. Moreover, the selective ethnic intolerance practised by voluntary organizations simply could not overcome stronger nativist sentiments stemming from increases in immigration and the latent anti-French sentiment of English Canadians.[17] Exposing the fissures in a society that had always barely concealed the class, gender, and racial dissonance lurking underneath a consensual exterior, the chaos in turn-of-the-century Canada illustrates just how fragile this constructed "liberal" social order was.

What I suggest in the following study is that voluntary associations played a critical role in the cultural, socio-political, and economic processes inherent in the construction of a liberal social order in central Canada during the nineteenth century. On the one hand, while the ideology of liberalism and the construction of the liberal order traditionally emphasized the triumph of the "individual," the liberalism intrinsic to voluntary organizations managed also to forge collective identities and mutual bonds among members in various associations. The liberal ideology preached in voluntary organizations simply refused to compartmentalize the public and private spheres, and focused instead on a "mutualist" approach to liberalism that contributed to a strong collective identity within various voluntary associations. These associations were also required to continually negotiate cultural space both within their own communities and within the larger Canadian community as a result of the tensions inherent in building these collective liberal identities. In essence, the true hegemonic effects of the liberal project promoted by Canadian voluntary associations rested on the conciliation between collective liberal identities and individualist liberal doctrines and – within the voluntary association movement itself – cultural negotiation between those enveloped by the liberal social order and the marginalized "other." As McKay suggests, Gramsci's theory of hegemony allows for an appreciation of the extent to which a given social group – such as the "liberal" voluntary association movement – exercises dominion over others by moving beyond its own corporate interests and taking into account other interests and classes.[18] *Uniting in Measures of Common Good* also attempts to present a more experiential reading of the liberal order in Canada by illustrating how ordinary individuals interacted with the cultural and social practices of liberalism within the voluntary association movement.

In the first half of the century, the term "voluntary" in describing certain societies and associations in Canada pertained to religious organizations who rejected state support and relied solely on the financial contributions of their members. In many respects, voluntarist religion constituted the first liberal revolution, as its advocates decried elite church establishment and the existence of religious ranks and orders, and emphasized personal spiritual experience rather than church attendance.[19] The following study adheres to a very similar definition of the voluntary association movement. All of the "voluntary" societies examined in this study attempted to eliminate elitist and "Tory" forms of organization, by opening their membership to all classes and occupations in the larger society and by forming their executive from those "volunteers" within the association. Similarly, the voluntary organizations under examination – while occasionally indulging in sectarian or political debates – did not restrict membership to members of a particular Christian religion or political party – although voluntary associations did place constraints on membership among Canada's ethnic population and among non-Christians in general. The one feature of the distinctive voluntary principle in dissenting religion that does not survive this examination of "secular" voluntary associations is the issue of state financial support. In fact, two prominent organizations examined in this study, Mechanics' Institutes and agricultural societies, both accepted liberal public support for their activities. However, far from undercutting their status as "voluntary" associations, this government support serves to illustrate that the much larger liberal project appearing in the structure of the growing state apparatus did choose to fund *some* distinct collective identities.

Uniting in Measures of Common Good concentrates on six specific voluntary associations for examination: Mechanics' Institutes, temperance societies, mutual benefit organizations, agricultural societies, the Dominion Grange and Patrons of Industry, and scientific and literary associations. Despite the rhetoric of interclass benevolence and inclusion of genders and ethnicities, all of these voluntary societies under investigation contributed to a unique collective "liberal" identity amongst their constituents, and in turn assisted in the construction *or* contestation of the liberal project in central Canada during the nineteenth century. For example, through efforts to provide adult education and literacy through the establishment of a library system, Mechanics' Institutes contributed both to an urban liberal and burgeoning industrial social order *and* to rural small-town liberal identities. Similarly, fraternal orders and mutual benefit societies attempted to construct a collective identity among the working class in central Canada, one that would weld skilled workers to the larger liberal project. Agricultural societies and the Dominion Grange/Patrons of Industry, for their part, actively engaged farmers and rural labourers in the construction of a collective agrarian identity that likewise welded *or* alienated the rural populace to liberal doctrines and practices. While temperance societies also tried to construct a temperate society in the larger rural and urban Canadian community, they experienced much more difficulty in supporting the larger liberal society than other associations did. Lastly, scientific and literary associations tended to foster a liberal collective identity among the professional classes, which in turn heralded the materialization of the corporate welfare state and the emergence of the bureaucratic "expert" in central Canadian society.

It must be acknowledged, however, that many of the voluntary organizations not chosen for this particular study either proscribed certain occupations from their ranks, or subscribed to an identifiable political or religious point of view. For example, while trades unions and Boards of Trade did forge collective identities – and in the latter case, a rather "liberal" collective identity – both tended to restrict membership to the skilled working classes or the mercantile populations, and were not generally inclusive to all members of the community. An examination of the Knights of Labor as an "open" trades union inclusive of all skilled workers would have made an interesting study of a specific collective identity, but their adversarial position toward capital rendered a collective "liberal" identity somewhat problematic.[20] Likewise, all churches and religious organizations, as well as political vehicles such as Liberal or Conservative clubs or the Equal Rights Association were not chosen for examination because of their adherence to specific religious and political opinions. On the surface, benevolent associations would be an excellent fit with the following examination of voluntary societies, given their status as precursors to state-regulated poverty assistance and their resulting contributions to the emerging liberal social order and the rendering of collective liberal identities. And yet benevolent associations also tended to create an impositional relationship with those under their aegis, forging patron/client connections with these individuals rather than liberal bonds of mutualism.[21] While some of the voluntary associations examined in this study shared to some extent one or all of these problematic "non-liberal" attitudes, they all included in their original constitutions the need for politico-religious and class inclusion in their membership, as well as the importance of taking their leaders from their own ranks to protect their societies from charges of elitism.

As an investigation of collective liberal identities in the Canadian voluntary association movement, this particular work employs a case study method rather than a thematic model. The six groups of voluntary associations examined are so diverse in their aspirations, membership composition, and operative functions that thematic comparisons would portray each organization in a rather one-dimensional fashion. Thus, *Uniting in Measures of Common Good* highlights the diversity of the Canadian voluntary experience, rather than considering particular activities as merely part of a common whole. In addition, while written largely as a cultural assessment of voluntary societies, this study also emphasizes the social experience of ordinary Canadians with the voluntary association movement. This investigation therefore attempts to bridge cultural and social history, in an effort to be attentive to the experiential elements of voluntary associations that would be lost in a thematic approach. Perhaps most important, the case study approach is essential to understanding the complex nature of the collective identities housed in the various associations discussed in *Uniting in Measures of Common Good*. The following work also focuses primarily on central Canada, using the French *société* in Lower Canada/Quebec as a counterpoint to the Upper Canadian/Ontario voluntary association. While I do not dismiss the significance of regional differences in Western Canada and the Maritimes, I found that the cultural identities of "*français*" and "English" provided more of a contrast for this particular study.

The following assessment of voluntary associations as a vehicle for collective liberal identities can also provide a framework for larger debates regarding cultural, political, and social structures and processes in the various societies of the North Atlantic triangle. The "consensual" nature of antebellum Americans – broken of course by the events of the Civil War – has largely been explained in terms of the intellectual currents inherent in republican principles of political economy and the emerging moral and political regulation of nascent state formation. And yet historians of the working class cannot accept any notion of "American exceptionalism," as, in their view, the American working classes have always demonstrated class consciousness in their attempts to reform political, cultural, and economic developments. Scarcely concealing the class, gender, political, and social discord simmering beneath the surface, any cultural or social transformation required constant negotiation and regulation.[22] By the late nineteenth century, leading American intellectuals had begun to redefine previously accepted liberal ideas about citizenship and the individual's relationship to the industrial state. This democratic challenge led in turn to intensified class discord as organizations such as the Knights of Labor and the Populist Alliance championed the plight of the labouring masses. Thus, it can be interpreted that the heightened "search for order" in the Gilded Age and in the Progressive era came as a result of the thinly veiled social, political, and economic uncertainty of the late antebellum years.[23] Voluntary associations would in this view therefore appear as highly significant organizations in this larger discussion on the nature of American society, contributing as agents of cultural, political, and social cohesion *and* as instruments of cultural reformation and social change.

Given the elaborate class system that reigned in Great Britain, debates on the theme of a consensual versus a more discordant model of society became far more protracted among British scholars than in the United States. The new "labour historians" such as E.P. Thompson attempted to correct a more liberal characterization of nineteenth-century Britain as an "age of improvement," an epoch of beneficial reforms, industrial and intellectual progress, and unrivalled economic prosperity. Focusing on issues of working-class political and institutional behaviour, expressions of craft culture, and the totality of the "working-class experience," these scholars of a Marxist bent put forward an image of British society teeming with social, political, and class tensions. While such explanations of class conflict in the years of the early industrial revolution resonated with historians of the working class, the relative harmony and concord of mid- to late Victorian British society frustrated those who saw an absence of class consciousness among waged industrial workers. While remaining focused on the experience and philosophies of the working classes and their radical middle-class allies, interpretations of this social phenomenon in Britain range from explanations of a labour aristocracy worried about keeping its occupational position, to the growth of a particularly submissive form of working-class reformism in both ideology and practice.[24]

Scholars examining middle-class formation claim, however, that the "consensual" nature of Victorian Britain came about as a result of middle-class hegemony, since the appearance of a confident and assertive bourgeoisie would not only moderate conflicts and discord between the classes but would also engineer consent to the emerging social order of industrial capitalism.[25] However, more recent explorations do not rely specifically on class analysis to explain the "consensual" social behaviour between the classes in Victorian Britain. Arguing that the notion of "class" itself was an illusory construction that engendered conflict and exclusiveness, the new social history concentrated on the flowering of an all-encompassing political tradition that created an awareness of the need for greater reforms. This discourse of popular radicalism portrayed an inclusive "vision of the people" that dictated the ideological tenets of liberalism throughout all interests in the Victorian era. Employing postmodern epistemologies, historians of the "linguistic turn" assert that class itself was a discursive construction, and merely one mode of analysis among a range of competing structures.[26]

Still other historians have hypothesized that British popular radicalism adapted with the times, and argue that liberalism merely continued the plebeian traditions of religious liberty, retrenchment, free trade, and reform of the electorate through the loose alliance of labour leaders, intellectuals, and free traders found in the British Liberal party. In their view, the political and social uses of the languages of class were mere smokescreens that masked the construction of *both* republican middle-class and radical/liberal political identities.[27] The cumulative work of these scholars on social and political discourse has managed to facilitate a significant reformulation of class identity. By refocusing on "occupational identities," these historians avoid socio-economic descriptions of an overly simplistic three-class model composed of workers, the "middling sort," and aristocrats. Instead, they have simply widened their vision of the interaction between the classes, noting that the Victorians themselves held rather wide-ranging views of occupational categories. Concluding that considerations of class were more about awareness than consciousness, their interpretation is that the "emergence of stability" in this period came from a shared intellectual matrix or a societal vision of co-operation, harmony, and goodwill among various classes.[28] Given this variety of historical perspective, the significance of voluntary associations on the nature of British "liberal" society is incalculable.

In stark contrast to the United States and Great Britain, historical debates over the conflict/consensus paradigm in early nineteenth-century central

Canadian society somewhat lacks the ideological fervour of British or even American scholars. Only recently have historians begun to examine the nature of the nascent political culture in Upper Canada as a foundation for both the contestation and construction of societal and cultural processes.[29] A similar pattern emerges in Lower Canada, where initial descriptions of society focused not on class formation, but on the burgeoning nationalism and political demands of the French-Canadian *Patriotes*, and their responses to social, economic, and cultural change. While there is some measure of debate about whether the rural *habitants* rebelled against an outmoded feudal system or against the developing capitalist commercial structure, there is a greater consensus that the tensions in the Lower Canadian countryside arose largely from socio-economic factors and anxieties related to cultural change. Still other scholars contend that the processes of early state formation contributed to the relative harmony in early Lower Canadian villages and towns.[30]

A surprising unanimity of opinion regarding mid-century socio-economic transformations in the colonies exists, however, among historians who have charted the transfer of economic power from paternalistic merchant and professional elites to an emerging liberal mercantile-capitalist social order. Indeed, the only debate remaining in regard to the socio-economic hegemony of the burgeoning social order is about the measure of historical agency granted to the "common people," individuals who were economically exploited and rendered powerless through political processes. Similarly, the development of expansionist sentiment, the exhibition culture of national consumerism, and the national geological surveys all contributed to the construction of the "Canadian nation," while new systems of education, civil law, and other organs of the emerging state provided the cultural, social, and political authority for administrative elites.[31] The engineering of consent in French-Canadian society became more a question of religious ideology and social practice, as the Catholic clergy were no less authoritative than other hegemonic agents of the commercial, professional, or mercantile middling classes. Forces of clerical opposition in Quebec, such the *Rouges* and the advocates of secular liberalism, would discover the effectual cultural and political authority of the Roman Catholic clergy.[32]

Despite the seemingly harmonious and consensual nature of liberal class relations at mid-century, the late nineteenth-century by contrast has often been described as a period seething with irreconcilable class, ethnic, and intellectual tensions. Labour historians such as Gregory Kealey and Bryan Palmer argue that while the persistence of a "producer ideology" exposed a lack of class-consciousness and political radicalism among Canadian industrial workers, the materialization by the 1880s of such class-conscious groups as the Knights of Labor greatly disturbed the precarious balance of the classes. Similarly, creeping urbanization, socio-economic changes in agriculture, and the emergence of the "populist" Patrons of Industry sowed class discord among the rural populace by the end of the century.[33] Intensified nationalism in Quebec also renewed cultural conflict between English and French in all provinces of Canada, while growth in immigration generated significant racial dissonance and discord. Even intellectual debates over secularization, innovative ideas of collective political economy, and the new social science threatened to overwhelm Canadian society from the mid-century "norms."[34] What *Uniting in Measures of Common Good* suggests is that the liberal collective identities that were negotiated through debate within the various voluntary organizations examined in this book not only reflected the broader trends of society as a whole but also in many respects contributed heavily to the larger liberal project.

In order to negotiate a collective liberal identity within their constituencies and establish liberal bonds of mutualism among members of voluntary organizations directors and members of voluntary associations formulated a clearly articulated rhetoric of "community." Although forged in a crucible of intersecting value systems, beliefs, and identities, certain ideological principles and assumptions about the significance of a liberal community surfaced which were common to all social classes and interests within these associations.[35] For Canadian voluntary associations, a collective liberal concept of "community" served a twofold purpose. By reinforcing the construction of a collective liberal identity, voluntary associations could employ the rhetoric of community both to forge a strong mutualist bond among their members *and* as a stratagem to eliminate opposition to liberal ideals. Expressions of "community" in various voluntary societies demonstrate in addition that these organizations were a unique phenomenon in central Canadian society, as they often provided a bridge between the larger liberal project of state and market, and the collective identities of family, church, and neighbourhood. Thus, the bonds of community illustrate how the interaction of individuals in the private and public spheres created a liberal ideology of the social self. Some historians interchange this notion of community with the middle-class "public sphere" and contend that the basic blueprint of this enlightened public sphere was the inclusive nature of participatory democracy, and the way the rise of public opinion established the parameters of an emerging liberal social order.[36] One might summarize by saying that in utilizing the concept of "community," voluntary associations attempted to fashion collective liberal identities and bonds of mutualism within a social order that focused on individualist doctrines inherent in the growth of liberal state and market structures.

In the liberal rhetoric of community advocated by voluntary associations, four primary doctrines and practices emerged which enabled their directors to communicate a sense of collective cultural identity and a sense of "community." The first was the conscious prescription to be inclusive toward every occupation and class interest. At the same time as accepting liberal notions of individual agency, equality, and respectability, the mutualist ideology preached in Canadian voluntary organizations emphasized *inter*dependence among the various social occupations in the larger community. Opening the doors of voluntary associations to all ranks and orders did tend to alleviate overt forms of class and occupational conflict, by maintaining an appreciation of how the liberal community fit together into a harmonious whole. By the final three decades of the century, however, the language of class interdependence intrinsic to the ideology of voluntary associations created more tension than it resolved. The language of class inclusion could also be exploited as a highly exclusionary discursive tool, as some organizations proscribed certain occupations from membership in their association, and thus from membership within the liberal voluntary community itself. Such proscriptive language arose most frequently in agricultural organizations such as the Dominion Grange and Patrons of Industry, while the rhetoric of temperance societies often excluded certain occupations from the protection of a temperate "community."[37]

A more troubling aspect for voluntary associations came as they attempted to integrate the "other," such as women and ethnic identities, into their organizations. The desirability of including all gendered and ethnic participants within the larger voluntary community generated a great deal of debate on the nature of the public and private spheres. Initial attempts to incorporate women and ethnic groups within voluntary associations were extremely problematic, for despite encouraging the *indirect* participation of women, men of colour and natives, voluntary associations clearly resisted their participation as equals. The resulting marginalization of women and ethnic minorities on the part of nineteenth-century voluntary organizations suggests that central Canadian liberalism was not only a class-based project but one that enforced a liberal patriarchy and notions of masculinity in the middle-class home as well as through the larger society.[38] And yet conscious efforts to include women in the voluntary association movement by late century did bear fruit in terms of membership and increased participation, as women were tentatively offered more direct roles. However, while the incorporation of women remained in the liberal vision of voluntary associations, any enthusiasm for women's inclusion was tempered by a continuing discourse of domesticity and adherence to female involvement along strict gendered lines. Furthermore, attempts to integrate ethnicity within voluntary associations had results ranging from overt segregation to selective intolerance, rather than genuine inclusion.[39]

A second facet of this liberal "community ethos" in voluntary associations manifested itself in the religious and political spheres, and entailed ending the politico-religious turmoil of the Rebellions and the subsequent dismantling of the Tory tradition. To further this aim, voluntary oganizations banned sectarianism and party politics from their activities, discussions, and discourses. Their purpose was to ensure fraternity, concord, and the construction of collective liberal identities among individuals of varying political and religious opinions. While measures to reduce politico-religious conflict within voluntary societies did tend to bolster the liberal nature of these societies, voluntary associations could rarely prevent political or religious discord from entering their organizations entirely.[40] As the century progressed, voluntary associations found it increasingly difficult to remain aloof from political processes and the effects of political partyism and sectarian discord, even though they maintained a "liberal" façade of political and religious neutrality. Despite efforts to enforce standards of political objectivity, the effects of urbanization and industrialization in the latter decades of the century forced some voluntary associations – agricultural organizations such as the Dominion Grange, the Patrons of Industry, and temperance societies in particular – to become more involved in the political sphere. The social attitudes and the political turmoil played out within voluntary associations suggest that political and religious perspectives and opinions continually required cultural negotiation and meditation.[41]

A third component of a liberal ideology of "community" expressed by promoters and members of the voluntary association movement came in the encouragement of the philosophy of honest industry and the political ecomony of hard work. The intellectual underpinnings of this ideology among liberal voluntary communities focused on seemingly irreconcilable stances: maintaining economic and commercial *inter*dependence among the classes while emphasizing the importance of individual diligence and hard work. Historians have initially portrayed this double-edged ideology as the liberal producer alliance, whereby the defeat of entrenched Tory mercantile elites in the early 1840s was arranged through a partnership of artisans and middle-class producers. The discourse of the liberal producer alliance also was fairly exclusivist, characterizing the "non-producing" and entrenched privileged mercantile elites as being outside the community of independent yeomen, artisans, and manufacturers.[42] The development of industrial capitalism revealed further tensions within cross-class voluntary associations. The unmasking of a producer *ideology* employed by both small producers and industrial capital to promote their own economic agendas forced voluntary associations to grapple with the question of class cleavages as never before. Even though the success of the producer ideology in creating economic consensus was clearly quite tenuous, given the debates over free trade and protectionism as well as the conflict engendered by the labour movement, it was incumbent on voluntary associations to try and limit the conflicts over economic science and create a liberal sense of community in the name of improvement and progress.[43]

This liberal ideology of "community" also appeared in the realm of leisure, as voluntary associations employed their entertainment activities to construct and maintain a spirit of liberal camaraderie and social concord within the voluntary association movement. As Lynne Marks suggests in her pioneering work on small-town Ontario, leisure is an effective prism through which to view how Canadians identified themselves. As with the concepts of non-sectarianism, antipartyism, and the theory of honest industry, the tensions involved in the interpretation of "proper" leisure were visibly perceptible in voluntary societies. Indeed, the categories of "rough" and "respectable" entertainment remained highly contested terrain for voluntary associations.[44] However, not only did the amusement activities promoted by voluntary societies help to define the collective liberal identity of their participants but in a very tangible sense, voluntary associations simply could not exist without these entertainment options. The revenues and interest generated by leisure activities within the larger or localized community frequently determined the success or the failure of its voluntary associations. While entertainment helped to sustain voluntary associations and their link to the liberal social order, toward the end of the century the rise of commercialized mass entertainment contributed to the demise of leisure activities within voluntary societies.

The annual report of the Lime Juice Club in 1894 noted that a distinguished man of science visited the Club to offer a lecture on the beauties of science and art. After his lecture, the learned professor boasted, "I trust that the words I have spoken will do much to elevate the hemisphere and usefulness of this great and noble institution, which I trust will continue to grow and flourish until it will control the destinies of mankind." As such useless flattery was anathema to the directors of the Lime Juice Club, the president ordered the kicker of the Club, "Pile Driver" Riley, to "escort" the man outside.[45] While this anecdote clearly mocks the inflated attitude of voluntary associations toward themselves, these institutions did in many respects held exactly such views for good reason. The history and the functions of voluntary associations were both far-ranging and essential to the development of colonial society, as voluntary organizations managed to construct a "liberal" vision of their societies which crossed rather ambiguous and fluid class, gender, and ethnic lines.

By the end of the century, attempts to abide by or conceptualize new philosophies among voluntary communities exposed the conflicts that had always been concealed in the ambivalances of in the Canadian liberal social order. Rivalries between rural and urban voluntary associations, the crisis between capital and labour, and ethnic tensions, as well as competing associations, philosophies, and political ideologies, simply could not be reconciled to the liberal ideology of "community" held by voluntary organizations at the end of the century. While the commonsense worldview shared by these voluntary associations enabled their promoters and members to negotiate some form of cultural, political, and social consent among their constituencies between the 1830s and the 1870s, the breakdown of a collectively liberal "community ethos" showed that cultural mediation and arbitration were still constantly demanded.

1

For a More Enlightened Citizenry

In the 1861 annual report of the Hamilton Mechanics' Institute, the directors lauded their association for being entirely inclusive of all classes within the community. They were committed to offering public lectures, adult education classes, and the amenities of their public library to all interested parties in Hamilton, and boasted about their influence: "[While] the professed object, as the name implies, is the improvement of our artisans and working classes of every grade, there is reason to fear that this design has in many instances been lost sight of, or perhaps we should say, *the original idea has been considerably amplified*, as other classes of the community rather than operatives constitute not unfrequently [sic] the majority of subscribers and attendants." While on the surface this pronouncement acknowledged the problems of the Hamilton Mechanics' Institute movement in bringing education to the working classes, the choice of the word "amplified" indicates clearly that the directors of the institute exulted in its cross-class allegiances.

Although the executive of the Hamilton Mechanics' Institute then promoted an inclusive ideology appealing for harmony between the classes in a co-operative venture of self-improvement, the middling-class directors had been exposed as hegemonic agents of the liberal social order very soon after the Institute's establishment in 1839. Not only were the Institute promoters in Hamilton most concerned with self-education as a means of keeping the working classes from committing crime and participating in trade unionism but a scant nine years after the incorporation of the Institute they tried to change its name to the more middling-class appellation of the "Gore Literary and Scientific Institution."[1]

The example of the Hamilton Mechanics' Institute is significant, given that promoters of adult education and the Mechanics' Institute movement attempted to establish a "liberal" cultural consensus by serving the needs of all interests in the community. Originally created to help working class adults further their education, early Mechanics' Institutes in urban central Canada offered scientific and practical lectures, night classes, and functioning libraries. In so doing, many Institutes began to promote an inclusive and collectivist ideology of liberalism that called for harmony and unity between occupational interests in a co-operative venture of self-improvement and education. To more fully accomplish this task, Mechanics' Institutes simply broadened their mandate to include all the diverse political, social, economic, and religious forces in the colonies in the pursuit of improvement and progress. However, involving and promoting these other forces more often constituted a desire of the manufacturing and commercial elites in burgeoning urban areas to establish cultural stability and engineer consent to an emerging liberal social order.

With the expansion of urban areas in the late decades of the century, Mechanics' Institutes continued this tradition of occupational inclusion by extending their services to include popular lectures, gymnasia, and other forms of recreation. And yet promoters of Mechanics' Institutes were also exposed as socio-economic agents of this by then rather outmoded liberal social order. While skilled workers continued to attend the night classes and reading rooms of urban Institutes, many allowed their memberships to lapse or failed to participate fully in Institute activities. The rapid decline of Mechanics' Institutes toward the end of the century in contrast to their popularity at mid-century is a function of the withdrawal of the working classes in conjunction with the growth of large-scale recreation, government-sponsored adult education, and the free library movement. Despite clinging to a liberal rhetoric of "community," in representing the obviously hegemonic forces of a new industrial social order urban Mechanics' Institutes had simply become irrelevant by the end of the century.

EARLY HISTORY OF MECHANICS' INSTITUTES

The Mechanics' Institute movement began its history in Great Britain in early nineteenth-century Glasgow, as education pioneer George Birkbeck established the Institutes for the diffusion of scientific knowledge in the mechanical arts among the artisan classes. In 1824 a Mechanics' Institute was founded in London under the patronage of Henry Brougham, who introduced lectures, a library, and night classes to the artisan community. Placing an emphasis on mutual instruction among skilled workers, Brougham introduced a small fee to keep the workers independent, although he also requested liberal financial support for the London

Mechanics' Institute from the mercantile classes.[2] The Mechanics' Institute movement in Britain quickly lost momentum, however, and debates abound in Great Britain over the motives behind the bourgeois ascendancy over the movement. With the rise of industrialization, Mechanics' Institutes became a focal point for the spread of such middle-class values as utility, morality, and thrift. Consequently, some historians conclude that middle-class tradesmen and professionals enforced strict social control over the operation of the Institutes to preserve the industrial social order. Conversely, labour historians of the working class argue that radical artisans simply ignored Mechanics' Institutes when their officers were usurped by the middle class. Skilled workers interested in the "pursuit of knowledge under difficulties" managed to preserve both their independence and their advocacy of working-class radicalism while profiting from the Mechanics' Institutes specifically to further their own educational needs.[3]

Another factor to consider is that Mechanics' Institutes in Britain also allowed both middle-class and artisan radicals access to new scientific theories, which elite scientists attempted to monopolize through the professional science associations such as the Royal Society of London and the British Association for the Advancement of Science. Therefore, "marginal men" in the Institutes could participate in the technological revolution while at the same time rebelling against the traditional scientific method of more aristocratic practitioners of science. The popularization of science through the Mechanics' Institute movement in Great Britain allowed the manufacturing and commercial middle classes – as well as the working classes – to carve out their cultural niche within an Old World society then in a state of social flux. Still other historians contend that Mechanics' Institutes were simply a consequence of the Industrial Revolution, where the formation of the middle classes was secured through the ascendancy of a new industrial social order. Along with literary societies, temperance organizations, reformed aristocratic scientific associations, and mutual improvement societies, Mechanics' Institutes became centres of cultural activity for bourgeois citizens in Great Britain.[4]

Canadian historiography regarding Mechanics' Institutes closely mirrors the work done on the Institute movement in Britain in concluding that the Institutes reflected the entrenchment of middling-class hegemony. Although some Canadian historians recognize that the working classes retained some agency in choosing whether or not to become members, they construe middling-class supremacy in Mechanics' Institutes as an impulse for social control, while more recent scholarship focuses on the Institutes as vehicles for both middle-class and state formation.[5] Canadian scholars are also fairly unique in their tendency to scrutinize the Institute movement by degrees, rather than examining the movement as a whole. Much of the literature on Mechanics' Institutes in Canada analyses them either as pioneers in adult education or as the precursors of the public library movement. United in their dismissal of the Mechanics' Institute as a constructive force, these scholars often present the failure of the Institutes to provide access to education for the working classes as a conundrum of high educational expectations lowered by the reality of limited resources and competing agendas.[6] And yet Mechanics' Institutes also addressed the needs of a fledgling colonial society, creating an enduring mandate for a cultural consensus of collective liberalism among the various classes. While the more "middling" founders of Mechanics Institutes leaned toward the establishment of such communal values as co-operation, mutual instruction, and inter-class harmony, urban Mechanics' Institutes were the most attuned to the sentiments of the liberal social order as a result of their financial ties with the emerging state.[7]

This is not to say that Mechanics' Institutes in developing urban areas did not try to imitate their counterparts in Great Britain by offering educational benefits to the skilled working classes. The earliest established Mechanics' Institutes appeared in Lower Canada, with the creation of the Montreal Institute in 1828 and the founding of the Quebec Mechanics' Institute soon afterward in 1831. The Quebec Mechanics' Institute stated that its main object was to improve the condition of the operative classes: "The instruction of Mechanics, at a cheap rate, in the principles of the Arts which they practice, as well as in all other branches of useful knowledge, is a measure calculated to improve extensively their condition and habits, and to add largely to the resources and prosperity of the Country."[8] The Montreal Mechanics' Institute incorporated this goal into their initial rules of association, legislating that two-thirds of the committee of management should consist of skilled workers. Chief Justice Thomas Aylwin explained the reasoning behind the high respect for of the mechanic in his inaugural address in the newly built Mechanics' Hall in 1854: "The mechanic is alike useful and necessary; he is the backbone of society, and its best interests are linked with him and his prosperity ... whatever tends, then, to improve and elevate mechanics as a class, directly contributes to our best interests, and urges on all the other classes to make similar efforts towards progress and advancement." Of course, such an appeal from one of the leading members of Montreal society underscores unspoken concerns over working-class violence and discontent in the city of Montreal, and the implicit need to incorporate the skilled artisan into the "liberal" social order.[9]

From its inception in 1831, the Toronto Mechanics' Institute gave a great deal of thought to the participation of the artisan population. In one of the first recorded meetings of the Institute, the directors noted that the diffusion of useful knowledge would "introduce to the notice of the Mechanics of this town a means by which their happiness and interest would be greatly promoted." During one board meeting, a member of the executive observed that the entire work of the Institute, from the lectures and classes to the library and the exhibitions should be "adapted to promote the advancement and proficiency of the Mechanics of this city."[10] A similar ideology emerged in the Mechanics' Institute of London, a "rising industrial town" that desperately required educated artisans and mechanics. In their request for a Mechanics' Institute, the London executive claimed that the mechanics and artisans in their locale were "highly respectable, and ... assist[ed] in a large degree by their industry, character and contributions to make up the aggregate of our public and common weal." As a result, the constitution of the London Institute stipulated that two-thirds of its management should come from the operative classes.[11]

Despite these efforts to promote education among skilled workers, operatives in urban areas often recognized that in many respects the day-to-day operation of Mechanics' Institutes rested in the hands of those who were *not* of the labouring class. Mechanics and other skilled workers would express their dissatisfaction with Institute boards of management through letters to city newspapers and riotous board meetings. The London Mechanics' Institute executive realized after their first year that radical artisans *and* the conservative merchant classes could both halt the progress of the Institute, as "fears were doubtless entertained by the overcautious, and prejudices by the doubtful; apathy by the lukewarm and indifference or animosity by foes."[12] However, liberal Institute executives could also articulate their frustration at the apathy among skilled workers and their dearth of education. The promoters of the Kingston Mechanics' Institute took the leading mechanics of the city to task for their lack of interest, as they had "ample opportunity" to form their own society before the "younger tradesmen" took the reins. An essay contest celebrating the completion of the Montreal Mechanics' Hall in 1854 also illustrated the disdain that liberal directors taken from the "middling sorts" held for their labouring confrères. In judging the fifth-place entry – an essay entitled *Labour Directed by Industry, the Source of all Wealth and Prosperity* – the judges condescendingly noted that it was "apparently the unostentatious effort of an uneducated mechanic, who, had he possessed the advantages of the other

Essayists, might have produced something worthy of a higher place in the report of the Committee."[13]

Despite these signs of occupational discord, the membership figures of Mechanics' Institutes at mid-century suggest that the Institutes were fairly successful in recruiting the skilled working-class element and suffusing the Institutes with a rather liberal worldview of progressive economic development. Membership figures recorded in many urban Mechanics' Institutes reveal a fairly solid and active skilled working-class constituency. In the Montreal Mechanics' Institute, skilled workers made up from 44 to 68 percent of the ordinary membership from the years 1856 to 1864. Similarly, when the London Mechanics' Institute received its charter of incorporation in 1852, nearly a third of its ordinary membership came from the skilled working classes.[14] The membership figures of the Toronto Mechanics' Institute reflect a similar pattern, as membership books document that a full 34 percent of the ordinary membership of the Toronto Mechanics' Institute at mid-century came from the operative classes of the community (see Table 1.1). However, a further examination of membership records illustrates that while a healthy proportion of members came from the operative classes, more than half of the members joining the Toronto Mechanics' Institute came from the "middling sorts." Evidently, securing the co-operation of various occupational groups in the educational and cultural activities of Mechanics' Institutes entailed building a collective liberal ideology that would appeal to all segments within the community, while simultaneously engineering consent to the liberal social order in urban locales. When controversy erupted in the hallowed halls of central Canadian Mechanics' Institutes, these disputes revealed that the harmonious relations so carefully constructed to favour the liberal social order in the Institute movement were in fact rather tenuous and fragile.

"A NOBLE FRATERNITY OF ALL CLASSES": LIBERAL INCLUSION AND CULTURAL AUTHORITY

Mechanics' Institute promoters recognized from the outset that the Institutes should not only benefit the operative classes, but should be as inclusive as possible toward the collective liberal community. Even though the directors of the Quebec Mechanics' Institute were quite clear that its aim was to improve the lot of the skilled worker, they also decreed that it should bring together "in one association men of different pursuits and acquirements" for the purposes of mutual improvement, enlarging the minds of

Table 1.1
Ordinary Membership by Occupation, Toronto Mechanics' Institute, Selected Years, 1855–1865

Occupation	Total	Percentage	Occupation	Total	Percentage
Carpenter	63		Merchants	55	
Printer	36		Dry Goods/Grocer	36	
Cabinet Maker	18		Chemist/Druggist	15	
Painter	16		Agent/Broker	13	
Baker	13		Bookseller/Stationer	12	
Tailor	13		Jeweller	11	
Bookbinder	12		Others++	31	
Founder	12		TOTAL BUSINESS	173	18
Surveyor	12		Student	38	
Marble/Stonecutter	12		Teacher	20	
Boot/Shoemaker	11		Barrister	13	
Others*	107		Architect	10	
TOTAL SKILLED	325	34	Engineer	10	
Clerks	190		Others+++	17	
Accountant/ Bookkeeper	42		TOTAL PROFESSIONAL	108	11
			TOTAL UNRECORDED	97	10
Others+	32				
TOTAL CLERICAL	264	27			

* Other occupations in the skilled category include: blacksmith, butcher, cooper, carriage/coach maker, mechanic, millwright, wire worker, boiler maker, joiner, turner, upholsterer, trunk/baggage maker, steward, hall keeper, dyer, watchmaker, mason, coppersmith, candle maker, soap maker, engraver, gas fitter, guilder, gunsmith, telegrapher, lithographer, moulder, paper hanger, piano maker, pattern maker, plumber, slater, decorator, saddler, tinsmith, artist, boat maker, bellhanger, brewer, bricklayer, machinist, builder, typographer, brass worker, brass finisher, labourer, waiter, and porter.
+ Other occupations in the clerical category include: bailiff, teller, cashier, collector, photographer, civil service, reporter, editor, postmaster, salesman, notary, and librarian.
++ Other occupations in the business category include: auctioneer, boarder, clothier, furrier, contractor, confectioner, lumber dealer, wool dealer, flour dealer, hatter, pawnbroker, manufacturer, and storekeeper.
+++ Other occupations in the professional category include: choir master, clergy, dentist, doctor, professor, and school superintendent.
SOURCE: Toronto Mechanics' Institute fonds, MTL, (L1), series E, vol. 2, membership lists, 1855–65, cross-referenced with Toronto city directories from the same years to ensure accuracy.

each member and tending "to the advancement of the interests of society generally, and this province in particular." The directors of the York Mechanics' Institute understood that interclass co-operation would broaden the influence of the Institute: "The combination of all classes in a great object of public good ... cannot fail, in the end, to enhance the power of the nation, and add to the happiness of individuals composing it."[15] the directors of the London Mechanics' Institute, at its incorporation in 1841, asserted that the dissemination of knowledge would not only strengthen the operative population, but would also serve the general good of all members of the liberal community. The management of the Ottawa Mechanics' Institute likewise saluted the fact that while the Institute originated with the mechanical class, it was now "extensively patronized by all classes, the most wealthy as well as the poorest." Extolling the virtues of their open library, the directors boasted that any member of the burgeoning manufacturing and commercial population could walk through its doors and acquire the specific volume needed to assist in his labours.[16]

However, early manifestations of the ideology of liberal class inclusion also camouflaged a rhetoric of consent to the liberal social order, as directors from the middling sorts in urban Mechanics' Institutes jockeyed for position with their skilled working-class constituencies. In the fifth annual report of the York Mechanics' Institute in 1836, the executive outlined its plan to offer monetary prizes, "premiums," to the mechanics of the city, to demonstrate their skills and labour to the general populace. And yet the directors of the York Institute also noted that such a display would benefit the mercantile and commercial elites, through the opening up of new avenues of profitable industry, promoting education, lessening crime, and elevating the character of the people. While the directors of the Hamilton Mechanics' Institute welcomed the membership of both young men and the "liberal and wealthy," they also complained that the labours of the Institute always depended "on the exertions of the few."[17] In a lecture to the York Mechanics' Institute in 1832, William (Tiger) Dunlop praised the Mechanics' Institute for housing "the combination of all classes in a great object of public good." Dunlop was even more forthright in his defence of the liberal social order, as he described how the emerging "middle classes" formed a communicating link between the propertied orders and the working classes, disseminating harmony throughout society. As a superintendent and land agent with the Canada Company, Dunlop would have envisioned himself as part of this liberal middling sort, for he was neither a propertied landholder nor a skilled worker. And yet his description of the liberal "middling classes" was a highly discursive construction, as he noted that, while only a minor portion of society could be men of "rank and influence," the middling classes reinforced a shared sense of emulation and ambition: "Every man sees that the door is open to him to possess these distinctions, and every man feels anxious to promote the good of the community."[18] Such rhetoric also heralded the end of the older Tory vision of "community," which divided society into ranks and distinctions, and the beginning of a more liberal vision that recognized the occupational diversity of central Canadian society.

By mid-century the directors of the Toronto Mechanics' Institute continued to forcefully preach these rather liberal values of class inclusion, as a consequence of the increasing presence of manufacturing elites and the commercial classes. And yet Richard Lewis, the future president of the Toronto Mechanics' Institute, clearly viewed society in traditionally binary terms when he noted that the Institute would only progress if "a noble fraternity of all classes, high and low, aristocratic and plebeian" worked together in harmony. The opening of the Mechanics' Hall in 1854 therefore provided for the education and refinement of the entire populace, inciting every branch of industry into "laudable amelioration" and "generous emulation." The firm of H. Rogers and Sons was only too glad to contribute to an institution that included all classes; the fact that not only mechanics but also merchants, professional men, and clerks were to be found within its ranks made it worthy of the support requested.[19] Although the directors of the Ottawa Mechanics' Institute cherished their labouring roots, they congratulated themselves on extending the benefits of the Institute to all members of their community, and particularly the middling sort. Indeed, the executive noted that some of the "best educated men" in Ottawa took a great interest in the progress of the Institute, and thus called on others of "liberal" wealth and influence – professional men, merchants, manufacturers, and master mechanics – to loosen their purse strings and donate books and other financial assistance. Obviously these men responded, as it was later noted in 1857, that the Institute was "not *merely* a Mechanics' Institute, but [was] also devoted to the higher branches of art and science, and number[ed] among its members and supporters professional men of distinguished ability and the first mercantile men of this section of the Province."[20]

The creation of the Board of Arts and Manufactures of Upper Canada/Canada West and the *Conseil des Arts* in Lower Canada/Canada East in 1857 solidified the connection between the manufacturing, mercantile, and commercial elites with the political order of the burgeoning liberal state. The *Conseil des Arts* was forthrightly a hegemonic undertaking of the liberal social order, for in a lecture to the Lower Canadian Association of Arts and Manufactures on "the Future of Canada," Dr. James Bovell, a prominent physician and educator, noted that "commercial necessities" provided cohesion and bonds of common interest, and that true homogeneity in the colony would occur through the erosion of commercial boundaries.[21] Similarly, the goal of the Board of Arts and Manufactures in 1857 was to both educate and encourage the entire manufacturing sector of the Upper Canadian economy, by stimulating "the ingenuity of Mechanics and Artizans by means of prizes and distinctions." The promoters of both the Board of Arts and Manufactures and the Mechanics' Institute movement intended that their institutions would break down the previous system of Tory "class" education, whereby one category of knowledge would be purveyed to the rich and another to the poor. Once again the discourse of inclusion and the levelling affect of the middling sorts arose in this liberal ideology, as the technical education provided by the Board was intended to have "the inevitable tendency of [giving] social and political power to the masses, the confusion and intermixture of ranks, in which the 'privileged few' are being pushed aside, and the bold and resolute of every rank take precedence." Despite assurances in the prospectus of the Board's *Journal* that such a scheme would elevate the artisan population, the liberal cultural and social authority inherent in the endeavours of the Board came through when the editors also mentioned that the Board would also enrich the manufacturer and swell the coffers of the state.[22]

Urban Mechanics' Institutes also attempted to embrace women in furthering the development of the Institute movement throughout the liberal community. The experience of the female members who participated in colonial Mechanics' Institutes was slightly different from that of the women in analogous improvement societies in Great Britain. Mechanics' Institutes in the Old World were particularly restrictive to women in their early manifestations, although by mid-century they had come – albeit rather grudgingly – to accept the regulated contribution of women.[23] Despite the continual preaching of the doctrine of domesticity in Mechanics' Halls, women were strongly encouraged to become members and participate indirectly in Institute activities. Their endorsement as members of these organizations resulted in their somewhat limited participation, however, as they only played token roles as figureheads and spectators. This dichotomy would later prove to be rather problematic for Institute promoters as they tried to broaden women's participation along fairly strict gendered lines. It seems that liberal masculine subjectivities would involve and include the presence of women, while simultaneously holding them at arm's length with an explicit discourse of female domesticity.[24]

Female participation and membership in Mechanics' Institutes was from the outset on the agendas of many Institute committee meetings. In the Montreal Mechanics' Institute, the directors encouraged women to attend Institute lectures and soirées, and as early as 1843 women were also permitted to join as members under the same category of privileges as apprentices and sons of members. Women were also admitted free to lectures in the Toronto Mechanics' Institute as early as 1835, and by 1845 there was at least one female on the roll of ordinary members – the confectioner Elisabeth Dunlop – indicating that there were no restrictions on membership based on gender. Similarly, in the London Mechanics' Institute in 1851, women were permitted to join as full members and at a reduced initiation fee. Unfortunately, it appears that only one female member took advantage of this original offer, a Mrs J. Monsarrat, according to the membership list compiled in 1852.[25] The Ottawa Mechanics' Institute lauded the efforts of women in the community in presenting a highly successful bazaar in 1854, as the proceeds added significantly to its financial reserves: "In fact the present flourishing state of the Institute is chiefly due – and acknowledged with pleasure by the committee to be due – to the cordial and generous co-operation and assistance of those Ladies who, on this occasion, as on all others, have been the foremost in lending the most active and successful aid in promoting the best interests of the community ... To these Ladies the Committee cannot adequately express the grateful sense which it entertains of their noble exertions and the magnificent result of these exertions for the Institute." Although the women of Ottawa greatly reduced the debt of the local Mechanics' Institute, however, their efforts did not garner them any greater privileges than free admission to the winter course of lectures.[26]

While women were encouraged to attend these "public" lectures, those who attended Mechanics' Halls listened to a reinforcement of the domestic ideal. When Thomas Keefer gave his lecture on manufacturing to the members of the Montreal Mechanics' Institute, he noted that the prosperity of Montreal did concern women, as it was "the annual balance sheet which determines the concerts and pianos, the summer jaunt and the seaside baths, the furs and the velvets, the silks and the satins, the parasols and the scent bottles, and all the innumerable and comprehensive elements which form a material basis for what is called domestic bliss." Likewise, the members of the Ottawa Mechanics' Institute heard an identical ideology described in two talks on the "Rights of Women" and "Domestic Affections," during a series of lectures in 1855.[27] Walter Eales, a painter by profession, in his lecture to the Toronto Mechanics' Institute, described women as a "valuable class of the community," yet envisioned women taking an even more confining role. To Eales, the only effort needed to recruit women members would be to include vocal music in the program of the Institute. And yet he acknowledged that their presence was crucial for the extension of the Institute into the community, for "without their courtesy and cheerful countenances at our Soirees, Tea Meetings, Pleasure Excursions and Lectures, we would be out of our element."[28]

THE PURGING OF POLITICO-RELIGIOUS DISCORD

Another fundamental approach to ensuring harmonious social relations and creating a collective liberal identity in urban Mechanics' Institutes was the elimination of sectarianism and political partyism. On the surface, this process was an attempt to develop an educated, liberal, and literate citizenry that transcended the apparent social, religious, and political divisions that marred social and cultural relations in the 1820s and 1830s. In this sense, Mechanics' Institutes reflected the desire for political normalization so prevalent in the political, social, and educational discourse that materialized after the Rebellions. Even though Mechanics' Institutes proved to be fairly adept at purging sectarian and political discord and engineering consent to their operations, by mid-century, conflicts between political and religious opponents did in fact arise with some frequency. The suppression of these sentiments, potentially damaging to the voluntary "community" inherent in Mechanics' Institutes, often determined the success of urban Institutes in central Canada.[29] As with the ideology of class inclusion, the close relationship between Mechanics' Institutes and the rise of the liberal state would ensure that political and religious conflicts were kept to a minimum.

The early history of the Montreal Mechanics' Institute from 1828 reflected a great deal of sectarian conflict between the members of the Church of Scotland and those of the Anglican faith, as well as discord between Reformers and Tories. When the Institute was reorganized in 1840, the need to abolish such quarrels was paramount in the thinking of Institute administrators and lecturers who hoped to sustain a liberal collective identity of an educated populace. The merchant William Bristow asserted in his 1850 lecture to the Montreal Mechanics' Institute that the spirit of party politics and a public spirit were quite different. The party spirit sought to further private or individual advancement and an ascendancy of one part of the population over the remainder, whereas a "liberal"-minded individual promoted the general welfare.[30] To avoid such sectarian conflict, the directors of the London Mechanics' Institute not only outlawed religious discussions in the Institute, but also decreed that no religious denomination be allowed to congregate in the new Mechanics' Hall. However, sectarian disagreements did occur when the Reverend William Bettridge – an Anglican clergyman – lectured to the London Institute in 1853. Bettridge denounced as a "dangerous influence the religious opinions [that] a certain class of the community was assuming." The Institute board, concerned on behalf of the members of the Institute who belonged to this unnamed religious body, stated that the lecture introduced "Religious Animosities ... and that therefore this Institute disclaim[ed] being identified with the promulgation of any such sentiments as destructive to its best interest and general advancement." Despite his breach of protocol, Reverend Bettridge was only mildly reprimanded by the board, as he had been unaware of the institute's policy on such matters.[31]

The Toronto Mechanics' Institute implemented the guiding principle of allowing no political or religious discussions in their assemblies, although it had members from every political faction. Its very first membership list reflects the diversity of political opinion, as prominent Tories W.B. Jarvis, George Denison, John Strachan, and John Macaulay met side by side with Reformers – and some future rebels – such as Charles Duncombe, John Rolph, William Dunlop, William Baldwin, and James Lesslie. The patron of the Toronto Mechanics' Institute, Governor-General Charles Thomson, Lord Sydenham, stated firmly in 1840 that the contentions of party politics had no place in an institution of liberal self-improvement. Demonstrating his love for the philosophy of utilitarianism, Thomson noted that Mechanics' Institutes were indispensable to the political process, as they refined minds, elevated characters, and made better citizens. Walter Eales, a painter by occupation, concurred, claiming that knowledge – particularly that knowledge taught in the Mechanics Institutes – purified the political process while simultaneously supporting principles of Christianity.[32] Religious toleration was also clearly essential, as the Toronto Institute library committee in 1852 ordered several books on religious subjects. Requesting books by Episcopalians, non-conformists, and authors of other denominations, the committee charged the purchasers with the simple caveat to "guard against works of a sectarian or polemical character." Another function of the library committee was to root out irreligion in the Institute and protect the Christian faith. A member subsequently wrote to the committee requesting the removal of a book on Christ that only offered "half-praise" and denied the divinity of scripture. The complainant asked for this exclusion in order to protect members from the influence of pernicious "freethinking" material.[33]

Despite assurances that the Toronto Mechanics' Institute would keep political and religious discussions at bay, an example of the simmering political undercurrents in the Institute surfaced in the case of the non-delivered lecture of printer A.A. Riddell in 1848. In November of that year Riddell requested permission to lecture on "The Rights of Labour," a discourse that highlighted the plight of the labouring classes. The general board of the Institute procrastinated for two weeks in deciding whether to allow Riddell to lecture, and then allowed the Lecture Committee itself to cast the determining vote. The committee resolved to allow Riddell to give his lecture, if he would alter certain parts that were considered objectionable. It is assumed that Riddell refused, as the lecture was never given to the Toronto Mechanics' Institute. In refusing to alter his discourse and "negotiate" certain standards, Riddell no doubt cemented the opinion of some board members on the argumentative nature of the skilled working classes.[34] Even though Riddell believed that the elevation of the artisan did not imply the degradation of the other members of the community, he also acknowledged that the notion of Labour and its rights was entirely a political question, and therefore addressed the subject of labour in a more political fashion rather than focusing it solely on the discourse of "class." In recognizing the potential pitfalls of political dissonance inherent in his lecture, Riddell offered a liberal introduction of inclusion that he hoped would defuse possible objections to his address:

> The subject I have chosen being considered by some persons a political one, and political observations being wisely excluded from this Institute, lest during and subsequent to the reading of any lecture bearing upon politics the passions of some get aroused and the prejudices of others become excited ... I have been constrained to confine my discourse within much narrower limits than I should have felt inclined to do had this been originally intended for anywhere else in order that I might not, in the slightest degree, violate the well determined regulations of the Institute – a place where men of all opinions have united together for the attainment of laudable objects, and where men of all creeds have met, and still continue to meet – in harmony and in love.[35]

On the surface, Riddell's lecture simply ruffled the codes of conduct inherent in the lecture system, but on a deeper level the lecture managed to question the entire "liberal" social and political order. Despite his protestations, Riddell's lecture was heavily political, studded with references to natural rights, liberty, and the discourse of popular politics employed by Upper Canadian radical reformers. It is also readily understood that Riddell himself realized that some portions of the lecture would not escape the committee censor's scrutiny. A reference to the famous reform agitator William Cobbett showed Riddell's true colours, and his unwillingness to completely remove his radical political references was evident in his marginal note: "I'd have seen them d_d before I'd left this out." The committee's hand was forced, and the lecture was turned down. However, the highly political undercurrents in Upper Canada also led conservatives, reformers, and Tories alike on the Board of the Institute to censure Riddell's lecture.[36] The episode of A.A. Riddell and the Toronto Mechanics' Institute is highly instructive on two fronts; first, Riddell's non-lecture to the Institute demonstrates the proximity of Mechanics' Institutes to the liberal social order. By regulating the "correct" standards of collective liberal behaviour of an enlightened citizenry, the directors of the Toronto Mechanics' Institute refused to give Riddell the opportunity to present his "divisive" lecture. Second, the Riddell episode illustrates that some individuals also attempted to use voluntary associations as a vehicle to question the entire social order, and the tenets of liberal doctrine advocated by those societies.

Even among seemingly like-minded board members innocent confrontations could explode into potential political conflicts, which in turn would lead to rifts within the collective liberal identity that urban Mechanics' Institutes were trying to construct. In an 1845 board meeting of the Toronto Mechanics' Institute, the vice-president, Rev. David Rintoul, accused the president of being governed by nabobs and men of wealth in the country, while he himself spent his days in furthering the education of the operative classes. As the cashier of the Bank of Upper Canada and a staunch Reformer, the president, Thomas Ridout, rejected this claim as much as he had supported the conservative Rintoul in the Riddell episode. While on the surface this episode simply seems to be a political disagreement between two opponents, Rintoul illustrated the rationale behind this remark when he demanded that Ridout step down on account of his inactivity in the presidency, to allow a truly concerned and professional educator to assist those desperate for self-improvement. In other words, Rintoul believed that, were he to be president, he would favour a more "liberal" public spirit of a "professional" educator, whereas Ridout would simply favour a particular political party and the mercantile elite. Unlike Riddell, Rintoul did not extol the virtues of the workingman, nor did he couch his discourse in the language of labour's natural rights; in his view, the education of the artisan was no more than compensation for an inferior life and work.[37] Evidently, the middling sorts also required some measure of negotiation among themselves as they sought to position their educational collective identity within the liberal social order.

LIBERAL POLITICAL ECONOMY, EDUCATION, AND THE EMERGING INDUSTRIAL STATE

Another approach to increasing "liberal" harmony and co-operation among occupational interests in Mechanics' Institutes was the advocacy of the philosophy of honest industry and the political economy of hard work. This entailed merging individualist liberal doctrines of diligence and productiveness, and promoting a mutualist philosophy that encouraged commerce and industry throughout Canadian society. It was incumbent on voluntary associations such as Mechanics' Institutes to limit conflicts over economic science in order to create a collective liberal consensus in the name of commercial progress. And yet urban Mechanics' Institutes and their ties to the state through Boards of Arts and Manufactures ensured that such a bond was not only authoritative in nature but would also promote a producer *ideology* of the emerging liberal state. However, the endorsement of this social order could not be assumed, as radical members of the working classes and their allies of the middling sort could contest these "accepted" notions of liberal political economy. In many respects, the principles of honest industry preached in Mechanics' Institutes were blatantly exposed as doctrines of a mercantile and manufacturing hegemony.[38] As both the operative classes and the middling sort were in a state of fluidity at mid-century, discussions about political economy were indeed highly discursive in nature; their tenets appealed to both occupational factions. Once again, conflicts over economic science erupted more as a political response in comparison to the socio-economic conflicts that emerged at the end of the nineteenth century.

Leading merchants Thomas Keefer and William Bristow gave prominent addresses with themes on economic science to the Montreal Mechanics' Institute. To these lecturers, the source of *collective* wealth in a community was *personal* hard work on the part of every member of society, as it was by "honesty, by industry, by prudence, by frugality, and by perseverance that individuals thrive ... The aggregate of these qualities in a people, joined to public spirit, form the basis of national prosperity."[39] Despite agreement on the means to achieve national prominence, members of Mechanics' Institutes were free to select the economic *policies* they imagined would best facilitate this process. Bristow claimed that only free trade and reciprocity with the United States would increase productiveness. In breaking down the artificial barriers of commerce, free trade would allow individual enterprise to thrive as "the good to the community is effected solely through self-interest, the most powerful stimulus that can be employed to excite the industry, and sharpen the intellect and ingenuity of man." Keefer stated that neither unencumbered free trade nor protectionism without modification was desirable, as both policies partook of the character of class legislation. As Canadians were "a practical people" in a practical age, Keefer's advice to the Montreal Institute was simply to encourage the rapid development of commerce and the arts in the colonies, and to increase the moral elevation of the people. While Keefer was rather vague on how this could be accomplished, he envisioned the rise of a liberal order to bring about economic prosperity. To this prominent railway promoter, the alliance of the producing classes and the co-operation of capital and labour were essential to overcoming national animosities and in furthering the economic advancement of the nation.[40]

The political economy of hard work and the liberal ideology of the producer alliance were particularly strong in the urban Mechanics' Institutes of Canada West. Peppered with references to honest ambition and industry, William (Tiger) Dunlop's address to the York Mechanics' Institute in 1832, for instance, illustrated how the growth of commerce and manufactures would help the colonies attain national prosperity. This discourse led to even more lectures in the Toronto Institute on political economy, with topics ranging from the difference between productive and unproductive labour to the benefits derived from life insurance and mutual benefit societies.[41] The prominent politician Robert Baldwin Sullivan gave two very influential lectures in 1847 and 1848, one in the Hamilton and the other in the Toronto Mechanics' Institute, which touched heavily on the values of "earnestness, energy and industry." Unlike his counterparts in Montreal, Sullivan believed that the correct approach to these objectives lay in the creation of home markets, and the protection of the manufacturing sector. Walter Arnold, in his lecture on banking to the Toronto Institute, explained that industry in Canada would be stimulated by the establishment of a domestic currency and direct taxation. A prominent barrister, Arnold also concluded that a free exchange of goods would be more efficacious than protectionism, which would become a barrier to the natural course of trade and commerce. Arnold labelled protection a refined system of fraud and a "law which seeks to despoil one class of the community of the fruits of their industry and give them to another, an intolerable violation of natural justice."[42]

Manufacturing and mercantile elites also enlisted the burgeoning liberal state apparatus to reinforce honest industry and the work ethic through the creation of the Board of Arts and Manufactures and the establishment of its *Journal*. In the prospectus of its first volume, the periodical stated as its main objective the encouragement of industry and home manufactures in Canada West. Not only would honest industry provide independence and security in the new land for all classes but the nation as a whole would receive the benefits, as the "wealth and progress of the community is in proportion to the well-directed industry of its individuals."[43] The values and morality of collective honest industry, when applied to economics and business, would indeed highlight a new liberal order flexing its economic capabilities, although the discourse of hard work would remain "inclusive" of the entire community. In an article on education in the *Journal*, Richard Lewis outlined how honest industry, when applied to commerce, could become completely open, liberal, and democratic:

> There is nothing so democratical as trade and commerce. Its ways are countless, and are open to the whole world, and its successes are dependant [sic] upon laws, simple and clear and practicable to all ... As a general rule, it is the fruit and reward of industry and skill; and because industry and skill lie more or less within the reach of all – because all can labour and all can cultivate to the necessary degree the faculties common to all men, and yet the chief ones needed for the acquisition of wealth – the power which wealth exercises is a just power.

Any "self-made man" who followed the collective liberal principles of honest industry, economy, and thrift could therefore, through hard work and business acumen, outstrip in opportunity those who were technically superior in education and capital.[44]

With liberal state involvement in encouraging of commerce and industry, the article continued, Canada's progress, prosperity, and improvement required the co-operation of all occupational interests in the Mechanics' Institute movement. Individual efforts from these various members of the voluntary community were insufficient; the editors of the *Journal* were quite forthcoming that no economic improvements could be made unless the "farmer, the manufacturer and the merchant look upon their respective interests as identical." As the editors noted: "It is a great pity that some means cannot be devised to do away with this continual conflict between capital and labour, the employer and his employee, on principles that will be just to both parties – especially as their interests are really identical, although to so many of them apparently the reverse."[45] An interesting and crucial tactic for achieving harmony and co-operation in society through the honest industry came with the launching of the co-operative movement in England. Many articles dedicated to this cause in the *Journal* lauded co-operatives as a corrective to the recurring conflict of labour and capital; workmen in the factory could represent both sides equally. As such, the ideology of co-operation was more of a *liberal* construct, as it combined the salient individual doctrines of hard work, thrift, and productiveness, with a collective ideology of mutual aid.[46]

Skilled workers also revealed a vested interest in the continuance of these liberal ideas, as noted in Riddell's non-lecture "The Rights of Labour," prepared for the Toronto Mechanics' Institute in 1848. The necessity of honest industry and labour was a recurrent theme in Riddell's address, as he claimed that labour itself was "enobling to those engaged in it, of great advantage to society, and highly acceptable to God, [requiring] no strainings on the many faculties of common men." Relying on a rather liberal rhetoric of self-help, Riddell insisted that the operative classes needed to elevate themselves and acquire independence by being attentive to business and being sober at all times. They also needed "to read and to think; to be upright and candid; to be at home when not at work, and last, but not least, to enrol [their names]among the members of the Toronto Mechanics' Institute." To Riddell, the artisan should likewise obey the individualist liberal principles of political economy outlined by Adam Smith and others, while recognizing that the classes were in fact mutually dependent: "The manufacturer, workman or labourer, is far from being a recipient of charity when he receives his wages ... It is nothing more than an *exchange* between two parties, calculated to be for the benefit of both. The labourer receives, in the place of the actual produce of his labour, its value in money or some other exchangeable article – the improvement in value of the master's material being his recompense for the outlay in wages. From this, it may be inferred, that both should be *equally independent of each other*, for both are *dependent* upon one another. No man can subsist without labour."[47] The painter Walter Eales expressed similar views on political economy in his lecture to the Toronto Mechanics' Institute. While recognizing that those rising to opulence and wealth did so through "perseverance and industry," Eales claimed that the future progress of the skilled worker "depends upon himself, and any degree of proficiency is within his reach through knowledge and hard work." Echoing Riddell's opinions, Eales stated that Mechanics' Institutes would elevate the intellect, cultivate a sense of domestic affection, foster domestic piety, and promote moral culture among the labouring classes.[48]

Of course, the noteworthy difference between the lectures of Eales and Riddell is that the Toronto Mechanics' Institute permitted Eales to deliver his discourse and denied that privilege to Riddell. Unlike Eales's thesis, Riddell's insistence on the liberal gospel of honest industry only faintly concealed his Clear Grit political radicalism. The radical notions inherent in the "Rights of Labour" were present at the outset of Riddell's discourse, as those who labour were "justly entitled to comfortable dwellings, substantial food, protection in their persons, their property and their religion, the right of private judgment sufficient for their support when sick or out of employment, and hours for recreation and improvement." While this statement was fairly innocuous, the lecture committee's censors crossed out a particular sentence proposing the elevation of the mechanic to being able to "partake plentifully of the fruits which [his] hands had earned." Even though Riddell recognized that the rights of the workingman included respect and esteem from the other classes, his radicalism was subsequently revealed in his marginalia: "Respect and esteem do not fill the belly, even in Canada."[49] While praising the truly "independent" individuals as the emerging manufacturing and commercial classes who came to their fortune through the fruits of their own industry, Riddell condemned the formerly privileged mercantile and professional elites and others of the "idle rich" throughout his lecture. In his appeals for skilled working-class rights and privileges, Riddell equated the apprenticeship of artisans with the studies of the professional classes, claiming with thinly veiled hostility that while the "artizan cheerfully assists the professionalist in the upholding of his rights, he is far from acquiescing in the arrogant pretensions this class seems anxious to assume." While Riddell's objections reflected a more politically sensitive discourse, the nascent class conflict inherent in his critique of the middling sorts foreshadowed the socio-economic discord of the late nineteenth century.[50]

RATIONAL RECREATION AND THE COMMUNITY CENTRE IDEAL

Mechanics' Institutes also served the vital function of a community centre for emerging urban populations. As Mechanics' Halls were often the first buildings erected for entertainment and educational purposes, many different associations took advantage of their facilities for their own meetings and community events. By mid-century, the Montreal, Toronto, and Hamilton Mechanics' Halls were all prominent social centres of their respective cities, providing leisure activities as a form of cultural identity. In this respect the Mechanics' Institute movement continued to foster an aura of occupational and socio-political inclusiveness, as the Mechanics' Hall became a place where members of all interests and occupational groups could congregate and participate in leisure activities. Of course, Institute promoters' insistence upon the rational and educational aspect of entertainment and leisure, as well as their persistence in regulating "community" standards of morality in their activities also revealed that the provision of leisure and amusement could be an effective instrument for engineering consent to the liberal social order. However, as with all other facets of Mechanics' Institutes, competing agendas, occupational discord, and the need to negotiate cultural cohesion limited the effectiveness of entertainment within the Institutes.[51]

Initial attempts by more "urban" Mechanics' Institutes to provide recreation for their members were of the intellectual sort, as lectures and debates were the main entertainment staple. By the early 1840s the Hamilton Mechanics' Institute directors recognized that lectures, debates, and scientific demonstrations were not enough to sustain public interest, and they organized an excursion to Niagara Falls. They soon discovered that activities of this nature not only generated attention for the Institute's educational activities but also could provide necessary revenue for their struggling institution.[52] Elsewhere as well, the leisure activities of Mechanics' Institutes expanded along with their educational influence throughout the communities they served. The London Mechanics' Institute extended its entertainment repertoire at the zenith of its influence, as its executive organized a debating society, a mutual improvement society, and a chess club – and even purchased a pianoforte for musical presentations. Nonetheless, the directors drew the line at theatre productions and a dancing school, proscribing them as useless to "the advancement of literary and scientific pursuits." The theme of intellectual recreation also informed decisions made by the directors of the Toronto Mechanics' Institute, and even tended to support the regimen of a collective liberal identity of an enlightened citizenry. Even though the Institute promoted a wide range of recreational options such as soirées, reunions, lectures, and excursions, the rationale behind these activities was to end the "temptations to idleness and self-indulgence" of the skilled working classes and to advance the "pleasures of rational and intellectual pursuits."[53]

The Ottawa Mechanics' Institute recognized that success in drawing an audience from the larger community depended upon entertainment and related fundraising activities. Less than a month after the incorporation of the Institute in Ottawa, the directors planned a soirée to raise funds for the newly formed library. The organization of similar events, from bazaars and exhibitions, to mechanics' festivals and soirées, served to reduce the debt of the Mechanics' Institute after the Ottawa Mechanics' Hall was built. Lectures were initially set up to be the main attraction, yet the directors soon discovered that additional inducements were necessary and included music, readings, and recitations with each lecture program. Supplemental amusements were considered critical in fostering the correct liberal spirit in the Institute, as instruction in the higher branches of science could be a time of friendly association instead of a time of sitting in the lecture hall "sour and sulky like old philosphorums."[54] Intellectual recreation was not only a means for interaction between various members but could also save the operative classes in Ottawa from ignorance and vice. The executive of the reorganized Mechanics' Institute recognized in 1853 that the cultural offerings of the Institute needed to be as attractive as less savoury amusements elsewhere in order to save the artisan from depravity:

> Having no other resource for the employment of the spare hours of our long winter evenings, he must continue to patronize those haunts of frivolity and vice where the sensual appetites are alone ministered to and where the growth of all that is pure and good in the nature of man is perverted. If the youth of Bytown should thus grow up in ignorance, vice and depravity, and inferior in their intellectual acquirements to those of the other towns of the Province, their excuse must be, that their superiors, whose duty it is to supply them lavishly with the means of mental cultivation, have chosen rather to leave them to the tender mercies of the Ball-Alley, Gambling Room, and places of still worse character.[55]

THE POST-CONFEDERATION SHIFT TO MIDDLE-CLASS COMMERCIAL EDUCATION

In the 1870s and the 1880s, a fundamental shift in the attitudes, actual membership, and operations of urban Mechanics' Institutes turned the Institutes in a very different direction. While they continued to offer limited opportunities for technical education to the skilled working classes, Mechanics' Institutes began by the 1870s to focus almost exclusively on commercial and business education. Although the working class patronized Mechanics' Institutes on their own terms, the modes of education accessible to the community in general tended to favour those interested in upward mobility and a "better position" in the mercantile and business spheres. After mid-century, clerks, bookkeepers, and other members of the lower middle classes frequently composed the vast majority of Mechanics'

Institute members.[56] Although the *Conseil des Arts* continued to manage adult education in Quebec, in Ontario both the Educational Department and the Industrial Arts Association took over the reins of technical education, while agitation for free public libraries led to the *Free Public Library Act* and the creation of the Hamilton and Toronto Public Libraries in 1883. Another factor contributing to the demise of Mechanics' Institutes in urban areas was the fact that differing clubs, societies, and free library proponents had to compete for rather limited municipal funds. The myriad corporate, commercial, and state interests realized that the Institute movement was by then outdated and outmoded, a relic of the mid-century social order.[57] The development of industrial capitalism forced Mechanics' Institute directors to grapple with the question of class cleavages as never before, particularly as the industrial working classes appeared to abandon Institutes in droves. While Institute promoters continued to employ the language of class inclusion in their educational undertakings, the unmasking of Mechanics' Institutes as representatives of an antiquated "liberal" social order signalled the death knell of the Institutes by the last three decades of the nineteenth century.

On the surface, Mechanics' Institutes in the late 1860s and beyond remained loyal to their original intent in offering educational inducements to the skilled working classes. In 1871 the *Conseil des Arts* counselled the provincial government to restrict the grant for adult education to Mechanics' Institutes and the *Institut des Artisans* in Quebec, illustrating their focus on improving the educational lot of the working classes. And yet the *Conseil* also defended its education policies in the name of the industrial state and economic progress: "Schools of art [would] train our industrial population in the artistic taste and knowledge which are necessary to obtain some degree of eminence."[58] Alarmed that the march of progress was leaving them behind, and condemning the seeming indifference of the *Canadien* artisan community, the Montreal branch of the *Institut des Artisans* offered a library, a museum, and night classes to instruct both masters and apprentices on practical mechanical knowledge. The hierarchy of the Catholic Church in Montreal clearly approved of this approach, as three prelates gave the principal lectures in the first five years of the Montreal *Institut*'s existence. As with the pronouncements of the *Conseil des Arts*, these Catholic clergymen attempted to frame their lectures in the discourse of the new industrial state, for the artisan was key to developing industry and to "enrich a country and guarantee its place in all the world markets." As for the artisan himself, l'abbé Desmazures noted, in language similar to that of Justice Aylwin a decade earlier, *québécois* artisans had "founded this Institute in order to make education, and particularly instruction in the fine arts, available to working man. In this way you will make them worthy of this most worthy title of Artisan, which means Industrial Artist."[59]

Concerned promoters of the Toronto Mechanics' Institute continued to preach the importance of mechanical instruction and "liberal" self-improvement for the industrial classes, and the Toronto Institute still offered technical education in its evening classes to those "engaged in the active and industrial pursuits of life." By 1862 an attempt was made to return to the roots of the Toronto Mechanics' Institute, as the executive suggested that a special class be held to discuss matters of practical interest to mechanics. These "mechanics' meetings" ran until 1865, the same year the secretary of the Institute polled the members according to occupation. The concern of the Toronto Institute's directors about the attendance of the skilled working classes was entirely justified, as secretary George Longman recorded that of 969 members of the Toronto Mechanics' Institute, only 151 were either mechanics or involved in the manufacturing arts. Accordingly, in 1866 the Library Committee of the Institute tried to establish a penny reading room that would afford "the means for mutual improvement to mechanics and the working classes generally."[60] J.E. Pell, a past president of the Toronto Institute, wrote a letter in 1876 to the Board of Directors concerning the industrial classes' lack of interest in the Institute. Noting that by this time only forty mechanics were members, Pell suggested a return to the promotion of industrial exhibitions and the prize system to bring them back. This suggestion apparently had no effect, for in a Toronto Mechanics' Institute board meeting held in 1880, it was alleged that only 49 members out of 1050 in the Institute were mechanics or artisans.[61]

The executives' anxiety over the lack of participation from industrial workers revealed a frustration as to why the operative classes did not take advantage of all that the Institute offered. In reading the annual reports describing the evening classes of the Toronto Institute, it becomes evident that the manufacturing middle classes endeavoured to provide education not only for the moral and intellectual benefits of the working classes, but also for the "manufacturing and commercial progress of this country." The Board of Arts and Manufacturers of Upper Canada endorsed a similar philosophy as the *Conseil des Arts*, in supplying "a more correct and uniform knowledge of scientific principles which apply to various pursuits." This "art culture" would not only benefit the artisan but would also prove to be "a sure foundation of manufacturing prosperity."[62] The Board of Arts and Manufactures also recognized that while liberal *public* provision was made for the education of those intending to pursue the learned professions, similar funds must be advanced to the education of the working classes, through the technical education it provided. By the late 1860s, although the Board remained committed to the liberal principle of occupational inclusion, its directors were even more forthright in describing how the education of the skilled working classes would benefit the industrial state in general:

> Your Committee deem it highly desirable, and conducive to the interests of the community, that every facility should be afforded the industrial classes, to make themselves more intimately acquainted with the physical, artistic and mathematical principles they are daily calling into action – thereby enabling them to economize raw material, shorten the process of production, and produce more elegance of design and accuracy of workmanship, in whatever they execute. Artisans so instructed, both as to the science and practice of their respective arts, would be more likely to establish manufactories amongst us, employing the idle youths of our cities and towns, and adding to the wealth of the country.[63]

Despite adhering to the doctrines of educational inclusion, a paternalistic and authoritative dialogue began to enter the discourse of institute executives. The increasingly middle-class directors of the Toronto Mechanics' Institute continued to exercise a "beneficial influence" among the youth of Toronto in the late 1860s and 1870s by "guiding the tastes and elevating the sympathies of supporters into legitimate and refining channels." Improving the lot of the working-class youth in Toronto apparently required a considerable measure of authoritarian control, particularly in the operation of night classes and the Institute library. In the institute's 1875 annual report, the directors assured the citizens of Toronto that with the "exception of two trifling complaints," the conduct of young patrons to the night classes was highly commendable. Furthermore, by "continuous supervision" and the removal of young troublemakers, the executive managed to reduce the number of persons improperly using the reading room, which in turn improved the safety and comfort of the actual members.[64]

In the London Mechanics' Institute, frustration on the part of the industrial classes over similar practices also led to conflict. In the 1870s an article in the local newspaper from "A Mechanic" decried the fact that mechanics could not attend the Institute in their work attire; nor was the London Institute under the direction of the industrial classes. While the letter writer condemned the notion of "class institutes," he was highly disturbed by individuals in the reading room who were "men of leisure or of business, clerks or annuiatants [sic] who have little or nothing to do, and who therefore take refuge from themselves and from *ennui* among the newspapers." Perhaps "a Mechanic" was entirely correct in his inference about the new industrial social order for, in lauding Molson's and the Bank of Montreal for their generous donations, the Institute stated: "It is hoped that other monetary institutions in the city who have a large staff of young men in their employ will see the advisability of contributing in like manner, so as to have some useful place of resort in which to spend their leisure hours."[65]

Skilled workers were "voting with their feet." Their relative absence from urban Mechanics' Institutes by the end of the century illustrates that the Institutes were not entirely for the benefit of the industrial classes. Now serving the lower middle classes and their impulse for upward mobility, as well as the stimulus of the industrial state, Mechanics' Institutes became a safe harbour for those seeking to improve their position through commercial education. As the membership rolls in the latter 1870s and early 1880s indicate, the clerical and business population made up a substantial 64 percent of the membership of the Toronto Mechanics' Institute (see Table 1.2).[66] As a result, the educational priorities of the Institute shifted from strict technical instruction to a broader commercial curriculum. Even though the Institute had provided "mechanics' meetings" for the technical benefit of the industrial classes in 1862, a scant four years later the management of the Institute envisioned the night classes as a "People's College," an institution ostensibly available to all members of the developing industrial community. The annual report of the Institute's night classes emphasized the math, bookkeeping, architectural, and penmanship classes over the mechanical arts, "Whether it is to supplement the deficiencies of early teaching in the solid attainments essential to active business life, or to supply the attraction of elegant accomplishments tending to refinement, these classes represent a provision not only personally beneficial to those availing of them, but calculated in time to exercise a very decided and wholesome influence on the social and material well being of the community at large."[67]

The Toronto Mechanics' Institute put their newfound admiration for commercial education into practice. They consistently drew more students to their grammar, bookkeeping, arithmetic, elocution, and language classes than to mechanical drawing, which had the lowest attendance. While the Toronto Institute directors continued to laud their night classes for their production of "artists" rather than artisans, they were just as pleased that

Table 1.2
Ordinary Membership by Occupation, Toronto Mechanics' Institute, Selected Years, 1876–1883

Occupation	Total	Percentage	Occupation	Total	Percentage
Builder	17		Merchant	138	
Carpenter	16		Grocer	21	
Printer	10		Agent	20	
Machinist	12		Manufacturer	17	
Watchmaker	7		Stationer	17	
Boot/Shoemaker	7		Jeweller	8	
Surveyor	6		Others+	20	
Baker	6		TOTAL BUSINESS	241	25
Engraver	6		Barrister	60	
Painter	5		Law Student	27	
Founder	5		Chemist/Druggist	19	
Stonecutter	5		Teacher	16	
Others*	60		Architect	12	
TOTAL SKILLED	162	17	Engineer	8	
Clerks	278		Surgeon	7	
Bookkeeper	34		Others++	19	
Traveller	17		TOTAL PROFESSIONAL	168	17.5
Salesman	15				
Manager	14		Gentlemen	16	
Others**	19		TOTAL PRIVATE		
TOTAL CLERICAL	377	39	MEANS	16	1.5

NOTES: Unlike Table 1.1, cross-referencing did not take place with city directories, as the volume of names provided in the membership list precluded such a search; only occupations recorded were used as data.

* Other occupations in the skilled category include: apprentice, mechanic, signmaker, steam fitter, turner, fisherman, boiler maker, trunk maker, carriage maker, pressman, mason, butcher, bricklayer, brewer, milliner, bookbinder, cabinet maker, soap maker, gas fitter, tailor, moulder, coach maker, draper, pattern maker, plumber, plasterer, draftsman, coppersmith, gunsmith, and artist.

** Other occupations in the clerical category include: bartender, operator, photographer, sheriff, police chief, collector, secretary, and inspector.

+ Other occupations in the business category include: bookseller, broker, hatter, storekeeper, hotelkeeper, clothier, auctioneer and confectioner.

++ Other occupations in the professional category include: homeopath, doctor, dentist, professor, writing master, headmaster, clergy, and judge.

SOURCE: Toronto Mechanics' Institute fonds, MTL, (L1), series E, vol. 13, membership list with occupations, 1876 and vol. 15, membership list with occupations, 1883.

clerks and bookkeepers attended the Institute, for "in some of the best counting-houses may be seen youths who obtained their first lessons in accounts in the Mechanics' Institute classes."[68] The industrial exhibition sponsored by the Toronto Mechanics' Institute likewise became less a display of skilled craftsmanship and more a response to the tastes of the larger manufacturing community. No longer solely an industrial exposition of manufactures and implements, it became a more open and inclusive display with such categories as "Free and Decorative Arts" and ladies' work. The directors of the reading room and the library also marked the transfer of support from the industrial classes to the lower middle classes and others in their 1873 motion to change the institute's name: "Many of our citizens think that this association is for the benefit of the working classes, with the exclusion of mercantile and professional people. For this reason they think it would be advisable to amend the name of the Institute, so as to read 'Mechanics' Institute and Library Association' as no harm could possibly arise from the amended name, and much good might follow."[69]

Similar pronouncements appeared in the Montreal Mechanics' Institute, as the decline of its artisan membership reached what the executive perceived to be critical proportions. Recognizing that the majority of members now came from the lower middle classes, the directors dramatically changed their strategy for recruiting new members. Instead of publicizing the advantages of technical education, reports of the Montreal Institute after 1878 tended to mention that the Institute was open to people of all classes, occupations, races, and religion. As with the Toronto Institute, the committee decided that any change of name would be undesirable; the original should be kept as being distinctive and worthy of remembrance. However, this sense of "inclusion" also veiled the ascendancy of the new industrial social order, for the directors reminded their readers that "the original appellation included mechanics in the widest sense possible," as the executive comprised representatives from the industrial, commercial, and professional classes.[70] In the 1872 annual report of the London Mechanics' Institute, the executive congratulated the members on the "steady increasing patronage it [had] received from all classes of citizens" despite the lack of interest from the industrial classes and the city's mechanics. Of course such "involvement" came at a price. When the president of the Institute tried to hold fast to the original constitution requiring that the management committee be made up of two-thirds mechanics, the other members of the board insisted that they had "at one time" been in the mechanical arts.[71]

The liberal discourse of classlessness reached its apogee in 1869 with the Ontario the provincial government's attempt to centralize the Institute movement by creating the Association of Mechanics' Institutes. In the annual report of the Association in 1875, a report from Thomas Davison – the president of the Toronto Institute – insisted that government grants for Institutes not be limited to "Mechanics" Institutes. In order to be as "inclusive" as possible, Davison suggested, every library association should be awarded a grant, "leaving it to the originators to name it Mercantile, Professional, Mechanical library or library association, so long as its object was to educate the public irrespective of creed, nationality or occupation."[72] Given that these reports were distributed to Institute Libraries, it is not surprising that the industrial classes in urban locales completely abandoned Mechanics' Institutes, given the attitude of the central Association directors. Five years later, in the 1880 annual report, President James Young concluded that while an increased presence of skilled workers in the institutes was desirable, it was "a mistake to suppose that the Institutes were created and Legislative grants given to one class of the community alone; and in the interest of these institutions, and even of the mechanical classes themselves ... Mechanics' Institutes should continue to be open to all classes on terms of perfect equality." The disclosure of the executive's authoritarian outlook became complete in the annual report of 1885, as secretary William Edwards claimed that Mechanics' Institutes not only kept the industrial classes from places of questionable resort, but they also "kept many from drifting away and leading lives of uselessness and crime, and their minds directed to nobler aims, becoming better and more intelligent workmen and members of society."[73]

The thinly veiled hegemonic undertones contained in the rhetoric of class inclusion became even more evident in the Association of Mechanics' Institutes, as witnessed in their sponsorship of a topical essay contest in 1876 on the best means of improving the Institutes. David Boyle, Elora's famed learned artisan, marked the continuation of an older tradition of artisan self-improvement by noting that improving the Institutes would require ending the practice of electing officials who did not represent the interest of mechanics in general. However, Boyle also remarked that when members of sundry classes such as farmers or clerks comprised the majority of attendants of a Mechanics' Institute, their interests and tastes ought to be considered first.[74] Many of the other essays in the Association's contest similarly employed the ethos of class inclusion as a vehicle for promoting the interests of the industrial state and the manufacturing middle classes. A particularly virulent essay exhibiting middle-class disdain for the industrial classes was interestingly penned by Richard Lewis, a school teacher and past president of the Toronto Institute. The importance of Mechanics' Institutes in restraining the potentially dangerous ignorance of the idle working classes was incalculable, as ordinarily they were "destitute of all intellectual tastes, weak in moral principle, yet strong in animal energies and passions, they must needs have occupation, and when freed from the labours of their daily life, they find their excitement and relief to their passions in lawless disorder, intemperance and even violence." Lewis observed that it was therefore essential for Mechanics' Institutes to embrace all classes of the burgeoning industrial community to curb this element: "It would be the worst policy to place the entire management of the Mechanics' Institutes in the hands of any one class. The influence, the sympathy, and the assistance of an educated and moneyed class are necessary to its success, especially in its higher educational objects. But it would be quite practicable and the best policy to associate *bona fide* working men and women in the management of any department especially introduced for their benefit and pleasure."[75]

INCREASED PRESENCE OF WOMEN AND CONTINUED ENFORCEMENT OF POLITICO-RELIGIOUS NEUTRALITY

Women's participation in the activities of late-century Mechanics' Institutes became more active as the Institute's traditional bases of skilled working-class support became eroded. In both the Toronto and the Montreal Mechanics' Institute, industrial exhibitions offered the first opportunities for women to participate more fully. Ladies' work and art creations were often prominent categories in the exhibitions, and yet women's role as providers of the refreshment and entertainment portion of the celebration remained most significant. Women did such a superb job that the Exhibition Committee of the Toronto Institute "rewarded" them by inviting wives and daughters of Institute directors in 1868 to form a Ladies' Auxiliary Exhibition Committee.[76] In 1875 the Library Committee of the Toronto Mechanics' Institute appropriated the boardroom of the Institute for a Ladies' Conversation room as an additional inducement to members of the opposite sex. The Montreal Institute quickly followed suit in 1878, specifying that a "special effort be made to cultivate the membership of ladies, and that a special room be set apart as a Ladies' Reading Room." The Toronto experiment ended in 1881, as the Institute encountered the same problem with women as it had with mechanics; female members simply did not use the room for the intended purpose and it was forced to close down.[77]

The promoters of the centralized Association of Mechanics' Institutes recognized the need to reach out to the female segment of the population, and thus many of the essays on the improvement of Mechanics' Institutes pleaded for the greater participation of women members. David Boyle's essay, already mentioned, petitioned for the creation of subcommittees "consisting wholly of women, to present the advantages of the Institutes to others of their own sex, state terms, show catalogues, give information regarding classes and lectures, and procure names for membership." Despite these innovative ideas, most of the essays continued to advocate the practices of domesticity for the female constituency. While E.F. Dickson, a signal officer from Goderich, encouraged the enrolment of young women in Mechanics' Institutes, he did not envision them learning anything but domestic economy, music or drawing, and other subjects "pertaining to their position in the world and society."[78] John Davy, the past secretary of the Toronto Institute, offered the suggestion that women members should elect two lady subscribers to seats on its general board of management, with reading rooms provided for their specific use. When the management of the Toronto Institute tried to put these ideas into practice, by creating female directors to work in concert with other committees, women members soon realized that such an assignment did not admit their gender into the corridors of power. Female directors were simply segregated and advised to confine their labours to matters pertaining to other members of their sex.[79]

Evening classes proved to be a most effective vehicle for providing young women with educational opportunities, and including them in the workings of the industrial social order. As early as 1865, the Board of Arts and Manufactures for Upper Canada gave women the opportunity to enrol in its classes and art schools, although not many female students took advantage of this offer. Boyle's essay in the 1876 contest reflected changing Canadian attitudes to the education of women, as he called for an increase in funding provisions and female class availability, in order to assist young "sewing girls and servant maids" in their educational endeavours. Considering working women's low rates of remuneration, Boyle suggested that women should be admitted to Ontario Mechanics' Institutes at reduced membership rates.[80] The Toronto Mechanics' Institute followed this suggestion, but, in an obvious throwback to mid-century domestic ideology, offered only music, drawing, and wax flower making for female students. A concerted attempt was made to enlist women in commercial education classes, by recommending prizes for the top female students and targeting women in their advertising. As a result, the attendance of women grew considerably, reaching nearly 13 percent of the student body in the peak year of 1879. Although it is almost impossible to discover the class backgrounds of many of these students, the median age in the night classes from 1877–81 was seventeen, suggesting that young working women did manage to profit from the educational opportunities of the Institute. Thanks to these educational successes, women subscribers to the Toronto Mechanics' Institute by 1881 comprised over 10 percent of the total membership.[81]

In Montreal, even though opportunities for women began to open up with the transfer of commercial education from the Mechanics' Institute of Montreal to the *Conseil des Arts* in 1870, women were far more marginalized in the *Conseil*'s educational endeavours than they were in Ontario's Board of Arts and Manufactures. In 1878 the *Conseil* offered an afternoon art class to women in Montreal, upon securing the services of an "exceptionally good teacher" and charging a small fee. The directors made it clear that this was merely an experiment, as the *raison d'être* for the art schools was the education of artisans, not women. We can infer that by 1880 the women's art culture classes were all but dead, as they had to lower the fee to three dollars to entice women back.[82] A petition of the Montreal Women's Club in 1895 indicates that the directors of the Board were simply not concerned with the education of women. In bringing the Board's attention to the fact that unmarried young women – through no fault of their own – were compelled to enter the workforce, the Women's Club expressed the hope that a government institution would not discriminate against any class of the community. The Board conceded that women had both the ability and capacity for industrial arts, but stated that not only was the demand limited but, it was also undesirable that men and women learn together. The Board also declared that domestic economy was a far more important subject for women to learn: "A serious danger arises from the fact that women show an aversion to house and home duties and wish to work in factories. The greatest safeguard of a nation is to protect the home, and the happiest homes are those in which women excel in the domestic virtues." Under pressure from the Women's Club, the Board soon relented and offered women the opportunity to join the schools, although the only classes offered to them were dress cutting, needlework and millinery, occupations fitting for their sex.[83]

During the last three decades of the century, the policies of political and religious neutrality continued to be championed by concerned Mechanics' Institute directors. And yet the monitoring of religious and political discussions in Mechanics' Halls became far more relaxed, and the creation of literary and debating societies and the establishment of "reunions" in concert with the Institutes allowed for more freedom of expression. In 1865 the Montreal Mechanics' Institute had offered to host a meeting of "Mechanics and Manufactures" in order to discuss the importance of protecting manufacturing interests in Canada East. Fearing political expressions of class discontent, however, the *Conseil des Arts* quickly cancelled the meeting as it did "not feel warranted in initiating any movement of a political character, with which it appears this one would resolve itself."[84] Little more than a decade later, it appeared that "class" objections to discussing questions of protectionism and free trade had abated. The annual report of the Montreal Mechanics' Institute noted in 1878 that the latest and best works of Political Economy were on the shelves in the library for the guidance of both Free Trade and Protectionist members of both parties. To the directors of the Montreal Institute, such a position was consistent with their mandate of being "absolutely free from influence sectarian or political."[85]

By the time "reunions" first surfaced as a function of the Toronto Mechanics' Institute in 1862, the rules regarding political discussion appear to have eased, as many of the debates and essays presented during these meetings delved into political themes. Not only did the Reunion Committee invite both the Reformer George Brown and the Conservative John A. Macdonald to speak as a means of illustrating their neutrality but they also debated such topics as annexation, political independence, and a stronger British union. In 1864, however, when some members proposed to debate the merits of Confederation, committee balked at the overt political nature of such discussions and cancelled the debate.[86] Although the reunions originated in the same year as the "mechanics' meetings," these gatherings catered to an entirely different class of individuals, young professionals. Led by the young lawyer J.D. Edgar, educator Richard Lewis, and the politician Robert Sullivan, these "social meetings" would offer mutual improvement through the refining of oratory skills and elocution. The middle-class nature of the enterprise manifested itself through the rules of these reunions, as each patron was expected to "behave with proper decorum, and use his or her best efforts to be agreeable to the company present." Not only would the reunions offer a "laudable emulation in the display of talent and taste" for the general public but the directors felt that "in time" these meetings would have a beneficial influence on Toronto Society in general.[87]

In London, while the Mechanics' Institute also continued to frown upon political discussions, a number of debates before the London Literary society – an offshoot branch of the Institute – were politically charged. Debates on such controversial subjects as the nine-hour day, universal suffrage, labour unions, prohibition, the benefits of free trade and annexation, as well as the likelihood of Canadian independence, were freely admitted in the discussions of the society. Nevertheless, this did not prevent tempers from rising – and controversies from arising – in the course of the meetings. In one gathering of the society the members condemned "unmerited criticism" as being injurious to the design of the club, as "carried to excess [it] could not but be attended by evil." Similarly, when the society attempted to establish a mock House of Commons during their meetings, passions over Canadian party politics boiled over, and the simulated Parliament was rather quickly discontinued.[88] The London Literary Society charged an entrance fee of ten cents, which some members regarded as a measure affecting the popularity of the meetings. However, the majority offered the opinion that the fee would lend more middle-class "respectability" to the society, while one member argued that ten cents was still not sufficient to stem the "army of juveniles numerous enough to storm the Sudan." In subsequent debates, the president maintained the ten-cent fee in the name of bourgeois respectability, in order, he said, to "destroy some of the comic element which of late has entered too freely in our entertainment."[89]

Of course, Mechanics' Institutes could also harbour more latent sectarian and political discord, particularly in the province of Quebec. Although the Montreal Mechanics' Institute insisted that its doors were open to all Montrealers regardless of race, colour, religion, or creed, the directors balked at provisions for a free public library, ostensibly for completely political and sectarian reasons. The executive feared that the municipal government would introduce certain conditions that would lead to the destruction of self-government, with the result that "an almost irresponsible power is set up, whose interests are not always identical with those of the members." This was evidently a swipe at the French element in Montreal, for the directors added: "While our Institute is open to persons of all races, colour and religion, it would be well perhaps to notice that we are principally supported by the English-speaking Protestant population."[90] Similarly, while the rules of the Montreal *Institut des Artisans* forbade religious and political questions, they did not prevent prominent Catholic priests from extending their support, or exhorting members never to turn their backs on the Mother church. Frédéric Colin, in a speech to the *Institut* on the state of the working classes, encouraged *Canadien* artisans to ignore the libertarian utopian ideals of the *Rouge* faction, for "their words would only lead to the "barricades." Colin added that *Canadien* artisans would find their rights from within the Catholic Church, an institution that respected their rights and advocated for their benefit:

> Working man, you have been delivered from the chains that enslaved you for centuries; your rights have been recognized, your dignity elevated, and your greatness and freedom proclaimed; and it is from Jesus Christ and His Church that you have received these blessings ... Love well this Church, give youself to its protective embrace, and it will guide you and lead you forward. Cleave to the Church and it will be

your protector and guardian in the formidable struggles that you must still undergo against the irreligion of philosophers and the ambition of political leaders.[91]

THE PRODUCER IDEOLOGY, UPWARD MOBILITY, AND THE RISE OF THE INDUSTRIAL STATE

With the growth of industrialization and urbanization, the ascendant industrial order continued the discourse of honest industry as a means of negotiating consent to emerging industrial capitalism. However, clerks, accountants, bookkeepers, and other members of the lower middle classes could also call on the ideology of honest industry to ensure upward mobility. In the 1860s the doctrine of the "self-made man" persisted as a philosophy that both the industrial working classes and the emerging middle classes could embrace. The editors of the *Journal of the Board of Arts and Manufacturers* continued to persuade the industrial classes to enrol in Mechanics' Institutes, to become "more intelligent workmen and worthier citizens." They also expected the industrial classes to learn their laborious tasks out of duty and responsibility, with a potential twofold reward: "It may enable him to rise to the top of his profession, or what is more probable, it may simply increase his stock of information sufficiently to enable him to do his work with less labour, fewer errors, and much more pleasure to himself and others."[92] Lectures from Catholic clergy to the Montreal *Institut des Artisans* also reinforced the work ethic of the industrial *and* the religious social order for *Canadien* skilled workers. To Abbé P.J. Verbist, the prosperity of the Quebec "*patrie*" depended almost entirely on the honest labour of its workmen, while Frédéric Colin expressed the notion that the hardworking artisan could become a man of progress, industry, and civilization. Abbé Desmazures contended that the Church supported the precepts of honest industry : as "The Church has always honoured industry in all efforts of human activity; the Church in fact has done more than just honour industry; in prescribing work, it is as if the Church has also prescribed progress."[93]

The new-found class complexities imprinted by the socio-economic developments inherent in industrial capitalism changed the rules of the game somewhat, particularly among the promoters of the industrial state. Not only were the Board of Arts of Manufactures in Ontario and the *Conseil des Arts* in Quebec prepared to instruct the industrial classes on their duties to the ideology of honest industry but they also began lecturing their employers as well. An article in the Ontario Board's *Journal* entitled

"Success in Business" extolled the virtues of economy and propriety in the self-made businessman, as half of all business failures resulted "from extravagance, from ostentation, from rivalry, from a love of ease and self-indulgence; one quarter from speculation, leaving only a small portion that can be termed unavoidable. This is encouragement for the careful and industrious, and ought to be a warning to others." In another article titled "Hints to the Workmen and their Employers," the editors of the *Journal* recognized that both employees and commercial men needed to conform to the tenets of honest industry, although most barbs were aimed at the industrial classes:

> I don't like to see a workman arrive a quarter of an hour or twenty minutes after his time in the morning, and then enter in a jaunty, defiant, independent style. I don't like to see him punctual in going to, but the reverse in coming back from his meals. I don't like to see a man as the clock strikes drop his work as though it burnt his fingers. I don't like to see him, after coming late to his work, unwilling to devote one precious minute of his own time to his employer's service ... I don't like to see an employer always dissatisfied on principle. I don't like to see an employer make familiar companions of his workmen one day and act like a tyrant the next.[94]

In the annual report of the *Conseil des Arts* in 1891, the president, J.W. Hughes, offered similar counsel to workmen and their employers; he advised workmen to avoid drink, idleness, lying, and robbing the employer of his time. He also directed the working man to be clean in body and spirit, and to "not be a loud, dirty talker or swearer. It is not manly; it is mean, low, degrading. No gentlemen does such things, and you are all gentlemen." However, Hughes also criticized employers who refused to pay the wages of his workers on time and made poor excuses for not doing so.[95]

As urban Mechanics' Institutes began to harness the ranks of the lower middle classes in the 1870s, the language of upward mobility appeared in sundry discourses within the Institutes. The president of the Toronto Mechanics' Institute, noted architect Frederick Cumberland, addressed the Class Committee about the advantages of a thorough commercial education. The "resources of the country were so great," he said, "that all who wished [to] take advantage of the opportunities afforded for obtaining lucrative situations might easily obtain a comfortable livelihood."[96] The discourse of upward mobility also surfaced in the essay contest sponsored by the Association of Mechanics' Institutes in 1876. Many of the submissions touched on the theme of honest industry, and ways in which Institutes could assist the self-made man to prosper in an industrialized Ontario. The eventual winner of the contest, Richard Lewis, wrote that the operative classes needed to labour diligently to improve their station, but also noted that employers had an interest in "getting skilled, educated and honest employees" by supporting their local Mechanics' Institute. In language similar to that of the Board of Arts and Manufactures, Lewis further stated that employers themselves had a measure of self-interest in the education of their employees, as the boss "who thinks it possible to make the whole mind of his servant slave to his interests and wishes, will sometimes have to suffer from fraud and dishonour, because he expected dullness to be honester [sic] than intelligence."[97]

However, two skilled workingmen also had their say about the importance of the ideology of honest industry as a means of improving Mechanics' Institutes. W.A. Walls, a millwright from Otterville, spent nearly twenty-five pages declaring that Mechanics' Institutes should demand self-restraint from the vice of indolence and should instruct mechanics in the principles of self-reliance. In a throwback to the liberal artisan philosophy of educational self-improvement, Walls peppered his essay with references to those who improved their position through the application of hard labour. Concluding that "indolence bars the way to success," Walls echoed the producer ideology: "Unlucky is a word that may be translated unwise; generally a man is lucky because he is wise, or has a good sense and uses it. Another man is unlucky because he is a fool and acts like one. Misfortune lives next door to stupidity. If there is no luck about the house it is because there is no common sense – no industry – no economy of either money or time."[98] And yet Walls also reserved some criticism for employers and their apparent neglect of the workingman's education. The reading of appropriate material was a habit to be established, and it was entirely impossible for employees to form these habits if they were engaged "from morn till late at night in stores, factories and workshops." As the "mind could not work with a fagged body," Walls called on employers to exercise self-interest by limiting their employees' work day and encouraging them to attend Mechanics' Institutes, as clearly "they would desire intelligent workmen in their factories."[99]

Alexander Gunn, a blacksmith from London, picked up on Walls' latter critique, decrying the prevalence of middle-class literature of the self-made man in Institute libraries. To make the Institutes more attractive to the working classes, Gunn requested a return to the liberal education of "the mechanical world," as all the improvements from libraries, museums, and "remodlin furniture" would be of little effect until Institutes removed the idle character of the books from their shelves. In his unschooled English, Gunn remarked that "the literature they read for the most part is light blue green and yellow but this is more the fault of the character of the age it demands ... for little or no labour and when it asends into a spiritual province it readily mirrors such dogmas as to offer the riches of heaven without noticing the ordley laws that leads thereto thus mandkind for the most part finds more delight in a story which brings some idler into great possessions without giving the equivalent labour than one who came possessed in a heavenly and orderly way."[100] Gunn also offered a socio-economic appraisal of Mechanics' Institutes, and censured Institute directors for promulgating class inclusion in the function of the Institutes. To Gunn, that philosophy should be rejected: "[It was] too often supposed to be a real step in human progress that is for a mechanick to be come capable of moving in the social circles of lawyers, doctors, clearks, &c. After Institutes repudiates all that is admirable in the above detail they may Easley see that its success is by no means confined to any one particular member or any few tools in the possession of all." In calling on the ethos of honest industry to contest Institute standards, Gunn exposed the producer ideology preached in the Institutes as being attuned primarily to the needs of the commercial and manufacturing middle classes.[101]

MASS COMMERCIAL RECREATION AND INSTITUTE ENTERTAINMENTS

By the final decades of the century, Mechanics' Institutes had lost their momentum as *the* driving force for culture and entertainment in the emerging industrial city. The most obvious contributing factor was the development of the urban Free Library movement, as competing forms of mass entertainment eliminated the need for an all-inclusive library and community centre. Similarly, the realization that Mechanics' Institutes served as agents of middle-class authoritarian control, particularly in the realm of leisure, drove many young industrial skilled workers from the urban Institutes.

No better example of these complications exists than that of the Ottawa Mechanics' Institute, an institution that never really did achieve a strong foothold in the hearts of the people in the Ottawa Valley. In 1868 the Institute experienced such apathy from the public that the directors, in frustration, stated in their very last report: "They regret most sincerely that an institution of so valuable a character receives so little support from the citizens generally, that its existence can be described only as a constant struggle with difficulties." The patently middle-class Literary and Scientific Society founded a year later did not attract any greater interest, and the Institute limped along into the 1890s without seriously attempting to provide recreational opportunities, content only to procure insufficient municipal grants for their reading room. They were so unsuccessful in this endeavour that they unceremoniously disbanded after the passing of the *Free Library Act* in 1895. The situation was so chaotic that when a group of carpenters formed the Ottawa Technical library in 1901, the whereabouts of the books of the Mechanics' Institute library were simply not known.[102]

In London, the new administrators of the reorganized London Mechanics' Institute evidently were determined not to fall into the same trap as their predecessors by relying solely on intellectual recreation, and opened up their premises for a variety of entertainment options. In 1871 a newly formed concert and recitation committee served to coordinate entertainment, and the London Literary Society first convened a year later. This allowed the directors to congratulate members in the annual report "on the steady increasing patronage it had received from all classes of citizens, when it is borne in mind the many sources of amusement and entertainments offered to its citizens the past winter." Apparently the London public was hungry for even newer and more exciting entertainments later in the decade, as the entertainment committee of the Institute debated the merits of placing a billiard table and a gymnasium in the London Mechanics' Hall. By the 1880s, the managers of the institute realized they were fighting a losing battle for the hearts and minds of Londoners. Competition from other voluntary associations and mass commercial recreation were blamed for a dwindling membership base. The London Institute tried to imitate the example of other urban Institutes by passing a free library bylaw in 1884, but Institute debts were so great that it was not until 1893 that the citizens of London had a free public library.[103]

Although the directors of the Toronto Mechanics' Institute remained committed to the philosophy of rational recreation, they also discovered the need to offer more leisure activities in order to extend the influence of the Institute. In their 1866 annual report, they maintained that the selected new attractions were strictly for the amusement of the public at large, as the Institute supported such recreational endeavours as *conversaziones*, bazaars, reunions, and even a Mechanics' Institute chess club. And yet the limits of good taste were stretched thin in the community with the advertisement of Negro minstrel shows in the Mechanics' Hall; Board members complained that such entertainments made the character of the Institute suffer.[104] The notion of "elevating and agreeable amusement" became increasingly ineffectual in drawing members from the Toronto community. As the directors noted in the 1870 annual report of the Institute, the difficulty of attracting citizens arose from the popularity of competing associations:

> The organization of various national and philanthropic societies and associations, having strong claims upon the active sympathies and efforts of so many of our fellow citizens, it appears to be a difficulty with which this Institute has increasingly to contend. Even in respect to a class of entertainments which originated in this institution, and which, for a time, were so successful, and have been copied extensively by other institutions in the province, the various churches and benevolent societies have taken them up; and by the peculiar claims of sympathy presented to their members and the public, have rendered the success of lectures and reunions in this Institute almost impossible.[105]

Apparently the cultural offerings of competing associations created a very real problem for Mechanics' Institutes across Ontario, as many essays on the improvement of Mechanics' Institutes in the contest sponsored by the Association of Mechanics' Institutes mentioned the importance of recreation and leisure as a means of enhancing their value. John Davy, the secretary of the Toronto Institute, claimed that the only effective method of improving the Institutes would be to combine their educational work with social attractions. He noted that "the success of societies for amusement, such as singing, skating, curling and many others, notwithstanding their great cost when compared with Mechanics' Institutes and the many amusements now very properly provided in private families, all converge to one point; the necessity for relaxation to the overworked brain of man." In order to be competitive with other associations, Davy and others advocated that Institutes establish conversation and smoking rooms, recreation rooms with checkerboards, chessboards, and billiard tables, as well as gymnasia and facilities for archery and cricket.[106] And yet many of the essays also reflected a more middle-class vision of Institute leisure as a means of assisting young workers to avoid saloons, "low groggeries and other places of social degradation." J. Pennington Macpherson, a clerk from Ottawa, advocated building Institute gymnasia, for they would "not only harden the muscles and improve the physique of our young men [but] would prove the greatest enemy the tavern keepers could have." The Reverend John Butler of King's College in Toronto rejected the notion that smoking or billiard rooms in Mechanics' Institutes would further the aims of mutual improvement. He went even further, deriding paid lectures from such figures as circus entrepreneur P.T. Barnum; while such lectures were amusing, he conceded, they were "not in the least conducive to any intellectual improvement, or any moral benefit."[107]

The Toronto Mechanics' Institute closely followed many of the suggestions from the Association of Mechanics' Institutes for improving the entertainment portion of their mandate. Ironically, the shift of priorities from rational recreation such as lectures and recitations to games and other leisure activities is illustrated by the name change of the Lecture Committee to the Recreation Committee in 1876.[108] Initial forays by the Recreation Committee into the realm of entertainment meant setting up a recreation room with chess, checkers, quoits, and a billiard table. A major clash occurred in the recreation room between members who viewed billiards as "an innocent amusement when disassociated with gambling dens and saloons" and those who believed billiards interfered with the educational pursuits of the Toronto Mechanics' Institute. Even these debates, and their consequences, illustrated a class paradigm, as the 1876 annual report of the Institute recorded: "The large number of persons who have voluntarily expressed their readiness to become members, when the smoking, conversation and games room is established fully convince your Directors of the ultimate success of the Institute; they believe with many of our citizens, that it will afford a great and powerful counterattraction to the many places of public resort, which, unfortunately, do not tend to the moral or mental improvement of the large number of young men in the city."[109] Although in the short term the innovations brought about an increase in working class membership, two well-known directors of the Institute, Thomas Maclean and Matthew Sweetnam, resigned from the Board of Directors as a result of the changes to the Recreation Room. Both Maclean and Sweetnam couched their objections in class language, complaining that the Recreation Room committee made the "real use" of the Institute subservient to a "very common branch." Sweetnam also objected to the selfishness of "a few of the frequenters of the Recreation room, and their special friends" who banded together in setting aside the interests of the majority, who were more interested in the true educational objects of the Institute as opposed to the Billiard Tables.[110]

Even though the primacy of adult technical education in the Montreal Mechanics' Institute had been adopted by the *Conseil des Arts* in 1870 – an event that led to a brief re-examination of priorities within the executive – the Institute was healthy enough to open a branch of its operations at Point St Charles in 1887. Evidently the Montreal Institute was not immune to the debates about the need to expand its membership base in the community. By 1878 it had increased its attractiveness by introducing debating and literary societies, and a ladies' reading room, and by renting the Mechanics' Hall to other community organizations. Endeavours such as these allowed this Institute to peak at 907 members in 1889, well after other large urban Institutes had succumbed to the Free Library movement.[111] Emboldened by their success, however, the directors soon lost their focus as a community centre and began to compete with the free government night classes, drastically cutting the fees for the use of the reading room and their membership dues. Once it had abandoned its winning formula of constructing the Institute on the community centre model, the Montreal Mechanics' Institute quickly faded into oblivion. Its fall from grace indicates that competing with the free technical classes offered by the *Conseil des Arts* was a desperate measure that fell short. By 1897 the Institute had barely 500 members on its membership rolls.[112]

The "pursuit of knowledge under difficulties" is certainly an accurate statement of urban Mechanics' Institutes' aims in central Canada. Although Institute promoters made concerted efforts to assist the skilled working classes to further their educational undertakings, the Mechanics' Institute movement in many respects represented the hegemonic forces of the liberal social order. By mid-century, the preponderance of directors of the "middling sort" had ensured that Mechanics' Institutes as institutions were participating in the collective liberal project, their communications couched in a discourse that advanced the cause of economic and social progress through the education of an enlightened citizenry. Thus, the values of social and cultural "inclusion" in Mechanics' Institutes masked the engineering of consent to a liberal social order in political, rather than economic terms.

After mid-century, however, the relative dearth of industrial workers in urban Mechanics' Institutes exposed the socio-economic fissures inherent in the Institute system of education. Although class conflict was minimized through adherence to collective liberal values such as the ideology of classlessness and the absence of religious and political discord, class tensions became manifest as the industrial class only haphazardly utilized the recreation rooms and libraries of these institutions, or simply allowed their membership to lapse. Exposing the Janus face of the emerging industrial middle class rendered Mechanics' Institutes highly ineffective by the end of the century. Other associations, government agencies, and the Free Library movement took over the role of providing education, recreation, and literature for all classes and interests at the dawning of the twentieth century.

2

Small-Town Mechanics' Institutes

Even though rural Mechanics' Institutes were quite similar in scope to their urban counterparts, some significant points of comparison do arise. While urban Mechanics' Institutes catered to the needs of the emerging manufacturing and commercial liberal social order, Institutes in the rural countryside attempted to solidify an alliance between agricultural interests and the emerging entrepreneurial commercial class. Despite the Institute's success in creating a collective "liberal" identity in small towns, these organizations likewise endured some politico-religious dissent in the course of their operations. After mid-century, socio-economic relationships in rural areas became even more fluid and complex than in urban areas, given the fact that the agricultural community tended to interact more frequently with the professional, commercial, manufacturing, and skilled artisan classes than in the urban environment. As with urban Institutes, skilled workers largely ignored the Mechanics' Institutes and, along with agricultural labourers, continued to be marginalized to some degree by Institute directors. And yet the "community centre" ideal fostered by the Mechanics' Institute movement clearly struck a responsive chord in less inhabited regions, as the Association of Mechanics' Institutes in Ontario reported a strong increase in the chartering of rural Institutes in 1883, even after many of their urban counterparts had disappeared.[1] Mechanics' Institutes in the countryside therefore appear to have carved out a much stronger collective liberal "community" and a greater sense of cultural identity for small-town inhabitants in the nineteenth century.

What was unique about the rural Mechanics' Institute movement was the flexibility and rapidity with which they acclimatized to the central Canadian experience. Even as the directors of urban Mechanics' Institutes endeavoured to adapt their educational voluntary associations to the particular needs of a liberal commercial/mercantile social order, the agrarian social order in rural areas similarly used the Institutes as a means of safeguarding a small-town cultural authority founded on the primacy of agriculture. However, unlike the case with urban Mechanics' Institutes, in rural Institutes the class dissonance was not nearly as pronounced in the last three decades of the century. Evidently, the cultural authority of the emerging small-town middle class was stronger in the rural setting, contributing to the more lasting success of a collective liberal identity. The following chapter on Mechanics' Institutes lays a foundation for further study of rural associational life as it compares to that of urban voluntary societies. From rural temperance organizations and small-town literary and scientific institutions to agricultural societies, voluntary associations displayed a marked affinity for the "liberal" rural social order well into the twentieth century.

THE LIBERAL ETHOS OF "CLASSLESS" EDUCATION

Most of the rather limited historiography related to early to mid-nineteenth century Mechanics' Institutes examines the predominance of the "middling sort," concluding that an emerging bourgeois hegemony existed in small-town Mechanics' Halls. In Great Britain, rural Institutes did not even present formalized educational training, but offered informal tutoring and unsystematically formed mutual improvement societies. Rural Mechanics' Institutes in the colonies were far more organized in their offerings of subscription libraries, lectures, and night classes.[2] Although in rural areas the plight of the uneducated mechanic did not escape the attention of Mechanics' Institutes, initial efforts to provide educational opportunities to the operative classes appeared to mirror the rather disorganized British experience. In southern Ontario, both the Mitchell and the Paris Mechanics' Institutes, for instance, lacked sufficient funds to appoint qualified instructors, and therefore relied on loosely organized mutual instruction classes rather than formal tutoring. In 1858 the Elora Mechanics' Institute opened a mutual instruction class whereby members could present papers and essays to their colleagues and then discuss the subject brought forward, a strategy that would be more effective than a mere debating society, and was "likely to enlist more in the cause of mutual improvement than the class system." And yet Institutes such as the *Institut des Artisans* in the town of Laprairie just outside of Montreal ran highly successful educational classes for its operative population. The annual report of the *Institut* in 1854 readily testifies to the import of these night classes, as the membership figures tallied thirty mechanics out of a total membership of sixty-five. As a prerequisite for receiving government grants in Canada East was to have functioning night classes, the Laprairie *Institut*'s focus on educational endeavours for its skilled workers is also entirely understandable.[3]

Although their experiences with adult education and night classes accomplished mixed results, in other respects Mechanics' Institutes in small towns and villages functioned just as well as their urban counterparts. With the opening of reading rooms, the extension of the lecture system, and the launching of subscription libraries, rural Institutes strongly contributed to the pursuit of knowledge despite the lack of conventional forms of training. However, in cases where Mechanics' Institutes focused on only one of the above functions or operations, they were less successful. A good example is the Lakeshore Subscription library, an association that failed to combine all the salient features of a Mechanics' Institute. Their exclusive concentration on the subscription library put the organization in jeopardy. The board seldom met. The vice-president noted that he had "entirely forgotten" to attend an 1859 meeting of the executive. The recording secretary – the lone representative at another meeting a few years later – put the writing on the wall: "It is probable that had there been any thing of consequence to transact, such inattention would not have occurred; however, such carelessness is evidently culpable, since such a course, if persisted in, cannot but ultimately prove injurious to the success of the library." Even the leisure activities provided by the library were ineffectual, "since all proceeds of this kind go for church affairs." The society survived a few more years, but eventually relinquished its books to the local temperance society library.[4]

Despite making overtures to the liberal education of the operative classes, the directors of rural Mechanics' Institutes identified their constituents in categories, and the vast majority were not skilled workers. The economy of early to mid-nineteenth-century central Canada was highly agrarian, with pockets of manufacturing concentrated only in relatively few urban centres. A settled and stable class of independent farmers largely represented the "middling sort," while in small towns, self-employed tradespeople formed the backbone of the local economy. However the rural social order was composed, the heightened interaction among various classes, made it more fluid and complex than its urban counterpart.[5] Rural Mechanics' Institutes' success was based on their reliance on the same liberal ideology of class inclusiveness that urban Institutes employed. In advertising the library of the Niagara Mechanics' Institute, for instance, the executive claimed that the townspeople could discover a goodly number of volumes "complete with instruction and information for all classes." The Paris Mechanics' Institute went even further, declaring that the lectures and library of the Institute were for the benefit of all classes and interests in the local community. While the library contained a limited range of volumes, the executive of the Paris Institute believed that no interest or class in the village would go "empty away from this Emporium of Knowledge providing they are not over hard to please."[6]

As a result, rural Mechanics' Institutes were even more obsessed than their city counterparts with the notion of a liberal "community" and the need to eliminate exclusivity in the scope of their operations. James Dallas, in a lecture to the Orillia Mechanics' Institute, claimed that if local communities nurtured their Institutes, knowledge would permeate the entire nation: "You cannot raise the standard of education, of knowledge, of intelligence among such individuals, without powerfully affecting those with whom such members associate."[7] Appeals to the goodwill of the liberal voluntary community could, however, illustrate points of contention among directors of Mechanics' Institutes, particularly if townspeople failed to use the amenities of the institution. The plainly frustrated directors of the Paris Mechanics' Institute could not understand why community members so sparsely attended such a valuable institution of knowledge as theirs. In their fourth annual report, they noted that they were "exceedingly sorry to have the painful duty of recording the seeming indifference that prevails toward so useful an Institution." Summoning the last vestiges of civic pride from the town, the executive boldly exhorted its members: "All eyes are upon Paris; when they see or hear Paris people carry off the palm of victory from their neighbours at curling, cricketing and music, they actually think that seeing we excel so well at these, that the field of the mind will not be left a moral waste, overrun with the rank weeds of ignorance."[8]

Directors of Institutes recognized that appealing solely to skilled workers would be a grave mistake and made significant overtures to the agricultural population. In accordance with this sensibility, the Guelph, Streetsville, and Fergus Institutes were all named "Mechanics' and Farmers' Institutes" by their founders and directors in order to unite the disparate members of the rural community. The Fergus Farmers' and Mechanics' Institute went as far as to require that two-thirds of its management be either working mechanics *or* farmers, while the Guelph Farmers' and Mechanics' Institute trumpeted the fact that its library held volumes for the education and the benefit of both the "Artizan and the Agriculturalist."[9] Along with these expressions of liberal interclass benevolence, however, the interaction of the various classes in small-town Institutes could also exacerbate nascent occupational tensions. The executive committee of the Mitchell Mechanics' Institute called on the municipal council for financial assistance, reasoning that the council should "place the mechanical and manufacturing portion of the community in at least as favourable circumstances as the agricultural." Comparable yet reversed frustrations occurred in the Guelph Farmers' and Mechanics' Institute, where the directors often berated local farmers for not appreciating the town's efforts to provide liberal education for the agricultural population. Three years after the formation of the Institute in 1849, the directors bemoaned the fact that "so few of the agricultural population of the vicinity [had] yet availed themselves of mutual improvement to be derived at a very trifling share." In 1859 the directors removed the appellation "Farmers" from the official name of the Guelph Mechanics' Institute, in response to the apathy of the farmers of the town and its vicinity.[10]

Given the limited number of male participants in rural areas, women were made particularly welcome in the reading rooms of Mechanics' Institutes. Much of the recent literature regarding women and rural life concludes that social events in towns and villages did offer opportunities for women to gain prominence in the public sphere, as the shared nature of agricultural work entailed more mutual social activities.[11] Both the Orillia Mechanics' Institute and the Laprairie *Institut des Artisans* encouraged women to attend any public meeting of the Institute, quite often free of charge. The management of the Paris Mechanics' Institute' was initially inclined to allow women to join the reading room for free, but was compelled by strained financial circumstances to charge the ladies five shillings a year as members. Policies such as this allowed women to take the initiative and join rural Institutes in more respectable numbers than in urban Institutes. The Niagara Mechanics' Institute welcomed its first female member in 1852, and by 1856, 20 percent of its new members were women. Similarly, out of ninety-four members tallied in the Mitchell Institute in 1866, three local women were prominently featured. And yet, mirroring experiences in urban Institutes, early participation of women in rural Institutes was limited to indirect involvement rather than complete and active membership.[12]

POLITICO-RELIGIOUS DISSENT AS NEIGHBOURLY DISCORD

Rural Mechanics' Institutes also enforced a strict injunction against sectarianism and party politics, as these subjects could create as much *dishar-*

mony in the rural setting as they could in the urban environment. In the context of small villages and towns, where dependence on neighbourly benevolence was paramount, disagreements between religionists and political opponents could also ruin the progress of a local Mechanics' Institute.[13] The bylaws of virtually all mid-century Institutes reflected the need to keep partyism and "polemical divinity" out of their members' conversations. Both the Paris and the Owen Sound Mechanics' Institutes levied a fine of sixpence on perpetrators who introduced political or religious subjects in any debates occurring in the Institute; an offending member who dared to attempt further discussions of this nature, risked expulsion. The Paris Institute also went to the extreme of creating a library censorship committee to regulate political neutrality and ensure the promotion of non-sectarian Christianity. In 1858 the committee acted quickly to remove two issues of the *Westminster Review* for articles leaning toward infidelity. Although the Guelph and Ennotville Mechanics' Institutes proscribed religious and political controversies from their meetings, they also mandated that "all the instructions delivered, whether by lectures or classes, under [their] sanction ... be based on the direct recognition of the authority of Divine Revelation."[14]

Still other Mechanics' Institutes attempted to ensure conformity to the ideology of liberal respectability in their operations, as embedded in the discourse of the rural social order. The Owen Sound Mechanics' Institute threatened to fine, suspend, or expel any member who introduced sectarian and political discord or engaged in "immoral or improper language or conduct." The library committee of the Elora Mechanics' Institute outlawed political and religious discussions and also prohibited talking, smoking, and other "annoying habits" from the reading room. Not to be outdone, the executive of the Elora Institute disqualified any member "guilty of disorderly or criminal conduct."[15] John Ardagh, a local physician, taught the principle of religious and political toleration as a unifying force in the community before the Barrie Mechanics' Institute in 1858:

> Our very constitution prohibits the introduction and discussion of those subjects which most speedily enlist the passions and disturb the harmony of mutual intercourse. To my mind it constitutes no small recommendation that we here possess a neutral ground, on which men of all parties may contend without rancour and bear away palms which do not cost their opponents one embittered or unhallowed feeling. We have common subjects on which all may agree, without being taxed with any interested compromise of opinion, and concerning which

they may differ, without alteration in mutual feelings, or diminution of mutual esteem. A bond of fellowship is thus frequently formed between those whom circumstances would otherwise have kept for ever asunder; and if men come at all into collision, they are actuated by feelings of generous rivalry, not so closely interwoven with the absorbing interests of life as to arouse the meaner passions of jealousy.[16]

Removing sectarian and political turmoil from Mechanics' Institutes would not only benefit the social order but would also secure harmonious relations within a newly literate and liberal community in the rural countryside.

The experiences of the *Institut des Artisans* in the Laprairie and Drummond counties in Canada East are perfect examples of the need to accommodate all political and religious views in the local Mechanics' Institute. While the Laprairie *Institut* insisted that political subjects were forbidden, "défendu dans les salles de cette société," the directors required that all lectures, debates, and transactions occur in the French language. And yet this condition was tempered by the fact that the majority of members were in fact *Canadiens,* and English members were heartily welcomed.[17] In Drummond County, even though the *Institut des Artisans* had originated among the English-speaking community, its directors took steps to ensure the continued participation of French members. When a prominent French member – physician Dr Vallée – spoke in French, an English member objected that a member of the *Institut* ought not to address meetings in both languages. President J.B. Eric Dorion, the noted *Rouge* supporter, decided "there was nothing to prevent the same speaker from speaking in two, or more, languages on the same question," thereby sustaining the decision of the council with a vote of seven to five. This set the tone for future meetings of the *Institut,* as the executive committee was often made up of four English and four French members. Correspondingly, the minutes alternated between French and English according to the mother tongue of the secretary, and provisions were made to purchase fifty English and fifty French books to establish the *Institut* library. By 1861 the conduct of a "libéral" and ethnically sensitive directorate ensured a great deal of success among the French population, as members of French origin reached a high of 60 percent in the Drummond *Institut des Artisans*.[18]

Although the *Institut des Artisans* in Drummond County illustrated considerable unanimity in the function of its operations, the *Rouge* and the Reformer background of many of its members clearly influenced the political tone of their debates. The topics debated in the *Institut* more often than not reflected the liberal *Rouge* political position, particularly when the winning votes were tallied. The winners overwhelmingly preferred republican government, representation by population, secret balloting, annexation, non-sectarian schools, and the removal of property qualifications for the vote; and their true colours were revealed when members voted unanimously that L.J. Papineau was the greatest statesman of his time. The *Institut des Artisans* in Drummond County imitated the *Institut Canadien* in Montreal, both in political ideology and in debating style.[19] Many of the debate topics focused on local politics and institutional reform, signifying deference to the liberal social order. Favouring such local political positions as the establishment of a common school, a levied tax for the erection of the town hall, and a building for the *Institut*, as well as local enforcement of prohibition, members of the Drummond County *Institut des Artisans* evidently supported local governance and the apparatus of nascent liberal state formation. And yet *Institut* members also critiqued local political processes, as they debated the merits of the entire municipal system, and the difficulties of the local *crédit foncier* – and even squashed a motion to establish a volunteer militia company in the district. Members of the *Institut* also were quite specific in protesting the actions of the Durham city council for decisions they considered improper or erroneous.[20]

A similar regard for the liberal respectability of the middling sort was evident in the workings of the Barrie Debating Society, the forerunner of the Barrie Mechanics' Institute. Even though the directors often proscribed politically charged topics for debate, whether about capital punishment, the merits of the 1837 Rebellion, or the best means to achieve Canadian independence, maintaining decorum and order was obviously paramount to the executive. The bylaws of the society enshrined directives for the proper conduct of the debates: "No improper or obscene language, no swearing or other offensive conduct and no personal offensive remarks."[21] As with the *Rouge* element in the Drummond County *Institut des Artisans*, the members of the Barrie Debating Society were either Reformers or political radicals; they favoured universal suffrage, the secret ballot, and the secularization of the Clergy Reserves. However, problems developed when the society held a series of mock parliaments in which the debates focused squarely on Canadian party politics. In September of 1854, the Speaker in the mock Parliament rose and resolved: "That this House disapproves of the course taken by the ministry in regard to the measures to be introduced as stated in the eighth paragraph of the speech, vis. [sic] the bill relating to the Rebellion of '37 and the one on the Rebellion Losses Bill. These topics are in all cases to be avoided as likely to be productive of ill-feeling among members of this club and therefore the House would severely censure the course taken by the ministry in bringing them in." But by November, just as the new Speaker was revelling in his newly acquired power to "end the chaos in our meetings," his joy was curtailed. The debating society was disbanded and a new Mechanics' Institute was chartered a month later.[22]

New-world politico-religious controversies could also invade a rural Institute, as the Carleton Place Mechanics' Institute discovered in 1849. The president of the Carleton Place Institute, John Gemmill, was a stonemason from Glasgow, who also operated a small family farm in nearby Lanark County. Gemmill's roots in artisan self-improvement must have been difficult to break, as he attempted to form a committee to petition the government in Canada West to "place Mechanics' Institutes on the same footing as agricultural societies."[23] Even more disturbing to the members of the Carleton Place Mechanics' Institute was Gemmill's attitude when the Governor-General, Lord Elgin, agreed to become the patron of the Institute. Apparently Gemmill's radical politics were exposed when he wrote asking the Civil Secretary to dismiss the "appointment" of Elgin as patron of the Institute: "As President of the Carleton Place Library Association and Mechanics' Institute, I have the honour to enclose your favour of 30 November and beg that you will inform His Excellency that a society of Scotchmen can exist without patronage." Appalled that one of their directors, "so-called loyal members of the Crown," would be so insulting, the other executive members summarily expelled Gemmill: "By such improper conduct has made himself wholly unworthy of remaining a member of this society constituted for the express purpose of improving the intellectual and moral condition of the community." This sectarian episode definitely affected the members of the Institute, for a few months later the Carleton Place Mechanics' Institute was disbanded.[24]

The collective liberal gospel of honest industry was preached in the halls of rural Mechanics' Institutes as vigorously as it was in urban settings. The value of honest industry was a theme that pervaded lectures and debates in Mechanics' Institutes as Institute members deliberated principles of political economy among themselves. Even though these Institutes were often a far distance from manufacturing centres, there was a fairly strong correlation between the promotion of honest industry and the need to boost the economic advantages of a village or town.[25] From the outset, the political economy of honest labour was a critical philosophy for rural inhabitants. Many lecturers maintained that liberal educational self-improvement among the citizenry was a sure recipe for economic progress. In a lecture to the Hemmingford Mechanics' Institute, the Anglican churchman Francis Fulford counselled members that the honest labour of individual effort contributed to the achievements of the rural community as a whole:

> But with regard to labour, what I want to point out to you is, that every man's labour belongs to the community, because as the community is befitted by the general wealth, they have by the same rule an equal interest in that which produces the wealth, viz., labour. So by the same showing society are losers when labour is misapplied ... But there is one great fact which should be ever present in our minds, that in whatever way we may apply our labour, unless we are actuated by a strict principle of honour and integrity, we can never hope to see our operation successful. And as with the wealth so with the character of nations, it of necessity takes its tone from individuals.[26]

Reliance on this type of resilient work ethic would lead not only to economic wealth but also to a more liberal and more interdependent community.

Lecturers addressing Mechanics' Institutes outlined the importance of commercial, manufacturing, and agricultural sectors, working together in the producer alliance for the prosperity of the community at large. William Merritt, in his lecture to the St Catharines Mechanics' Institute, rather bluntly stated that the petty jealousies and rivalries existing between Quebec, Montreal, and Toronto ruined trade. In the opinion of this Reformer and rising commercial baron, if the competing commercial interests in Canada could unite in one common effort, the country would surpass the United States in prosperity. A united endeavour of this sort would benefit every class in society; the farmer and manufacturer would enjoy cheaper transport rates and the merchant would be able to seek a larger market for his goods. In spite of the prohibition of political discussion in the Institute, such a proponent of free trade as Merritt could not resist stating that reciprocity would place the manufacturing and commercial sector on the same footing as their flourishing American rivals. On the other hand, visiting lecturer Francis Fulford, in his speech to the Hemmingford Institute, recognized his farming constituency in particular when he asserted that all classes of society should focus on the improvement of agriculture: "The interests of the manufacturer and the farmer are not conflicting, but ... they are mutually interested in developing their respective trades; for it is only by bringing about a higher state of farming that we can hope to see machinery more generally used in cultivation."[27]

RECREATION AND RURAL COMMUNITIES

The importance of Mechanics' Institutes as community centres in small villages and towns cannot be underestimated. Unlike their urban counterparts, the most profitable and flourishing rural Institutes were those that went beyond the basic class, library, and lecture system of operation. While amusements did not guarantee success for individual Institutes, through their community-building activities they did provide unity and identity for rural villages.[28]

As long as the received limited grants from government funds, Mechanics' Institutes were able to function fairly well with the lecture, class, and library configuration. The Paris Mechanics' Institute found itself in such a prosperous condition through the government grant and lecture system that it was able to build a Mechanics' Hall in 1858. Less than a year later, however, the government in Canada West rescinded the grant, and the directors strained to restore the missing income. A series of canvassing drives, town concerts, and a mechanics' festival were soon suggested as ways to help ease the Institute's financial burdens. Unfortunately, due to the "unrivalled depression, [a]ffecting equally the mercantile and operative portions of the community," these plans went awry and the hall was soon sold.[29] The Niagara and the Mitchell Mechanics' Institutes also suffered from the loss of the grant and struggled to find alternative funding. Initially the efforts of both institute directors were rather meagre attempts to shore up a flagging membership base, with canvassing drives, the solicitation of former members, and the raising of membership fees. The directors of the Mitchell Institute half-heartedly gave their approval to a series of concerts, but since these performances reflected the attitude of the executive they were dismally attended by the citizens of Mitchell. The Institute continued its precarious existence, with the directors debating almost every year whether to shut the doors of the reading room.[30]

While the success or failure of rural Institutes did not entirely depend on recreation, a comparison between the Elora and the Fergus Mechanics' Institutes illustrates that entertainment in the Institutes could ensure some measure of longevity. The Elora Mechanics' Institute enjoyed considerable success, primarily thanks to the willingness of the people of Elora to embrace educational self-improvement and to the leadership of such men as David Boyle and Charles Clarke. The directors of this Institute were also more creative than most in promoting rational recreation; they organized a debating society, reunions, a Shakespeare festival, and a *conversazione*.

This philosophy allowed their Institute to remain in operation long after many other Mechanics' Institutes had closed their doors.[31] Just down the road in Fergus, the opposite approach was taken, with very different results for the population of that town. Even when under financial stress, the directors of the Fergus Institute did not shift their priorities toward entertainment so as to provide the community with much-needed recreation or to employ cultural events as revenue-generating ventures. When the board of directors staged a concert for the Queen's birthday, large numbers of townspeople enthusiastically attended. When a member of the executive desired to present another concert during the year, however, the other members of the board rather condescendingly responded: "The committee think it derogatory to the respectable standing of a Mechanics' Institute, to aid its funds by a second concert within twelve months." Consequently, the next mention of a soirée to assist the treasury of the Institute occurred only four years later, a delay that caused much pecuniary hardship to the executive when the grants were removed.[32]

Mechanics' Institutes in rural areas also endeavoured to ensure respectability in the function of their leisure activities. The Mitchell Institute endured several "acts of annoyance" and interruptions during lectures and debates in the early 1860s. These disturbances would lead to a statement from the board of directors, regretting that "personal remarks derogatory to any of the officers or members of the Mechanics' Institute should at any time have been made by either Officers or Lecturer, and [resolving] that for the future the presiding chairman will be expected to put an immediate stop to any proceeding of this kind at any Public meeting or lecture." Evidently one of the reasons for the rowdiness of the crowd came from the fact that "competent lecturers [were] not easily obtained" in Mitchell and the majority of lectures offered to the Institute were given by local clergymen. As a result, the executive of the Mitchell Institute called upon the Board of Arts and Manufactures to furnish them with written lectures, already prepared for presentation.[33] In the Niagara Mechanics' Institute, the younger members apparently caused the most distress as the directors attempted to place the Institute upon a liberal and "a proper footing." During a lecture on Electric Magnetism in December of 1855, the local sheriff had to quiet the disturbance in the Mechanics' Hall. It was recorded that "the assembly was then addressed by Sheriff Kingsmill on the impropriety of the Boys making a noise in the Hall when the Lecture was being delivered [and] his remarks were very appropriate and praiseworthy."[34]

THE RURAL MIDDLE CLASS, CIVIC INTEGRATION, AND RELATIONS WITH THE STATE

From the late 1860s to the end of the century, while urban Mechanics' Institutes either succumbed to the Free Library movement or limped along in a less than flourishing condition, their rural counterparts remained impressively strong. Often one of few resources available to offer adult education, a subscription library, and a community centre, a local Mechanics' Institute served many interests in a town or village. However, as recent studies indicate, they largely benefitted the emergent rural middle class, made up of self-employed businessmen, stable and settled farmers, storekeepers, and rural professionals. The ideology of liberal self-improvement, education, and a collective cultural identity struck a receptive chord in the rural social order even during the last three decades of the century.[35] Although Mechanics' Institutes continued to preach the values of liberal class inclusion, religious and political neutrality, and honest industry, it became evident that Institutes favoured the formation of a strong rural middle class. And it is interesting that the class diversity observable in Mechanics' Institute movement in the rural countryside exemplified a social order more adept at collective liberal consensus than its urban counterparts.

One of the obvious dissimilarities between rural and urban Mechanics' Institutes in the latter stages of the nineteenth century was their disparate relationships with the incipient industrial state. While urban Institutes enjoyed the ongoing support of the Board of Arts and Manufactures in Canada West/Ontario and the *Conseil des Arts* in Canada East/Quebec, rural Institutes did not experience such luxury. While the *Conseil* remained fairly consistent – if somewhat economical – with its grants to the *Institut des Artisans*, the government in Canada West had by 1859 committed itself to a course of financial retrenchment and discontinued government grants to Mechanics' Institutes. This "mistaken economy" was of such grave concern to the directors of the Guelph Farmers' and Mechanics' Institute that they entered this cutting statement into the 1860 annual report:

> The Committee of the Guelph Farmers' and Mechanics' Institute ... would express their feelings of congratulation in view of its highly prosperous and successful condition notwithstanding the apathy of a portion of the public in giving it practical continuance of support and the continued deprivation of the grant so judiciously bestowed in former years by Parliament; but withdrawn, your Committee would venture to

say, though a highly erroneous idea that "retrenchment" so called, in every branch of Public Expenditure or appropriation, regardless of the merits or wants of any almoner of the public purse, while winning vulgar popularity, was therefore unobjectionable and praiseworthy.

This discourse was couched, however, in the language of the liberal rural social order. The directors of the Guelph Mechanics' Institute went on to say: "The experience and readings of every true statesman must produce the conviction that to promote scientific enquiry, diffuse useful knowledge and encourage literary taste, the whole being based on a sound moral foundation, [is] to render a people happy and distinguished – whilst to cripple and retard efforts and objects of this character is calculated to delay their advancement in the scale of nations."[36] But petitions such as this fell on deaf ears in the legislature, and Mechanics' Institutes suffered much financial hardship as they struggled to replace the withdrawn revenue.

With the creation of the Association of Mechanics' Institutes in Ontario in 1869, a new relationship developed between rural Mechanics' Institutes and the liberal industrial state, which led to government grants for Institutes being restored by legislation. Although the chartering of new Mechanics' Institutes did in fact marginally increase as a result, however, the functionality of Institutes – principally in the realms of adult education for the skilled working classes – did not immediately improve. The Reverend Walter Inglis praised the labours of the Kincardine Mechanics' Institute in making it "no longer permitted or satisfactory to pick out a few sons of genius and educate them, leaving the dull mass alone." Unfortunately, Inglis's rhetoric was stronger than the ability of the Institute's directors to bring adult education to the operatives of Kincardine, as it took nearly a decade to get evening classes started in the Kincardine Mechanics' Institute.[37]

With the incorporation of the Peterborough Mechanics' Institute in 1868, the directors attempted to establish functioning evening classes by offering subjects such as mathematics, geometrical drawing, English, and practical Mechanics. However, subsequent annual reports reveal a litany of difficulties with the evening classes, from exorbitant fees and a lack of competent teachers to a deficiency in students and particularly a lack of interest from the Peterborough community. By 1878 the problems were so acute that the board of directors sent the president to a meeting of the Association of Mechanics' Institutes with the intent of securing more financial assistance. W.H. Trout, a member of the board, expressed the view that the advertised practical benefits of the Institute required both the revenue and the liberal support of the state: "We are now passing through a period that tries every institution in our country; now is the time to find easily the weak places and strengthen them; and plans for further advancement are not so likely to be impractical and visionary in these days when our minds are held so closely down to the mighty dollar."[38]

When Mechanics' Institutes came under the aegis of the Agriculture and Arts Association of Ontario and the Education Department in 1881, stronger bonds of association were formed between Institutes and the apparatus of industrial state formation. The Education Department made a more concerted effort to foster adult education in all Mechanics' Institutes in Ontario by offering grants based on the existence of functioning evening classes. Adam Crooks, the Minister for Education, in his introduction to a special report on Mechanics' Institutes, noted that the majority of Institutes were still in rural areas, and thus proved to be less effective in the education of the skilled operative classes. Employing the discourse of liberal class inclusion, Crooks stated that these classes could still be constructive, if the sons of farmers and others were given "opportunities for obtaining such practical knowledge of agriculture, chemistry and mechanics as would enable them to better understand the properties and capabilities of the soil and improved modes of cultivation." Even a staunch opponent of the report, Otto Klotz, recognized that while the night classes were crucial to the success of Mechanics' Institutes in general, villages were simply ill- equipped to handle the assignment because of a limited and roving population.[39]

What occurred as a result of this new grant system and subsequent attempts to bind Institutes to the liberal industrial state were rather cynical and half-hearted efforts to create night classes for very limited numbers of rural skilled workers. Many Institutes replicated the experience of the Kincardine Mechanics' Institute, an association that in fact had little interest in setting up night classes despite the attractiveness of the government grants. When the directors realized in 1881 that the grant was dependent on providing adult education, in a surge of ambitious energy, they established evening classes in such subjects as bookkeeping, spelling, composition, writing, math, and practical geometry. However, a scant six months later the classes were discontinued on account of "poor attendance."[40] A comparable experience occurred in the Ingersoll Mechanics' Institute, and in 1881 the directors petitioned the Ontario government to allow them to spend the entire grant on the library rather than on night classes. This request was apparently turned down, for the next year the Ingersoll Institute instituted a drawing class for the artisans of the town. Justifying their concentration on only one drawing class in the name of liberal industrial progress, the Ingersoll directors boasted that "in addition to many others, a considerable number of artisans availed themselves of the opportunity to obtain a knowledge of drawing, and acquired the use of the pencil skill that must be of great benefit to them in their various trades."[41]

A great example of this administrative shift in educational priorities can be found in the Elora Mechanics' Institute. In the 1870s the Elora Institute structured its night classes along more "proper" lines, introducing lessons in English, math, and bookkeeping. Financial difficulties put the scheme on hold for some years, and when the classes did begin, poor attendance forced the directors to enlist the aid of several ministers to extol the virtues of the Institute from their pulpits.[42] In focusing solely on the operation of the Institute library, the directors of the Elora Institute did not concern themselves with adult education again until a Dr May personally visited the Institute on a lecture tour in 1881. In the 1882 annual report the directors noted that these endeavours were obviously unappreciated by artisans in Elora, as only one youth in the entire community put himself forward to join the classes. And yet the Institute administrators did manage to add that the library was available to all, for "amusement and useful instruction." Elora's encounter with adult education would soon come full circle. In 1884, in the face of the complete failure of its night classes, the administrators called for the creation of a literary club or circle, whose object would be the educational improvement of its members through mutual instruction.[43]

Despite such impediments to launching evening classes, chartered Mechanics' Institutes in somewhat larger manufacturing towns did manage to achieve some success in their educational endeavours, as executives began to focus on more liberal middle-class values such as self-improvement, respectability, and upward mobility. In 1886 the Peterborough Mechanics' Institute held a series of successful drawing and mechanical classes, and fifteen of the sixteen students enrolled, came from the skilled working class. Although these workers attended the courses of their own volition, the Institute's program of evening classes undoubtedly reflected the needs of that emerging industrial town. In advertising the courses, the directors of the Peterborough Institute deployed the motto of upward mobility, "Learn More to Earn More," claiming: "No mechanic need stay away from the class because of his lack of education, as the classes are for the purpose of assisting those who desire to better themselves."[44] Similarly, the Napanee Mechanics' Institute expressed "surprise and regret" that mechanics and others did not avail themselves of the advantage it offered, particularly since "Napanee [was] rapidly becoming a manufacturing centre with its Glass Works and Brush Factory and the Institute [might] become extremely useful to the largely increasing artisan class." And yet their program was unmistakably a liberal middle-class enterprise; the "gentlemen comprising the Board of Management represent some of the best element in town." It appears that the Napanee Mechanics' Institute suffered the same fate as urban Institutes, for when their skilled workers recognized the hegemony of the commercial and manufacturing classes employed in the operation of the Institute they stayed away in droves.[45]

Although Mechanics' Institutes did *attempt* to offer educational opportunities for artisans and the skilled working classes, Institutes came increasingly to be operated by, and for, the rural middle classes. The files of newly created Mechanics' Institutes created by the Ontario Ministry of Education reveal a decisive pattern of middle-class participation in rural Institutes. These statistics show the diversity of the rural social order, as middle-class farmers and manufacturers, commercial representatives, and professionals worked side by side in small-town Institutes. They also support the contention that these Mechanics' Institutes represented a considerable impetus for middle-class formation. As with the urban situation in the second half of the century, the low participation of the skilled working classes was also a fact of life for rural Institutes (see Table 2.1).[46] Consequently, the rhetoric of liberal class inclusion preached by small-town Mechanics' Institutes concealed the authority of the middle classes in Mechanics' Halls. The preponderance of storekeepers, commercial retailers, and clerks among the members of small-town Mechanics' Institutes necessitated a subtle shift toward "commercial education" in rural Institutes. The directors of the Barrie, Niagara, and Collingwood Mechanics' Institutes expressed the belief that a "commercial class" teaching general business education was "far more practical," while the Guelph Institute tried to provide both commercial *and* manufacturing education for its members.[47]

Even up to the turn of the century, small-town Mechanics' Institutes initiated programs that would promote a sense of liberal civic integration. Class inclusiveness, coupled with an intellectual boosterism also encouraged discussion on the merits of changing the name of the Institutes. The Clinton Mechanics' Institute claimed that the appellation of "Mechanics' Institute" was not "sufficiently comprehensive, and [was] to some extent misleading" and thus changed their name to a Public Institute, hoping to illustrate that the "benefits of the public Library, Reading Room, Evening Classes and Museum [were] open to all persons on reasonable terms." Similarly, the 1886 annual report of the Orillia Mechanics' Institute appealed to its members' sense of the importance of civil integration:"It is your Institute; and the advantages it has brought to you, might be enjoyed by every-

Table 2.1
Occupations of Petitioners to Establish Mechanics' Institutes in Rural Ontario Towns, 1887–91

Occupation	Total	Percentage	Occupation	Total	Percentage
Blacksmith	15		Merchant	121	
Butcher	12		Agent	18	
Carriage maker	10		Hotel keeper	11	
Shoe maker	10		Druggist/Chemist	10	
Carpenter	9		Manufacturer	7	
Builder	9		Publisher	6	
Labourer	9		Banker	5	
Harness maker	7		Jeweller	5	
Tailor	6		Others++	25	
Others*	62		TOTAL BUSINESS	208	31
TOTAL SKILLED	149	22.5	Teacher	33	
Clerk	41		Doctor	27	
Bookkeeper	9		Clergy	17	
Postmaster	8		Barrister	10	
Others+	11		Student	9	
Total Clerical	69	10	Others+++	7	
Gentleman	16		TOTAL PROFESSIONAL	103	15
TOTAL PRIVATE MEANS	16	2.5	Farmers	82	
			Miller	11	
			Others^	17	
TOTAL WOMEN ^^	15	2.5	TOTAL AGRICULTURAL	110	16.5

NOTES: The petitioners of the Camden East, Baden, Cornwall, Dundalk, Highland Creek, Fronthill, Eastner, Alliston, Bothwell, Erin, Glen Morris, Highgate, Grand Valley, North Gower, Oil Springs, Pickering, Russell, Shedden, Sparta, Thamesville, Thessalon, Tisbury, Tilsbury East, Liverton, Tweed, Victoria, Walpole, and Woodville Mechanics' Institutes. Many of the Institutes not chosen for this sample had either unreadable listed occupations or simply did not include them in the petition to the Ministry of Education.
* Other occupations in the skilled category include: wagon maker, joiner, steam fitter, baker, bricklayer, cook, printer, baggage man, barber, cooper, saw maker, mason, undertaker, tinsmith, saddler, surveyor, founder, mechanic, seaman, machinist, telegraph operator, cabinet maker, oil operator, plasterer, watchmaker, cutter, conductor, carter, foreman, lumberman, operator, and milkman.
+ Other occupations in the clerical category include: newsman, bailiff, policeman, commissioner, traveller, notary, salesman, scribe, and registrar.
++ Other occupations in the business category include: manager, grocer, clothier, confectioner, contractor, and dealer.
+++ Other occupations in the professional category include: editor, engineer, and dentist.
^ Other occupations in the agricultural category include: farmers' son, flax dresser, starch maker, livery, stockbreeder, teamster, gardener, and cheese maker.
^^ Women's "occupations" included: married, young woman, spinster, wife, music teacher, seamstress, and housekeeper.
SOURCE: Ministry of Education files, AO, MS 5635, RG 2-42-0-2313 TO RG 2-42-0-2366.

one without any diminution of your own personal pleasure ... [It is incumbent on us] to place our beloved Institute on a more solid basis, that it may better fulfill the great object ... the elevation of that important class composing the workers in the great hive of humanity."[48] Larger manufacturing towns such as Peterborough lauded their Mechanics' Institute as a "counterpoise to the many places of resort, which are always to be found in every town, not calculated, to say the least of them, to elevate the mind or improve the body." In promoting the virtues of the liberal industrial state, the directors called on the larger community in Peterborough to maintain the Institute, and requested "the united and cordial support of all Christians and lovers of their country, in order that it may, under the blessing of an all-wise Providence, be the means of building up [in] our good town, an intelligent, sober and industrious class of people."[49]

The *Institut des Artisans* in rural Quebec also underwent significant change in the function of its operations, reflecting a transfer of support from the operative to the middle classes analagous to that of Mechanics' Institutes in Ontario. By the 1880s the Laprairie *Institut des Artisans* had transformed its institution into a *cercle littéraire* along the lines of the *Institut Canadien*, by applying the title *Société Littéraire de Laprairie* to their organization. While it is somewhat difficult to ascertain the actual membership of the *Société*, its appeal to the rural professional classes was manifest in their reports on the activities of the Montreal Natural History Society and the Ottawa Literary and Scientific Society.[50] The Drummond County *Institut des Artisans* also adjusted quickly to the needs of its occupational and ethnic constituency when the circumstances warranted. After the *Institut* was reorganized in 1878, the representation of the French element in Drummond County increased to a high of 73 percent in three years. By 1881 the agricultural middle classes had basically taken over the reins of the *Institut*; membership records indicate that a full 80 percent of the members were farmers, agricultural labourers, or journalists for agricultural periodicals. It comes as no surprise that in 1880 the *Institut* promoted several lectures on agricultural subjects and was renamed L'Association littéraire et agricole." However, the artisan population in Drummond County did not submit quietly to this usurpation of their rights by the agrarian middle-class. *Institut* members some months later called a public meeting "to consult a lawyer to defend the cause of the Institute, with the intent of depriving the artisans of their property."[51]

The provision of debates and the establishment of literary and debating societies in concert with Mechanics' Institutes also reflected the development of a rural middle class. When the Napanee Mechanics' Institute introduced debates as part of their curriculum in the late 1870s, they were ostensibly open to all members of the town on an equal basis. And yet inherent in this discourse of liberal class inclusion was an unspoken expectation that the future municipal leaders of Napanee would come from the commercial middle classes:

> Whereas many intelligent and well informed men are often in public meetings unable to express their views on important subjects and from their ignorance in conducting public business are often put to great inconvenience, and often public business suffers in consequence. Therefore be it resolved that the members of this association use every effort to try while attending the meetings to so fit themselves by taking part in debates, and observe how business is conducted and try in every possible way so to improve ourselves both in knowledge of public affairs generally and publickly expressing our views that if ever we are called upon to fill places of trust we can do so with credit to ourselves.

The middle-class majority in the Napanee Mechanics' Institute certainly came from the commercial and business sector. The Institute debated such topics as "Trades Unions are injurious to the Country and to the members themselves" and "The Credit system of doing business adopted by business men generally in this country is advantageous for the larger part of the community."[52] In some of the larger towns, the professional middle classes also participated in Mechanics' Institute debating activities. In 1880 members of the Peterborough Mechanics' Institute tried to establish a literary and scientific circle along the lines of the town's more famous Fortnightly Club, in order to study such subjects as botany, chemistry, and mineralogy. And an alliance with sundry professional middle classes was solidified in 1884, when the directors of the Peterborough Mechanics' Institute were made honorary members of the nearby Dufferin Literary Society.[53]

Although Mechanics' Institutes remained receptive to all classes and interests on terms of perfect equality, Institute directors often imposed middle-class standards of respectability and decorum in small-town libraries and reading rooms. Both the Peterborough and Orillia reading rooms banned smoking and loud talking in their precincts, requiring their patrons to observe "strict order and decorum." The Orillia Institute even went to the lengths of of disallowing "the juvenile element" from enjoying the reading room, as they not only defaced walls, books and newspapers but were "generally destructive and ill-behaved." Unfortunately, some patrons nevertheless defied the cultural authority of the reading room committee, as the committee noted a year later, "a petty pilfering of some of the smaller illustrated papers." Their response was well considered: "Your directors hope that the thief will be ashamed of such conduct or that he will be brought sooner or later to punishment."[54] Concerns over the regulation of libraries in rural Institutes also spilled over into judgment about exactly *what* materials patrons were perusing in the reading rooms. In 1883 the managing executive of the Peterborough Mechanics' Institute appeared somewhat apprehensive about the amount of fiction available on the shelves of the Institute library. In response to queries as to why the board purchased so many fictional works, the library committee retorted: "It is simply to retain the membership! While the taste of the public calls for fiction, it must be supplied or we should lose our members." And yet the directors consoled themselves over their choice of this course of action, claiming that any youth reading fictional literature "for the story" soon acquired a taste for reading and a "liberal" thirst for knowledge.[55]

INCREASED ROLES FOR WOMEN IN RURAL INSTITUTES

Female participation in small-town Mechanics' Institutes had grown by the end of the nineteenth century, and many of the Institutes realized that the inclusion of women members would entail extensive changes. Despite the inadequacy of available space, the directors in Elora and Peterborough were willing to experiment with setting up ladies' reading rooms to increase membership and support. The Orillia Mechanics' Institute envisioned the possibility that a strict observance of the rules of courtesy might permit lady members to co-operatively enjoy the benefits of association in the reading room of the Mechanics' Institute as they could in other Institutes:

> Your committee[,] still anxious for further improvement, would request that the Board prohibit smoking and loud talking during reading hours [for] as long as the reading room laws are being trampled with impunity, we cannot expect the attendance of lady members in the evenings. This your committee much regret, and consider it a serious loss to the growth and prosperity of the Institute. It is usual in other Institute towns to see ladies and gentlemen members reading together and discuss literary and other questions of the day. We were much pleased to notice this in other towns, and regret that ... Orillia should be an exception. Moreover, the influence which the presence of ladies exert[s], and the deference paid them by gentlemen, we would

think, place our Institute on a much higher plane, and relieve it of the monotony which now exists.[56]

When the Ingersoll Mechanics' Institute experienced financial hardship in maintaining their reading room, the local chapter of the Women's Christian Temperate Union (WCTU) stepped in and offered to match the Institute dollar for dollar on books for the library. The only thing the WCTU asked in return was that reading material on "Temperance, Heredity and Hygiene" be placed in the Institute library. This partnership proved so successful in Ingersoll that the two parties jointly established a recreation room in the Mechanics' Hall. The more middle-class WCTU's influence on the Institute was clearly a lasting one, as a posting in the amusement room read: "The following practices are strictly prohibited; betting, gambling, profanity, smoking, spitting, whistling, boisterous, noisy or improper conduct of any kind."[57]

Women's participation in Mechanics' Institutes rose in direct proportion to the administrative success they achieved through the rather limited roles they were offered. In the Guelph Mechanics' Institute, female participation was low until 1878, when the women of the town were asked to hold a strawberry festival to raise funds. The resulting net gain of $140 to the coffers of the Guelph Institute was entirely welcome, as the Institute's financial situation was so precarious that it had suspended payments to its creditors. When the strawberry festival committee – composed entirely of women – met with the directors of the Guelph Institute, the board suggested that "besides the appointment of officers and directors ... a few ladies be appointed Patronesses of the Institute."[58] In June of 1884, the Barrie Mechanics' Institute altered its bylaws to allocate four positions in the board of management to female members. The reasons for this change become apparent in the 1883 annual report; the female-dominated Philharmonic Class had helped the Institute with its fundraising entertainments to the tune of $800. Similarly, women in the Niagara Mechanics' Institute did not hold prominent positions until 1880, when the board of directors appointed a ladies' subscription committee to solicit members for the Institute. Evidently the women were very successful, as shortly thereafter a Miss Cavansham was elected general secretary of the Niagara Mechanics' Institute – with a paid salary – along with three other female officers, including the president of the entertainment committee.[59]

Several small-town Mechanics' Institutes followed the advice given by Dr May in his report on the Institutes and appointed young single women as librarians and custodians of the library. By 1895 the Orillia, Orangeville,

Drayton, Niagara, and Peterborough Mechanics' Institutes had all hired female librarians to operate their reading rooms. For the most part, directors were fairly pleased with their female employees. Miss Boise of the Orillia Institute was praised as "an expert librarian and courteous official." The Peterborough Institute was even more generous with accolades for its librarian, Miss Shaw, who had "made herself popular with all, by her zeal and attention to the interests of the Institute and her uniformly polite and obliging manner to all members."[60] In the fourth annual report of the Peterborough Institute in 1872, the directors registered a concern: "Lady readers have complained that many of the Books added have been of a class of reading for which they care little." The rather blunt response was that government grants were dependent on the purchase of scientific works for the education of the skilled working classes, and not novels for female members. However, by the 1880s this touch of condescension had mellowed out considerably. The managers of the Institute had discovered that the general public – and not only women – became members when the library shelves were stocked with novels.[61]

Even though the participation of women in Mechanics' Institutes increased, a domestic ideology was still reinforced in small-town Mechanics' Halls. Women were permitted to join evening classes, but the Barrie and Elora Mechanics' Institutes also arranged for female teachers to come and tutor students in the Institute. However, these female instructors only taught the more "womanly pursuits" such as Music and Free Drawing classes.[62] The directors of the Peterborough Mechanics' Institute encouraged young women to join classes, as they viewed the evening classes as a "powerful auxiliary" to the provincial school system. The board members of the Peterborough Mechanics' Institute also focused on the education of the "mechanics' wife," although the instruction offered served to buttress male patriarchy through an emphasis on the domestic ideology. In the opinion of board member W.H. Trout, the "importance of her education for her duties and position which are both onerous and responsible is hardly secondary to that of her partner. The mechanic's wife is to a great extent the businessman for the family; she deserves a good rudimentary business education, a thing which would never be amiss but often wonderfully helpful in every man's wife. So we should certainly provide for our girls and young women a good English and business education."[63]

A perfect example of this dichotomy involved in sanctioning higher levels of female participation and reinforcing the liberal ideology of domesticity is found in the auxiliary organization to the Barrie Mechanics' Institute, the Barrie Literary Society. In the early 1880s the organization discussed at length whether to admit females to their society. The directors decided to form a committee to "secure the attendance of as many ladies as might be conveniently be persuaded to come." According to the management of the society, the biggest drawback to inviting female members was the absence of the "normal" male members when several women of the town did come to the meeting. Perhaps the presence of women was fairly dispensable to the society, as the very next debate held by the society was on the subject of women's mental inferiority to men, in the course of which it was concluded that women were decidedly less intelligent.[64] A short while later the society held a debate on whether women should receive the electoral franchise. Only male members participated in the debate, in which one member argued – utilizing a liberal discourse of domesticity – that women should receive the vote on the basis that their "presence at election contests would banish all the rougher features which at present characterize them." James Hunter, a later president of the Mechanics' Institute and an admirer of noted liberal Goldwin Smith, pointed out that men and women were designed to occupy separate spheres and such a change would destroy the sacredness apparent in Canadian homes. Hunter concluded that "women would necessarily be placed in opposition to men and consequently all the deference and respect paid to them would forever vanish. [Furthermore] enfranchisement of women shouldered them with responsibilities and duties which they were not able to endure." Hunter won this particular debate with these arguments, but in 1893 an identical debate decided in favour of allowing women the vote, thereby presaging the coming changes in Canadian society.[65]

POLITICO-RELIGIOUS TOLERANCE, THE PRODUCER IDEOLOGY, AND MIDDLE-CLASS RESPECTABILITY

Not only did rural Mechanics' Institutes maintain the same liberal standards in outlawing party politics and sectarianism from their institutions as they had done in previous decades but they also attempted to monitor controversies in their reading rooms, debates, and other Institute functions. The Claude Mechanics' Institute apparently borrowed its bylaws from the Guelph Institute, insisting that no religious or political controversies be introduced; yet "all instruction shall be based on the distinct recognition of the authority of Divine Revelation."[66] Although the Kincardine Mechanics' Institute ostensibly discouraged sectarian conflict, it allowed debates on such questions as "Does Science induce Scepticism?" and "Is the Intellectual Development of the World more due to Religion than Science?"

The domination of local clergy over the Kincardine Institute would result in a strong "victory" of the Christian religion over science. Similarly, the cultural authority of the clergy was guaranteed in the library by the board's decision to allow clergymen of the Institute "to ballot for books by proxy; such proxies to have equal privileges with the members present." However, the directors of the Elora Mechanics' Institute did not always enjoy such favourable relations with local clergymen. They had a running battle with the Reverend James Middlemass in the pages of the *Elora Express* in the winter of 1883 over what the good reverend considered to be scandalous material in the library of the Institute. Of course the Elora Institute was duty-bound to restore honour and place in the community by forcefully contradicting the clergyman's allegations.[67]

Small-town Mechanics' Institutes also resembled their urban counterparts when it came to allowing significantly more freedom of expression in political and religious debates in the late nineteenth century. Many debates resembled those in the early Drummond County *Institut des Artisans* and the Barrie Mechanics' Institute, where topics of local interest were paramount. In the Kincardine Mechanics' Institute, members deliberated the feasibility of building a harbour and whether the continuation of the local Grammar School was advisable, while in Napanee the Institute debated the local uses of credit. The Napanee Mechanics' Institute also established a mock Parliament through which the local leaders of the burgeoning manufacturing district revealed their true colours in the resolution: "That the advisors of your excellency have not seen proper to advise your excellency to introduce a measure to grant such an increase in the Tariff as will afford protection to the various industries of this country!!"[68] A quite contrasting position was taken in the debates before the Barrie Literary Society, an auxiliary to the Mechanics' Institute established in 1881. Although its bylaws were silent regarding political debates, the Barrie Literary Society posted strong injunctions against "theological questions of a sectarian nature" and the insulting use of "personalities and indecorous language." Unlike the manufacturing interests in Napanee, members of the Barrie Literary Society remained true to the Reformer heritage of the original society, favouring commercial union, universal male suffrage, and reciprocity. However, the presence of the middle classes and their insistence on decorum and respectability ensured a measure of non-partyism. While members of the Society debated such controversial subjects as commercial union, Canadian independence, capital punishment, and the single tax, one assumes that many of debates and speeches presented appeared as a forum on the National Policy, lauded for its "non-political character."[69]

Despite efforts to limit potential conflicts in village Mechanics' Institutes, variance of opinion occurred more frequently than in the urban environment, reflecting the diverse nature of the rural social order. The directors of the Fergus and Elora Institutes squabbled for months over the payment of the Fergus Concert band for performing during a joint excursion. Some years later the president of the Fergus Institute had to call a meeting to order when a "long and fiery discussion" was taking place among members over a proposition to substitute the *Daily Globe* for the evening edition. Not to be outdone, the Ennotville Mechanics' Institute board of management argued among themselves in a series of meetings in June about whether to sanction dancing during the annual picnic.[70] Nowhere was *ad hominem* conflict more apparent than in the Drayton Farmers' and Mechanics' Institute in the 1890s. A motion by the board to move the reading room and the library to another location apparently caused some rancour in the executive. Secretary Isaac Brown reported that the discussion "degenerated in some instances to mere insolent personalities against the Secretary." When others tried to smooth over the difficulties, Brown smugly wrote in the minutes, "Some feeble effort was also made to thank the Secretary but as thanks were neither merited or appreciated this was promptly suffocated." At the next meeting a month later, the directors objected to these scandalous minutes, claiming that some of the phraseology recorded too much detail. Both Brown and the president of the Institute promptly tendered their resignations, and the work of the Institute moved forward with scarcely a ripple.[71] Despite the prohibition of politico-religious controversy in the halls of small-town Mechanics' Institutes, neighbourly quarrels could not be outlawed.

In the late 1860s and 1870s the liberal doctrines of honest industry and the political economy of hard work remained staple principles in rural Mechanics' Institutes. In 1867 John Lynch, a brewer and real estate agent, gave a lecture to the Brampton Mechanics' Institute in which he claimed that Canada was a nation full of "spirited, industrious and enterprising people." In his opinion, the future prosperity or privation of the newly united Canada was dependent solely upon how the people used the resources "Divine Providence" gave them. However, Lynch's lecture also reflected the tenets of the producer ideology inherent in the manufacturing, commercial, and agricultural middle classes: "There are three sources of wealth and prosperity which are desirable in a country – Agriculture, Commerce and Manufactures – and a country which possesses reasonable facilities for the pursuits of these branches of industry, and is inhabited by a good, industrious and a united people must and will be a good, prosperous country."[72] In 1866 a local clergyman, Walter Inglis, delivered a similar lecture at the Kincardine Mechanics' Institute. Hearkening back to the days of religious paternalism, Inglis recommended the Institute as a "den for the young and thoughtless, [as we] must have something to compete with the Bar-room and Billiard Table." Inglis claimed that only the re-invention of Christian charity and relief programs would bring workmen back to the Church: "Kindness commands man and beast. Never preach or talk to a hungry, starving man. Feed him, warm him and then say, poor fellow! Want of attention to this is one great cause why multitudes of citizens, workmen, have drifted away from the Church and the Bible."[73]

Since rural Mechanics' Institutes emphasized lectures less than their city counterparts, it is more difficult to ascertain how much they stressed honest industry. And yet the records of debates in rural Mechanics' Institutes as well as their library catalogues reveal an active interest in the science of political economy. The topics of debates held in the Napanee Mechanics' Institute, from the uselessness of the credit system to the detrimental effects of trades unions, tell of an Institute more in tune with manufacturing and commercial interests. Similarly, the Peterborough Mechanics' Institute advertised its night classes as a means of competing in the "arts of peace," rather than the arts of war. Replicating the discourse of more urban Institutes, the Peterborough directors acknowledged the value of educating the skilled worker in the name of economic progress: "In this peaceful struggle with our powerful neighbours the result will as largely depend upon the educated head and skilfully trained hand of the mechanic as upon the workers in many other departments. Let us do what we can to assist him."[74] As with urban Mechanics' Institutes, much of the literature appearing in reading rooms of manufacturing towns consisted of the standard works of liberal political economy. From the complete works of John Stuart Mill, Adam Smith, and Samuel Smiles, the discerning reader could find much to justify a "liberal" social order oriented toward the rural middle classes.[75]

However, debates and library catalogues also reveal occasional tensions and a questioning of a liberal social order, particularly in relation to the manufacturing dominance of larger towns. The Barrie Literary Society chose topics related to a more Reform-oriented and "agrarian" social order, debating more than once the benefits of commercial union, annexation, unrestricted reciprocity, and the merits of the single tax. In comparison to the debates held in Napanee, the discussions in the Barrie Literary Society illustrate an agrarian and commercial middle-class dominance rather than a manufacturing priority. Indeed, a slant toward more "populist" literature appears in the reading room catalogue of the Barrie Mechanics' Institute, which advertised works from authors such as Arnold Toynbee, Henry Fawcett, John Ruskin, and Henry George, as well nascent socialist literature such as Sidney Webb's *Socialism in England*.[76] Rural audiences seemingly appreciated perusing both the traditional tomes and the more "current" authors of social and political science. While few records exist in rural Institutes to indicate whether individual members actually read these works, an artifact of the Peterborough Mechanics' Institute confirms that political economy was fairly popular with readers. In 1872 the Peterborough Institute placed a "request book" in the reading room so that members could petition the library committee to purchase particular books. Members solicited a rather eclectic collection of works on political economy, from Samuel Smiles' *Life and Labour*, Henry Fawcett's *Lessons in Political Economy*, Rogers' *Political Economy*, and Charles Paisley's *Chronicles of Political Economy* to William Ashley's *English Economic History* and Henry George's *Perplexed Philosopher*.[77]

RECREATION AS A MEANS OF GENERATING REVENUE

Although government grants for Mechanics' Institutes were restored by the 1870s, the withdrawal of the earlier grants had forced Mechanics' Institutes to realize the importance of entertainment rather than lectures as a means of opening the institution to the larger community and providing much-needed revenue. The Niagara Mechanics' Institute initiated a bold plan in the 1870s to improve its revenue stream by advertising a variety of activities. The 1871 annual report noted that the financial position of the association was stronger than ever, thanks in large part to "keeping its claims constantly before the public by promoting lectures, concerts, excursions and readings." Many rural Mechanics' Institutes emulated this example, and provided opportunities such as picnics, musical presentations, and tea-meetings for both recreation and the generation of revenue. By the late 1880s, the Drayton and Niagara Institutes had both formed entertainment committees, the directors in Ennotville had created a ball and picnic Committee, and the executive in Barrie had established Chess, Concert, and Music committees to handle the recreation workload.[78]

The grand re-opening of the Kincardine Mechanics' Institute in 1881 consisted of an improved entertainment program, complete with short addresses, readings, and recitations along with vocal and instrumental music. Lectures were clearly no longer the primary Institute attraction. In 1884, when the Institute lost $20 in inviting a Reverend Wilds to lecture, although poor weather might have been a factor the directors acknowledged there was "a decided lack of interest in lectures of any description." They went on to conclude that "lectures as a means of raising funds must be regarded as things of the past" as they believed "concerts and excursions might possibly prove more successful." Evidently these were very lucrative, for the entertainment committee of the Kincardine Institute regularly showed a profit from its recreational activities.[79]

When the Ingersoll Mechanics' Institute was re-organized in 1880, its management committee also recognized the importance of providing the larger community with recreation options. During an early meeting of the board, a general discussion took place on the best means to "awaken a greater interest, and secure a larger patronage and support of the Institute." What is highly significant is that the recruitment drive landed in the hands of the Entertainment Committee, which planned a Jubilee concert, a strawberry Festival, and several musical presentations. These amusements proved fairly successful in promoting the image of the town, although their success was not reflected in membership numbers. To further encourage the citizens of the town, the Ingersoll directors set up an amusement committee in preparation for the opening of a gymnasium and amusement room with checkers, chess, dominoes, quoits, an air gun, and croquet. Unfortunately these campaigns came to naught, as the Ingersoll Public Library quietly became a reality in 1890.[80]

The Windermere Mechanics' Institute coupled its need for patrons with a promotion of the tourist possibilities of the Muskoka district. Before the directors even mentioned the Mechanics' Institute itself in their advertising circular, they pointed out the "first rate" fishing, bathing, and scenery in the area. In promoting the benefits of the Institute, the circular listed dominoes, chess, and literary recreation. When the library itself was mentioned, the directors took pains to emphasize the sportsmen's collection. Its statement that books "relating to hunting, angling and camping out in Muskoka will be procured for the benefit of those of sporting proclivities, who may visit us in summer" cemented the relationship between town boosterism, tourism, and the village Mechanics' Institute.[81]

Not all Mechanics' Institutes recognized the benefits of promoting recreation and entertainment, and continued to concentrate solely on their reading rooms, libraries, and evening adult education classes. These Institutes either perfected their ability to procure municipal grants by the end of the century, or had to quickly fold or transform their operations into a free public library. The Orangeville Mechanics' Institute focused solely on the function of the reading room and the library, and consequently spent its funds only on books, fire insurance, rent, and wages for librarians. From 1879 to 1887, a typical year's revenue in the Orangeville Institute came to $450 from municipal and provincial grants, $100 from members' dues, and often less than $20 from lectures, concerts and other entertainments.[82] Similarly, the Caledon Mechanics' Institute limited its cultural offerings to lectures and the occasional concert, relying solely on provincial and municipal grants. The lowest point in Caledon's entertainment efforts occurred when a Dr Lees lectured to the Institute and the door committee received only $2 in fees, of which $1.25 went to the lecturer for his expenses. The incorporation of the Erin Mechanics' Institute occurred late, and its directors constantly struggled to obtain government money, despite the executive's refusal to provide free evening night classes. By 1895 the directors gratefully acknowledged the passing of the *Free Library Act* and passed the reins of the library over to the municipal council.[83]

Once again, a comparison between the Elora and the Fergus Mechanics' Institutes is of interest. It illustrates the contrast between the community centre approach and the approach of procuring provincial and municipal grants in rural Institutes. The Elora Institute followed the community centre program to perfection in their attempts to provide the citizens of Elora with entertainment and amusement activities. With the reorganization of the new Elora Mechanics' Institute in 1871, the board of management evidently appreciated the fact that members of the community were drawn to the Institute through its entertainment and recreational activities. The 1874 annual report applauded the board for its efforts, and observed that the Institute was flourishing thanks in large measure to the entertainments provided for the local community. Art exhibitions, musical performances, excursions, picnics, and tea meetings, as well as an "Old Folks Concert," were just some of the amusements offered by the entertainment committee during the final decades of the century. The amusement committee furthermore understood the needs of the Elora community and did not hold events during the skating and curling seasons. And yet the directors were under no illusion as to the financial benefits of these community events. They acknowledged in 1885 that the Amusement Committee had "provided for the public ample means of intellectual and social improvement and ... thereby been enabled to assist materially in keeping the Treasury supplied with funds."[84]

The Fergus Institute, on the other hand, was among the Institutes left scrambling when the government grants were cut in 1859. When the grants were restored in the 1870s, it almost completely abandoned its efforts to provide entertainment for the community, and focused on petitioning both the provincial and municipal governments for funds. The directors were very proficient in obtaining grants from both levels of government, as we can see from the annual report of 1887, where the Institute noted its receipt of $50 from entertainments, $85 from membership fees, $300 from provincial grants, and $100 from the village council. The transition from a Mechanics' Institute to a free public library in 1895 was relatively smooth, as the municipality was already one of the strongest supporters of the Institute.[85] A similar experience occurred with the Guelph Institute, which was converted into a free library as early as 1883. The Guelph Mechanics' Institute was never particularly well received by the local populace, and the addition of entertainments and recreation likewise did not attract any attention. With the discontinuation of the government grant in 1859, the directors of the Institute realized they had to turn to fundraising activities, and held Shakespeare festivals, art exhibitions, excursions, and musical performances. Few of these activities met with financial success until the directors decided to hold a strawberry festival in 1878. This was an extremely profitable exercise, and with the funds raised the Institute was able to purchase a billiard table and establish a smoking and chess room for its members. Despite the effectiveness of the strawberry festival, the public did not respond to the further entertainment options that it provided, and the Guelph Mechanics' Institute became a free public library in 1883, the same year in which the transition occurred in many urban Institutes.[86]

The Peterborough Mechanics' Institute's approach to fundraising was to simply take an old formula for raising funds – the lecture circuit – and repackage it for its members and townspeople. The directors fashioned the innovative scheme of inviting famous speakers such as Matthew Arnold, Mrs Charles Watson, and Horatio Parker to give readings and recitations rather than lectures. When their popularity proved rewarding to the coffers of the Peterborough Institute, the directors expanded the range of entertainments by sponsoring billiard tables and a chess room in the Institute. Of course, such amusements served the liberal middle-class views of the executive "both in the way of keeping the young men of the town from places where the surroundings are objectional [sic], and in the way of being a source of income to the Institute."[87] Nonetheless, the Peterborough Mechanics' Institute soon suffered from the same setbacks as urban Institutes, to the extent that other entertainment alternatives became available to the inhabitants of the town. In the 1885 annual report, the directors explained the situation facing the Institute: "Our fair town is now rapidly approaching the dimensions of a city, and in consequence counter-attractions are much more numerous than formerly, the result being that the membership has slightly decreased during the year." Unlike in urban Institutes, however, Peterborough's directors stepped up their efforts to bring entertainment to the public, rather than agitating for the free library. In the last decade of the Peterborough Institute's existence before it became a free library in 1895, the directors still continued to invite popular entertainers such as P.T. Barnum, to perform and even improved the Institute museum.[88]

As elsewhere, Institute promoters also wanted to ensure that all activities in the Institute were open to all members of the liberal community. The supervision of amusement rooms, leisure activities, and public concerts ensured that nothing untoward occurred, protecting small-town Mechanics' Institutes as liberally "inclusive" institutions. The Guelph Mechanics' Institute specifically pinpointed troublemakers in their billiard room, decreeing that "no young men under twenty years of age be allowed to enter the Billiard Room without the written consent of their parents or guardians."[89] The Elora Mechanics' Institute not only hired the local constable to "keep good order" for its Old Folks concert in 1879 but comically advertised: "It is not seemlie for Big Men or Littell boys to whistle inside a house, nor to make greate noyses like unto ye yells of Wilde Indians, but it does not seem necessary to tell this to ye people of Elora, because thai alwaies behave themselves well in publicke places." The local constable would also regulate proper relations between the sexes, as he would "keepe a sharp looke-out, and see that no courting or sparking goeth on." In a rather delicate touch, a further request was issued: "As ye younge women singers are shamefaste ye younge men are desired to looke awaie from them while thai sing."[90]

As a result of their very diverse class base, small-town Mechanics' Institutes were fairly inclusive, reflecting the collective liberal cultural identity of the rural social order. In the last three decades of the century, the Mechanics' Institute movement in rural areas took on even more significance as they outlived Institutes' demise in the cities. Rural Institutes that became centres for community events provided a necessary service in promoting the virtues of a town or village not only for outsiders but also for the inhabitants themselves. And yet the records of Mechanics' Institutes reveal the cultural authority of the rural social order, both in the "liberal" nature of the mid-century movement, and in late-century processes of rural middle-class formation. Despite experiencing difficulties in reaching the operative classes through their functions, small-town Mechanics' Institutes attracted professional men, farmers, commercial men, self-employed businessmen, and women to the liberal cause of self-improvement. In constructing a community-centre vision for often-isolated towns, Mechanics' Institutes managed to persist in their efforts toward mutual improvement and rational recreation until they were legislated completely out of existence by municipal directives in Quebec, and by the *Free Library Act* of 1895 in Ontario.

3

Continuity and Change in Temperance Societies

Temperance as a moral, political, and social issue has often overshadowed the temperance society itself as a harbinger of cultural change, and yet temperance organizations displayed remarkable resiliency in central Canada. Temperance societies not only offered the wider community membership in a seemingly inclusive organization of like-minded individuals but they also adapted extremely well to the changing circumstances related to the war on liquor traffic. As a result, the ideology of temperance supporters evolved from a vision of moderation in the consumption of alcohol in the early 1800s to teetotalism by mid-century, and then to complete prohibition by the final decades of the nineteenth century.[1] Even though the longevity of the temperance movement rested on an appeal that crossed gender and class lines, conflicts over just how to fulfil the objective of a dry Canada unmasked the rather exclusive nature of these societies. While early temperance societies and temperance fraternal orders liberally recruited women and members of the working classes to fill their ranks, sectarian and political turmoil from within soon revealed division within the temperance "community." By the end of the century in the more urbanized areas of central Canada, temperance had come under the influence of the Alliance movement, a network of temperance unions and leagues united in their attempts to find a legalized solution to the liquor problem. Culminating in the creation of the Dominion Alliance for the Total Suppression of the Liquor Traffic in 1877, the Alliance was one of the more successful organizations in centralizing temperance efforts. And yet by focusing all their labour on accomplishing political prohibition, urban temperance and prohibition advocates tended toward exclusivity and the entanglements of political controversy, while rural temperance supporters of all classes continued to rely on temperance fraternal orders.

The differences between the two approaches in the campaign against alcohol also reflected the competing visions of temperance held by rural and urban inhabitants.

From the formation of earliest temperance societies in the 1820s to the introduction of temperance fraternal orders at mid-century, temperance ideology modelled itself largely on individual efforts to rescue drunkards from the grip of alcohol. Temperance pledge societies focused on temperance as a simple matter of moral agency, and applied "moral suasion" in their attempts to reclaim the inebriate into the natural – and liberal – order of the community. Coinciding with other ideologies such as evangelicalism, the rationale behind the outpouring of temperance sentiment has often been explained as the desire of the early "middling sorts" to impose discipline, social order, and hegemonic respectability upon a radical working class that was difficult to control. Conversely, temperance also became a vehicle for master artisans and the lower middling classes to express their dissatisfaction with a backwoods commercial aristocracy.[2] As a result, early temperance societies would try to pattern their organizations along the lines of institutions wedded to the cultural authority of the governing social order. Unlike Mechanics' Institutes and agricultural societies, however, temperance associations were not as closely allied with the emerging liberal state. Attempts to reconcile various classes, orders, and interests into a harmonious, united, and collectively "liberal" temperance community became a precarious balancing act for temperance societies. Even though temperance organizations employed a liberal rhetoric housed in an ideology of "community" – the values of inclusion, politico-religious neutrality, and honest industry – their insistence on creating a *temperate* community often put them at odds with an emerging liberal social order.

AN EMERGING LIBERAL/EVANGELICAL SOCIAL ORDER AND TEMPERANCE PLEDGE SOCIETIES

The earliest temperance societies envisioned that their organizations would embrace an all-encompassing membership composed of all those who were willing to abide by the temperance pledge. One of the first temperance societies formed in Canada was the Montreal Temperance Society, the organization that published the *Canada Temperance Advocate* from 1835 to 1849. Founded on the principle that the vice of intemperance was highly detrimental to every class in the community, the *Advocate* called on everyone, "whatever may be his opinions, prejudices, profession, occupation or pursuit; whether he be religious or irreligious, temperate or intemperate, old or young, rich or poor," to awaken to the danger of alcohol. Whatever the nationality, creed, or character of the potential candidate, the Montreal Temperance Society would welcome that member with open arms to the ranks of its temperance army. In Upper Canada, the Toronto Temperance Reformation Society similarly declared that membership in the society required only the signing of the pledge, without distinction of sex, creed, political party, or condition of life. As a result, the Toronto Society proudly proclaimed that men of all occupations, classes, ranks, and orders of the community were to be found in attendance. While this rhetoric appears to be exceedingly *in*clusive, however, membership in the earliest pledge societies remained extremely *ex*clusive and somewhat elitist, restricted in practice to the evangelical constituency of the "urban" commercial and mercantile middling classes.[3]

Temperance pledge societies also recognized the need to target specific portions of the community in their membership drives, as both skilled workers and the wealthy elites could influence the cause of moderation in their own fashion. A perusal of the *Canada Temperance Advocate* reveals an avid interest in workmen's temperance societies such as the Washingtonian movement, a Baltimore organization founded by six pledge-taking artisans that had a substantial membership from the skilled working classes. And yet early temperance societies felt that workingmen were the major source of intemperance. Articles such as "The Ruined Artizan" and "The Dangers of the Tavern" portrayed the dangers of skilled workmen frequenting public houses.[4] As a result, the evangelical middling sorts in the Montreal Temperance Society infiltrated the burgeoning facilities of the liberal municipal social order in Montreal and would frequently contest the granting of liquor licences to taverns and inns. When politicians in Lower Canada reduced the number of licences in the aftermath of the Rebellions, the *Advocate* hailed the measure as a harbinger of things to come: "Every tavern is, in our opinion, a nuisance, and the way to deal with a nuisance is not to 'reduce' it, but to remove it." The granting of liquor licences continued to be an aggravation for the Montreal Temperance Society, as they held liquor licence inspectors "morally responsible" for the degraded sociability, functions, and operations of the working-class public house.[5]

The Montreal Temperance Society took an analogous approach to the older privileged elites – the wealthy merchant and professional classes – by calling on them to provide monetary support and show a good example in the moderation of their drinking habits. One of their earliest resolutions included the statement that the continued use of alcohol by the "higher classes" promoted the greatest evil in the community. The *Advocate* also carried an article on the aborted formation of a young workingmen's temperance society in the city, which recounted how a noted clergyman, lawyer, and judge refused to aid the fledgling society with either financial or moral support, citing peer pressure as the motivating factor.[6] Of specific concern to the evangelical directors of the Montreal Temperance Society was the conduct of the professional classes, particularly ministers of religion. Scarcely two months after the *Advocate* launched its attack on working-class taverns and public houses, the editors of the temperance paper condemned a group of clergymen in Montreal for attending a public dinner where wine was the beverage of choice. Their criticism alleging lack of judgment on the part the clergy in this instance reflected the often-turbulent relationship of the mostly evangelical Montreal Temperance Society and the more conservative clergymen in the city. Such episodes reveal an emerging liberal social order in conflict with an established Tory and High Anglican political and religious structure.[7]

The rhetoric of class inclusion employed by temperance organizations was an ideological strategy to ensure that all community members were made to feel welcome in the cause of moral suasion. When the Anglican Reverend Henry Patton addressed the citizens of Kemptville who were congregating to form a temperance society, he commented that the cause of temperance affected the farmer, merchant, clergyman, and mechanic equally. Another clergyman, the Reverend James Byrne, in a lecture on temperance societies to the Young Men's Literary Association in Montreal, reinforced the goal of inclusiveness: "In the pledge of our society we have a plain, honest, undisguised declaration, suited to all characters, situation and sex; a declaration at once benevolent and philosophical. There is no separation between the rich and the poor; but justice, humanity and religion are wisely balanced."[8] And yet this discourse of liberal inclusion also masked the designs of evangelical temperance supporters, who tended to view society in moral and religious terms. In a sermon promoting the Perth Temperance Society, the Reverend T.C. Wilson suggested a stark division between those who supported the temperance cause and those who did not. To Wilson, those who joined in condemning temperance societies were not the respectable members of the community, "the sober, the industrious, the benevolent, the good," but rather "the drunkard, the profligate, the profane, the infidel, the Sabbath-breaker, the gambler, and such like." One of the first tracts printed by the Montreal Temperance Society appealed to the "sense of community" held by Montreal inhabitants who promoted the temperance ideal. However, it became clear that this petition was made in the interests of the liberal/evangelical middling sort, when the society maintained that all the wealth expended on spirituous liquors could "pay all the expenses of civil government, thoroughly school every child in the province, provide all its inhabitants with the ministrations of the Gospel, and maintain all the poor, who would then be diminished by one-half."[9]

In their attempts to develop into a comprehensive force in the larger community, temperance societies heavily conscripted women to endorse the temperance ideal. Much debate regarding women's participation in temperance societies centred around the theme of domesticity and how temperance issues allowed women access to the public sphere. Indeed, many scholars conclude that female involvement in temperance – even at this early stage – framed the early impetus for women's rights. The first annual Toronto Temperance Reformation Society meeting in 1840 recorded a female membership of 45 percent.[10] Temperance soirées and picnics were often lauded as being highly inclusive of females, unlike the dram shop, where men "would even exclude their own mothers, sisters, wives and children, or in other words, three-fourths of the community from their enjoyments." In a report of a Ladies' Soirée of the Montreal Temperance Society, directors contrasted their dinner with other social functions. Elsewhere, "the ladies were kept away, they must be domestic [but] we propose another plan; we want the ladies with us; we count them as stars to ray out on the gloom of the world." Such lofty expressions of inclusion were soon exposed as rather empty rhetoric, however, as women were not allowed to hold early temperance society executive positions; nor was their participation in temperance campaigns more active than a supporting role of giving temperance bazaars and tea parties. In relegating women to spectators and figureheads, temperance pledge societies mirrored the inequalities and conflicts that existed within the "liberal" temperance movement itself.[11]

The connection of temperance societies with evangelical Protestant religion led to more sectarianism, and increasing calls for the endorsement of legal sanctions to alcohol brought about greater political discord than in many other voluntary associations. Although on the surface, objectivity over political and sectarian issues may have been a creed for the country's leading temperance paper, the *Canada Temperance Advocate*, its position was by no means neutral. In an article entitled "The Temperance Movement is Unsectarian," temperance supporters extolled the virtues of a movement that united men of all religious persuasions in a common cause. However, if the Montreal society practised evangelical principles regarding temperance, they undoubtedly supported the established churches in matters of religion.

The editors of the *Advocate* repeatedly warned temperance proponents not to react violently against churches that refused to sponsor the temperance cause, particularly when lecturers contracted by the society falsified claims of being recovered tipplers, played impious music, and put forward poor champions of the cause "without character, [who hurl] at Christianity darts poisoned with infidelity."[12]

The veil of sectarian concord within the temperance movement was exceedingly thin, and the neutral ground that it covered became increasingly contested. The Reverend Joseph Abbott, an Anglican minister in Montreal, complained that "innovation and Heresy in Religion" were starting to establish a foothold in the community of believers. He also likened the good Christian men of the temperance movement to dissenters such as Wesley and Watts, who erred on points of vital importance to the established Church of England. Similarly, at the inaugural meeting of the Kemptville Temperance Society in 1830, the Reverend Henry Patton called on all men, without distinction of party or sect, to aid in the common cause of temperance. As a High Churchman, Patton visualized the temperance movement being led by the institutional Church of England, not voluntary churches, and his discourse was therefore naturally couched in the language of sectarianism.[13]

When placed in historical context, it can be seen that a great deal of this sectarian and political discourse reveals a rising liberal social order bent on ending the politico-religious turmoil of the Rebellions and sweeping away the vestiges of an older Tory hierarchical order. Joseph Abbott, in his pamphlet against dissenting temperance societies, represented an older privileged order railing against liberal society, as he "exposed" an evangelical minister's friendship with members of the American Temperance Society as proof of his "radical" tendencies. The Reverend Robert Murray, an established Church of Scotland minister, charged temperance societies with sapping the foundations of civilized society and fostering an unchristian spirit. Ironically, Murray utilized the discourse of a liberal "community" to censure temperance societies: "The minister of religion, the merchant and the mechanic, who were not members of the temperance society, were all exposed alike to its undermining and malicious influence ... induced by such a distorted state of society, and such a system of public persecution, under the pretext of promoting morality and religion."[14]

John Knowlson, a former rum seller and merchant, took umbrage with Murray's charges, and in a lecture before the Cavan Temperance Society criticized clergymen who objected to their cause on "frivolous grounds." Knowlson represented new evangelical temperance associations that contested established churches and their religious monopoly, and disagreed with Murray that the Church embodied the "true" temperance society. Echoing many evangelical arguments, Knowlson asked: "What sound reason can be given why the laity should not be allowed to act in concert with the Clergy, or by themselves, for the suppression of vice, and the promotion of virtue?" Of course the larger ramifications of the temperance debate between Murray and Knowlson came in debates over political "loyalty," as Murray's lecture was published by the noted Toronto Tory press, the *British Colonist*, while Knowlson's reply was published by the more "liberal" press of Egerton Ryerson, the *Christian Guardian*.[15]

While impartiality in politics was a mandate of the Montreal Temperance Society, oblique political statements offered in the *Canada Temperance Advocate* testify to temperance supporters' difficulty in remaining politically objective. During the rebellions in Lower Canada, the editors of the *Advocate* equated the rising political passions of the people with mounting intemperance in the countryside. Evidently the more "evil and turbulent" individuals in the community were highly attracted to the public house, as supporters of the Rebellion offered free liquor to those attending seditious meetings.[16] As temperance increasingly became an issue for the differing political parties, the *Advocate* warned its supporters: "No great moral cause has ever yet been able to withstand party spirit, that political maelstrom which engulfs all that come within its reach. The Temperance cause, in the violent commotions of the two great political parties, had well nigh been swallowed up, and that too, by the party zeal of its friends – and had it been any other than the temperance cause, we should despair of a resuscitation." When the *Advocate* delved into political matters in their displeasure over the election of John Molson – the city's most notorious brewer – the paper pleaded self-defence in thrusting temperance principles into politics. To the editors of the *Advocate*, the Molson election episode illustrated that politics could also be rudely pitted against temperance principles.[17]

Just as Mechanics' Institutes had done, early temperance societies also vigorously touted the benefits of honest industry and individual labour. These societies followed the more evangelical social order by accusing loafers and spendthrifts of contributing nothing to the "liberal" community, while those who laboured for their own support became the foundation of society itself. Temperance groups also accepted the labour theory of value: "Labour levels all distinctions, and gives the poor man an inheritance in this world, more certain, though not so extensive as the rich, in his own talents, faculties and capacities. By making all welfare and acquisition depend on labour, all mankind is provided for, and monopolies, in effect, done away." Temperance societies blamed the curse of idleness on the blight of intemperance, as the inebriated labourer was seen to halt the spread of honest industry. Statistics produced by the society illustrated that hundreds of families were living in liquor-induced conditions where industry, respectability, and morality were simply impossible.[18] Accordingly, the alcohol trade itself was considered an aberration from normal laws of "liberal" political economy and a hindrance to national prosperity, as it wasted financial reserves and other resources, and killed the labour incentive. In viewing the liberal public as an aggregate body, temperance social economy included the development of industry, the proper rewards of labour, the diffusion of property, and measures integral to the protection of society against those evils – such as the liquor traffic – that were destructive to the peace and prosperity of a nation.[19]

As with other voluntary associations, sociability played a rather significant role in building the collective ideology of a temperate "community." The entertainment endeavours of early pledge societies were designed to help former tipplers turn from their degraded former lives by offering them social alternatives to the public house. Providing "cheerfulness and social comfort" to all without the temptations of alcohol, temperance picnics, soirées, tea parties, and other entertainments would create social cohesion through various leisure activities. Indeed, the *Canada Temperance Advocate* proclaimed that teetotallers were the "most joyous part of the community": "Against no class of men could the charge of diminishing innocent pleasures be brought with less propriety."[20] While the Montreal Temperance Society became involved in large-scale entertainments such as soirées, temperance picnics, and suppers, the smaller rural societies had to be content with simpler fare. These amusements were of the rational variety, temperance lectures and essays, singing, recitations, debates, and spelling matches being the most common. Public lectures and presentations of temperance papers were often delivered by local clergymen, to ensure their accordance with principles of morality and also because of their low cost. For example, the Toronto Temperance Reformation Society insisted that its Temperance Hall be used solely for public meetings of a moral and useful purpose, regardless of the organization renting the Hall.[21]

THE SKILLED WORKING CLASSES, LIBERAL INCLUSION, AND TEMPERANCE FRATERNALISM

By the 1840s many temperance supporters believed that pledge societies had lost their effectiveness in encouraging temperance within central

Canadian society. Skilled working-class temperance supporters in particular stressed the need to strengthen the moral assault on the liquor trade. Appreciating the advantages of mutual benefit fraternalism, skilled workers enthusiastically joined new temperance orders from the United States such as the Sons of Temperance and the Independent Order of Good Templars (IOGT). The most popular temperance fraternal lodges were those of the Sons of Temperance, an organization that entered Canada in 1848. Intent on reclaiming the drunkard through self-help, self-improvement and alternative social diversions, the Sons recruited heavily from the ranks of the working class. Although temperance fraternalism was theoretically open to all classes, the extension of mutual benefits in these organizations ensured a large constituency from the skilled working classes, who were engaged in creating their own collective identity and enhancing their own vision of respectability.[22] Indeed, the traditional producer alliance of artisans and yeoman farmers comprised over 60 percent of the initial membership of three rural divisions of the Sons of Temperance in Canada West (see Table 3.1). Farmers and skilled workers also managed to have strong participation in the executive of these temperance fraternal orders.[23] With working-class aspirations toward liberal respectability through mutual aid and the simultaneous shift of temperance ideology from moral suasion to legislative prohibition, accommodation between temperance societies and a "liberal" governing social order became increasingly difficult by mid-century and beyond.

Nonetheless, both the Sons of Temperance and the IOGT tried to forge a sense of interclass unity within the bonds of temperance fraternalism. The Sons' executive board hoped that temperance fraternal orders would have a more liberal and levelling effect on the larger community. In the Sons of Temperance division room, all stations, ranks, and classes ceased to exist, as the "high born" elite stood on the same level as the "base born peasant."[24] By the early 1860s the competition for lodge or division members had become so strong, that accessibility of temperance fraternal orders to all members of the community became a key selling point. Lodges of the IOGT therefore also included all "grades and conditions of society – the minister of the gospel, the cultivated man of letters, educated and refined ladies, mingling as equals with the weather bronzed tiller of the soil, the toiling mechanic, the working girl and the bashful apprentice."[25] Temperance societies now called on the legislators of the land to halt liquor traffic as a threat to public welfare, and to wage war against the private interests of alcohol dealers. Likening society to a body, they considered each member of the community to be essential to its welfare and protection – except for

Table 3.1
Occupations of Initial Members of Three Rural Sons of Temperance Divisions, 1850–58

Occupation	Total	Percentage	Occupation	Total	Percentage
Labourer	29		Merchant	14	
Blacksmith	26		Clothier	7	
Carpenter	20		Druggist	2	
Wagon maker	12		Hatter	1	
Tailor	12		Bookseller	1	
Cooper	11		TOTAL BUSINESS	25	7
Shoemaker	8		Clergy	8	
Cabinet maker	7		Doctor	5	
Tinsmith	5		Student	5	
Others*	38		Teacher	4	
TOTAL SKILLED	168	49	Barrister	2	
Clerk	6		TOTAL PROFESSIONAL	24	7
Bookkeeper	1		Farmers	92	
TOTAL CLERICAL	7	2	Yeomen	16	
			Others^	10	
			TOTAL AGRICULTURAL	118	35

* Other occupations in the skilled category include: joiner, baker, brickmaker, printer, painter, mason, chairmaker, pumpmaker, butcher, millright, tinsmith, saddler, founder, watchmaker, moulder, artist, cabinet maker, saddler, sawyer, carter, operative, peddlar, and harnessmaker.
^ Other occupations in the agricultural category include: miller, millermaker, teamster, and tanner.

SOURCE: Occupations of the initial membership of the Norfolk Division, Sons of Temperance, NAC, MG 29 D8/24, M-282, reel 9, minute book, 1850–54, 12340–12538 and the Norwich Division, AO, Harold Williams Collection, MS 301, item 4, minute book, 1851–60, pasted at the end and the Orono Division, AO, MU 2879, membership list, 1850–58.

"the man who attempts to fasten himself upon the community, and who, through indolence or some other cause, refuses to contribute something to the common stock." That man, of course, was the rum seller, who contributed nothing to society and deserved no protection in return.[26]

It became even more problematic for temperance organizations to incorporate those marginalized by liberal society, such as women, natives and people of colour. In a predicament similar to that faced by the Oddfellows (see chapter 4), Sons of Temperance members' admiration for the liberal temperance community was tempered by the American National Division's prohibition of black members. Temperance went hand-in-hand with antislavery in both the United States and Britain, and Canadian Sons of Temperance members felt uncomfortable about the American Division's policy of prohibiting "the most respectable portion of the community" from joining their order. Even a noted supporter of the Sons such as the *Canada Temperance Advocate* was angered when in the city of Kingston a coloured gentleman was denied membership in the Canada

West Sons of Temperance. The *Advocate* stormed: "We cannot believe that in a free country, any association would dare to offend public opinion so grievously, as to introduce sentiments or distinctions peculiar to slave territories; and we are confident that Temperance men would be among the last to tolerate them for a single moment." When even the *Canadian Son of Temperance and Literary Gem* traced their lack of membership to "inconsistencies in the order by the exclusion of men of colour," the Grand Division in Canada West wrote to the National Division in Baltimore requesting that the ban on blacks be rescinded, as it denied their claims of humanity and religion, and was at variance with the spirit and letter of the Sons' own constitution. It may be the case, however, that much of this discussion served mainly to justify creating a separate Canadian Division of the Sons of Temperance, rather than expressing true concern over the plight of blacks and natives in the order.[27]

Nowhere was the inclusive/exclusive liberal paradigm of temperance societies more in evidence, than in temperance fraternalism's recruitment and treatment of women members. Initially the Sons of Temperance refused to allow women members, and instead sponsored a branch order called the Daughters of Temperance. While women were patronizingly permitted to form the executive of various unions, much of their work came under the direction of nearby male-dominated divisions. When the Sons tried to breathe more life into the order by becoming a more gender-neutral body, their initial attempts fell short because they did not offer full membership to female members. Designated as "lady visitors," women who joined the Sons of Temperance were not allowed to vote, hold executive positions, or profit from the benefits system except as widows.[28] Sons of Temperance divisions such as the one in Nithburg in Canada West were perfectly satisfied with this arrangement, as female visitors often provided entertainment and refreshments for division meetings, as well as participating in relief and visitation committees. And, by encouraging the contributions of women, the Nithburg Sons of Temperance increased the membership of "lady visitors" to nearly 40 percent of the total attending division functions. However, this scenario continued to marginalize women in the domestic roles of spectator, hostess, and purveyor of refreshments.[29]

Even after the Grand Division of Canada West had agreed "generally" with the principle of admitting women as full voting members in 1856, the Orono division of the Sons of Temperance began to debate the issue a scant month later. Noting that women had a tendency to awaken sociality within a division, directors decided to encourage female participation by eliminating women's initiation fees. When the directors of the Orono division reinforced a ban on female members, a disgruntled Brother reported a "conversation with a lady who thought about joining the division [but he said] that he could not conscientiously recommend a lady to join the Sons." The issue of female membership continued to arise in Orono, but it was not until 1870 that women were allowed full membership in the Orono Sons of Temperance. When directors contrasted the state of the Sons to that of the Good Templars in a retrospective of the order printed at mid-century, they attributed the success of the former to the admission of women as full members while the Sons had excluded them.[30] The Independent Order of Good Templars had realized the importance of women to the temperance movement, and made great strides in recruiting women to the cause. From its commencement, the IOGT had not only allowed women to join in full fellowship but had also permitted them to fill executive positions. In the fierce competition for members among the temperance fraternal orders, the IOGT highlighted their society's inclusion of women in contrast to the discriminatory policies of other fraternal temperance orders such as the Sons of Temperance.[31]

SECTARIAN TURMOIL AND THE POLITICS OF PROHIBITION

Despite proclamations against political partyism and sectarianism, the political and sectarian tensions simmering behind the issue of temperance became even more pronounced among temperance fraternal orders. On the surface, both the Sons of Temperance and the IOGT supported the liberal concept of "community," remaining committed to the principles of religious and political neutrality. While the Sons of Temperance was not a political or religious movement, it exhorted its members to be more "individually active in the field of general usefulness" by becoming better citizens and Christians. The Independent Order of Good Templars held a similar disdain for sectarianism and partyism, outlawing any interference with the political or religious preferences of any member. As one director of the IOGT proposed: "While we may differ in our opinions, let us bear and forbear with each other, suppressing all undue strife and contention – debating only to make our varied presentations acceptable, having in view, in all we do, the best interests of our noble fraternity."[32] Notwithstanding such statements of collective liberal neutrality, establishing political and religious toleration in various temperance lodges proved difficult for temperance fraternal orders.

Thanks to the strong working-class component of temperance fraternal orders, some measure of working-class reformist dialogue did in fact creep into their ideology, a discourse that tended to censure the privileged commercial aristocracy. A lecture by the noted Reformer and member of the International Order of Rechabites, T.S. Brown, took aim at the drinking "*snobs* of society" and sounded the rallying cry to all temperance orders: "Let all our batteries of reproach, derision and exposure be directed against the liquor loaded tables of the rich, and the drinking usages of so-called fashionable society." The Sons of Temperance also joined the working-class radical culture in blaming a "SELFISH GENTEEL CLASS" for increased intemperance in the community. If the skilled working classes had a better example of moderation placed before them from the influential members of society, they claimed, the use of alcohol in the community would be eradicated. Other tracts printed by the Sons praised the organization's inclusive nature at the same time as delivering transparently cloaked taunts at the elite classes: "We are aware that a prejudice exists amongst the higher classes against uniting in the temperance movement, because of the supposed necessity of mingling too much with men of inferior station. Happily, however, such a result is by no means necessary. Retain if you will all your exclusiveness. Shun as much as ever all intercourse with the *vulgar*. We are by no means fastidious on such minor points; but abandon the wine-cup, abandon it forever; and henceforth let the influence of your example be thrown on the side of humanity, of benevolence, of virtue."[33]

No finer example of radical political temperance exists than the prominent Charles Durand, editor of the *Canadian Son of Temperance and Literary Gem*. A lawyer and supporter of the original Reform party of Mackenzie, suspicious of the Liberal/Tory alliance, and yet no friend to the Clear Grits, Durand often used the supposedly neutral ground of his temperance newspaper to stir up political and religious controversy. Originally, Durand echoed the "liberal" sentiments of the Order in general, claiming that his paper would brook no religious or political controversies. When a local division petitioned the Grand Division to censure dancing as entertainment, for instance, Durand responded from a liberal perspective: "The order was based upon a wider foundation than a mean and beggarly sectarianism, which would establish a censorship over every man's private judgement, in religious and social conduct. The moment we narrow ourselves to that limit, we are not a world order, but one of isolation. We were established to promote temperance and humanity, not religious creeds."[34]

Despite this statement of non-sectarianism, however, Durand attacked the Clergy Reserve question with Reformer enthusiasm, as well as making quite unprovoked attacks on Roman Catholics. In an article on the Know-Nothing party in the United States, Durand declared unequivocally: "We would say to all Catholics, we hate not you but it is your system, your errors, your delusions ... Give us the reign of the French Goddess of Reason, bad as it was, before the blackness of minds enslaved by Popish priestcraft."[35]

Durand further rationalized the political nature of his temperance publication by quipping that if there were not such a great disposition in the Canadian press to truckle to class interests, he would be less inclined to comment upon political matters. As it was, Durand associated temperance issues with the older Reform party, slamming liberal conservatives such as Malcolm Cameron with equal vehemence as "High Tory" conservatives. From July to August of 1853, Durand held a running battle in the *Canadian Son of Temperance* with "traitors" to the Reform cause such as Cameron and William Macdougall, politicians whom he accused of selling out to the liberal-conservative Francis Hincks for "a mess of patron pottage." Macdougall responded in kind, reproving Durand for making the Sons too political, and therefore less popular with the skilled working classes. Of course, Durand always qualified his attacks by saying that he respected an honest Tory as much as a Reformer; it was just "double faced Tories, temperance and political trimmers" that he heartily detested. Durand's privileging of Reform issues over temperance promotion came to a head by 1855, when he announced that he would replace the *Canadian Son of Temperance* with a paper entitled the *Crisis*, which would be a emphatically a Reform paper, of a fearless independent kind.[36]

While the Good Templars avoided this kind of political controversy, they became embroiled in a far more serious sectarian debate in 1858, which led to the creation of the British American Order of Good Templars (BAOGT). Reverend James Scott of London, objecting to the removal of the Son and Holy Ghost from IOGT rituals to suit American Unitarians, attempted to forge a National Temple independent from the United States. To Scott, such an organization would neither be bounded by geographical distinctions nor bow to any theological dogma.[37] In the end, the Grand Temple wished the British American Templars well in their temperance crusade but denied them membership in the IOGT. However, when BAOGT recruiter N.C. Gowan tried to aggressively campaign in IOGT Temples, the IOGT's *Good Templar* went on the offensive. Responding to the worn-out charge of disloyalty in following the creed of an American temperance order, the editors stated: "We do not boast of loyalty, we allow deeds to speak for themselves. Loyalty is something like religion, the genuine possessor of either of them boasts not of them. Show us a loudmouthed religionist and loyalist, and we will show you a hypocrite and a coward." The discord between the two groups died out after 1865, when the IOGT adopted a motion to allow members of the British Order back into the Good Templar fold.[38]

The rather "illiberal" politicization of temperance became even more manifest in Canada during the early 1850s, when the Maine Laws came into effect in the United States. Championed by temperance crusader Neal Dow, these laws effectively legalized the prohibition of alcohol in Maine and led to further laws against the liquor traffic in other American jurisdictions.[39] Convinced that moral suasion was no longer effective, Canadian Sons of Temperance supporters now called on the government to protect the community from the "immense pecuniary sacrifices, the mental and physical maladies, the outrages of life and property, and the moral contamination" of the liquor traffic. Underscoring this shift in temperance politics, the Most Worthy Patriarch of Canada West Sons of Temperance nonetheless employed a liberal rhetoric of the "public good" in rationalizing the need for prohibition:

> Should it be urged that, in so doing [agitating for Prohibition] we would transcend our appropriate limits, and be interfering with politics, I answer that the subject of Temperance is one of vast *political* importance. I use the term "political" not in the narrow, contracted sense, which would bring the work of great moral reformation into the arena of party strife, or array a class of men, whose object is, or should be, to elevate their fellow men, and purify society, from a desolating and corrupting evil, into a political party, to strive with others for the loaves and fishes of office; but in that higher and nobler meaning in which politics is the science of government – a science which teaches to advance the general welfare and the aggrandizement of the whole community.[40]

The official periodical of the IOGT recognized that moral suasion had run its course, and that "to its aid legal enactment must be called in at last." While the *Good Templar* condemned "mealy-mouthed reformers" content to compromise with vice and wrong, it also conceded that: "Public opinion needs first to be aroused to a proper sense of the great social and moral evils which the prevailing drinking usages of the day [are] bringing upon the country, and when that is done, there will be no difficulty in obtaining and enforcing a Prohibitory liquor law."[41]

While prohibition became a rather difficult principle for temperance supporters who favoured liberal governance, those who challenged the authority of the liberal state utilized a political discourse to justify it. Durand, a noted Reformer as well as a Sons of Temperance enthusiast, employed the language of liberal popular politics on several occasions to voice his support for prohibition. The public evil of alcohol pervaded all ranks and orders in society, he said, and for that reason legal suasion could abate the situation "constitutionally, [in accord] with individual liberty." Furthermore, Durand echoed radical/populist pleas for political vigilance, claiming that freemen, to preserve their liberty, "have to be watchful, for if they [are] not, the selfishness of cliques will circumvent them in some way. Ever and anon combinations will be formed to overthrow the people and circumscribe their rights."[42] And yet, paradoxically, the shift to political prohibition also appears to be one of the subtle factors inherent in the reaction of cross-class collaboration in temperance societies. Even Durand noted that if temperance became a political question, the labouring classes needed to be included in the political process. In the opinion of Durand and other radical political temperance agitators, the natural desire of the working class for freedom and liberty would be offended by legal suasion.[43] However, the withdrawal of the skilled working-classes from central Canadian temperance societies involved more than calls for the legal prohibition of alcohol within the larger society.

THE MUTUAL BENEFIT SYSTEM AND FRATERNAL BONDS OF SOCIABILITY

Temperance fraternal orders also grasped the concept of liberal honest industry as a philosophy essential not only to national prosperity but also to the success of the temperance enterprise. As many early members of the Sons of Temperance were also from the skilled working class, much of the ideology expressed in their temperance publications emphasized the dignity of labour, the labour theory of value, and the fact that "labouring men [were] the props and sinews of all communities." However, the liberal values of thrift and economy also began to be accentuated along with the importance of emulating the economy of one's employer. As expressed in the *Good Templar*:

This temperance journal proposes to advocate the right of the producer to an equitable share of what they produce, and discuss the various social questions in which workingmen are directly interested. This is much needed, and we trust it will also live to succeed in convincing the laborious portion of the community that they have more to do than work, eat and sleep, in order to enjoy that happiness, social enjoyment and domestic comfort, which constitute the great end of their mundane existence. To do this effectually the workingman must be convinced that to procure happiness, he must not only get his proper share of the production, but take care of, and put to proper use what he gets.[44]

From this point of view, the liquor trade was anathema to the laws of political economy. Not only did it waste national resources but it was the enemy of respectability, the opponent of industry, and the adversary of every man's prosperity. Despite the sizeable presence of skilled workers in temperance fraternalism, sufficient numbers of the evangelical middling sort remained to continue negotiation with the liberal social order in regard to temperance doctrines.[45]

Temperance fraternalism offered an appealing array of benefits for the temperate skilled workingman, such as sickness insurance, funeral benefits, and a widows' and orphans' fund, all dependent upon the continuing sobriety of the applicant. The expansion of the benefits system by fraternal temperance orders helped disseminate the collective liberal gospel of honest industry through the doctrines of temperance, self-help, and mutual assistance. The summation of the relationship between the mutual benefit system and honest industry appeared in an article by Durand, then the Worthy Secretary of the Canada West Sons of Temperance, in the *Canadian Son of Temperance*. Durand pointed out the spin-off of sobriety unequivocally: "Poverty cannot exist amongst us, for with us all must be sober, industrious and honest, and the really deserving – the sick, the orphan, the widows of our order – have hearts of love, upon which they can always depend."[46] While the system of benefits maintained by the Sons of Temperance and other fraternal temperance orders fulfilled the mandate of the individual work ethic and collective mutual aid, however, the working classes found the financing of mutual assurance far more difficult. Not only were lodges and divisions susceptible to over-claiming on benevolent funds but problems such as creative bookkeeping and outright embezzlement of division monies created periodic funding crises. Delegates to the

1853 annual meeting of the Sons of Temperance of Canada West held in Kingston recognized that the order had fallen inward through the introduction of the benefit system, as those interested only in monetary rewards left as quickly as they joined.[47]

As a result of such funding difficulties, the Grand Division of the Canada West Sons of Temperance experimented with a partial withdrawal from the benefits system. During the 1854 semi-annual session it was suggested that poorer divisions discontinue mutual assurance, as their monies were "entirely exhausted by incessant drafts for benefits." When delegates floated the notion of equality between non-benefit and benefit members in 1856, it was not surprising that, as the Grand Worthy Secretary reported in the 1857 annual session, those divisions dropping the benefits were the most successful. This advantage did not stand the test of time, however. The number of Sons of Temperance divisions in both Canadas went from a high of 400 in 1852 to lower than 300 in 1862, and from 18,000 contributing members to fewer than 7,000.[48]

It would seem no coincidence that the meteoric rise and fall of the Sons of Temperance in Canada coincided with the re-emergence of the Independent Order of Oddfellows over the same period of time. Many prominent Sons and their supporters viewed the Oddfellows, Masons, and Orangemen as viable competitors to their association. Noting that Oddfellowship cost nearly two or three times as much as membership in the Sons, Durand found it particularly galling that the Orange Order, based simply on the protection of Protestantism and consumed with vice and intemperance, claimed more adherents than either. If the Orange order was "partly a political movement," he asked, "why should not the Order of the Sons, which is not political, and has only the test of strict temperance superadded, succeed equally well? Does the fact of this last test injure it with the masses? It would really seem so, as society is now constituted."[49] While the advocacy of prohibition was somewhat to blame for the loss of working class support from temperance societies, it was the mismanagement and eventual removal of the benefits system that most contributed to the waning of support among the mid-century skilled working classes.

Fraternal temperance lodges and divisions grasped the significance of sociability in forging brotherhood and associational ties. Temperance fraternal associations acknowledged the importance of rational recreation to their members, sanctioning temperance lectures, essays, and recitations while establishing libraries and debating societies for mental and social improvement. In announcing their peak enrolment of 11,000 members during the annual session of the Grand Division in 1855, the executive of the Sons of Temperance in Canada West observed that success in recruitment could be attributed to the introduction of the social feature in temperance work. To N.C. Gowan, the Grand Secretary of the BAOGT, the primary advantage of the Templar lodge was the happiness acquired through the formation of new acquaintances. No matter if Good Templars had been strangers before, they could "in a short time get acquainted with each other; reserve and restraint are laid aside; all are brothers who never part but with regret, because of the many pleasant and profitable hours spent together."[50] Division and lodge social activities also had a far more practical purpose; to raise much-needed funds for the actual temperance crusade. Tea meetings, soirées, excursions, and other diversions entailed an entrance fee, but they also required the presence of the entire town or village to be successful. As the continuing existence of temperance fraternal lodges rested on a rather precarious financial footing, the failure of temperance lodges to provide revenue through social events is evident from their slashing initiation fees, levying fines for non-attendance of officers, and tinkering with the entire mutual benefit system.[51]

Although temperance fraternal orders were largely composed of skilled workers and yeomen farmers, they were also remarkably far more circumspect about disrespectful or profane behaviour in their leisure activities than the earlier pledge temperance societies of the evangelical middling sort. One of the earliest constitutions of the Sons of Temperance in Canada West decreed that members needed to avoid both "personalities and indecorous language" during recreational debates, and censured individuals who disturbed fellow Sons while they were speaking. Some divisions went even further; the Norwich division fined individuals who used disrespectful language or spat on the floor, and even expelled Sons found gambling. The Nithburg Sons of Temperance went as far as to ban the use of tobacco by its members.[52] Debates over the appropriateness of fraternal temperance activities were common. One of the first meetings of the Norfolk division of the Sons determined that no meeting of the division would be succeeded by a public dance, in order not to give offence to "serious minds." The issue of dancing also came before the Canada West Grand Temple of the IOGT in the early 1860s, when the Warpath lodge suspended some individuals for participating in a temperance social that permitted dancing. While the executive of the Grand Temple condemned dancing as a rather dubious entertainment option, they also reinstated the dismissed members and censured the Warpath lodge for creating disharmony over such a question. This episode illustrates that ensuring recreational respectability was a rather sensitive matter when dealing with liberal standards, particularly in relation to events open to the entire community.[53]

Temperance societies therefore had to ensure that their external activities not only promoted the temperance ideal but also offered recreation that was both respectable and reputable. In the summer of 1860, the directors of the Gananoque lodge of the BAOGT organized an excursion to visit the Thousand Islands region. After the proprietors of the chartered boat forced the Good Templars to share their accommodations with a group of drunken revellers, the lodge executive abruptly concluded that excursions were not conducive to the welfare of the order. Concerns about what constituted respectable leisure affected the Norfolk division of the Sons of Temperance to such a degree that they even counselled their members to avoid entertainments that did not have a direct bearing on the temperance question:

> That this Division, while deprecating any attempt to put forms or strenuous constructions on its constitution or bylaws which could have a tendency to interfere with or control the private rights of its members for the purpose of hurting the feelings or prejudices of individuals and while condemning movements having for their object the setting up of a particular standard of worldly or other matters unconnected with temperance, would at the same time strongly and feelingly recommend to the membership the propriety of wholly abstaining from practices calculated even remotely to bring the noble order with which we are connected into disrepute, among which practices this Division include the frequenting of the Ball Alley at present in operation in this place.[54]

To the "respectable" working class, policing the leisure choices within fraternal temperance orders – ensuring their acceptability to the rest of the liberal community – while respecting the individual rights of each lodge or division member became a delicate operation.

THE LATE-CENTURY URBAN PROHIBITION MOVEMENT AND TEMPERANCE UNION SOCIETIES

In the last three decades of the nineteenth century, the tone of temperance societies changed dramatically, as they shifted their emphasis from promoting moral suasion to advocating complete legalized prohibition. As a result, a large influx of middle-class members decided to affiliate themselves with both rural and urban temperance associations. Historical explanations for the growth in numbers of middle-class temperance supporters range from the augmented presence of women in temperance societies to the desire of the emerging commercial, industrial, and manufacturing classes to impose capitalistic discipline through legal restrictions on the sale and consumption of alcohol.[55] In order to centralize the prohibition work of the various churches and temperance societies, temperance activists in 1877 established the Dominion Alliance for the Suppression of the Liquor Traffic. By the 1880s, the prohibition movement had achieved consensus among middle-class temperance advocates as the preferred solution to society's ills, but the internal dynamics of urban prohibition created discord among the major players by the turn of the century. Conflicts between evangelicals and social gospellers, political partisanship, and disputes among social reformers, radicals, and conservatives served to fracture the prohibition alliance. However, the shift in temperance support from the skilled working classes to the emerging middle classes illustrates that collective liberal identities in voluntary associations were in a constant state of flux throughout the nineteenth century.[56]

Although not overtly exclusive to the middle class, the prohibition union movement became far more attuned to middle-class sentiments than the traditional fraternal temperance orders. It originated in the 1850s with the Canadian Prohibitory Liquor Law League, and took on many forms before its most successful manifestation, the Dominion Alliance for the Total Suppression of the Liquor Traffic. Patterned after the United Kingdom Temperance Alliance, temperance union associations developed simply out of a desire to amalgamate support for prohibition among diverse groups consisting of fraternal temperance orders, churches, and others willing to invest in so great a cause.[57] The Ontario Branch of the Dominion Alliance claimed that it would not enter into any competition with existing temperance organizations but would only relieve them of the work of legislation, so that they could "prosecute their reformatory work with unremitting vigour." As rival to none and helper to all, the Dominion Alliance aimed to combine temperance forces for political action, creating both a bond of union and a centre of action in amalgamating the efforts of the temperance community. While the success of the Alliance movement as a cohesive force for prohibition is debatable, even Frank Spence, the secretary of the Dominion Alliance, recognized that the work required organizing temperance supporters of diverse types. Utilizing the editorship of the *Camp Fire* as his platform, Spence argued that the existence of separate temperance associations was an extravagant waste, demonstrating weakness, division, and dilution of purpose. He pleaded for a centralized apparatus to achieve political prohibition, noting with frustration that there was too great an array of societies: "Knights and leagues, circles and lodges crowd upon us with bewilderment."[58]

Taken at face value, temperance union associations continued to foster a liberal ideology of inclusion, as they opened their doors to all temperance supporters irrespective of race, creed, class, or colour. Indeed, the Quebec Temperance and Prohibitory League claimed that the only way to effect the temperance revolution would be to harvest the unanimous support of all classes and interests within the community. The League was aware of the importance of recruiting both the commercial middle classes and their workers and instructed agents of total abstinence societies to approach both groups in establishing their associations. These union associations also emphasized the need to raise the leading members of society to higher standards of propriety, as those individuals wielded a most powerful influence on the rest of the community. The Dominion Alliance embraced middle class groups such as the Women's Christian Temperance Union (WCTU) and various church synods, yet also made overtures to working-men's associations such as the Trades and Labour Council (TLC). As Council member and labour reformer Daniel O'Donoghue noted, the TLC and the Alliance held the same goals of the moral and social elevation of both the industrial workers and the community, for if the "temperance workers and the workingmen joined hands for a common object, no liquor power would be able to resist them."[59]

It was also evidently seen that the ability to connect with French Canada would be an invaluable asset, as the Dominion Alliance professed to be an organization representing all of the Canadian provinces. The alliance between French and English Canada in the cause of temperance seems to have thrived during a string of successful challenges to the *Canada Temperance Act*, or *Scott Act*, in Quebec in the late 1880s. As the *Canada Citizen and Temperance Herald* triumphantly proclaimed: "Let Protestant Ontario know, for the encouragement of her moral community, and a warning for the liquor advocates, that Catholic Quebec has suffered from intemperance to the limits of endurance, and she, too, may be counted upon to do her part in the hard conflict upon us."[60] During the 1898 plebiscite on prohibition, however, Quebec was noticeably out of step with the rest of the country in defeating prohibition by a wide margin. However, the Dominion Alliance did not impugn French Canadians and their drinking habits, but rather attributed the failure of the prohibition cause to political considerations peculiar to Quebec. Prohibition advocates claimed that since only 330 liquor licences had been granted in some 933 municipalities, the province was essentially dry to begin with.[61] Initiating prohibition work within the liberal community also required the presence of women temperance supporters. By working in tandem with such organizations as the WCTU, Dominion Alliance executives such as Frank Spence, William Burgess, and J.W. Bengough caught the suffragist fervour through association. Although female suffrage only became part of the Alliance agenda in 1890, the 1894 plebiscite in Ontario convinced many prohibition militants to endorse votes for women. The first vote given to Ontario women of property resulted in a nearly 85 percent support of prohibition, and convinced Alliance members of the potential advantage of women to the movement. The Dominion Alliance would later mourn the fact that women were not permitted to vote in the national plebiscite on prohibition in 1897.[62]

Notwithstanding these efforts toward liberal inclusion, the temperance union movement was far more consciously a middle-class movement than its counterparts in fraternal temperance societies. Even at its inception in the form of the Canadian Prohibitory Liquor Law League, temperance union promoters recognized that such movements would not be very well attuned to the value system of the masses. John Dougall, the noted temperance figure from Montreal, stated emphatically that the existence of the League would rest solely on the zeal, energy, perseverance and *money* of a small minority.[63] The Quebec Temperance and Prohibitory League was even more audacious in its conscription of liberal members from the middle classes in Quebec. As its directors proclaimed: "The middle classes of the community are those from whom we must expect the largest support; not from the highest or lowest. The middle classes, strong and stalwart in their views of right and wrong, are the exponents of public opinion. They are such as no Governor, or body of rulers, dare for any length of time to set at defiance; for these reasons the efforts of the League should be directed at the middle classes."[64] The *Canada Citizen and Temperance Herald* therefore highlighted the drinking habits of the skilled working classes, denying that temperance was a movement designed by the rich to crush the poor. To the editors of the *Canada Citizen*, prohibition would put an end to the cycle of perpetual poverty caused by intemperance. Editorials in the official organ of the Dominion Alliance likewise censured the big business of alcohol in the name of the middle class, noting that hotelkeepers neglected to fund *Scott Act* challenges "for the benefit of metropolitan capitalists who are building up large fortunes and palatial residences, regardless of the indisputable fact that their enrichment must mean the impoverishment of the community at large."[65]

Another example of the influence of urban middle-class temperance supporters on the prohibition movement is the creation of joint stock temperance businesses. The advertisement pages of the *Canada Citizen and Temperance Herald* included strong endorsements of the Temperance and General Life Assurance Company, along with a bevy of public notices for a variety of other temperance insurance companies. The Temperance Colonization Society, a joint stock venture, offered shares in a landholding company with aims to colonize tracts of land where liquor could not be manufactured, sold, or imported. This company was unmistakably a middle-class enterprise, for out of thirty-six original investors thirty-five listed their occupation as merchant, lawyer, clerk, or minister of religion.[66] The Canadian Temperance League showed its colours by embracing the coffee house movement that originated with the Toronto Coffee House Association in 1882. In order to offset the influence of the workingman's tavern, coffee house advocates particularly urged the poor and unemployed to frequent these establishments. The coffee house movement was clearly not only a philanthropic venture but also a middle-class business proposition. The objects of the Toronto Coffee House Association were to provide "a check upon the use of intoxicating drinks as well as being financially viable to the shareholders."[67]

By the end of the century prohibition had become a hotly contested political issue, and it was increasingly difficult for urban temperance union societies to eradicate the influence of party politics from their operations. And yet a semblance of liberal political and religious objectivity was essential to launch temperance unionism, given the diversity of religious and temperance groups associated with the movement. The Canada Temperance Union not only worked in unison with other temperance groups to stimulate prohibition sentiment but it triumphantly claimed that it was able to avoid sectional and national feuds or jealousies. The Quebec Temperance and Prohibitory League worked co-operatively with the Roman Catholic segment of the population, in the firm conviction that religious differences should not prevent unanimous support of the great social question of temperance reform.[68] And initial Dominion Alliance declarations on the subject of political and religious neutrality mirrored this discourse in an attempt to shelter various church synods, fraternal temperance orders, and other groups from destructive disputes unrelated to prohibition. As to the editor of the *Canada Citizen and Temperance Herald* brought to his readers' attention, the evidence of non-partyism in the Dominion Alliance could be witnessed in the co-operation and unity displayed by the president of the Alliance, a Conservative senator, and the president of the Ontario Branch, S.H. Blake, a noted Reformer.[69]

The subsequent politicization of the temperance movement came via the ballot box, as prohibition advocates wrestled with the thorny problem of electing temperance men into office. The Canada Temperance Union documented this shift in ideology, as its policy was to assist both the drunkard and the moderate drinker with moral suasion, while driving the rumseller "from his entrenchments by the avenging power of righteous legislation." The result of this twofold strategy was a division and a weakening of the "liberal" temperance power, as temperance politics could easily be overwhelmed by party rivalry and private speculation. Even when such associations as the Quebec Temperance and Prohibitory League espoused the ideology of an independent temperance political party, they were heard lecturing temperance men to throw off the shackles of party bondage. Philip Carpenter, a member of the Quebec Temperance and Prohibitory League, also levelled a direct criticism at the ruling Conservatives, who as a result of the Pacific scandal were "deprived of power, not so much because the policy of the party was distasteful to the community, as because its leaders were involved in corrupt practices."[70] The Young Men's Prohibition Club of Toronto clarified the developing sense of liberal temperance community, which was by no means above using the political process to achieve its overall objectives:

> That it is neither right nor politic for the State to afford legal protection and sanction to any traffic or system that tends to increase crime, to waste national resources, to corrupt the social habits and to destroy the health and the lives the people. That the traffic in intoxicating beverages is hostile to the true interests of individuals, and destructive of the order and welfare of society, and ought therefore be prohibited. That the total prohibition of the liquor traffic is in perfect harmony with the principles of justice and liberty, is not restrictive of legitimate commerce, and is essential to the integrity and stability of government and welfare of the community.[71]

Favourable pronouncements by the Dominion Alliance on the Prohibition Party in the United States initially served as a wake-up call to both the Conservatives and Liberals; if the politicians would not legislate prohibition, the Dominion Alliance *could* correspondingly take matters into its own political hands. While conceding the problematic fact that many party temperance men would vote for their party every time, the vast majority of temperance men from both parties wanted to prevent a third party with a prohibition platform, for it would be "defeated beyond all redemption" and create undesirable party divisions.[72] Although Frank Spence envisioned that the mere threat of a new party was enough to alarm politicians, he was obviously not in favour of a new prohibition party himself, given his leaning toward a liberal state: "[Temperance politicians,] are wise enough to see that the better class of the community is beginning to get impatient of the indifference shown towards a matter of the most intense and vital importance to our country's welfare, and they see, in the near future, unless something is speedily done to avert this awful catastrophe, the disturbing political element of a CANADIAN PROHIBITION PARTY." Spence's true colours came to the fore when, in 1888, he criticized the New Party, a prohibition party that was created by the one-time editor of the *Canada Citizen*, William Burgess, and a Dr A.H. Sutherland. Objecting vociferously that building a political party around a single platform was simply nonsensical, Spence proceeded to condemn the party's formation as being dissonant to the general temperance community.[73]

As early as 1886, during an annual meeting of the Dominion Alliance, discussion about the possibility of creating a independent political party based on principles of prohibition had degenerated into a partisan debate over the merits of the Liberal platform. Many delegates accused Spence and others of conducting a Reformer convention rather than a prohibition meeting, particularly after one delegate stated categorically that there was no need of a third option, as the Liberals were clearly the party of prohibition.[74] Allegations such as this would haunt Spence throughout his tenure with the Dominion Alliance, particularly in his dealings with the executive of the Royal Templars of Temperance. Complaining that the Dominion Alliance criticized the Patrons of Industry for adopting prohibition as a political ploy while avoiding the obvious parallel with Liberal plebiscites, the *Templar* eagerly reported the establishment of the Patron Prohibition Alliance. The official organ of the Royal Templars called on all members to support the new movement, and "publicly proclaim [their] protest against the present unholy alliance between Toryism-Grittism and liquordom, and refuse to belong to either camp, as long as both lack the courage to raise the Prohibition standard." In an obvious endorsement of the Patron platform, the *Templar* echoed the more radically populist *Canada Farmers' Sun* in opposing the liquor traffic, class legislation, monopolies, taxes on labour, corrupt politics, hidebound partyism, and cowardly politicians.[75] After these articles appeared in the *Templar*, Spence angrily denied charges of political favouritism in a council meeting of the Dominion Alliance. Despite his denunciation of the *Templar*, he refused to investigate the affair, a refusal that some council members took as an admission that he feared the truth. The council also questioned Spence's motives when both he and Liberal MP G.W. Ross opposed the nomination of W.W. Buchanan – an independent prohibition candidate in Wentworth – as the election eventually went to the Liberal candidate. The Montreal chapter of the Royal Templars therefore withdrew its support from the Dominion Alliance "until such time as its officers [were] prepared to carry out its platform" by rising above party considerations.[76]

In their scrutiny of the liquor traffic, temperance union societies also exhibited a middle-class mentality by examining the economic benefits of prohibition through the professionalized science of political economy. The liquor trade not only destroyed the national economy and contravened legitimate commerce, they asserted, but it failed to execute the primary function of capitalization. As the executive of the Canada Temperance Union pointed out, the greater the investment in the liquor traffic, the greater the injury, the lower the availability of employment of skilled and unskilled labour, and the closer one came to an utter loss of any profit whatsoever.[77] The Dominion Alliance concurred, reiterating the age-old argument of temperance societies that the liquor traffic interfered with legitimate commerce and the nation's economy. In one plebiscite circular, the Alliance insisted that trade in alcohol disrupted normal political economy, as the great amount of capital invested in the liquor traffic employed comparatively few men and also kept out other investments that would employ more people, pay higher wages, and benefit the people instead of making them poor.[78] Some urban temperance supporters also aligned themselves with new and innovative principles of political economy in denouncing the evils of the liquor traffic.

William Burgess, former editor of the *Canada Citizen*, Congregationalist minister, member of the Dominion Alliance, and co-creator of the New Party, illustrated this new political economy in his 1887 book, *Land, Labor and Liquor: A Chapter in the Political Economy of the Present Day*. In many ways, this tome was faithful to the liberal tenets of honest industry and the political economy of hard work. In discussing the differences between productive and unproductive labour, the labour theory of value, and the evils of idleness, Burgess also taught the important principle of co-operation between labour and capital, as "the gain of either the capitalist or the workman is not necessarily the loss of the other." And yet lauding the Knights of Labor for abolishing class distinctions, the co-operative system, profit sharing, trade unionism, and Henry George's nationalization schemes, Burgess also heralded change in the political economy of temperance.[79] Calling on his working class audience to recognize the real enemy of the distillery, the brewery, and the saloon, Burgess deployed a typical temperance argument; if the legislative suppression of the liquor traffic occurred, the stimulus for honest industry would be assured amongst a dry populace. In the prohibition scheme, labour would come at a premium, wages would be fair, and no willing hands would be idle. To Burgess, the responsibility of the liquor traffic for pauperism, disorder, accidents, and the subsequent financial ruin of society was obvious, but, he wrote: "Social reformers and political economists who recognize the terrible burdens and afflictions under which the masses groan and suffer, and yet ignore the intimate relation of the liquor traffic to every form of social depression and woe, are simply baling out water from a leaky ship while its timbers are being rotted and scuttled."[80]

While the temperance union movement did not entirely frown on the use of entertainment as an additional device to further the cause of prohibition, amusements were not a high priority for the directors of union societies. The Young Men's Prohibition Club in Toronto initially realized the necessity of offering entertainments to its members. Consequently, the directors established a reception, concert, and musical committee to help raise funds for the political work of the Club. Highly elaborate activities were planned, from a comedic slide presentation by the noted satirist J.W. Bengough, to excursions and concerts. When the expenses for Bengough's presentation ran too high, the appetite for entertainment began to wane. After the concert committee had reneged on a promise to hold a summer concert, the directors began to hold rather fruitless meetings on the financial state of the Club. By 1890 a special committee meeting on the finances of the Club reported that "some discussion took place with reference to the financial affairs of the club, but no conclusion was arrived at." Similarly, in an entertainment report of the Hall committee of the Toronto Temperance Reformation Society in 1886, no mention was made of possible new leisure activities. Instead, the Hall committee merely reported its refusal to allow dancing parties, theatrical companies, Negro minstrels, immodest exhibitions, infidel lectures, and electioneering meetings within the hallowed walls of the Toronto Temperance Hall.[81]

POST-CONFEDERATION TEMPERANCE FRATERNALISM AND AN EMERGING MIDDLE-CLASS SENSIBILITY

In small towns, despite a transferral of temperance support from skilled workers to the middle classes, temperance fraternalism remained a vital force among all interests toward the end of the century. Much evidence for this change illustrates an ideological swing to middle-class temperance rather than a literal shift, as recent studies demonstrate a strong continuing presence of skilled workers in rural fraternal temperance orders.[82] Although temperance fraternalism in small towns worked closely with organizations such as the Dominion Alliance in promoting the prohibition ideal, the attention of many such associations was taken by their own local battles to control the liquor traffic. As with organizations such as the Dominion Grange and the Patrons of Industry, tensions between middle-class temperance supporters who favoured a more liberal position and those favouring a more "populist" stance indicate that attitudes to political prohibition and other principles relating to temperance were difficult to reconcile.[83] Just as the issue of prohibition had a propensity to expose latent disagreements in the urban prohibition alliance, the dissimilar prohibition strategies of rural and urban fraternal temperance supporters likewise highlighted the regionally delineated visions of temperance as well as the breakdown of the mid-century "liberal" social order.

Conventional cross-class membership and the rhetoric of class inclusion in fraternal temperance societies reveal a lingering liberal "community" ethos among traditional orders such as the Sons of Temperance and the IOGT. In 1898 an article in the *Sons of Temperance Record and Prohibition Advocate* recalled the history of the Order, candidly recounting various controversies over both coloured and female membership. That battle had clearly been won: "[The Sons now have] no privileged classes; it enrols under its tricoloured banner all ranks in society ... It recognizes no distinction on account of race, sex, colour, or former condition, but all are alike equal, and all join in the common purpose of promoting the public weal and overthrowing the wrongs of intemperance from which the world suffers." The official organ of the IOGT, the *Camp Fire*, appealed to its readers on the basis that the lodge was an aggressive force for good, and nothing would be as effective in uniting all classes in a community for warfare against the liquor traffic.[84] Even though the boundaries of class were often crossed in the course of these appeals, evidence of an ideological shift to the middle class appears in some of the condescending discourse of the traditional fraternal temperance orders. Rather than embracing the radical worker subculture of their mid-century forbearers, both the Sons and the IOGT engaged in a more exclusionary dialogue despite the continued presence of skilled workers. For example, while lauding the honest and noble workingman, the *Camp Fire* also condemned the "drones in the hives of industry, the loungers in the street, whose useless hands are stretched to take."[85]

Traditional fraternal temperance orders continued to recognize the necessity of being inclusive by opening up lodges, divisions, and councils to women. By late century, female participation in the WCTU, in the prohibition movement, and in temperance orders in general involved so much more than just the issue of achieving prohibition. Women's suffrage, the social purity movement, moral reform, and scientific temperance would be the hallmarks of female contributions – and additions – to the temperance movement.[86] Much of the work to augment female presence in fraternal temperance societies was done in response to the threat to their membership posed by groups such as the WCTU. For example, both the *Templar*, the pro-Patrons of Industry temperance organ of the Royal Templars, and the *Camp Fire*, the pro-Liberal paper of the IOGT edited by Frank Spence, came out in favour of votes for women. Of course espousal of female suffrage on the part of most prohibition supporters represented quite simply a desire to unleash the potential power of temperance women into the electorate to achieve prohibition.[87] The Sons of Temperance also followed the lead established more than a decade earlier by the IOGT, in allowing women to become officers in their lodges. By the end of the century, two rural divisions of the Sons of Temperance had appointed women to their highest office, that of Worthy Patriarch. All temperance lodges, divisions, and councils similarly attempted to encourage the enlistment of female members through reduced fees and other inducements. Although some local lodges rebelled against this practice and just as quickly hiked female initiation fees, the decision to appoint women as debate leaders and as chairmen of various entertainment committees in some measure aided the cause of female recruitment.[88]

And yet women continued to have secondary status in fraternal temperance orders, as the female secretary in the Plantagenet council of the Royal Templars of Temperance discovered during a discussion on the lack of women in the entertainment committee. This shortcoming met with disapproval of one of the Brothers, who justly thought that the "fairer sex" should have better representation. With some disdain at the lack of progressive thinking in the council, the secretary wrote: "Evidently the Council did not approve of the suggestion of the upholder of [women's] rights as the amendment was carried with the proportion 4:1 in favour of mankind."[89] In the Williamstown Council of the Royal Templars, the executive censured some brothers for unruly behaviour, ostensibly for an affront to some of the sisters in the council. In a contrasting example, in the Orono division of the Sons of Temperance, the secretary recorded on one occasion that "a general giggle broke out among the sisters," which disturbed the meeting. The secretary was not as inclined to reprimand the women and reported a more tolerant response: "Shame on them, the Brothers chimed in, and for a few minutes a social time was royally enjoyed. These are bright spots in our gatherings which make our work more enjoyable." Efforts to fully include women in fraternal temperance orders eventually came to naught, however, as the WCTU could offer women complete autonomy in the function of their operations.[90]

The Royal Templars of Temperance adhered strictly to traditional temperance society values of liberal inclusion, proclaiming as their objective the promotion of temperance, morality, and industry among all classes. And yet the Royal Templars – another U.S.-based temperance fraternal order that reached a zenith of popularity in the 1870s – also echoed the more exclusionary discourse of radical temperance societies such as the mid-century Sons of Temperance. As one of their ritual odes made clear, real labouring men did not include:

They who creep in drives and lanes,
To rob their betters of honest gains;
The rich that stoop to devour the poor,
The tramp that begs from door to door;
The rogues that love the darkened sky,
And steal and rob and cheat and lie;
The loafing wights and senseless bloats,
Who drain their pockets to wet their throats!

Not only did the Royal Templars return to a denunciation of both upper and lower class drinking patterns, but editorials in their official temperance paper, the *Templar*, lauded the TLC for supporting complete prohibition. The editors praised the TLC for acknowledging that the saloon was the enemy of the workingman, and urged that steps be taken to protect industrial workers from its influence.[91] Similarly, one of the more popular entertainments of the Royal Templars was known as the pauper party, where participants could either come dressed in rags or be fined for wearing expensive items. Attendees were charged five cents for a watch and chain, pearl necklaces, and diamond tiaras, and two cents for rings and other light jewellery, and all the proceeds were either given to the poor or used to advance the cause of prohibition. At the same time, it appears that the increasing popularity of the Royal Templars was buoyed by a return to the older and liberal political economy of producerism, through the restoration of the benefit system of fraternal temperance.[92]

The popularity of the Royal Templars both with the rural working classes and with the urban industrial classes seemed to be more a function of their providing insurance and sick benefits to members than their sustaining of a new political economy. In order to improve the moral, intellectual, social, and physical condition of its members, the Royal Templars instituted a "magnificent system" of protection from sickness and from the hardships associated with the passing of a relative. Underscoring the intense competition for customers in the insurance and mutual benefits field, fraternal temperance orders advertised a more comprehensive and economical benefits package: "Total abstainers are less liable to sickness and accident, live longer than non-abstainers, and suffer injustice when classified with such inferior risks in insurance companies or benefit societies." The Royal Templars managed to capture their share of working class members. After subtracting female members and occupations not listed, labourers and farmers made up 58 percent of one rural council in Ontario, while 56 percent of the membership in the North Toronto Council of the Royal Templars came from skilled workers (see Table 3.2). Traditional fraternal temperance orders were quick to take advantage, as by the 1880s the IOGT had established a fund for mutual assistance in case of disability, sickness, or death. Evidently this feature served to lure many skilled workers back into the fraternal temperance fold, particularly in small towns.[93]

In maintaining their system of benefits, fraternal temperance orders continued to respect the liberal precepts of honest industry, mutual aid, and the individual work ethic. In individuals, intemperance led to idleness, profligacy, and vice; in a liberal community, the liquor traffic damaged legitimate businesses by laying unwanted financial burdens upon society. As the IOGT summarized the economic argument: "Drinking habits mean idleness and unthrift. Drunkness seriously impairs the ability of the people to indulge in the luxuries, sometimes even in the necessities, of life. The drink waste is a serious interference with the purchasing power of the people, and therefore, an impediment to wealth production ... All this poverty, crime, and suffering impose additional financial burdens upon the community. As a whole, we are taxed heavily, we suffer keenly, as the outcome of a system under which some gratify their appetites and a few others grow rich at the general expense."[94] Fraternal temperance orders reproduced statistics illustrating the devastating impact of the liquor trade, and many fraternal temperance lodges, divisions, and councils held debates and discussions on the relationship between temperance and liberal political economy. Whether debating the merits of Commercial Union, freer trade, or commercial trade versus agriculture, all fraternal temperance societies were in agreement about the detrimental economic effects of alcohol upon society.[95]

Table 3.2
Ordinary Membership by Occupation, Royal Templars of Temperance, Selected Years, 1886–1906

Brooklin Council #102			North Toronto Council #104		
Occupation	Total	Percentage	Occupation	Total	Percentage
Trackmen	5		Carpenter	8	
Mason	3		Plumber	3	
Tinsmith	3		Shoemaker	2	
Labourer	2		Painter	2	
Boot/Shoemaker	2		Printer	2	
Others*	7		Others*	13	
TOTAL SKILLED	22	21	TOTAL SKILLED	30	25.5
Clerk	4		Bookkeeper	3	
TOTAL CLERICAL	4	3.5	Clerk	2	
Agent	4		TOTAL CLERICAL	5	4
Merchant	3		Merchant	2	
TOTAL BUSINESS	7	6.5	Others^^^	7	
Minister	11		TOTAL BUSINESS	9	7.5
Teacher	3		Student	18	
Others**	3		Doctor	3	
TOTAL PROFESSIONAL	17	16	Lawyer	2	
Farmers	18		TOTAL PROFESSIONAL	23	19
TOTAL AGRICULTURAL	18	16.5			
			TOTAL UNRECORDED	20	16.5
TOTAL UNRECORDED	10	9.5			
			TOTAL WOMEN^^	33	27.5
TOTAL WOMEN^	29	27			

* Other occupations in the skilled category include: baker, blacksmith, builder, carpenter, tanner, artist, bricklayer, conductor, driver, guilder, harness maker, telegraph operator, pump maker, and watchmaker.
** Other occupations in the professional category include: doctor, student, and veterinarian.
^ Female occupations listed in the Brooklin Templars include: twelve teachers.
^^ Female occupations listed in the North Toronto Templars include: bookkeeper, domestic, dressmaker, student, housekeeper, and tailoress.
^^^ Other occupations in the business category include: druggist, florist, grocer, and real estate agent.

SOURCE: Records of the Brooklin Council, Royal Templars of Temperance, in the John Whitford papers, AO, MU 7825, membership list, 1895–1906 and records of the North Toronto Council, Royal Templars of Temperance, in the John Linton fonds, AO, MU 7276, file #2, petitions for membership, 1889–1900.

On the surface, the pronouncements of the more urban IOGT organ, the *Camp Fire*, continued in an earlier and more radical condemnation of the non-producing classes and the proprietors of public houses in the name of the respectable workingman. As one editorial summed it up: "The public house and the private house cannot both thrive. The earnings of workingmen are not sufficient both to supply the wants of their own homes, and support an army of lazy landlords and well-fed landladies." However, such rhetoric could also have stemmed from a liberal producer *ideology* of the middle class, as still another article in the *Camp Fire* acknowledged that "the awakening commercial appreciation of the injury [alcohol] inflicts upon all legitimate business interests."[96] This was a far cry from the censure heaped on the "genteel upper class" for their drinking habits a few decades earlier. Urban fraternal temperance orders now focused instead on how workingmen became idle wastrels as a result of drinking. In an editorial slamming the *Licensed Victuallars Gazette*, an anti-prohibition newspaper in Toronto, Frank Spence severely criticized the paper for not understanding that "many workmen who are now idle because of their drinking habits, under prohibition would be industrious and thrifty." In a lecture to the Grand Division of the Sons of Temperance in Canada East, Mrs L.M. Sherlocke called on the working class to be more temperate so as to gain the world's respect and a greater portion of their own productions. Conceding that the working class had suffered more wrongs than any other class in existence, Sherlocke invited workers to concentrate on the real enemy: King Capital indeed chastened them with whips, but King Alcohol punished them with scorpions.[97]

Although rural fraternal temperance orders were interested in promoting prohibition on a national scale, they placed more attention on efforts to control the liquor traffic closer to home. By now acknowledging that the temperance question was of necessity a political one, local temperance societies offered both financial and moral support to the Dominion Alliance. The Williamstown and Fergus councils established a plebiscite committee to handle all the campaign work, while the Fergus Royal Templars took the direct route by protesting to their MP over a treaty to admit French wines.[98] Similarly, the Fergus council of the Royal Templars went so far as to ask the village constable to pay special attention to the Sabbath closing of barrooms, and to infractions such as the sale of alcohol to minors. The Orono division of the Sons of Temperance often had complaints about the way inspectors handled the licence acts, and offered to pay for the prosecution of taverns under the *Dunkin Act*. By the end of the century, the Orono Sons of Temperance had concluded that the most effective means of securing a dry Orono was to have a Son appointed to the office of Tavern inspector.[99] Although these rural temperance societies were more than willing to assist the urban prohibition alliance with their efforts toward national prohibition, they gave far more prominence to mutual assistance through the benefits system and their own local efforts to halt the spread of the liquor traffic.

Changes in the political landscape also explained the renewed interest in prohibition on the part of temperance fraternal orders in rural areas at this time. Despite the fact that prohibition in the urban environment upheld middle-class values, the rural experience was that temperance and prohibition could also empower the marginal to censure the accepted social order. In this context, fraternal temperance orders also participated in a populist critique of politicians, big government, monopoly capitalism, and the professional classes.[100] Even though the Grand Temple of the IOGT decreed in 1875 that fraternal temperance orders should concentrate their energies on obtaining adherents from all parties, irrespective of their creed or politics, the surest means to achieve prohibition was for temperance men to act politically. However, the IOGT also effectively criticized liberal governments for their failure to carry the subject immediately before the electorate:

> While we are not a political party, and leave every man free to vote with his party and for such men and principles as he may prefer, we do protest against men being nominated for office who are not known, beyond question, to be competent and reliable moral men, who will not disgrace the country by habits of personal intemperance, or debauch the public conscience and corrupt public morals by favouring measures unfriendly to temperance reform, or defeat our cause by refusing to support and enforce such laws as are calculated to protect society against the evils of the liquor traffic. That if political parties will persist in putting forward men who are unworthy of our confidence, they must take the responsibility of any divisions or defeats that may result in our refusing to support them.[101]

Although fraternal orders supported the middle-class–dominated Dominion Alliance in their prohibition efforts, these societies often held their own populist agendas. More than one response to the Alliance expressed the intent of this poorly spelled reply from the Cherry Valley Royal Templars: "Acknowleging our councils cooperation with all truly temperance sentiment [we will] work with zeal to gain such a majority for Proabition as will maik Politions stand agast."[102]

By the 1890s, when the Royal Templars of Temperance officially came out in support of the newfound alliance of urban workers and rural farmers through the Patrons of Industry, the connection between temperance and populism was complete. The Royal Templars undoubtedly knew their prospective temperance audience; one Royal Templar ode entitled "We'll Make the Retreat, Boys" lauded the true temperance and prohibition reformers from the "tilling and toiling" labouring classes:

> The horny handed workmen, the ploughmen from the farms;
> And diggers from the gold mines, have come to shoulder arms.
> With us they shoulder arms, boys, while drums by quakers beat;
> Shall cheer us on, till victory's won, we see the foe retreat.[103]

The *Templar* tried to fulfill the mandate of an "aggressive Christian temperance order": Christianity, if applied in the community, it claimed, would purify politics, destroy monopolies, wipe out class privileges, and establish the brotherhood of man. The *Templar* published articles on Henry George's single tax, J.W. Bengough's views on tax reform, social purity issues, and the views of the Christian Socialist movement. Among its claims was that competition was cruel and anti-Christian in forcing businessmen to grind the poor. To the Grand Council of the Royal Templars, such concerns were the foundation of a populist response to an elitist political economy: "[A] science which often traces want and misery, enforced idleness and brutalizing conditions to monopoly and privilege ... is not likely to make progress till it has become popularized. How shall we be fed? Wherewithal shall we be clothed? These are the questions with which political economy attempts to deal, and since food and clothing are the first requisites of life, political economy is the basis of social science."[104]

THE CHALLENGES OF SOCIABILITY IN LATE NINETEENTH-CENTURY TEMPERANCE FRATERNALISM

In the late 1860s temperance fraternal orders did not adjust well either to their new middle-class constituency or to the changing circumstances surrounding temperance societies, particularly when it came to leisure and entertainment options within the lodge or division. The recreation offered by the Good Templars and Sons of Temperance in this period continued to be of the rational variety – speeches, recitations, songs and music, and debates as well as mathematics or spelling matches. As the *Canada Digest*, the handbook of the IOGT, proclaimed, once the rigid rules necessary for the business portion of a meeting were over, with the observance of order and decorum, the members might be invited to seek relaxation in social intercourse and *intellectual* repasts. The *Digest* also continued to stress liberal "respectability" within its membership, forbidding the attending of horse races and cock fights, the smoking of tobacco, gambling, and the playing of cards.[105] After a series of cancelled tea meetings, the Gananoque lodge of the BAOGT perceived that weak turnouts resulted from a lack of anything instructional or interesting in lodge meetings, and so organized debates, lectures, and an anniversary soirée to bring the cause of temperance to the community. These plans clearly came to naught, however, as the last meeting of the Gananoque lodge contained a debate on whether the lodge was of any benefit to its members or the public.[106]

By the late 1860s and early 1870s, the printing of temperance dialogues became a growth industry for temperance presses, and they were disseminated as means of alleviating the boredom of fraternal temperance lodge and division meetings. With such titles as *The Teetotaller's Companion* and *Light for the Temperance Platform*, these collections of temperance skits, songs, recitations, and readings were designed to help temperance societies to produce *worthy* entertainment for their members.[107] Regrettably, these amusements and leisure activities could not guarantee a healthy temperance society or banish ennui. Despite the best efforts of the Greensboro Temple in Caledon to provide quality "intertainments," sarcastic commentaries in the minute book by the secretary, William McLaren, illustrate the true nature of the troubles within the lodge. Recognizing that disturbances during lodge meetings resulted from the initiation ceremonies' being "dry as parched beams," McLaren quipped that one of the officers had to leave the ceremony temporarily to check his pulse. These sentiments were later echoed in a poem entered into the minutes: "The Lodge then closed in prayer. / And all went home to those most dear; / and also glad to get away from here." The Worthy Patriarch of the Orono division of the Sons of Temperance in 1870 called members' attention to the arrival of a disease in Orono, which he termed the "dry rot." This disease, he said, manifested itself through "indifference and lack of interest, and these things tend to the death of any community that is infested with them ... shun this disease and the best way not to contract it [is] to strive to keep the divisions interesting by short addresses, singing, recitations, etc."[108]

Attempts to cut out the "dry rot" from fraternal temperance societies led to further struggles in communicating the temperance crusade to those in the larger community. The motivation behind proposed amusements was twofold: to bring in more revenue to fund the temperance crusade, and to stir up interest in the society itself. As early as 1863, the *Good Templar* had noted that the competition for leisure within villages and towns already had claimed some casualties among lodge members: "[They seek] amusements and pleasure for [them]selves, desert our Lodge rooms, and thereby run the risk of some newly reclaimed member follow[ing] the example, with this fearful indifference, while [they] seek for enjoyment at a social tea-party, or singing and debating club."[109] Consequently, many Good Templar lodges and Sons of Temperance divisions would make tentative plans to bring sundry entertainments to their town or village, ranging from picnics, concerts, and open lodges, to tea-meetings and anniversary socials. The timing of these plans in the 1870s was rather poor, as the economic depression in central Canada made the public ill-disposed to spend tight funds on temperance entertainment. The Orono Sons of Temperance had originally been very enthusiastic about public entertainment and solicited advice on how to proceed. However, entertainment committee in Orono met with a great deal of resistance from the general membership in the 1870s. In fact, when it asked for guidance from the membership body in 1878 on how to handle public leisure, the members voted to disband the committee.[110]

The general public tended to shy away from temperance-sponsored entertainment, and many lodges and divisions simply did not explore the revenue-generating possibilities of leisure and amusements. As a result, most lodges of the Good Templars during the 1870s struggled to maintain their enthusiasm for temperance on a shoestring budget. The executive of the Hampton lodge did not hold any public entertainments from 1873 to 1876, prompting some of the members in 1875 to discuss "money and other matters" in the lodge meeting, which "amounted to nothing." Less than a year later the lodge met to consider the advisability of surrendering their charter, as their membership had dropped from a high of nearly eighty in 1870 to a low of under forty. The Forest Home lodge of the Good Templars in Minesing was initially very successful in its public entertainments, and accumulated sufficient funds to consider building a temperance house in Barrie. Enthusiasm for tea meetings, excursions, and concerts waned, however, as the lodge executive pondered the feasibility of supporting a Temperance Hotel and offering direct support for various temperance demonstrations. The injudiciousness of ignoring public amusements readily became apparent to the board, when membership figures fell from a high of seventy to a mere nine.[111] The exclusive focus on the work of prohibition and the temperance crusade brought a waning interest for the society among its own members and soon spelled the end of the Good Templars in Minesing and in other rural areas of central Canada.

By the end of the century, the picture had again changed. Fraternal temperance orders experienced a marked revival of interest in small towns, particularly in the realms of entertainment. The Eugene division of the

Sons knew that leisure would secure a greater attendance from the public and tried to make their amusements more attractive to outsiders.[112] Most of the entertainments remained of the rational variety, and lodges, divisions, and councils again established committees to devise new and interesting ways to organize their social gatherings. Among the innovative amusements were contests, such as the one the Summerville division of the Sons of Temperance in Peel County initiated to recruit members. Two teams were chosen from among their membership, and points were awarded on a sliding scale, from a low of two points for simple attendance to a high of fifteen for recruiting members and composing temperance essays, with the loser treating the winner to an oyster supper. These contests also stimulated some temperance societies to bolster the reputation of their locale, as nearby towns or villages responded to challenges in order to defend the dignity and honour of their town. The Summerville division, for instance, offered to duel the Cooksville division of the Sons in a tug of war, while the Cherry Valley Royal Templars challenged a neighbouring council to a debate.[113]

Successful lodges, divisions, and councils were those that approved of amusements both as a way of offering enjoyment and as a means of raising revenues. Concerts, strawberry festivals, oyster suppers, and picnics encouraged the participation of all members of the community in the activities of the temperance society. The longevity of a fraternal temperance order in a community came in direct proportion to the quantity – and the quality – of entertainment offered to local inhabitants. The Orono division of the Sons of Temperance staved off extinction for several decades through its activities for the community.[114] The Williamstown council of Royal Templars managed only an erratic membership base that often dipped into single figures from its establishment in 1892. When the council invited neighbouring councils to visit, held taffy parties, reunions, and other social events, the resulting enthusiasm for entertainment spread into the executive. From January to August 1898, the Williamstown council established music, entertainment, picnic, excursion, and concert committees to make the arrangements. The Eugene Sons of Temperance also became overloaded with entertainment committees, and their events were so lucrative that a motion was passed to do away with most of the initiation ceremony as it took up too much time from the entertainment portion of their meetings.[115]

Not all fraternal temperance societies had successful leisure programs or experienced entertainment as a cohesive force in their society. The Fergus Royal Templars initially offered a wide array of entertainment options to members and the village in general, ranging from balls, picnics, and concerts to open meetings and excursions. With such a program their attendance fluctuated from a low of forty to a high of ninety-one. As the council began focusing more exclusively on the issue of prohibition, attendance quickly plummeted to single digits. The last straw for the Fergus Royal Templar executive came when an open meeting in 1895 had to be postponed because of conflicting schedules, a poorly outlined program, and lack of interest. Competition from other leisure activities could also disrupt the meeting schedule of temperance orders. A speech by a Mrs Manners in the Eugene division of the Sons of Temperance on the subject of croquet critiqued the sport for keeping members away from meetings.[116] Sociability in the lodge, division, or council room could also create *dis*order and conflict. Debates were often thinly veiled accusations of impropriety, as in the ease of the Williamstown council of the Royal Templars, where the women of the council discussed whether card playing was worse than smoking tobacco. Another episode in the Orono division of the Sons of Temperance merely demonstrated a new director flexing his authority. The worthy Patriarch indicated during a division social that "he wanted to have good order and was going to have it, and hoped the members would in future conduct the discussions in the division in a more Brotherly manner than he had seen several times of late."[117]

Urban spokesmen for fraternal temperance societies in particular recognized the difficulty in initiating entertainments within the urban lodge, division, or council. The *Quebec Good Templar* hoped that entertainments held in Quebec Good Templar lodges would only have two purposes: to alleviate debt and to promote prohibition, as "such united public gatherings show a strong centre and front to the community, and could not but give strength to our common cause."[118] An editorial in the *Camp Fire* complained that temperance societies in the more populous cities and towns of central Canada "were crowded out by the pressure of other institutions" while they retained their hold over the rural community. In another *Camp Fire* editorial, Spence urged that every division, every lodge, and every Prohibition club should have a picnic or outdoor party to bring prohibition to the community. He added, however, that every such gathering required "short, pointed addresses on our political position and duty." The politicization of entertainment in urban societies came full circle in Spence's analysis: "What shall we do to save the lodge? This is the wrong question. What shall the lodge do to save the people? If the lodge does nothing in this direction it isn't worth saving. If it goes actively to work it will save itself."[119]

Early temperance orders employed the temperance ideal to construct a liberal *and* temperate community free from alcohol and inclusive of all classes and creeds. The erosion of this ideal in mid-century temperance societies can be measured by the unconditional acceptance of legislative prohibition, and the political and religious squabbling that accompanied temperance discourse. Likewise, early temperance associations could be quite flexible in the construction of liberal identities, given the preponderance of the evangelical middling sort in early temperance orders, and the large constituency of skilled workers in temperance fraternalism.

Despite protestations to the contrary, the injection of political discussion into the question of temperance in the latter decades of the nineteenth century ensured that the conflicting philosophies of rural and urban temperance and prohibition ideologues would create fissures in central Canadian society that would continue into the twentieth century. Temperance societies in particular illustrate the contested nature of Canada's liberal project, given the changing strategies and adherents of the temperance crusade. Not only did the dry utopia envisioned by temperance supporters of all classes in the late decades of the century fall short of the ideal but, in attempting to fashion such an idyllic world, temperance societies hastened the demise of a liberal temperance community so carefully constructed throughout the early Victorian period.

4

A Spirit of Candour, Moderation, and Open Generosity

The early history of the Independent Order of Oddfellows (IOOF) in Canada from the 1840s to the 1870s tells us that it was an organization very much concerned with both the external and internal behaviour of its membership. Oddfellows set up "committees of character" to examine potential candidates and kept "black books" to exclude those of questionable moral fibre. Among themselves, they attempted to maintain fraternal courtesy in all their conversations and to conduct themselves in a "spirit of candour, moderation and open generosity," proposing that "all personal allusions or sarcastic language be dropped."[1] To judge from the abundance of names in the black books of mid-century lodges, however, regulating the behaviour of its membership proved to be a difficult task for the Oddfellows. The list of names in the Phoenix Lodge's "register of rejected candidates" in Oshawa was so long that the executive in 1847 counselled its members to be more careful in advocating members, as the resulting rejections were "causing a heavy expenditure in postage and station[e]ry." The Industry Lodge of the IOOF in Haldimand expelled existing members and rejected potential Oddfellows for many reasons, including being "Subject to Fitts," practising immoral conduct, and not paying their dues. Suspensions and fines for "conduct unbecoming an Oddfellow" in IOOF lodges were similarly harsh; the Imperial Lodge in Burford, for instance, fined an Oddfellow two dollars for intemperance and suspended him for three months. One of the most severe examples of moral regulation occurred in Blenheim, when the Rondeau lodge of the IOOF in 1863 gave an Oddfellow a six-month suspension for making derogatory statements about a fellow lodge member.[2]

In contrast, Henry Telford's 1874 trial over his membership in the St Clair Lodge of the IOOF in Point Edward reveals a slightly different motive behind concern with an Oddfellow's behaviour. The St Clair lodge executive accused Telford, a brakeman and relatively new Oddfellow, of conduct unbecoming a member of the lodge for "the purpose of evading the law for the crime of seduction and attempt of abortion." The St Clair lodge's initial reaction to the case was fairly consistent with earlier patterns of moral regulation, as one executive member, a Brother O'Neill, moved before the assembled Oddfellows to immediately expel Telford from the lodge. Even though O'Neill, an engine turner, conceded that "there was not a young man at Point Edward whom he thought anything more about than he did of Brother Telford" and "felt sorry for him in his trouble," he would still vote for Telford's expulsion on the basis of "the effect it was likely to have on the minds of people not connected with the society if [Telford] should be returned in the order after being guilty of such a crime."[3] However, Telford's case received more a sympathetic hearing when a Brother W.J. Spettigue, an engineer, asked O'Neill to withdraw his motion for a week. This would allow Henry Telford a chance for a character trial or the opportunity to resign his membership before he was expelled from the IOOF in Point Edward. What is highly significant to note – and completely dissimilar from the approach of the IOOF a few years previously at mid-century – is that Spettigue's defence of Telford's conduct, as recorded in the lodge's minute book, reflects a greater fraternal concern with the individual Oddfellow under examination than with maintaining the respect of the community:

> But as Brother Telford had always borne a respectable name and was generally highly thought [of] wherever he had accompanied him and as no crime of that kind had ever been brought up against him before, and as the woman in question was gilty [sic] of the same at some former period he thought Bro. Telford had been induced by her to fall instead of him inducing her ... Bro. Telford had been placed in such trying circumstances and to such temptation it was almost contrary to human nature to resist. And he did not think there was one member sitting in the Lodge at that time but only for good luck might have been in the same fix, "He excepted none." He [Spettigue] said when a young woman would come into a man's bedroom after all had gone to bed in the house and she knowing that he was alone, and ask him to share a part of that bed with him, he did not see how any young unmarried man was likely to keep clear of the trouble that Bro. Telford was in at present. And he hoped the lodge would deal as leniently with the case as they could possibly afford to.[4]

The case of Henry Telford was a trying experience for the executive of the St Clair lodge of the IOOF, even though the directors did in fact vote in favour of his expulsion. A week after ostensibly deciding Telford's fate, the executive of the lodge met again to reconsider their harsh punishment. When Spettigue recommended a suspension rather than expulsion, Brother O'Neill was so incensed that he asked for his withdrawal card from his fellow directors. Apparently this discussion was indeed rather combative, as Spettigue rose and pleaded for forgiveness, in that "he had opposed Bro. O'Neill as much as any he knew in the Lodge, but he had done so thinking in his own mind he was right. But if he had said anything that was directly the cause of Bro. O'Neill's resigning he was willing to humbly beg his pardon, as he had always entertained Bro. O'Neill with the highest respect as an *Oddfellow.*"[5] O'Neill, determined to cultivate respect from the community, recommended a four-month suspension, against Spettigue's proposal of a two-month ban. The importance of this episode lies not in the fact that Telford was given a four-month suspension for his misdeeds but rather that his sentence was for an offence that would earlier have guaranteed a lifetime expulsion from many mid-century IOOF lodges. It is even more interesting to note that in 1879 the rehabilitated Telford joined his erstwhile nemesis Brother O'Neill on the board of directors of the St Clair Lodge in Point Edward.[6]

The differences between mid-century approaches to the ideology of moral regulation in fraternal orders and mutual benefit societies and those found in the late century reveals an evolution of sorts within fraternal orders. The proliferation of fraternal orders and mutual benefit associations throughout this period was a function of the security they provided against sickness, accident, and death and the bonds of unity and brotherhood they forged through their stylized rituals and myriad lodge activities. More than any other voluntary associations, fraternal orders remained fairly consistent in terms of embracing a skilled working-class membership base, illustrating that the construction of collective liberal identities was indeed a task that crossed all class lines. However, some orders became tainted with a brush of selectiveness for their membership strictures along colour, gender, and nationalistic lines, and fraternal orders such as the Orange Order, the Sons of England, and the *Société St Jean-Baptiste* are historical models of the *ex*clusivity of fraternalism rather than any ideology of a liberal and *in*clusive "community." While this vision of fraternalism is to some extent justified, associations such as the Oddfellows, the Independent Order of Foresters, and the Ancient Order of United Workmen did attempt to provide inclusive environments. By the close of the nineteenth century, fraternalism and mutual benefit associations had become bastions of the skilled working classes, as mutualism in Canada remained a potent force well into the twentieth century.

Fraternalism and mutual benefit societies are highly contested territory for historians as they debate the merits and the meanings of fraternal orders and the social services they provided. Most of the work on mutual benefit fraternalism has concluded that these societies were essential to the forging of bonds of brotherhood, self-help, and the culture of mutuality in the skilled working classes. Despite a considerable working-class presence within fraternalism, others have argued that while working-class bonds were reinforced through mutualism, it was the focus on differences of gender, race, and nationalities that whittled away at class consciousness. Reinforcing the hegemonic order of early industrial capitalism, fraternalism accepted only "respectable" workers who held the commercial and liberal values of thrift, self-help, and independence.[7] Other scholars have contested the seeming preponderance of working-class members in fraternal orders, claiming that the lower middle class and the commercial business class held equal proportions of members in mutual benefit societies. Cross-class membership in fraternalism thus muted class consciousness within the skilled working class, tending instead to further commercial and mercantile interests and the ideology of the liberal social order. Taking this analysis still further, some historians claim that fraternalism and mutual benefit societies became a chief component in the formation of the middle class itself.[8] In this particular examination of fraternalism I maintain that the earliest manifestations of mutualism served the machinations and purposes of a fledgling liberal social order, rather than serving only the agendas of the skilled working classes or the commercial/mercantile middling sort.

By the final three decades of the nineteenth century, fraternal orders and mutual benefit societies had begun to serve as vehicles of self-definition and collective identity for the skilled working classes. Unlike the case with Mechanics' Institutes, temperance societies, and scientific associations, the consolidation of industrial capitalism ensured that the class composition of fraternal orders and mutual benefit societies would reflect a very resilient working-class element. While the former associations could serve the interests of the industrial classes, they could simultaneously mask the inequalities inherent in the capitalist system. By focusing on the male role of protecting home and hearth, fraternal orders cultivated a ritualized sense of brotherhood within the lodge that allowed members to define themselves through the values of bravery, independence, and self-reliance thought to be inherent in respectable manhood.[9] One of the more recent strains of fraternal historiography explores the relationship between mutual benefit societies and the nascent welfare state. While not discounting the importance of cultural factors within fraternalism, historians such as George and J.C. Herbert Emery and David Beito conclude that the most critical function of mutual benefit orders came in their provision of sickness, accident, and life insurance for those who desperately needed it. The dread of dependence, coupled with a strong liberal ethic of thrift enabled the "young men's benefit" societies to become universally popular with a young skilled working class constituency and paved the way for the growth of the welfare state.[10] Consequently, mutual benefit societies and fraternal orders sponsored a collective identity among skilled workers, an identity that could simultaneously support *and* critique a liberal social order that was on the verge of collapse.

One of the major difficulties in examining fraternal orders or mutual benefit societies arises from the varieties of fraternalism available. Ritual societies, mutual benefit and insurance groups, and ethnic societies all competed fiercely for clients throughout this period. As a result, historians conclude that all fraternal orders practised some form of exclusion, whether along class, gender, religious, or ethnic lines. This is particularly true of mutual benefit orders such as the Sons of Scotland, St George's or St Andrew's societies, or the *Société St Jean-Baptiste*, associations that used tests of ethnicity as requirements for membership. The Orange Order is an exceptionally useful example of this category of fraternal order, as its propensity to sectarian violence and exclusiveness is well documented.[11] This examination of fraternal orders will also not analyse Freemasonry, for despite their more egalitarian beginnings, Masons by mid-century and beyond had become quite elite institutions, pandering exclusively to the commercial middle classes and business elites. Nor will this study examine the Knights of Labor, although their tendency to support the producer ideology, fraternal rituals, and co-operative ventures falls in line with an ideology of a liberal "community." However, the Knights also promoted a strong craft-worker identity and a plebeian culture in spite of opening the movement to workers of all stripes, thereby leading to episodes of class conflict and an antagonistic relationship with industrial capital.[12] The fraternal orders that remain after this "exclusivity" assessment were in fact among the most popular ritualized insurance societies such as the Independent Order of Oddfellows, the Independent, Ancient and Canadian Order of Foresters, and the Ancient Order of United Workmen. The evolution of fraternal orders would also reflect the transformation of Canadian society itself by the dawn of the twentieth century.

THE LIBERAL AND BOURGEOIS ROOTS OF EARLY ODDFELLOWSHIP

While the official birthplace of Oddfellowship in central Canada is heavily disputed, Montreal unmistakably was the area where the Oddfellow movement put down its strongest roots in the early 1840s. Both the IOOF, based on the Baltimore rituals with headquarters in the United States, and the Manchester Unity, based on the British model, settled in the Montreal area, setting up lodges all around the island by 1843. A few years later, the British North American Lodge established the *Odd Fellows Record*, the official organ of the IOOF in central Canada. Numerous articles in the *Record* outlined the importance of ensuring liberal inclusiveness and classlessness in the lodge room, as fraternal concord would link men of different ranks and classes in bonds of harmony. The editors of the *Odd Fellows Record* believed complete equality occurred in the Oddfellow lodge room, where "no diversity of rank impresses awe on weaker members." To the majority of Oddfellows, fraternity was the ultimate goal of the movement, and this could only take place with the elimination of "honours and distinctions, [except] such as are based on merit."[13] Christopher Dunkin, the well-known Montreal lawyer and ardent Oddfellow, proclaimed that the lodge room united all disparate members of the broader community by doing away with ranks and classes, and "every other artificial demarcation that can separate man from man." Albert Case, the Grand Sire of the IOOF, offered an address to the Oddfellow lodge in Stanstead, Canada East, in which he stated: "[Oddfellowship] brought men of all parties together, and consolidated them into a union that has been efficient in banishing discord and contention from the community, and establishing the reign of friendship and good will."[14] Of course, this dialogue would also tend to critique the more traditional "Tory" order of ranks and classes that "liberal" voluntary associations would attempt to do away with by mid-century.

And yet the discourse of class inclusion preached by these early Oddfellows in Montreal harboured a nascent liberal outlook that was favoured by the middling sort. The class composition of the Oddfellows centred in Montreal was initially formed mainly by the professional, mercantile and commercial middling-class elements in the city. Even the institutional *History of Oddfellowship* called these early Oddfellows "aristocratic," as they were all leading statesmen, members of Parliament, prominent merchants, and manufacturers – the "very *elite* of Canadian society." The failure of Oddfellowship in Canada East was directly attributed to the nature of this membership base, as these organizations soon dismissed the mutual benefit system so integral to the skilled working classes in favour of the more fashionable elitism of Freemasonry.[15] Many of the articles in the *Odd Fellows Record* confirm a rather liberal bias in the ideology of the early Oddfellows in Montreal. Claiming that their mutual benefit system buttressed the needs of both the middling and working classes of the community, the *Record* was fairly condescending to the labouring classes and condemnatory of the elite classes in the tone of many editorials. In one article bemoaning Montreal's crime rate, the editors blamed the lower orders for committing the actual crimes, while blaming the "rich" for their failure to set the proper example of religion, education, and industry. Despite the fact that Oddfellows were ostensibly social equals, the *Record* called for an increased recruitment drive among the commercial classes, as the "humble and poor look up to rank and wealth." Such individuals could also add more to the Widows and Orphans fund than the less elevated in societal status could.[16]

When the Grand Lodge of British North America of the IOOF dispatched three missionaries to Canada West in 1846 to establish new lodges, the pretensions of the liberal middling sort travelled with them. When setting up an IOOF lodge in Peterborough, the Montreal deputation was glad to see that their membership reflected those of "the first standing" in Peterborough society. After visiting the lodge in Kingston, the missionaries were conversely dismayed to see that a lodge of the Manchester Unity of Oddfellows was busily encroaching upon their territory. The deputation found it even more upsetting that the Manchester lodge had "for its objects the absorbing of the most respectable portion of the community." Safeguarding Oddfellowship for the most respectable – and financially well-off – members of the community became an axiom for these early Oddfellows, as both the Port Hope lodge and the Phoenix lodge in Oshawa set up committees to examine applicants' standing in society before approving them for membership.[17] However, the liberal outlook of the middling sort also demonstrated a degree of class conflict in mid-century IOOF lodges. The Phoenix lodge in Oshawa, for instance, convened a disciplinary council for a Brother Clark, overheard in conversation complaining of the many mechanics who were joining the lodge. Clark, a doctor by profession, was duly charged by John Martin, an axe maker, with sowing discord and wounding the feelings of certain brothers in the lodge.

Even though Clark was later exonerated of this charge, these early Oddfellows were evidently quite sensitive to any allegation of class intolerance within the lodge.[18]

After the British North American chapter of the IOOF collapsed from neglect in both Canadas, a resuscitation of sorts occurred. Dr Thomas Reynolds attempted in 1853 to revive the order with the help of the Grand Lodge of the IOOF in the United States. The success of this Oddfellow resurrection was largely attributed to the fact that all groups in the community regardless of station or position, could engage in its liberal benevolent purposes. In the view of the officers of the Grand Lodge of Canada West, the sooner Oddfellow lodges took root in the province, the sooner "all distinctions in society, all differences of blood, of class and of creed [would] be buried together in the dust."[19] A more radical discourse clearly followed the reorganization of IOOF lodges in Canada West, as more skilled workers began to join lodges to complement a sizeable business, clerical, and professional class membership. These changes can be measured not only through a shift in ideology but empirically as well, in a comparison between membership lists at mid-century in the Cobourg lodge and those of a decade later in the Forest City lodge of London. Even though half the members in both lodges came from the middling classes, ten years later the working class component in the London area had increased by 7 percent over that of the Ontario lodge in Cobourg, and members of the lower middle classes such as clerks had experienced a jump of nearly 13 percent (see Table 4.1). What caused this sudden resurgence in working-class interest in mutual benefit fraternalism? Evidently it was the financial benefits and protection accrued through the insurance system intrinsic to the principles of Oddfellowship that encouraged the skilled working class to join lodges in increasing numbers by the 1860s. It is also no coincidence that working class membership in the IOOF intensified after temperance associations such as the Sons of Temperance in Canada West discontinued their mutual benefits systems.[20]

Although the wider liberal "community" tried in a limited way to include women in voluntary associations, the values of "respectable manhood" inherent in fraternalism were unambiguous; women had no place in the lodge rooms of fraternal orders in North America. Women unmistakably represented the marginalized "other" in these liberal fraternal orders.[21] Early IOOF fraternalism had no qualms about banning females from associational life in Montreal; the spouses of male members were only invited periodically to lodge activities and socials. These Oddfellows justified their exclusion of women on the grounds that women had more "appropriate

Table 4.1
Occupations of Initial Members in Two Independent Order of Oddfellow Lodges, 1846–65

Ontario Lodge #12, Cobourg, 1846-60			Forest City Lodge #38, London, 1857-65		
Occupation	Total	Percentage	Occupation	Total	Percentage
Carpenter	7		Carpenter	8	
Machinist	4		Shoemaker	7	
Saddler	3		Tailor	7	
Painter	3		Painter	6	
Others*	42		Others*	41	
TOTAL SKILLED	59	35	TOTAL SKILLED	69	42
Clerk	12		Clerk	26	
Others**	4		Others**	11	
TOTAL CLERICAL	16	10	TOTAL CLERICAL	37	22.5
Merchant	19		Merchant	19	
Others^	30		Others^	12	
TOTAL BUSINESS	49	30	TOTAL BUSINESS	31	19
Gentlemen	4		Schoolteacher	4	
TOTAL PRIVATE MEANS	4	2	Doctor	4	
			Others^^	11	
Engineer	5		TOTAL PROFESSIONAL	19	11.5
Others^^	10		Farmers	3	
TOTAL PROFESSIONAL	15	9	Miller	2	
Farmers	19		Others^^^	3	
Others^^^	3		TOTAL AGRICULTURAL	8	5
TOTAL AGRICULTURAL	22	14			

* Other occupations in the skilled category include: blacksmith, coachmaker, builder, printer, joiner, baker, fireman, fitter, mason, butcher, millwright, upholsterer, roofer, cigar maker, mechanic, cordwainer, dyer, tinsmith, bricklayer, founder, watchmaker, plasterer, artist, cabinet maker, cooper, shoemaker, marble cutter, brewer, musician, gunsmith, conductor, and wagon maker.
** Other occupations in the clerical category include: bailiff, bookkeeper, sheriff, collector, notary, accountant, bartender, and photographer.
^ Other occupations in the business category include: agent, bookseller, distiller, manufacturer, tailor, hotel keeper, grocer, tobacconist, saloon/tavern keeper, auctioneer, jeweller, hatter, confectioner, stationer, chemist, and furrier.
^^ Other occupations in the professional category include: clergyman, engineer, student, barrister, dentist, schoolmaster, editor, architect, and surveyor.
^^^ Other occupations in the agricultural category include: miller, tanner, yeoman, and groom.

SOURCE: Occupations of the Initial membership of the Coburg Lodge #12, Cobourg, International Order of Oddfellows, MTL, L36, Proposition book of new members, 1846–60 and of the Forest City Lodge #38, London, RCL, Box 4150, membership list, 1857–65.

and important duties" than attending lodge events. As an article in the *Odd Fellows Record* entitled "The Beauty of Woman's Helplessness" explained, not only did women need the financial benefits afforded them but the moral respectability inherent in the doctrines of Oddfellowship would help their male family members learn to become better protectors, companions, and guardians of the household. To make this philosophy more palatable to women, Albert Case praised the female members of his audience for being virtuous already: "We do not close our lodge doors against your sex because we distrust your faithfulness or your truth; but we do so because we wish to cultivate our moral natures, and arise to the standards of your own."[22]

Early IOOF lodges in Canada West fostered an identical ideal in regard to women, promoting the importance of protecting female family members in the home, while restricting their privileges in the lodge room. However, Canada West IOOF lodges also recognized the value of including women in their social outings, as the executive of the Port Hope lodge demonstrated when they instructed their members to invite as many female friends as possible to an open meeting in order to broaden interest in the lodge. The Industry lodge in Haldimand invited a brother visiting from Wisconsin to speak, and he advised his Canadian brethren that in his experience, "the admission of females tended very much to increase the interest in the Order."[23] Even the Grand Lodge of the IOOF in the United States recognized the need to establish a female auxiliary, creating the Rebekah degree for women. We know that Oddfellows in Canada were not apathetic to the possibilities of the degree, as Reynolds wrote to the Grand Sire about establishing Rebekah lodges in Canada West as one of the first steps in reorganizing the Oddfellows. The first mention of an attempted Rebekah lodge in Canada West occurred in 1857 in the town of St Thomas, where the Grand Lodge lauded the fact that "wherever the influence of women is exerted in a labour of love, good is exerted." The history of the Rebekah degree is marred, however, by the refusal of the Grand Lodge to allow Rebekah lodges to have autonomy from local male lodges or to include female members other than the immediate family of a male Oddfellow. In the view of the *Canadian Journal of Oddfellowship*, these constraints virtually guaranteed the failure of the Rebekah degree, and the editors suggested that Oddfellow lodges offer women more general membership privileges instead of simply segregating them.[24]

While elements of ethnic and religious exclusivity did in fact occur within fraternal and mutual benefit orders, attempts at compliance with the liberal ideology of "community" also transpired in many lodge rooms. By translating their lectures and addresses into French, and by inviting the St Patrick's Society and the *Société St Jean Baptiste* to social functions, the Oddfellows endeavoured to provide a welcome environment for potential French and Roman Catholic members. As Dunkin explained, Oddfellows united all men, who were separated by "artificial demarcations" such as race, religion, and "unfortunately even by language." Even when the Bishop of Montreal, Ignace Bourget, forbade Roman Catholics from entering "secret societies," the Oddfellows in the British American Lodge did not think that such a policy included them, as they took no oaths. Indeed, Oddfellow appeals for a French Catholic lodge in Montreal merely intensified after Bourget's pronouncement.[25]

The "coloured question" in fraternal orders is largely characterized as one of complete exclusivity, as most fraternal lodges and mutual benefit societies permitted only "free white males" as members. And yet the exclusion of blacks, Chinese, and natives by the IOOF and other fraternal orders is far more complex and problematic, particularly in the central Canadian context. It is clear avoiding non-white membership in Oddfellow lodges at mid-century was a largely American concern that reflected racial struggles in the United States. During the reorganization of the Grand Lodge in Canada West, the lack of a race stipulation in Canada attracted the attention of the Grand Sire in the United States. He quickly wrote to Reynolds advising him to "be careful not to overlook the all-important question whether there be any *colored* members in these lodges."[26]

Fraternal orders and mutual benefit societies had an understanding of the correlation between fraternal harmony and the eradication of sectarian and political discord, but putting that understanding into practice was a challenge. Early Oddfellowship in Montreal during the post-rebellion era was fertile ground for such discourse as Oddfellows tried to avoid the religious and political violence of the previous decade. Several articles and editorials in the *Odd Fellows Record* fervently recommended abstaining from political and religious discussions in the lodge room in the hope that "all causes of discord and ill-will" that ruled the hearts of men in the "outside world" would not enter their fraternal sanctuary. As Albert Case, a leading Oddfellow lecturer, noted, Oddfellowship came to fruition thanks to the work of individuals who "saw that men were divided in feeling, alienated by party prejudices and sectarian animosities, and saw the necessity of an Institution where they could meet as brothers, where at the door of entrance they should lay down all sect and party, and enter as into a safe retreat from temptation, pollution and schism."[27]

However, given the more middling sort composition of these early Oddfellows in Montreal, this rhetoric of politico-religious toleration in fact demonstrated acceptance of a more liberal social order. The editors of the *Odd Fellows Record* claimed that the only political feeling Oddfellows experienced was love of country, the desire to be true to the Government and obedient to its laws, while the only religious impulses acted upon was a love of God, morality and charity. Case added that sceptics would find that Oddfellows "were not all agreed in politics, but ... required no political test, savouring more of party than this – that we will be true to our Government, obedient to its laws, and moral citizens."[28]

However, particularly as their relations with the Oddfellows of the Manchester Unity show, there was inevitably a gap between hopes and reality. The IOOF based in the United States and the Manchester Unity seemed to have secured a fair amount of co-operation between their organizations at first. The IOOF and the Manchester Unity were both brought to Montreal thanks to the efforts of John Hardie, a Baltimore painter. Attitudes of co-operation seemingly transferred to Canada West, as the Ontario lodge in Cobourg offered to share rooms with its Manchester Unity counterpart, while the *Odd Fellows Record* in Montreal besought the executives on both sides to patch up their "little differences."[29] What is more remembered about these early Oddfellows, however, is the fierce competition between the two groups for a fairly limited clientele. At the heart of these disputes was the political nature of "loyalty," as the Toronto and Montreal lodges of the Manchester Unity proclaimed themselves to be "Loyal" Oddfellow lodges after the British model. Despite flaunting this British rather than American loyalty, the Montreal lodge of the Manchester Unity claimed: "[We meet] in Friendship, transact our business in Harmony, and depart in Peace. Political or religious disputes are never permitted among us." And yet the Loyal Montreal lodge enlisted the support of the Attorney General of Canada East, who advertised that lodge as a "very loyal, moral, useful and praiseworthy institution." The "missionaries" of the Grand Lodge of the IOOF responded in kind when they visited Kingston, accusing the Oddfellows of the Manchester Unity in Kingston of having an "extraordinary jealous disposition" regarding their visit to Canada West.[30]

The reorganization of the IOOF's Grand Lodge in Canada West posed new problems for the two factions, as they struggled to supplant one another and recruit members to their respective causes. In 1853 the Grand Sire of the IOOF in Baltimore counselled Reynolds to keep public discord at bay in the interests of harmony between the two groups, yet he privately crowed about the zeal with which IOOF representatives "rolled up" the Manchester Unity organization in Canada West. Similarly, Reynolds delivered a veiled barb at the Manchester Unity in the 1856 annual report of the IOOF, insisting that *his* organization "ignored all party and political views, and endeavoured to unite all in a cause in which honesty of purpose is a prominent characteristic, a bond of union which requires not traditional lore to give antiquity to its origin, for in all ages those alone have been recognized *Oddfellows* who have proved themselves *honest men.*" The rivalry filtered right down to the local lodges. When the Loyal London lodge of the Manchester Unity ultimately resigned itself to accepting the U.S. Grand Lodge charter in 1853, the last entry in the minutes – "God Save the Queen and preserve the MU, for man can't do it in this Canada" – epitomized the feelings behind these loyalty squabbles.[31]

Relations with the Manchester Unity and the IOOF did improve shortly after these events, when the Manchester Unity met in Toronto to discuss the possibility of reciprocal relations with the IOOF Grand Lodge in the United States. Nevertheless, as late as 1863, a communication from the Grand Lodge of Canada to the Grand Master of the Manchester Unity outlining a plan for union still noted: "I may be mistaken, but can conceive of no hindrance to union, aside from petty national prejudice on the part of a few." Only with the cessation of such sentiments were the two groups able to construct a more formal reconciliation in 1865.[32]

MUTUALISM, THE LABOUR THEORY OF VALUE, AND FRATERNAL CONCORD

As with many other voluntary associations, fraternal orders and mutual benefit societies encouraged the personal work ethic as a means of promoting a collective liberal ideology within the larger community. The credo of the Oddfellows consisted of self-reliance, the necessity of labour, and the prevention of idleness, and Oddfellows attempted to abide by these precepts. However, the theme of honest industry was also a conduit for the ideology of the liberal social order. In lauding the merits of the developing middling commercial classes, the editors of the *Odd Fellows Record* stated that it was among the middling orders that one could find "sobriety, honesty, industry and a general rectitude of conduct." Almost in the same breath, the *Record* both condemned the inherited wealth of the upper classes as a means of promoting idleness and reviled the lower orders – the "ignorant and the untutored" – for being "frequently engaged in brawling and crime."[33] Along with temperance societies, Oddfellows also associated sobriety and temperance with industriousness, and thus encouraged their lodges to be moderate in their drinking habits. Many lodges of the IOOF and the Manchester Unity included temperance regulations in their bylaws and fined or expelled members for habitual drunkenness. As Case expressed it, Oddfellows needed to confine their revenues to charity and mutual benefit work: "We do not squander them in convivial parties at the festive board; we allow no part or tittle of them to be expended to furnish the Lodge with indulgencies such as bacchanalians use."[34]

Not only were prospective Oddfellows required to accept these core values of liberal honest industry and temperance but, they needed to actively pursue them through some form of livelihood. In both Canada West and East IOOF logdges themselves observed the values of frugality, economy, and retrenchment in the conduct of Oddfellows business. In an effort to cut back costs, the Thames Lodge in Mitchell bought a cord of wood for the members; they also asked the secretary to print their bylaws as "quickly as possible and as cheap." Insofar as fraternalism lived by the values of self-help, self-reliance, industry, and toil through the assurance system, in its early "liberal" phase and in its later manifestation as a vehicle for the skilled working class it embodied the ideals of honest industry.[35] As these values shifted with the establishment of the mutual benefit system, the focus turned toward the economic protection, rights, and support of the individual. Early Oddfellowship considered life and sickness insurance as the wisest political economy, one that offered security and stability in times of want. Financial benefits in cases of need would thereby offer the Oddfellow an amelioration of his condition, and lessen "the ills and miseries incident on human life." When a brother in the Hope lodge in Port Hope fell seriously ill, the lodge stepped in when a discovery committee found he was "destitute of means wherewith to help himself with." This same economic philosophy would be in effect upon the death of an Oddfellow, so that he could die happy knowing that his wife and children would receive assistance and support that was no longer his to bestow.[36]

Even though these early Oddfellows expressed genuine feelings of liberal mutual benevolence, they also took pains to explain that the financial benefits they offered were their due, and not a charity: they were "given to all considered worthy, rich or poor, as a *right*, not as a *gratuity*." Critics of fraternal orders nevertheless raised the charge of exclusivity, pointing out that the IOOF was concerned only with helping their own rather than the larger community. Oddfellows countered this accusation by explaining that while they could not save everyone in their poverty, they would go about it "a little at a time." And Case was quick with his rejoinder: "Oddfellows are generally as charitable and public spirited as any members of the community, and give as much for relief to every object of charity as their neighbours do."[37]

Unfortunately, economic depression, limited revenue, financial insolvency, and outright embezzlement of lodge monies plagued many Oddfellow lodges. The most frequent offence leading to expulsion in

Oddfellow "black books" was the non-payment of dues and fines. In 1856 the Imperial lodge in Burford realized the problems inherent in non-payment of dues, and threatened suspension for any Oddfellow still in default by a specific date. Although the widows' and orphans' fund was particularly sacrosanct as a means of providing monies to those of the most worthy poor, payments to widows caused the most difficulty. The Ontario lodge in Cobourg experienced so much hardship in paying its obligations to widows that it was obliged to make a difficult decision: "This Lodge finding it impossible to sustain its expenses with the present limited number of members, deem it an act of Justice among other retrenchment[s], to declare that the widows pension can no longer be paid."[38]

Many early bylaws of both the IOOF and the Manchester Unity particularly highlighted the expulsion of members caught making false claims, thereby defrauding the widows and orphans of deceased Oddfellows. In these cases suspension was not a harsh enough punishment; those found guilty of "abusing the benevolent intentions of the order" faced immediate expulsion. In the Loyal London lodge, although a brother was suspended for three months for intemperance, when the executive found out he was also guilty of fraud they instantly expelled him from the lodge. Another brother in the Loyal London lodge faced expulsion for cheating his fellow members, but his sentence was commuted to a six-month suspension if he made complete financial restitution to the lodge.[39] At an early meeting of the Grand Lodge of Ontario the directors condemned the charlatans and fraud artists who contravened the collective liberal ethos of honest industry through embezzlement, fraud and deception: ["The] disbanding of Lodges, defalcations in Treasurers, and embezzlements that have taken place in different sections show that there have been unprincipled men in our Order. Men who, regardless of every sense of honour, of the obligation of the most solemn vow, stole into our lodges, intent upon nothing but the pecuniary advantage that gleamed in the future, and if Providence blessed them with health, that they could not obtain the funds under the false pretence of sickness, would conspire with a kindred spirit, and, regardless of bringing ruin upon a lodge, and mocking the hopes of the widows and orphans, would rob it."[40]

Fraternal lodges also generated a strong sense of liberal sociability through elaborate rituals and lodge activities. While the mutual benefit system kept fraternal orders such as the Oddfellows well stocked with clients, members needed more than lodge business, initiation rituals, and the monthly paying of dues to keep them coming to lodge meetings. To these early Oddfellows, attendance at lodge gatherings offered social situations that allowed men to unite in friendship, harmony, and peace. Under early liberal management from the middling sort, Oddfellowship required members not only to be possessed of sobriety, moral character, and industriousness but also to have "prudence and self-command, which are indispensably necessary to social intercourse." To ensure respectability, subordinate lodges could not plan activities such as balls or other forms of public entertainment without the expressed permission of the British North American Grand Lodge.[41] During the period of reorganization in Canada West, the recreation menu consisted of national pleasures: lectures, recitations, speeches, and music. Imitating the philosophy of institutions such as Mechanics' Institutes regarding liberal self-improvement, Oddfellows established reading rooms both helped to educate members and to promote the objectives of Oddfellowship. Entertainment also fulfilled the sociability requirements of the order, as evidenced in the request of the Ontario lodge in Cobourg that the "committee on sociall enjoyment ... envite Industry lodge to participate in Brotherly love" through a joint entertainment venture.[42]

Most of the early Oddfellow lodges in the city of Montreal held anniversary socials to celebrate the existence of the order and publicize its benefits, as well as to raise money for the construction of the Montreal Oddfellows' Hall. Inviting other nationalist societies such as the St Patrick, St Andrew and St Georges' societies and the *Société St Jean Baptiste* to Oddfellow anniversaries benefited fraternal union and also added to their coffers.[43] Oddfellow lodges in Canada West used both rationales in holding open lodge functions for all the citizens of a town, village, or city. The social committee of the Ontario Lodge in Cobourg organized open lodge meetings simply to introduce the neighbourhood to the advantages of Oddfellowship, while the Phoenix lodge in Oshawa held a community ball and concert to raise funds to erect an Oddfellows Hall. The Loyal London lodge of the Manchester Unity, in a more flourishing urban centre, held an anniversary parade and a ball concert for the inhabitants of London. While these public amusements were designed to publicize the work of the Oddfellows in the town, an oyster supper served to replenish the depleted Widows and Orphans fund.[44]

FRATERNALISM AS COLLECTIVE IDENTITY: SKILLED WORKERS AND LATE-CENTURY FRATERNAL ORDERS

While fraternalism at mid-century largely supported a more liberal social order, by the late decades of the nineteenth century the mutual benefit system and the insurance schemes offered by these societies attracted a much larger constituency of skilled workers. While ritualized sociability, mutualism, and fraternal harmony continued to appeal to individuals of all classes and interests, more recent historiography illustrates that the principal members of these fraternal orders were young men of the skilled working classes. Although late-century fraternalism remained fairly responsive to the ideologies, culture, and social practices of "liberal society," in reality it also revealed the duality inherent in Canadian society insofar as it reinforced differences of class, gender, race, and nation.[45] Despite these seeming contradictions, the ideology of a liberal fraternal "community" continued, and the socio-economic factors inherent in the "consolidation of capitalism" made the services provided by benevolent societies invaluable to skilled workers who were economically marginalized in society. Even though fraternal orders constructed a vastly different collective liberal identity than such voluntary associations as Mechanics' Institutes and temperance societies, adherence to the ideology of the liberal "community" remained strong in Canadian fraternal orders.

Empirical evidence suggests that skilled workers comprised the vast majority of members in Oddfellow lodges, particularly in large towns and villages in Ontario. Research conducted in Thorold, Campbellford, Ingersoll, and Point Edward confirms that skilled workers not only joined Oddfellow lodges in great numbers, but managed to secure executive positions as well.[46] In towns with large working-class populations, the membership would reflect the personnel of some of the largest employers in that town. The St Clair lodge in Point Edward, a railway town, where over 60 percent of Oddfellows were railway employees, is an excellent case in point. Similarly, if an Oddfellow lodge established roots in rural areas in Ontario such as Kerwood or Fergus, farmers, agricultural labourers, and members of other occupations housed in a small village would join the Oddfellow lodge (see Table 4.2). Whatever the occupational composition of a lodge, individuals who joined the Oddfellows were in most cases in need of the financial benefits of mutualism for their families' protection. As a result, many lodges teetered on the edge of financial insolvency, as they ususally were dependent on the contributions of members with rather limited means. IOOF financial secretaries employed several strategies to overcome deficits in lodge funds, from living off the various benefit funds and placing the monies in savings banks to other practices that at times constituted overt fraud. These secretaries could also prove to be the complete downfall of a lodge, through their acts of embezzlement or poor accounting.[47] Often the first fund to go

Table 4.2
Ordinary Membership by Occupation in Three Oddfellow lodges, Selected Years, 1871–1899

Egremont Lodge #207, Kerwood (Rural)			Fergus Lodge #73, Fergus (Rural)		
Occupation	Total	Percentage	Occupation	Total	Percentage
Boot/Shoemaker	5		Carpenter	8	
Carpenter	4		Machinist	3	
Others	9		Others	21	
TOTAL SKILLED	18	20	TOTAL SKILLED	32	24
Clerk	1		Clerk	4	
TOTAL CLERICAL	1	1	Others	3	
Merchant	6		TOTAL CLERICAL	7	5
Others	3		Merchant	5	
TOTAL BUSINESS	9	10	Others	11	
Teachers	5		TOTAL BUSINESS	16	12
Others	4		Teacher	5	
TOTAL PROFESSIONAL	9	10	Others	18	
Farmer	49		TOTAL PROFESSIONAL	23	17
Others	3		Farmer	48	
TOTAL AGRICULTURAL	52	59	Others	8	
			TOTAL AGRICULTURAL	56	42

St Clair Lodge #106, Point Edward (Town)

Occupation	Total	Percentage	Occupation	Total	Percentage
Fireman	29		Merchant	6	
Brakeman	19		Others	7	
Rail Engineer	18		TOTAL BUSINESS	13	8
Others	60		Others	5	
TOTAL SKILLED	126	80	TOTAL PROFESSIONAL	5	3
Clerk	8		Farmer	2	
Others	4		TOTAL AGRICULTURAL	2	1.5
TOTAL CLERICAL	12	7.5			

NOTE: These statistics largely confirm those compiled by Emery and Emery in *A Young Man's Benefit*, 35–8.

SOURCE: Records of the St Clair Lodge #106, Point Edward, RCL, box 4318, question book, 1873–98; Fergus Lodge #73, Fergus, WCA, A.996.24, series 3, subseries 2, file 1, membership book, 1871–99 and Egremont Lodge #207, Kerwood, RCL, recent acquisition, membership book, 1877–92.

bankrupt was the widows and orphans fund, as executives wrestled with providing benefits to those unable to reciprocally contribute into the fund. The St Clair lodge in Point Edward instituted a lump sum payment to widows instead of monthly instalments to ease the lodge's financial burdens. The Wardsville lodge of the IOOF actually named the widows Murphy and Frickelton as the individuals responsible for the bankruptcy of the lodge's widows and orphans fund.[48]

Despite such financial pressures, the liberal dichotomy of inclusion/exclusion continued to be an axiom of mutual benefit societies during the zenith of Oddfellow influence, and interclass co-operation and fraternal harmony remained strong. As the Oddfellowship movement was dedicated to the moral improvement and elevation of the human character, it continued to commend itself to the "high, the low, the rich and the poor" of society: "On the floor of the lodge room social distinctions are unrecognized. No man's wealth entitles him to particular privileges; no man's poverty debars him from attaining the highest offices."[49] The rhetoric of liberal egalitarianism would prove to be the greatest selling point of mutual benefit societies to the members of the skilled working classes. However, toward end of the century, the Oddfellows saw themselves extensively as a working-class institution. The *Canadian Journal of Oddfellowship* conveyed its sense of gratitude that the middle classes viewed the Oddfellows as a worthwhile institution, something workingmen had known for years. When the Grand Sire of the IOOF came to Toronto in 1880 and visited the Industrial Exhibition, his speech, in which he declared that the power, prosperity, and happiness of a nation rested on its industrial workers, was plainly aimed at his own working-class constituency. To Henry Outram, the Grand Master of the Manchester Unity of Oddfellows, the greatest priority of the Oddfellow movement was to provide skilled labourers with the opportunity for self-help in providing insurance protection for their "helpless families" in the event of sickness or death.[50]

The Oddfellows were not alone in their attempts to ensure class concord within their fraternity. The various manifestations of the United Foresters also agreed in principle with the liberal ideology of interclass co-operation. The *Canadian Forester*, the official organ of the Canadian Order of Foresters, observed that war against prejudice and intolerance, and the removal of the "fictitious and factitious distinctions of society" were essential in bringing men into closer relations in fraternal brotherhood. In working toward this harmonization in Forester courts various directors and officers had to reduce the initiations of individuals prominent in social, business, or political arenas. By elevating such men before the general court, Foresters would be guilty of acting "contrary to that feeling of equality which is the true basis upon which all fraternal Orders rest."[51] The ritual of the Canadian Order of Foresters was likewise instituted so that "no dissentions mar our joy, no distinctions here employ, and oppression here destroy" the classless nature of the Forester court. Even more specifically, the Canadian Order of Foresters stated emphatically that their institution fostered a spirit of co-operation in all departments of labour and commerce. Unfortunately, such explicit references to occupation could also lead to exclusionary practices in the insurance aspect of mutual benefit societies. The Independent Order of Foresters introduced a list of proscribed occupations that included alcohol dealers, coal miners, and workers in explosives, while the IOOF disqualified saloonkeepers, bartenders, and professional gamblers from the benefits of membership.[52] Exclusionary dialogue of this sort protected the collective identity of the "true" workman from falling into disrepute among mutual benefit societies.

Both the Canadian and the Independent Order of Foresters conveyed a strong impression in the pages of their respective periodicals of their associations rested on solid working-class foundations. The *Canadian Forester* said that fraternal orders in general reached the "energetic, industrious, influential citizens, who constitute[d] what Lincoln called the 'plain people.'" The *Independent Forester* lauded the IOF's participation in the 1896 Labour Day parade in Toronto, noting that the workingman was essential and vital to the overall success of the order. In spite of these protestations from Forester periodicals, however, many historians view the Foresters as having a larger middle-class constituency than the Oddfellows or the United Workmen. In reality, the Foresters, like the Oddfellows, managed to attract a consistent working-class membership both in a rural setting such as Listowel and in a large-town environment such as Peterborough (see Table 4.3),[53] whereas other fraternal orders, particularly the Ancient Order of United Workmen (AOUW), encouraged working-class members to join their associations. Recruitment appeals in AOUW literature focused on low-waged individuals, to whom the spectre of leaving family members destitute upon their eventual passing was very real. Records held in some Ontario AOUW lodges illustrate the need for insurance among their members; the AOUW lodge in Madoc, for instance, initiated skilled workers to 36 percent of its membership, with an additional 32 percent of members being either farmers or agricultural workers.[54]

Even though fraternalism limited the conflict between the urban and rural visions of a liberal "community" that plagued institutions such as temperance societies and agricultural associations such as the Dominion Grange/Patrons of Industry, some subtle shifts toward a more urban middle-class ideology of fraternalism did occur. Urban fraternalism seems to have come full circle to early "bourgeois" Oddfellowship, as the *Canadian Forester* noted that the order had increased in favour with the "best classes of the community." Even as the *Dominion Oddfellow* out of Napanee praised

Table 4.3
Occupations of Proposed Members, Canadian and Independent Order of Forester Lodges, 1883–98

COF Court Peterborough #29, 1883–86			IOF Court Listowel, 1891–98		
Occupation	Total	Percentage	Occupation	Total	Percentage
Labourer	7		Carpenter	4	
Carpenter	7		Printer	2	
Printer	4		Harness Maker	2	
Machinist	2		Others*	6	
Foreman	2		TOTAL SKILLED	15	43
Others*	14		Clerk	4	
TOTAL SKILLED	39	62	Others^	2	
Clerk	6		TOTAL CLERICAL	6	16
Others^	2		Agent	3	
TOTAL CLERICAL	8	12.5	Others^^	4	
Agent	2		TOTAL BUSINESS	7	19
Others^^	6		Doctor	2	
TOTAL BUSINESS	8	12.5	TOTAL PROFESSIONAL	2	5
Barrister	1		Farmers	5	
TOTAL PROFESSIONAL	1	2	Others^^^	2	
Farmers	4		TOTAL AGRICULTURAL	7	19
Others^^^	3				
TOTAL AGRICULTURAL	7	11			

* Other occupations in the skilled category include: brickmaker, barber, butcher, roofer, tinsmith, shoemaker, canoe builder, carriage maker, cabinet maker, harness maker, engraver, plasterer, tailor and framer, carter, and nightwatchman.
^ Other occupations in the clerical category include: bookkeeper, accountant, and customs official.
^^ Other occupations in the business category include: bookbinder, grocer, druggist, chemist, merchant, restaurant owner, confectioner, and piano dealer.
^^^ Other occupations in the agricultural category include: tanner, miller, and teamster.

SOURCE: Proposed candidates for membership of the Canadian Order of Foresters, Peterborough Court #29, PCMA, Acc. 96-065, box 1, series 1, minute book, 1883–86 and Listowel Court # AO, MU 7175 #23, minute book, 1891–98, membership list at the back.

that town's lodge as a place where all classes could meet on the basis of social equality, the editors noted that such an association tended to level men upward as "it [gave] men of ordinary calibre and position an opportunity of mixing with the most refined, intelligent and illustrious in the community."[55] As the bureaucracy of the mutual benefit society became more centralized and run more like an insurance company, the urban offices of the Foresters and the Oddfellows developed into large-scale business operations. After the IOOF had built their spacious Oddfellows Hall in Toronto complete with corporate offices, the Independent Order of Foresters put up a sizeable building of their own – the new Foresters Temple, which was the "equal in completeness of any public building in Toronto." In addition, the Foresters created the new Foresters' Island Park, where all Foresters and their families could go for recreation and entertainment.[56] Fraternal orders also formed associations not unlike Boards of Trade or Chambers of Commerce to promote their own interests. The Association of Fraternal Orders provided co-operation and assistance among Foresters, Oddfellows, United Workmen, and other societies on such matters as government legislation and medical practices, thereby tending to "professionalize" the mutual benefit society field. Although urban mutual benefit associations demonstrated a more middle-class ehos in the course of their insurance operations, fraternalism itself remained popular with the skilled working classes, as evidenced by the large number of individuals who had joined fraternal organizations by the turn of the century. In 1899 the Independent Order of Foresters and the AOUW each would report a membership of over 30,000 members in Ontario alone, and the Oddfellows close to 24,000.[57]

THE CHALLENGES OF GENDER AND ETHNICITY IN FRATERNAL ORDERS

Even though the "mostly male worlds" of respectable masculinity were indeed a prominent hallmark of fraternal orders, a more refined analysis reveals a quite complex pattern of female participation in these associations. The demarcation of gender was not always so apparent in fraternal orders, particularly in rural areas where the accepted – yet limited – participation of women in other voluntary associations was an accomplished fact.[58] The St Clair lodge in Point Edward, for example, had a strong history of incorporating females into its activities, despite restrictions on their actual membership. An entertainment put on jointly by the Ladies Aid Society of the Methodist church and the lodge demonstrated that when women took charge, the social events were far more successful. A few years later, in 1884, despite the continuing exclusion of female members, eight women formed the very first entertainment committee of the St Clair lodge. Even though the committee was composed only of the spouses of prominent members, thanks to their work, the number and quality of social events held in the lodge increased dramatically. And yet women continued their traditional onlooker and provider roles in IOOF lodge activities.[59]

By 1886 enough changes had occurred in Canadian society that Rebekah lodges of the IOOF had become completely autonomous. And by 1891 lodges accepted any unmarried women into the Rebekah degree. Acknowledging that it was "narrow-minded men with deep seated prejudices" who had delayed the development of the Rebekah degree, the executive of the Grand Rebekah lodge expressed their gratitude when the Grand Lodge of Ontario returned the relief work of Oddfellowship to the sphere of women by permitting the Rebekah sisters to open an orphans' home in 1895. As Emily Bowden, the first president of the Grand Rebekah Lodge stated in 1892: "It is only within the last decade since the Degree was placed entirely under our control, that its success has been so marked. It only requires that the sisters should have the opportunity given them to ensure the success of the Degree of Rebekah."[60] In spite of this liberal rhetoric, the Ontario Grand Rebekah lodge had only recruited 1,800 sisters by the turn of the century, and the Grand Lodge in Quebec reported meagre numbers of just over three hundred. Obviously these numbers could not match those of a completely self-sufficient organization such as the WCTU, and the tone of Oddfellow publications gives an indication of why this was so. While writers extolled the virtues of American temperance supporter and suffragette Frances Willard, they cautioned the sisters of the Rebekah degree to remember the advantages of the order rather than agitate for women's electoral suffrage. Furthermore, even as the Grand Rebekah Lodge appreciated the notion that women need not be confined solely to their domestic chores, they also considered it unseemly for women to do the labour "of the keenest masculine intellect."[61]

Gender issues in fraternal orders and mutual benefit societies became a highly contested sphere in the competition for female insurance clients. The creation of the female Independent Forester auxiliary – called the Companion Court – can be directly attributed to the work of the editor of the *Independent Forester*, the Mohawk doctor Oronhyatekha, who noted as early as 1885 that "in this enlightened and progressive country we shall be fearfully handicapped until we shall remove the defect in this respect from an otherwise perfect organization." With the establishment of the Companion auxiliary court, the fraternal women's auxiliary provided not only a parallel ritual degree but corresponding benefits as well. As the *Independent Forester* stated, insurance benefited a family upon the death of a mother, as well as the death of a father.[62]

Another gender-inclusive fraternal order was the Canadian Order of Chosen Friends, an organization that permitted women to join their association on terms of "perfect equality" with their male brethren. Women could equally participate in all council rituals and also receive all the mutual benefits offered by the order. And yet if the records of the Antrim Council #245 are any indication, the Chosen Friends must have continued to marginalize women to some degree. The only mention of female involvement in the affairs of the order came in the preparation of council refreshments, by "young ladies from around [the] vicinity who are always rejoiced to be able to help on such occasions."[63]

A similar difficulty arose in mutual benefit societies as they moved toward incorporating various ethnic groups. The failure of Oddfellows to attract French Catholics in Quebec in the early years of the movement did not bode well for later attempts to enrol Catholics in the ranks of Oddfellowship. But the difficulties were not entirely one-sided since the Catholic hierarchy often put the Oddfellows and other fraternal orders on the proscribed list of secret societies. Despite this evidently uneasy situation in Quebec, however, a large French Catholic market for mutual benefits and fraternal insurance was ready to be exploited, and the Catholic Order of Foresters arose in Chicago. Many historians viewed this association merely as a collection of disgruntled Catholics who, upset with the second-class status afforded them in the Independent Order of Foresters, segregated themselves into an entirely new order to make sure that their members did not associate with any group condemned by the Roman Catholic Church. What is apparent is that the Catholic Order of Foresters filled a void created by the absence of fraternalism in Quebec, as they amassed a total of eighty-five lodges in the province by 1892.[64] Such remarkable growth of fraternalism among the French Canadian populace did not go unnoticed by the parent association, the Independent Order of Foresters. In the highly competitive atmosphere of mutual benefit fraternalism, the IOF did not hold back in their attempts to attract French clients. By translating their constitution and the *Independent Forester* into French, and inviting the *Société St Jean Baptiste* and well-known Catholic clergymen such as Paul Bruchesi to their social functions, the IOF was able to attract prominent French Catholic members such as Wilfrid Laurier into its ranks. By 1897 the success of this approach could be measured in the thirty-three subordinate IOF courts established in Quebec, nearly half of which functioned in French.[65]

In barring African-Canadians, natives, and Chinese, as well as most Roman Catholics and Jews from membership, most fraternal orders were less than subtle in their racism and intolerance to those who were not white Protestants. Although this racist depiction of mutual benefit societies in this period is indeed warranted, David Beito's portrayal of fraternalism as being selectively intolerant rather than exclusively racist also makes a fairly convincing point. On the other hand, the treatment of Asians by mutual benefit societies on the west coast of Canada was overtly racist. This dichotomy of liberal inclusion and exclusion regarding the "other" in Canadian fraternalism in the late nineteenth century exemplifies the contradictions inherent in the making of class, gender, and racial boundaries.[66] In reality, strictures on black membership were not published in central Canadian lodge constitutions until well into the 1870s. By 1875 the debate over black Oddfellows in the General Board of the IOOF in the United States had reached a critical juncture, as the segregation of coloured lodges in the United States became strict IOOF policy. It is therefore understandable that the first mention of the "free white males" clause in the Grand Lodge of Ontario's constitution occurred only in 1876.[67] Nevertheless, even among Oddfellows who accepted the decree of the IOOF regarding the segregation of black lodges, some approved of associations of coloured individuals. The Worthy Grand of the Zephyr lodge was excited to discover in Nipissing "gentlemen of coloured persuasion in rapport with principles of Oddfellowship" and was highly encouraged by their success. Outram, the Grand Master of the Manchester Unity, visited a lodge of black Oddfellows in Toronto, and found it "as well conducted, as respectable and in every way equal to the Lodges of their paler brethren."[68]

Critics of the exclusion policy often employed the ideology of a liberal "community" to express their disillusionment with the American Grand Lodges' decision to bar natives and African-Canadians from IOOF lodges. The *Canadian Journal of Oddfellowship* printed a letter from a Canadian Oddfellow who lamented the exclusion of men of colour: "Is it not uncharitable for us to put our foot on the head of those who are different from us in colour? Why not grant them the same privileges that we enjoy? Why not let them work with us side by side? Why not give them our hand and clasp them as brother grasps brother's?" An American Oddfellow periodical in New York noted and took exception to this tirade, and printed a response justifying the exclusion of Native Americans and blacks. Ironically, the *Heart and Hand* used a similar discourse of "community" to justify the prohibition of non-white Oddfellows from American lodges:

> While civil, political and religious equality may be, and are extended to the black or red man, it is a well established fact that, save in rare instances, social equality is not. And in the white race, even, those of different nationalities and religions, select their associates and friends from their own. The Day may come when all men of every race shall be equal socially, as well as otherwise, but one thing is certain and positive; THEY ARE NOT SO NOW, and we would be introducing dissen[s]ion, discord and trouble, to endeavor to precede public opinion and custom upon this point.

The editors of the *Canadian Journal of Oddfellowship* were incensed by the high-handed manner in which the *Heart and Hand* attempted to preclude discussion on the "coloured question." The editorial indignantly asked "Is it because he thinks that we foreigners in Canada should be sufficiently thankful for our connection with an Order whose headquarters are in the United States, without presuming to criticize any of its enactments?"[69]

The theme of the exclusion of non-whites in fraternal orders recurs largely in mutual benefit societies originating in the United States, as the Canadian Grand Lodges and Councils of the AOUW, Knights of Pythias, and the Order of Chosen Friends all barred non-whites from joining. However, the Independent, Ancient and Canadian Order of Foresters was quite unique in the central Canadian experience, as it removed all references to race restrictions in its constitutions and bylaws.[70] This became quite a selling point for the Foresters in a highly competitive insurance market, particularly after Oronhyatekha became the Chief Ranger of the IOF. As a living testament to the ethnic inclusiveness of the Foresters, the Mohawk physician from Brantford appeared more and more frequently in the pages of the *Independent Forester* to illustrate true Forester fraternalism. Festivals held in his honour, with Mohawk children singing hymns in their native language, demonstrate how the IOF took advantage of the selection of Oronhyatekha as Chief Ranger to construct a fraternal identity that would *attempt* to integrate the entire community. The advertisement of ethnic diversity in the Forester court came full circle with the publication of a biography in the *Independent Forester* of the first Chinese Forester, Brother Moy Loy. Transparently capitalizing on the racially restrictive policies of the Knights of Labor, Oddfellows, and the AOUW, the Foresters managed to uncover a niche in the mutual insurance market – at least in Ontario and Quebec – that secured a significant ethnic-based membership for the IOF.[71]

POLITICO-RELIGIOUS TOLERANCE AND THE FUNCTIONS OF THE MUTUAL BENEFIT SYSTEM

With the "political" troubles of the Manchester Unity behind it, the IOOF in the 1870s became even firmer in its determination to remove sectarianism and party politics from the lodge room. As the *Dominion Oddfellow* recorded, the lodge offered a retreat from the "wild waves of party spirit and the zealot's controversy," as its principles and doctrines were more about life and conduct than about dogma and creed. Edwin Lander, in his *Exposé of Oddfellowship*, equated strife and discord with party and sect, and proposed that banishing dissension from the Oddfellow lodge room would benefit all mankind:

> Based upon certain truths which are like axioms among all nations, tongues and creeds ... sacred tolerance presents a nucleus, which by its gentle influence gathers within its orbit antagonistic natures, controls the elements of discord, stills the storm and soothes the spirit of passion, and directs in harmony man's united efforts to fraternize the world. Strife and discord, party and sect, which create heart-burnings and divisions among men, are banished by our laws ... the great principle of universal love, that goes behind all distinctions of sect, party and nation, recognizes all men as brothers, and bids us do unto others as we would have them do unto us. The neglect or violation of this principle is the source of all the social evils that afflict mankind and disturb the general harmony.[72]

Both at the Grand Lodge and the local level, Oddfellows diligently practised what they preached in efforts to religious and political controversy in their association. During the visit of Grand Sire to London, a large crowd gathered to hear his address, illustrating the preached truth that politics had no place in Oddfellow assemblies, since they met as brothers and co-labourers in a glorious cause. Attentiveness to the requirement to abstain from politics was demonstrated by the Charity lodge in Sunderland, which expressed disapproval of a recent circular by a group of Oddfellows "using our order in a political way" during the previous year's election campaign.[73]

By the end of the century, one of the greatest sectarian controversies surfacing among skilled working-class Oddfellows was that of *ir*religion – agnosticism and atheism. In justifying the exclusion of the "infidel," the *Canadian Journal of Oddfellowship* acknowledged that the Oddfellows followed the universal religion of nature, the "cement which unites in one band, men of the most discordant opinions." While sectarianism divided men, Christianity, presumably a "cement," would bring them even closer together in an integrated brotherhood. This philosophy would remain in force even as late as 1899, when the Grand Lodge of Ontario proclaimed: "No man should offer himself for membership in our Order who has not this belief; no one should be accepted without it; and no member who loses faith in such a supreme being can honestly and consistently remain with us."[74] Irreligion and the neglect of the basic tenets of Christianity would not be tolerated at the local lodge level, as the St Clair lodge in

Point Edward discovered in 1880. When a Brother Wilson from the Eastern Star lodge in Whitby visited the lodge, his remarks on procedure were recorded: "[He] called the lodges['] attention to the fact that he had passed through all the Chairs and had visited several lodges but had never seen a lodge opened or closed without prayer and urged it strongly as part of our duty. The noble grand acknowledged our neglect and said we had no excuse to offer but supposed it was never too late to mend." A lack of spiritual enlightenment in the St Clair lodge was further exposed three months later by a Brother Rogers, who was expelled from the order for conduct unbecoming an Oddfellow. He had stated in no uncertain terms that he would "not sit in a lodge of sons of bitches, liars and thieves."[75]

Other fraternal orders likewise stressed the importance of avoiding sectarian and political turmoil among their members. The rituals of both the Canadian and Independent Order of Foresters emphasized the significance of remaining politically and religiously neutral. As John King, an executive with the Knights of Pythias observed, while nothing of a political or sectarian character could enter the portals of its lodge room, Knights were to enforce liberal toleration in religion, obedience to law, and loyalty to government.[76] In response to a predicament similar to that faced by the early IOOF and the Manchester Unity, the Canadian Order of Foresters (COF) separated from the IOF in 1883 to secure more national autonomy. Unlike the Oddfellow debates over the Baltimore or Manchester rituals decades earlier, these disputes were not as politically charged, reflecting more of the competitive nature of the fraternal insurance business. Rather than questioning each other's loyalty, both the COF and the IOF cast suspicion on the business practices of their rival, from expressing reservations about the actual figures of financial surpluses to reporting embezzlement. The rancour was therefore not as insurmountable, and by the end of the 1880s the two groups had restored their co-operation.[77]

Executives and members of fraternal orders in the last three decades of the century still fully accepted the mandate to spread the collective gospel of honest industry and individual hard work. Counselling Oddfellows to remember their economic responsibilities to the general community, noted Oddfellow author Edwin Lander invited them to consider their duty to the common weal, to strive to promote general prosperity, and to remember that profit was to be found in all labour and that an idle soul was an encumbrance to the earth. This philosophy found its way into the character books of the order, as the interrogation of each prospective member included asking him if he possessed a reputable means of support and industrious habits.[78] Even by the mid-1890s, the liberal producer ideology, with its distinctions of productive and non-productive labour, appeared in the discourse of the official organ of the IOOF, the *Dominion Oddfellow*: "When all are educated to understand the true effect of idlers in a community, all will see that it is a matter of self-interest that not only those who desire work should be given it, but that those who are engaged in useless occupations, or who are making their living in dishonest or vicious ways, should join the ranks of true labourers – that is, the ranks of those who, by their hands or brains, or both, are doing their share of the legitimate work of the community."[79]

Members of the IOOF also debated the merits of temperance as a means of upholding the precepts of honest industry and hard work. As the most pernicious of all vices, intemperance caused an individual to neglect his business and property, inducing idleness, vagrancy, and crime among the respectable working class. Unlike temperance societies, who were gripped by prohibition fever, Oddfellows did not accept the doctrine of total abstinence, but tended to listen to the voice of liberal public opinion. As the Grand Lodge put it: "Oddfellowship cannot afford, even if no higher end were to be served, to lag behind public sentiment on this question, and if we would command the respect of the public, improve our members morally and intellectually, and fulfill the mission of the Order by warring against vice in all its forms, we must adhere closely to the wise and wholesome restrictions which have been thrown around us in regard to the use of intoxicating liquors."[80] Unfortunately, at the local lodge level, fraternal orders often honoured temperance more in the breach than in the observance. Illustrating the IOOF's disdain for total abstinence, when a Dr Gilles proposed a Brother Stewart for membership in the St Clair lodge in Point Edward, the only failing that surfaced in his interrogation was that he took an occasional glass of liquor, "occasionally, but nothing to hurt, and thought he had quite stopped it too." Stewart passed muster and became an Oddfellow. However, some months earlier a Brother Mann had been suspended for three months when a character committee discovered that he had been "labouring under the influence of intoxicating liquor for one week." Ensuring standards of temperance and respectability remained fairly important well into the 1890s. A Brother Currie was denied his health insurance benefits from the St Clair lodge when it was discovered that he did not conduct himself as a proper Oddfellow, "his disability proceeding from Drunkenness and Debauchery[,] his insanity immediately following the same."[81]

Other fraternal orders likewise required their members to have steady, industrious habits as well as a "reputable calling." The Foresters not only taught the importance of toil and labour but also encouraged frugality and thrift, instructing their members to acquire provident habits. However, with their large working-class constituencies, fraternal orders could also reinforce the socio-economic tenets of populism and its criticism of industrial capitalism. One editorial in the *Canadian Forester* reminded readers that it was "men who work, not politicians who talk, [who] are the builders of our national fortunes. The problem over which deep thinkers are pondering is being solved by active Canadians who plough, sow, reap and gather in the harvest, and whose toil is the architect of our destiny."[82] Some fraternal orders also moved away from an attitude of blaming those without work as "willing idlers" to an understanding that the duty of mutualism included giving aid to brothers in distress from lack of employment. The Foresters and the Canadian Order of Chosen Friends all counselled their members to help brothers, particularly those afflicted by "adverse fate," to find gainful employment. Although the *Canadian Forester* clearly blurred the boundaries between luck and labour – individuals with a strong work ethic would eventually turn up some work – they also recognized that the day of liberal individualism was over, as mutual aid and co-operation went hand in hand with the ideology of producerism. The Foresters therefore made it an order of business to enquire after the employment needs of any member of the court.[83]

Similarly, the notion that mutual aid relieved the suffering of those in distress while providing economic protection for family members was essential in recruiting the working class element. As late as 1895, the *Dominion Oddfellow* reiterated that the financial benefits accumulated by members were not a charity but a right that one earned by paying into the fraternal insurance scheme. As a Brother Ayers in the St Clair lodge noted, such a policy was entirely inclusive, as, "being an Oddfellow over 30 years ... the benefits accrued from this [were] the same for all members."[84] Moreover, incorporation for fraternal orders became a necessity as the government began attempts to regulate the fraternal insurance industry. Both the Oddfellows and the Foresters welcomed the new *Insurance Act*, and mimicked the kind of populist discourse employed by early reformers in condemning speculative banking and other "non-productive" enterprises. In the view of the special committee commissioned by the Ontario Grand Lodge of the IOOF to investigate the new act, the legislation would prove an effective restraint on the "paper societies and fraternities, duping the people with worthless certificates of life and accident insurance."[85] The constitution of the AOUW stated unequivocally that the order was formed primarily for the protection of family members dependent on a workman's income. The obligation of a workman was to provide for his family: "He who provideth not for his family is worse than an infidel. See the result of the careless life, in which there was no love, no prudence, no foresight. A heritage of poverty is the gift of such a man to his children." The Canadian Order of Foresters used a similar rhetoric; the motto of the *Canadian Forester* was "A good man leaveth an inheritance to his children." Similarly, the COF recognized that man could not prosper on his own but needed the assistance of a united fraternal brotherhood. As a result, a man could ensure that his family enjoyed he benefits of mutualism from beyond the grave; he had the liberty of choosing whether to leave his family "in partly independent circumstances or in poverty."[86]

WORKING-CLASS SOCIABILITY IN FRATERNAL LODGES

According to the *Canadian Journal of Oddfellowship*, fraternal sociability made it possible that the Oddfellows, instead of a being mere life assurance company, would become an influential source for good among all men. Oddfellows therefore continued to encourage wholesome leisure activities until the end of the century. The *Dominion Oddfellow*, for instance, lauded the fact that the order taught men to enjoy relaxation and social outings without excess. The more urban publications of the IOOF such as the *Oddfellow Gazette* out of Montreal came full circle to earlier middling class pronouncements on sociability, by urging the brethren to "cultivate their social graces."[87] Oddfellow lodges continued to sponsor reading rooms and museums for the liberal and moral self-improvement of their members. Even as late as 1891, the *Digest of the Laws of the IOOF* in Ontario expressed approval of libraries and reading rooms as an acceptable expense for Oddfellow lodges. The lodge in Wardsville even combined entertainment and amusement with the establishment of an Oddfellow library and reading room, as they held a ball and concert to raise funds for purchasing books.[88]

These entertainments were not enough to hold the attention of members for long, however, and lodges had to search for new and appropriate ways to entertain Oddfellows over the long haul. The evolution of entertainment in the Egremont lodge in Kerwood, for example, began with the standard fare of music, recitations, speeches, and readings. Opportunities for further amusement in Kerwood graduated slowly to debates and paid lectures, to fruit soirées, strawberry socials, and turkey suppers as the membership increased accordingly. The entertainments of the Zephyr lodge in Nippissing were evidently not all met with enthusiasm, as the secretary skeptically recorded that he "was counting chickens before they were hatched, though they might turn out ducks."[89] The many lodges who set up entertainment, concert, or ball committees within their executive were much more successful in promoting the benefits of Oddfellowship. The directors of the St Clair lodge in Point Edward did not initially realize the importance of providing public entertainments as such a "request caused some of the Brothers to cast off their usual artificial humanity and gave their faces their more natural ... very long and pale appearance." But by the 1880s, the lodge had created an entertainment committee to handle picnics, moonlight excursions, balls and concerts, and its establishment neatly coincided with an increase in membership. However, Oddfellows continued to insist that entertainments within the lodge abide by the liberal philosophy of moral respectability. The entertainment committee of the Cypress lodge in Bradford, for example, wanted members to invite their friends to lodge meetings, but three individuals were barred from attending: "If we admit such as these we would soon have their friends and associates, some of which are of a very low order, socially and morally speaking." Four months later, the directors forced the entertainment committee to resign, and the lodge limped along a few more years before suspending operations.[90]

Both the Independent and the Canadian Order of Foresters advocated principles of sociability within Forester courts, in order to foster affection and friendly relations. In permitting "neither wrangling nor dissen[s]ion to mar [their] harmony," Forester courts encouraged the "moderate enjoyment of social intercourse and ... the *temperate exchange of social feeling*."[91] The Juvenile Canadian Forester court in Peterborough followed this formula to perfection, offering readings, singing, spelling matches, and refreshments for their young men, to "help make their meetings more interesting." The Independent Foresters in Shelburne enjoyed paid entertainment in their court; they hired elocutionists and lecturers, and even paid for an oyster supper out of their general funds. It appears the Shelbourne Foresters did not mind coming up with additional dues for entertainment purposes, as the general membership accepted supplementary fees to cover their amusement expenses. However, it appears that not all courts appreciated the exhortations to social intercourse, as the Listowel court of the IOF did not hold any entertainments for the first four years of its existence. Even after the directors recognized the importance of entertainment to relieve the monotony of court meetings, it took them a further two years to come up with a court entertainment. Unfortunately, by the time a picnic was decided upon, the court had to fold for lack of funds in 1897.[92]

In bringing entertainment to the larger community, Foresters offered open courts, excursions, concerts, balls, picnics, and festivals. The purpose of such public entertainments was of course twofold; to promote the Forester order within the town and to raise much-needed revenue. The Canadian Order of Foresters in Peterborough hoped that their annual excursion would "be looked to with interest by a large portion of our citizens," and combined that activity with raising funds for a new Forester Hall. The Shelburne IOF became so proficient at providing public amusements for the townspeople that they created in short order excursion, concert, and general entertainment committees.[93] In urban areas, as a result of the growing business aspect of mutual benefit fraternalism, the entertainments from the Independent Foresters were more elaborate spectacles. These events, advertised in the *Independent Forester* under the caption "Foresters in a Social Sense," frequently included comedy sketches, dancing, and grand concerts for public consumption. The dedication of Foresters' Island Park marked this new phase of urban fraternal entertainment, as members could now bring their families into a carnival-like atmosphere at the park.[94]

Like many voluntary associations examined in this study, mid-century fraternal orders promoted the principles of an inclusive, "liberal" social order in central Canada. As largely cross-class organizations, fraternal orders mirrored associations such as Mechanics' Institutes and temperance societies in supporting the social and cultural agenda of the middling classes. However, mutual benefit societies and fraternalism did not suffocate early working-class consciousness as some suggest; rather they cemented the bonds of comprehensive mutual aid through the nascent yet active participation of skilled workers in fraternal orders. By the 1870s, as socio-economic boundaries began to be noticeably demarcated in many Canadian voluntary associations, fraternal orders came largely under the patronage of skilled workers. As a result, mutual benefit societies focused heavily on the needs of their working-class constituency.

Although they had a very different social composition than other voluntary societies, fraternal orders in many respects advanced the ideology of a liberal "community" much more fully than other central Canadian voluntary organizations. Some mutual benefit societies harboured a latent nationalism and a tendency toward exclusion through ethnicity tests, but on the whole, fraternal orders such as the Independent Order of Oddfellows, the Independent, Ancient and Canadian Order of Foresters, and the Ancient Order of United Workmen attempted to create a collective identity built on liberal values of mutuality, openness, and fraternal harmony. Despite the occasional language of occupational exclusivity and a necessary focus on their working-class constituencies, Canadian fraternal orders and mutual benefit organizations successfully employed the discourse of "community" in constructing a strong fraternal identity within the understanding of liberalism.

5

Elevating the Cultivators of the Soil

The isolation resulting from establishing a homestead in the rural countryside of Central Canada often strengthened the resolve of the agricultural community to promote association and create opportunities for social and cultural interaction. Farmers' clubs, agricultural societies, and the agricultural press provided forums for farmers to air their views and also fostered the means to stimulate their sociability and economic independence through fairs, exhibitions, and public gatherings. As a result, farmers often perceived themselves as a breed apart from the rest of society, and this conviction at times produced a rather striking discourse of exclusivity in agricultural associations, tinged with a strong sense of class superiority. And yet farmers' dependence on the produce of the land also cultivated an acute awareness in the agricultural population of their *inter*dependence on the rest of society as a whole, producing a liberal agrarian counter-discourse of interclass solidarity within the larger community. By the late nineteenth century, wealthy and large commercial farmers would effectively become the voice of Canadian agriculture, particularly when government involvement increased from mere financial support for agriculture societies to the actual establishment of associations such as the Farmers' Institutes in Ontario and the *cercles agricoles* in Quebec.

At the same time, some Canadian farmers voiced a radical, "populist" discourse of agrarian discontent, protesting their economic and social neglect relative to other classes in the community. From the Clear Grits in Canada West to the Anti-Seigneurial Tenure League in Canada East, mid-century expressions of agrarian discontent gave way to acute socio-economic dissatisfaction among farmers in the final three decades of the century, as manifested in the Dominion Grange of the Patrons of Husbandry and the Patrons of Industry. The combination of these various attitudes fostered a rather paradoxical and contested liberal agrarian identity amongst central Canadian farmers.

The early history of agriculture in the North American triangle is a story of changing market conditions from subsistence to commercial farming, and the way the subsequent transition affected farmers as a class. A hallmark of this historical writing, particularly in the United States, is its focus on the conflicts arising from farmers' reactions to nascent forms of capitalism and a new liberal commercial and mercantile order.[1] The rise of agricultural societies, farmers' clubs, and the agricultural press reflected the response of leading farmers to the threat of mechanized development and the destruction of a rural way of life. These societies preached the message of agricultural improvement and emulation, as the progressive farmer would utilize new scientific techniques and methods to further the cause of agriculture. Many historians thus conclude that such movements were highly elitist, generating clashes between the "landed gentry" and "gentlemen farmers" on the one hand and independent yeomen and tenant farmers on the other. Such disputes also lingered into the late years of the century, as farmers faced governmental intrusion into what they perceived as their own sphere of influence.[2] However, the agricultural community also held internal and rather complex pastoral visions of rural culture, from the idyllic and romantic image of the independent yeoman depicted in art and architecture to a vision of the stabilizing influence of agrarian communal interaction through various social activities and networks. These multifaceted impressions of the farming population are crucial to understanding the emergence of a contested agrarian identity in the rural countryside both in North America and Great Britain.[3]

The Canadian colonial experience with agriculture has also received significant scholarly interest, although the focus of consideration and debate has been the economics of farming and the structure of home markets. The pre-eminence of agriculture in the economic development of Upper Canada/Canada West is unquestioned, although historian's assessment of how the dominance of agriculture occurred range from emphasizing the importance of the wheat staple for export to focusing on the formation of strong internal markets. In Lower Canada/Canada East, explanations for the apparent lack of agricultural production of the French-Canadian *habitants* vary from the lack of a staple crop, to the *habitants'* reluctance to adapt to modern farming methods, to the weaknesses of the seigneurial system and the lack of rural capital to improve active internal markets.[4] More recent historiography tends to mirror themes explored in the United States, emphasizing an interpretation that rural areas were wrought with tension and conflict over increasing commercial and manufacturing interests. Historians with this sense see the meagre financial resources of the colonial government as being desperately needed not only to improve the condition of agriculture but also to buttress a rural social order of "gentlemen farmers" and merchants, and their liberal notions of agricultural improvement. The perception of agrarian voluntary associations such as agricultural societies, farmers' clubs, and the exhibitions they sponsored is that of a public/private sphere hybrid, capable of inclusive access to farmers of all stripes, but limited in scope by the extensive patronage of elitist farmers and the intervention of state funding agencies.[5]

As a result of this perception, the supposedly open and inclusive agricultural associations are viewed as elite groups of gentlemen farmers banded together to foster their own interests. The early agricultural societies created by Lord Simcoe in Upper Canada and by Lord Dalhousie in Lower Canada in the 1790s were modelled along those in Great Britain – gentlemen's clubs organized to solidify a code of gentility and to modify tensions between the "landed gentry" and rural merchant elites. When these private agricultural clubs became public institutions by mid-century, despite governmental accountability their privileged character was unabated, as "gentlemen farmers" remained titular heads of these organizations. Nascent state formation simply usurped the authoritative role of the pre-rebellion economic elite, sculpting a rudimentary liberal social structure through the medium of government-supported agricultural associations. Thus, a new commercial and politically active agricultural class conspired to create a commonality of interest based on economic prosperity in agriculture.[6] And yet the collective agrarian identity embraced by farmers of all socio-economic circumstances took into account the complexities of a farmers' life, refusing to agree that the public and the private spheres of agriculture should be compartmentalized at all. This vision, coupled with a resilient ideology of an agrarian liberal community, permeated the philosophy of central Canadian farmers.

Although many farmers turned to agricultural societies and farmer's clubs for support, by far the most important voice of the rural populace was the agricultural periodical. The farming press solicited advice and contributions from practical farmers as well as offering special rates to agricultural societies and farmers' clubs, in the quest to improve agriculture and scientific husbandry in the colonies. Scholarly insight on the agricultural press observes that many working farmers subscribed to and read these publications despite some of the rather dubious scientific advice offered in their columns, and the petty bickering that occurred between various publications.[7] And yet the agricultural press – more than the periodicals of any other voluntary associations – would also tend to reinforce rather contested collective liberal identities within a highly diverse agrarian constituency. Since agricultural newspapers relied heavily on financial subsidies from the emerging state apparatus, farming periodicals in many ways reflected the more "elitist" agricultural societies of gentlemen farmers in their support for the liberal social order in rural areas. However, some agricultural periodicals such as George Brown's *Canada Farmer* and William Evans' *British American Cultivator* also harboured a burgeoning "populist" outlook that highlighted agrarian discontent and the concerns of the agricultural population.[8] Rival agendas and images among these periodicals mirrored competing philosophies among gentlemen farmers, independent yeomen, and tenant farmers and would preclude unity on many issues facing farmers throughout the nineteenth century.

"FAIR PLAY AND NO FAVOUR": INTERCLASS CO-OPERATION AND AGRARIAN SUPREMACY

Members of the agricultural community saw themselves as a vital component of the liberal social order, and implicit in this vision was an understanding that society could not function without other producing classes labouring together in a co-operative fashion. The Lower Canadian Agricultural Society, for instance, in submitting its bylaws to the "community of all classes," proclaimed itself to be a "Society of the People," and consequently open to all rural inhabitants. An editorial in the society's *Agricultural Journal* outlined its egalitarian ideals: "By mutual co-operation, the different ranks and classes assist and urge on one another, each link in the community profits by the exertions of the other, each has a mutual connection with and a dependence on the other's welfare, which is essential to the harmony of society and the advancement of the general good." Given that the executive of the society comprised several prominent professionals such as the lawyers A.N. Morin and L.H Lafontaine, Chief Justice Thomas Aylwin, and businessmen such as Jacob de Witt, pronouncements on the classless nature of the Society masked an underlying preference and support for the liberal social order.[9] The Oro agricultural society, for one, claimed to be a farmers' society interested in encouraging agriculture, but also "would rejoice to see the whole community co-operate heartily in the work, [and] then we might see greater results." The directors of the Peterborough agricultural society noted that, with only sixty-seven members on its rolls in 1863, something need to be done to awaken the interest of the farmer, mechanic, and the community in general in the society. The Colchester agricultural club near London, Canada West emphasized that inclusion of all classes demanded obedience to the rural social order, as only those "who may not be considered objectionable" could become members of the club.[10]

Farmers of all socio-economic circumstances were cognizant that every downturn or upswing in farming or general trade affected all of society, not only themselves. Poor wheat crop yields in Wellington County caused the Guelph agricultural society to complain that not only the farmer but also "every class in the community" experienced debilitating effects. A comparable depression in agriculture appeared in Peterborough around the same time, and society directors concluded that such economic upheavals brought an awareness of *inter*dependence between the farming class and other members of the community. Correspondingly, the farmer tilling the soil should "particularly see that his prosperity depends in a great measure upon that of the rest of the community ... if one member suffers, all suffer."[11] Confirming this interdependence, agricultural exhibitions in the rural hinterland, as well as being crucial to local commerce, also provided sporadic opportunities for social interaction. Many agricultural societies such as the Peterborough agricultural society, in a rural marketplace, welcomed the increasing interest of farmers, mechanics, and others in their exhibitions, as it would prove to be financially prosperous to the whole community. In advertising fairs and exhibitions to the municipality, associations such as the Guelph agricultural society often noted the significance of the presence of patrons who were not tillers of the soil.[12]

The agricultural press clearly articulated the obligation of farmers to contribute to the ideology of a liberal agrarian "community." William Evans, in his agricultural paper the *British American Cultivator*, claimed that not only would agriculture be advanced without "injustice" to any other class but the agricultural population would rejoice to see the other classes in a prosperous condition. It was impossible, he wrote, "to advance the prosperity of agriculture, without promoting in some degree, the interests of almost every other individual that compose[s] this community." And the *Canadian Agriculturalist* judged that the tendency of one class to exaggerate its importance over the others was inappropriate: "In this respect, all the great pursuits of life in a civilized community may be deemed of equal importance, because they have each and all for their object to supply some one of the great wants of our nature; because each is necessary, to some extent at least, to the prosperity of every other; and because they are all brought by the natural sympathies of our being into a harmonious system, and form that noble and beautiful whole which we call civilized society."[13] The promotion of agriculture was indeed a function of agrarian newspapers, yet they also assured their audience that agriculture advancement could only benefit all other members of liberal society.

The creation of the Board of Agriculture of Upper Canada in 1852 solidified growing ties between the nascent liberal state apparatus and farmers, just as the Board of Arts and Manufactures managed to do between the burgeoning urban commercial and mercantile middling classes and the Mechanics' Institutes. The centralization of liberal government forces behind agricultural improvement in agricultural societies would beget "a friendly and harmonious feeling, and infuse a spirit of enterprise and independence amongst all classes." One of the chief methods of achieving this independence was the art of scientific husbandry, as the the presence on the Board of University of Toronto professor of agriculture, William Buckland, and the noted Reform politician William McDougall, editor of the *Canadian Agriculturalist,* confirms. The Board of Agriculture therefore endeavoured to provide grants to agricultural societies, develop experimental farms, and promote agricultural education. As noted agricultural engineer W.J. Charnock explained, these efforts would tend to accommodate the liberal social order: "A good feeling between thinkers and workers is always of advantage to the latter in every department of action, especially so in agriculture."[14] As a result, the Board continued to hold a rather binary vision of the "high and low" in societal relations, particularly when it came to categorizing different classes of farmers in Canada West. In a Board of Agriculture lecture on Practical Farming, James Croil outlined the differences: "Farmers are divided into two classes; those who practice agriculture with a view of earning a livelihood by it, and those who follow it as an amusement or recreation. The former are divided into as many classes as there are different systems or kinds of farming, such as grain farmers, sheep farmers, dairy farmers, &c. These are what we call practical farmers. These are the men who provide food for the million to who the nation look up next to Providence for the supply of their daily food. The other classes of farmers are divided into such distinctions as these; the experimental, the theoretical, and the gentlemen farmer."[15]

Although the bonds of an interdependent rural community were fairly durable among members of the agricultural population, many farmers did envision themselves as *the* fundamental and productive class. The reasoning behind these rather exclusive assertions was multifaceted and intricate, yet farmers' confidence in the art of husbandry framed their belief that agriculture was the cornerstone of prosperity for an emerging nation, an understanding that was not far from the truth. Reports of the Peterborough agricultural society, highlighted the belief that agriculture was the earliest and the most interesting and necessary of pursuits: "A profitable agriculture is considered the basis of national prosperity and as such the success of every organization which in any measure tends to improve the husbandry of a country must be viewed with interest to every true patriot." Employing parallel language, the management of the Lower Canadian Agricultural society maintained that agriculture was the first and principal means of production, setting the whole machinery of national wealth into active and prosperous motion.[16] Another crucial consideration in the mentality of farmers was the necessity to combine seemingly rather exclusive practices for mutual improvement and protection. The 1858 annual report of the Oro agricultural society stated that it was effectively a "Farmers' Society," instituted solely for the encouragement of agriculture in the region. Similarly, the *Transactions* of the Lower Canadian Agricultural Society boldly stated on its masthead that the journal would promote scientific husbandry among rural inhabitants, since agricultural improvement was "the only means that [could] give permanent support to commerce, manufactures, and all other business and professions, and for the payment of revenue."[17]

Agricultural societies also tended to criticize both the older Tory tradition and the emerging commercial and mercantile classes for the perceived injustice that those elite merchant classes, deemed "non-producers," often surpassed farmers in social status. Stating that all farmers wanted was "fair play and no favour," the directors of the Lower Canadian agricultural society pointed out that the agricultural population grew weary of being the "hewers of wood" for the less productive classes. Likewise, the directors of the Peterborough agricultural society rebuked both the politician and the philanthropist for being interested solely in the "upheaving [sic] and overturning of powers and dynasties replete with tyranny and the debasement of mankind" while the farmer laboured "in the prospect of all these events being turned to good as the precursor of improved agriculture and ... reclaiming and properly cultivating lands naturally fertile but now laying waste and at most scarcely half tilled."[18] Articles in the *Transactions of the Board of Agriculture* followed closely on this theme, as the editors examined the stumbling blocks to improved scientific husbandry in Canada West. Following a more populist critique of banks and specie speculation, the president of the Agricultural Association of Ontario in 1859 gave a speech condemning speculation and the "quick score," directing much of his venom to the "dishonest banks." Correspondingly, a report from the Bruce

County agricultural society in 1860 blamed the actual credit system and the banks for the rampant speculation in Bruce County: "[The] division court act at the present time is the most abused law in the Canadian statute book; it is the sheet anchor of all tinkers, peddlers, pettifoggers and speculators of all descriptions."[19]

Agricultural periodicals were also fairly united in their exalted estimation of the importance of farming. To the editors of the *Canadian Agricultural Journal,* appearing out of Montreal, the question of agricultural improvement and prosperity was "vastly more importan[t] to the inhabitants of this country, than all political questions put together."[20] The *Lower Canadian Agriculturalist* added to the discourse: the progressive farmer would not only utilize scientific farming but would recognize that "with agriculture the prosperity of Canada was largely identified; and it was the interest of all Canadians, in whatever rank of society they moved, or whatever class they belonged, to promote agriculture." The significance of scientific husbandry and agricultural improvement to all members of the liberal community surfaced in Buckland and McDougall's joint publication, the *Canadian Agriculturalist.* Emphasizing the noble calling of the farmer, Buckland and McDougall crowed that agriculture was "the fountainhead of all the streams of a country's resources." An essay by noted agriculturalist John Lynch signalled the coming socio-economic changes in agrarian society from the earlier binary model of the Tory tradition toward the "liberal" social order: "The pursuit of agriculture may be considered as desirable to the higher classes, or the affluent, as a source of healthful recreation and rational enjoyment; profitable to the middle classes as the best means of acquiring and retaining a competency; and necessary to the lower classes, as affording a means of subsistence, and almost the only pursuit by which they can ever hope materially to improve their condition."[21]

The rather exclusive nature of this discourse of agrarian supremacy did in fact lead to expressions of discontent in agricultural periodicals, over the status of the Canadian farmer, which led to criticism of the commercial and professional classes. The *British American Cultivator* called on all classes in the liberal community to become more respectful of agriculture, for while farmers would rejoice in the prosperity of other members in society, it would only occur "provided their own interests are protected and put upon an equal footing with [those] of other classes." The *Canadian Agricultural Journal* was even more forthright in denouncing the merchant and commercial classes, remarking that farmers "can never accumulate great wealth, by appropriating a large share of the labour of others for themselves, as other classes do. Indeed, they receive less remuneration for their labour and capital than would satisfy any other class of the community."[22] Similarly convinced that the commercial middling classes, banks, and the entire credit system in Canada benefited the financial speculator more than the agricultural population, the *British American Cultivator* attributed the lack of agricultural credit to the failure of government to support enterprise, to the monopoly of banking institutions, and to the overall preference for speculative ventures rather than agriculture. While the *Lower Canadian Agriculturalist* approved of manufacturing and industry as well as agriculture, they were zealous in their condemnation of the commercial classes:"Let tradesmen, nineteen out of twenty, turn from their unhallowed, unproductive, speculative pursuits, to the honest, useful, healthy business of farming ... when this shall be, man's inhumanity to man will be lessened, and the world will be turned in the direction of the millennial age."[23]

An excellent example of this agrarian ideology relating to other classes within the community can be found in Buckland and McDougall's *Canadian Agriculturalist*. McDougall, the editor of these periodicals and an erstwhile supporter of the Clear Grit party in Canada West, frequently commented on the subordinate position of farmers in his editorials and in the articles chosen to represent agrarian views. Lauding the swift proliferation of farmers' clubs in Canada West, McDougall pointed out why they were necessary: "The time has come when farmers *must* meet together and discuss questions relating to their own interests, and adopt means to carry their wants and wishes into effect, or they will be pushed aside by others and made the stalking horse of less important by more active classes." Condemning speculation and the "tricks" of merchants and lawyers, McDougall claimed that agriculture on the other hand edified the people: "[It] prevents their acquiring that spirit of artifice and cunning, which in all countries is so apt to degrade the character of those engaged in the inferior branches of commercial employment."[24] However, McDougall's partnership with Buckland, and the *Canadian Agriculturalist*'s increasing ties with the Board of Agriculture tempered this discourse of agrarian discontent into a tacit approval of the liberal social order. Not only were the pages of the periodical replete with articles and editorials on the importance of "improvement" and "emulation" but one later editorial even criticized farmers for censuring other classes, as lawyers, merchants, and doctors worked just as hard as the tiller of the soil. Even McDougall himself linked agricultural improvement to liberal governance, blaming the agricultural population themselves for many of their tribulations:

[McDougall] would be exceedingly glad to see a go-ahead spirit take possession of the farmers of Canada, to hear them expressing their determination to avail themselves of all those means of improvement in their noble calling, which were eagerly laid hold of by the other classes in society. While they remained indifferent to their own interests, they must expect to be overlooked and neglected, and instead of laws promotive [sic] of agricultural advancement, to find the statute book teeming with enactments for the protective of others at their expense.[25]

RURAL DOMESTICITY AND THE AGRARIAN WOMAN'S SPHERE

In the rural hinterland, it proved even more crucial than elsewhere to include women in any discussion of a liberal "community," particularly in the agrarian context. The intricate footwork involved in ensuring that gender boundaries remained intact, while at the same time recognizing women's economic contributions and interdependence in agriculture, became an elaborate balancing act for agricultural society promoters. The gradual recognition of women's work both inside and outside the domestic sphere permitted even greater involvement for women in agricultural circles, while at the same time reinforcing the domestic ideology. Female participation in agricultural exhibitions endowed women with greater assertiveness in demanding representation in other public spheres.[26] Early exhibitions in Canada invited women's contributions by establishing Ladies' Departments of artwork, domestic manufactures, and dairying. To encourage female entrants, many societies offered to waive the usual entrance fee. However, many societies nevertheless mirrored the Oro Agricultural society's vision of women's work as simple utility: "Very dry would be our bread, though made with the finest of wheat, without the good wife's butter; and cold would be our hands and feet, at this inclement season of the year without our daughters' mitts and socks." Other agricultural societies valued female entries in the category of fine and fancy artwork, complimenting women's creations for their great taste and skill, and comparing them favourably to the fine arts in more urban exhibitions. Such displays illustrated to the community that women's talents were not confined to the "wash-tub and the spinning wheel."[27]

Female roles in agricultural exhibitions achieved even greater prominence when agricultural society directors realized that to "properly classify" the articles in ladies' departments required the co-operation of female judges. Still, the majority of the women judges in agricultural exhibitions were wives of agricultural society directors or female superintendents appointed to be in charge of ladies' departments. Even though women were not invited to judge the more "manly" exhibits of stockbreeding, coarse grains, and agricultural implements, women could and did have entries in the stock and grains categories, and on occasion even won.[28] And yet, unlike the case with other voluntary associations such as temperance societies, female membership in agricultural societies and farmers' clubs was simply nonexistent. While the main features of agricultural exhibitions were in the "manly arts" of livestock, agricultural implements, and the actual produce displayed, women's contributions earned the less than laudatory comment from the Peterborough agricultural society directors, that they illustrated the "intelligence, industry and perseverance" of female entrants. Similarly, the Norwich ladies' department earned the female entrants no more than a rather paltry tribute from the director that their work exhibited "taste, skill and economy."[29]

The paradigm of adhering to the ideal of female domesticity in women's participation in the agrarian public sphere became even more apparent in the editorials of the agricultural press. Even though agricultural periodicals in many ways initiated "feminist" forums in the pages of their domestic departments, they also reinforced gender stereotypes and the division of labour. Many of the articles in these ladies' departments indeed highlighted the domestic sphere as the place where women could exert their primary influence as mothers and homemakers. Agricultural periodicals mirrored the opinion of the *Lower Canadian Agriculturalist* that "the highest, noblest lot of woman is her home mission, and the most superior place for the exercise of her power is the quiet home in the country."[30] The appeals that agriculture periodicals made for improved education for farmers' daughters ostensibly proposed an increased presence of women in the public sphere, but the *British American Cultivator* stated unequivocally that female education should be "moral, religious, intellectual, social and practical." The editors of the *Canadian Agriculturalist* covered all the bases: women's education on the farm would simultaneously benefit both the domestic sphere and the larger liberal community, as female forays into education would "enable her to discharge her duties to her husband, to her children, to her parents, to her other relatives, to the neighbourhood in which she lives, to the community at large, and to her God."[31]

And yet the editors of agricultural periodicals also acknowledged both the economic and the social contributions that agricultural women made both on the individual farm and in the agrarian community. An article in the *Lower Canadian Agriculturalist* reported on an agricultural family in New York that consisted of seven daughters who worked equally on the farm with their father. The article did more than report with satisfaction that women could become practical farmers; it was positively glowing in its description fo the benefits to be derived: "Plowing dragging, sowing, rolling, planting, hoeing and harvesting will become the pleasant, healthful and remunerative occupation of women as well as men. Their effort is above all praise, and deserves and will receive the hearty approval of all who truly seek to elevate the race by improving the health and elevating and ennobling the character of woman."[32] An article in the *Canadian Agriculturalist* entitled "Woman and her Toils" concurred, and lauded farm wives for their sacrifice: "[The farm wife] saved, by ceaseless, wearying toil, hundreds of dollars for her husband, and he has lost – what money is powerless to recall – the companion of his youth, the one who has walked beside him through life's most thorny paths." Despite acknowledging that women indeed assisted with agricultural labour, the same editorial in the *Canadian Agriculturalist* confirmed that the majority of women's work on the farm remained in the domestic sphere. Counselling farmers to appreciate their wives, the editorial particularly praised women's dedication in stressful circumstances: when their "weak, exhausted frame was suffering from disease, induced by overexertion; the hours stolen from needed slumber and devoted to labour; the numberless household duties performed with a fretful infant on her arm; the immense amount of time spent in cooking over a hot fire, and the many sleepless nights passed in anxious watching over sick children."[33]

THE TRIBULATIONS OF RELIGION, POLITICS, AND AGRICULTURE

According to many farmers, the great divide in Canadian society was the sectarian and political turmoil that faced society in the aftermath of the failed Rebellions in both Upper and Lower Canada. Directors of agricultural societies and farmers' clubs therefore required their members to lay aside all distinctions of "party, sect and country" for the sake of agricultural improvement. However, in many agricultural associations, particularly those that were coupled with the liberal state apparatus, this discourse of an agrarian "community" also harboured an unspoken consent for the liberal social order. According to the Board of Agriculture in Canada West, agricultural associations came together for the general advancement of agriculture and the nation in general, and their meetings were sacrosanct:

"a time when men of every religious denomination, of every nationality and colour, can meet together upon one common ground, freed from every political or religious bias and opinion, for mutual benefit, for exchanging views and comparing opinions upon the leading and important interests whereby we are mutually improved." Debates in local farmers' clubs and agricultural societies were similarly guarded against indecorous discussion; in the Colchester agricultural club, for example, members were encouraged to confine their remarks to purely agricultural topics, and to not stray from the subject under consideration.[34] Unfortunately for many agricultural society directors, such rhetoric could not hide the reality of simmering political discord that was rippling just beneath the surface in many agricultural associations.

Political and religious discord appeared to be a constant source of frustration for those labouring in agricultural societies in Lower Canada/Canada East, although on the surface liberal political harmony appeared to be a *fait accompli*. At the executive level, the Lower Canadian Agricultural Society was very successful at excluding political discussions and all debates that were "not of a useful character," especially by avoiding questions pending in the Canadian legislature. One of the key political questions concerning agriculture was whether to abolish seigneurial tenure, and the board of directors of the Lower Canadian society was remarkably in accord with supporting its removal. Given that the executive was dominated by Reform politicians Thomas Aylwin, Thomas Boutiller, and P.J.O. Chauveau, along with members of the Anti-Seigneurial Tenure League such as Jacob De Witt, A.N. Morin, and L.H. Lafontaine, uniformity on the issue was to be expected. When agricultural meetings on seigneurial tenure reached the level of the ordinary membership, however, the executive lashed out against "party politics" and called on members of the agricultural community to "extend their views beyond their own direct and personal interest, and the interest of parties with whom they may be connected."[35]

The editors of the Lower Canadian *Agricultural Journal* decried political partyism, as it precluded unity among the agricultural population on important political issues. "[They] have constantly regretted to witness, that if there is a meeting called for any party question or discussion, all the world is assembled, and quite excited and interested, in a matter, perhaps, that is not of any importance whatever to the country generally, but if an agricultural meeting is called, it is quite another affair, and it would appear because there is no question of its vast importance to the country, that no one feels the slightest interest in the matter, and would go anywhere, rather than take any part in what was not to promote party views." One can safely conclude from this episode that not all members of the Lower Canadian agricultural society were in complete agreement with advocating the removal of seigneurial tenure.[36]

Agricultural associations did experience measured success in the struggle against sectarianism, as they were very conscious to avoid interfering with religious opinions, and promoted accommodation with various religious groups in buttressing a liberal social order. Lower Canadian agricultural society directors welcomed the assistance of the Roman Catholic clergy in promoting the improvement and prosperity of Canadian agriculture. Far from retreating from the Catholic Church's sponsorship and patronage, the executive praised the Catholic clergy for supporting the society more than any class in the community, and encouraged priests from other denominations to follow their example.[37] A comparable appreciation for Protestant Christianity and the liberal social order appeared in agricultural societies in Canada West, as witnessed in a lecture by the Reverend Cooper to the Toronto District agricultural society. While concurring that agricultural societies were worthy of support, Cooper also intoned that farmers' dependence on divine Providence was not something to take lightly if agrarian prosperity was to continue. Consequently, the directors of the Peterborough agricultural society reminded their constituency that "man may plow and reap and sow but the increase must be from God."[38]

The agricultural press also advocated the eradication of party strife and polemical religion, although agricultural periodicals at times reflected the disunity of political partyism and sectarianism more than the agrarian associations they supported. In Canada East, the *Canadian Agricultural Journal* called on farmers to display a more "liberal" public spirit by ignoring the selfish demands of party and sectarian religion; it can be inferred that the *Journal* expected agricultural improvement to be the result of this neutral course.[39] The *Canada Farmer* in Canada West echoed the *Journal*, and pleaded for more "noble, generous and patriotic impulses" to abolish party feeling and religious animosity. Its first editorial also noted that the climate had indeed changed after the Rebellions: "The lines of demarcation between sections and parties, which have hitherto been so plain to every eye, so offensive to, and so regretted by every generous well wisher of his country, are becoming shadowy and indistinct." And yet agricultural newspapers could not escape charges of political meddling, as different governments subsidized friendly periodicals and offered discounts through the agricultural societies themselves. Thus the *Canada Farmer*'s neutrality became a bulwark in their accusation that the *British American Cultivator* maintained just such a "church and state connexion" with various agricultural societies, an accusation that led to a rather protracted controversy between the two agricultural papers.[40]

The competing agendas of agricultural periodicals tended to overshadow the rhetoric of all-encompassing ideologies and the calls for political harmony from within the agricultural population, as organs such as the *British American Cultivator* condemned the lack of farmers and the consequent absence of a united agricultural voice in Parliament. Even though the *Cultivator* did not advocate a farmer's political party, the editors were highly concerned by the fact that political parties tended to ignore agricultural interests in their quest for votes.[41] Conversely, the *Canadian Agriculturalist* largely buttressed the governing social order. Buckland and McDougall began their prospectus by stating their non-partisan intentions: "[We shall] scrupulously study to keep our pages clear from party politics and polemical theology. As we shall write for the people of Canada – for the common good of our common country, we can know of no distinctions as colour, party, race or creed – our readers must judge of the sincerity of these professions by the character of our deeds." While the readers of the *Canadian Agriculturalist* could not ignore McDougall's political affiliation as a Clear Grit, he succeeded to some extent in steering clear of the Clear Grit platform – apart from his advocacy of free trade. The political rhetoric was further toned down after 1858 when the *Canadian Agriculturalist* won the right to publish the *Transactions* of the Board of Agriculture and Agricultural Association of Upper Canada. This development presumably transpired as a result of Buckland's political connections with Robert Baldwin and his successor, Francis Hincks, who had gained prominence over McDougall's radical Clear Grit cronies, who had a difficult time staying in office.[42]

THE PRODUCER ALLIANCE AND THE INDEPENDENT YEOMAN FARMER AS CULTURAL ICON

The independent yeoman farmer was a popular rural image that celebrated honest industry and the interdependence of the producer alliance among the agricultural population. And yet hardworking and independent farmer was also glorified by middling class apologists in order to foster social cohesion and the hegemony of the liberal state. The emulation of liberal values and producerism bolstered the community in general and also created a society of self-interested producers who would maximize their own production for material profit.[43] Early agricultural societies endorsed the motif of the industrious farmer by lauding the intelligent, enterprising, and energetic tiller of the soil who exerted his physical and mental energy to furnish material plenty and abounding wealth. Other classes could even visualize the efforts of the hardworking farmer in the landscape. The Oro agricultural society praised its members for their "patience and perseverance, with the hope of success to sweeten our labour, [which] encouraged us to toil on, [so that] now instead of one unbroken forest may be seen the comfortable homesteads, with barns respectably filled." Even the centralized Board of Agriculture in Upper Canada recognized that it was the "hardy and ennobling pursuit of Agriculture which has transformed these vast forests into green pastures," and that it was the "unswerving industry" of the agrarian population that produced material prosperity in Canada.[44] To the directors of agricultural societies, this illustration would provide a stimulus for further exertion and diligence among members of the agrarian community.

It was also a significant endeavour of agricultural societies to diffuse a greater liberal spirit of emulation, as directors visualized no other method of teaching practical farming to young farmers. Membership in an agricultural society was therefore not a matter of profitable speculation, but a matter of "exciting an innocent emulation in a community" and promoting liberal agrarian improvement. The development of agriculture required the intelligence, energy, and enterprise of all the farming population, and these were judged by honest industry: "From the perseverance manifested in the first march of improvement, namely the removal of those great impediments to thorough tillage, stumps and stones ... the farmer is in a position to adopt the other improvements of the day, such as deep and thorough plowing, high manuring, draining, rotation of crops, &c." Although a practical farmer could not imitate his rich neighbour by purchasing livestock, the directors of the Oro agricultural society did envision improvement for the small farmer: "[By] a little tact, tak[ing] the hint, and by indefatigable exertions [he] may make a gradual improvement and very soon it will be perceptible in his stock, and in his farm, and in a little time the man's style of farming will be raised several degrees."[45] Farmers also should educate themselves on the operations of the business aspect of farming and familiarize themselves with "social and other economies" integral to their survival. Farmers understood that the business of agriculture did not depend solely on the harvest and a hardy work ethic, as a scarcity of labour, want of capital, and a lack of economy could impinge on their sometimes meagre fortunes. As the directors of the Oro agricultural society noted, farmers needed to better balance the machinery of supply and demand, as the commercial and manufacturing sectors did. It would be more to the advantage of the farmer to raise costly wool and flax to clothe the community, for example, than to focus all their energies on the cultivation of inexpensive wheat and thus beggar themselves.[46]

The agricultural press likewise advanced the values of honest industry and the labouring ethos of hard work. Praising the "benefits of industry" in the colonies, the *British American Cultivator* proclaimed that every true-hearted Canadian should be proud that theirs was a nation where "labour is respected and richly and liberally rewarded." Even though the profits of the farm were small, skill and industry "moderately exercised" would ensure happiness in an agrarian people. The editors of the *Canadian Agriculturalist* applied this vision to society in an article entitled "Vice vs. Labour": "Virtue, industry and wealth, whether viewed in an individual or in a collective or national light, have always been considered synonymous terms; and so have immorality, idleness and poverty. Such is Nature's irrevocable fiat, pronounced against every race and against every social rank of the human family."[47] Honest industry was the great divider of the community, separating those who were flourishing materially from those who were not. The agricultural press also counselled the agrarian population to constantly improve their farms, and emulate more prosperous farmers. The *Canadian Agriculturalist* encouraged farmers to "stick with the farm" and also to make it more productive, and "less expensive to work, by availing [themselves] of every available improvement." The *Canada Farmer* denounced the farmer who grew poorer every year because he would not improve his farm, preaching that the "best fertilizer of any soil is the spirit of industry, enterprise and intelligence."[48]

Another important facet of the gospel of honest industry was thrift and economy, and the need for farmers to safeguard their resources and not get caught up in the accumulation of wealth. Distrust for those who did not practise economy and thrift – individuals such as financial opportunists and speculators – spilled into many agricultural periodicals. While much of this discourse was a subtle condemnation of the commercial and mercantile class, most farmers concurred that only the kind of labour practised on a farm could bring peace and contentment while speculation could only bring avarice and oppression.[49] Editors of the agricultural press also stressed the importance of being prudent and frugal on the farm, in a recurring motif that contrasted the prosperous thrifty farmer and the poverty-stricken spendthrift farmer. The thrifty husbandman diligently followed a three-step program: he did everything in its proper time, converted everything to its proper use, and put everything in its proper place.

The press characterized the idle tiller of the soil as lazy, often inebriated, one who bought all his equipment on credit and blamed all his troubles on ill fortune instead of his own misdeeds. The *Canadian Agriculturalist* took the middle road: the largest class of farmers were those who were "neither thrifty or unthrifty, neither industrious or tidy, nor dissolute or idle, but ... wholly indifferent to appearances, and whose farms are liable to be mistaken for the residence of Mr. Unthrifty." And yet the major differences between "Mr. Thrifty" and "Mr. Unthrifty" were based not on their wealth but on their standing in liberal society: the former "lives respected, and dies regretted as a useful man and a good Christian," while the latter "is a poor farmer, a poor husband, a poor father, and a poor Christian."[50]

Many agricultural journals also respected the apparently finite laws of political economy, and their editors advised their readers to study this science in order to further their profession. In order to make agriculture more profitable, farmers needed to understand the laws of business and capital, supply and demand, and other principles of political economy. Discussions on the subject invariably became debates about the merits of reciprocity and tariff protection. Since their policies limited political deliberations, farming journals would rarely favour one position over the other. On the contrary, many of these early journals called either for protection from the state, *or* for full, free, and unrestricted trade, as equality demanded that no industry be favoured above another. This discourse of "fairness" in trade practices harboured a restrained critique of the mercantile, manufacturing, and commercial classes for their espousal of trade doctrines favourable only to their own interests. As the *Canadian Agricultural Journal*, a paper that strongly favoured reciprocity, stated in one of its editorials: "We never did advocate, and do not wish that any one class should be protected, or favoured at the expense, or the injury of any other. We would rejoice to see all restrictions on trade removed, and the productions of the earth, and of man's industry allowed to circulate as freely as the wind; but we have always been opposed, and ever shall be, to partial, or one-sided free trade, that will allow freedom only in agricultural productions, while there is ample protection and encouragement to all other productions."[51] The editors of agricultural periodicals were obviously well acquainted with the divided loyalties of their clientele, and refused to alienate any part of their agrarian constituency.

Social interaction among farmers through recreation was a major element in the development of an agrarian identity, and promoters of agricultural associations recognized the importance of combating isolationism in a rural populace. Agricultural exhibitions, ploughing matches, soirées, and concerts were therefore community-based events that brought rural people together for mutual improvement and social concord.[52] Social intercourse among the agricultural population required the unity and co-operation of farmers' associations, for the development of social, mental, and moral culture within their constituencies. As Major Lachlan, a "gentleman farmer" and the president of the Western District agricultural society noted: "The increased and expanded congenial feeling[s] produced by such institutions, naturally tend to draw closer the bonds of social intercourse among the inhabitants of a neighbourhood, and to lay the foundation of valuable friendships and endearing associations and connexions."[53] The earliest attempts to provide intellectual events and activities for the agrarian community were efforts on the part of directors of agricultural societies to procure lecturers, organize discussions on agricultural subjects, and provide annual dinners during the exhibitions. But the pre-eminent means for agricultural societies to provide amusement and entertainment in the community was the ploughing match. Attended in large numbers by neighbouring farmers and other interested parties, ploughing matches brought in large revenues, often by charging fees for both participants and spectators. When the match was enlarged into a spectacle, the gate revenue increased; but, when directors of both the Carleton and Peterborough societies, for instance, presented just a simple ploughing match, both the crowd and contestants were sparse. The president of the Carleton society was puzzled by the apathy of the ploughmen, as the economic rewards in the prize list had been upgraded.[54] Prize money and competition were indeed motivations for some of these events, but their success ultimately depended on a vision of expanding rational recreation within the larger community.

Directors of agricultural societies also tried to ensure that all their activities conformed to liberal standards of cultural and social regulation. In the 1861 annual report of the Addington County agricultural society, the executive directed that "some responsible person, or persons shall give a guarantee for the safety of articles exhibited, and that *good order* shall be observed" during the annual exhibition. The directors even insisted that the dinner connected with the exhibition be conducted according to principles of temperance.[55] The Norwich agricultural society's exhibitions were very popular as community events as well as being financially successful. However, while these accomplishments garnered much praise, the directors found it a challenge to keep good order. In order to prevent certain individuals from sneaking onto the exhibition grounds, the executive in 1861 hired several constables and gatekeepers to enforce the payment of entrance fees. A few years later the directors of the Norwich agricultural society took a J. Chambers to court, in an attempt to recover the five-dollar fine levied on him during the previous year's exhibition because he had "forced his way upon the Exhibition Ground during the last exhibition of this society, and conducted himself in an improper manner while on the ground."[56]

The focus of agricultural societies in Lower Canada/Canada East on economic utility and the practical aspects of agriculture did not allow them to contribute to the leisure activities to the same extent as farmers in Canada West. In deliberating on the demise of agricultural societies in Canada East at mid-century, some historians have argued that the neglect of successive Quebec governments to appreciate the exhibition movement was *the* major cause of agricultural societies' failure to provide significant change and improvement to provincial agriculture. The bureaucracy of the liberal state in Canada East was partly to blame. The administation was simply not partial to exhibitions, and conflicts between English and French members in the Board of Agriculture and the *Conseil des Arts* were too daunting. And yet agricultural societies in Canada East themselves refused to provide the kind of community events that would attract a larger audience than a simple exhibition from surrounding rural areas. Many societies concentrated solely on improving agricultural schools, model farms, and libraries and on increasing the prize lists for agricultural exhibitions. One of the important innovations of Lower Canadian agricultural associations was to award prizes to the most progressive and cultivated farms of a district, in order to stimulate emulation among farmers. Such contests involved taking prizes to the community, rather than creating a social event for the village or town.[57]

CONTESTED AGRARIAN IDENTITIES AND LATE-CENTURY RURAL MIDDLE-CLASS FORMATION

Although methods of agriculture underwent a significant transition in the post-Confederation decades, commercial farming as *the* foundation of economic activity in central Canada remained stable until the twentieth century. Even though most farming families in Ontario reached a stable level of economic self-sufficiency by the 1870s, many farms did even better, producing varying levels of market surpluses. While these surpluses were not considerable by any means, they provided stability, respectability, and a decent productivity level for most family farms in Ontario. In Quebec continued reliance on the production of the family farm did not guarantee great prosperity, but most farms in the province generated a measure of stability for agricultural families.[58] Many farmers relied heavily on the wheat and other cereal products grown on their own acreage or even on rented plots of land, as the significance of generating commercial surpluses for participation in "agrarian capitalism" prompted many agricultural families to promote alternative market strategies. Therefore, the escalation of mixed agriculture – with an ever-increasing emphasis on the large-scale commercial farming found in livestock and dairy products and a strong focus on the respectability of "ownership" – tended to illustrate the various socio-economic approaches taken by the agricultural population in rural Ontario and Quebec to attain an elusive middle-class status. Tillers of the soil, coupled with larger commercial farmers, did in fact represent the sizeable development of rural middle-class formation, and became one of the main stimuli for sustained cultural and social stability in the central Canadian countryside.[59]

Although successful farmers comprised a good majority of the middle-class in both Ontario and Quebec, a considerable amount of evidence demonstrates that agrarian conditions were not rewarding to all tillers of the soil. In some areas of the country, a profoundly structured "hierarchy of the soil" emerged, in which widespread poverty, inequality, and limited opportunities for development were socio-economic norms for the agricultural population. While the relative prosperity of agriculture in Ontario alleviated in some degree these pressures of economic disparity, studies reveal contested agrarian cultural identities amongst farmers in the rural hinterland, particularly in Quebec and the Maritimes. Small producers and tenant farmers tended to be materially marginalized, as they could not afford to experiment with new, improved, and more expensive agricultural processes. This led to increased conflict between family, commercial, and tenant farmers, conflict that also highlighted the plight of the landless agricultural labourer.[60] Large commercial farmers of a liberal stripe who either embraced or reacted with indifference to the market system of industrial capitalism found themselves at odds with marginal farmers who felt highly circumspect toward urban monopoly capitalism. Although escalating urbanization and industrialization were often an issue of perception, as Ontario remained largely agricultural by the turn of the century, less fortunate commercial farmers, subsistence farmers, and agricultural labourers reacted with trepidation to the socio-economic changes inherent in large-scale commercial agriculture.[61]

These contested cultural visions of the tillers of the soil would endure among farmers from the waning of the "liberal" social order in the 1870s to the beginning of the twentieth century. On the whole, large commercial farmers generating large marketable surpluses tended to favour the continuation of the market system in selling their agricultural products. Farmers in this group were also predisposed to favour government intervention in agriculture, from the establishment of experimental farms, the establishment of university chairs in agronomy, and the acceptance of governmental patronage of Farmers' Institutes in Ontario and *cercles agricoles* in Quebec. The centralization of farmers' organizations ensured that large commercial farmers led both agricultural societies and government associations, and also that ordinary or "practical" farmers avoided them in droves.[62] Materially excluded small agricultural producers and tenant farmers were therefore far more likely to support farmer organizations that critiqued monopoly capitalism and market-driven agriculture while expressing preference for radical agrarian populism and economic doctrines such as co-operation. Farmers of this ilk drifted toward the Dominion Grange of the Patrons of Husbandry and the Patrons of Industry, associations that viewed farmers as the downtrodden class of society. What is significant about these competing images of agriculture is that tillers of the soil all along the economic continuum could either accept or reject these diverse and contested – yet also highly "collective" – cultural identities of the central Canadian farmer.[63]

Continuing support for a liberal ideology of class inclusiveness in agricultural societies became even more crucial by the end of the century, as agrarian associations in rural villages and towns began to expand and embrace some of the new commercial and industrializing classes. The membership base of agricultural societies reflected these changes, with many subscription lists reproducing the results of the Missisquoi agricultural society, whose directors recorded that between 29 and 48 percent of the paying members of the society during the years 1884 and 1896 were not working farmers.[64] As a result, the liberal philosophy of "classlessness" often harboured some measure of consent for the rural social order, which was increasingly composed of large commercial farmers, merchants, and manufacturing interests. In their 1893 annual report, the directors of the South Wellington agricultural society acknowledged the contributions of other classes in the community during the exhibition: "We cannot speak too highly of the unselfish effort of those merchants, manufacturers and others, who, at considerable expense for advertising and other purposes, displayed their products during the exhibition, and would tender them our sincerest thanks for their share in contributing to its success." Even a specialized agricultural association such as the Guelph Fat Stock Club, made up of large commercial farmers, recognized the importance of remaining accessible to the entire community. The city of Guelph clearly managed to provide liberal public support for the club, as its president noted: "The country had the hearty co-operation of the city in any undertaking. Their interests were pretty much identical and they should work together for mutual benefit."[65] The increasingly diverse occupational identity in small-town Ontario is similarly reflected in the membership lists of the Elora, Metcalfe, and Glengarry agricultural societies (see Table 5.1).

Despite this liberal appreciation for other classes in the community, farmers in agricultural associations continued to perceive agriculture as the backbone of society, and wondered why they remained the subordinate class. While asking why farmers remained inferior to other classes, the Oro agricultural society concluded that since "the great mass must depend on the products of the soil, consequently ... agriculture is and will be the great mainstay of Ontario and will increasingly be so for years to come."[66]

On the other hand, many large-scale commercial farmers held their less successful agrarian brethren responsible for many of the socio-economic changes transforming agriculture, rather than the machinations of other classes or urban industrial capitalism. Wealthy commercial farmers, who could afford to purchase livestock in the Guelph Fat Stock Club, often despaired at the apathy of the ordinary farming population in Guelph who withheld support from the activities of the club. Similarly, the South Wellington agricultural society criticized the county council when its members, "composed principally of farmers ... by their vote cut off the small grant given towards institutions in which they should take so great an interest and do all in their power to foster. We trust the council for 1881 will be more liberal, and in future do all they can to encourage their own profession." Walter Riddell, an influential commercial farmer and member of the Northumberland society, also squarely blamed ordinary farmers themselves for their inferior position in society:

> On the whole the benefits derived from Agricultural societies, Farmers' Clubs and Institutes, and the labours of patriotic individuals have not been commensurate with the exertion put forth. The fault rests mainly with the farmers themselves. A little more public spirit, a little less jealousy and a little more liberality would greatly conduce to the better working of all our agricultural institutions. It is not enough for any farmer to give only pecuniary support. That is needful, and good so far as it goes, but every farmer ought to be willing to give of his time and thought to every scheme that seeks to improve the farmers' condition.

Table 5.1
Ordinary Members of the Metcalfe, Glengarry and Elora Agricultural Societies, 1892–99

Glengarry (1892)

Occupation	Total	Percentage
Farmer	268	
Others*	4	
TOTAL AGRICULTURAL	272	81
Carriage Maker	3	
Blacksmith	2	
Others**	10	
TOTAL SKILLED	15	4
TOTAL CLERICAL	3	1
Merchant	15	
Hotel Keeper	12	
Others^	7	
TOTAL BUSINESS	34	10
Doctor	5	
Others^^	7	
TOTAL PROFESSIONAL	12	4

Metcalfe (1893)

Occupation	Total	Percentage
Farmer	40	
Others*	3	
TOTAL AGRICULTURAL	43	74
Printer	2	
Others**	2	
TOTAL SKILLED	4	7
Merchant	5	
Hotelkeeper	3	
Others^	2	
TOTAL BUSINESS	10	17
TOTAL PROFESSIONAL	1	2

Elora (1899)

Occupation	Total	Percentage
Farmer	91	
Others*	25	
TOTAL AGRICULTURAL	116	47
Blacksmith	6	
Others**	16	
TOTAL SKILLED	22	9
TOTAL WOMEN	7	3

Occupation	Total	Percentage
Merchant	28	
Hotelkeeper	15	
Others^	28	
TOTAL BUSINESS	71	29
Clerk	8	
TOTAL CLERICAL	8	3
Barrister	5	
Others^^	16	
TOTAL PROFESSIONAL	21	9

* Other occupations in the agricultural category include: horseman, florist, gardener, beeman, teamster, saw miller, seeds man, miller, cheesemaker, and livery man.
** Other occupations in the skilled category include: carter, founder, labourer, lumberman, carriage maker, brewer, plasterer, carpenter, weaver, marble cutter, barber, butcher, shoemaker, harness maker, printer, tinsmith, and bartender.
^ Other occupations in the business category include: agent, traveller, manager, undertaker, hostler, banker, manufacturer, jeweller, and grain buyer.
^^ Other occupations in the professional category include: barrister, politician, teacher, editor, postmaster, and dentist.

SOURCE: Glengarry Agricultural society papers, in the McGillivray Family fonds, LAC, MG 24 I 3, vol. 21, file 2, subscription list, 220–29; Metcalfe Agricultural society papers, Township of Metcalfe fonds, LAC, MG 9 D8/52, minute book, 1889–1902, membership list at the back; and Elora Agricultural society fonds, WCA, A1982.70, series 9, subseries 1, file 1,minute book, 1896–1907, list of members 1899.

These are not the days that farmers can afford to lie on their oars, they must be up and doing if they do not wish to lag behind their more enterprising neighbours.[67]

The pronouncements of the Middlesex agricultural society provide an excellent example of these contested agrarian identities. Initial declarations from the society reflected its proximity to the burgeoning urban area of London, as the 1872 annual report expressed gratitude for "the prosperity of all classes in society." Another statement related to the 1877 exhibition lauded the fact that the products of the agricultural, mercantile, and manufacturing sectors were all in one place, "thrown in the common fund for the benefit of all."[68] Despite this liberal discourse of class concord and harmony, however, later assertions from the Middlesex agricultural society directors echoed the more adversarial language of farmers as the downtrodden class of the community. Reporting that "farmers are not quite satisfied with the subordinate position in society that has hitherto been assigned to them by others," the Middlesex executive proposed a more proactive strategy for dealing with other class interests:

> We believe that this habit of [e]ntrusting our public affairs entirely to other men or other classes of the community is a serious fault in the character of our farmers. We cannot have the agricultural interests of the Province properly attended to, unless we ourselves take hold of it. It is an old saying that "he who by the plough would thrive, himself must either field or drive." This is just as applicable to public affairs, as to our own private interests, and until we, as individuals, awake to the necessity of paying more attention and devoting more time to the advancement of our common interest as farmers, we shall never be able to unite to secure that power or even to obtain that respect to which our numbers and wealth would certainly entitle us.

In 1892 the Middlesex agricultural society went even further and decried an executive election where "boys, hotel keepers and a mixed crowd" voted for positions on the board, instead of the more respectable farmers of the district. This episode illustrates that not every farmer was pleased with the merger of agriculture and urban industrial interests. The dichotomy of providing *in*clusive agricultural services with an *ex*clusive vision of the farming community was evidently a difficult one for some members of the agricultural population.[69]

Contested agrarian identities also arose when the liberal industrial state attempted to strengthen agriculture by augmenting financial grants and sponsoring organizations such as Farmers' Institutes in Ontario and the *cercles agricoles* in Quebec. Among the overtures of Oliver Mowat's Liberal government to Ontario farmers, Farmers' Institutes were centralized in 1887 and became even more overtly and exclusively concerned with the rights of the tillers of the soil. The first object of the Central Board of Farmers' Institutes was to further the material interests of farmers, ostensibly by encouraging agrarian education and offering protection from encroachments that emanated from other class interests. The Central Board also claimed that it would conserve and secure farmers' rights in relation to "legislators, corporations and individual industries." It is no surprise that unlike the membership of agricultural societies at the same period in time, farmers comprised well over 98 percent of the entire executive of Farmers' Institutes in Ontario.[70] Successive presidents of the Central Institute took pains to illustrate to farmers that it was their skill and industry that made Ontario prosperous. In 1889 the motto of the Central Institute became "justice to the farmer," with the implication that the interests of agriculture were the most neglected in the community, whereas in reality they were critical to the welfare of society at large. It therefore appears that increased government involvement in the lives of Ontario farmers created even more exclusivity and a greater sense of class superiority than the limited grant system of the early years.[71]

The tillers of the soil in Farmers' Institutes had a fairly volatile relationship with the forces of socio-economic transformation that were taking place in agriculture, and a strongly antagonistic discourse arose in the Institutes regarding other classes in the community. The Farmers' Institute movement made sure that ordinary farmers came to acknowledge their contribution – that "upon their welfare rested the welfare of the whole community," even though their "interests [had] been the most neglected of any class" in society.[72] And many farmers agreed with the thought expressed by the South Wellington Farmers' Institute: "[The] altered condition of agriculture generally, together with the avaricious exactions of some classes, [makes] concerted action ... absolutely necessary to enable us to hold our own." To the directors of the Northumberland Farmers' Institute, combinations of commercial men and manufacturers permitted a situation whereby the few benefited at the expense of the many, to the extent that a corresponding combination of farmers was necessary to counteract the monopoly of industrial capitalism. The executive of the North Lanark Institute argued that banding together as farmers was entirely defensive: "We do not say that farmers should not organize to defend their commercial rights. Nay, when he is pocket-picked by the sharpers of every class, not to defend himself would be culpable cowardice."[73]

The larger commercial farmers and their allies in the Farmers' Institute movement tempered this language of agrarian subjugation with a vision of liberal class inclusion and a call for reform among farmers themselves. In the 1889 report of the Central Board of Farmers' Institutes, the Board recognized that farmers themselves were stumbling blocks to agrarian concord, as they lacked the "adhesive properties" of other classes. When the future premier of Ontario E.C. Drury visited the Frontenac Farmers' Institute, he blamed farmers for forgoing their influence both socially and politically: "The chief reason was that they had no respect for themselves, and appeared slovenly and ill-attired ... Farmers should dress well and show that their position called for respect, and then they should demand their rights, because no man had reason to be prouder than the man who tilled the soil."[74]

The influence of large commercial farmers over the affairs of Farmers' Institutes can also be measured in their rules and regulations. Executives were admonished to "bring the rank and file of the farmers into touch with the most successful local men, that the masses may become more conversant with the best and most profitable methods of farming, stock raising, dairying, fruit culture, and all branches of business connected with the industry of agriculture." Similarly, the directors of the Oshawa Farmers' Institute publicized their debate on Commercial Union as "fair and open," inviting members of the entire community to participate. A few over-exuberant farmers tested this resolve when a Mr Larke, a regional manufacturer, rose to defend the National Policy. One farmer objected that Larke was not a farmer, had no interest in farming, and had no right to speak to the assembly. However, the chairman of the Institute responded that he "had a great respect for Mr. Larke and was glad to have him address the meeting. He hoped he would be given a hearing, especially as he was a member of the Institute."[75]

Contested agrarian attitudes toward liberal class inclusion and the ranking of agriculture among other interests in the community also surfaced in the parallel *cercles agricoles* movement in Quebec. As with the Farmers' Institutes in Ontario, large commercial farmers encouraged "book farming," model farms, and agricultural instruction, along with their tacit support for the rural social order and the industrial state. A government pamphlet promoting the *cercles agricoles* recognized that Quebec lagged far behind

English Canada in agricultural prosperity, and implicitly blamed the problem on the ordinary, uneducated farmer. To the Department of Agriculture in Quebec, "neither climate, soil, means of communication, nor markets are wanting. What then? It is the insufficiency of agricultural instruction which prevents our appreciation, at their true value, of the advantages with which Providence has blessed us." With such governmental backing, the movement appealed to all segments of rural society, as witnessed in the *cercle agricole* in the *paroisse* St Francis du Lac, where over half of the composition of the executive included *notaires* and *registrateurs*.[76] However, the *cercles agricoles* in Quebec also reaffirmed the ideology of class dissonance and class superiority inherent in the discourse of the rural agrarian population. In the *Almanachs* of the *cercles* published by the Ministry of Agriculture and Colonization, editorials lauded the agricultural profession as an "inexhaustible source of national wealth, a bulwark against chaos, a guarantee of social harmony, a source of prosperity and happiness for nations as well as for individuals." Another editorial in the *Almanachs* also derided other classes in the community for placing all their confidence in "l'industrialisme et le commercialisme" and the promises of industrial capitalism. Despite the sponsorship of the industrial state, the article decried an exclusive focus on manufactures and commerce as an "economic mistake, and speculation, which is called monopoly, is a crime; in reality it is theft instituted by the state of the system. This is a warning for all who are concerned with social reform."[77]

By far the most influential agricultural newspaper in Canada during the late nineteenth century was the *Farmers' Advocate*, printed in London, Ontario, and edited by William Weld, a "gentleman farmer" who wrote articles almost exclusively on the plight of agriculture. Saddled with a business dependent on advertising revenue from merchants and manufacturers, Weld epitomized the contested nature of farmers, alternating between support for the rural social order and an acknowledgement of agrarian subjugation by other classes in the community. On the one hand, Weld outlined a vision of liberal class inclusion in his periodical, espousing the values of interdependence and harmonious relations among all the classes in society. Demanding "fair play and fair treatment" for the farmer in his economic relations with other classes, Weld reiterated that there should be no clash of interests between farmers and businessmen. He refused to set class against class; his paper would "uphold the rights and just claims of farmers, [but] not wage war upon others."[78] He also suggested that ordinary farmers should appreciate both the larger commercial farmer, for establishing good markets in Ontario, and the experimental farmer, for his inventions and leadership in agricultural associations. The experimental stations and model farms in Ontario, he asserted, illustrated to ordinary tillers of the soil that if experiments were economically and practically conducted, "intelligent farming [could] be made profitable." The *Ontario Farmer* concurred: "Farming in this Province should become, and with many it is fast becoming, every year less a mere matter of manual drudgery, and more an occupation where education and intelligence, earnest experiment and scientific research should assert their claims, and make themselves felt as a necessity to success." The reliance of the *Ontario Farmer* on government subsidies to support its publication would of course make such pronouncements fairly predictable.[79]

As an "ordinary farmer" himself, however, Weld also outlined numerous problems both with governmental influence in agricultural associations and with the liberal market system. While he appreciated state efforts in manning model farms and experimental stations, he felt that practical farmers needed to be more involved in the operations of these facilities. Not only did government involvement in agriculture stifle private incentive, but the lack of success in government enterprises led Weld to conclude that governments should limit themselves to protecting and encouraging private agrarian interests. Agricultural triumphs required practical farmers: "What is a purely scientific man? Is it a man who is most thoroughly acquainted with one or more sciences, and who is acquainted with nothing else? If so, then of course a purely scientific man cannot make farming pay or anything else pay. Farming is an art as well as a science."[80] Practical farmers were in his estimation the backbone of the community in a socio-economic sense, and thus a discourse of class superiority emerged in the pages of his agrarian periodical. Lauding agriculture as the most important profession, Weld glorified the independent farmer as "one of the most ancient and honourable occupations known; it takes the lead in the world; it is the backbone and sinew of every country; it has made nations, caused them to become mighty, and when neglected have collapsed; it must take the lead of all employments; it is the impetus that sets everything in motion."[81]

This language of class supremacy spilled over into vitriolic assertions about other classes in the community in the pages of the agricultural press. The transformations that had taken place in agriculture as a result of industrial capitalism and large-scale commercial farming led Weld to conclude that farmers were surrounded by enemies from all classes, with the result that the farmer was "born a king, and made a slave." He particularly singled out the politicians, who made class laws injurious to ordinary farmers while picking their pockets with taxes on roads, postage, and transportation.[82] Although the *Ontario Farmer* received the bulk of its support from the Ontario government, it likewise promoted an adversarial discourse between the farmer and other classes in the community. In an article entitled "The Scourge of Speculators," the *Ontario Farmer* in 1869 condemned land speculators and asked if there was "not some way that the poor and honest farmer, who wishes land and a home, may escape the grasp of the middle-men, the land-sharks, those who come between the Creator and the tiller of the soil." That publication also compared the healthy, invigorating, honourable, and independent occupation of farmer with the "effeminate" position of store clerk, an emerging commercial reality in small towns and villages in the rural countryside. Condemning the fact that young farmers were abandoning agricultural pursuits for clerking jobs, the *Ontario Farmer* satirically demanded that such young men take a good look at themselves: "Answer this query if you can, ye dyspeptic specimens of humanity, attired in man-millinery, who listlessly lounge behind the counters of drapery establishments – occupying the places that nature intended for the weaker sex – and whose greatest physical strength seems to be exerted in the blandishments of a smile, when some fair customer condescends to make a purchase. Answer it, pale clerk, doomed to the desk day after day, to whom a breath of heaven, cooling the throbbing brow and wasting cheeks, is a luxury seldom enjoyed."[83]

THE CONTRIBUTIONS OF WOMEN TO A COLLECTIVE AGRARIAN IDENTITY

The experiences of women in agricultural associations not only mirrored the transformations of late nineteenth-century agriculture but they also reflected the dichotomous position of women in central Canadian society itself. The increased presence and responsibilities of female members in agricultural associations highlighted the growing participation of women in the agrarian community as a whole, and showcased their unique talents and contributions. However, male directors of agricultural organizations also continued to marginalize women, keeping them from market involvement in agriculture and direct participation in agrarian associations, confining their efforts to the domestic sphere and less challenging agricultural pursuits such as horticulture and gardening.[84] It became acceptable for women to participate only in a limited fashion but female members did not even appear on most society records until well into the 1870s. Most societies experienced a rather fluctuating presence of women. The

Guelph agricultural society, for instance, recorded female membership numbers as low as 3 percent in 1873 to a high of 27 percent in 1896. Not only were these figures fairly minimal compared to the membership of women in temperance societies at the same period but women were simply absent from the rolls of agricultural society directors.[85]

Exhibitions sponsored by agricultural societies also gave expanded opportunities to women in the agrarian community, as female judges were promoted from merely judging women's entries to judging dairy products and horticulture. Despite the rising prestige of the ladies department in exhibitions, the prizes for ladies were less rewarding, and more than one executive echoed the faint praise of the Oro agricultural society to the effect that "the domestic manufactures and fancy work show the ladies to be fully alive to the interests of their side of the farming economy."[86] However, when it came to making protests in agricultural exhibitions, women were largely placed on the same footing as other members of the community. In many cases of women's protests, society directors simply attempted to redress the grievance quietly; for example, giving a donation of one dollar to two ladies who had their cheese stolen at the Cardwell agricultural society exhibition. The executive of the Erin agricultural society conversely chose to ignore a protest against a prominent teacher who was simply uninformed about the rules of competition in the Erin agricultural fair. Negligence on the part of male agricultural society directors in dealing with protests also caused female exhibitors to flex their symbolic muscles. The executive of the South Wellington agricultural society received letters from two incensed women, one suing for damages to her taxidermy specimen, and the other going to the extraordinary lengths of hiring a lawyer to collect her eighteen-dollar prize.[87]

The inclusion of women into the Farmers' Institute movement followed a pattern identical with other agricultural associations under examination. Farmers' Institutes purported to incorporate women through recreation, entertainment, and lectures on domestic subjects and many Institutes called on local women to provide recitations, singing, and instrumental music for revenue-generating concerts and soirées. By the second half of the 1890s, concerted efforts were made to secure special ladies' meetings with female lecturers. However, the continued marginalization of women in the lecture system, is evident from the fact that Farmers' Institutes would only provide lectures for women on more "feminine" agrarian topics such as domestic economy, fruit growing in the garden, happy homes, and domestic requirements.[88] The absence of women from the executive councils of individual Institutes, and the apathy of rural women about becoming members of the Institutes led Adelaide Hoodless in 1897 to explore the possibility of establishing a separate Institute experience for women. Intending a similar experience to the WCTU and temperance societies, the Women's Institutes of Ontario met the needs of rural women by providing education and affordable sociability, while at the same time allowing agrarian women the opportunity to construct their own identity and run their own programs.[89]

The views of the agrarian press on female contributions to agriculture reflected a similar paradigm, as the language of domesticity counterbalanced appreciation for the assistance of women in agrarian pursuits. While the *Farmers' Advocate* did consider women in the countryside as practical farmers in their own right, advocating that "plowing, dragging, sowing, rolling, planting, hoeing and harvesting ... become the pleasant, healthful and remunerative occupation of women as well as men," a balance needed to be struck between the desirability of female participation in the agricultural sphere and the acceptability of heavy labour to the gentler sex. As the *Farmers' Advocate* suggested, outdoor agricultural work for women needed to be as light as possible, for "weak is the pulse of a nation where [women] are regarded as slaves, instead of companions."[90] As a result, by the late 1870s the pages of the *Farmers' Advocate* devoted more space to women as wives and mothers in the domestic sphere than to their participation in agriculture. The measure of a woman's effectiveness in the home, according to "Minnie May's" advice column in the *Advocate*, was her cultivation of the finer arts of sociability, economy, and fashion in dress, keeping the family home neat and attractive, and ensuring that love and order prevailed.[91]

According to the agrarian press, the contributions of women in agricultural associations reinforced the ideologies of liberal gender inclusion *and* the domestic ideal. Weld, of the *Farmers' Advocate*, severely criticized male agricultural society directors for neglecting their female constituency, as the "ladies have too little to say, particularly when financial questions, or questions on political economy are discussed." Unfortunately Weld's proposed solution would only serve to marginalize women in the domestic sphere, as he called for a "portion of the evening [to be] set apart for their special benefit, during which such topics as they are most interested in should be considered. There should be domestic economy, home ornamentation, relations of parents to children, education, woman's rights, influence, sphere, duties, etc." The editors of the *Ontario Farmer*, for their part, stated that farmers' clubs and agricultural societies would be vastly improved "if the presence of ladies were secured, as woman was meant to be man's companion and helpmeet in all walks of life. Much of the hard work of the farm falls to her share, and we believe such meetings might be made of interest to the fairest portion of the human family." The *Ontario Farmer* also observed condescendingly that "if ladies attended, the proceedings might be enlivened with music, which would be a very pleasant addition, delightfully varying the more practical engagements of the evening."[92]

AGRICULTURAL ASSOCIATIONS AND RELATIONS WITH THE EMERGING INDUSTRIAL STATE

The contestation of agrarian identities continued in agricultural societies, particularly as these organizations attempted to buttress the rural social order by masking political and religious differences amongst their constituents. The Puslinch farmers' club prided itself on being an inclusive institution: "Any question bearing directly on the agricultural interests of the whole community shall be decreed a legitimate subject for discussion." The Oro agricultural society showed its unwillingness to favour one religious denomination over another by deciding not to lease land that it owned to a church.[93] However, as a result of socio-economic transformations in agriculture, farmers also recognized that party politics could erode the bonds of unity that should exist among tillers of the soil. Walter Riddell, in a lecture to the Northumberland agricultural society, recommended that government legislation should be made for "the general public interest, and not for *classes*," adding that farmers had been "much too long blinded by party political opinions against their own interests – were they to work together and do as other classes do[,] their interests would soon receive more attention at the hands of our rulers."[94]

With the grant system for agricultural societies and the creation of Boards of Agriculture and experimental farms, the public and private spheres were as blurred in the realm of agriculture as in education. The liberal dichotomy of being dependent on the state for financial support and yet remaining free from religious and political conflict did in fact lead to a reduction of anti-sectarian and anti-political rhetoric in agrarian associations. This situation has led many historians to conclude that agricultural organizations were agents of state hegemony and actively participated in the construction of middle-class values.[95] When the government became more involved with the Agriculture and Arts Association in 1869, President David Christie decried the move as one of "political necessity." Calling on the government to keep the association free of politics and party considerations, Christie praised what the association had previously accomplished: "In the management of this institution we have steadily abjured politics; if we had not done so we would never have accomplished anything. This is common ground, on which we can all meet; and it is refreshing to have such a rendezvous. Let us say to every political meddler, no matter who he may be, 'This is sacred ground.'" Christie's address clearly masked simmering political tensions within the Board. As a conscientious Clear Grit, Christie simply could not tolerate the politics of Sandfield Macdonald's Liberal/Tory administration.[96]

As a result of their subsidies from the liberal state, directors of Farmers' Institutes in Ontario and *cercles agricoles* in Quebec took great pains to distance themselves from party squabbles of the day. The bylaws of Farmers' Institutes insisted that all Institutes organized had to be "strictly non-partisan and non-sectarian in every phase of their work, and [that] no Institute shall be operated in the direct interest of any party, sect or society, but for the equal good of all citizens and the farming community." Furthermore, local directors were to avoid promoting wares or schemes in which any member would receive direct or even indirect pecuniary reward.[97] O.E. Dallaire called the *cercles agricoles* a "legal association" and a "deliberative body," created for the purposes of contending "against prejudices, egotism, political and other causes of disunion" among farmers. Accordingly, many editorials in the *Almanachs des cercles agricoles* advised farmers to prevent political and religious "dissensions" and "jalousies" by remaining on good terms with the parish priest. Such a policy ensured that prominent Roman Catholic clergy such as Archbishop Taschereau in Quebec and Archbishop Laflèche in Trois-Rivières would support both the government of Quebec and the *cercles*. One circular even quoted a prominent clergyman, Bishop Antoine from Sherbrooke: "I ask the parish priests in my diocese to kindly help me, to the extent that they are concerned with the agricultural classes, to give proper guidance to the *cercles* that will form under this government, in my diocese."[98]

In Ontario, despite the pacifying and hegemonic influence of the liberal industrial state, Farmers' Institutes became intensely politicized in the late 1880s over the merits of Commercial Union. As the executive of the East Peterborough Farmers' Institute discovered, while discussions on politics were important to farmers, debates on Commercial Union were useless "as the electors of today were too set in their party lines to change easily." Finding unity on the doctrines of Commercial Union was also a great problem for Farmers' Institutes, as farmers simply did not hold monolithic views regarding its implementation. As the West Kent Farmers' Institute reported, Commercial Union was "strongly recommended by some" and "bitterly denounced" by others.[99] Discord and disharmony took over

Commercial Union debates, to the extent that the Central Institute president forbade further discussion on the topic of politico-economic relations with the United States:

> I am bound in all honour and all conscience and anxiety for the future of the Institutes throughout the country, to say that I believe that in those Institutes that have passed and put on record, after due deliberation, their convictions with reference especially to this question, its further discussion will lead to discord, and on anything relating to the farmers' interests we should be united. The result of keeping politics or a quasi-political matter under discussion in a collective body would bring about discord. This country is cursed with politics ... I say it is the duty of the farmers of this country to look to the welfare of the country first, and look to the welfare of political parties afterwards. You have been a tool in their hands.

With these discussions on Commercial Union came the exposure of an agrarian population deeply divided, both in material circumstances and in political ideology. The Board of the Central Institute in 1888 issued the terse commentary that the Institutes "will be wrecked if we continue to discuss any subject that is based upon or relates to the politics of this country."[100]

The image of the independent yeoman farmer unburdened by party and sectarian constraints was fostered and protected by Weld's agricultural paper, the *Farmers' Advocate*. Boasting that no paper had "ever existed for such a length of time without being the tool to some sect, body or party of politicians," Weld claimed that readers of his periodical would not have their religious or political creeds interfered with. But this political neutrality came at a price, as Weld noted that both George Brown's *Canada Farmer* and William Clarke's *Ontario Farmer* were in receipt of government aid and "bound to the political system." Weld's denunciation of Brown was far more heated, given that Brown was the leader of the Reform faction in Upper Canada and used the *Canada Farmer* as a Clear Grit/Liberal party organ. Weld was also a strong supporter of London Tory John Carling, a role that further heightened his critique of George Brown's Reform party.[101] Although a friend of Carling's, Weld was skeptical about the entire political process, condemning a system in which voters opted for political entities and parties rather than expressing preference for individuals. Weld encouraged farmers to ignore the two principal political parties and vote for a "free, untrammelled and independent man" in their riding, and particularly, if he "has common sense, and real, unencumbered property,

[to] prefer him to any fettered slave." One method to guarantee autonomous members in the Parliament of Canada would be to send more farmers to Ottawa, a theme recurring in Weld's editorials. Barring such an extreme step, farmers needed to concentrate on political matters that affected agriculture, rather than on simple party questions.[102] Weld's tirades against party politicians illustrate both a lack of political cohesion and a consistent bout of Liberal/Toryism among tillers of the soil.

As noted earlier, Weld became the most outspoken opponent of government involvement in agricultural matters. Foreshadowing the problems that Christie envisioned in his address to the Agricultural and Arts Association of Ontario, Weld accused the serving president of the Association, James Johnson, of trying to interfere with the Middlesex Agricultural Emporium in an overbearing and tyrannical manner. In Weld's view, Johnson's difficulties with the Emporium arose from looking at the project from a "political point of view, and aiming at higher offices." While Weld's distaste for government-run agricultural projects was also a function of his lukewarm appreciation for the Tories and his disapproval of Oliver Mowat's Reform clique, this episode also illustrated his "independent" status, as Johnson was also a Tory and an opponent of free trade.[103] Government involvement in other projects, such as the Experimental Farms and the Agricultural College in Guelph, caused Weld further consternation as he noted the haphazard methods employed by their directors. Convinced that practical farmers could manage the Experimental Farms more efficiently, Weld asked the Mowat government to turf out the "political hangers-on" and partisan hacks administering the affairs of the model farm. He was also very critical of Farmers' Institutes for the same reason, as governmental patronage of agricultural associations threatened the independence of the farmer. Much of Weld's discontent seemed to stem from his opposition to Commercial Union, which he claimed was a policy of conflict and disharmony. However, he also blamed the Liberal government's patronage for the fact that such policies had a forum in agricultural associations at all.[104]

In many agricultural societies, the ideology of honest industry was best served by the large commercial farmer, who utilized this philosophy as a unifying set of values in upholding the rural agrarian order and liberal market agriculture. In the 1872 annual report of one of the largest agrarian associations in the province of Ontario, the Middlesex agricultural society, the directors lauded the prosperity "of all classes in society" and the improvement of agriculture in the region. Honest industry brought about this transformation, they implied, as "it was not waiting with arms folded that these happy changes have been accomplished; means must be used if the end is to be attained."[105] Riddell remarked in his history of the Northumberland agricultural society, that the "mere possession of capital" or even the ownership of a good farm did not qualify anyone to be a good farmer, but there must be "diligence, integrity and a thorough knowledge of the business." Philippe Landry, the president of the Montmagny agricultural society, also called on the members of his society to contribute "their energy and their love of their country," commenting that "merit and work, and not wealth, [would] ensure success."[106]

Large commercial farmers continued to preach the value of liberal emulation in the agricultural marketplace as a means of sustaining their hegemony in agrarian matters. To Thomas McCrae, a prominent farmer and member of both the Guelph agricultural society and the Fat Stock Club, the defining purpose of agricultural exhibitions was to emphasize hard work and liberal emulation in the larger community. McCrae exhorted the farmers of Guelph with evangelical fervour: "Let the successful look well to their laurels and wear them modestly. Let the unsuccessful *try again* as those who manfully persevere are sure of ultimate success. Let those who have only been onlookers say 'Here are lessons for me to go and do likewise' and may we all be ready and willing to do our best for our own and our country's good, going forward in the march of improvement until the waste places of this land be made fruitful and the wilderness blossom as a rose."[107] And yet chinks in the armour of agrarian emulation were discovered when the Fat Stock Club tried to sell subscriptions in Guelph – it was "a hard matter to squeeze money out of the farmers." After the Fat Stock Club held a show in 1885 without prize money, the executive fully recognized its mistake in promoting pure emulation without material reward: "The farmers of today are not so flush with cash that they will take their cattle to a show merely for the sake of a red, white or blue ribbon." For similar reasons, the directors of the Glengarry agricultural society received a letter of resignation from an ordinary farmer named John Tobin in 1891, who asked the executive: "Pleas take my name of the Agriculture Society book as I do not wish to subscribe to it aney longer for I have nothing to show by so doing."[108]

Careful not to upset the balance among competing visions of political economy in the agrarian population, many directors simply invited the government and the manufacturing sector to improve and develop home markets for their produce. Even when the rules were bent, as they were in Riddell's pro-reciprocity lecture to the Northumberland agricultural society, it was done in the interests of equality and in the name of the liberal community. To Riddell, the economic doctrines of protectionism engendered a forced tribute from farmers and workmen to the manufacturers and also conveyed the impression that Ontarians were "less skilful, less industrious, and less energetic" than their American counterparts. Although Riddell was a large commercial farmer, his criticism of protectionism also employed the discourse of agrarian discontent, with the complaint that farmers were taxed to support other classes in the community: "No one can see the palatial private residences, and large splendid factories erected by our highly protected manufacturers without feeling that they have either wronged the workman of his fair share of wages, or robbed the farmers, by charging him more for his manufactured articles than they were worth." Comments on political economy echoed those of the South Wellington agricultural society, whose executive claimed that the real National Policy for farmers should consist of improved husbandry, and not a reliance on "fluctuating and uncertain markets."[109]

The concepts and principles inherent in the creed of liberal honest industry were increasingly stressed as the government became more involved in agricultural associations. The Centre Wellington Farmers' Institute retained its appreciation for the doctrines of emulation, counselling ordinary farmers to become "more conversant with the best and most profitable methods of farming, stock raising, dairying, fruit culture, and all branches of business connected with the industry of agriculture." The South Leeds Farmers' Institute also associated honest industry directly with the rural social order: "If any should ask in after years for the monuments of your labours, you have only to say 'look around' to secure and happy homes, a pervading mental culture and public order. These kindly fruits of intelligent labour are fit and speaking proofs of the industry, skill and virtue of this and the rising generation of the farmers of South Leeds."[110] However, debates on Commercial Union in Farmers' Institutes illustrated division among the agricultural population along material *and* representative lines. Large commercial farmers who were sympathetic to the continuation of the market system of agriculture believed that Commercial Union would open larger markets for their agricultural goods. Conversely, the directors of the South Wellington Farmers' Institute invited members of the Commercial Union Club to speak at their meeting, to demonstrate that liberal free trade would also serve more radical tenant farmers in helping them "resist the encroachments upon our rights of unscrupulous combines."[111]

Promoters of the *cercles agricoles* movement in Quebec were vociferous in their defence of honest industry, as they encouraged their members to improve agriculture through vigorous and intelligent labour. Concerned advocates of the *cercles agricoles* also preached the importance of a strict economy and the avoidance of the credit system. Farmers were counselled to hold an "exam of conscience" at the end of the year, to evaluate their use of time and resources, and to ensure that their expenses were lower than their revenue, this being the only principle of political economy needed.[112] Convinced that the country family was the foundation of the French-Canadian nation, supporters of the *cercles agricoles* recommended the rural life as a defence against disorder and a guarantee of social peace – arguments that were clearly thinly veiled propaganda for the Quebec government's colonization drive. Furthermore, the advantages of agriculture and the *cercles agricoles* would eventually trickle down to the whole community. Noting that agriculture was free from the disastrous fluctuations of commerce and industry, rural life would "improve man by preserving in him simple customs, a righteous heart, habits of thrift, a taste for hard work, the love of justice, and an abundance of joy, camaraderie, and familial love, a prosperity founded on the moderation of desires."[113]

These attitudes lingered in the agricultural press well into the final decades of the century, although the gospel of hard work in relation to agriculture was tempered by the recognition that agrarian prosperity could only be achieved though hard labour *and* scientific husbandry. Weld claimed that the successful cultivator regarded husbandry as both an art and a business, and that adherence to the *Advocate*'s motto "Persevere and Succeed" would ensure the farmer's fortune. And honest industry remained the ultimate gauge of a successful farmer, as *Miller's Canadian Farmer's Almanac* promised: "Let a man be sober, healthy and industrious, not afraid of hard work, and one can scarcely conceive how he should fail in his career."[114] William Clarke, the editor of he *Ontario Farmer*, also believed that hard work was the key to material success: ["Canada is] no country for the frivolous, idle or the dissipated. People of this sort usually blame the country for their want of success, instead of blaming themselves, which they ought to do." The *Ontario Farmer* also suggested that farmers combine mechanical and agricultural science with physical labour to achieve prosperity in agriculture. This approach would manifest itself in the liberal agrarian community, as "the general prosperity, the rapid increase of population, the accumulation of wealth, the enterprise and activity everywhere seen throughout the country, where bodily labour, so far from being considered degrading and the badge of slavery, is honoured and respected."[115]

In this period the agrarian press continued to keep away from discussions on issues of free trade and protectionism, as they recognized how highly divided the agricultural population was over these economic doctrines. As with earlier agricultural periodicals, Weld shied away from advocating a favoured economic policy, as he was mindful not to upset any paying customer of the *Farmers' Advocate*. And yet Weld at the same time claimed that an unfettered and "unjobbered" reciprocity with the United States would benefit the nation as a whole, and he did lean toward free trade as an accepted economic solution for farmers. He was therefore circumspect enough to blame the failures of the National Policy on the political parties themselves, rather than on protectionism itself. A correspondent to the *Ontario Farmer* agreed with this assessment, claiming that he was no friend of protectionism, although he noted that since the United States had imposed tariffs on Canadian products many positive changes had occurred. Not only did protection result in the construction of the railway, but it contributed to liberal honest industry by "developing in a thousand ways the means of self-help." If reciprocity were to occur between Canada and the United States, the terms needed to be just, fair and equitable, as it was "a question of mutual advantage, not of mendacity on the one side, and generosity on the other."[116]

EXHIBITION CULTURE AND THE SIGNIFICANCE OF RURAL RECREATION

By the late nineteenth century the provision of entertainment to the public had become a focal point for agricultural association directors, although conflicts over what was perceived as "vulgar entertainment" and pandering to public opinion often strained relations within an executive. This transformation in exhibition culture from the education to the entertainment of the farmer was variously described as a struggle for hegemonic control between agricultural societies and the weight of public opinion, or a clash between the proprieties of the liberal social order and the "transgressions" of alternative forms of amusement.[117] This gradual change can best be perceived through the medium of the agricultural press, who recognized the need for farmers to set aside some time for leisure, whether it be for family, or social or public gatherings. Editors of agrarian periodicals recognized the importance of relaxation to the agrarian population in a community setting, and encouraged expanding the opportunities for social networking to include picnics and excursions as well as exhibitions. And yet these editorials also stressed the importance of *rational* recreation, cautioning farmers not to carry their revelry to excess. As the *Farmers' Advocate* observed, "Light amusements when taken in moderation, have a tendency to relieve, lighten and cheer the mind after being busily engaged from day to day in the active and monotonous pursuits of life."[118] By the 1880s the escalation of entertainment in agricultural exhibitions would suggest that the rational had no place with the recreational.

Despite rather generous government grants, directors of agricultural associations promoted recreation in rural exhibitions and fairs as a method of generating more revenue. The Niagara agricultural society recognized that entertainment was a successful formula for financial security. Over the space of five years revenues increased dramatically when it introduced a horseracing track, bicycle races, high jump competitions, concerts and a skating rink to its agricultural fairground. The Ottawa agricultural society rented out its fairgrounds for purposes of public recreation and amusement, noting that with the erection of swings, "the attractions of the grounds and their surroundings, will doubtless secure in the future a considerable revenue as their popularity as a health giving summer resort is now fully established."[119] Other agricultural societies offered attractions such as wire walking, trapeze and balancing acts, comic singing, and dancing at their agricultural exhibitions. The rural population appear to have welcomed these attractions, as many societies debated the merits of having two-day fairs, restricting the first day to agricultural competition and reserving the next for amusements and entertainment. Many directors noted from this experiment that the "educational" portion of the agricultural fair was sparsely attended, while the public visited the fairgrounds in droves for the entertainment portion of the festivities.[120]

Despite the success of recreation in agricultural exhibitions, some associations insisted that amusements and attractions be left out of exhibition or show programs, but the societies who did so often complained about the lack of patronage to their events. The history of the Guelph Fat Stock club is full of grievances from the executive that the agricultural community refused to sustain the club's efforts to improve the livestock of the region. Overtures to the general public were rather superficial; the promoters of the club insisted that building attractive pens and stalls, and giving fuller explanations of the judging results would ensure that "the trouble [was not] from the want of interest, but space enough to accommodate the people." Unfortunately the Guelph Fat Stock club only reached out to large commercial farmers and not to the public at large; as late as 1894 the directors confirmed that "the encouragement to the improvement of the livestock of our community and country is, we may say, the sole object of the Club."[121] And the Middlesex agricultural society – no doubt influenced by Weld – insisted in 1880 that while they had "no balloon ascensions, races or regattas" to amuse the crowd during the Western fair, the solid yeomanry of the district appreciated the instructive and useful character of the exhibition and attended in decent numbers. The directors insisted that when entertainment became the chief purpose of an agricultural fair, "people soon come to look upon it something like a circus, and a real circus can beat them on that line in spite of all they can do." Yet, in two short years the desires of the larger community for more frivolous recreation forced the promoters of the society to change their vision of the exhibition for the sake of "the People":

> From the greatly increased attendance at our Western Fair last fall, in consequence of those extra attractions, and from the eagerness of the crowds to see the sports in the horse-ring, we are convinced that the great majority are in favour of combining pleasure with profit, and while we acknowledge the paramount importance of the agricultural and industrial departments, we see that it is necessary to the financial success of the Society that a variety of attractions should be provided to meet the public taste. Such being, as we believe, the opinions of the great majority of the people, it becomes the duty of your directors to carry their wishes into effect, as we recognize the fact that your officers are not placed in their position as rulers or censors of public opinion, but merely as representatives and servants of the public, and their highest merit is implicit obedience to the voice of the people when clearly expressed.[122]

Not every agrarian advocate was pleased with this stated preference to please the larger community, and opponents of spurious attractions at agricultural exhibitions had Weld as their spokesman. Weld believed amusements were to educate and edify an audience, and the combination of the race course and other "demoralizing influences" was evil and pernicious. The Industrial Exhibition in Toronto was a prime example of exhibition managers "stooping to the demands of the masses," who expected "amusements and pleasures without stint" as a condition of their attendance. Weld stated that such large fairs were inimical to the interest of the farmer, as the liberal emulation principle of agriculture was far more important than money and popularity. Even his successors to the editorship of the *Farmers' Advocate* agreed, criticizing attractions at agricultural fairs as worthless to the education of young farmers, and a waste of both time and money. Despite the seeming exclusivity of this position in relation to mass opinion, the difficulties experienced in various agricultural fairs led many directors to examine the value of inconsequential entertainments in the agrarian community. Some agricultural societies went so far as to petition their municipal governments to arrest scalpers and remove gaming licences for the duration of an exhibition.[123]

In 1889 the executive of the South Wellington agricultural society held a special meeting to debate the merits of recreation as part of their annual agricultural fair. Many directors agreed with Thomas Laidlaw, who conceded that there was nothing immoral or wrong with attractions, but felt they simply were not in keeping with the goals of liberal emulation housed within an agricultural show. And yet the majority opinion among the members of the executive was similar to the more pragmatic view of McCrae: "[There were] two alternatives, to supply the demand or not keep up the show ... a purely agricultural exhibition could not be run without outside attractions, [as] they brought out the city people, and the country people as well."[124] Increased interaction with other classes compelled agricultural societies to provide amusement to the larger community, although uneasiness over the attractions would continue. The Guelph Ministerial Association protested the "brutality, frivolity and vice" of some of the attractions, while one farmer complained, that "it was impossible to imagine any connection existing between circus performances and the interests of agriculture." The editors of the *Guelph Mercury* reminded readers that it was through universal consent that exhibitions were seen as part of the holiday season, and thus "multitudes gather for business, no doubt, but for relaxation and pleasure as well, and if the business were only thought of, not one in ten of those who assemble would come, and nothing like the same amount of good would be accomplished."[125]

The recreation aspect of agricultural exhibitions proved to be so lucrative that some agricultural societies established specifically dedicated entertainment committees. When financial setbacks forced the Elora agricultural society to merge with the Centre Riding and the Peel agricultural societies, the entertainment committee took matters into its own hands, and held annual concerts with a dinner, lectures, recitations, and music. They also increased revenue by spicing up the exhibition with driving and riding contests, so that the executive quite crowed at one exhibition: "Good weather, good crowd, good sport, good show."[126] Many societies charged a special rate for families, while the Elora agricultural society asked town ministers and teachers to provide a special class for the children on fair day. The entire point of the exercise was to build liberal community spirit and feeling: "The farmer that has a real pride in the farm will take great interest in the local exhibition, and will exhibit the best products of farm life in the boys and girls, who are interested exhibitors. The day at the exhibition should be a social one, everyone making it a point to meet many neighbours and others with a pleasant word."[127]

Even with the increased presence of the liberal state in Ontario Farmers' Institutes, recreation and social interaction among the farming population remained a strong component of Institute meetings and socials. Many Farmers' Institutes also used recreational activities such as concerts, dances and picnics to increase their revenue streams and publicize their existence. The combination of sociability and practical agricultural discussions was seen by the executive of the South Leeds Institute to be highly desirable: "Monthly or semi-monthly reunions like these will strengthen many social bonds, and enlarge the sympathies as well as the ideas of those who avail themselves of these advantages."[128] A great local example of the merging of agricultural dialogues with entertainment is that of the South Wellington Farmers' Institute. The directors continually emphasized the importance of coming to Institute meetings to hear lectures and share experiences on scientific and practical husbandry, as all were invited to attend and participate: "Don't hide your light under a bushel. Come out and let us learn something from your experience. You may also learn something. Farmers who know most of their profession, are usually the most anxious to learn more." However, the South Wellington directors placed equal emphasis on sociability, and the success generated from the 1888 annual entertainment of the Institute filtered out to all in the community. "As is usual on all such occasions the hall was filled by a large gathering and the programme provided took the audience from the start. It had been usual to depend on giving speeches and filling in with songs and recitations, but this year the evening was entirely given up to lighter amusement."[129]

In Quebec agricultural societies and *cercles agricoles*, the endorsement of practical farming and a corresponding disregard for recreation and entertainment would persist well into the last third of the century. The Montmagny agricultural society not only organized premiums for the most cultivated farm but it also established a model farm to introduce enhanced methods of agriculture. The stated aim of these efforts was to "promote the cause of agriculture in this country," through the practical improvement of agriculture; the society simply ignored the entertainment option. The Missisquoi agricultural society followed an identical pattern, as they offered premiums for cultivated farms, the purchase of livestock for stud, and the distribution of flax seed to society members. Apparently this was adequate for the needs of the farmers, as society directors rejected a plan to hold a two-day agricultural fair with a ploughing match in 1869. It was not until 1887, well after Ontario agricultural societies and Farmers' Institutes had begun to experiment with community entertainment, that driving competitions and other amusements were offered to the public in Missisquoi.[130] Unlike the Farmers' Institutes in Ontario, the *cercles agricoles* in Quebec concentrated solely on practical discussions related to the improvement of agriculture and scientific husbandry. According to the literature from the government of Quebec, the sole purposes of the *cercles agricoles* were to cultivate the love of farming, to replace routine with scientific agriculture, and to create a unity of action among farmers for the development of the art of husbandry.[131]

Despite the rather contested identity of farmers and their divisions over political, economic, and even social issues, central-Canadian tillers of the soil constituted a formidable collective agricultural presence throughout the nineteenth century. And yet, while a strong state involvement in agriculture may have provided for a renewed defence of the liberal social order in agricultural associations, it also created further conflicts and disharmony among farmers. Competing visions of agricultural "improvement" in turn highlighted the differences in the agricultural population, and the increasing socio-economic gulf between "gentlemen farmers" and independent yeomen.

By the final decades of the century, state-sponsored agricultural associations such as Farmers' Institutes had become even more exclusive, even as agricultural societies were increasing their availability to all classes in the rural countryside. While farmers all along the economic continuum could support these agricultural associations, large commercial farmers in many respects formed the backbone of these organizations. As a result, many of the statements and activities of agrarian associations continued to support the rural social order, although there remained voices of agricultural discontent. Recognizing the divided state of the agricultural class, promoters of farming interests turned to new agricultural associations to further the cause of agriculture. While attempting to unite farmers as a class, the executive of the both the Dominion Grange and the Patrons of Industry employed methods that leaned toward exclusivity of the agrarian "community" and further conflicts between farmers and others in central-Canadian liberal society.

6

The Dominion Grange and Patrons of Industry

On 2 June 1874 the first meeting to organize the Dominion Grange of the Patrons of Husbandry was held in London, Ontario. One of the first enthusiastic supporters of the Grange, William Weld, was also the publisher of Ontario's most prestigious agricultural newspaper, the *Farmers' Advocate*. Acting as the Dominion Grange's first steward, Weld praised the new order in *Advocate* editorials for creating unity, harmony, and strength among farmers and for forging new associational ties in the rural population. However, a year later, Weld resigned his office in the Dominion Grange, stating that he preferred to remain an unfettered member. Already sensing potential problems in the Dominion Grange, Weld believed that in giving up his office he could freely criticize the order if they should "misuse their powers." By 1880 Weld expressed that the business ventures of the Dominion Grange were "petty and selfish" and based more on pecuniary gain and the elimination of the commercial class than on fostering mutual understanding between farmers and other classes. Commenting that the principle of economic co-operation was a perilous foundation for the Grange to stand upon, Weld accused the Patrons of Husbandry of "severing the connection that should exist in a complex community, making the farmer storekeeper, shipper, speculator, and everything else."[1]

Weld was not the only agricultural critic to abandon the possibilities of late nineteenth-century agrarian protest. The meteoric rise and fall of both the Dominion Grange and the Patrons of Industry indicate that many farmers shared Weld's initial fascination and eventual disillusionment with agrarian associations that emphasized agricultural protest and economic co-operation, rather than liberal class collaboration. As discussed in the previous chapter on agricultural societies, even though farmers often complained about their weak social, political, and economic position in society through comparison with other classes, the goal of economic co-operation was held out as *the* solution to the dilemmas facing the agricultural population. Initial enthusiasm for the co-operative principle was founded on the possibility of connecting farmers in liberal bonds of economic mutualism. Through bulk purchasing and united commercial retailing, the co-operative ventures of the Dominion Grange and Patrons of Industry served to bring buyer and seller into more direct contact. Conversely, however, co-operation could also alienate farmers accustomed to dealing directly with established market forces and with large-scale commercial farmers unwilling to change their modes of operation. Entrenched ideological differences about the merits or shortcomings of the co-operative principle in the Dominion Grange and Patrons of Industry came to highlight the socio-economic tensions and conflicts intrinsic to the varied philosophies and collective agrarian identities of the farmers themselves.[2]

Explanations for farmers' waning interest in both the Dominion Grange and the Patrons of Industry range from inter-associational strife to ideological conflicts between farmers and other social classes. As the rise of both the Grange and the Patrons of Industry occurred during the period of rapid urbanization and industrialization, a great deal of early historiography related to these two agrarian movements focused on the dynamics of the relationship between farmers and urban labourers. As a result, the failure of both the Patrons of Husbandry and the Patrons of Industry mirrored that of organizations such as the Knights of Labor, as both farmers and the larger community were simply ill prepared for the radical rhetoric of agrarian class-consciousness.[3] More recent scholarship highlights the palpable conservatism of Ontario's farming population as a justification for their rejecting the militant platform of both the Grange and the Patrons of Industry. Mirroring the work done on Western prairie farmers by Jeffrey Taylor and Bradford Rennie, historians such as Kerry Badgely assert that it was farmers' ideological disagreement over market agriculture and the co-operative system that precluded unity and collaboration over larger issues affecting the farming population. While these agrarian protest movements indeed questioned the position of farmers in the larger society, they lacked coherence on how to solve fundamental economic, political, and social concerns of the rural tillers of the soil.[4]

While the ideological conflicts and tensions inherent in the construction of collective agrarian identities certainly hampered the fortunes of the Grange and Patrons of Industry in Ontario, material inequalities among the agricultural population contributed largely to these philosophical differences. Not only were the majority of farming families able to reach a fairly enviable level of self-sufficiency by 1860 but they also managed to produce commercially viable market surpluses. Even though these surpluses were by no means considerable, such "scanty fortunes" provided stability and ensured a decent productivity level for most family farms in Ontario by 1871. As mentioned in the previous chapter, the escalation of mixed agriculture with an increased emphasis on livestock and dairy products, as well as renewed interest in gardening and horticulture, illustrates various approaches by farmers to attain the often-elusive middle *class* status.[5] While the relative prosperity of agriculture in Ontario to some degree alleviated the pressures of economic disparity, however, other studies reveal a fractured social structure in the rural hinterland. The many social, cultural, and economic conflicts between small farmers working their family farms, large commercial agrarian enterprises, and tenant farmers, in addition to the dissatisfaction of the marginalized agricultural labourer, illustrate that the rural populace was indeed highly divided along socio-economic lines. Although escalating urbanization and industrialization may have been a perception issue, as Ontario remained largely agricultural by the turn of the century, small-scale and subsistence farmers as well as agricultural labourers reacted with apprehension to the changes in commercial agriculture.[6]

Thus, the two main currents of thought regarding agriculture – the accommodation of liberal market forces through acceptance of the industrial capitalist system, and the rejection of that system through the co-operative approach – appeared to be fairly irreconcilable. By actively participating in the formation of agricultural societies and exhibitions, farmers who embraced the liberal market system and commercial agriculture represented a new commercial and politically active class conspiring to create a commonality of interest based on economic prosperity in agriculture. As noted, agricultural associations and agricultural colleges also buttressed the cultural formation of the rural liberal order, which was divided among increasingly commercial farmers, self-employed businessmen, professionals, and retailers.[7] The participation of farmers in other voluntary associations also demonstrated their contribution to a cultural and social identity in small villages and towns. By partaking liberally of associations with a strong cross-class membership, farmers managed to negotiate their own space within an increasingly complex rural social structure. Their presence in fraternal organizations like the Oddfellows and other mutual benefit societies, as well as Mechanics' Institutes and temperance societies, indicates that farmers were quite active in the construction of a rural middle-class cultural identity.[8]

However, as observed in the previous chapter, farmers not only reinforced but at times also criticized the liberal socio-economic order, as they expounded a radical, "populist" discourse that exposed the material inequalities inherent in monopoly capitalism. Drawing on populist traditions of castigating corporate, political, and social privilege, this particular strain of radical agrarianism at once embraced and critiqued the concept of producerism and the labour theory of value. Even though this socio-economic outlook had many adherents in both the Dominion Grange and the Patrons of Industry, it tended to hold a more negative view of other classes in the larger community. Seeing society as divided between useful producers and slothful, parasitical non-producers, some members of the Dominion Grange and the Patrons of Industry fostered adversarial sentiments among the less prosperous members of the agricultural population by focusing on issues of their material, political, and even social exclusion. However, what is noteworthy regarding this antagonistic class rhetoric of agrarian protest is that farmers advocating the continuance of market agriculture and those supporting the co-operative system both maintained hostile relations with individuals they deemed non-producers.[9]

It would be fairly simplistic to suggest that prosperous farmers adhered solely to an economic ideology of market and commercial agriculture, while their less fortunate peers all reacted with apprehension to the workings of modern industrial capitalism in advocating a co-operative system of market relations. A purely deterministic approach to the complexities of agrarian economic and social ideology would be erroneous, as farmers could express preference for either market agriculture or the co-operative system from anywhere on the agricultural economic continuum. What the following evidence does suggest, however, is that it was the tensions inherent in the differing material circumstances, *in combination with* various representational visions of agriculture, that made it simply impossible for the Dominion Grange and the Patrons of Industry to sustain a collective agrarian identity for any length of time within a deeply divided agricultural population. The initial success of both agrarian protest movements in Ontario displayed at least a willingness on the part of farmers to bond together for united action, and would ultimately influence a twentieth-century agricultural enterprise, the United Farmers of Ontario. However, their collapse into irrelevancy by the turn of the century also revealed endemic the ideological, cultural, social, and economic fissures within Ontario's rural populace. The difficulties within the Dominion Grange and the Patrons of Industry also illustrate the breakdown of the "liberal" social order after the

1870s, and the difficulties of sustaining collective liberal identities among central-Canadian farmers.

"PROMOTING THEIR COMBINED INTERESTS": THE DOMINION GRANGE AND AGRARIAN IDENTITIES

In the late 1860s a rather minor civil servant in the U.S. Department of Agriculture named Oliver Kelley established the Patrons of Husbandry, a new agricultural association to unite farmers. Drawing on his experiences as the president of an agricultural society and director of an experimental farm, Kelley insisted that his organization was an ideal association to improve agriculture and provide sociability and education for rural inhabitants. After gaining a strong foothold in the United States, the Patrons of Husbandry in 1872 formed a local Grange in Missisquoi, Quebec. By 1875 the Dominion Grange proudly noted that there were 500 subordinate Granges and well over 20,000 members in Canada.[10] Only recently have historians of the Dominion Grange examined the movement in a much larger context, within a continuity of agricultural movements throughout the nineteenth century. While some describe the Grange as a rather hidebound agrarian movement that was highly suspicious of modernity, others see it as the culmination of a republican ideology of virtue and liberty. As a result, scholars of the Grange in the United States describe the association as the direct antecedent of the People's Party and the Farmers' Alliance. In Canada, the Dominion Grange has been firmly linked with the Patrons of Industry and the Farmers' Institute movement, as well as the United Farmers of Ontario.[11] What is certain is that the Dominion Grange was an organization committed to the unification of farmers by providing commercial, educational, and social opportunities for all of its members.

Consequently, the initial thrust of the Dominion Grange was to provide occasions for Canadian farmers to end their isolation by uniting in "friendly intercourse" with other Grange members, and to promote their combined interests. The Patrons of Husbandry, comparing the Grange to trades unions, guilds, boards of trade and law societies, claimed that their association advanced the calling and fortune of the agricultural population. Observing that their interests conflicted less than any other business, the Dominion Grange executive realized that farmers "rarely make their plans in unison, but each man lays out and executes his work by his own light, without advice or council from his neighbours." While recognizing that farmers' clubs and agricultural societies helped counteract this individualism, they were only partially successful, insofar as they omitted the elements of "union and secrecy" needed to hold such bodies together.[12] The discourse of uniting farmers under one organization became a rather prominent feature of the Patrons of Husbandry and their early supporters, particularly Weld and the *Farmers' Advocate*. In Weld's opinion, the principle of secrecy and selectiveness inherent in the rituals and function of the Dominion Grange was entirely necessary to create a "bond of honour" among different parties of farmers. Equating the Grange with other voluntary associations such as the Oddfellows, Masons, and Orangemen, Weld argued that each had their private bonds and secrets, and that through associational ties came unity, harmony, and strength.[13]

Despite this rhetoric of agrarian unanimity, Grange directors firmly believed that they strove for the general good and not only for the advancement of their own interests or "without any regard to the welfare of other classes." Dominion Grange members were encouraged not to extol the virtues of their occupation above others, as their platform was based on broad and *liberal* principles that respected and acknowledged the necessity of every legitimate profession.[14] Respect apparently was a reciprocal virtue, as Patrons of Husbandry were encouraged to remember that all legitimate trade, the arts and sciences, and various other professions were parts of a great whole, "weak when taken alone, strong when united in bonds of social brotherhood." The Grand Master address of the fifteenth annual meeting of the Grange emphasized this point by noting that the "highway of advancement is broad enough for all to run, and our hope of ultimate success depends more on our own progress than the retarding of others." The Dominion Grange also tried to moderate the stance taken by the National Grange in the United States, which stipulated that all its members must be engaged in farming pursuits: "It is not safe to open the Grange to any others, as it is emphatically a Farmers' Institution, and the base must rest on the farmers alone." The Dominion Grange therefore tempered its initiation rules to include not only those directly interested in agricultural pursuits but also those who had no commercial interests conflicting with the Grange.[15]

A detailed investigation into the background of those who attended the very first meeting of the Dominion Grange reveals, however, a group of farmers far more attuned to the sentiments of the upper levels of the rural social order than to the troubles of subsistence farmers and agricultural labourers. The census records of nineteen of the original twenty-five attendees indicate that six of these members were not even listed as farmers: Henry Hanson, a doctor; William Brown, a professor of agriculture at the

University of Toronto; Thomas Dyas, a surveyor and engineer and later a journalist; Henry Weld, a grain dealer and son of William Weld; Enos Scott, a pork dealer; and Henry Bruce, a retired army officer.[16] Furthermore, the remaining thirteen Grangers, who were listed as farmers, were noticeably the more wealthy commercial farmers in the province. With only two of the thirteen listed as tenant farmers in schedule three of the 1871 census, the average acreage was 225 acres of land, well above the average for a large commercial farm. These thirteen farmers also reported an average of five buildings on their land and nine agricultural implements per household.[17] Thus, the concern over "classlessness" in the Dominion Grange was apparently an ideological façade that not only masked the economic inequalities of the officers compared with those of the rank and file membership, but would also soothe the sensibilities of the other members of the liberal social order.

And yet certain pronouncements by the Grange reflected rather negative sentiments toward other members of the rural middle-class. While politicians were not new targets for agricultural critics, the Dominion Grange visualized an adversarial "professional coalition" of politicians, lawyers, and doctors as the prime assassins of class relations within the larger community. The *Granger* was quick to point out that while lawyers, doctors, and other professionals were indeed requisite to the welfare of society, the surplus of professionals – that portion which was not "necessary to the well- being of the community" – caused great distress to farmers and society as a whole.[18] According to the Patrons of Husbandry, the greatest disruption to societal relations was the commercial class. The problem itself was not merchants or commercial activities *per se*; what angered the Grange was the "tyranny of monopolies" or big capital. Corporations and large-scale industries were thought to ruin the honest farmer and oppress the people by robbing them of their just profit, with a system that "built up Princes, men in idleness, who do nothing, who won't do anything and who never have done anything ... have never done a hand's turn ... never plowed or sowed, reaped or mowed, nor even teamed a load of produce into any market." With the opening of the Ontario People's Salt Company in 1883 near Kincardine, the Dominion Grange refused to sell stock to commercial dealers and businessmen, allowing only subordinate Granges and farmers to purchase salt, as it was they who suffered the most from monopoly and tyranny.[19]

This discourse of exclusion was clearly the antithesis of harmonious class relations in the rural hinterland and contradicted the pronouncements of liberal class concord articulated in the early years of the Dominion Grange. The rhetoric of large commercial farmers from one section of the province had undoubtedly begun to wear thin with the escalating number – and subsequently the stronger influence – of subordinate Granges by the end of the 1870s. An examination of the background of ten members of the first executive of the Knock Grange in Simcoe County is extremely revealing in this regard. Admittedly, the first officers of the Knock Grange were from the most prominent agricultural families in the region, not at all subsistence farmers. However, the agricultural returns of the 1871 census illustrate that 20 per cent of the directors were tenant farmers, with all farmers reporting an average acreage of just over 100 acres, roughly three buildings per lot, and five agricultural implements per household.[20] And yet on the surface, the executive of the Knock Grange was just as interested in maintaining the "liberal" social order of the rural community as the officers of the Dominion Grange. In 1875 the Knock Grange suspended the initiation of labourers and labourers' wives until the Dominion Grange ruled on the possibility of allowing non-farmers equal privileges as members. This decision exposes a divisiveness within the agricultural population and demonstrates the desire of Knock farmers to achieve liberal "respectability" by denying the status of membership to others. Correspondingly, in an address to the Acadia Grange, the Grand Master impressed upon his audience that farmers in the Grange demanded respect and equal consideration from other members of the community, to escape the "odium of being considered mere workers, the 'mud-sills.'"[21]

In order to maintain their standards of prosperity, farmers in the Knock Grange and other subordinate Granges enthusiastically supported the co-operative system in their locales. While the more affluent members of the Dominion Grange could use the liberal ideology of classlessness to camouflage their higher status in the range of material inequalities, smaller subordinate Granges could likewise use the co-operative system as a means of blaming the commercial classes for their economic misfortune. One of the primary functions of the co-operative system was to bring producers and consumers, as well as farmers and manufacturers, into more direct working relationships. The *Granger* tried to reassure merchants and manufacturers, that farmers did not want to usurp established rules of trade or make all other interests subservient to their own. This was no declared war on middlemen, it affirmed; Grangers recognized the necessity of the commercial class by assisting the creation of their businesses and helping mercantile retailers succeed. And yet Grangers also criticized most retailers for their excessive salaries, high rates of credit and interest, and elevated rates of profit. Furthermore, if the commercial class proved unable to enact the changes required by farmers in Canada, then farmers needed to unite and restrain the reins of government, rail monopolies, the courts, banks, and the entire mercantile system of capital.[22]

Supporters, allies, and officers of the early Dominion Grange movement soon recognized that censuring the commercial classes was a rather retrograde step that would soon erode the rural social order and commercial bonds forged through liberal interclass co-operation. Weld offered a word of caution to the Grange as early as 1875, stating that it was not a "judicious policy" to array class against class in their business activities, or to attack manufacturers or merchants for making a living. By 1880, convinced that the Dominion Grange not only singled out the "patent right men, tree agents, notion agents, and shoddy agents" for reproach but condemned the entire mercantile sector, Weld distanced himself completely from the Grange. In calling for the Patrons of Husbandry to end their crusade against the commercial and mercantile retailers, Weld was safeguarding his own business and his advertising revenue from commercial ventures and also upholding the liberal vision of classlessness preached by the original Dominion Grange.[23] In a remarkably candid retrospective on the Patrons of Husbandry presented at the twenty-third annual meeting of the Grange in 1898, the Grand Secretary admitted that many of the outlined mistakes resulted from discord over the exclusivity of its business practices. Noting that the whole country was aroused in opposition to the new movement out of surprise and alarm for its power and influence among farmers, he added that class antagonism also transpired when early Grangers attracted "a class so sordid and selfish that money was all they looked for." These individuals were plainly uninterested in the pleasures of social intercourse or the advantages of meeting together to discuss their noble calling, but focused exclusively on furthering their own pecuniary interests.[24]

The participation of women was a significant factor in the rise of the Dominion Grange, as the Patrons of Husbandry attempted to create a more respected role for both men and woman within liberal society. The alliance of the Grange with early American suffrage movements and the WCTU in the movement toward an increased presence of women in the public sphere is well documented. However, the Grange also reinforced women's domestic roles within society, a position that tempered the quest for mutuality and sisterhood within the Patrons of Husbandry.[25] One of their more notable achievements – more so than any other voluntary association examined in this study – was to incorporate women into their actual rituals, necessitating the presence of women at Grange meetings. The inclusion of women into the Grange corresponded with its ideology: "[The] interest, the social relations and the destiny of man and woman are identical. She was intended by her Creator to be the helpmeet, companion, and equal of man." Creating the offices of Pomona, Flora, and Ceres to represent Faith, Hope, and Charity would remind women of the high position assigned to them and encourage them to be worthy of it. The editors of the *Canadian Granger* regretted that woman's instinctive perceptions of righteousness and purity had been lost to society, and determined that the Grange was the organization to re-introduce rural women to the larger community. The Grange acknowledged that while man "generally improves in knowledge and business ability after he enters active life, [and] woman too frequently retrogrades," their role within the Grange would assign women equal powers and privileges. Ending the seclusion of women from society would not only liberate females from confining pursuits but would allow men and women to universally elevate their social selves.[26]

The Dominion Grange also reflected the coming changes to agriculture with a more gendered realignment of farm work. Even though Grange rituals recognized that women were still required to labour "side by side" with their producer husbands, the nature of female agricultural work evolved substantially with the onset of commercial agriculture. Christina Moffat, in her pamphlet outlining the female offices of Flora, Ceres, and Pomona, surprisingly employed the masculine language of the husbandman in her description of Ceres, the "protectress of agriculture." And yet in her portrayal of Flora, the goddess of flowers and Pomona, the goddess of fruit gardens, Moffatt emphasized that these branches of agriculture were the prerogative of women alone. And in her essay on the decorative importance of flowers Moffat reinforced a domestic ideology: "How pure and refreshing plants appear in a room watched and waited on as they generally are by the gentler sex; they are links in many pleasant associations, they are cherished favourites of mothers, wives, sisters, and friends not less dear, and connect themselves in our minds, with their feminine delicacy, loveliness, and affectionate habits and sentiments."[27]

POPULAR POLITICS, CO-OPERATION, AND GRANGER POLITICAL ECONOMY

One of the central tenets of the Dominion Grange stated was that no Granger, "in keeping true to his obligations," could discuss political or religious questions, call political conventions, nominate candidates, or discuss the merits of any political contestant. It was no crime to have a variance of beliefs, for the "progress of truth is made by difference of opinion," but disharmony resulted through the bitterness of political controversy. Paradoxically, however, the executive of the Dominion Grange bemoaned the "utter extinction" of liberal independence from the political parties while simultaneously lauding the stability of the Grange, which itself arose from the exclusion of sectarian and political turmoil.[28] As the Grange established a tentative hold on the imaginations of farmers, William Weld and the *Farmers' Advocate* trumpeted the need for a Farmers' party to listen to their concerns. The Dominion Grange agreed with this assessment, and, while they did not form a "Farmers' Party," they encouraged members to take an active role in the liberal politics of the country in the preservation of the public good:

> The principles we teach underlie all true politics, all true statesmanship, and, if properly carried out, will tend to purify the whole political atmosphere of our country ... It is [the Granger's] duty to do all he can in his own party to put down bribery, corruption, and trickery; and see that none but competent, faithful, and honest men, who will unflinchingly stand by our interests, are nominated for all positions of trust; and to have carried out the principle which should always characterize every Grange member, that THE OFFICE SHOULD SEEK THE MAN, AND NOT THE MAN THE OFFICE.[29]

As with the liberal philosophy of classlessness, the effort to eliminate any discussions of party politics was also a blatant attempt to amalgamate a group of farmers under the hegemonic influence of the Dominion Grange executive.

Complications arose when the National Grange, prompted by the influence of subordinate Granges, attempted to purify the political process through political means, rather than following outlined liberal notions of party independence. Initial forays by the Dominion Grange into the political realm occurred as early as 1875, when Parliament consulted the national body on the possibility of raising duties on agricultural productions. Experiences such as this led several prominent Grangers, such as Worthy Grand Master Squire Hill, W.M. Blair, and Charles Drury, to join the Mowat Liberals in provincial politics. The defection of prominent Dominion Grange officers to Mowat, the ultimate party politician, proved to be a great detriment to the integrity of the movement.[30] Subordinate Granges such as the Knock Grange illustrated the divergence of opinion over political action, as they contemplated the necessity of becoming involved in the political sphere. While debating the merits of cumulative voting and the possibilities of referenda, the Knock Grange became more intent on taking up the political banner when it began sharing premises with a local chapter of the Patrons of Industry.[31]

And yet farmers who promoted commercial agriculture and the preservation of market forces could discover in the Grange a popular version of classic collective liberalism, which admired the ethos of honest industry and adhered strongly to the philosophy of the producer alliance. The glorification of the hardworking and independent farmer illustrates the Grange's participation in an ideology that not only fostered social cohesion but also buttressed the rural hegemonic social order. The early Dominion Grange did in fact appreciate the importance of individual diligence, honest industry, and self-reliance, as evidenced by their motto, "Put your shoulder to the wheel; fortune helps those who help themselves." The vast majority of Granger songs, such as "God Speed the Plow," "Work," and "Sowing and Reaping," underscored the significance of honest labour for the husbandman, as a liberal harvest would only be secured through toil and exertion. As the song "Dignity of Labor" chorused:

Tis toil that over nature gives man his proud control;
And purifies and hallows the temple of his soul.
It startles foul diseases with all their ghastly train;
Puts iron in the muscle and crystal in the brain.
The Grand Almighty Builder, who fashioned out the earth,
Hath stamped his seal of honor on labor from her birth.[32]

While some conclude that the majority of farmers within the Grange favoured economic protection, many of its publications were either ambivalent about or fully supportive of freer trade. As with most agrarian associations, the Patrons of Husbandry were far more concerned with ensuring equality of opportunity within the community when it came to trade practices, than with advocating a particular economic position. To the editors of the *Granger*, the question of tariffs was all about equal rights for farmers, and thus they demanded protection for agricultural products *or* unrestricted free trade. A subtle defence of free trade was then offered in the *Granger*: "All any government can do for the farmer, as a class, is to merely let them alone, and to give no undue advantage to other classes ... not that we believe that any such assumed advantages by protection or taxation can, in the end, benefit any class of the community, as has been pretty conclusively shown by the experience of the late depression." The *Canadian Granger* echoed this position by claiming that protection, or any "trade or commerce that prevents the continuance of the demand for labour," injured every class in the community, from the workers and the farmers to the commercial sector.[33] The stand taken by the Dominion Grange once again exemplifies divisions among farmers and the difficulties of forming a collective agrarian identity, as the executive could not risk offending any member of its constituency by advocating one economic position over another.

The development of monopoly capitalism in the final decades of the nineteenth century further revealed intrinsic tensions within the agricultural community. While large-scale commercial farmers and those devoted to liberal market principles used the rhetoric of producerism and debates over tariffs to mask economic disparity, still other tillers of the soil, in their own desire for respectability, could accentuate the co-operative system to highlight the evils of capitalism. It is therefore no contradiction that some view Granger disdain for monopoly and capital as a radical departure from established ideas of popular political economy.[34] The Dominion Grange gradually introduced the co-operative system as a form of collective mutual aid that would enhance the dependence of capital upon labour and ensure "harmony and confidence" between labourers and employers. The systematic application of commercial association was designed to promote the well-being of liberal society, as the truest principles of co-operation included brotherly kindness and the inculcation of peace among nations – the answer to most of the "practical problems appertaining to human life." As these commercial principles tended to protect and succour the weak and keep the strong in check, co-operation was a logical extension of popular liberalism, which eschewed commercial conflict and encouraged the interdependence of classes: co-operation "touches no man's fortune; seeks no plunder; causes no disturbance in society; gives no trouble to statesmen; needs no trade union to protect its interests; contemplates no violence; subverts no order; accepts no gifts, nor asks any favour; keeps no terms with the idle, and breaks no faith with the industrious; it means self-help, self-independence, and such share in the common competence as labour can earn, and thought can win."[35]

Campaigns to introduce co-operative doctrines into the Knock Grange began as early as 1875, when speeches to the Grange on the benefits of co-operation were met with enthusiasm. Buoyed by this initial fervour, the Knock Grange began purchasing items in bulk from various retailers – from farm books to gypsum, from carriages to scales – and then offering reduced prices on those items to its members.[36] In supporting the Grange's wholesale retail operations, its insurance ventures, and most of all, the Ontario People's Salt Company, Knock Grange directors were explicit in their explanations for their patronage of the Grange's commercial activities; it quite simply came from a hatred for monopoly capitalism. In 1887 the Knock Grange "condemned in the strongest terms" the salt manufacturers of Ontario for offences ranging from price fixing, price gouging, and particularly the practice of selling lightweight barrels to unwary farmers. In resolving never to patronize a manufacturer or salt dealer that engaged in defrauding their members, the directors determined to purchase their salt from the Grange's Salt Company, organized to protect farmers from the grinding effects of the salt ring. This was a drastic measure, but a necessary one: "At first it was thought by some that a little agitation would be enough to open the eyes of the monopolists and induce them to meet us on equitable grounds, but experience has shown us otherwise, and the longer matters go on so, the firmer becomes the compact and less liable to dismemberment; it is now next to impossible to purchase salt except through a secretary of the ring, by whom the price and all conditions of sale are fixed, and the supplying of orders apportioned to the different wells in proportion to their capacity." Further evidence to illustrate the fact that this manoeuvre was aimed squarely at monopoly capitalism came as the Ontario People's Company denied their stock to dealers and businessmen, keeping it solely in the hands of subordinate Granges and farmers themselves.[37]

Agricultural critics – and even supposed allies – found the principles of co-operation to be a hazardous underpinning for the Dominion Grange to build upon. Weld, the spokesman for liberal farmers advocating free market agriculture, agreed that co-operation was indeed the foundation of society as a whole. However, he was also of the opinion that the Grange misapplied the principle, as mutuality between various classes should occur only in social relationships and not in economic ones: "The snag upon which the boat has sunk is summed up in one word, co-operation. This, taken in one sense, is essential to the welfare of society – indeed, it is the foundation of society – but then, if co-operation is so essential, is not division equally so? Could society exist without co-operation in social relations and division in regard to labour? But the co-operation of the Grange included moral, social, commercial and everything else. Thus, whilst the aims of the society were good, in inducing farmers to meet together in their social relations, it was likewise violating a known law in political economy, that civilized society had to exist through a division of labour."[38] Of course, the fact that Weld's business and advertising revenue depended on the goodwill of all occupations within his locale, doubtless shaped his thinking on co-operation. And yet many farmers shared his influential views, with the result that there was tension between the advocates of the co-operative principle and the farmers who preferred the existing market system.

Some of Weld's prophecies related to co-operation did come true in the organization of Dominion Grange commercial ventures, as economic conflict often erupted between Grangers and the officers of co-operative institutions. Commenting upon his relations with the Dominion Grange, D.S. McKinnon of the Co-op Sewing Machine Company noted that he should receive "thanks instead of abuse" for selling his machine at a lower price. Calling on the Grange to remember their principles of bringing manufacturers and farmers into more direct contact, McKinnon asked farmers to send in their orders to "show the Dominion Grange is a reality, and not a myth." Similarly, the Grange Wholesale Company demanded prompt payment from the secretaries of individual Granges, as cash payments were a "plank in their platform." The problems of debt among various Granges was so great that, unless they agreed to payment in advance, the Grange Wholesale Company would decline filling their orders explaining that it would "surely be disastrous to yourselves as well as us to continue under the present system." Even the most enthusiastic supporters of co-operation, most notably the Knock Grange, experienced difficulty with the co-operative principle. Orders from the Knock Grange to the Ontario People's Salt Company often remained unfilled, or arrived exceedingly behind schedule, leading to a frustration with the Grange's salt company comparable to what the Knock directors had experienced with the original salt monopolists.[39]

THE DOMINION GRANGE AND RURAL SOCIABILITY

The Dominion Grange experienced an early surge in membership growth, thanks largely to the social and recreational activities offered to rural inhabitants. Even a hardened critic such as Weld recognized the potential of social events in promoting brotherly feeling, allaying local animosities, and bringing together entire neighbourhoods through Grange picnics and other events. In Weld's view, if the Grange abandoned the solid structure of liberal sociability for economic prosperity with the extension of the co-operative principle, it was doomed to failure.[40] Noting that the Grange was primarily a social institution, members expressed their belief that the "old, selfish system of isolation" was giving way to this new "invigorating sociality" whereby the agricultural community could develop themselves as social beings. The majority of the Grange's rituals and music would emphasize this feature, as one opening song proclaimed:

> We have come to the Grange, where 'tis joyful to meet
> Our friends and companions in unity sweet;
> Now our labour is done, and to rest and repose
> We bid a fond welcome at day's weary close.
>
> Then Patrons, in joy, come gather around,
> Concord and harmony with us be found!
> Down with the spite and the hate that estrange,
> And long live the peace that we find at the Grange.[41]

Local Granges quickly grasped the importance of this liberal doctrine of sociability, and provided members with a number of entertainment options. Many of these activities emulated the social functions prominent in agricultural societies, such as ploughing matches, agricultural debates, and discussions along with musical interludes, recitations, *conversaziones*, and literary readings. Culinary events such as oyster suppers and tea excursions were highly successful; one such event in the Knock Grange led the executive to crow: "All enjoyed themselves, with the good things provided, and social chat flowed freely round."[42] It would soon become apparent that Granges focusing on entertainment as a means of increasing their revenue streams were far more successful than their counterparts. Both the Minesing and the Knock Granges sold tickets to their tea parties and oyster suppers, while the Knock Grange held a concert for the villagers that resulted in a sizeable profit. As a result, both of these assemblies managed to remain intact well into the twentieth century. Conversely, the Brougham Grange left the entertainment in the hands of its female members with limited support, while providing agricultural lectures as the only supplementary amusement to Grange meetings. The Royal Oak Grange likewise made only half-hearted attempts to arrange a festival to raise funds, focusing exclusively on the merits of the co-operative functions of the Patrons of Husbandry. Each of these Granges lasted only four years, and the Brougham Grange was forced to return more than three hundred dollars to its members, funds that had been earmarked for the construction of their Granger Hall. The final entry of the Royal Oak minute book recorded despondently: "This was the last of the Royal Oak Grange; it died a natural death just like all."[43]

THE PATRONS OF INDUSTRY: AN ALLIANCE OF TILLERS AND TOILERS

Another factor contributing to the decline of the Patrons of Husbandry was the appearance of the Patrons of Industry in the early 1890s. The Patrons of

Industry in many ways emulated the Populist movement and the Farmers' Alliance in the United States, associations that have received a great deal of scholarly attention. Interpretations of the American Populist "moment" range from seeing it as a radical agrarian response to monopoly capitalism to seeing it as agricultural class-consciousness finding political expression. Current studies on the Populists conclude that the movement merely attempted to redress old agrarian grievances associated with capitalism and the ever-present isolation of the agricultural community.[44] The Patrons of Industry are viewed either as an agrarian retreat into classic economic liberalism or as harbingers of radical social change as farmers confronted industrialism with collectivized solutions to the problems of modern monopoly capitalism. More recent treatments of the Patrons suggest that the agrarian protest movement followed in the tradition of Clear Grit agrarian radicalism, providing a continuity of farmers' movements of agrarian protest well into the twentieth century.[45] What becomes evident through an examination of the ideology of the Patrons movement is that it was far more attuned to the radical sentiments of the agricultural population than its immediate predecessor, the Dominion Grange. The spectre of rural de-population continued to haunt Ontario's farmers, although by the turn of the century it was more reality than perception; urban dwellers for the first time outnumbered their rural counterparts. Commercialized mixed farming continued to compel the subsistence family farmer to adapt to new methods of agriculture or be swept under. Likewise, the "consolidation of industrial capitalism" amplified agrarian discontent and fostered a more militant ideology in the Patrons of Industry.[46] As a result, the agricultural community within the Patrons movement began to seek out new allies outside the accepted rural economic and social order, and they discovered one in the similarly outcast industrial labourer. While this coalition posed its own problems for farmers, renewed tension between those supporting a liberal middle-class position within a more radicalized agrarian association presaged disaster for the Patrons of Industry in Ontario.

Founded in Port Huron, Michigan, the Patrons of Industry began as a politico-economical association of farmers with tentative overtures to the emerging industrial class. Within a few months of the initial meeting of Patrons in Sarnia, Ontario, in 1891, the Grand Association of the Patrons of Industry of Ontario established its headquarters in Strathroy. By 1893 the Patrons had nearly 100,000 members in Ontario, with over two thousand active associations.[47] Right from the outset, the directors of the Patrons of Industry intended to establish a more radical producer alliance of "tillers and toilers." Promoting the interests of industrial workers and farmers, the Patrons' main aspiration was to "advance the interest of the suffering masses." In doing so, the Patrons of Industry understood that all members would enter a mutual agreement to elevate the moral, intellectual, social, political, and financial position of toiling workers and farmers. In aiding these individuals, who provided the subsistence to all life and the advancement of the prosperity of all nations, the Patrons were convinced that the community as a whole would benefit.[48]

Even though the Patrons were of a radical shade, they also moved quickly to dispel illusions that their association would disturb the existing liberal social order. The directors of the Patrons of Industry therefore took great pains to explain that their organization existed to protect individual members, not to unfairly curtail the rights or privileges of other groups and classes. Even though the Patrons decreed that farmers were vital to society as a whole, they allowed that society was interdependent on all occupations to provide the necessities of life, "be they manufactural [*sic*] to prepare fabric from his cotton fields or the back of his animals, or implements and utensils from his forests and mines; commercial, with its monetary medium of convenience, to effect the desired exchange of productions of the various departments and the different parts of his extended realm; educational to develop and mould the character and accumulate knowledge for the more successful prosecution of his labours; or governmental, to formulate and administer his will in prudence and justice."[49] A biographical sketch of George Wrigley, the editor of the *Canada Farmers' Sun,* the official organ of the Patrons, noted that his influence was successful in preventing the Patrons from becoming merely a class movement. Likewise, the president of the Grand Association of the Patrons of Industry of Ontario, C.A. Mallory, viewed with satisfaction that the Patrons had received the liberal political support of all classes, races, and creeds, stating: "Our platform is so broad that all may stand upon it."[50]

Consequently, the Patrons attempted to rectify the conflicts over commercial retailers experienced by the Dominion Grange by limiting adversarial discourse that condemned the commercial class itself. A year after the writing of the Patrons' constitution, Mallory insisted that while understandable antagonism between Patrons and merchant retailers did exist, such prejudice was just as quickly being eroded. Editorials in the *Canada Farmers' Sun* confirmed this observation, as farmers attempted once again to exempt all "legitimate" merchants and manufacturers from derision. Unscrupulous travelling sales agents who extorted high profits from hardworking farmers earned the wrath of the Patrons, but not conscientious businessmen. This message apparently trickled down to the local level, for when the Victoria Lodge expelled a merchant from its ranks, it was not for commercial activities *per se*, but for being a travelling peddler.[51] The president of the Bronson Lodge of the Patrons of Industry, J.P. Mullett, took things a little too far when he suggested that all residents of villages and towns be excluded from the order. Noting that such a practice would be "antagonistic to the spirit and principles" of the Patrons of Industry, an editorial in the *Canada Farmers' Sun* underscored that the Patrons' aim was to "secure justice and improve social conditions for all; to abolish rather than emphasize and intensify class and caste distinctions [for] injustice suffered by one class always reacts upon a community."[52]

And yet the Patrons also demonstrated their more radical colours, in their unequivocal denunciation of other classes. By excluding not only candidates of an immoral character, but also lawyers, doctors, merchants, liquor dealers, manufacturers, party politicians, and "minor members of families of persons as above mentioned," the Patrons exhibited a fairly condemnatory vision of the non-producing class.[53] By the mid-1890s, the resentment of the Patrons had kindled far more animosity against the professional class of doctors, lawyers, and politicians than the commercial classes. Patrons of Industry complaints against the medical profession are well documented; they viewed the medical practices of members of the Canadian Medical Association as catering only to the educated elite and found the fees charged by medical colleges to be akin to tariff walls that ensured the continuation of the special privileges of medical doctors. For similar reasons they made a concerted effort to limit the entrance fees charged by the Law Society, to do away with the monopoly of lawyers and the "laws made for the few at the expense of the many."[54] Clearly all forms of monopoly were repugnant to the new radicalized version of agrarian discontent represented by the Patrons of Industry.

The extent of women's participation in the Patrons of Industry movement rivalled that of the Dominion Grange in scope; women were incorporated in their rituals with the creation of the Demeter and Minerva degrees. The pages of the *Canada Farmers' Sun* were often filled with editorials advocating the increased presence of women in colleges and universities, or lauding the Council on Women and the work done by women factory inspectors. The connection of the Patrons of Industry and the WCTU was also very intense, as the Patrons not only became leaders in the temperance cause but also agreed to make female suffrage a plank on the Patrons' platform if the subordinate associations were in agreement. (Despite these calls for an escalation of women in the public sphere, columns in the *Canada Farmers' Sun* entitled "With the Fair Sex," "Just for the Ladies," "Sunlight for Women," and "Facts for Housewives" continued to affirm the domestic ideal for women witnessed in other agricultural associations.[55]) Women obviously felt comfortable joining their menfolk at Patrons' meetings, as the Galetta, Victoria, and Willow Vale lodges reported that between 23 and 33 percent of the membership were women. And yet the contribution of women in the Willow Vale Lodge took the limited form of a committee of women authorized "to buy blines [sic] for the house." Under these conditions the wife and daughter of John Strumm refused their appointments as Minerva and Demeter, and a few months later the Willow Vale Patrons slashed entrance fees for women from ten cents to five. The Victoria lodge had the highest concentration of female members, and consequently two women received an invitation to sit on the committee on bylaws. Gender conflicts soon erupted, as a motion was put forward to restrict the rights of women to vote on Lodge business. Given the high percentage of women members, the two men putting forward the motion had to apologize in writing for "depriving the ladies of their right to vote."[56]

"POWER TO THE PEOPLE": AGRARIAN POLITICS, POPULAR POLITICAL ECONOMY, AND CO-OPERATION

Initial proclamations from the Patrons condemned the practice of introducing partisan and sectarian discourse in both the Ontario executive and their subordinate associations. In reinforcing the edict by fining, suspending, or expelling any repeat offender, Patrons attempted to unite a very diverse group under one agriculturally hegemonic banner. Many prominent Patrons such as Grand Association of Ontario president C.A. Mallory traced all the evils of the times back to partyism, as the modern age required "free men" to break the shackles of the party whip.[57] To relieve the pressures of party conflict, the Patrons proposed a solution that kept within the liberal traditions of popular politics. Recognizing that partyism introduced class legislation and influence, Patrons demanded that the people – the source of all political power – be afforded the opportunity to make their own laws and to initiate legislation in Parliament. Accomplishing this task necessitated limiting election spending and introducing referenda into the political process. Limiting the spending of political parties would ensure that independent men free from party ties would be elected, men who would "serve the whole community" rather than class interests. In supporting the referendum movement, Patron leaders argued that if decisions were left to the electorate, "no party, no elections, no political enmity or strife, yet a thoroughly responsible and popular government" would result. Joining the political process was clearly key even at the local level, as the Willow Vale lodge of the Patrons of Industry encouraged its members to run as candidates in the local municipal election.[58]

By 1891 the Patrons of Industry launched the rather liberal "London platform," which consisted of such political platitudes as the maintenance of the British connection, the independence of Parliament, rigid economy in every branch of the public service, civil service reform, and the abolition of the Senate. To counteract the perceived sluggish pace of reform, the Patrons decided to test the waters on independent political action by fielding a candidate in the riding of North Bruce in an 1893 by-election. When the "People's candidate" was successful in the election, the Grand Association determined to field other candidates in the 1894 Ontario election, all using the London platform as a guide.[59] In an attempt to steal the Patrons' thunder, the consummate politician Oliver Mowat "exposed" the Patrons as an *exclusively* agricultural political party that was hostile to the accepted rural social order. Mowat therefore appealed to more liberal farmers, proclaiming in the North Bruce by-election: "The Reform party has always been specially a farmers' party, *while faithful to every other class as well*; and ... the Reform Party is the true farmers' party." Similarly, when Liberal critics accused the Patrons of Industry of acting like any other political party, Patron claims of political independence were soon exposed: executives had made voting for the Patron candidate an obligation for lodge members. Perceived Patron hypocrisy over the party system came full circle just a year after noted labour journalist Phillips Thompson had lauded the Patrons for an absence of party hierarchy, when the Patrons of Industry in the Ontario legislature organized both a party secretary and whip.[60]

As with other voluntary associations mentioned in this study, the Patrons of Industry recognized the primacy of the Christian religion to its members: "We, the farmers and employees of the Province of Ontario, believing that Almighty God, as the source of all power and the ruler of nations, should be acknowledged in all constitutions of societies, do hereby with due reverence to Him, associate ourselves together ..."[61] Notwithstanding Patrons' insistence on religious tolerance and neutrality, one of the greatest difficulties they experienced during the 1894 election came as Liberals and Tories both tried to paint them as closet supporters of the Protestant Protective Association (PPA), a conservative anti-Catholic pressure group. Denying any affiliation with an organization concerned solely with racial and religious questions, Patron directors insisted that Roman Catholics were "quite as loyal members and good subjects as those of other creeds. We believe in equal rights for all." Despite rejoinders that the claim of a

Patron/PPA connection came only from the partisan press, confusion over party positions within the Patron movement contributed both to their defeat at the polls and to a loss of credibility as a group devoted to social, moral, and intellectual improvement.[62]

While offering economic critiques consistent with the popular liberalism of the times, the Patrons of Industry also went against the producer ideology by proposing radical new solutions to age-old agrarian concerns. Historians of the Patrons of Industry and the Populist "moment" in the United States have both debated these points of political economy, concluding either that these rural protesters suggested "socialist" responses to industrial capitalism or were simply a part of popular radicalism that often challenged the hegemony of the marketplace.[63] And yet farmers of an ideologically liberal bent could find much to approve of in the socio-economic thought of the Patrons of Industry. Boasting that the prosperity of Canada was due to the "untiring industry of the toiling masses," the Patrons envisioned the hardy work ethic of the stout Canadian yeoman as the panacea for all of society's ills. The true aims of the Patron movement were lofty: to "build, not palaces, but men; to exalt, not titled stations, but general humanity; to dignify, not idle repose, but assiduous industry; to elevate not the few, but the many." Unlike the Dominion Grange, which furthered agrarian diatribes that pinpointed bankers and speculators as *the* cause of depression and economic hardship, the Patrons kept this discourse at a minimum, although they did recognize that bankers were part of the "privileged class" that supported large monopolies over the small producer, and that the usury practised by the large banks was a "direct tax on the community." Similarly, the Patrons threatened to expel any member who purchased goods at a reduced price to sell in speculation. Oddly enough, neither bankers nor speculators were mentioned by name as occupations barred from membership in the Patrons of Industry.[64] These examples demonstrate that commercially influential farmers who favoured less antagonistic relations with the commercial class remained a viable force in the constituency of the Patrons of Industry.

While there is some disagreement over whether the Patrons under the guidance of Mallory or the *Canada Farmers' Sun* under the editorship of George Wrigley agreed with the doctrines of reciprocity, the tone of Patrons' pronouncements throughout their history indicated approval, at least in principle, of free trade.[65] What is certain is that the Patrons disapproved specifically of the National Policy and tariffs in general, calling them also a "direct tax" on the community. Patrons blamed the National Policy for almost everything wrong with the economic outlook of the nation, from the proliferation of monopolies and combines to the reality of young men leaving Canada to seek their fortunes in the United States. Perhaps the most damning indictment of tariffs was based on the liberal principle of honest industry. As the *Canada Farmers' Sun* noted: "The average Canadian gets no Government aid to enable him to live. He would be ashamed to have his neighbours taxed for his benefit."[66] Several other articles in the *Canada Farmers' Sun* under Wrigley's editorship came out strongly in favour of reciprocity with the United States. In July of 1893 the Patron periodical reprinted a lecture by Nathaniel Burwash on political economy, in which he denounced protection as a detriment to the economy and a help only to the manufacturing sector. Burwash then concluded that free trade was the only economic principle guaranteed to bring about prosperity for all classes. It is also very interesting to note that the paper edited by a socialist sympathizer contained not only platitudes on Henry George's Single Tax but also articles on free trade by one of George's harshest critics, Goldwin Smith.[67]

Upon closer inspection, the Patrons of Industry were fairly ambivalent on the question of free trade, sharing with the Dominion Grange and other agricultural associations concerns about not receiving equitable treatment in trade practices. Complaining that the rights of the farmer were "determined largely by the equal rights of others," Patrons appeared to disparage protection only when it was inaccessible to farmers and reserved for the infant manufacturers of Ontario. Patrons therefore insisted that reciprocity with the United States was the most impartial economic policy as it ensured justice and fair play among all occupations and classes. The Patrons also insisted that free trade should become the preferred economic policy of organized labour for similar reasons.[68] In objecting to the favoured status that protection afforded manufacturers and the commercial sector, the London platform of the Patrons nevertheless called for tariffs as a means of increasing revenue for the government coffers. Mallory attempted to justify tariffs under the banner of equal rights for all classes in the community, stating that they would increase the revenue not only of the Canadian government but of other countries as well. Mallory also claimed that the majority of small producers, farmers, and industrial workers preferred a reasonable tariff, and that, as the Patrons of Industry were the "people's party," such a stance on a controversial issue like the tariff was fully defensible.[69]

Despite adhering to these liberal principles of honest industry, the Patrons also discussed a new radicalized scenario whereby "toilers" in agriculture and industry would receive a more appropriate share of the wealth that they themselves created. This suggestion required the Patrons of Industry to combat charges of being "anarchists and socialists," as they called on the producing class to receive "more of the leisure that rightfully belong[ed] to them; more society advantages; more of the benefits, privileges and emoluments of the world." However, it was the farmers' view that Patrons were simply demanding "those rights and privileges necessary to make them capable of enjoying, appreciating, defending and perpetuating the blessings of good government."[70] In order to secure a more prosperous future, many Patrons were prepared to abandon normative ties to the rural social order by forging new bonds with the Knights of Labor and the Trades and Labour Council (TLC). In early 1893 the TLC and the Patrons assembled as a "conference of workers in city and country" to construct a community of "field and factory." Even though this was a short-lived partnership – in 1895 the TLC banned Patrons from joining their organization – the temporary coalition did produce agreement on such issues as monopoly and direct political action. In 1895, when the Patrons formed a political committee in the Ontario Legislature, the TLC sent representatives to encourage the Patrons to vote for "laws fully protecting the public interest and those of employees in the charters asked for by electric railway companies." Unfortunately, the disparity of economic conditions between a group that traditionally formed the rural middle-class – no matter how radical they appeared on the surface – and an increasingly "class-conscious" group of industrial workers simply could not sustain unifying interests.[71]

Even more than the Grange, however, the Patrons of Industry recognized that the new industrial capitalist with his monopoly and combines was the rising threat to the producing classes. It was the duty of the agricultural and industrial classes to correct the imbalance that monopoly capitalism and the new breed of large-scale industrialism created. As one opening ode of the Patrons, "Labour's Tribute," confidently proclaimed:

> Ye noble sons of labor, and daughters fair and true,
> Truth's bright and gleaming sabre at last is drawn for you.
> The minions of aggression, monopoly and trust,
> Dread bulwarks of oppression, we'll trample in the dust.
>
> Our fathers met to battle with this tyrant's proud array,
> And 'mid the din and rattle they nobly won the day.
> They hurled the proud oppressor from off his lofty throne,
> And made themselves possessors of rights they'd justly won.

Now generations later, this haughty grasping lord,
By effort even greater, with power of his hoard;
Is gathering up each valley and riverside and plain,
Oh sons of freedom rally and drive him back again.

The tillers of the soil for many ages past,
Have bent the knee in toil before the tyrant's mast;
Then rally 'round your standard and by your colors stand,
And paint upon your banner the equal rights of man.[72]

While many of these sentiments echo those of farmers in Canada throughout the nineteenth century, the Patrons introduced collectivized solutions that were indeed unique for an agricultural association. Stating that the interests of the Patrons were those of the "suffering masses," President Mallory cited the personal opulence of the capitalist as the real menace of society. An editorial in the *Canada Farmers' Sun* suggested that combines and trusts be made "criminal," and that monopolies be placed under public control.[73]

As with the Dominion Grange, the Patrons of Industry maintained that the principle of co-operation would solve all agricultural economic malaise. Not only would co-operation bridge the gulf between capital and labour but it would address the imbalance of trade between the commercial class and the labour-farmer alliance. As noted, the Patrons exercised restraint in employing the language of co-operation, emphasizing the necessity of the commercial class, particularly the honourable occupation of the village storekeeper. To the Patrons, co-operation would simply protect the farmer from the effects of the "super" market, and from the power of monopoly combines.[74] The Patrons of Industry followed stringent co-operative doctrines at the local level, buying livestock, dairy products, grains, and seeds on a strictly co-operative basis. The Willow Vale lodge focused so much on the co-operative system that they sent a delegation to their township trade association to "bring up the market question" with other commercial representatives. Local Patrons even established a co-op store in Bismarck with like-minded merchants of the town, demonstrating that not all co-operative efforts necessarily fostered antagonistic relationships with the commercial classes.[75]

Once again less radical farmers who favoured the prolongation of the market system had their say, and conflicts often erupted over co-operation and the hazards it presented. Although William Weld had passed away by the time the Patrons of Industry rose in force, the *Farmers' Advocate* under the direction of his son John Weld initially found much to praise with the Patron platform, as William had done with the Dominion Grange. The junior Weld entreated farmers to forgo party politics and join with this "national organization" of farmers and workers dedicated to combatting the double evils of monopoly and class legislation. However, John Weld also recognized that the Patrons went against the producer ideology with the co-operative system, as he believed the only remedy to economic depression was the liberal solution of retrenchment and thrift. Co-operatism, he said, also severed the rural social and economic order: "The farmer cannot do without the merchant and the middle man, any more than the merchant can do without the farmer. The one is dependent on the other."[76] Not unlike the case of the Grange, by offering a radical modification of the accepted popular political economy of economic liberalism, the Patrons risked alienating market-based farmers from their organization.

"MAKING RURAL LIFE ENJOYABLE": PATRONS AND AGRARIAN SOCIAL INTERACTION

As with other agricultural associations, the Patrons of Industry tried to prevent isolation by offering occasions for social interaction to rural inhabitants. The Grand Association of the Patrons in Ontario sponsored many events – from picnics, excursions, baseball matches, *conversaziones*, and literary entertainments, to shooting matches and garden parties – to increase the sociability of farmers. John Miller, travelling lecturer and vice president of the Grand Association, noted that the main object of the Patrons of Industry was to "develop ... social relations by meeting as brethren and visitors on a common level and to cultivate and improve the talents with which we have been endowed." Many Patrons reported the kind of success of a Brantford picnic, where the promoters proclaimed enthusiastically: "Another Patron event makes rural life enjoyable." Even the *Canada Farmers' Sun* attempted to imitate the style of the most thriving agricultural periodical, the *Farmers' Advocate*, by widening its appeal to a larger readership than just the agricultural population. By the end of 1892, the *Sun* contained serial novels and other prose, as well as a children's section with short stories, puzzles, games, and attractive homilies. Catering to a youthful audience, the *Canada Farmers' Sun* established "For the Young People" and "Chat for Children" sections as late as 1895.[77] However, it was at the local lodge level that the Patrons of Industry proved to be most beneficial as a source of sociability for rural villages and towns.

Patron lodges quickly learned that in order to attract and maintain members, lodge meetings needed entertainment to keep them enjoyable for new recruits. The decision of the Victoria lodge to hold debates, singing, and mouth organ selections for amusement purposes, but only when the "normal business was concluded," corresponded perfectly with recruitment drives in the neighbouring village. When its executive offered only lukewarm support for a union picnic with the nearby Grove Lodge, the Victoria lodge closed with little fanfare after a scant nine months in operation.[78] The Willow Vale lodge of the Patrons of Industry lasted much longer, and a healthy dependence on entertainment as a necessary part of the functions of the lodge aided in this process immeasurably. Readings, instrumental and vocal music, recitations, speeches, and debates were all featured in the "literary part" of the lodge meetings, and a picnic was held with the Bismarck lodge for fundraising purposes. While a motion to acquire some literature for the lodge as part of a Patron library was defeated, it was one of the few decisions against entertainment made by Willow Vale lodge directors. In a debate on whether to procure an organ for musical programs in the lodge, Brother John Strumm argued against the purchase, stating, "business was more important than pleasure, and [he] thought business took up all our time." Although the Willow Vale Patrons actively participated in the co-operative system, the amusement portion of lodge activities was obviously just as important, and the organ was purchased.[79]

The rapid materialization of agrarian protest in the late nineteenth century and its equally abrupt disappearance from the rural landscape was a difficult lesson for Ontario's farmers to learn. Their experience with the Dominion Grange and the Patrons of Industry would also be repeated in the twentieth century with the meteoric rise and fall of the United Farmers of Ontario.[80] While the leadership of the Patrons of Husbandry and the Patrons of Industry offered ideological visions of class harmony, the promise of united political action through anti-partyism, and the assurance of material prosperity to Ontario's farmers, the history of agrarian protest can be viewed as one of broken promises and unfulfilled expectations. Even though farmers could blame monopoly capitalism, the professional classes, and the unfair business practices of commercial retailers for the difficulties experienced by their members, in reality the class divisions among farmers themselves played a large part in the failure of both the Dominion Grange and the Patrons of Industry.

And yet these agrarian movements also united farmers as never before in a collective liberal identity, with the growth of an inclusive organization, wide-ranging social activities, integrated economic mutualism, and combined political action. Simply put, the complexities of varied material circumstances and representational differences among the farming population precluded agreement on any issue confronting them. While the Dominion Grange and the Patrons of Industry made an admirable attempt to unify an easily alienated agrarian class, sustaining harmonious relationships in a very combustible economic and ideological environment proved far too problematic for either group. It was the pressures from within agrarian protest, rather than from without, that would eventually be the undoing of both the Dominion Grange and the Patrons of Industry.

7

A Feast of Popularized Science and Literature

Whereas the Mechanics' Institute movement encompassed elements of the commercial and manufacturing classes, the directors of agricultural associations served the needs of farmers, and fraternal orders offered a refuge to the skilled working classes, scientific societies and literary organizations catered to a vastly different constituency – the professional middling/middle classes. Originally created to promote the advancement of scientific knowledge for an enlightened citizenry, scientific and literary societies established an alliance with the liberal social order by opening up avenues for utilitarian science and literature for the entire community. Despite occasional tensions between "professional" men of science and literature and the emerging manufacturing, mercantile, and commercial middling sorts, their literary and scientific coalition showed some resilience in the mid-nineteenth-century. However, by the 1870s the "professionalization" of the scientific and literary elite had transpired, gradually phasing out the "non-expert" from the various learned societies. Although the segregation of the recreational scientist and literary figure within these societies did augment friction between the professional classes and other groups, many scientific and literary societies remained conscious of the need to involve the entire community in their affairs. By consciously encouraging a dichotomy between the authority of the expert and the appeal of the popular, the professional classes used the ideology of a liberal "community" to their advantage to firmly establish their supremacy in scientific and literary endeavours.

In many respects, the culture of scientific and literary associations in central Canada mirrored the experiences of similar associations in Great Britain and France, albeit with some rather noticeable differences. The scientific and literary establishment in these European nations was culled from the aristocratic classes who viewed their intellectual pursuits as amateur endeavours rather than vocations. The leadership of such organizations as the French *Académie des Sciences* and the British Royal Society was entirely drawn from the upper aristocratic classes.[1] As rather passive guardians of scientific and literary culture, amateur scientists, historians, and poets were not pleased when "professional" scientists and the mercantile/commercial elites began to demand membership in the hallowed aristocratic halls of science. Despite the tensions inherent in the discourse of science and literature, those who were interested in the advancement of scientific and literary knowledge did attempt to achieve some form of consensus. In reality, the reform-oriented commercial elite, the aristocratic upper classes, and even scientific-minded artisans, marched behind the banner of scientific and literary improvement to further their own political, social, or economic agendas. The "popularization" of early scientific organizations therefore assumed a variety of connotations for different groups within scientific and literary societies in Europe.[2]

Unlike the aristocracy of science and literature in the British and French settings, the early promoters of scientific and literary culture in central Canada comprised the mercantile and the professional elite. With an overwhelming majority of members in these associations from the upper middling classes, tensions did erupt in scientific and literary societies between elite executives and reform-minded critics during the 1820s and 1830s. In a way comparable to the sectarian and political squabbles that accompanied the creation of agricultural societies, early scientific and literary societies had rather turbulent beginnings.[3] Despite the social discord inherent in these early scientific and literary societies, however, the interaction of the elite leadership solidified a scientific and literary alliance between the liberal social order and the professional classes. The parallel expansion of learned societies during this phase of commercial and mercantile development also underscores the highly hegemonic nature of this middling-class enterprise. While conceding the overwhelming popularity of utilitarian and popular science during this period, some "professional" scientists and literary figures were unnerved by these developments. Preferring to focus on the pursuit of knowledge for its own sake, some members of scientific and literary societies chided their mercantile and commercial compatriots for their willingness to override "pure" science for its practical applications. The political debates related to the significance of the Geological Survey headed by William Logan typified many of these disagreements.[4]

POPULAR/PROFESSIONAL SCIENCE AND LIBERAL CLASS INCLUSION

The genesis of this dichotomy between "popular," commercially applied, versions of knowledge and purely academic interest highlights the importance of voluntary learned societies and their role in the liberal community. Despite the largely commercial and professional elite leadership in early scientific and literary societies, the rhetoric of liberal class inclusion was fundamental to their development. Two of the earliest, the Literary and Historical Society of Quebec (hereafter the LHSQ) and the Montreal Natural History Society (hereafter the MNHS) illustrate from their inception the significance of liberal social interaction among all classes and interests. In the early annual reports of the LHSQ, the executive noted that the establishment of the society invited no feelings of an exclusive nature, and that the society existed for the benefit of all ages and conditions. Similarly, a year after the creation of the MNHS in 1828, the directors confirmed that the object of the society's founders was to foster a general public spirit of scientific and literary research. As a result, the society's membership was inclusive, on "a most liberal basis, being open to all ranks of the community, the sole gratification being a desire to promote the cause of science and country."[5]

The discourse of liberal class inclusion took on a new meaning in Montreal, with a solidified membership coalition of the commercial elite and the professional middling sort that was determined to end the domination of Tory elites in the MNHS. Robert Lachlan, one of the founders of the MNHS, observed with satisfaction in 1852 that over half of the supporters of the society were mercantile men, a third were doctors, and the rest were lawyers and members of the clergy. Recognizing that "experts" still administered the governance of the society, Lachlan noted that a mixed membership of commercial, mercantile, and professional men did improve their scientific meetings. He also emphasized that while "men of learning may be required to lead the way in the more abstruse and unfrequented paths of research, so intimately are science and philosophy in one way or another united and interwoven with the ordinary pursuits and occupations of life, that, in a society aiming at *mutual instruction*, it is in the power of almost every reflecting, moderately educated man, to bear a part in the practical illustration of some subject or other."[6] Prominent members of the MNHS such as William Eyre and John William Dawson perpetuated this liberal philosophy during this period. In the April 1858 edition of the

Canadian Naturalist and Geologist, Eyre lauded the MNHS for cultivating intellectual pursuits that were not restricted solely to the *litterati* or any other particular class. In 1863 Dawson closely followed this theme in his address to a general audience at the first annual *conversazione* under his tenure. The MNHS was open to the whole liberal community, he affirmed: "Our philosophy is not of that kind which shuts itself up in pedantic exclusiveness. We regard the study of nature as the common heritage of all."[7]

A similar philosophy of scientific education emerged in the most recognized scientific society in Canada West, the Canadian Institute. In 1852 a group of land engineers, surveyors, and architects gathered in Toronto to form a scientific organization to meet their professional needs. A few months after their original meeting, prominent members such as surveyor Sandford Fleming and chemist Henry Youle Hind recognized that this professional designation would restrict the growth and development of the Institute. Accordingly, when the directors of the Canadian Institute incorporated their charter, they widened the intended membership to include all members of the community, from the "enterprising manufacturer and scientific farmer" to the "enquiring mechanic." In announcing this change, the executive acknowledged that they had satisfied their own professional needs before turning their thoughts to a provision for the liberal public. And yet the paradigm of encouraging professional scientific activity and opening the society to the community emerged in many of the early meetings of the Institute. In a report in the *Canadian Journal*, the directors noted with satisfaction that both professional and amateur scientific objectives could be served. Meetings in the Institute not only afforded "opportunity for closer communication between scientific and professional men" but they could also serve to link all classes within the community.[8]

The directors of the French-language counterpart to the Canadian Institute, the *Institut Canadien* of Montreal, aggressively campaigned for an inclusive membership of all classes, albeit in the literary rather than the scientific domain. The expressed purpose of the lectures and literary meetings of the *Institut* was to improve the liberal mind of the community at large and to enhance the "theatre of public life." As a result, the *Institut Canadien* quickly became the centre of cultural and intellectual life for French Canadians in Montreal.[9] In 1852 the prominent Montreal lawyer and president of the *Institut*, Joseph Doutre, opened the course of lectures for the season with an address promoting the very theme of liberal inclusion. In Doutre's vision, the mission of the *Institut Canadien* to fashion an enlightened citizenry in Montreal simply required public awareness and the interest of all classes of the community. The liberal interclass objectives of the *Institut Canadien* were reiterated in the annual report of the *Institut* in 1861, in which President Dessaules declared: "Our *Institut* has become a Palladium [a veritable music hall] for all, lacking exclusion, devoid of censure, and our individual conscience, as well as the eternal laws of morality, truth, justice, and charity will be our only guides and our sole judges." Of course, descriptions of "liberality" in the *Institut Canadien* were often deployed as rather large sticks with which to subdue the controlling influences of the Roman Catholic Church in French society.[10]

By mid-century, interclass co-operation in learned societies included accommodation with the liberal state, given the centrality of both the Lower and Upper Canadian Boards of Arts and Manufactures. Although a merger never occurred between the Quebec Mechanics' Institute and the LHSQ, its possibility was constantly before the two executives from 1841 to 1844. And one of the founders of the MNHS, the Reverend Henry Esson, was also the key individual behind the formation of the Montreal Mechanics' Institute a year later. As a result, the MNHS and the Montreal Mechanics' Institute often shared rooms, museum space, and classes, and likewise discussed amalgamation on several occasions until dropping the project in 1841.[11] The usefulness of the Canadian Institute in augmenting the prosperity of the nation through scientific husbandry, commerce, and manufacturing was acknowledged even in the title of their official organ, *The Canadian Journal: A Repository of Industry, Science and Art*. The prospectus of the scientific periodical proclaimed its desire to support other societies dedicated to the promotion of science among all classes of society: "The objects of this Journal are essentially of a useful character ... by supplying such a publication as will afford a medium of communication between all engaged or interested in Scientific or Industrial pursuits; will assist, lighten and elevate the labours of the mechanic; will afford information to the manufacturer, and generally minister to the wants of that already numerous and still increasing class in British America, who are desirous of becoming acquainted with the most recent inventions and improvements in the Arts, and those scientific changes and discoveries which are in progress throughout the world."[12]

RAISING THE TONE AND STANDARD OF LIBERAL SOCIETY: LEARNED SOCIETIES AND THE PROFESSIONAL MIDDLING CLASSES

In many respects, the intended liberal class inclusiveness of scientific and literary societies existed only on a rhetorical level, as the professional middling classes retained their influence as cultural guardians of "pure" science and literature while exerting their superiority over their "amateur" counterparts. The directors of the MNHS anticipated a very small initial list of members for, unlike their aristocratic British counterparts in the Royal Society, the MNHS existed in a land where "wealth is comparatively little, [and] where no opulent endowments take off the necessity of securing a livelihood, and where in consequence the attention is directed into channels very different from scientific research." And yet the MNHS executive also recognized that those elite few comprised the commercial, professional, and mercantile elite, the eminent, respectable, and intelligent gentlemen of Montreal.[13] The LHSQ faced an equivalent dilemma in the function of its scientific and literary mission, as the majority of members worked in the professional, commercial, and agricultural spheres. As a result, the LHSQ recognized the "difficulties to overcome which are peculiar to its situation," noting that unlike Great Britain, "society, besides being comparatively less extensive, is so constituted, that those who have leisure for scientific enquiry are far from numerous, and there are perhaps none who are so circumstanced as to be able to devote the greater part of their time to the acquisition of knowledge." Nevertheless, most of the early executive was formed from the elite circle of founder Lord Dalhousie and other prominent Quebec mercantile men and professionals.[14]

The desires of the professional middling-class executive of the MNHS to attract more distinguished and expert scientific men to their institution intensified by the 1850s, despite continued attempts to reach out to the larger community. While clinging to a discourse of liberal scientific inclusion, MNHS directors endorsed the view of Major Lachlan, who in an 1852 lecture recommend the participation of leading members of the community, as theirs was "an intellectual institution whose unceasing aim should be to *lead*, as well as elevate the tone and standard of the public mind." President Abraham De Sola's explanation of the trickle-down effect of the Society's rather elitist attitudes in a lecture to the 1864 annual meeting echoed these lofty aims. As the MNHS embraced members of high reputation and standing, "it could, and did, command that sort and degree of respect which gave weight to its proceedings [so as] to render services of greatest value to the whole community, by being instrumental in bringing these resources more and more into notice."[15] One way of giving prominence to their resources was to bring the annual meeting of the American Association for the Advancement of Science (AAAS) to the city of Montreal in 1857. The directors of the MNHS coveted the annual AAAS meeting to not only showcase their own scientific talent, but also to increase the stature of the Society through the visit of distinguished scientific men, and they enlisted "influential" members of the community such as William Logan and William Dawson for the cause. Contrasting the learned constituency of the MNHS with the liberal community in general, the Executive Council noted after the visit of the AAAS that they had "sufficient reason to feel satisfied with the struggles of a Society like this placed by its very nature, so far in advance of our crude national state."[16]

Even though in Canada West it was the stated aims of the Canadian Institute's charter of incorporation in 1854 to include all classes and occupations, the original mandate of the Institute only provided avenues of association for land engineers, surveyors, and architects. A few months after the first meeting of the Institute, the executive assured scientists that the Institute had extended its original objects and would embrace members of all grades and pursuits. Despite such high flown rhetoric, out of the original fourteen members of the Canadian Institute, only one listed his occupation as a civil engineer. The others listed in the original membership were all members of the elite professional class, including four "gentlemen," four university professors, two barristers, two doctors, and a judge.[17] Although the Institute did expose the larger society to scientific pursuits, in reality it remained restricted to the eminent men of science, the "active minds of the community." By 1860 the close co-operation between the Canadian Institute and the Mechanics' Institute movement came to an abrupt end when government retrenchment ended the funding for both organizations. To the directors of the Canadian Institute, the fact that the government compared them with the working-class educational efforts of the Mechanics' Institute was an affront to an eminently superior scientific and learned society such as theirs. Arguing that the Canadian Institute was a professional scientific institution of a "purely public and Provincial character," the executive debated whether to change their name so that future governments would not confuse them with the more proletarian Mechanics' Institutes.[18]

The Montreal *Institut Canadien* discovered a comparable dichotomy between their mission to open their association to all members of the community, and their quest for authority and influence. Not only would the *Institut* provide intellectual improvement for the larger community but it would also teach the working classes, for "the education of the working classes has become the greatest need of our time and the primary civilizing element on our continent."[19] However, the executives of the *Institut* also considered themselves to be a society analogous to such groups as the *Société Française* and other *sociétés savantes* like the MNHS and the LHSQ. As a *learned* voluntary society on a par with these other associations, the *Institut* would no doubt produce "les hommes des lettres canadiennes" and other men of literary or scientific distinction. Therefore, despite the discourse of class inclusion, the educational endeavours of the *Institut Canadien* of Montreal focused fairly exclusively on young men entering the liberal professions. Meticulous research conducted by Yvan Lamonde on the occupations of the *Institut*'s membership supports this argument, as he notes that between 1855 and 1900, almost 80 percent of the ordinary membership of the *Insitut* came from the liberal professions and the mercantile/commercial classes.[20]

As with other voluntary associations, the introduction of women into scientific and literary societies strongly illustrated this inclusive/exclusive paradigm, as these organizations opened up new avenues for women while simultaneously maintaining a strong ideology of domesticity. While upperclass men indeed dominated the scientific landscape in Great Britain, middling-class women could find a voice writing popular science books and exploring the "simpler" life sciences such as botany.[21] It appears that the marginalization of women in central-Canadian scientific and literary societies became even more pronounced, as women were relegated to minimal participation at lectures, soirées and social events, while providing revenue-generating bazaars and refreshments to complement the efforts of these associations. The degree of their participation depended on the organization: as early as 1832 women became subscribing members of the York Literary and Philosophical Society of Upper Canada, while at the LHSQ they were allowed to attend lectures only in 1859. Whatever measure of involvement women found in scientific and literary societies, the male directors were highly dubious as to the seriousness of life contributions females could make to scientific or literary advancement. While this attitude underwent some changes in the late decades of the century, many lecturers echoed the attitude of Major Lachlan, who begged the "indulgence of the fair portion of the audience," and hoped they would not be bored during the presentation of his remarks.[22]

"NO FEELING OF AN EXCLUSIVE NATURE":
POLITICO-RELIGIOUS TOLERATION IN LEARNED SOCIETIES

In attempting to offer the educational benefits of science and literature to the larger liberal community, scientific and literary societies endeavoured to slay the twin dragons of sectarianism and political partyism. To the directors of the LHSQ, the scientific undertakings of the society invited the co-operation of all Quebec citizens: "Within these walls there exists no feeling of an exclusive nature; party distinctions are unknown; political and religious feuds cease on crossing the threshold." Apparently the LHSQ was highly successful in banishing sectarian and political turmoil from its institution, as they reported in their 1838 annual report that despite the storm of rebellion and the "distractions of political changes" they had managed to pursue their peaceful course of scientific exploration and discovery.[23] The same could not be said of the Toronto Literary Society, in spite of its efforts to control the emergence of political or religious controversy. Although the Society had many members from the Tory Family Compact – men such as John Spragge and John Strachan – it also welcomed Reform supporters like William Lyon Mackenzie and the Ridouts. Unlike the Toronto Mechanics' Institute, the mingling of party factions in the Toronto Literary Society created a great deal of conflict and discord. Perhaps some political squabbling in the society resulted from the topics for discussion: a March 1836 debate on "Should the law support a combination of workmen?" surely would have touched a nerve with the Reform faction. Similarly, in discussing about whether manufactures were prejudicial to national mores, the statement made by one side that businessmen were "the best body in the nation, generous, sober and charitable" would also have sparked some heated debate between Tories and Reformers.[24]

Constraints on the presentation of political or religious questions in the MNHS initially appeared to be problematic, given that one of the original founders of the Society, the Reverend Henry Esson, engaged in sectarian disputations that necessitated the closing of the Montreal Mechanics' Institute. While the Tory and elitist composition of the MNHS ensured that comparable sectarian difficulties did not arise, the political stresses of the immediate post-Rebellion period forced it to disband for a time. The brief recession of the early 1840s is often blamed for closing the Society's doors, but at least one director blamed the failure of the Montreal Mechanics' Institute, the Library, and the MNHS to join forces, which would have allowed potential French members to "get rid of those narrow sectional feelings and prejudices."[25] With the reorganization of the MNHS in 1845 came a new determination to eliminate sectarian and political discord from among the membership, and to open the society's doors to the entire community. As President Major Lachlan noted, the executive of the MNHS from then on cordially invited the heads of all "churches, and seminaries, and professions and callings, for the liberal Republic of letters knows no narrow distinctions of races, creeds, classes or political parties." The Canadian Institute similarly trumpeted its society as being inclusive and harmonious, with the aim that "men of all shades of religion or politics may meet on the same friendly grounds."[26]

Although both the MNHS and the Canadian Institute did rise above sectarian and political conflict within their organizations, they continually attempted to create ties with the emerging liberal state. When the MNHS received an award of a thousand pounds from the legislature in 1860, President Dawson took great pains to safeguard the annual grant from the retrenchment ethos of the Reform element in Parliament. Not only did Dawson praise politicians for "emulating the wise liberality of older countries" in offering financial support for the Society but he also recognized – as did Logan – that preserving the "nobility" of pure science required practical and utilitarian applications for the larger community. In justifying the expenses of the MNHS, Dawson reiterated the Society's aim: to "mingle the pursuit of merely utilitarian objects in the development of the resources of this country, with higher and more philosophical conceptions of nature. In the midst of many perturbed social and political elements, we are studying things that make for peace, and which are for the common benefit of all."[27] From its inception, the Canadian Institute took similar action to secure government funds for its scientific mission. The legislature's liberality in providing assistance was not unrecognized by the Institute, particularly as many of their directors, Hind, Logan, Henry Lefoy, and Sandford Fleming, for example, owed their appointments to government largesse. When the annual grant to the Institute was threatened by the economic recession of the 1850s, the Canadian Institute marshalled its forces to defend the commercial and utilitarian uses of science. The editors of the *Canadian Journal* emphasized that the influence of science could be measured throughout the liberal community, from its applications to agriculture, commerce and manufactures to "the administration of justice [and] to each art of domestic life."[28]

Although a period of political and religious normalization for many scientific and literary societies occurred at mid-century, the *Institut Canadien* in Montreal was a notable exception because of its affiliation with the reformist *Rouge* element. The experience of the *Institut* is fairly unique, in that sectarian and political disagreements erupted between members of the same class, as the leading conservative Roman Catholic clergy and most of the *Institut Canadien*'s members all came from the liberal professions. However, the *Institut* had originally acknowledged the importance of eliminating divisive sectarian and political turmoil. This turn toward liberal beliefs reached a peak in 1850 when the *Institut Canadien* modified its bylaws to permit English-speaking Protestants to become active members of the *Institut*. Its executives encouraged the majority constituency of French Canadian Catholics to be tolerant of differing political and religious opinions and boasted that they had finally achieved liberty of thought and discussion, as well as freedom from exclusion and censure in their operations.[29] During the 1860s Dessaules gave several speeches on the religious and political tolerance realized under his presidency of the *Institut Canadien*. He had guaranteed peace and harmony within the *Institut*, he said, by welcoming Anglo-Protestants with open arms and ending the exclusionary practices of religious fanaticism. Dessaules painted a portrait of the *Institut* as "toutes les opinions, soit religieuses, soit politiques" and being committed to eradicating political and religious discord: "[The] field is open to all, without consideration of origin or creed."[30]

In reality, the well-known history of the Montreal *Institut Canadien* was a cacophony of political and religious conflict, as members of the same professional class fought for the loyalty of their fellow-citizens. In supporting the 1848 return of Louis-Joseph Papineau from exile and politicizing their journal, *L'Avenir*, with *Rouge* liberalism, the *Institut Canadien* immersed the institution in the controversies simmering between liberals and the more conservative Roman Catholic order. An excellent example of the politicization of the *Institut* occurred in 1853 when the executive resolved to build a monument to those who had lost their lives during the 1837–38 rebellions in Lower Canada. Acknowledging that passions over political issues and "national hatreds" had lost their intensity, the *Institut* felt free to express its sympathy for all those killed in the struggle. However, undercurrents of controversy erupted because the directorate repeatedly referred to the dead as "political victims" and emphasized the current battles for French nationalism.[31] The connection of the *Institut Canadien* with the liberal *Rouge* element became even more pronounced when Dessaules took on the presidency of the *Institut*. Praising the *liberal* religious and political tolerance of the *Institut* while deriding Ignace Bourget and the Catholic clergy for their *illiberal* religious exclusivity, Dessaules in fact exacerbated the sectarian and political tensions between the two factions. Even as he claimed that the politics of liberalism recognized the power of the "communauté" and the people, his insistence on censuring conservative Catholic elements also alienated those who would have been inclined to support the *Institut*. Although Dessaules claimed that his remarks were always defensive in nature, by engaging in an adversarial discourse between the *Institut* and Roman Catholic ultramontanes he not only went against his own institution's policy against religious and political discussions but he also helped to perpetuate nationalist tensions within Quebec society.[32]

UTILITARIAN POLITICAL ECONOMY, THE LIBERAL STATE, AND THE CULT OF HONEST INDUSTRY

Scientific and literary societies also recommended honest industry and the individual work ethic, thereby solidifying the connection between the emerging liberal state and voluntary learned societies. Their thinking was that political economy was a liberal science that organized society, just as science itself organized the workings of nature. However, the liberal political economy of science could also foster adversarial positions among classes, political entities, and ideologies. The commercial possibilities of science and technology could also represent contested terrain relating to various interest groups.[33] In the first half of the nineteenth century, however, central Canadian scientific and literary societies demonstrated a consensual accommodation with the liberal social order, through their qualified acceptance of the precepts of honest industry. Even though there were some points of divergence regarding political economy both from within learned societies and from without, on the whole, literary and scientific societies tried to solidify consent between their own professional class membership and the liberal social order.

Most scientific and literary societies demonstrated their professional biases and an accommodation with commercial and mercantile interests, particularly in their debates regarding the political economics of the labouring poor and the necessity to provide workhouses for the "proper employment" of those less fortunate. To the Robin Hood Society, an English-speaking debating club in Montreal, Houses of Industry would not only teach a liberal work ethos but would also provide maintenance for both the working poor and those too disabled to provide for themselves. In a debate regarding the propriety of workhouses, debaters mentioned the growing evil of begging and stealing, whereby young people were getting "habituated to idleness and vice, and never wish to acquire the means of subsistence by honest industry." Significantly, a reiteration of this argument occurred nearly thirty years later in the LHSQ, when the distinguished lawyer E.A. Meredith urged the members of the LHSQ to fight for educational improvements that would teach children industrious habits. Meredith argued that such teaching was needed early in children's development, in order to save the government the expense of establishing Houses of Refuge.[34] Debates over political economy in scientific and literary societies could also highlight the political fissures just underneath the surface, particularly in the societies formed just before the Rebellions, such as the Toronto Literary Society. One of the earliest debates of that society illustrates the promising partnership of the professional and elite middling classes of the older Tory tradition, as the Family Compact – dominated Society debated whether manufactures were prejudicial to the national morality. The Society concluded that they were not, given that there was "no evidence that vice and immorality [was] more prevalent among these people, considered as a class, than among any portion of the community in the same station." It appears that other debates on political economy were not as well received, as a later debate in the Toronto Literary Society on workmen's combinations exposed the fault lines of political discord between its Tory and Reform factions.[35]

The alliance between the liberal order and the professional members of scientific and literary societies became even more pronounced, principally in their espousal of the desirability of honest industry and the utilitarian connection of science to commercial endeavours. In a lecture to the Literary and Historical Society of Toronto in 1845, W. Scott Burn outlined the connection between great literature and the commerce of the middling sort in an essay that celebrated the demise of the Family Compact and the rise of a liberal social order:

> With the full development of society comes the diffusion of wealth, with wealth comes the desire of luxurious ease, and luxurious ease passes naturally into indolence. Were this tendency to remain unchecked, exertion of mind would become hateful; the desire of acquiring knowledge would be lost, or cultivated only as a subsidiary to ornament and the gratification of the senses. A retrograde movement would commence, science would be frittered away into elegant quibbles, and literature dwindle into nothing more important than a sonnet. But here the commercial spirit steps in and arrests the progress of decay; it keeps society in constant motion, elevating the low and depressing the lofty, filling every rank with new claimants for distinction, and keeping all on the watch that they may not, during a season of forgetfulness, be elbowed out of the way, and lose their position.

Given that Burn was first a merchant, then a bookkeeper and teacher of accounting, his love of commerce and its capacity for allowing social mobility within the middling class is understandable.[36] While the correlation between scientific societies such as the MNHS and the Canadian Institute and a utilitarian political economy has been amply demonstrated, disagreements between the advocates of "pure" science and those of the "applied" science represented *political* differences, not mere distinctions of *economic* philosophies. Both the MNHS and the Canadian Institute plunged headlong into "industrial and scientific pursuits" and mingled practical science with the "lofty philosophies of nature." While extremists on both sides of the debate remained firmly entrenched in their political ideologies, the official stance of both these scientific organizations was to support a political economy that also regarded science as a national resource to be exploited.[37]

Although these organizations achieved remarkable consensus on the principles of honest industry and liberal political economy, in order to eradicate political partyism from their ranks, scientific and literary societies offered their members complete autonomy in their chosen economic policy. This neutrality would not always be observed in the lectures given before such bodies, as evidenced by William Hincks's 1862 address to the Canadian Institute entitled "An Inquiry into the Natural Laws Which Regulate the Interchange of Commodities between Individuals and Nations, and the Effects of Interference with them." While the lecture was a rather long-winded treatise on free trade, Hincks nevertheless employed the liberal discourse of the labour theory of value, maintaining that almost all goods were "obtained by our own labour employed upon it, or by an exchange for it of the produce of our labour otherwise employed." As a clergyman and professor at the University of Toronto, Hincks had also lectured against the factory system while a university professor in England, solidifying his views on the labour question. In reinforcing his arguments for freer trade, Hincks likewise appealed to the larger community: "Restrictions on commerce have the effect of monopoly, in abling [*sic*] a class to live by a tax on the rest of the community, added to the fair natural price of the commodity, which is to prove that common justice, as well as wise policy, requires the utmost attainable freedom in trade."[38]

However, scientific and literary societies also gave ample space to frequently contrary views of commercial and mercantile men in their lecture halls. In 1866 the Secretary of the Quebec Board of Trade, T.H. Grant, gave a lecture to the LHSQ on the future commercial policy of British North America, with a subheading "Protect Industry and it will Prosper." Grant argued that young Canadian manufactures required tariffs both as a protection against cheap American produce and as a support for industries directly affected by the lack of capital to be found in British America. And yet Grant employed similar language to Hincks in his lecture, justifying his position on the basis of the political economy of honest industry and the significance of popular political economy to liberal society at large. To Grant, tariff protection was analogous to the labour theory of value in benefiting the whole community: "If the skilful artisan, the respectable mechanic, and the inventive genius of our race, whether emigrant or native born, are to be induced to settle permanently in British America, we must protect the means by which the fruit of their skill and labour my be made profitable to them."[39]

The *Institut Canadien* in Montreal similarly acknowledged the importance of honest industry and the political economy of labour; the *Institut* employed mottoes such as "Le Travail Triomphe de Tout" and "Travail et Concorde" intermingled with work-related images of beehives and beavers in their periodicals. The reading room of the *Institut* also housed volumes related to political economy all along an ideological continuum in its stated desire to aid its patrons find answers for "all the great questions of social interest, both public and private." Even the educational aims of the *Institut* reflected principles of honest industry, as P.R. LeFrenaye noted: "To make our country even more great, beautiful and stronger, and to position it at the level of our competitor nations in industry, commerce, and prosperity, it is absolutely necessary to promote education that is both useful and practical."[40] Of course the political economy supported by the *Institut Canadien* accentuated the tenets of liberalism preferred by the executives of the *Institut*. Not only did the *Institut* hall house the offices of the liberal anti-seigneurial league but many *Institut* directors such as J.B.E. Dorion openly favoured the more Reformist position of free trade. In a lecture to the *Institut* in 1852, Dorion employed the liberal discourse of honest industry in defence of reciprocity, claiming that not only were tariffs a tax on the community to support a certain class, but also: "In regard to commerce, and everything related to it, I am in favour of a *laisser-faire* policy, or of the greatest possible freedom, for that is the spirit, the nature, the soul, and the life of business."[41]

LEARNED SOCIETIES AND RATIONAL RECREATION

The rationale that scientific and literary organizations used for their recreational activities showed their active interest in bringing their endeavours to the larger community. The MNHS and the Toronto Literary Society did attempt to enliven their presentations and meetings by introducing prize essay contests and a lecture series – entertainments that were fully open to the general public. These activities did not, however, generate much revenue or interest for either society, as both the MNHS and the Toronto Literary Society languished in the immediate aftermath of the Rebellions.[42] Reliance on rational sociability alone could hamper the effectiveness of a scientific or literary society, particularly in rural settings where more "social" community events were a necessity. Despite discussions of fairly interesting topics such as women's rights, protection vs free trade, and the injurious morality of novel reading, the Brockville Debating Club suffered from poorly attended meetings, repetition of topics, and a lack of interest from both the general membership and the community at large. As a result, in January of 1853 the secretary called a special meeting to consider "the propriety of continuing or dissolving the society." Apparently the latter view prevailed, as the next meeting did not take place until 1855 under the banner of the Brockville Young Men's Association, an organization that lasted only seven meetings before it was "adjourned until further notice."[43]

The directors of learned societies also recognized the vital role of sociability in bringing members and non-members closer together. In a report of the first *conversazione* of the Canadian Institute in 1852, it was noted that while the actual work of the Institute brought together scientific and professional men, it was the social aspects that welded "an agreeable and profitable link uniting those who, although engaged in widely different paths of business, possess congenial tastes and interests." Although the *conversazione* only offered the audience scientific papers and addresses, it did attract a fairly large group containing such luminaries as John Strachan and Egerton Ryerson.[44] The *Institut Canadien* in Montreal also, organized *séances* with debates, readings and recitations for members and non-members. But the *Institut* did not depend solely on these rational recreations. They also arranged concerts and other musical events, which culminated in a combined social evening with the Montreal *Société St Jean Baptiste* in 1856. The Montreal *Institut Canadien* also focused on entertainment as a means of raising revenue for their literary society, particularly in 1858 in their efforts to erect a monument for the political victims of the 1837–38 Rebellions. In order to pay off the debts accrued during the construction of the monument, the directors organized a concert and a *promenade* for the citizens of Montreal.[45]

The excitement of holding *conversaziones* gripped the directors of both the MNHS and the Ottawa Natural History Society (hereafter the ONHS). *Conversaziones* helped member and non-member alike to realize the beauties of natural history through the reading of scientific papers, and also provided avenues of sociability for all participants. The soirées and picnics organized by these scientific societies therefore coupled an appreciation for natural science with opportunities for social contact, a combination that increased attendance at social gatherings, particularly among the women of Ottawa and Montreal. Such outings combined a more "popular" science with professional scientific papers, demonstrating that science could cross gender and class boundaries, and that the study of nature could be a pleasurable activity.[46] However, the entertainment offered by scientific societies also foreshadowed the late-century separation of popular science from professional scientific endeavours. In 1861 the MNHS inaugurated the Sommerville Lectures, a series of public and popular scientific addresses that targeted a more general audience. Undoubtedly this was a very conscious division of scientific work within the society, as the directors noted with enthusiasm that these free general lectures of a "popular character" were well attended. Unfortunately, the monthly meetings of the MNHS, where papers on "very able and scientific subjects ... its really scientific work" were presented, experienced sparse crowds and indifference from the general populace. It was an acknowledged that greater attendance would require "increasing desire on the part of the citizens of Montreal generally for the attainment of knowledge of Natural history and its kindred sciences."[47]

THE DOMINION OF LETTERS: THE PROFESSIONALIZATION *AND* THE POPULARIZATION OF SCIENCE AND LITERATURE IN THE LATE NINETEENTH CENTURY

Scientific and literary societies experienced a very subtle shift from the 1870's to the turn of the century, as they increasingly operated under the auspices of professional scientists and scholarly literary figures, and amateur naturalists and literary enthusiasts were increasingly marginalized in this new "Dominion of Letters." This process occurred somewhat earlier in the United States and Great Britain, where increasing state involvement in the sciences and other intellectual endeavours necessitated the presence of university-sponsored professionals in several organizations. The ideology of "professionalism" therefore crossed disciplinary boundaries in a pedagogic quest for authority and influence in scientific and literary affairs.[48] And yet learned societies also cultivated an even greater sense of liberal inclusion, as the popularization of science and literature reached its zenith by the end of the century. Although science was characterized at this time as a discipline of intense specialization and professionalization, this period was also an era of mass-market science textbooks, radical popular science, and increased accessibility of scientific and literary knowledge to the general public. As a result of conscious efforts to bring the fruits of science and literature to the larger community, these societies could not be elite monolithic creations, as professionals were obliged to negotiate cultural space within a multiplicity of social groups, including women, amateur scientists, and the skilled working classes.[49]

As literary and scientific associations wrestled with the specialization and the professionalization of their disciplines, the organization of consent around the authority and influence of the experts occurred in many scientific and literary professions, from the civil service to engineers, and from the hallowed groves of academe to the teaching professions. Similarly, learned associations came to be dominated less by voluntary societies such as the Canadian Institute and the MNHS than by the Royal Society of Canada, which was highly selective in its invitations to membership. The ascendancy of the Royal Society signified the emergence of a professional and intellectual elite with the aim of honouring academic and scholarly achievement and establishing a national academy similar to the Royal Society of London and the *Institut Français*.[50] Despite this renewed focus on pure and comprehensive research, popular lectures and the dissemination of natural science remained key objectives for these associations, as they endeavoured to serve all members of the community. It was therefore no contradiction to find a scientific luminary such as John Macoun – the Dominion botanist and leader of the 1881 Geological Survey– involved in collecting natural history specimens for the Ottawa Natural History Society.[51] By intentionally emphasizing both the authority of the expert and the allure of the "popular," the emerging professional middle class would assert its superiority in scientific and literary endeavours, and solidify its collective liberal identity.

In principle, scientific and literary societies continued to advocate an ideology of liberal classlessness within their institutions, in promoting their societies throughout the larger community. Organizations such as the Royal Astronomical Society in Toronto were proud of their inclusive membership. "The society desires to be popular in the best sense of the word and therefore cordially invites to membership anyone who takes a sincere interest in astronomical and physical matters, be his or her scientific qualifications what they may." Similarly, the Canadian Institute remained open to all classes in the community, an institution "completely catholic and not restricted to the éminent" residents of the province of

Ontario. Although the Institute's main objective remained the encouragement of original scientific research, the executive came to the conclusion that "they should endeavour at the same time to promote the spread of popular science."[52] In the 1880 *Transactions* of the Ottawa Field-Naturalists Club, the directors welcomed the enlarged membership rolls, observing that the club was "day by day more widely known and popular." By the end of the century the ONHS remained committed to the principle of inclusion. In the 1896 edition of the *Ottawa Naturalist* the editors extended an invitation to the whole community. "Our membership is by no means restricted, as might be thought by some, to those who in the professional sense of the term be called scientists. We are certainly particularly fortunate in having among our members many who are devoting their time exclusively to the study of scientific problems ... Nevertheless, we invite all to join us." Thus the ONHS organized popular lectures, collecting excursions and picnics, in order to broaden the appeal of scientific endeavours to the inhabitants of Ottawa. As a result of these activities, the *Transactions* of the ONHS could proclaim: "Science is no longer a lifeless abstraction floating above the head of the multitude. It has descended to earth and mingles with men."[53]

The MNHS directors' insistence on referring to the society as a popular institution continued into the 1870s, as the society remained committed to the popular Sommerville lectures and to its *conversaziones*. In the annual report in 1868, President Abraham de Sola made an appeal for increased membership, as he remarked that the MNHS represented all classes within the larger liberal community: "[None should] hesitate to join us, because he may be diffident as to his qualifications to do so. In addition to moral and mental culture, we insist on no other qualifications for membership than a love for knowledge and sincere desire for its advancement. We believe that eminent scientific acquirements are not necessary in every case to make one a useful member of the society, and that though an individual may not have means or leisure for original investigations, he may yet render himself serviceable in many ways to the cause."[54] The MNHS therefore encouraged members to abandon technical jargon during the course of regular meetings in order to make them more accessible to the layman. The value of the Sommerville lectures to the community was incalculable, given the "feast of popularized science, without reference to age, sex, social position or any other distinction." *Conversaziones* would also allow all members of the community to experience the joys of science, bringing them together in sociability and friendly co-operation. To Sir William Dawson, the *conversaziones* were "a great way of popularizing science in the city ... the programme of the conversazione is most alluring, and as all its promoters express their intention of avoiding dry details in explanation, the pill of science will be successfully sugar-coated."[55]

Despite this lofty discourse of liberal inclusion, the professional middle *classes* became even more entrenched in scientific and literary societies. In a history of the LHSQ written in 1874, D.R. Macleod recognized that while the Society attracted men of a great variety of occupations, they by and large came from the professional classes. Contributors to the *Transactions* included "members of high classical attainments, its votaries of science, its travellers, and its lovers of historical research, its antiquitarians, and its lovers of fine arts, its financiers, and its statisticians, its pioneers and its navigators, the church and the ladies, the army and navy, the bench and the bar, statesmen and scholars, the chemist, the surveyor, bankers and merchants, the civil service and the press, MD's and LLD's, and BA's and MA's." The profusion of professionals was also reflected in the ideology of these societies, as noted in a letter from American W. Leconte Stevens to prominent MNHS director T. Sterry Hunt. As one of the "experts" in scientific culture, Stevens regretted the lowering standards of the American Scientific Association, as there was an "aristocracy of brains and personal culture, the exclusiveness of which is based on its inherent nature."[56] No longer content to simply negotiate their own space, the professional middle classes began to revel in their position of cultural authority in scientific and literary associations.

Even though the executive of the MNHS was at the forefront of science popularization, it remained conscious of promoting the association as a centre of original scientific research executed by competent and expert scientists. Recognizing the gap between the amateur and the professional, the *Canadian Record of Science* – the official periodical of the MNHS – in 1890 reprinted an article by the president of the AAAS, T.C. Mendenhall, entitled "Relations of men of Science to the General Public." Mendenhall deplored the turbulent relationship between men of science and the general public: "[This relationship] is not what it should be in the best interests of either. In assemblages of the former, it is common to hear complaints of a lack of appreciation, and proper support on the part of the latter, from whom in turn, occasionally comes with expressions of indifference, now and then tinctured with contempt for men who devote their lives and energies to study and research, the results of which cannot always be readily converted into real estate or other forms of taxable property."[57] To MNHS luminaries like Sir William Dawson, the society cultivated high culture and a "healthy scientific tone," avoiding the temptation to delve into sensational science as practised by charlatans. Although Dawson highlighted the popularization of science in the MNHS, his appreciation for the "expert" exploration of the more professional members of the Society was clear: "I would not underrate what we have accomplished for the popular diffusion of knowledge, by means of our museum, our excursions and popular lectures, but the original investigations which we have given to the world constitute our best claims and title to regard as a scientific association."[58]

The Canadian Institute also resisted an increasing concentration on utilitarian science, as it began to focus more exclusively on professional scientific applications. In accomplishing this task, the Canadian Institute as early as 1863 began to delegate its overall work into different sections: a strong medical section, an architectural section, and others such as geology and mining. In 1869, when a Bill came before the Ontario legislature for a Medical Act that would place homeopaths and eclectics on the same footing as licensed medical practitioners, the professional elements in the Canadian Institute's medical section sprang into action. Calling the bill "degrading to the profession," the section launched a formal protest to the government in the name of their profession: "We as a *liberal profession* [are] unwilling to violate our clearly defended principles by associating with any sect holding views and theories we consider to be absurd and false." While the action of the Canadian Institute's medical section did not obstruct the passage of the Bill, it did contribute to the eventual merger of the eclectics with the regular medical board by 1874.[59] The increasingly "authoritative" voice of the Canadian Institute's various sections emboldened other members of the Institute to emphasize the scientific aspect of the Institute's work. To such luminaries, the Canadian Institute functioned as a learned society, not as an association for the mere dissemination of knowledge. As Arthur Harvey, the noted statistician, author, and president of the Canadian Institute stated: "[The Institute's] prosperity was not to be advanced by courting popularity ... the Institute of the future should have nothing to do with anything but the consideration and discussion of the subjects which were brought before it. It was on these lines that other important and valuable societies worked."[60]

As a result of such pronouncements, the Canadian Institute became rather ambivalent about the possibilities of popularized science. Unlike the MNHS, the directors of the Canadian Institute remained wary of the amateur members of the Institute, and their leanings toward utilitarian science. James Loudon, a mathematics professor and president of the Institute in the 1870s, lamented the mid-century utilitarian age with its concentration on the commercial applications of science, and called for more altruistic *and* expert scientific explorations. However, Loudon's vision of popular science included only the cultivated classes of the community in the Institute's lectures. "The sympathy of such men is not without value to us; moreover, amongst them are to be found many of high culture and great influence who are particularly fitted to discuss philosophical questions of great interest." And yet in regard to the Institute's popular lectures, the guidance from the Canadian Institute included stipulations that "they should not be popular in the same sense alluded to previously of conforming to the supposed popular taste for the sensational and the trifling to the exclusion of the useful and solid."[61] Edward Meek, a well-known lawyer and author of several books on Canadian law, went even further in his essay to the Canadian Institute on the Canadian parliamentary system. He opined that not all classes, persons, societies, or interests needed to have representation in the government system, as the objects of government were "to give the greatest power and influence to the most intelligent, the most progressive, the most industrious, the most enterprising and the best elements in the community." Clearly Meek envisioned an aristocracy of brains and intellect, a society run by professionals and experts, which would banish the amateur to the sidelines not only in such associations as the Canadian Institute but in Canadian society as a whole.[62]

Although the prominence of utilitarian science did in fact gradually diminish in scientific societies, the importance of practicality in science did linger. In a lecture to the Ottawa Field-Naturalists' Society, Macoun lauded the "practical good" that arose from scientific exploration, in a thinly veiled advertisement for the Geological Survey. The president of the Literary and Scientific Society of Ottawa, H.B. Small, followed up this lecture with a paper on Hugh Miller – the "workingman's scientist" – in an attempt to illustrate that many of nature's mysteries could be discovered "amidst the hard struggle of a laborious life." Similarly, in 1884, the executive of the Canadian Institute insisted that its mission included the promotion of utilitarian science to benefit the entire liberal community: "Nowadays, each new discovery is at once communicated in clear and precise language, not only to those whose training has fitted them to understand the technicalities of science, but also so far as possible to the general public ... No sooner has a new truth been discovered or a new law been established than a hundred acute minds are ready to seize upon it and turn it into practical utility – discovery and invention go hand in hand, and the door of the laboratory opens into the workshop."[63] Despite Small's adultation of Hugh Miller, he also recognized that exploration in practical science required experts and professional scientists: "We are too apt to confine ourselves to matters of importance of today, without regard to their bearing on the future, when their commercial bearing may be most marked. The scientific result of specialists should be discussed by men of general knowledge or science, before they can become available to all." Even as the Canadian Institute directors approved the relationship between invention and discovery, they also warned Institute members to beware the scientific pretender with his useless wares, and a reliance solely on practical science.[64]

The elite professional middle classes were similarly represented in the Royal Society, an organization dedicated to literary and scientific scholarship, and the intellectual achievement of eminent Canadians. Founded by the Governor-General Marquis of Lorne in 1882, the Royal Society of Canada would, in Lorne's opinion, promote a sense of academic emulation among Canadian scholars and *litterati* and would exhort them towards enhanced intellectual development. As Carl Berger discovered, this mandate ensured that the original membership of the Royal Society would consist mostly of professional academics, clergymen, civil servants, and journalists.[65] What makes the Royal Society so unique in this study of voluntary associations is its unabashed *illiberal* exclusivity and restricted membership. All Royal Society fellows elected were men of scholarly distinction, and limiting the number of fellows to twenty in each of the four sections of the Society assured that only the most distinguished intellectuals became members. The electoral procedures for Royal Society fellows indeed would smack of professional elitism and selectivity, and the directors did not shy away from acknowledging this fact. T. Sterry Hunt, a professor in the sciences at McGill and a prominent member of the MNHS, reinforced this new stance in his address to the Royal Society in 1882: "[The] world's intellectual workers are, from the very nature of their lives of thought and study, separated in some degree from the mass of mankind. They feel, however, not less than others the need of human sympathy and co-operation, and out of this need have grown academies and learned societies devoted to the cultivation of letters and science."[66]

As the antithesis to other Canadian "voluntary" associations, the more judicious and selective Royal Society of Canada did have a sizeable number of detractors and critics. Its most vocal critic, the noted liberal Goldwin Smith, accused the Royal Society of nepotism, cliquishness, and ignoring popular opinion, charging that its exclusivity "repelled the spirit of Canadian society." The exposure of the Royal Society as an elite group of academics and other professionals put its directors on the defensive, and they attempted to shield themselves from such attacks on their election procedures through the employment of the liberal community ethos. Sir

William Dawson recognized that the Royal Society embraced "selected and representative" intellectuals, adding that without this selectivity the Society would be "a great and popular assemblage whose members would be characterized by mere receptivity than by productiveness. In this sense it must be exclusive in membership, but inclusive in that it offers its benefits to all."[67] By way of offering the benefits of the Royal Society to the larger community, the directors invited selected delegates from other scientific and literary societies across Canada to its annual meetings. Despite numerous charges of elitism and favouritism, many associations reacted positively to invitations from the Royal Society. H.H. Lyman, president of the Montreal branch of the Ontario Entomological Society, spoke of the "honour of being elected as a delegate and attend[ing] the meeting of that distinguished body." As John Bourinot, the secretary of the Royal Society stated, while the Royal Society was not a literary or scientific "picnic" available to all, it was "aristocratic in the sense that there are certain men and women who have won fame and stand on a pedestal above their fellows, but it is the world, not of a class, but of all ranks and conditions, that has agreed to place them on that pedestal as a tribute to their genius which has made people happier, wiser and better."[68]

The rather contradictory nature of the exclusive/inclusive paradigm in the Royal Society of Canada reached a peak with the meeting of the Royal Society in Montreal in 1891. Organizers of the meeting worked actively to secure the co-operation of the larger community in the successful conclusion of the meeting. For example, all the citizens of Montreal were invited to the garden parties arranged around the event, and as a special incentive to the common branch, "all persons interested in science and literature may become associates for the meeting."[69] And yet the elitist nature of the Royal Society's Montreal meeting also crept into the local committee's preparation, as they planned to "extend to the distinguished literary and scientific men who will then visit ... a reception ... worthy of the eminent position occupied by that body." Many of the replies sent by other learned associations such as the Ottawa Literary and Scientific Society lauded the intellectual feast "among Gentlemen eminent in art, science and literature" while confirming their own attendance at the meeting. Subtle reservations about the elitism of the Royal Society emerged, however, in the refusal of some citizens to support the meeting. Warren King, the owner of a foundry in Montreal declined the offer of the citizens' committee to assist in preparations for the Royal Society, as "other objects which I am interested in occupy my time very fully." And Lyman, a former delegate at the Royal Society's annual meetings, had his doubts about the usefulness of the visit: "The smallness of the attendance of members of that Society at their meetings, hardly ever exceeding forty, I think the Montreal Natural History Society has very magnificent ideas to think of squandering any such sum as $10,000 upon the meeting."[70]

INCREASED ROLES FOR WOMEN IN SCIENCE AND LITERATURE

By the end of the century, scientific and literary societies appeared to follow societal trends in Canada by actively recruiting women and assigning more roles to them. In reality, these associations were simply catching up to Britain, where women's participation in life sciences such as botany, anatomy, and entomology was exploited. In Britain, the enlistment of women to the cause of scientific advancement and the appreciation of literature illustrates that the forces of scientific popularization did not shy away from crossing gender boundaries. But in central Canada, the situation was quite different; a noted scientific association such as the MNHS could postpone having women as active members until as late as 1867.[71] However, by the final years of the century, scientific and literary societies had begun to harness the potential contribution of female members to their associations. Daniel Wilson, the president of the Canadian Institute, gave a lecture in 1869 regarding women in higher education, concluding that once prejudice was eliminated, women would be included in the higher halls of academe. Women were particularly given a warm reception in rural scientific societies such as the Guelph Scientific Society, where they outnumbered the men nearly two to one by 1889. This circumstance no doubt occurred as a result of slashing the membership fees for women in half, merging the Society's interests with the Women's Literary Association, and encouraging women to attend their excursions, lectures, and collecting trips around the Guelph area.[72]

The expanded role of women engendered some discord in these organizations, however, as the increased visibility of female members clashed with a continued ideology of domesticity. In the ONHS, not only did women attend excursions, *conversaziones,* and lectures but by 1881 a female member of the Society, Miss Harman, taught botany to a class filled with other young women. In 1888 Macoun, the president of the ONHS, led a discussion on the "eligibility of ladies as officers," and decided in March of 1890 that three ladies would be nominated as members of the Executive Council of the Club. This led to the election of the first woman vice president of the ONHS in 1892, although wrangling over female officers appears to have taken its toll, as a Miss Mills refused to take up the appointment.[73] Even though female members of the ONHS managed to enter the corridors of power, they were unmistakably relegated to the popular aspects of science, rather than the "professional" scientific endeavours. In an 1890 editorial of the *Ottawa Naturalist*, the editors welcomed the new female officers, as they wanted to make the excursions and other proceedings of the society "more agreeable to this most important part of our membership." However, in the same paragraph they added: "It has always been understood that our club, while working hard at scientific development, at the same time wishes to be recognized primarily as an institution for teaching, popularising and making attractive the by-ways of knowledge." Similarly, in 1894 the *Ottawa Naturalist* printed an article entitled "Popular vs. Scientific Ornithology," by Mrs Miller, an amateur bird-watcher. When a devoted reader wrote to the journal pleading that Miller place some of her more important discoveries in "an accredited scientific journal," she demurred, claiming that she had no bent toward serious scientific exploration.[74]

While the MNHS prided itself on its modern approach and openness to women members in 1867, they made the change only after the ladies' decorating committee had done "such a fine job" at an annual *coversazione*. The Ottawa Camera Club elected a woman vice president and secretary in 1894, while Miss Mather, an amateur photographer, continually took home the top prizes for photography in the annual shows. And yet its counterpart in Toronto, the Toronto Camera Club, only permitted women members to join in 1895, stating: "It is hoped that now this regulation is passed a large number of ladies will apply for membership." While women were originally allowed to vote and hold office in the Toronto Camera Club, this privilege was soon taken away by the fairly reactionary executive council, and the annual report in 1896 reported – unsurprisingly – that only three women joined the club that year.[75] Because of their limited membership base, rural scientific and literary societies in particular augmented roles for women within their associations. The Hampden Literary and Scientific Society allowed women to lead their debates, while the Guelph Scientific Society not only permitted women to hold official positions, but also invited several women to give scientific papers to the society. Although one presenter, Miss Vale, appeared to be quite shy in actually reading her papers to the society, she was often elected to the executive council and she also held the singular honour of being selected the first honorary member of the Guelph Scientific Society. Despite women's majority presence in Guelph, dominating scientists from the Experimental Farm continued to expect the "sisters" to provide refreshments and collection interludes for popular science, rather than encouraging them to explore professional natural science. For example, the directors unceremoniously dropped Miss Henderson's series of lectures to the Guelph Scientific Society in 1890 on the "science" of phrenology. More than likely a previous lecture some months before by the professional "Dr." Lett on the lack of correlation between the shape of a man's skull and his intellect had defused the enthusiasm for such amateur "quackery" as phrenology in the society.[76]

"ALL SHADES OF OPINION": POLITICS AND RELIGION IN LATE-CENTURY LEARNED SOCIETIES

Scientific and literary associations such as the MNHS and the ONHS continued to preserve strictures and bylaws against sectarianism and political partyism, in order to maintain a sense of decorum and minimize discord in their societies. The Jewish rabbi and president of the MNHS, Abraham de Sola, extolled the advantages of eliminating sectarian strife and political agitation within the society, as the directors "loved science for its sake alone." When George Wardwell of Buffalo asked for information on Canada from the ONHS, "especially such as may bear on the question of its annexation to the United States," the directors sent a book on the mineral resources of the Dominion with the disclaimer that other matters did not come within the province of the club. The Perth Literary and Debating Society barred religious discussions and the use of quotations from the Bible, while the Fortnightly Club in Peterborough forbade questions on denominational theology and Canadian party politics.[77] As D.R. Macleod observed in his history of the LHSQ: "As all religious discussion is excluded, the conservative Catholic, and the liberal Dissenter, the English Episcopalian and the Scotch Presbyterian, alike help to swell the *Republican* role of the Society's associate members." Similarly, Louis Turcotte on the twenty-seventh anniversary of the *Institut Canadien* in Quebec commended the *Institut* for its availability to the entire politico-religious community: "It is neither a political club nor a gathering of the chosen few. On the contrary, it is open to all respectable persons, without regard to their politics or social status."[78]

Despite being proponents of unity through the elimination of political and religious discussions, literary and scientific associations nevertheless did immerse themselves in the political and religious culture of central Canada. Of course, the most extreme example of the politicization of literary societies came in the case of the *Institut Canadien* of Montreal. The *Institut's* sympathy for *Rouge* liberal doctrines merely exaggerated religious and political conflict in Quebec, as the directors of the *Institut* continued to adhere to the anticlerical and adversarial doctrines of L.A. Dessaules and Henry Lacroix. As an "armée de penseurs," the *Institut* continually battled "fanatic and religiously intolerant" ultramontane Roman Catholics in their attempts to sever what they saw as an intolerable alliance of Church and State.[79] In 1869 the political and religious struggles between the *Institut Canadien* and the ultramontane Bishop Bourget intensified when the Catholic clergy denied Joseph Guibord, a faithful member of the *Institut*, burial in a consecrated cemetery. This incident touched off a series of legal, constitutional, and sectarian disputes as the *Institut* pleaded its case for Guibord's burial all the way to the Privy Council. Despite its victory in the courts, the *Institut Canadien* never recovered its momentum among Montreal's French-Canadian professionals, particularly after the noted English Protestant John Dougall used the Guibord affair to utterly condemn the Roman Catholic Church. The complete politicization of the *Institut* during the Guibord affair turned moderate Liberals away from the organization, while exposing the *Institut* to characterization as a mere political lobby group, rather than a literary society of renown. Repositioning the *Institut Canadien* away from its original mandate clearly amplified the irrelevancy of the *Institut* by the late 1870s.[80]

The *Institut Canadien* of Quebec managed to avoid the political and sectarian struggles of the Montreal chapter. Louis Turcotte boasted of the Roman Catholic clerical connections of the Quebec *Institut*, and how they managed to maintain excellent relations with the clergy throughout their history. However, camaraderie with local Catholic clergy did not come without a price, as by the 1880s the clergy appeared to occupy full-time lecture seats of the *Institut Canadien* in Quebec. Not only did members have the opportunity to hear a discourse on "L'église, le progrès, et la civilisation" by abbé Begin but they also endured a lecture by Archbishop Taschereau on how the literature placed on the index of forbidden books was simply an example of how the Church looked after its own, as a mother to her children.[81] The presence of Roman Catholic clergymen did not encumber political discussion in the Quebec *Institut Canadien*, as Hector Fabre, a Quebec lawyer and moderate Liberal politician, would find out in 1871. In a lecture entitled "Confédération, Indépendence, Annexion," Fabre outlined the various struggles French Canadians endured for their national rights, language, and culture. He condemned Confederation as merely a political ploy to benefit Ontario economically and denounced Quebec independence as a pipe dream, advocating commercial union with the United States as the only hope for the province of Quebec. Camouflaging this rather *Rouge*-like doctrine under the banner of economic prosperity for all Québéçois, Fabre argued that since nearly half a million French-Canadians had already emigrated to the United States, catching up to their economic successes required commercial union.[82]

English Canadian literary and scientific associations also began to scrutinize the political culture of the surrounding community. Leigh Gregor, a professor of languages at McGill University, delivered a lecture to the LHSQ on the "new Canadian patriotism." Like Fabre, in his lecture to the *Institut Canadien* of Quebec, Gregor simply ignored the protocols on avoiding political discussions and presented the LHSQ with an oration on the need for an enhanced imperial federation. The Montreal Parliamentary Debating Society was established in 1884 simply to expand the influence of the Montreal Free Trade Club, and debates on Canadian party politics were the order of the day. Organizing a mock Parliament with representation from the major political parties, the Society discussed such matters as Commercial Union, customs tariffs, the Senate, votes for women, and other political questions of relevance.[83] Led by the venerable Sandford Fleming, the Canadian Institute in 1893 invited the general public to submit essays to a contest on how best to rectify Canadian politics and the Parliamentary system. Mindful that such a contest would have to follow the guidelines of the Institute's neutrality in political affairs, Fleming argued: "While non-political in its corporate character, [the Institute] is representative through its members of all shades of opinion. The object expressed was to awaken an interest in a difficult problem, which vitally concerns the whole community, in the hope that some practical and beneficial solution may be obtained." Fleming's vexation with the entire Canadian Parliamentary system came from his concern that ordinary Canadian citizens could not find adequate representation or accountability from the current political parties. Fleming feared that Canadian politics did not represent the entire community, a theme that he touched on during his presidential address to the Royal Society in 1890.[84]

The essay submissions indicate Canadians' growing fascination with the doctrines of populism, a movement that espoused politics for the people, the destruction of the party system of politics, and more accountability from elected leaders. Imitating populist discourse, Fleming blamed the ills of the Canadian political organization on the liberal party system, an evil, he said, that led to divisiveness and factionalism, while ignoring policies for the greatest public good. To Fleming, Canadian party politics, and Parliament in particular, was simply not responsive or representative of Canadians, and thus the Institute offered a thousand dollars to the essayist who found "the best workable measure, which if made law, would give the whole Canadian people equal representation in Parliament and each elector, due weight in Government through Parliament."[85] Many of the essays picked up on this theme, offering populist critiques of the party system and the entire political process. One essayist claimed in populist language that the people of Canada were the origin and source of all political power and authority, and that regrettably too many citizens – including women – were left "without any voice in state affairs, [a situation that] exercises an undesirable influence and constitutes a grave political injustice to the great bulk of the community." The author of the essay "New Occasions Teach New Duties" offered the panacea of referenda as a means of obliterating politicians who placed party above the nation. The author of "Southern Cross" counselled Canadian voters to elect only those individuals who considered what was best for the community as a whole, and who, by "calling on men to co-operate rather than to fight for mastery and spoils" could lead the people to "rectify Parliament and to purify politics."[86]

Upon closer inspection, Fleming's concerns and many of the essays collected by the Canadian Institute both reflected Canadian intellectuals' quest for a new social science and an appreciation for the doctrines of corporatism, rather than upholding the tenets of populism. The new study of political economy and social science at universities like Queen's and Toronto, social Christianity, and the new vision of the state held by Ottawa's civil service intellectuals appeared to have greatly influenced the essay competition at the Canadian Institute.[87] Some essays in the compilation favoured corporatism as the means to achieve greater representation, and Fleming himself went even further, recommending that the removal of the party system would bring about the positivist state. Instead of "successive faction fights and interminable struggles," politicians and the civil service would be forced into "generous efforts to determine who would accomplish the greatest public good." The noted lawyer Edward Meek and the University of Toronto political economist William Ashley took umbrage at Fleming's critique of the party system in the name of the emerging corporate state. They both disputed Fleming's claim that the party structure in Parliament was not representative of the people, contending that political parties prevented stagnation, educated the voter, and eliminated despotism. Echoing Fleming's desire for the positive state, Meek stated that "a good government is one which not only preserves order in the community but which develops, promotes and stimulates industry, invention, progress, intelligence – in short, a higher civilization." The further unmasking of the Canadian Institute's contest as a political exercise rather than a populist one came in the judging aspect, as the essays were adjudicated "by a tribunal composed of men of the highest standing in their several spheres, comprising persons learned in political science, law and practical politics."[88]

A comparable situation arose in the learned halls of the Fortnightly Club, a debating and literary society in Peterborough, Ontario. Given the titles of some of the papers presented before the club, the Fortnightly Club was evidently a hotbed of small-town populist radicalism, as the members listened to presentations on Christian Socialism, the life of John Ruskin, Censorship in the Press, Social Evolution, and the Phases of Modern Thought. In a speech to the club on the progress of Canada, one author described the levelling effect of populist doctrines, for a feature of the modern age was the "education and the intelligence of the so-called WORKINGMAN." This author also preached the necessity for a populist vision of the *inter*dependence of classes: "We all need to produce a unity and fraternity of sentiment amongst ALL CLASSES OF THE COMMUNITY that shall rise above the discord of conflicting interests and unequal culture, and hold us all together in the recognition of the truth that we are all, in the performance of our duty, working for the common good, the man who breaks stones for the road as well as the Mayor of the Town."[89] The club also delved into social Christianity, as the Reverend Herbert Symonds, a rector of the Church of England in Peterborough, offered a paper on Thomas Carlyle that criticized religion as being unresponsive to the needs of the workers. Utilizing populist discourse, Symonds and others insisted that the problem of religion and the workingman rested with religious institutions: "Churches have hitherto tended to follow the line of least resistance, and to grow into societies for the demarcation and the consecration of class. The more they have done so, the more distasteful they have become to the workingman. The master who goes to worship where only other masters are, does his best to alienate himself from his people, to lower religion in their eyes, and to bring on the SOCIAL REVOLUTION, for the only salt that can preserve society is sympathy and communion in the most serious things of the spirit between all classes."[90]

Despite this rather populist-sounding discourse, many members of the Fortnightly Club held similar outlooks as other learned societies in their vision of social investigations, social science, and the function of the corporate state. In a discussion regarding the book *Merrie England* by Robert Blatchford, which favoured the co-operative system, some members of the Fortnightly Club acknowledged that humans were not independent beings but that the "individual must be subordinated to society." Citing examples such as roads, the police, and schools as state-run institutions that benefited entire communities, these club members saw society as a corporate body "of which every part must do its duty in order that its life may be what it should be ... The spirit of the age would teach us to live, not for ourselves, but for the good of all."[91] Similarly, Symonds' paper on social Christianity was at once an advertisement for the social gospel *and* a critique of Christian sociology for neglecting the spiritual needs of the whole community:

> Someone once drew a distinction between religiousness and religiosity. The former is a strong faith and reverence, which permeates all life, the latter is kind of a fussy interest in sermons and services, in clubs and societies, without any regard for the weightier matters of the law ... The church should in the very process of fulfilling her duty do two things; first, teach men of all classes to be in the highest sense religious men in all their offices, trades and relations; and secondly, bring men of all classes together as men, and make them know each other, and look at his own questions with the others' eyes.

The social composition of the learned Fortnightly Club's executive also revealed a decided lack of enthusiasm for populist thought, as Cortez Fessenden, president and an educator and Conservative politician, Symonds, vice-president and rector of the Church of England, and James Hall, the secretary and local sheriff, all would have tended to uphold the small-town liberal social order rather than question it with the ideology of populism.[92]

HONEST INDUSTRY, POPULISM, AND THE NEW POLITICAL ECONOMY

Literary and scientific societies also had a fascination for the science of political economy, particularly the liberal gospel of honest industry and the ideology of producerism. Many speeches to the *Institut Canadien* in Ottawa reinforced a middle-class emphasis on liberal respectability and the importance of the work ethic to effect occupational mobility. Both P.J.O. Chauveau, the famous Quebec politician and educator, and Alphonse Benoît, president of the Ottawa *Institut,* offered lectures on the significance of moral and intellectual improvement in relation to material success. Joseph Tassé, a classically educated journalist who assisted the passage of the Royal Society's bill of incorporation in the House of Commons, spoke to the *Institut Canadien* in Ottawa on the subject of "Cercles des Familles." Tassé encouraged the entire *Institut* family to work tirelessly for their own success, as "what makes great men produces great things."[93] As with the *Institut Canadien* in Montreal, the library of the *Institut* in Quebec was filled with books on political economy for the *Institut*'s discerning readership. Although the Quebec *Institut* did not incur the wrath of the Roman Catholic Church like its counterpart in Montreal, Quebec members undoubtedly favoured a similar economically liberal policy of free trade. Books by notorious free traders such as Leon Say, Frédéric Bastiat, Michel Chevalier, John Stuart Mill and Adam Smith dominated the political economy section of the *Institut* library.[94]

Late nineteenth-century literary and scientific societies also delved into new theories of political economy, particularly those dealing with social Christianity and welfare reform. The discussion of these doctrines was often highly eclectic, given the motley collection of labour reformers, Christian socialists, and the followers of Henry George's single tax who were granted a platform for their ideas. While not ideologically consistent, many of the philosophies espoused by these reformers concluded that Canada's basic social structure was fundamentally flawed.[95] Even a learned society such as the Canadian Institute debated the merits of George's land policies and other points of this "new" political economy. William Houston, a former journalist for George Brown's *Globe* and Ontario's parliamentary librarian, delivered a paper on George's *Progress and Poverty*. Houston initially found much to praise in George's work, yet concluded that George's greatest error was to head a movement back to the land, as this simply could not function in an increasingly "complex industrial community." Perhaps more significantly, the Canadian Institute invited W.A. Douglas, an ardent Georgite and single-tax advocate, to give a series of lectures on political economy at the Institute. Douglas presented two papers on George's philosophy: "Land and Labour" – obviously on George's land tax scheme – and a paper on "The Distribution of Wealth," a discussion of the single tax. Douglas also criticized John Stuart Mill's theory of wages, claiming in Georgite discourse that the labourer and capitalist were mutually dependent and worked concurrently to produce wealth, and thus should divide equally the fruits of their labour.[96]

Upon closer inspection, the professional composition of learned societies such as the Canadian Institute tended to disparage advocates of George's philosophy, harking back to more "accepted" class, social, and economic relations in liberal society. Edward Miall, a prominent civil servant, delivered a lecture to the Ottawa Literary and Scientific Society in which he argued that the classification of society was fairly simple and based on the liberal producer ideology: "[It] always has been, and always will be composed of various classes, and these may be massed under three distinctive heads, capitalists and labourers and those who are partly both." The political economy of corporatism also reared its head in the Canadian Institute, as Houston presented a paper on the "Genesis of Capital," in which he maintained that the trickle-down effect of capitalism benefited society as a whole. However, Houston also argued that large-scale capitalists should be assessed a monopoly tax and a succession tax, to return some of their funds back to the larger community.[97] The responses of Canadian Institute members to Douglas's lectures on George's doctrines are also informative in illustrating literary and scientific associations' confidence in "conventional" political economy. George Murray, a barrister and poet, contended with Douglas over his theory on wages, stating unequivocally that capital and labour regulated themselves, while wages "must be a free agreement between employer and employee." Alexander Marling, a lawyer and deputy director in Ontario's Department of Education, disputed Douglas's claims that the single tax would produce wealth, as "he did not see any objection to men like Vanderbilt accumulating wealth. He [Marling] thought they were an acquisition to the country."[98]

Perhaps it would be instructive to give the last word to Douglas himself, for despite his support for George's single tax principles, he also bought into the more liberal labour theory of value, and the principle of honest industry. In "Land and Labour," where he discussed George's land policies, Douglas condemned the practice of urban land speculation in the name of honest industry: "Instead of taking revenue from the rewards of idleness, we are now doing everything in our power to diminish the reward of labour." Although Douglas worshipped George as an individual who brought "humanity a Christian science of political economy," that Christian science required a hearty Protestant work ethic. As Douglas explained: "Nature is a coy maiden, and will be wooed only by the hand of industry. Idleness she abhors as she abhors a vacuum, and the idler she punishes with weeds, poverty and death. Man's tenure on this planet depends on his industry; nature knows no compromise; her decree is short, sharp and decisive; toil or death. The first of nature's laws is producer to the producer only." Although Douglas's discourse censured the parasitical landlord and his drones in the name of the community of producers, it was not entirely dissimilar to the dialogue of the school of Manchester liberalism of such luminaries as Goldwin Smith.[99]

Controversies over the "new" political economy did not escape small-town learned societies such as the Peterborough Fortnightly Club. They actively discussed such topics as the eight-hour day, Chinese labour, the

Knights of Labor, Christian socialism, and the theory of co-operation during their meetings. As noted, much of their discourse was indeed somewhat radical, as they approved in principle of any doctrine that worked for the "amelioration of the social relations existing between the different sections of the community, and especially between capital and labour, master and man." Symonds's paper on Christian socialism purported to solve society's malfunction through social investigations, as social discontent was rampant among the social classes through injustice in the economic system.[100] And yet members of the Fortnightly Club were hesitant to accept more revolutionary economic doctrines if they contravened traditional conventions of liberal honest industry. One member of the Club critiqued the co-operative system in a review of Blatchford's *Merrie England*, where he stated his concerns with socialism in general: "The ideal man is he who stands upon a free soil himself free, not merely as a citizen, but free to make full use of the natural opportunities before him ... if however, distinctions are to be made and degrees of labour or of reward are to be created we shall then be in as bad a position as ever for the man who can do most will receive most, and the lazy man and the loafer will suffer just as they do at the present time." Another member of the Fortnightly Club agreed with this assessment, and stated his preference for a political economy that was completely utilitarian, one that would ensure the greatest good for the greatest number. From this member's viewpoint, studying the social questions of the day would be the only antidote, as the poor would always see the rich as greedy and avaricious, while the rich would likewise consider the poor as simply lazy and shiftless.[101]

POPULAR SCIENCE AND LITERATURE IN AN INFORMAL SETTING: RECREATION IN LEARNED SOCIETIES

Literary and scientific associations in the late century retained their enthusiasm for leisure activities as a continued means of bringing science and literature to the entire community. Their ideology of entertainment continued to be the promotion of popular science and literature in less imposing social settings. Despite their various responsibilities at McGill University and the MNHS, both Sir William Dawson and T. Sterry Hunt used their role as members of the MNHS Conversazione Committee, to ensure that the *conversaziones* kept their "popular, scientific and social character." Along with the museum and the Sommerville lectures, Dawson maintained, such activities would bring the entire community together: "One of the functions of the society was to bring together in friendly co-operation all who were cultivating any branch of science and all those who took interest in such work."[102] Scientific and literary societies also tried to preserve the sanctity of rational recreation, by providing entertainment that would prove instructive as well as enjoyable to the larger community. In advertising a series of popular lectures, the directors of the Ottawa Literary and Scientific Society declared that sociability in turn produced a love of learning among its members: "That social element, the attrition of thought and intellect by intercourse among the members, requires fostering, for neither the library nor the reading room affords such opportunity. Thinking men without some social tie are starved intellectually."[103]

Both the ONHS and the MNHS offered annual soirées, *conversaziones*, field days, and excursions as means of providing social connections for members as well as opportunities for improving their knowledge of natural science. Both scientific institutions recognized that rational recreation simply was not enough to sustain the interest of their members and the general public. Correspondingly, the ONHS included oral and instrumental music on its soirée program, and tried to provide specific themes for its *conversaziones*. The Conversazione Committee of the MNHS organized a music and decoration subcommittee to handle the "non-scientific activities" of the annual *conversaziones*, from oral and instrumental music to refreshments. Of course, a significant aspect of the amusement presentations of both the MNHS and the ONHS was their monetary benefit.[104] The *Institut Canadien-Français* in Ottawa also discovered that increased entertainment alternatives meant a rise in membership figures and in financial proceeds. By 1876 *Institut* soirées included music and recitations, and the directors also organized bazaars, theatre productions, and concerts to augment their revenues. In 1893 the *Institut*'s success in raising funds culminated in their building a hall, which fittingly contained billiard rooms for *Institut* members. Scientific societies could also stumble accidentally upon entertainment, as in the case of the Montreal Branch of the Ontario Entomological Society. Although the society organized several excursions to collect insects in the Montreal environs, they discovered that "healthful and innocent recreation" could follow them to their meetings, where the president "very kindly refreshed the members with a cup of excellent coffee and cakes, with which finished up one the most agreeable and interesting meetings we have had yet."[105]

Even more so than their urban counterparts, rural associations needed entertainment and leisure to sustain the interests of their rather limited membership base. The Guelph Scientific Society decided to liven up its scientific presentations and papers with sundry social events, when the directors noted that competition for members was acute in Guelph, with "numerous attractions elsewhere." The Guelph Scientific Society therefore organized excursions to Elora and Puslinch to collect natural history specimens, and established a "question drawer" of interesting scientific queries for the learned men of science in the society. Unquestionably the members of the Guelph Scientific Society understood the differences between scientific enquiry and sociability, at the end of the inaugural meeting of the Guelph Botany Club "the meeting then assumed a social character and discussed the refreshments bountifully provided by the ladies for the occasion."[106] Even a non-descript literary society such as "Mrs. Jones' Improvement Class," a youth-oriented debating society in Belleville, appreciated the need for entertainment and leisure activities for its members. A typical program for the class included the reading of essays, recitations, debates, and music, while the teacher, Mrs Jones, offered to provide the class with a free supper when the attendance reached fifty. This small group also used leisure activities to raise funds: "A conversazione was given by the class, in the lecture room of the Church, and was a complete success, both in attendance and in a pecuniary point of view, the programme was well carried out." However, Mrs Jones also harked back to the earlier views of rational recreation, when it was recommended in a later meeting that "the selections for the program be chosen with a view to a little more improvement and a little less amusement."[107]

While many literary and scientific societies expanded their entertainment repertoire, still others felt that providing leisure weakened the "professional" nature of their institutions. Although the directors of the Ottawa Literary and Scientific Society, for example, appeared to sanction the usefulness of the "social element," they also recognized the essential value of scientific lectures: "They represent not so much the popular and entertaining side of the Society's work, as that more technical and *substantial* side, to which special importance has always been attached by those who have had the administration of the Society's affairs at various stages of its history."[108] The eminent members of the professional middle class in the LHSQ rejected any forms of entertainment other than the reading of scientific or historical papers. In 1873, when some members petitioned the executive to purchase a chess board, the opponents of the scheme went to the absurd lengths of getting George Stuart's legal opinion:

> Should the Society pass an order for the introduction of Chess into its rooms, there would be two objections to it; First, that games or amusements were not contemplated by the founders of the Society and do

not fall within the terms of the Charter; and as a natural consequence, Secondly, the application or appropriation of the Rooms of the Society for this purpose, would be a misapplication of property; and should there be added the purchase of tables, chess boards and other conveniences for chess players, there would be a diverting of funds of the Society, from their *legitimate* destination to the purposes of private amusement; either of which objections, I am of the opinion would be well-founded, and therefore the introduction of Chess into the rooms of the Society would be repugnant to, and in violation of the Charter.

Some twenty years later, the former president of the LHSQ, James LeMoine, raised a similar objection when he argued that the inclusion of popular novels in the library of the LHSQ overstepped the original scientific, historical and literary objectives of the Society.[109]

A perfect illustration of this dichotomy between the "professionalization" of leisure and entertainment for amusement's sake can be witnessed in a comparison between the Ottawa Camera Club and its counterpart in Toronto. The Ottawa Camera Club evidently appreciated the importance of entertainment to its members, as they organized not only photographic exhibitions, but also euchre parties and slide interchanges to enhance their meetings. During a photographic exhibition in 1897, the directors invited two women members to provide a piano recital and vocal music, and this led to the decision to have music during all of their meetings. These programs were so successful that only the 1895 exhibition was not a money maker: "[The] annual entertainment was not as financially successful as it otherwise would have been had not the elements set up two counter attractions – the large fire and the great storm."[110] Initially the Toronto Camera Club arranged curling matches and lantern shows as well as photographic excursions and exhibitions for the members and the general public. Apparently singing was also a feature of the club's meetings, as the recording secretary reported: "From a musical standpoint the general verdict was that our Club nightingales could challenge comparison with those of any similar organization." And yet the Toronto Camera Club was far more concerned about its professional image than its counterpart in Ottawa, as they limited their membership to 175 in an attempt to keep the amateurs out. The club also kept a strict regimen for their photographic rooms, asking for a particular member's resignation when they discovered he "abused his privileges" by bringing young women into the rooms late at night. Similarly, in keeping with a more professional society, the executive of the Toronto club "appointed a Dunce Committee, who with the assistance of a thick stick [was]on the trail of those members who habitually leave the club rooms in a state of chaos and desolation after their cyclonic visits." The Toronto Camera Club's insistence on professional decorum comes as no surprise, as they began their existence as the photographic section of the Canadian Institute.[111]

Although many scientific and literary societies continued well into the twentieth century, they had reached the pinnacle of their influence in the Victorian age. With the "rise of professional society," the antiquated scientific and literary voluntary society no longer met the needs of experts from universities, the civil service, and a host of other professional groups.[112] Even though literary and scientific associations for the most part successfully navigated the separation between the professional and the commercial/industrial amateur within their halls of learning, the widening gulf between the two forces proved irreconcilable by the end of the century. The professional middling sort largely managed to eliminate potential conflicts between these various interest groups in learned societies, so as to sustain the dominance of these associations over scientific and literary endeavours until the 1870s.

After Confederation, although the professional classes continued to effectively negotiate their cultural authority over science and literature within these societies and through such bodies as the Royal Society of Canada, this authority would increasingly manifest itself *outside* the learned voluntary association. As a result, while the hegemony of the professional learned classes over scientific and literary affairs remained constant into the twentieth century, their reliance on the learned voluntary society as a cultural vehicle for their ascendancy was arrested sharply by the end of the century.

Conclusion

In the year 1872 the noted liberal demagogue Goldwin Smith delivered lectures on "The Labour Movement" to the Montreal Mechanics' Institute and the Literary Society of Sherbrooke. At the height of the influence of the liberal social order, Smith employed a discourse praising the inclusive nature of the "liberal" community. Much like a sledgehammer being applied to the "props of privilege" of upper-class merchant elites and advocates of the older Tory tradition, Smith hammered home his vision of a society that incorporated all the diverse elements of a successful "liberal" community of interests, free from sectarian and political turmoil:

> Aided by the general awakening of social sentiment and of the feeling of social responsibility, it has practically opened our eyes to the fact that a nation, and humanity at large, is a *community*, the good things of which all are entitled to share, while all must share the evil things. It has forcibly dispelled the notion, in which the rich indolently acquiesced, that enjoyment, leisure, culture, refined affection and high civilization are the destined lot of the few, while the destined lot of the many is to support the privileged existence of the few, by unremitting, coarse and joyless toil. Society has been taught that it must at least endeavour to be just.[1]

As a self-confessed "liberal of the old school," Smith had spent his life in efforts to eliminate "Old Privilege," whether by annihilating the hereditary social orders of the aristocratic elite and the religious elitism of church and state connections, by advocating the political emancipation of the middle classes, or by seeking the termination of mercantile privilege through the medium of free trade. Even as late as 1884, Smith – Canada's unrepentant liberal – continued to embrace the idea of a liberal order, which was by then under assault from more corporate and statist principles. He stated candidly that he looked for "improvement" not in the authority of governments, but in the "same agencies, moral, intellectual and economical, which have brought us thus far": "Unless we have renounced our faith in liberty and its fruits," he said, "we must all hold that the narrower is the range of coercion, the wider that of free action, the better for each man and the community it will be."[2]

In addition to extolling the liberal virtues of political, religious, and class inclusion in his lecture on the labour movement, Smith also recognized that economic liberalism rested on the "firm ground of genuine respectability and solid comfort." The importance of individual honest industry was a recurring theme throughout his lecture to the workmen in the Montreal Mechanics' Institute: "The hardest of all labour is idleness in a world of toil, and the bitterest of all bread is that which is eaten by the sweat of another man's brow." Although conceding that liberal honest industry rested on the foundation of the individual work ethic, Smith claimed that economic power rested in the collective liberal community itself. While he accepted that the *voluntary* association of workmen into unions resulted in the economic emancipation of the working classes by placing them on equal footing with their employers, he noted that the iron laws of political economy dictated that "the *community* purchases their work; and though the master, when hard pressed may, in his desperation, give more for the work than it is worth rather than at once take his capital out of the trade, the community will let the trade go to ruin without compunction rather than give more for the article than it can afford." In Smith's opinion, liberalism improved the very nature of leisure itself, as "leisure well spent is a condition of civilization; and now we want all civilized, not only a few."[3] For us, Smith's lecture highlights the strength of liberal doctrines and principles that were manifest in voluntary associations during the Victorian era, then at its peak.

Some forty-six years later, in 1918, William Lyon Mackenzie King published his *magnum opus* of social planning and industrial relations, which he entitled *Industry and Humanity*. Written at the worst moment of the difficulties foretold by Smith in regard to industrial society, *Industry and Humanity* attempted to explain the dynamics of industrial conflict and to propose solutions for class antagonism. While King's notion of a mutualist "community" was a function of the collective liberal mindset regarding the interdependence of classes and interests, King also strongly believed in the need for regeneration within the community as the essential means for bringing about the "secular" Paradise envisioned in *Industry and Humanity*. "It is the *Community*, organized in various ways, which maintains government and foreign relations, secures law and order, fosters the arts and inventions, aids education, breeds opinion, and promotes, through concession and otherwise, the agencies of transportation, communication, credit, banking and the like, without any production, save the most primitive, would be impossible." Although forged by King's experience as a young activist in Wilfrid Laurier's new Department of Labour, and by his vision of "Christian sociology," *Industry and Humanity* nonetheless hearkened back to the era of interclass benevolence found in the liberal ideology of political, social, religious and class inclusion. To King, the elimination of class enmity and politico-religious distrust was in the realm of possibility: "When ... men look no longer to the passions that divide, but rather to the sympathy that unites, recognize the common sway of like impulses and feelings, of like endeavours and aspirations, then will the way be opened to a better appreciation by each of the many difficulties of the other, and a long stretch be taken on the road that leads to common understanding, mutual forbearance, and peace."[4]

And yet King's *Industry and Humanity* also set out new boundaries for the type of "community" assumed by leading intellectuals and politicians in the twentieth century. Unlike the ideology of community held by nineteenth-century visionaries, who praised voluntarism and activities that crossed between public and private spheres, King's vision of community leaned heavily toward the principles of the corporate state and the governance of the bureaucratic "expert." Indeed, he himself recognized that the individualist liberal order of the previous century had collapsed, noting that in the twentieth century, "the point of view of obligation toward social and industrial conditions shifts from an individualistic attitude to one of collective responsibility, and an organic view of society."[5] While many of King's pronouncements echo statements inherent in the collective liberalism featured in this study, in reality he viewed community more as a corporate construction. In fact, King believed that the community was more than mere class interdependence: "It is not only something more; it is something different. It is, in reality, a separate and distinct entity." As a result, he declared that the *community* was more than the simple sharing of interests between capital and labour; his ideological concept of the community provided for social co-operation and, ultimately, social order and social control. Although King envisioned that the community would use voluntary methods of reason to effect change among differing parties, he also recognized that coercion would be necessary if voluntary alterations in behaviour failed. The power of the corporate state – or the Public might of the Government – would need to be unleashed in circumstances when private rights became public wrongs: "Is not this the principle underlying law and order in all civilized communities? Is it a principle from which communities can depart without inviting anarchy? It cannot be contended that what is a matter of grave concern to the public is a matter of exclusive concern to private parties. There is no right superior to that of the community as a whole."[6] For King, the voluntary "limits of liberalism" would end where the compulsion of the corporate state began.

It comes as no surprise, then, that by the beginning of the twentieth century voluntary associations were very much in a state of flux. Although many Canadians continued to embrace aspects of the "liberal" voluntary movement well into the next century, it was not with the enthusiasm exhibited a few decades before. Mutual benefit and insurance societies like the Oddfellows and the Foresters, as well as temperance associations such as the WCTU and the Dominion Alliance, continued to be extremely popular, and the United Farmers of Ontario and Alberta managed to once again unite the agricultural population into a progressive force by the time of the First World War. However, as if anticipating the coming changes in society, institutions such as Mechanics' Institutes as well as the Dominion Grange, the Patrons of Industry, and the Sons of Temperance, simply disappeared from the landscape. Evidently Canadians were rather circumspect when it came to supporting voluntary associations by the twentieth century, and renewed state involvement in social services and an innovative vision of the corporate state took a toll on what had been a vibrant voluntary association movement. As an added complication, the ideological definition of a liberal "community" changed radically as the intersecting identities of nation, province, and municipality – as well as those of class, gender, and ethnicity – competed for attention from a citizenry divided in its loyalties.

It was the development of corporatism more than any other event that sealed the fate of voluntary associations. To many intellectuals, the divisive nature of class interests, ethnic discord, and progressive socio-economic ideologies created an aura of instability within the body politic that only a reconstituted, functioning, and inclusive nation-state could remedy. Rather than by means of the enlightened amateur social philosopher sermonizing his way into the Athenaeums and lecture halls of voluntary associations, the salvation of an enlightened citizenry would be found through "professional" sociology and governmental social service. A cadre of experienced and enlightened civil servants, university professors, and other intellectuals would replace the inefficiency of voluntarism with social planning, government institutions, and state welfare. Even traditional institutions such as the Christian church and the family could not escape this re-ordering of society, although such groups managed to propose new solutions to social reform by utilizing familiar ideologies and perspectives.[7] Similarly, in distancing themselves from the previous century's ideology of honest industry, self-help, and the producer alliance, more Canadians began to accept increasing government involvement in non-traditional economic spheres. Particularly in the realms of transportation, public utilities, and communications, government-sponsored monopoly and the big business of industrial capitalism began to replace the small producer economy of the previous century. The popular political economy preached in Mechanics' Institutes, mutual benefit societies, and agricultural associations throughout the nation also suffered the indignity of being co-opted by the "modern" intelligentsia. As twentieth-century reformers established chairs of political economy in such institutions as the University of Toronto and Queen's University, a new philosophy of "collectivized liberalism" also found its way into the civil service in Ottawa.[8]

Clearly, to speak of the late nineteenth century as the "age of transition" is no misnomer, as these corporate and statist changes did not arrive unheralded or unforeseen. However, during the formative years of voluntarism, voluntary associations were invaluable not only for the variety of services they offered but also for their role the construction of a viable and at times collective ideology of a liberal "community" that permeated their sphere of influence. On one level, the principles intrinsic to the construction of collective identities within voluntary associations did in fact validate the larger society, and provide some measure of cultural consensus. By fostering an aura of inclusiveness, voluntary associations involved the entire community in their efforts regardless of sectarian origin or political preference. By adhering to the ethic of honest industry and the importance of individual work, voluntary associations often forged a sense of occupational interdependence as they negotiated consent over economic and social issues. Furthermore, in providing leisure activities to their members and communities, voluntary associations displayed a "public spirit" and a sense of camaraderie that brought together diverse social elements within the broader community.

Despite the manifestations of class, ethnic, and gender conflicts that materialized in the late nineteenth century, the larger society remained in many respects remarkably free from widespread expressions of socioeconomic discontent. Even though industrial capitalism had the ability to create rather formidable class cleavages, central Canadian society also managed to build some degree of cultural consensus and hegemony. These phenomena can be explained as the results of continued ideological attempts to build the Canadian "nation" or as perhaps the influence of shared cultural practices and unifying social identities. Central Canadians, although recognizing the socio-cultural complexities of the wider community and the limitations of assumptions based on "monolithic" cultural practices, rituals, and symbols, in some measure shared an implicit series of liberal values, ideologies, and beliefs that intersected through their numerous competing identities.[9] Given the points of divergence between a more collectivist ideology and a developing emphasis on the corporate state, it would be inaccurate to describe these unifying values among voluntary associations as a literal continuation of the "liberal" philosophy of the mid-nineteenth century. And yet the persistent popularity of voluntary associations indicates that these organizations provided mutually satisfying cultural experiences for their various constituencies, despite the growing demarcations of class, ethnic, and gender boundaries.

On a deeper level, however, while many of the principles and doctrines of this liberal community were to some extent cultural assumptions shared among almost all voluntary associations, each standard was highly contested within every conceivable interest group. Due to the proliferation of these organizations in both the urban and the rural environment, the intersection of class, religion, politics, and gender made complete cultural consent over the nature of collective liberal identities simply impossible. While embracing the concept of inclusiveness, voluntary associations could also be highly exclusive, as witnessed in the class discord inherent in agricultural organizations, the "professionalization" of scientific and literary societies, the "selective intolerance" of fraternal orders, and the tensions over gender issues in temperance societies. Debates over the election of "agricultural men" or "temperance men" in the Grange/Patrons of Industry and temperance societies also underscored the political tensions within society, and the interference of evangelical religion in the temperance movement played havoc with pronouncements of sectarian neutrality. Similarly, discussions and debates over the merits of free trade and protectionism, the primacy of agriculture over an emerging manufacturing sector and the advent of a "collectivized political economy" exposed conflicting interpretations of the mantra of honest industry in many voluntary societies. Likewise, disputes over the significance of rational recreation and the importance of bringing "respectable" leisure to the larger community often surfaced in the entertainment activities of these associations.

What this study of voluntary organizations and the subsequent preaching of the ideology of "community" within these societies has suggested is that the limited success of the "liberal" agenda championed by the voluntary association movement during the apogee of the liberal social order from 1830 to 1870 simply could not be sustained by the last three decades of the century. Although politico-religious conflict, the exclusion of women, and ethnic discord rendered the accomplishments of an inclusive liberal ideology in voluntary societies highly debatable and problematic, there is no question that these associations were extremely successful in establishing some measure of cultural consensus and engineering consent to a liberal social order both in burgeoning urban settings and in rural communities. As the boundaries of class, gender, and ethnicity became more inflexible, voluntary associations responded to socio-economic and cultural changes by shifting the contours of the collective liberal "identity" debate. Even though the voluntary association movement contributed in large measure to working-class, agricultural, and middle-class consciousness, it did not greatly affect measures of capitulation to the socio-economic hegemony of industrial capitalism, nor did it radically alter fundamental social, economic, cultural, or political relationships.

And yet voluntary associations managed to introduce what became, in effect, a sense of class *segregation* into late nineteenth-century central Canadian society. By emphasizing an ideology of class awareness, the various manifestations of voluntary associations did in fact contribute to the isolation of various socio-economic interests. Smaller farmers interested in the promotion of a more radical agrarian "identity" would feel at home both in agricultural societies and in the Dominion Grange/Patrons of Industry, while large-scale commercial farmers could also find support for the "liberal" social order in the same agrarian voluntary associations. Similarly, the skilled working classes could remain entrenched in the membership of fraternal orders, while simultaneously disregarding the blandishments of liberal self-improvement offered by both rural and urban Mechanics' Institutes. The professional middle classes could also experience cultural expressions of class identity in scientific and literary societies, as the "professionalization" of Canadian science and literature occurred with the diminishment of the voluntary principle in leading learned societies such as the Royal Society of Canada. What emerges from this study of voluntarism, then, is a portrait of an extremely vibrant movement of highly fractured and secluded class interests each hunkering down behind its own increasingly parochial organization. This picture corroborates the fact that this era is characterized as a rather factional and splintered period in

Canadian history, and makes it quite understandable that intellectuals in the early decades of the twentieth century looked to the welfare state, the ideology of social science, and the stability of corporatism for solutions to the problems of central-Canadian society.

Voluntary associations therefore bridged a significant gap between the limited social services offered by the developing colonial society of the early nineteenth century, and the origins of the Canadian welfare state nearly a hundred years later. These associations also functioned so as to define the way the larger community was ordered, and were also upheld as models of what an inclusive, "liberal," open, and harmonious society should be. When cracks in the armour of this liberal "community" began to appear in the final decades of the century, the liberal community ethos so carefully constructed in voluntary associations could not withstand the penetrating gaze of new class structures of an urban professional elite, industrial skilled workers, or "neglected" rural farmers.

Even though the ideology of collective liberalism remained viable and strong in rural areas well into the twentieth century, the influx of new ideas regarding the role of the state apparatus and social planning spelled the end of "amateur" voluntary organizations in central Canada. The ideology of an all-inclusive, ethnically interdependent, and genderless society secured through the removal of political and religious strife and the ethics of small producerism practised through associational life simply was no longer functional by the turn of the century. While the construction and contestation of what constituted liberal "community" were still in process at the dawn of a new century, the principal players and philosophies would change dramatically enough to completely redefine the contours of these debates over liberal doctrines, as new ideologues, philosophers, and institutions began to focus instead on the merits of the corporate welfare state.

Notes

INTRODUCTION

1 For the Lime Juice Club's lampooning of mutual benefit societies, see the scrapbook of the Lime Juice Club, PCMA, Acc. 67–004, folder 1, clipping of 28 April 1894, 118; 8 June 1895, 198; and 18 April 1896, 284. On temperance societies, see 16 June 1886, 1; 26 June 1886, 4; and 1 June 1895, 198. On science and literary pursuits, see the clippings of 19 Jan. 1887, 42; 4 March 1894, 108; and 5 May 1894, 120.
2 See the scrapbook of the Lime Juice Club, PCMA, Acc. 67–004, folder 1, clipping of 22 Sept. 1886, 21; 30 March 1887, 50; 21 Jan. 1888, 70; 2 March 1895, 180; 18 May 1895, 194; 30 May 1896, 296; and 8 Aug. 1896, 310.
3 For voluntary associations in the United States, see the work of Theda Skocpol, "The Tocqueville Problem," 455–80; Skocpol and Crowley, "The Rush to Organize," 813–29; as well as Gamm and Putnam, "The Growth of Voluntary Associations in America, 1840–1940," 511–57. In Britain, see Dentith, *Society and Cultural Forms*, 39–63; and especially Clark, *British Clubs and Societies*. For French voluntary associations, see Baker, *Fraternity Among the French Peasantry* and Harrison, *The Bourgeois Citizen in Nineteenth-Century France*. For Canada, see McNairn, *The Capacity to Judge*, 63–115; Calnan, "Blessed Be the Tie that Binds"; Ferry, "On Common Ground"; and Burr, *Canada's Victorian Oil Town*, 123–57.
4 On initial working class-efforts at voluntarism in Great Britain, see E.P. Thompson, *The Making of the English Working Class*, 441–68; Gosden, *Self-Help*; Kirk, *The Growth of Working Class Reformism*, 132–73; and particularly the recent work of Simon Cordery, *British Friendly Societies*. In the United States, see Faler, *Mechanics and Manufacturers*, 28–52; Wilentz, *Chants Democratic*; and Coavares, *The Remaking of Pittsburgh*, 98–154.

5 For voluntary associations as a process of middle-class hegemony in Britain, see Hall and Davidoff, *Family Fortunes*, 416–49; Koditschek, *Class Formation and Urban Industrial Society*, 293–319; Morris, *Class, Sect and Party*; Gorsky, *Patterns of Philanthropy*; Gunn, *The Public Culture of the Victorian Middle-Class*, 84–105; Lewis, *The Middlemost and the Milltowns*, 248–86; and Roberts, *Making English Morals*. For the United States, see Doyle, *The Social Order of a Frontier Community*, 119–93; Ryan, *Cradle of the Middle Class*, 105–44; Gilkeson, *Middle-Class Providence*, 136–74; and Blumin, *The Emergence of the Middle Class*, 192–229.

6 On voluntary associations as expressions of interclass collaboration, civic engagement, and social capital, see Clawson, *Constructing Brotherhood*; Ryan, *Civic Wars*, 58–93; Skocpol, "The Tocqueville Problem," 455–80; Gamm and Putnam, "The Growth of Voluntary Associations"; and Beito, "To Advance the Practice of Thrift and Economy," 585–612; as well as Clark, *British Clubs and Societies*. Jason Kaufman, in *For the Common Good*, argues that the notion of social capital is somewhat overrated, given that American voluntary associations produced socio-economic segregation and collective group identities, rather than civic integration.

7 For working-class associational life, see the work of Kealey, *Toronto Workers Respond to Industrial Capitalism*, 98–153; Palmer, *Working-Class Experience*, 95–100; and Palmer, "Mutuality and the Masking/Making of Difference," 111–38. On voluntary associations and the formation of a middle-class identity, see Sutherland, "Voluntary Societies and the Process of Middle Class Formation," 237–64; McDonald, *Making Vancouver*; and Holman, *A Sense of Their Duty*, 105–29.

8 On voluntary associations as vehicles of liberal state formation, see Fecteau, "État et associationnisme," 134–62, and Little, *State and Society in Transition*, 83–118. Elsbeth Heaman, in *The Inglorious Arts of Peace*, argues that the cultural roots of Canadian nationalism fuelled voluntary associations, while McNairn, in *A Capacity to Judge*, 63–115, contends that voluntarism was a product of emerging notions of participatory democracy in Upper Canada.

9 Antonio Gramsci pioneered the theory that cultural hegemony was a reciprocally negotiated phenomenon; see Hoare and Smith, *Selections from the Prison Notebooks*, 5–23. For an excellent article on the application of cultural hegemony in the nineteenth century, see Lears, "The Concept of Cultural Hegemony," 567–93. For Canadian examples of cultural hegemony see Anstead, "Fraternalism in Victorian Ontario"; Marks, *Revivals and Roller Rinks*; and Bouchier, *For the Love of the Game*.

10 The following cultural examination of voluntary associations is heavily influenced by an article suggesting that power structures are both material in nature, and culturally constructed through representations and symbols; see Braddick and Walters, "Grids of Power," 1–42. On the new "cultural history," see the work of Peter Burke, *Popular Culture in Early Modern Europe*; many of the essays in Darnton, *The Great Cat Massacre*; and particularly the essays in Chartier, *Cultural History*. For

Canadian examples of going "beyond class" and discursively examining cultural forms, see Valverde, *The Age of Light, Soap, and Water*; Anderson, *Vancouver's Chinatown*; McKay, *The Quest of the Folk*; and Walden, *Becoming Modern in Toronto*.

11 See Chartier, *On the Edge of the Cliff*, 2–27. Critics of Chartier claim that he underestimates the complexities in societal and cultural processes; see Dewald, "Roger Chartier and the Fate of Cultural History," 221–40. However, some historians have successfully attempted to bridge the gap between empiricism and discourse analysis; in the British context, see Lawrence, *Speaking for the People* and Epstein, *In Practice*. See also the work of Marks, *Revivals and Roller Rinks*; Loo, *Making Law, Order and Authority in British Columbia*; and Burr, *Spreading the Light*.

12 While the historiography of the "liberal" social order is in its infancy in Canada, it appears most often in the work of historians studying governmental processes and state formation. See the work of Bruce Curtis, *Building the Educational State* and his masterful *Politics of Population*; Fecteau, *Un nouvel ordre des choses*; Loo, *Making Law, Order and Authority in British Columbia*; Morgan, *Public Men and Virtuous Women*; Little, *State and Society in Transition*; Samson, "Industry and Improvement"; McNairn, *The Capacity to Judge*; McKay, "The Liberal Order Framework," 617–45; Christie, "Family, Community and the Rise of Liberal Society," 3–20; and particularly Fecteau, *La liberté du pauvre*.

13 For a discussion of these liberal doctrines, see Roy, *Progrès, Harmonie, Liberté*, 47–57; Samson, "Industry and Improvement"; McKay, "The Liberal Order Framework," 625–36; and Fecteau, *La liberté du pauvre*, 53–6. Fecteau also argues effectively in *La liberté du pauvre*, 78–82, that the apogee of the liberal social order in Canada occurred between 1830 and 1870.

14 See Fecteau, *La liberté du pauvre*, 54–62, 69–75 and 78–81. Tina Loo argues that the state could also prescribe the correct conditions for individualist liberal doctrines and ideologies to flourish in *Making Law and Authority in British Columbia*, while Nancy Christie states that liberalism found a "home" in familial discourse and the construction of liberal society; see Christie, "Family, Community and the Rise of Liberal Society," 3–15. Alternatively, Martin Petitclerc argues that doctrines of mutualism could also be used by marginalized workers as a concept to avoid the blandishments of mid-century liberalism in Canada East; see his "L'association qui crée une nouvelle famille," 259–92.

15 See McKay, "The Liberal Order Framework," 625–7.

16 Much of this discussion is heavily influenced by the arguments contained in the essays in Thompson, *Customs in Common* and Wharman, *Imagining the Middle Class*. A similar discussion of Canada's moral economy and resistance to the social order can be found in Palmer, *Working-Class Experience*, 42–9, and Cadigan, *Hope and Deception in Conception Bay*. For arguments on the "identity" conflicts within Canadian society at the apogee of the liberal social order, see Wilton, *Popular*

Politics and Political Culture; Perry, *On the Edge of Empire*; Sandwell, "The Limits of Liberalism," 423–50; and Petitclerc, "L'association qui crée une nouvelle famille."

17 For the history of working-class formation see Palmer, *A Culture in Conflict*; Kealey, *Toronto Workers Respond to Industrial Capitalism*; Kealey and Palmer, *Dreaming of What Might Be*, and Burr, *Spreading the Light*. For the awakening of the agricultural class, see Cook, "Tillers and Toilers," 5–20, and Ferry, "Severing the Connections in a Complex Community," 9–47. On middle-class formation, see McDonald, *Making Vancouver* and Holman, *A Sense of Their Duty*. On anti-French and Catholic sentiment in Canada see Miller, *Equal Rights* and Gaffield, *Language, Schooling, and Cultural Conflict*. On nativist attitudes in general see Avery, *Dangerous Foreigners*; Ward, *White Canada Forever*, and Palmer, *Patterns of Prejudice*. On late-century gender issues, see Valverde, *The Age of Light, Soap, and Water* and Kealey, *Enlisting Women for the Cause*.

18 See McKay, "The Liberal Order Framework," 626–31. For a further discussion of the concepts of cultural hegemony, see Gramsci, *Selections from the Prison Notebooks*, 5–23; and Lears, "The Concept of Cultural Hegemony," 567–93.

19 On the liberal principles of "dissenter" religion, see Westfall, *Two Worlds*; Gauvreau, "Personal Piety and the Evangelical Social Vision," 9–47; and Gauvreau, "Covenanter Democracy," 55–83. J.I. Little, *Borderland Religion*, argues that even though this "radical" voluntary principle came with American settlers, it was overshadowed by more "established" religious traditions.

20 Alternatively, there are already some very fine studies of the Knights of Labor in Canada; see Kealey, *Toronto Workers Respond to Industrial Capitalism*; Palmer, *A Culture in Conflict*; Kealey and Palmer, *Dreaming of What Might Be*, and Burr, *Spreading the Light*.

21 For example, see the work of Lapointe-Roy, *Charité bien ordonnée*; Morgan, *Public Men and Virtuous Women*, and especially Varty, "A Laudable Undertaking." Martin Petitclerc, in his article "L'association qui crée une nouvelle famille," argues that mutual benefit associations actually held adversarial relations with these benevolent associations, as they tended to "humiliate" and emasculate working men in Quebec.

22 For the conflicts inherent in American society, see Gutman, *Work, Culture and Society*; Wilentz, *Chants Democratic*; Cmiel, *Democratic Eloquence*; Montgomery, *Citizen Worker*, and particularly the work of Burke, *The Conundrum of Class*. For examples of American intellectual consensus in the antebellum era, see Foner, *Free Soil, Free Labor, Free Men*; Rodgers, *The Work Ethic in Industrial America*; Gunn, *The Decline of Authority*; Sellars, *The Market Revolution*; Livingston, *Pragmatism and the Political Economy of Cultural Revolution*; and Howe, *Making the American Self*. For arguments illustrating that American society experienced episodes of conflict *and* consensus, see Laurie, *Artisans into Workers* and Greenberg, *Worker and Community*.

23 On changes in late-century American society, particularly the replacement of the "island community" of family and voluntary associations with the state apparatus, see Wiebe, *The Search for Order*. On the reordering of liberal ideals in the Gilded Age, see Baker, *The Moral Frameworks of Public Life*; Skalansky, *The Soul's Economy*; and Cohen, *The Reconstruction of American Liberalism*. On agrarian populism and working-class consciousness, see Goodwyn, *Democratic Promise*; Fink, *Workingmen's Democracy*; Voss, *The Making of American Exceptionalism*; Weir, *Beyond Labor's Veil*; and particularly Sanders, *Roots of Reform*. For socio-economic conflicts in American associations see Kaufman, *For the Common Good?*

24 For examples of liberal and "Whiggish" history, see Houghton, *The Victorian Frame of Mind* and Briggs, *The Age of Improvement*. For the new labour history, see Thompson, *The Making of the English Working Class*; Foster, *Class Struggle and the Industrial Revolution*; and Williams, *Culture and Society*. On the labour aristocracy, see Gray, *The Labour Aristocracy in Victorian Edinburgh*; Crossick, *An Artisan Elite in Victorian Society*; and Prothero, *Artisans and Politics*. For descriptions of working class reformism, see Kirk, *The Growth of Working Class Reformism*; Claeys, *Machinery, Money and the Millennium* and his *Citizens and Saints*. See also Thompson, *Customs in Common*; Green, *From Artisans to Paupers*; Gray, *The Factory Question and Industrial England*; Prothero, *Radical Artisans in England and France*; and Kirk, *Change, Continuity and Class*.

25 On middle-class paternalism and hegemony see Joyce, *Work, Society and Politics* and Koditschek, *Class Formation and Urban Industrial Society*. For the significance of nationalism in reducing class conflict at mid-century, see Finn, *After Chartism*. See also Seed, "From Middling Sort to the Middle Class," 114–35; Morris, *Class, Sect and Party*; Gorsky, *Patterns of Philanthropy*; Gunn, *The Public Culture of the Victorian Middle Classs;* Lewis, *The Middlemost and the Milltowns*; and Roberts, *Making English Morals*.

26 See Jones, *Languages of Class* and his article "Rethinking Chartism," as well as the work of Patrick Joyce in *Visions of the People*, his *Democratic Subjects* and his crowning work, *The Rule of Freedom*. See also the work of Vernon, *Politics and the People* and Wharman, *Making the Modern Self*.

27 On the connection of plebeian traditions with Gladstonian liberalism, see the work of Eugenio Biagini, *Liberty, Retrenchment and Reform* and his edited collection with Alastair Reid, *Currents of Radicalism*. See also Haggard, *The Persistence of Victorian Liberalism*. On republican middle-class identity, see Wharman, *Imagining the Middle Class* and Taylor, *The Decline of British Radicalism*.

28 In many ways, W.L. Burn pioneered this pattern of thinking with his *The Age Of Equipoise*; see also the collection of essays in Hewitt, *An Age of Equipoise?* See also Crossick, "From Gentlemen to the Residuum," 150–78; Hewitt, *The Emergence of Stability in the Industrial City*; Lawrence, *Speaking for the People*; and Epstein, *In*

Practice. David Cannadine, in his book *The Rise and Fall of Class in Britain*, argues effectively that there were no shared perceptions of class identity in Victorian Britain.

29 On the ideological debates about "loyalty," see Read, *The Rising in Western Upper Canada*; Errington, *The Lion, the Eagle, and Upper Canada*; Mills, *The Idea of Loyalty in Upper Canada*; Westfall, *Two Worlds*; and Morgan, *Public Men and Virtuous Women*. See also Read, "Conflict to Consensus," 169–85; Noel, "Early Populist Tendencies in Ontario Political Culture," 173–87; McNairn, *The Capacity to Judge*, and particularly Wilton, *Popular Politics and Political Culture in Upper Canada*.

30 On the predominance of nationalist ideology in early Lower Canada, see the work of Ouellet, *Lower Canada, 1791–1840*. For the economic stresses – or the lack thereof – in rural Lower Canada, see the work of Allan Greer in *Peasant, Lord, and Merchant* and *The Patriots and the People*. See also Courville, *Entre ville et campagne*. On the emergence of embryonic state formation and social authority in Quebec, see Fecteau, *Un nouvel ordre des choses*; Bernier and Salée, *The Shaping of Quebec Politics and Society*; and Little, *State and Society in Transition*.

31 On the mid-century socio-economic shift from the "moral economy" of paternalism to a nascent capitalist order in Canada, see Palmer, *Working Class Experience*, 40–73; many of the essays in Samson, *Contested Countryside*; the work of Cadigan, "Paternalism and Politics," 319–47, and his *Hope and Deception in Conception Bay*. On the relatively recent historiography on the liberal social order, see Samson, "Industry and Improvement"; McKay, "The Liberal Order Framework," 617–45; Christie, "Family, Community and the Rise of Liberal Society," 3–20; Sandwell, "The Limits of Liberalism," 423–50; and Fecteau, *La liberté du pauvre*. On the ideology of nation building, see Owram, *The Promise of Eden*; Zeller, *Inventing Canada*; Heaman, *The Inglorious Arts of Peace*; and Perry, *On the Edge of Empire*. On the predominance of supporting a weak state apparatus as the main consideration of the governing order, see Curtis, *Building the Educational State* and his *Politics of Population*.

32 For the overshadowing influence of the Roman Catholic clergy in mid-century Quebec, see Eid, *Le clergé et le pouvoir politque au Québec*; Lapointe-Roy, *Charité bien ordonné*; Bellavance, *Le Québec et la Confédération*; and Hardy, *Contrôle social et mutation de la culture religieuse au Québec*. For the comparatively weak liberal opposition forces in Canada East, see Bernard, *Les rouges*; and Lamonde, *L.A. Dessaules*.

33 On the reformist tendencies of the producer ideology and the overall absence of class-consciousness in Canadian workers before the Knights of Labor, see Kealey, *Toronto Workers Respond to Industrial Capitalism*; Palmer, *A Culture in Conflict*; Kealey and Palmer, *Dreaming of What Might Be*; and Burr, *Spreading the Light*. On the Patrons of Industry, see Cook, "Tillers and Toilers," 5–20; and Ferry, "Severing the Connections in a Complex Community," 9–47.

34 On creeping secularization, see McKillop, *A Disciplined Intelligence*; Cook, *The Regenerators*; Marshall, *Secularizing the Faith*. On the new ideologies of corporate political economy and social science, see Ferguson, *Remaking Liberalism*; Burke, *Seeking the Highest Good*; and Christie and Gauvreau, *A Full-orbed Christianity*. On French/English conflict, see Miller, *Equal Rights* and Gaffield, *Language, Schooling, and Cultural Conflict*. On nativist attitudes in general, see Avery, *Dangerous Foreigners* and Valverde, *The Age of Light, Soap, and Water*, 104–28.

35 For the use of community as a conceptual device, see particularly the revised and extended version of Anderson's *Imagined Communities* and Garrioch, *Neighbourhood and Community in Paris*. Interchanged with the ideology of "community" is the notion of national identity; see Colley, *Britons* and, for a Canadian example, see Perry, *On the Edge of Empire*. For the contours of the debate, see Walsh and High, "Rethinking the Concept of Community," 255–74; and Christie, "Family, Community and the Rise of Liberal Society," 3–15. Other colonial societies also "constructed" their communities on the basis of the "liberal" social order; see Fairburn, *The Ideal Society and Its Enemies* and Raby, *Making Rural Australia*.

36 On the bourgeois public sphere, see the work of Jürgen Habermas, *The Structural Transformation of the Public Sphere* and, in the Canadian context, see particularly McNairn, *The Capacity to Judge*, 6–10 and 63–115. For the American context of the rural community, see Osterud, *Bonds of Community*; Pederson, *Between Memory and Reality*; and Hansen, *A Very Social Time*. For the Canadian small-town context, see the pioneering work of Marks, *Revivals and Roller Rinks*; Wilson, "Reciprocal Work Bees and the Meaning of Neighbourhood," 431–64; and the work of Paul Voisey in *Vulcan* and *High River and the Times*.

37 See Ferry, "To the Interests and Conscience of the Great Mass of the Community," 137–63 and "Severing the Connections." For working-class use of the ideology of interdependence to integrate non-skilled and skilled workers in associational life, see Kealey and Palmer, *Dreaming of What Might Be*; Cook, "Tillers and Toilers"; and Burr, *Spreading the Light*. On the middle-class use of "inclusion" for their own agendas, see Sutherland, "Voluntary Societies and the Process of Middle Class Formation"; Marks, *Revivals and Roller Rinks*; Heaman, *The Inglorious Arts of Peace*, and Holman, *A Sense of Their Duty*.

38 Building upon Hall and Davidoff's masterful work, *Family Fortunes*, John Tosh suggests that Victorian masculinity and notions of manliness reinforced the "white" British middle-class through such groups as clubs and voluntary associations; see Tosh, *A Man's Place*, 132–8 and his recent collection of essays, *Manliness and Masculinities in Nineteenth-Century Britain*, 1–9 and 41–51. For the Canadian context see also Sutherland, "Voluntary Societies and the Process of Middle Class Formation," 243–50; Palmer, "Mutuality and the Masking/Making of Difference"; Morgan, *Public Men and Virtuous Women*, 198–218; McNairn, *The Capacity to Judge*,

63–115; and particularly Perry, *On the Edge of Empire*. Carmen Varty, in "A Laudable Undertaking," argues that while women in benevolent societies were granted access to the public sphere in the course of their relief work, they were still regulated by a liberal, patriarchal society.

39 On the more symbolic yet crucial inclusion of women in late nineteenth-century voluntary associations see Marks, *Revivals and Roller Rinks* and particularly Christie, "Family, Community, and the Rise of Liberal Society," 3–15, and Varty, "A Laudable Undertaking." On the completely exclusive nature of fraternalism in reference to non-white races see Palmer, "Mutuality and the Masking/Making of Difference"; Emery and Emery, *A Young Man's Benefit*, 26–30; and Holman, *A Sense of Their Duty*, 105–29. David Beito argues convincingly that fraternalism practised selective intolerance; see his *From Mutual Aid to the Welfare State*, 17–40.

40 Political normalization has most often been associated with state formation and the post-rebellion system of education, although more recent scholarship acknowledges the resulting construction of a liberal social order. See Read, "From Conflict to Consensus"; Curtis, *Building the Educational State* and his *Politics of Population*; Little, *State and Society in Transition*; Samson, "Industry and Improvement"; McKay, "The Liberal Order Framework"; and Fecteau, *La liberté du pauvre*. On the continuing tensions of politico-religious conflict in Quebec, see Bernard, *Les rouges* and Lamonde, *L.A. Dessaules*. In Ontario, see Morgan, *Public Men and Virtuous Women*; Wilton, *Popular Politics and Political Culture*, 10–15; McNairn, *The Capacity to Judge*, 63–115; and particularly Gauvreau, "Covenanter Democracy," 55–83.

41 On the involvement of the Grange, Patrons of Industry, and temperance societies in the political culture of central Canada in the late nineteenth century, see Ferry, "Severing the Connections" and "To the Interests and Conscience." See also Cook, "Tillers and Toilers" and his masterful work *The Regenerators*; Marshall, *Secularizing the Faith*; Christie and Gauvreau, *A Full-orbed Christianity*; Ferguson, *Remaking Liberalism*; and Burke, *Seeking the Highest Good*.

42 See MacDonald, "Merchants Against Industry," 266–80; Acheson, *Saint John*; and Hewitt, "Science, Popular Culture and the Producer Alliance," 243–75. Tina Loo makes an interesting argument that classical liberalism and state intervention in the economy were not exclusive concepts; see her *Making Law, Order and Authority*. See also the essays in Samson, *Contested Countryside* and his new work, *The Spirit of Industry and Improvement*.

43 On the producer ideology and industrial capitalism, see Palmer, *A Culture in Conflict*, 97–122; Kealey, *Toronto Workers Respond*, 124–50; Craig Heron, "Factory Workers," 480–515; and Heaman, *Inglorious Arts of Peace*. Both Burley in *A Particular Condition in Life* and Holman, *A Sense of Their Duty* argue that small producers and self-employed entrepreneurs formed the backbone of the late Victorian

small-town economy, using the rather flexible producer ideology for their own purposes.

44 There is a fine literature on the importance of leisure in constructing the identity of its patrons as well as the tensions inherent in competing visions of proper and respectable entertainment. For Britain, see Bailey, *Leisure and Class in Victorian England*. For some American examples see Rosenzweig, *Eight Hours for What We Will* and Hansen, *A Very Social Time*. For the Canadian context, see Marks, *Revivals and Roller Rinks* and particularly Nancy Bouchier, *For the Love of the Game*.

45 See the scrapbook of the Lime Juice Club, PCMA, Acc. 67–004, folder 1, clipping of 5 May 1894, 120.

CHAPTER ONE

1 See the report of the Hamilton Mechanics' Institute, *Journal of the Board of Arts and Manufacturers* vol. 1 (April 1861), 106–7, and also the records of the Hamilton Mechanics' Institute, Hamilton Public Library, Special Collections, minute book, 1839–51, 24 Feb. 1840; 28 Feb. 1844; 28 Feb. 1845; 5 April 1848, and annual meeting, 22 Feb. 1850. On education as a vehicle to control working-class propensities to crime, see Prentice, *The School Promoters*. For a discussion of the middle-class nature of the Hamilton Mechanics' Institute, see Palmer, *A Culture in Conflict*, 49–52.

2 See Tylecote, *The Mechanics' Institutes of Lancashire and Yorkshire*, particularly chapters 1 and 2, and also Royle, "Mechanics' Institutes and the Working Class," 305–21.

3 See Shapin and Barnes, "Science, Nature and Control," 31–74, and Garner and Jenkins, "The English Mechanics' Institutes," 139–52. See also Thompson, *The Making of the English Working Class*, 817–20; Johnson, "Really Useful Knowledge," 75–102; and particularly Rose, *The Intellectual Life of the British Working Classes*, 58–91.

4 Ian Inkster has pioneered the work in this field; see Inkster, "Aspects of the History of Science and Culture in Britain," 3–14, and particularly the edited collection of his own articles on British Mechanics' Institutes in *Scientific Culture and Urbanization in Industrializing Britain*. See also Cooter, *The Cultural Meaning of Popular Science*; Wach, "Culture and the Middle Classes," 375–404; Morris, *Class, Sect and Party*, 161–203; and Winter, *Mesmerized*.

5 For explorations of the social control thesis, see Keane, "A Study in Early Problems and Policies in Early Adult Education," 255–74, and also Robins, "Useful Education for the Workingman," 20–34. The subject of Mechanics' Institutes as a vehicle for middle-class hegemony and state formation is covered in Hewitt, "Science as Spectacle," 91–119; Heaman, *The Inglorious Arts of Peace*, 3–20; and Ramsay, "Art and Industrial Society," 71–103.

6 On the adult education side, see the work of Keane, "Priorities and Resources in Adult Education," 171–87. For Mechanics' Institutes as the first public libraries, see Eadie, "The Napanee Mechanics' Institute," 209–21; Blanchard, "Anatomy of Failure," 393–8; Curtis, "'Littery Meritt', 'Useful Knowledge,'" 285–311; and Bruce, *Free Books for All*, 3–70. The following presentation emulates the work done on Mechanics' Institutes in the parallel colonial experience of Australia; see the essays in Candy and Laurent, *Pioneering Culture*.

7 On the growth in industrialism during the 1840s and 1850s in Canada, see Tulchinsky, *The River Barons*; Kealey, *Toronto Workers Respond to Industrial Capitalism*, 18–36; and particularly the work of T.W. Acheson, *Saint John* and Samson, "Industry and Improvement." On the growth of a "liberal" social order, see McKay, "The Liberal Order Framework," 617–45; Christie, "Family, Community and the Rise of Liberal Society," 3–20; and particularly Fecteau, *La liberté du pauvre*.

8 See *Rules of the Quebec Mechanics' Institute*, 3–4 and 28, as well as the *Catalogue and Rules of the Library and Reading Room of the Quebec Mechanics' Institute*, 1–2.

9 Aylwin, *Inaugural Address*, 6–11; *Report of the General Committee of the Mechanics' Institute of Montreal* and *Constitution and Laws of the Montreal Mechanics Institution*, 3–7. Aylwin likely wanted to avoid expressions of Irish worker discontent such as the Lachine Canal strike a decade earlier; see Boily, *Les Irlandais et Le Canal de Lachine*.

10 See the records of the Toronto Mechanics' Institute, AO, MU 2020, vol. 1, minute book, 1831–36, 5 March 1832 and 19 Feb. 1836, as well as vol. 8, 1848 and 1851 annual reports and the Toronto Mechanics' Institute fonds, Baldwin Room, MTL, L1, series B, vol. 1, board meeting minute book, 1840–48, 13 Nov. 1848.

11 See Judd, *Minutes of the London Mechanics' Institute*, 96 and the London Mechanics' Institute records, London Public Library, vol. 1, minute book, 1841–50, Constitution and bylaws, as well as the meeting of 8 March 1842.

12 Judd, *Minutes of the London Mechanics' Institute*, 104 and the London Mechanics' Institute records, London Public Library, vol. 1, minute book, 1841–50, first annual meeting, 3 Jan. 1842. For class discontent in the Toronto and Hamilton Mechanics' Institute, see McNairn, *The Capacity to Judge*, 96–9 and Palmer, *A Culture in Conflict*, 51. Similar sentiments emerged in Maritime urban areas; see Hewitt, "Science, Popular Culture, and the Producer Alliance," 243–75.

13 Aylwin, *Inaugural Address*, 14–15; the *British Whig* (Kingston), 11 March 1834, and particularly James Reilly, "The Political, Social and Economic Impacts on the Emergence of the Kingston Mechanics' Institute."

14 For the membership figures of the Montreal Institute, see Kuntz, "The Educational Work of the Two Montreal Mechanics' Institutes," 222–9 and Robins, "Useful Education for the Workingman," 31–4. For London, see Judd, *Minutes of the London Mechanics' Institute*, 62–4.

15 See the Toronto Mechanics' Institute fonds, MTL, L1, series M, folder n.d.–1851, unbound papers, annual report, 4 Jan. 1833; see also *Rules of the Quebec Mechanics' Institute*, 3–4, and *Catalogue of the Quebec Mechanics' Institute*, 1–2.
16 The Ottawa Mechanics' Institute and Athenaeum fonds, LAC, MG 28 I 1, vol. 2, meetings of trustees and members, reorganization meeting, Jan. 1853, and annual reports, 19 March 1861. See also the records of the London Mechanics' Institute, London Public Library, vol. 1, minute book, 1841–50, annual report of 1841 and vol. 2, minute book, 1851–65, library committee minutes, 13 Jan. 1851, and annual report of 1857.
17 See the records of the Hamilton Mechanics' Institute, Hamilton Public Library, Special Collections, minute book, 1839–51, 24 Feb. 1840 and 28 Feb. 1844, as well as the Toronto Mechanics' Institute fonds, AO, MU 2020, vol. 1, minute book 1831–36, 5 March 1832 and 19 Feb. 1836.
18 Dunlop, *An Address Delivered to the York Mechanics' Institution*, 6–7 and 14–15. These beliefs were similar to those of the rising industrial interests; see Hewitt, "Science, Popular Culture and the Producer Alliance"; Heaman, *The Inglorious Arts of Peace*, 3–28; and Ramsay, "Art and Industrial Society."
19 The Toronto Mechanics Institute fonds, MTL, L1, series M, unbound papers, 1852–63, letter of H. Rogers to the Institute, 20 Nov. 1852 and the report on the laying of the cornerstone on the Mechanics' Hall, 17 April 1854. See also Lewis, "Lecture on Education," in the *Journal of the Board of Arts and Manufacturers of Upper Canada* vol. 2 (Nov. 1862), 338–9; the *Annual Report of the Toronto Mechanics' Institute for 1855*, 7–8 and 11; as well as the *Annual Report for 1860*, 10–11.
20 See the Ottawa Mechanics' Institute and Athenaeum fonds, LAC, MG 28 I 1, vol. 2, meetings of trustees and members, Jan. 1853 and 27 March 1857.
21 Bovell, *A Lecture on the Future of Canada*, 1–3 and *Conseil des Arts* fonds, ANQ, Micro #1640, 4 Jan. 1858. On the connection between a liberal social order and the state, see McKay, "The Liberal Order Framework" and Fecteau, *La liberté du pauvre*, 53–88.
22 See the Board of Arts and Manufacturers of Upper Canada fonds, AO, MU 280, vol. 3, Letterbook of the Secretary, 1 April 1860, 33–4; and particularly the *Journal of the Board of Arts and Manufacturers of Upper Canada* vol. 1 (Jan. 1861), 1–7.
23 Tylecote, *The Mechanics' Institutes of Lancashire and Yorkshire*, 17–25; Radcliffe, "Mutual Improvement Societies in the West Riding of Yorkshire," 2–8; and especially Purvis, *Hard Lessons*. A more recent article illustrates that women did have a role, although limited, to play in adult education in Britain; see Jones, "A Woman's Contribution to Nineteenth-Century Adult Education," 1–17.
24 See the work of John Tosh, *A Man's Place*, 132–8 and his collection of essays, *Manliness and Masculinities in Nineteenth-Century Britain*. For this paradoxical view of women in voluntary societies such as temperance associations, the exhibition

movement, and other voluntary organizations see Noel, *Canada Dry*, 89–102; Morgan, *Public Men and Virtuous Women*, 208–18; Heaman, "Taking the World by Show," 599–631; Ramsay, "Art and Industrial Society," 87–9 and Varty, "A Laudable Undertaking."

25 The records of the London Mechanics' Institute, London Public Library, vol. 2, minute book, 1851–70, 27 Jan. 1851, and Judd, *Minutes of the London Mechanics' Institute*, 64. See also the Toronto Mechanics' Institute fonds, MTL, L1, series E, vol. 1, membership list, 1833–48, and Kuntz, "The Educational Work," 229–30, 447–8.
26 See the Ottawa Mechanics' Institute and Athenaeum fonds, LAC, MG 28 I 1, vol. 2, minutes of meetings of trustees and members, 6 Dec. 1854 and 28 Feb. 1855.
27 Keefer, *Montreal and the Ottawa*, 3, and also the records of the Ottawa Mechanics' Institute, LAC, MG 28 I 1, vol. 3, managing committee minutes, 23 Nov. 1855.
28 Eales, *The Benefits to be Derived from Mechanics' Institutes*, 9–12, 15–16. Such activities no doubt reinforced the emerging hegemony of the middle-class patriarchy; see Hall and Davidoff, *Family Fortunes*.
29 Education and expressions of state formation are often viewed as agents of middle-class hegemony and harmonization; see many of the essays in Radforth and Greer, *Colonial Leviathan*; Prentice and Houston, *Schooling and Scholars*; Curtis, *Building the Educational State*; and Heaman, *The Inglorious Arts of Peace*. And yet some Institutes did become immersed in political and sectarian conflicts; see Keane, "A Study in Early Problems and Policies in Early Adult Education"; Palmer, *A Culture in Conflict*, 49–52; and Ramsay, "Art in Industrial Society."
30 See Bristow, *The Commercial Prospects of Canada*, 24–5; Bovell, *A Lecture on the Future of Canada*, 1–2; and Keefer, *Montreal and the Ottawa*, 23, 31–2. The sectarian disagreements of the early Montreal Institute are mapped out in Kuntz, "The Educational Work," 79–90; see also the *Constitution of the Montreal Mechanics' Institution*, 12.
31 Reverend Bettridge chose a rather unusual location to lecture against voluntarism, although accusations like this were typical of the sectarian battles of the time; see Fahey, *In His Name*, 202–5. See also the record of the London Mechanics' Institute, London Public Library, vol. 1, minute book, 1841–50, 4 March 1843, and the 1850 annual meeting, as well as vol. 2, minute book, 1851–70, 24 Jan. 1853.
32 Eales, *The Benefits to be Derived from Mechanics' Institutes*, 12–13; Toronto Mechanics' Institute fonds, MTL, L1, Board minutes, 1840–48, series B, vol. 1 (10 Sept. 1841) and Special meetings, 1854–83, series B, vol. 7 (4 Oct. 1854), as well as the records of the Toronto Mechanics' Institute, AO, MU 2020, vol. 1, minute book 1831–36, membership lists. See also the article by Radforth, "Sydenham and Utilitarian Reform," 64–102, which illustrates that individualist liberal doctrines could inform the direction of state and other institutions.

33 Toronto Mechanics' Institute fonds, MTL, L1, Board meetings, 1848–54, series B, vol. 2, report of the Library Committee, 9 Feb. 1852 and series M, folder 1864–77, letter of W.T. Withrow to the Institute, 1864.
34 See Heaman, *The Inglorious Arts of Peace*, 20, 330. For the details of this episode see the Toronto Mechanics' Institute fonds, MTL, L1, series B, vol. 1, Board minutes 1840–48, 15 Nov., 21 Nov. and 5 Dec. 1848; series M, folder n.d.–1851, letter of A.A. Riddell, 13 Nov. 1848.
35 Riddell, "The Rights of Labour," in the MTL, unpublished lecture, 1848, 1–6, 16–18.
36 Riddell was a staunch friend of noted radical Charles Clarke, who shared these philosophies; see Dewar, "Charles Clarke's *Reformator*," 233–52. Prentice and Houston discovered that Riddell followed in the artisan tradition of self-improvement, becoming first a school inspector and then a doctor after his printing days were over; see Prentice and Houston, *Schooling and Scholars*, 231 and Riddell, "The Rights of Labour," 4–8, 18.
37 The Toronto Mechanics' Institute fonds, MTL, L1, series B, vol. 1, Board meetings, 1840–48, 15 May 1845. For Rintoul's view on education, and how this fit into the prevalent educational theories of the day, see his *Lectures on Rhetoric to the Toronto Mechanics' Institute*, 43–8 and Prentice, *The School Promoters*, 94–6. See also Wilton, *Popular Politics and Political Culture in Upper Canada*, 194–230.
38 On the producer alliance, see MacDonald, "Merchants Against Industry," 266–80 and especially Hewitt, "Science, Popular Culture and the Producer Alliance," 243–75. For the producer ideology, see Kealey, *Toronto Workers Respond to Industrial Capitalism*, 124–50; Palmer, *A Culture in Conflict*, 97–122; Ramsay, "Art and Industrial Society," 74–95, and Heaman, *The Inglorious Arts of Peace*, 21–7.
39 See Bristow, *Commercial Prospects of Canada*, 10–11, and 25; Brown Chamberlain, *Our Country and Our Duty to It*, 13–14; and Keefer, *Montreal and Ottawa*, 5–6. Manufacturers and merchants in Ottawa likewise viewed their city as a commercial power, and lectures were often presented on economic subjects in the Ottawa Mechanics' Institute; see Cortlandt, *An Epitome of a Lecture on Ottawa Productions* and Perry, *The Staple Trade of Canada*.
40 Bristow, *Commercial Prospects of Canada*, 5–9; Keefer, *Montreal and the Ottawa*, 6–8, 23–32; Bovell, "A Lecture on the Future of Canada," 1–4; and see also the Reverend John Cook's lecture in the Quebec Institute, "The Advantages of Life Assurance to the Working Classes," 3–6.
41 Dunlop, *An Address to the York Mechanics' Institution*, 3–6, 12–14, and the Toronto Mechanics' Institute fonds, MTL, L1, series B, vol. 1, Board minutes, 1840–48, 2 Dec. 1842, 22; 7 April 1843, 32, and 3 Jan. 1844, 40. See also Hugh Baker's lecture to the Hamilton Mechanics' Institute, *A Lecture on Life Assurance*.

42 Arnold, *Money and Banking*, 1–4, 30–4, 45–8. See also Sullivan, *Address on Emigration and Colonization*, 3–8 and Sullivan, *The Connection between Agriculture and Manufactures of Canada*, 4–12, 32–6. See also the lecture of the Reverend Adam Lillie, *Canada, Its Growth and Prospects*, 12–16, 37–9.

43 See the Board of Arts and Manufactures fonds, AO, MU 279, minute book, 1857–67, 1861 annual report, and *Journal of the Board of Arts and Manufactures of Upper Canada*, vol. 1 (Jan. 1861), 1–9, and (March 1861), 60–1 and 74; vol. 2 (Oct. 1862), 289–90 and (Dec. 1862), 359; vol. 5 (Aug. 1865), 199–202, and vol. 6 (Jan. 1866), 25–7.

44 See *Journal of Arts and Manufactures of Upper Canada* vol. 2 (Nov. 1862), 338–9; vol. 4 (March 1864), 94–5; vol. 5 (Nov. 1865), 284 and vol. 6 (Jan. 1866), 25–7. See also Hewitt, "Science, Popular Culture and the Producer Alliance," 245–58; Ramsay, "Art and Industrial Society," 74–81; and Heaman, *The Inglorious Arts of Peace*, 21–7.

45 *Journal of the Board of Arts and Manufactures of Upper Canada* vol. 1 (July 1861), 184–5 and (Oct. 1861), 257–9; vol. 3 (Jan. 1863), 13–15, and vol. 5 (March 1865), 57–9.

46 *Journal of the Board of Arts and Manufactures of Upper Canada* vol. 4 (Oct. 1864), 305; vol. 7 (Jan. 1867), 27–8, and (March 1867), 57–8, as well as (May 1867), 117–18, 123–5.

47 See Riddell, "The Rights of Labour," 5–8, 19–22.

48 See Eales, *The Benefits to be Derived from Mechanics' Institutes*, 4–7, 16–18. These arguments also appeared among skilled workers in the Maritimes; see Hewitt, "Science, Popular Culture, and the Producer Alliance," 243–75.

49 As noted, this philosophy borrowed heavily from Canadian forms of mid-Victorian radicalism; so despite his adherence to the producer ideology, Riddell's lecture was rejected. See Riddell, "The Rights of Labour," 10–16, 18–23, and 35–6; Prentice and Houston, *Schooling and Scholars*, 231; Dewar, "Charles Clarke's *Reformator*," 243–52; and Wilton, *Popular Politics and Political Culture*.

50 See Riddell, "The Rights of Labour," 10–12. Populism did not emerge only in the class turbulence of the 1890s, as its tenets were present throughout Ontario's earlier history as well; see Cook, "Tillers and Toilers," 5–20, and especially Noel, "Early Populist Tendencies in Ontario Political Culture," 173–87.

51 For the British context, see Bailey, *Leisure and Class in Victorian England*; Cooter, *The Cultural Meaning of Popular Science*; Wach, "Culture and the Middle Classes"; and Morris, *Class, Sect and Party*, 161–78. For leisure in the mid-century Canadian Mechanics' Institutes, see Hewitt, "Science as Spectacle."

52 See the records of the Hamilton Mechanics' Institute, Hamilton Public Library, Special Collections, minute book, 1839–51, 28 Feb. 1844; 11 Aug. 1844 and 28 Feb. 1845; the records of the Toronto Mechanics' Institute, AO, MU 2020, vol. 1,

minute book, 1831–36, 19 Feb. 1836 and *Constitution and Laws of the Montreal Mechanics' Institution*, 3–4.

53 The Toronto Mechanics' Institute fonds, MTL, L1, series B, vol. 2, board meeting minute book, 1848–54, 7 Jan. 1851; Eales, *The Benefits to be Derived from Mechanics' Institutes*, 14–15; the London Mechanics' Institute fonds, London Public Library, vol. 2, minute book, 1851–65, 12 Jan. 1852, 8 July 1852, 2 May 1853, 2 Feb. 1857, 3 March 1859; and also Judd, *Minutes of the London Mechanics' Institute*, 110.

54 See Friel, *Inaugural Address at the Opening of the Winter Course of Lectures*, 8–9 and the Ottawa Mechanics' Institute fonds, LAC, MG 28 I 1, vol. 1, minutes of general meetings, 17 Feb. 1847 and vol. 2, meetings of trustees and members, 25 Aug. 1853, 7 Feb. 1855, and 28 Feb. 1855.

55 The Ottawa Mechanics' Institute and Athenaeum fonds, LAC, MG 28 I 1, vol. 2, meetings of trustees and members, Jan. 1853.

56 For the change in education and class composition of urban Institutes in Britain, see Hemming, "The Mechanics' Institutes in Lancashire and Yorkshire," 18–31 and Laurent, "Science, Society and Politics," 585–619. In Canada, see Blanchard, "Anatomy of Failure," 396–8; Heward, "Industry, Cleanliness and Godliness," 87–128; Eadie, "The Napanee Mechanics' Institute," 215–20; and Ramsay, "Art and Industrial Society," 89–101.

57 On working class formation in the latter decades, see Palmer, *A Culture in Conflict*, 97–122; Kealey, *Toronto Workers Respond to Industrial Capitalism*, 124–50; and Heron, "Factory Workers," 480–515. For the process of middle-class formation, see McDonald, *Making Vancouver*; Holman, *A Sense of Their Duty*, and Heaman, *Inglorious Arts of Peace*. On the growth of a larger community vision of grand entertainments, see Rosenzweig, *Eight Hours for What We Will*; Walden, *Becoming Modern in Toronto*, 247–91; and Heaman, *The Inglorious Arts of Peace*, 106–40. For changes in education and in the library system, see Bruce, *Free Books for All*, 70–93 and Prentice and Houston, *Schooling and Scholars*, 310–44.

58 See the *Conseil des Arts* fonds, ANQ, P543, Microfilm #1640, minute book, 4 Nov. 1873, 27; 17 Nov. 1873, 35; 16 Feb. 1876, 185–7; and 12 May 1879, 213–15. See also the *Thirty-Ninth Annual Report of the Montreal Mechanics' Institute*, 5–6.

59 "[Les artisans québécois ont] fonté cette Société pour répandre l'instruction et en particulier l'étude des Beaux Arts parmi les Ouvriers. C'est ainsi que vous les rendrez dignes de ce titre si noble d'Artisans, qui veut dire Artistes de l'industrie." See the lectures of Desmazures, *Entretiens sur les Arts Industriels*, 2–4 and 19; Colin, *Discours sur l'Ouvrier*, 2–6; and Verbist, *Projet d'Organisation d'une Académie des Beaux Arts à Montréal*, 3–5. These clergymen probably wanted to keep some form of religious control over the *Institut*, to avoid the conflictual model of Ignace Bourget and the *Institut Canadien*; see Bernard, *Les rouges*.

60 The Toronto Mechanics' Institute fonds, AO, Misc. file #6, and also the Toronto Mechanics Institute fonds, MTL, L1, series M, Folder 1862, unbound papers, letter of J. Pearson, 12 May 1862 and series D, vol. 24, Library minute book, 1866–77, 6 July 1866.
61 See the Toronto Mechanics' Institute fonds, MTL, L1, series B, vol. 6, Board Meetings 1878–83, 30 July 1880 and *Annual Report of the Toronto Mechanics' Institute for 1880*, 6–7. See also the Toronto Mechanics' Institute fonds, MTL, L1, series B, vol. 7, Special Meetings 1854–83, Letter of J.E. Pell to the Institute, 14 Feb. 1876.
62 The Toronto Mechanics' Institute also harboured a love of "industrial art," as did the *Conseil des Arts*; see Ramsay, "Art and Industrial Society." See also the *Annual Report of the Toronto Mechanics' Institute for 1868*, 7–8; Board of Arts and Manufacturers fonds, AO, MU 280, vol. 2, committee minute book, 1857–68, 27 Oct. 1864 and the *Journal of the Board of Arts and Manufacturers*, vol. 6 (June 1866), 170.
63 See the Board of Arts and Manufacturers fonds, AO, MU 280, vol. 2, committee minute book, 1857–68, 27 Oct. 1864 and *Journal of the Board of Arts and Manufacturers*, vol. 7 (July 1867), 168–72.
64 As noted earlier, this actual membership mostly comprised the lower middle classes; see *Annual Report of the Toronto Mechanics' Institute for 1866*, 17–20; *Annual Report of the Toronto Mechanics' Institute for 1875*, 6–9; and *Annual Report of the Toronto Mechanics' Institute for 1876*, 2–3.
65 See the records of the London Mechanics' Institute, London Public Library, vol. 4, minute book, 1871–76, clipping pasted on the front; annual report of 1871 and annual report of 1872, as well as vol. 5, minute book, 1876–95, annual report of 1882. Similar problems occurred in the Hamilton Mechanics' Institute; see Palmer, *A Culture in Conflict*, 49–52.
66 Clerks and bookkeepers also became regular patrons in the Montreal and London Mechanics' Institutes; see Robins, "Useful Education for the Workingman," 32–4 and Judd, *Minutes of the London Mechanics' Institute*, 65–71. In the late Victorian period, clerks embraced an ideology of respectability similar to that of their employers; see Holman, *A Sense of Their Duty*, 75–96, and Spurr, "Those Who are Obliged to Pretend that They are Gentlefolk."
67 See the Toronto Mechanics' Institute fonds, MTL, L1, series B, vol. 7, Special Meetings, 1854–83, minutes of the 1866, 1867, and 1868 annual reports.
68 Toronto Mechanics' Institute fonds, MTL, L1, series D, vol. 24, Library and Lecture Committee minutes, 3 April 1872, and for the class attendance figures, see series D, vol. 11–15, particularly vol. 13 for the year 1877.
69 See the Toronto Mechanics' Institute fonds, MTL, L1, series D, vol. 26, Exhibition Committee minutes, 1859–68, general meeting on 14 July 1868, and series B, vol. 5, committee of the Reading Room, 17 April 1873. The importance of exhibitions in forging cultural consent and consensus among an industrial people is

examined in Rydell, *All the World's a Fair*; Greenhalgh, *Ephemeral Vistas*; Heaman, *Inglorious Arts of Peace*, 3–27; Ramsay, "Art and Industrial Society," 88–95; and Walden, *Becoming Modern in Toronto*.

70 See the *Thirty-Ninth Annual Report of the Montreal Mechanics' Institute*, 3–6; *Forty-Second Annual Report*, 3–4; and *Forty-Third Annual Report*, 3–6.

71 The records of the London Mechanics' Institute, London Public Library, vol. 4, minute book, 1871–76, annual report of 1871, and annual report of 1872.

72 The Association of Mechanics' Institutes fonds, AO, MU 2021, copy of sessional paper no. 5, 6 Oct. 1869 and the seventh annual report, 23 Sept. 1875.

73 See the Association of Mechanics' Institutes fonds, AO, MU 2021, twelfth annual report, 22 Sept. 1880, 8–11, and the seventeenth annual report, 15 Sept. 1885, 4–6.

74 The Association of Mechanics' Institute fonds, AO, MU 2021, prize essays contest folder, Boyle, "Arole," 1–2 and 13, and Donald, "Perseverance is Better than Talent," 1–2. See also Killan, *David Boyle*.

75 The Association of Mechanics' Institute fonds, AO, MU 2021, prize essays contest folder, Lewis, "To Make the Man a Better Mechanic, and the Mechanic, a Better Man," 7–12; Hutchinson, "Non sine labore," 1–3; Dickson, "Rex," 4–5; Davison, "To Make the Mechanic a Better Man; the Man, a Better Mechanic," 1–4. Lewis clearly followed a newer "hegemonic" element of bureaucratized state education; see Curtis, *True Government by Choice Men?*

76 Exhibitions illustrated the dichotomy of women appearing in both the public and the domestic sphere more than any other Institute activity; see Heaman, "Taking the World by Show" and the Toronto Mechanics' Institute fonds, MTL, L1, series D, vol. 26, Exhibition minutes 1847–49, meetings of the Exhibition Committee and series D, vol. 26, Building and Reunion minutes, 1859–68, Ladies' Committee meeting of 14 July 1868. For a similar dichotomy, see the fine work of Carmen Varty, "A Laudable Undertaking."

77 See the *Thirty-Ninth Annual Report of the Montreal Mechanics' Institute*, 15, and also the Toronto Mechanics' Institute fonds, MTL, L1, series D, vol. 24, Finance, Library and Lecture Committee minutes, Library Committee, 9 June 1875.

78 Association of Mechanics' Institute fonds, AO, MU 2021, prize essay contest folder, Dickson, "Rex," 7–8; Lewis, "To Make the Man a Better Mechanic," 8–9; and Boyle, "Arole," 13–14.

79 Many women simply refused to become directors under these conditions; see *Annual Report of the Toronto Mechanics' Institute for 1876*, 3–4, and *Annual Report for 1879*, 9. See also the Association of Mechanics' Institute fonds, AO, MU 2021, prize essay contest folder, Davy, "Suum Cuique," 3.

80 See the Association of Mechanics' Institute fonds, AO, MU 2021, prize essay contest folder, Boyle, "Arole," 13–14, and the Board of Arts and Manufacturers fonds, AO, MU 279, general committee minutes, 1857–67, annual report of 1865.

81 In 1877 women comprised 11 percent and in 1878, 9 percent of the student body; see the statistics in the Toronto Mechanics' Institute fonds, MTL, L1, series D, vols. 13, 14, and 15, Evening classes membership lists. For the membership statistics, see *Annual Report of the Toronto Mechanics' Institute for 1881*, 4–5.

82 See the records of the *Conseil des Arts*, ANQ, P543, Microfilm #1640, minute book 1869–1881, annual report for 1878; 12 May 1879, 201–4, and the annual report for 1880, 370–2.

83 *Conseil des Arts* fonds, ANQ, P543, Microfilm #1640, minute book 1887–1904, petition of Women's Club, 376–8 and 395 and the Board's response, 10 June 1895, 396–8, and 15 Nov. 1895, 423–5. Contesting the gendered hegemonic order often occurred near the turn of the century and beyond; see Burke, *Seeking the Highest Good*, 28–40, and especially the work of Nancy Christie, *Engendering the State*.

84 See the *Conseil des Arts* fonds, ANQ, P543, Microfilm #1640, minute book, 1857–1869, 7 Aug. 1865, 194. For political expressions of class discontent, see Kealey, *Toronto Workers Respond to Industrial Capitalism*, 154–74, and Palmer, *A Culture in Conflict*, 97–122.

85 *Thirty-Ninth Annual Report of the Montreal Mechanics' Institute*, 4–5, and for the protection/free trade debates in this period, see Forster, *A Conjunction of Interests*.

86 Toronto Mechanics' Institute fonds, MTL, L1, series D, vol. 28, Reunion and Lecture Committee minutes, 1862–66, 15 Oct. 1863, 28 Nov. 1864, and 26 Jan. 1866.

87 See the Toronto Mechanics' Institute fonds, MTL, L1, series D, vol. 28, Reunion and Lecture Committee minutes, 1862–66, 11 Aug. 1862, and series M, Unbound papers, folder 1863, report of the Reunion Committee, from William Calley.

88 For some of the more controversial debates, see the records of the London Literary Society, London Public Library, minute book, 1872–74, 11 Nov. 1872, 23 Dec. 1872, 3 March 1873, 2 June 1873, 10 Dec. 1873, 7 Jan. 1874, 25 Feb. 1874, and 7 Oct. 1874; see particularly the meeting of 24 March 1873.

89 See the records of the London Literary Society, London Public Library, minute book, 1872–74, 21 Feb. 1872.

90 See the *Thirty-Ninth Annual Report of the Montreal Mechanics' Institute*, 3–4; *Forty-Second Annual Report of the Montreal Mechanics' Institute*, 3; and *Forty-Third Annual Report of the Montreal Mechanics' Institute*, 3–5.

91 "Ouvrier, tu es delivré des chaînes qui te retenaient depuis des siècles dans l'esclavage, tes droits sont reconnus, ta dignité est relevée, ta grandeur et ta liberté proclamées, et c'est de Jésus Christ et de son Eglise que tu tiens ces bienfaits ... Aime-la bien cette Eglise, jette-toi dans son sein' elle te conduira et te fera progresser. Attache-toi bien à elle, car elle sera ta protrectrice et ta gardienne dans les lutes formidables qu'il te reste encore à soutenir contre l'impiété philosophique et l'ambition des meneurs politiques." Of course, such

assertions by the French Catholic clergy would ensure that the ultramontane religious order in Montreal would not be disturbed; see *Constitution de l'Institut des Artisans*, 16; Desmazures, *Entretiens sur les Arts industriels*, 5–6; and particularly Colin, *Discours sur l'Ouvrier*, 7–9. See also Eid, *Le clergé et le pouvoir politique au Québec*.

92 See *Journal of the Board of Arts and Manufactures* vol. 5 (Jan. 1865), 2–4 and (Aug. 1865), 201–5; vol. 7 (May 1867), 118–21; and (Sept. 1867), 225–6.

93 "L'église a toujours honoré l'industrie et les efforts de l'activité humaine; elle a bien mieux fait que de les honorer, elle a prescrit le travail *c'est comme elle avait prescrit le progrès*" (emphasis mine). See the lectures of Desmazures, *Entretiens sur les Arts Industriels*, 5; Verbist, *Projet d'Organisation*, 3–4; and Colin, *Discours sur l'Ouvrier*, 17–19.

94 *Journal of the Board of Arts and Manufactures*, vol. 4 (Oct. 1864), 305, and vol. 6 (Jan. 1866), 25–6.

95 *Conseil des Arts* fonds, ANQ, P543, Microfilm #1640, minute book, 1887–1904, 8 April 1891.

96 See the Toronto Mechanics' Institute fonds, MTL, L1, series D, vol. D24, Library and Class Committee minutes, 1866–77, 11 April 1867 and 3 April 1877; see also series M, Unbound papers, 1864–77, folder 1864, report of the class committee for 1864.

97 See the Association of Mechanics' Institute fonds, AO, MU 2021, prize essay contest folder, Lewis, "To Make the Man a Better Mechanic," 16–18; see also Hutchinson, "Non sine labore," 1–2 and Davy, "Suum Cuique," 1–2.

98 Walls's philosophy would echo the Scottish tradition of common sense of individuals such as David Boyle, another essayist in the contest; see Killian, *David Boyle and the Association of Mechanics' Institute* fonds, AO, MU 2021, prize essay contest folder, Walls, "Tell me not in mournful numbers, Life is but an empty dream," 1–15.

99 The Association of Mechanics' Institute fonds, AO, MU 2021, prize essay contest folder, Walls, "Tell me not in mournful numbers, Life is but an empty dream," 20–1.

100 See the Association of Mechanics' Institute fonds, AO, MU 2021, prize essay contest, Alexander Gunn, "Progression, extermination and repudiation," 1–3. On the widespread use of "Horatio Alger" self-made man literature, where the working class hero seems to achieve his fortune rather providentially, see Rodgers, *The Work Ethic in Industrial America*, and Blumin, *The Emergence of the Middle Class*.

101 Association of Mechanics' Institute fonds, AO, MU 2021, prize essay contest, Gunn, "Progression, extermination and repudiation," 2–3.

102 See the Department of Education Special Files, AO, MS 5635, RG 2-42-0-2287, 16 Oct. 1901, and RG 2-42-0-2369, 29 Aug. 1895; the Ottawa Mechanics'

Institute fonds, vol. 2, meetings of trustees and members, 1868 annual report, and the Ottawa Natural History Society fonds, LAC, MG 28 I 31, vol. 1, minute book, 1879–85, 25 March 1879.

103 For this episode, see Bruce, *Free Books for All,* 90–1 and the London Mechanics' Institute fonds, London Public Library, vol. 4, minute book, 1871–76, 9 Sept. 1871 and 1872 annual report; vol. 5, minute book, 1876–95, 6 Nov. 1877; annual report of 1879; 8 May 1882; and annual report of 1884.

104 Toronto Mechanics' Institute fonds, MTL, L1, series B, vol. 4, Board meetings, 1862–72, 6 March 1863; the *Annual Report of the Toronto Mechanics' Institute for 1866,* 7–8, 8–12, and the *Annual Report for 1862,* 11–12.

105 See the *Annual Report of the Toronto Mechanics' Institute for 1870,* 11–15.

106 The Association of Mechanics' Institutes fonds, AO, MU 2021, prize essay contest folder, Davy, "Suum Cuique," 1–3; Donald, "Perseverance is better than talent," 5–9; Macpherson, "Perserverantia omnia vincit," 14–17; and Davison, "To Make the Mechanic a Better Man," 2–3.

107 The Association of Mechanics' Institutes fonds, AO, MU 2021, prize essay contest folder, Butler, "Union is Strength," 20–2; Macpherson, "Perserverantia omnia vincit," 17; Donald, "Perseverance is better than talent," 4–6; and Davison, "To Make the Mechanic a Better Man," 4.

108 See the Toronto Mechanics' Institute fonds, MTL, L1, series D, vol. 24, Lecture and Recreation room minutes, 1876–78.

109 See *Annual Report of the Toronto Mechanics' Institute for 1876,* 18, and the Toronto Mechanics' Institute fonds, MTL, L1, series M, unbound papers, folder 1879–192–, letter from the Alymer Mechanics' Institute, 11 March 1878; letter of John Langrell, 22 Jan. 1879, and the unpublished manuscript of E.S. Caswell, "History of the Toronto Mechanics' Institute."

110 The Toronto Mechanics' Institute fonds, MTL, L1, series M, unbound papers, letter of M. Sweetnam to the Board of Directors, 10 July 1878, and letter of Thomas Maclean, 15 July 1878.

111 See the *Thirty-Ninth Annual Report of the Montreal Mechanics' Institute,* 6–8, 15; *Forty-Seventh Annual Report,* 4–6; and *Fiftieth Annual Report,* 3–7.

112 *Thirty-Ninth Annual Report of the Montreal Mechanics' Institute,* 3–4; *Fifty-First Annual Report,* 10–12; and *Fifty-Eighth Annual Report,* 3–5.

CHAPTER TWO

1 In 1876 54 Mechanics' Institutes were affiliated with the association; by 1884 over 104 had joined, and there were over 140 working Mechanics' Institutes in the province of Ontario. See the Association of Mechanics' Institute fonds, AO, MU 2021, Annual reports, 1876–84. For the purposes of this particular study, the

rubric "rural" was utilized for small towns and villages, in order to provide a stronger contrast to the urban Mechanics' Institute environment.

2 There is scant literature on British Mechanics' Institutes in rural areas; see Radcliffe, "Mutual Improvement Societies in the West Riding of Yorkshire," 2–8; Watson, "The Origins of Mechanics' Institutes of North Yorkshire," 12–25; and Rose, *Intellectual Life of the British Working Classes*, 61–72. See also the essays in Candy and Laurent, *Pioneering Culture*. For the Canadian context, see Donald Akenson's study of the Gananoque Mechanics' Institute in *The Irish in Ontario*, 218–22; Curtis, "'Littery Meritt,' 'Useful Knowledge,'" 285–311; and Wood, *Making Ontario*, especially chapter 4, "Building a Social Structure," 50–83.

3 See the records of the *Société Littéraire de Laprairie*, Elisée Choquet fonds, ANQ, P60, box 20, file 4.174 and file 4.180, the annual report of 1858. See also the Elora Mechanics' Institute fonds, WCA, MU 60, minute book, 1857–70, 21 and 30 April 1858; the Mitchell Mechanics' Institute fonds, Stratford-Perth Archives, minute book, 1854–70, 11 March 1854 and the records of the Paris Mechanics' Institute, AO, MS 359, reel 2, minute book, 1843–62, 9 Jan. 1846 and 6 Dec. 1847.

4 Lakeshore Subscription library fonds, MTL, minute book, 1850–77, 19 March 1850, 25 Aug. 1850, 4 Aug. 1856, 11 Jan. 1859, and 8 Feb. 1877.

5 Douglas McCalla argued that economic development in Ontario was fuelled by the complex nature of markets in rural areas; see his *Planting the Province*. See also Darroch, "Scanty Fortunes and Rural Middle-Class Formation," 621–59; Fair, "Gentlemen, Farmers, and Gentlemen Half-Farmers"; and Burley, *A Particular Condition in Life*. For the importance of rural markets in Quebec, see Courville, "Un monde rural en mutation," 237–58.

6 See the Paris Mechanics' Institute fonds, AO, MS 359, reel 2, minute book, 1843–62, second annual meeting, 2 April 1842 and fifth annual report, 7 April 1846. See also the Niagara Mechanics' Institute fonds, AO, MU 2022, MS 566, vol. 1, minute book, 1848–62, 11 Nov. 1857, 14 Nov. 1857.

7 Dallas, *A Lecture on the Aims and Usefulness of Mechanics' Institutes*, 3–7, and Lewis, *Lecture Delivered before the Brockville Mechanics' Institute*, 3–5, 16–17. Rural Mechanics' Institutes followed the "familialist" model of other organizations like church congregations and temperance societies; see Nancy Christie's introduction, "Family, Community, and the Rise of Liberal Society," 3–20.

8 See the Paris Mechanics' Institute fonds, AO, MS 359, reel 2, minute book, 1843–62, fourth annual meeting, 2 April 1844, 7 April 1846, and 7 Jan. 1857.

9 Fergus Public Library fonds, WCA, A993.36, MU 281, series 2, subseries 2, minute book, 1857–96, meeting of 21 Aug. 1857 and the Guelph Public Library fonds, Guelph Public Library, Farmers' and Mechanics' Institute minute book, 1850–72, 28 Jan. 1856.

10 See the Guelph Public Library fonds, Guelph Public Library, Mechanics' Institute minute book, 1850–72, 14 Jan. 1852, 17 Jan. 1854 and 11 Jan. 1859; and the Mitchell Mechanics' Institute fonds, Stratford-Perth Archives, minute book, 1854–70, 21 Jan. 1861.
11 Osterud, *Bonds of Community*, 247–74, and Hansen, *A Very Social Time*. For the Canadian context, see Van Die, "The Marks of Genuine Revival," 524–63, and in particular, Wilson, "Reciprocal Work Bees and the Meaning of Neighbourhood," 431–64. Of course, just permitting women to join Mechanics' Institutes did not overly disturb the rural social order.
12 Niagara Mechanics' Institute fonds, AO, MU 2022, MS 566, vol. 1, 19 Nov. 1852 and 20 Nov. 1856; and the Mitchell Mechanics' Institute records, Stratford-Perth Archives, minute book, 1854–70, 15 Oct. 1866. See also the Paris Mechanics' Institute fonds, AO, MS 359, reel 2, minute book, 19 Jan. 1856 and 14 Feb. 1856; J.E. Curran papers, LAC, MG 30 C85, vol. 4, Orillia Mechanics' Institute minute book, 1864–72, bylaws of 1864 and the records of the *Société Littéraire de Laprairie*, Elisée Choquet fonds, ANQ, P60, box 1, file 4.180, the annual report of 1858.
13 Curtis, "'Littery Meritt', 'Useful Knowledge,'" 285–311 and Bruce, *Free Books for All*, 3–70.
14 Of course, such regulation occurred often in these societies and in the liberal state itself; see Marks, "Railing, Tattling, and General Rumour," 380–402 and Fecteau, *La liberté du pauvre*. See also the Paris Mechanics' Institute fonds, AO, MS 359, reel 2, minute book, 1843–62, bylaws, 15 May 1858; and the Mitchell Mechanics' Institute fonds, Stratford-Perth archives, minute book, 1854–70, 9 Jan. 1854. See also the *Bylaws of the Owen Sound Mechanics' Institute*, 14; the *Constitution, Rules and Regulations of the Guelph Farmers' and Mechanics' Institute*, 4; and the records of the Ennotville Mechanics' Institute, WCA, MU 106, series 1, subseries 1, file 1, minute book, 1856–1900, 2 Nov. 1859.
15 See the *Bylaws of the Owen Sound Mechanics' Institute*, 14; Elora Mechanics' Institute fonds, WCA, MU 60, minute book, 1857–70, constitution pasted on the front, and 7 Jan. 1858; and the Niagara Mechanics' Institute fonds, AO, MU 2022, MS 566, vol. 1 (18 Dec. 1855).
16 Ardagh, *An Address Delivered Before the County of Simcoe Mechanics' Institute*, 19–20 and Dallas, *A Lecture on the Aims and Usefulness*, 6–7.
17 See the records of the *Société Littéraire de Laprairie*, Elisée Choquet fonds, ANQ, P60, box 20, file 4.173, constitution et règles, 1853.
18 Menard, "L'Institut des Artisans du Comté du Drummond 1856–90," 207–18, and the Drummond County *Institut des Artisans* fonds, LAC, MG 28 I 142, vol. 1, minute book, 1856–58, 26 Dec. 1856, 10 Sept. 1857 and 3 Dec. 1857.
19 Drummond County *Institut des Artisans* fonds, LAC, MG 28 I 142, vol. 1, minute book, 1856–58, 26 Dec. 1856; 8 Jan. 1857; 12 Feb. 1857 and 14 Jan. 1858, as

well as vol. 2, minute book, 1858–1890, 3 June 1858 and 9 Jan. 1862. For more on *Rouge* political beliefs, see Bernard, *Les rouges*.
20 See the Drummond County *Institut des Artisans* fonds, LAC, MG 28 I 142, vol. 1, minute book, 1856–58, 15 Jan. 1857, 26 March 1857, 27 May 1857, 15 Oct. 1857 and 7 Jan. 1858, as well as vol. 2, minute book, 1858–1900, 27 Jan. 1859 and 6 Dec. 1860. For similar responses to institutional reform in the Eastern Townships, see Little, *State and Society in Transition*.
21 Barrie Debating Club and Mechanics' Institute fonds, SCA, minute book, 1854–56, bylaws of the debating club, and the debates of 23 Jan. 1854, 27 Feb. 1854 and 14 July 1854.
22 See the Barrie Debating Club and Mechanics' Institute fonds, SCA, minute book, 1854–56, bylaws of the debating club, 27 Feb. 1854, 9 Aug. 1854 and 27 Sept. 1854; the first meeting of the Barrie Mechanics' Institute transpired on 7 Dec. 1854. On Reformer/radical political ideology, see Dewar, "Charles Clarke's *Reformator*," 233–52.
23 Carleton Place Mechanics' Institute fonds, LAC, MG 9, D8/4, minute book, 1846–49, 10 March 1849. For the ideological roots of artisan self-improvement in Ontario, see Killian, *David Boyle*, 2–39. I am indebted to Jane Errington for information about John Gemmill's occupation and activities in Lanark County.
24 It seems that President Gemmill was caught up in the radical political and religious controversies in the Scottish church; see Gauvreau, "Covenanter Democracy," 55–83. See also the Carleton Place Mechanics' Institute fonds, LAC, MG 9, D8/4, minute book, 1846–49, 7 May 1849, 32, and 12 May 1849, 33.
25 Even though the prevalence of commercial and mercantile elites in the urban Mechanics' Institute was not as evident in those of the small-town Institutes, the producer ideology still held full sway. See Burley, *A Particular Condition in Life*, particularly chapter 5, "The Making of the Self-Made Man," 170–97, and McCalla, *Planting the Province*, 217–39.
26 Fulford, *The Misapplication of Labour*, 8 and 25–6. See also Dallas, *Lecture on Aims*, 3–7; Ardagh, *An Address Delivered before the County of Simcoe*, 2–6; and Lewis, *Lecture Delivered before the Brockville Mechanics' Institute*, 3–5.
27 See Fulford, *Misapplication of Labour*, iii–iv, and also Merritt, "A Lecture Delivered by William Hamilton Merritt," 11–12, 17–18.
28 This was all part of the "community-building" process in small towns examined by Hansen in *A Very Social Time*, and in the Canadian context see Bouchier, *For the Love of the Game*, as well as Wilson, "Reciprocal Work Bees and the Meaning of Neighbourhood," 431–64.
29 See the Paris Mechanics' Institute fonds, AO, MS 366, reel 2, minute book, 1841–62, 6 Jan. 1859, 19 March 1859, 13 Dec. 1859, 28 Jan. 1860, 23 Jan. 1861,

and 21 March 1861, as well as the Guelph Public Library fonds, Guelph Public Library, Mechanics' Institute minute book, 1850–72, annual report, 1860.
30 Mitchell Mechanics' Institute fonds, Stratford-Perth Archives, minute book, 1854–70, 20 Feb. 1860, 9 Oct. 1865, 15 Oct. 1866, 1 April 1867, 17 May 1867, and 11 Oct. 1869; and the Niagara Mechanics' Institute fonds, AO, MU 2022, MS 566, vol. 1, minute book, 1848–62, 9 Nov. 1858, and 21 April 1859.
31 See the Elora Mechanics' Institute fonds, WCA, MU 60, minute book, 1857–70, 12 Feb. 1858, 21 April 1858, and 10 Dec. 1860; and also Killian, *David Boyle*, especially chapter 3, "Elora's Intellectual Awakening," 40–69.
32 See the Fergus Mechanics' Institute fonds, WCA, A993.36, MU 281, series 2, subseries 2, minute book, 1857–96, 3 April 1860, 16 April 1860, and 18 Jan. 1864.
33 Mitchell Mechanics' Institute fonds, Stratford-Perth Archives, minute book, 1854–70, 24 Aug. 1859, 18 May 1864, and 28 Nov. 1864. See also the Paris Mechanics' Institute fonds, AO, MS 359, reel 2, minute book, 1843–62, sixth annual report, April 1848.
34 Once again the problem appears to be with a local clergyman lecturer, a Reverend Burns; see the Niagara Mechanics' Institute fonds, AO, MU 2022, MS 566, vol. 1, minute book, 1848–62, 18 Dec. 1855.
35 See Eadie, "The Napanee Mechanics' Institute," 209–21; Marks, *Revivals and Roller Rinks*, 125–6 and Holman, *A Sense of Their Duty*, 121–9. These ideas would also find an ideological home among self-employed businessmen and farmers; see David Burley, *A Particular Condition in Life* and Gordon Darroch, "Scanty Fortunes."
36 Guelph Public Library fonds, Guelph Public Library, Mechanics' Institute minute book, 1850–72, annual report, 1860 and box 10, folder 21, papers from 1860 and the Niagara Mechanics' Institute fonds, AO, MU 2022, MS 566, vol. 1, minute book, 1848–62, 4 Nov. 1862.
37 Inglis, *Our Village and Mechanics' Institute*, 5–8, and the records of the Kincardine Mechanics' Institute, Kincardine Public Library, Jan. 1868 and 10 Jan. 1876. A similar circumstance arose in Fergus; Fergus Public Library fonds, WCA, A993.36, MU 281, series 2, subseries 2, minute book, 1857–96, 24 Sept. 1874, 14 Feb. 1878, and 8 Nov. 1878.
38 See the Peterborough Mechanics' Institute fonds, LAC, MSS 1995–2005, series C1, box five, folder 4, correspondence of the Board, letter from W.H. Trout to George Shaw, 28 Dec. 1878; and series A, folder 2, circular from the Clinton Mechanics' Institute, 1870. See also the Peterborough Mechanics' Institute records housed in the PCMA, 59–028/1, minute book, 1868–86, 23 Oct. 1873, 18 May 1874, and 21 May 1877.
39 Klotz, *A Review of the Special Report on the Mechanics' Institutes of Ontario*, 3–7, and *Special Report of the Minister of Education on the Mechanics' Institutes*, x–xii. For the

change in administration over rural Mechanics' Institutes, see Bruce, *Free Books for All*, 56–8.
40 See the records of the Kincardine Mechanics' Institute, Kincardine Public Library, minute book, 1866–89, 10 Oct. 1881 and 13 March 1882; for a similar experience with a rural Institute's night classes, see the Erin Public Library fonds, WCA, A1996.56, MU 308, minute book 1891–1945, 30 Nov. 1892, 8.
41 See the Ingersoll Mechanics' Institute fonds, RCL, M-581, minute book, 1880–90, 26 June 1883 and Marks, *Revivals and Roller Rinks*, 125–6.
42 Elora Mechanics' Institute fonds, WCA, MU 60, minute book, 1857–70, 21 and 30 April 1858; Elora Public Library fonds, A1984.5, series 1, subseries 1, file 1, minute book, 1871–78, 27 Nov. 1871, 7 Nov. 1873, 5 Dec. 1873, and 3 Nov. 1876.
43 Similar attitudes to evening classes emerged as early as 1858; see the Elora Mechanics' Institute fonds, WCA, MU 60, minute book, 1857–70, 21 and 30 April 1858, as well as the Elora Mechanics' Institute fonds, WCA, MU 60, minute book 1878–1887, 16 Sept. 1881, 113; 8 May 1882, 133–4, 14 May 1883, 166, and 12 May 1884, 210.
44 Peterborough Mechanics' Institute fonds, LAC, MSS 1995–05, series E, box six, folder 19, Publicity and Promotion, broadside of 1895 and series C3, box 5, folder 12, Reports of the Teachers, 30 April 1878 and 23 March 1886.
45 See Eadie, "The Napanee Mechanics' Institute," and the Lennox and Addington Historical Society fonds, LAC, MG 9 D8/18, M-229, Napanee Mechanics' Institute records, annual report of 1886, 34120–3 and letter to Adam Crooks, 21 Sept. 1881, 34037.
46 On small-town middle-class formation and hegemony, see Burley, *A Particular Condition in Life*; Marks, *Revivals and Roller Rinks*, 125–6; Darroch, "Scanty Fortunes," and Holman, *A Sense of Their Duty*, 121–9.
47 Guelph Public Library fonds, Guelph Public Library, Mechanics' Institute minute book, 1872–85, 1 Sept. 1874; the Collingwood Public Library fonds, SCA, Mechanics' Institute minute book, 1894–95, 24 Oct. 1894; Niagara Mechanics' Institute fonds, AO, MU 2022, MS 566, vol.2, minute book, 1866–95, 2 Nov. 1881; and the Barrie Mechanics' Institute fonds, SCA, Acc. 981–31, minute book, 1871–84, 2 Oct. 1879 and 25 Nov. 1880.
48 Orillia Mechanics' Institute fonds, Wallace family collection, SCA, Acc. 993–13, the 1886 annual report and *Resolution of the Board of Directors of the Clinton Mechanics' Institute*, 1–2.
49 To construct "a sober and industrious people," the Peterborough Institute forbade members to use improper language, gamble or "introduce intoxicating liquors" to other members. See the Peterborough Mechanics' Institute records, PCMA, 59–028/1, minute book, 1868–86, 8 June 1869, 47, and 5 June 1868, 18–19.

50 For the professional classes' fascination with scientific and literary societies, see chapter 7, "A Feast of Popularized Science and Literature." See also the records of the *Société Littéraire de Laprairie,* Elisée Choquet fonds, ANQ, P60, box 1, letter of 21 Oct. 1889 and box 20, file 4.180 and file 4.182.

51 See the *Institut des Artisans* fonds, LAC, MG 28 I 142, vol. 2, minute book, 1858–82, 4 Nov. 1880 and 12 Nov. 1880 as well as Menard, "L'Institut des Artisans," 211–6.

52 Lennox and Addington Historical Society fonds, LAC, MG 9 D8/18, M-229, Napanee Mechanics' Institute records, 12 April 1877, 34517–8, and Oct. 1877, 34548–9, as well as the Elora Mechanics' Institute fonds, MU 60, minute book, 1878–87, annual report, 12 May 1884, 210–1.

53 See the Peterborough Mechanics' Institute records, PCMA, 59–028/1, minute book, 1868–86, twelfth annual report, 17 May 1880, 258, and 10 Oct. 1884, 352–4.

54 The annual reports of the Orillia Mechanics' Institute, Wallace family collection, SCA, Acc. 993–13, reading room committee report, 1888, and annual report of 1887. See also the Peterborough Mechanics' Institute records, PCMA, 59–028/1, minute book, 1868–86, library bylaws, 5 June 1868, 27.

55 Peterborough Mechanics' Institute fonds, LAC, MSS 1995–05, series C2, box 5, folder 6, the library committee report, April 1883; and the Kincardine Mechanics' Institute fonds, Kincardine Public Library, minute book, 1866–89, 14 Oct. 1884.

56 Orillia Mechanics' Institute records, Wallace family collection, SCA, Acc. 993–13, reading room committee report, 1889; see also the Peterborough Mechanics' Institute fonds, LAC, MSS 1995–2005, series C2, box 5, folder 5, board and committee reports, 16 May 1881 report; and Elora Mechanics' Institute fonds, MU 60, minute book 1878–87, 11 June 1885.

57 The involvement of the WCTU reinforced the middle-class nature of the enterprise; see Cook, *Through Sunshine and Shadow.* See also the Ingersoll Mechanics' Institute fonds, RCL, M-581, minute book, 1880–90, 25 Oct. 1886, 14 Dec. 1887, and 3 June 1889.

58 See the Guelph Public Library fonds, Guelph Public Library, Guelph Mechanics' Institute minute book, 1872–85, 28 May 1878, 5 July 1878, 22 May 1879, and 6 June 1879, as well as the Ennotville Public Library fonds, WCA, MU 106, series 1, subseries 1, file 1, minute book, 1859–1896, 10 Nov. 1892.

59 Niagara Mechanics' Institute fonds, AO, MU 2022, MS 566, vol. 2, minute book, 1866–95, 2 Sept. 1880, 4 May 1883, 5 May 1890, and 1 Oct. 1891. See also the Barrie Mechanics' Institute fonds, SCA, Acc. 981–31, minute book, 1871–84, 25 Nov. 1880, 22 May 1884, and 10 July 1884.

60 See the *Special Report on the Mechanics' Institutes in Ontario,* 74–6, and the Peterborough Mechanics' Institute fonds, PCMA, Acc. 59–028/1, minute book, 1868–86, 4 Aug. 1881, 296, and 15 May 1882, 313. See also Orillia Mechanics'

Institute records, Wallace family collection, SCA, Acc. 993–13, reading room committee report, 1889; and the Orangeville Mechanics' Institute fonds, DCA, AR 2096–994, minute book, 1888–96, 20 May 1890, 28 May 1891, and 16 May 1892.
61 Peterborough Mechanics' Institute fonds, PCMA, Acc. 59–028/1, minute book, 1868–86, 1872 annual report and their records in the LAC, MSS 1995–2005, series C2, folder 11, April 1883 report.
62 See the Barrie Mechanics' Institute fonds, SCA, Acc. 981–31, minute book, 1871–84, 11 Dec. 1878 and 2 Oct. 1879, as well as the Elora Mechanics' Institute fonds, WCA, MU 60, minute book 1878–87, 29 Aug. 1884, 227.
63 Peterborough Mechanics' Institute fonds, LAC, MSS 1995–2005, series A, box 1, folder 21, letter from George Ross, Sept. 1886; and series C, box 5, folder 4, correspondence of the board, WH Trout to George Shaw, 28 Dec. 1878.
64 See the records of the Barrie Literary Society, in the Barrie Mechanics' Institute fonds, SCA, Acc. 981–31, minute book, 1881–89, 23 Feb. 1882 and 16 March 1882.
65 Barrie Literary Society records, Barrie Mechanics' Institute fonds, SCA, Acc. 981–31, minute book, 1881–89, 26 Oct. 1883, and minute book of the Mechanics' Institute, 1890–93, 21 Feb. 1893. For further reading on the domestication of politics see Ryan, *Women in Public*, Isenberg, *Sex and Citizenship in Antebellum America*, and for its rural perspective see Baker, *The Moral Frameworks of Public Life*, especially chapter 3, "Feminine Virtues and the Public Life," 56–89. For the Canadian context, see Bacchi, *Liberation Deferred?* and Kealey, *Enlisting Women for the Cause*, 15–42.
66 See the *Claude Mechanics' Institute Constitution and Bylaws*, 3–4, and the Peterborough Mechanics' Institute fonds, PCMA, Acc. 59–028/1, minute book, 1868–86, 5 June 1868, 18.
67 The directors of the Fergus Institute exercised self-censure in banning a tome entitled *Creeds of Christendom* on the grounds of its being a pernicious book; see Fergus Public Library fonds, WCA, A993.36, MU 281, series 2, subseries 2, minute book, 1857–96, 31 Oct. 1879. See also the Elora Mechanics' Institute fonds, WCA, MU 60, minute book, 1878–87, 10 Feb. 1883; the Kincardine Mechanics' Institute records, Kincardine Public Library, minute book 1866–89, 7 Nov. 1866, 14 Nov. 1866, and 19 Jan. 1867. For the ideology of church regulation, see Marks, "Railing, Tattling and General Rumour."
68 Lennox and Addington Historical Society fonds, LAC, MG 9 D8/18, M-229, Napanee Mechanics' Institute records, 12 Oct. 1877, 34557, and annual report of 1878, 34582. See also the Kincardine Mechanics' Institute records, Kincardine Public Library, minute book, 1866–89, 3 Sept. 1866 and 7 Nov. 1866.
69 See the records of the Barrie Literary Society, Barrie Mechanics' Institute fonds, SCA, Acc. 981–31, minute book, 1881–89, constitution of the society, 22 Oct. 1881, 27 April 1883, and list of debates from 1881–89.

70 Ennotville Public Library fonds, WCA, MU 106, series 1, subseries 1, file 1, minute book, 1859–96, June 1892; see also Fergus Public Library fonds, WCA, A993.36, MU 281, series 2, subseries 2, minute book, 1857–96, 3 Feb. 1893; and Elora Mechanics' Institute fonds, MU 60, minute book, 1878–87, 2 Oct. 1878.

71 See the Drayton Farmers' and Mechanics' Institute fonds, WCA, A987.36, series 1, subseries 1, minute book, 1884–1905, 9 Feb. 1891, 9 March 1891, and 16 March 1891. A similar episode in the Orillia Mechanics' Institute revealed inter-committee strife; see the records of the Orillia Mechanics' Institute, Wallace family collection, SCA, Acc. 993–13, annual report of the Institute, 1887.

72 On the prevalence of the nascent producer ideology in this period, see Palmer, *A Culture in Conflict*, 97–122; see also Lynch, *Canada, Its Progress and Prospects*, 11–16.

73 Inglis, *Our Village and Mechanics' Institute*, 9–11.

74 See the records of the Peterborough Mechanics' Institute, LAC, MSS 1995–2005, series C, box 5, folder 4, correspondence of the board, WH Trout to George Shaw, 28 Dec. 1878, as well as the Lennox and Addington Historical Society fonds, LAC, MG 9 D8/18, M-229, Napanee Mechanics' Institute records, annual report of 1886, 34120–3.

75 *Catalogue of the Point Edward Mechanics' Institute Library*, Political Economy section; *Catalogue of Books in the Newburgh Mechanics' Institute Library*, Economics section; and *Catalogue of the Elora Mechanics' Institute Library*, Political and Social Science section.

76 See the records of the Barrie Literary Society, Barrie Mechanics' Institute fonds, SCA, Acc. 981–31, minute books, 1881–89 and 1890–93, list of debate topics and also *Catalogue of Books and Magazines in the Barrie Mechanics' Institute Library*, Economics section. On the appeal of commercial union to farmers in the late nineteenth century, see chapter 5, below; on the influence of populism in small-town Ontario, see Ferry, "Severing the Connections in a Complex Community," 9–47.

77 Peterborough Mechanics' Institute fonds, PCMA, 59–028/2, request book, 1872–84. See also *Catalogue of the Elora Mechanics' Institute Library*, Political and Social Science section and *Catalogue of Books in the Mechanics' Institute of Orillia*, Social Science section.

78 See the Niagara Mechanics' Institute fonds, AO, MU 2022, MS 566, vol. 2, minute book, 1866–95, 14 Nov. 1871 and 5 Jan. 1881; Barrie Mechanics' Institute fonds, SCA, Acc. 981–31, minute book, 1871–84, 12 Nov. 1873, 14 Oct. 1882, and 5 May 1884; the Drayton Farmers' and Mechanics' Institute fonds, WCA, A987.36, series 1, subseries 1, minute book, 1884–1905, 7 Jan. 1888, 56, as well as the Ennotville Public Library fonds, WCA, MU 106, series 1, subseries 1, file 1, minute book, 1856–1900, 16 Oct. 1882 and 2 May 1889.

79 See the Kincardine Mechanics' Institute fonds, Kincardine Public Library, minute book, 1866–89, 25 Feb. 1881, 6 May 1884, and 20 Jan. 1885.

80 Ingersoll Mechanics' Institute fonds, RCL, M-581, minute book, 1880–90, 5 March 1883, 7 June 1883, 23 May 1884, 26 June 1885, 3 June 1889, and 21 Oct. 1889.
81 See the circular *To the Friends of Literature and Mental Culture and Recreation*. On the importance of leisure in boosting a town, see Nancy Bouchier, *For the Love of the Game*.
82 Orangeville Mechanics Institute fonds, DCA, AR 2096–994, minute book, 1888–96, 5 April 1890 and 4 March 1897, as well as the Institute Treasurer's book, 1879 to 1887.
83 See the Erin Public Library fonds, WCA, MU 308, A1996.56, minute book, 1891–95 and the Caledon Mechanics' Institute fonds, AO, MU 2018, minute book, 1884–96, 1 May 1888 and 30 April 1891. See also the Highland Creek Public library fonds, AO, MU 2121, miscellaneous collection, 1889 #6.
84 Elora Public Library fonds, WCA, A1984.5, series 1, subseries 1, file 1, minute book, 1871–77, 5 Oct. 1874 and 18 March 1875; Elora Mechanics' Institute fonds, WCA, MU 60, minute book, 1878–87, 12 May 1879, 32–3; 8 Oct. 1880, 71–2; 9 May 1881, 98; 14 May 1883, 166; and 11 May 1885, 252.
85 Fergus Mechanics' Institute fonds, WCA, A993.36, MU 281, series 2, subseries 2, minute book, 1857–96, 18 Nov. 1881, 26 May 1882, 6 Feb. 1886, and 1887 annual report.
86 See the Guelph Public Library fonds, Guelph Public Library, Guelph Mechanics' Institute minute book, 1850–72, 30 April 1864, 25 Oct. 1865, and 3 April 1866; and minute book, 1872–83, 28 March 1878, 22 May 1879, 3 Oct. 1879, 4 Dec. 1879, 9 Aug. 1881, and 16 May 1882.
87 Peterborough Mechanics' Institute fonds, LAC, MSS 1995–2005, series E, folder 13, special events and series C2, folder 5, 1881 annual report. See also the Peterborough Mechanics' Institute fonds, PCMA, 59–028/1, minute book, 1868–86, 17 May 1880, 258, and 16 May 1881, 290.
88 Peterborough Mechanics' Institute fonds, LAC, MSS 1995–2005, series E, folder 13, special events; and the Peterborough Mechanics' Institute fonds, PCMA, 59–028/1, minute book, 1868–86, 12 May 1884, 341, and 18 May 1885, 363–5.
89 See the Guelph Public Library fonds, Guelph Public Library, Guelph Mechanics' Institute minute book, 1872–83, 4 Dec. 1879; and the Ingersoll Mechanics' Institute fonds, RCL, M-581, minute book, 1880–90, annual report of 13 May 1889.
90 For an excellent discussion on the middle-class regulation of leisure, see Marks, *Revivals and Roller Rinks*. See also the Elora Mechanics' Institute fonds, WCA, A993.33, MU 279, Circular of the Old Folks Concert, 13 Nov. 1879.

CHAPTER THREE

1 For the evolution of temperance from moderation to prohibition in the United States see Tyrell, *Sobering Up*; Blocker, *American Temperance Movements*; and

Pegram, *Battling Demon Rum*. In Britain, see the classic by Harrison, *Drink and the Victorians*, and Shiman, *Crusade Against Drink in Victorian England*. For the Canadian context, see Clemens, "Taste Not, Touch Not, Handle Not," 142–60; Dick, "From Temperance to Prohibition," 530–52; Noel, *Canada Dry*; Holman, *A Sense of Their Duty*, 130–50; and Ferry, "To the Interests and Conscience of the Great Mass of the Community," 137–63.

2 That early temperance was led by an evangelical commercial aristocracy bent on social control and creating a capitalistic hegemony. See Tyrell, *Sobering Up*, 34–70, and Dannenbaum, *Drink and Disorder*, 32–62. For Britain, see Harrison, *Drink and the Victorians*, 25–30, 115–78, and for Canada, see Dick, "From Temperance to Prohibition," 530–5. Other historians have argued that a labour aristocracy and master artisans led temperance societies. See Lambert, *Drink and Society in Victorian Wales*, 32–40 and 87–113, as well as Holman, *A Sense of Their Duty*, 130–7. A more recent and compelling argument is that both the middling sort and the working classes used temperance in different periods of time to further their own agendas. See Shiman, *Crusade Against Drink*, 15–40; Blocker, *American Temperance Movements*, 3–60; and Pegram, *Battling Demon Rum*, 25–41. In Canada, see Clemens, "Taste Not, Touch Not, Handle Not," 142–60; Barron, "Damned Cold Water Drinking Societies," 11–28; and Noel, *Canada Dry*, 105–46.

3 See the *Canada Temperance Advocate* vol. 2 (1 Nov. 1836), 49–50; vol. 9 (15 May 1843), 23, and vol. 17 (15 May 1851), 157, as well as the *Eighth Report of the Toronto Temperance Reformation Society*, v and 8. For the membership of the evangelical middling classes in early temperance societies, see Noel, *Canada Dry*, 105–46, and Ferry, "To the Interests and Conscience of the Great Mass of the Community," 137–42.

4 *An Appeal to the Inhabitants of Lower Canada*, 11–12. See also the *Canada Temperance Advocate* vol. 2 (1 July 1836), 9; vol. 7 (1 June 1841), 40; vol. 7 (1 April 1842), 182; vol. 8 (15 Aug. 1842), 118; vol. 8 (1 Oct. 1842), 172; and vol. 14 (15 Aug. 1848), 241–2. On the skilled working-class roots of the Washington movement, see Tyrell, *Sobering Up*, 135–44.

5 *Canada Temperance Advocate* vol. 3 (1 Jan. 1838), 78; vol. 4 (1 Jan. 1839), 68–9; vol. 10 (15 April 1844), 112–3; vol. 10 (15 June 1844), 185–7; vol. 12 (2 Jan. 1847), 11–12; and vol. 17 (1 March 1851), 72. On the authority of a nascent liberal social order in Montreal, see the work of Fecteau, *Un nouvel ordre des choses* and his *La liberté du pauvre*.

6 *Canada Temperance Advocate* vol. 2 (1 Dec. 1836), extra supplement, 3. See also vol. 9 (15 June 1843), 50; vol. 12 (16 Nov. 1846), 344; and vol. 16 (15 March 1850), 90.

7 *Canada Temperance Advocate*, vol. 12 (1 Aug. 1846), 230–1, and vol. 16 (15 March 1850), 90–1. On the sectarian turmoil relating to temperance in Montreal, see

Noel, *Canada Dry*, 64–88, and particularly Abbott, *Strictures on the Remarks of the Rev. J Reid*, 3–5 and 25–7. Similar problems occurred in Upper Canada and the Maritimes with an emerging liberal social order; see Clemens, "Taste Not, Touch Not, Handle Not," 144–50, and Acheson, *Saint John*, 138–45.

8 Byrne, *The Claims of Temperance Societies*, 6–10, 20, and also Patton, *An Address for the Purpose of Forming a Temperance Society*, 4–5.

9 See the first tract of the Montreal Temperance Society, *An Appeal to the Inhabitants*, 10–12. See also the *Constitution of the Kingston Temperance Society*, 3, and Wilson, *A Sermon Preached on Behalf of the Perth Temperance Society*, 12–13.

10 *Eighth Report of the Toronto Temperance Reformation Society*, v and 18–19, and the statistics in the *Canada Temperance Advocate* vol. 6 (1 July 1840), 20, as well as the encouragement of women petitioners in vol. 2 (1 April 1836), 91. The Vaughn Anti-Bacchanalian Society recorded twenty-three women out of a membership of fifty-eight; see their records, AO, MU #2111, minute book, 1852–3, April 1852. More recent historiography focuses on the emergence of women in the public sphere as a result of temperance agitation, despite a rather public vision of domesticity. See Blocker, *American Temperance Movements*, 61–94; Noel, *Canada Dry*, 89–102; Ginzberg, *Women and the Work of Benevolence*, and Mattingly, *Well-Tempered Women*.

11 See the *Canada Temperance Advocate* vol. 9 (1 Aug. 1843), 104–5 and vol. 13 (16 Oct. 1847), 314–5; and Morgan, *Public Men and Virtuous Women*, 208–18.

12 *Canada Temperance Advocate* vol. 1 (1 Oct. 1835), 43; vol. 1 (1 Jan. 1836), 65; vol. 6 (1 Feb. 1841), 86; vol. 11 (1 April 1845), 101; and vol. 17 (15 May 1851), 57. Although this study focuses mainly on Protestant Christianity, Catholics also joined the temperance crusade; see Noel, "Dry Patriotism," 27–42.

13 The Reverend Joseph Abbott was a High Churchman who held a virulent hatred for dissenters; see his *Strictures on the Remarks of the Rev. J. Reid*, 3 and 25, and his entry in the *Dictionary of Canadian Biography* vol. 9, 3–4. Similarly, despite his enthusiasm for increased participation by the laity, Henry Patton believed in voluntarism from like-minded Church of England men, not other Protestant dissenters. See his *Address Delivered in the Village of Kemptville*, 11–13, and Fahey, *In His Name*, 183, 243–7 and 273–4.

14 See Abbott, *Strictures on the Remarks of Rev. J. Reid*, 21–2. See also Murray, *A Course of Lectures on Absolute Abstinence*, preface and 65–6. Educated in Glasgow, Murray most likely came under the influence of Thomas Chalmers, who believed in an institutionally led reform movement rather than in laity-dominated voluntarism. See Gidney, "The Rev. Robert Murray," 195–204, and Brown, *Thomas Chalmers and the Godly Commonwealth*, 152–95.

15 Knowlson, *An Address of Total Abstinence*, 3–5 and 11–14. On the established churches and the concept of loyalty, see Mills, *The Idea of Loyalty in Upper Canada*.

For the new liberal evangelicalism, see Gauvreau, "Personal Piety and the Evangelical Social Vision," 48–97.
16 Of course, such pronouncements signified support for a more liberal "middling" social order; see the *Canada Temperance Advocate* vol. 3 (1 Dec. 1837), 70–1; vol. 3 (1 Jan. 1838), 78; vol. 3 (1 Feb. 1838), 86–7; and vol. 4 (1 Dec. 1838), 60–1.
17 On the election of Molson in Montreal, see the *Canada Temperance Advocate* vol. 10 (1 March 1844), 71; vol. 10 (15 March 1844), 88; and vol. 10 (1 April 1844), 106.
18 See the *Canada Temperance Advocate* vol. 8 (15 July 1842), 96; vol. 9 (1 Jan. 1843), 271; vol. 13 (2 Aug. 1847), 238; and vol. 15 (1 June 1849), 166. See also *An Appeal to the Inhabitants of Lower Canada*, 6–7, and *Facts and Figures for the People*, 4–5.
19 Much of this sentiment echoed the ideology of the early producer alliance, whereby the "non-producing" and entrenched privileged mercantile elites were viewed as being outside the community of independent yeomen, artisans, and manufacturers. See MacDonald, "Merchants Against Industry," 266–80; Acheson, *Saint John*; and Heaman, *The Inglorious Arts of Peace*, 21–7. See also the *Canada Temperance Advocate* vol. 9 (1 July 1843), 71–2; vol. 11 (15 Jan. 1845), 24–5; vol. 11 (16 Nov. 1845), 344; and vol. 18, (15 Nov. 1852), 348–9.
20 *Canada Temperance Advocate* vol. 2 (1 Dec. 1836), 61–2; vol. 7 (1 May 1841), 4; vol. 9 (1 Aug. 1843), 104–5; and vol. 17 (16 Aug. 1851), 267.
21 See the records of the Vaughn Anti-Bacchanalian Society, AO, MU 2111, #5, minute book, 1852–53, 20 April 1852 to 7 June 1853, and records of the Toronto Temperance Reformation Society, John Linton fonds, AO, MU 7280, series A, file #14, act of incorporation for the society, 30 Aug. 1851, 1–2.
22 Dannenbaum, *Drink and Disorder*, 41–56; Blocker, *American Temperance Movements*, 45–57; and Acheson, *Saint John*, 148–54. Jan Noel argues that the Sons of Temperance formed a radical working-class subculture in Canada West, formulating their own concepts of respectability; see *Canada Dry*, 105–19 and 141–50.
23 In the Ameliasburgh Division of the Sons of Temperance from 1850–54, nine yeomen, five carpenters, 2 blacksmiths, a tailor, and a cooper became directors. See the records of the Ameliasburgh division, AO, MU 2085 #1, minute book, 1850–54, preamble.
24 See the *Canadian Son of Temperance and Literary Gem*, 22 April 1851, 74; 12 Aug. 1851, 195 and 26 Aug. 1851, 214.
25 See the *Good Templar*, 6 Jan. 1863 and 10 Feb. 1863. See also the *Ritual of the British American Order of Good Templars*, 13–14. Temperance societies therefore operated on a "familialist" model of society, where the local group acted as an extended family for members. See Christie's introduction, "Family, Community, and the Rise of Liberal Society," 3–20, and Marks, "Railing, Tattling, and General Rumour," 380–402.

26 *Canada Temperance Advocate* vol. 8 (15 July 1842), 88, and vol. 20 (1 June 1854), 172. See also *Proceedings of the Grand Division Sons of Temperance, Canada West*, Semi-annual session, (May 1852), 44, and Semi-annual session, (May 1854), 10.

27 A parallel difficulty existed in the United States; see Fahey, "Blacks, Good Templars, and Universal Membership," 133–61. See also the *Canada Temperance Advocate*, vol. 15 (1 Aug. 1849), 233–4; *Canadian Son of Temperance and Literary Gem*, 12 July 1853, 220–1 and 16 Aug. 1853, 260; and the *Proceedings of the Grand Division, Sons of Temperance, Canada West*, Annual session, (Oct. 1854), 19. The *Canadian Son of Temperance and Literary Gem* also reported a native division, with the chief of the tribe acting as the Worthy Patriarch; see 9 Aug. 1852, 238. On similar anti-slavery impulses inherent in evangelicalism, see Stouffer, *The Light of Nature and the Law of God*.

28 *Constitution of the Leading Star Union #33, Daughters of Temperance*, 3–25, and *The Sons of Temperance: Its Origins, History, and Influence*, 16–17.

29 See the Nithburg Division records, AO, MU 4734 #6, minute book, 1857–60, 7 April, 14 April, 21 July, 1858; 12 Jan., 9 Feb. and 2 March 1859. See also Noel, *Canada Dry*, 89–102 and Morgan, *Public Men and Virtuous Women*, 208–18.

30 Orono Sons of Temperance fonds, Archives of Ontario (hereafter AO), MU 2879, minute book #2, 1854–59, 6 Jan., 1 Sept. 1858; and also the Orono minute book #3, 1863–64, 23 Sept. 1863. This is a great local example of the kind of debates held at the Grand Division level about female membership; see *Proceedings of the Grand Division of the Sons of Temperance, Canada East*, Annual session (June 1864), 5; Annual session (June 1867), 14–15; and Annual session (June 1868), 6 and 18.

31 See the *Proceedings of the Grand Temple, IOGT*, Annual meeting (April 1861), 12–13, and the *Good Templar*, 6 Jan. 1863 and 7 April 1863. See also the *Ritual of the British American Order of Good Templars*, 13–14.

32 *Proceedings of the Grand Temple, IOGT*, Semi-annual meeting (Oct. 1860), 9; see also the *Good Templar*, 26 May 1863 and 28 July 1863, as well as the *Degree Book of the IOGT*, 6–7 and 15. See also the *Proceedings of the Grand Division Sons of Temperance, Canada East*, Annual session (July 1863), 5–6.

33 See Brown, *Speech of T.S. Brown at the Union Tent*, 2–3; *An Appeal to Men of Wealth and Influence*, 3–8; and also the *Canadian Son of Temperance and Literary Gem*, 13 May 1851, 90, and 5 July 1853, 212.

34 *Canadian Son of Temperance and Literary Gem*, 11 March 1851, 28; 18 Oct. 1851, 275; 5 Jan. 1852, 20, and 17 April 1852, 123.

35 *Canadian Son of Temperance and Literary Gem*, 18 Jan. 1853, 22; 7 Jan. 1854, 5; 22 April 1854, 97; and 2 Sept. 1854, 211–2. On anti-Catholic sentiment in Canada, see the excellent article by Miller, "Anti-Catholic Thought in Victorian Canada," 474–94.

36 See the *Canadian Son of Temperance and Literary Gem*, 9 Sept. 1851, 230; 6 May 1854, 108; 13 May 1854, 115; 26 July 1853, 235; 2 Aug. 1853, 244; and the prospective of *The Crisis*, 13 Jan. 1855.
37 See the *British American Order of Good Templars, The Documents, Reasons and Proceedings*, 6–8, 10–14; *Ritual of the British American Order of Good Templars*, 10; and Gowan, *The Advantages of Membership in the Order of British Templars*, 4–5.
38 *Proceedings of the Grand Temple, IOGT*, Annual meeting (April 1860), 10–11, 27, and Semi-annual session (Nov. 1865), 47–8; the *Good Templar*, 3 May 1864 and 17 May 1864.
39 For the efficiency of the Maine Laws in enforcing prohibition in the United States, see Dannenbaum, *Drink and Disorder*, 69–99; Blocker, *American Temperance Movements*, 70–9; and Pegram, *Battling Demon Rum*, 39–45.
40 See the *Proceedings of the Grand Division, Sons of Temperance, Canada East*, Annual session (June 1854), 8–10, and the *Proceedings of the Grand Division, Sons of Temperance, Canada West*, Semi-annual session (May 1852), 9 and 44; Semi-annual session (May 1853), 9–10 and Semi-annual session (May 1857), 3–4.
41 Appeals to "public opinion" often shrouded the authority of the social order; see McNairn, *The Capacity to Judge*. See also the *Good Templar*, 20 Jan. 1863, 26 May 1863, 14 July 1863, and 4 Aug. 1863.
42 On the language of popular politics in this period, see Wilton, *Popular Politics and Political Culture in Upper Canada*. See also the *Canadian Son of Temperance and Literary Gem*, 16 Dec. 1851, 372–3; 5 Jan. 1852, 7; and 12 June 1852, 188–9.
43 *Canadian Son of Temperance and Literary Gem*, 6 Dec. 1851, 357, and 15 Nov. 1853, 360. See also the *Proceedings of the Grand Division, Sons of Temperance, Canada West*, Semi-annual session (June 1861), 10–11. Many historians view the reallocation of interest to political prohibition as the mitigating factor in the removal of working class support from temperance; see Tyrell, *Sobering Up*, 230–40; Blocker, *American Temperance Movements*, 50–5; and Holman, *A Sense of Their Duty*, 140–50.
44 See the *Good Templar*, 3 Nov. 1863, 4, and 12 April 1864. See also the *Constitution of the National, Grand and Subordinate Divisions of the Sons of Temperance*, 20. See also the *Canadian Son of Temperance and Literary Gem*, 26 Feb. 1851, 12–13, and 26 Aug. 1851, 211–13.
45 The Sons of Temperance also enforced an edict that each member needed to have a visible means of support; see the *Constitution of the National, Grand and Subordinate Divisions of the Sons of Temperance*, 20. See also the *Canadian Son of Temperance and Literary Gem*, 26 Feb. 1851, 12–13, and 26 Aug. 1851, 211–13.
46 *Canadian Son of Temperance and Literary Gem*, 24 June 1851, 142, and the *Constitution of the National, Grand and Subordinate Divisions of the Sons of Temperance*, 16, 21–3. See also Leach, *An Address on Rechabitism*, 6–9, and the *Revised Constitution, General Laws and Bylaws of the Knights of Temperance*, 3–4.

47 See the *Proceedings of the Grand Division, Sons of Temperance, Canada West*, Annual session (Oct. 1853), 6–7, and 16. For an example of a treasurer absconding with lodge or division funds, see the records of the Ameliasburgh Sons, AO, MU 2085 #1, minute book, 1850–54, 4 Oct. 1851 to 21 Feb. 1852.

48 *Proceedings of the Grand Division, Sons of Temperance, Canada West*, Annual session (Oct. 1852), 53; Semi-annual session (May 1854), 11–12; Semi-annual session (May 1856), 6–7; Annual session (Dec. 1857), 37–8; and Semi-annual session (June 1862), 12–13.

49 See the *Canadian Son of Temperance and Literary Gem*, 18 Oct. 1853, 332, and the *Canada Temperance Advocate* vol. 16 (15 Jan. 1850), 22. The International Order of Rechabites made similar comments about non-temperance fraternalism; see the *Canada Temperance Advocate* vol. 15 (1 May 1849), 132. For the rise of other mutual benefit societies in this period, see Palmer, "Mutuality and the Masking/Making of Difference," 111–38, and Peticlerc, "L'association qui crée une nouvelle famille," 259–92.

50 Gowan, *The Advantages of Membership in the Order of British Templars*, 1–2 and 5. For the formation of temperance libraries and debate societies, see the Nithburg Sons of Temperance fonds, AO, MU 4734 #6, minute book, 1857–60, 12 Jan. 1859; record of the Ameliasburgh Sons, AO, MU 2085 #1, minute book, 1850–54, 18 Jan. 1851. See also the *Proceedings of the Grand Division, Sons of Temperance, Canada West*, Annual session (Oct. 1855), 6–7, and *Constitution and Bylaws of the St. Lawrence Division*, 27–8.

51 See the *Proceedings of the Grand Division, Sons of Temperance, Canada West*, Annual session (Oct. 1852), 19 and 53; Semi-annual session (May 1854), 11–12; and the Semi-annual session (May 1856), 6–7. See also the Orono Sons of Temperance fonds, AO, MU 2879, minute book, 1854–59, 21 March 1855, 6 Jan. 1856, 9 April 1856, and 16 July 1856; Norwich Sons of Temperance fonds, Harold Williams collection, LAC, MS 301, minute book, 1851–60, 4 June 1851, 22–3; and Nithburg Sons of Temperance fonds, AO, MU 4734 #6, minute book, 1857–60, 29 Sept. 1858.

52 See the Nithburg Sons of Temperance fonds, AO, MU 4734 #6, minute book, 1857–60, 11 Aug. 1858; the Norwich Sons of Temperance fonds, Harold Williams collection, LAC, MS 301, minute book, 1851–60, 4 June 1851, 21–3; and especially the *Constitution of the Sons of Temperance of North America*, 42–5.

53 *Proceedings of the Grand Temple, International Order of Good Templars*, Semi-annual session (April 1860), 25–6, and Norfolk Division, Sons of Temperance, Norfolk Historical Society fonds, LAC, MG D8/24, M–282, reel 9, minute book, 1850–54, 20 May 1850, 12344.

54 Concerns over rational recreation infused the world of skilled workers as well as the middle class; see Blocker, *American Temperance Movements*, 45–52; Acheson,

Saint John, 146–51; and Noel, *Canada Dry*, 105–19 and 141–50. See also the Norfolk Division, Sons of Temperance, Norfolk Historical Society fonds, LAC, MG D8/24, M–282, reel 9, minute book, 1850–54, 6 Nov. 1850, 12374, and the records of the Gananoque lodge, British American Order of Good Templars, MTL, minute book, 1860–61, 15 May 1860, and 29 June 1860.

55 Most historians have identified middle-class involvement with temperance as a result of increased interest in political prohibition. See Blocker, *American Temperance Movements*, 51–6; Dannenbaum, *Drink and Disorder*, 172–8; Tyrell, *Sobering Up*, 223–40; and Dick, "From Temperance to Prohibition," 548–52, as well as Harrison, *Drink and the Victorians*, 220–9, and Sendbueler, "Battling the Bane of Our Cities," 30–48. Feminist historians view this shift as a result of the amplified participation of middle-class women in organizations such as the Women's Christian Temperance Union. See Bordin, *Women and Temperance* and Cook, *Through Sunshine and Shadow*.

56 On the convoluted atmosphere of urban prohibition associations in the United States, see Blocker, *Retreat from Reform* and Kerr, *Organized for Prohibition*. Decarie has noted the complexity of urban prohibition movements in Canada; see Decarie, "Aspects of Prohibitionism," 154–71.

57 This would be the credo of many temperance union societies: see *Canadian Prohibitory Liquor Law League*, 2–3; *Proceedings of the Second Session of the Canada Temperance Union*, 4–5; *Proceedings at the Third Annual Meeting of the Ontario Temperance and Prohibitory League*, 3; and *Third Annual Meeting of the Quebec Temperance and Prohibitory League*, 4–5.

58 See the *Camp Fire*, 1 Sept. 1895 and 1 April 1896. See also the records of the Dominion Alliance, John Linton fonds, AO, MU 7270, file #13, miscellaneous Ontario Branch records, letter from WH Howland, no date, 1, and *Second Annual Meeting of the Ontario Branch of the Dominion Alliance*, 3–4.

59 Dominion Alliance records, John Linton fonds, AO, MU 7269, file #10, minute book, 1877–99, 2 June 1886. See also the *Third Annual Meeting of the Quebec Temperance League*, 13, and 28–9, and *Fourth Annual Meeting of the Quebec Temperance and Prohibitory League*, 3–4.

60 See the Dominion Alliance records, John Linton fonds, AO, MU 7269, file #10, minute book, 1877–99, 1881 annual meeting, 141. See also the *Canada Citizen and Temperance Herald*, 25 July 1884, 40; 17 April 1885, 494; and the *Third Annual Meeting of the Quebec Temperance League*, 13–14.

61 The Alliance not only set up a successful French Branch but a few years later the Ontario Branch of the Alliance requested a French lecturer from Quebec to assist in the recruitment of Franco-Ontarians. See the Dominion Alliance records, John Linton fonds, AO, MU 7269, MU 7270, file #19, minute book of the Ontario Cam-

paign Executive committee, 27 Oct. 1893 and 10 Nov. 1893, and file #5, council meetings, 14 July 1897.
62 The records of the Dominion Alliance, John Linton fonds, AO, MU 7269, file #10, minute book, 1877–99, 19 Sept. 1887; *Yearbook of the Dominion Alliance 1884*, 12; and also the *Canada Citizen and Temperance Herald*, 12 Dec. 1884, 278–9, and 4 Nov. 1887, 4. See also Decarie, "Aspects of Prohibitionism," 169–71; Bacchi, *Liberation Deferred*, 72–5; and Cook, *Through Sunshine and Shadow*, 64–6.
63 *Canadian Prohibitory Liquor Law League*, 18 and 30, and also *What Does It Cost? Statistical Report of the Canada Temperance Union*, 4–5.
64 *Second Annual Meeting of the Quebec Temperance and Prohibitory League*, 3, and *Third Annual Meeting of the Quebec Temperance League*, 13–14.
65 See the *Canada Citizen and Temperance Herald*, 29 Aug. 1884, 98; 26 Sept. 1884, 121 and 18 Nov. 1887, 2.
66 *Charter and Bylaws of the Temperance Colonization Society*, 4–5 and 9, as well as the *Canada Citizen and Temperance Herald*, 12 Sept. 1884, 121, and 31 Oct. 1884, 206.
67 Toronto Coffee House Association fonds, AO, MU 2120, #10, miscellaneous papers, 1882–99, first annual report, Nov. 1882, and ninth annual report, Nov. 1890. See also the *Constitution and Bylaws of the Canadian Temperance League*, 3 and 6–7.
68 *Second Annual Meeting of the Quebec Temperance and Prohibitory League*, 14–15, and *Third Annual Meeting of the Quebec Temperance League*, 12–13. See also *What Does it Cost? Canada Temperance Union*, 5–6, and *Proceedings of the Second Session of the Canada Temperance Union*, 20.
69 See the *Canada Citizen and Temperance Herald*, 11 Nov. 1884, 241–2, and the records of the Dominion Alliance, John Linton fonds, AO, MU 7269, file #10, minute book, 1877–99, Sept. 1877 and 2 June 1886. See also the Young Men's Prohibition Club, John Linton fonds, AO, MU 7281, file #18, constitution and bylaws, 1886.
70 *Fifth Annual Meeting of the Quebec Temperance and Prohibitory League*, 69–73, and *Proceedings of the Second Session of the Canada Temperance Union*, 27 and 49–50.
71 See the records of the Young Men's Prohibition Club, John Linton fonds, AO, MU 7281, file #18, constitution and bylaws, 1886; *What Does It Cost? Canada Temperance Union*, 16; *Fourth Annual Meeting of the Quebec Temperance League*, 8; and *Dominion Alliance Yearbook for the Year 1882*, 13–14.
72 *Canada Citizen and Temperance Herald*, 8 Aug. 1884, 61; 6 June 1885, 607; and 28 Nov. 1887, 4. See also the records of the Dominion Alliance, John Linton fonds, AO, MU 7269, file #9, responses from temperance politicians to Frank Spence, from P. Macdonald, 27 June 1888; from James Innes, 28 June 1888; and from E. Holton, 28 June 1888.
73 *Canada Citizen and Temperance Herald*, 18 July 1884, 9; 23 March 1888, 5; and 30 March 1888, 4.

74 See the records of the Dominion Alliance, John Linton fonds, AO, MU 7269, file #10, minute book, 1877–99, 2 June 1886.
75 The *Templar*, 21 June 1895, 8 Nov. 1895, 22 Nov. 1895, 29 Nov. 1895, and 6 Dec. 1895.
76 Spence would also receive censure for his lukewarm condemnation of the Liberals after the failed plebiscite of 1898. See the records of the Dominion Alliance, John Linton fonds, AO, MU 7269, file #5, Dominion Alliance council meetings, 24 July 1896, and the *Annual Council Meeting of the Dominion Alliance*, 16–17.
77 *What Does it Cost? The Canada Temperance Union*, 4 and 13–14. See also the *Second Annual Meeting of the Quebec Temperance League*, 42, and records of the Young Men's Prohibition Club, John Linton fonds, AO, MU 7281, file #18, constitution and bylaws, 1886.
78 Records of the Dominion Alliance, John Linton fonds, AO, MU 7269, file #10, minute book, 1877–99, Sept. 1877.
79 Burgess, *Land, Labor and Liquor*, 21–6, 30–2, 51–5, 82–95, 102–11, and 114–18. For these "new" ideas of political economy, see Ferguson, *Remaking Liberalism*; Burke, *Seeking the Highest Good*; and Burr, *Spreading the Light*.
80 See Burgess, *Land, Labor and Liquor*, viii, 41–3, 122–6, 174–82, and 228–40. Burgess also argued against compensation for the liquor traffic with the introduction of prohibition. "They have rendered no service to the country, nor placed the public under any obligation or indebtedness ... the whole community is placed under tax to meet the ravages of the unholy business." See Burgess, *The Liquor Traffic and Compensation*, 4–6 and 20–1.
81 Miscellaneous files, John Linton fonds, AO, MU 7280, file #14, Bylaws of the Toronto Temperance Reformation Society, 1886. See also the records of the Young Men's Prohibition club, John Linton fonds, AO, MU 7281, file #19, minute book, 1889–90, 16 Feb. 1889, 6 and 18 April 1889, 16 July 1889, and 26 Sept. 1889.
82 Several studies on small-town Ontario fraternal temperance societies confirm a diverse membership base, including a healthy portion from skilled workers. See Anstead, "Fraternalism in Victorian Ontario," 325–40, and Cook, *Through Sunshine and Shadow*, 22–9. See particularly Marks, *Revivals and Roller Rinks*, 85–95 and 246–9, and her work on temperance in Thorold, Campbellford, and Ingersoll.
83 Marks, *Revivals and Roller Rinks*, 85–9; Holman, *A Sense of Their Duty*, 139–50; Anstead, "Hegemony and Failure," 163–88; and Ferry, "Severing the Connections in a Complex Community," 9–47.
84 See the *Camp Fire*, Feb. 1895, 4, and 1 Nov. 1897, 3. See also the *Sons of Temperance Record and Prohibition Advocate*, Feb. 1898, 2; July 1898, 3; and Sherlocke, *Present Aspect of the Temperance Movement*, 4–7.

85 *Camp Fire*, 1 Nov. 1895, 2–3; 1 Dec. 1897, 2; 1 Feb. 1898, 3; and the records of the Orono Division of the Sons of Temperance, AO, MU 2880, minute book #6, 1877–81, 4 Sept. 1878, 98.
86 On the increased involvement of women in temperance after mid-century, see Blocker, *American Temperance Movements*, 61–94; Pegram, *Battling Demon Rum*, 44–70; and Bacchi, *Liberation Deferred?* chapter 5, "Temperate Beginnings," 69–85. That the WCTU was an exercise in proto-feminism, see Bordin, *Women and Temperance* and Mattingly, *Well-Tempered Women*. For the WCTU, scientific temperance, and the moral purity movement, see Cook, *Through Sunshine and Shadow*. Daniel Malleck makes a very compelling argument that the WCTU focused on education, moral purity, evangelicalism, and prohibition as the local context warranted. See Malleck, "Priorities in Development in Four WCTU's in Ontario," 189–208.
87 A debate held in the council room of the Cherry Valley Royal Templars of Temperance came out in favour of votes for women; apparently the sisters managed to persuade their male colleagues. See the records of the Cherry Valley council, Royal Templars, AO, MU 7793 #3, minute book, 1892–1900, 22 March 1893, 11. See also Sherlocke, *Present Aspect of the Temperance Movement*, 18–22; the *Camp Fire*, 1 March 1895; the *Quebec Good Templar*, 1 May 1892, 125–6; and the *Templar*, 8 Nov. 1895.
88 The lowering of fees caused a rather cantankerous debate in the Hampton lodge of the IOGT; see the Henry Elliot fonds, LAC, MG 28 III 41, vol. 13, financial secretary's record, 1871–73, and minute book, 1873–76, 26 April 1875, 75; and the *Constitution of the Grand Temple*, 21–2. For women as Worthy Patriarchs, see the records of the Summerville Sons, Peel Region Archives, M78.0006, minute book, 1890–91, 2 Jan. 1891, and minute book, 1891–94, 6 Jan. 1893; records of the Hobart Sons, SCA, Acc. 975–92, minute book, 1897–1900, 27 Sept. 1899.
89 See the records of the Plantagenet Royal Templars of Temperance, AO, MU 7793 #2, minute book, 1892–94, 11 Nov. 1892.
90 This was also the conclusion of Sharon Cook, *Through Sunshine and Shadow*, 24–9. See the Orono Division, Sons of Temperance fonds, AO, MU 2880, minute book #7, 1881–91, 30 May 1888, 428; records of the Williamstown Royal Templars, F.D. McLennan papers, AO, MU 7914, file #8, minute book, 1891–92, 29 May 1891; and file #9, minute book, 1893–94, 7 April 1893.
91 See the *Templar*, 21 June 1895 and 6 Dec. 1895; *Royal Templar Platform: A Collection of Readings and Recitations*, 63–6; and *Trumpet Notes of the Temperance Battlefield*, 19.
92 See the *Templar*, 8 Nov. 1895, 13 Dec. 1895, and *Trumpet Notes for the Royal Templars*, back page. See also the records of the North Toronto council of the

Royal Templars, John Linton fonds, AO, MU 7276, file #2, petitions of membership, back page, and *Manual of the Select Degree and Ceremony of Installation*, 10–11.

93 *Constitutions of the Grand, District and Subordinate Order of Good Templars*, 13–15, and the *Camp Fire*, 1 Sept. 1895. The statistics compiled by Marks and Anstead in the towns of Ingersoll, Campbellford, and Thorold are also invaluable in this regard, although neither focuses on the benefits offered by the IOGT and the Royal Templars as an explanation for their popularity among skilled workers. See Anstead, "Fraternalism in Victorian Ontario," 325–40; Cook, *Through Sunshine and Shadow*, 22–9; and Marks, *Revivals and Roller Rinks*, 85–95 and 246–9.

94 See the *Camp Fire*, 1 Oct. 1895, 1 April 1895, 1 June 1898, and 1 Sept. 1898, as well as the *Quebec Good Templar*, 1 June 1893, 144.

95 Bradley, *Facts and Figures Dedicated to the People of Canada*, and the *Camp Fire*, 1 Aug. 1898. The Williamstown Royal Templars, in the F.D. McLennan collection, AO, MU 7915, file #1, minute book, 1894–1903, 24 March 1893, and the Orono Division of the Sons of Temperance, AO, MU 2879, minute book #5, 1870–77, 11 Jan. 1871.

96 *Camp Fire*, 1 April 1897 and 1 Feb. 1898. On the producer ideology in the late nineteenth-century, see Kealey, *Toronto Workers Respond to Industrial Capitalism*; Palmer, *A Culture in Conflict*; and Burr, *Spreading the Light*.

97 See the *Camp Fire*, 1 Feb. 1895 and 1 Dec. 1897. See also the *Sons of Temperance Record and Prohibition Advocate*, 1 Feb. 1898 and 1 July 1898, and particularly Sherlocke, *Present Aspect of the Temperance Movement*, 4–7, 16–17.

98 Decarie in "The Prohibition Movement in Ontario," illustrates that prohibition sentiment was strongest in rural Ontario. See also the records of the Cherry Valley Royal Templars, AO, MU 7793 #3, minute book, 1892–1900, 1 Aug. 1894 and 16 May 1898; Williamstown Royal Templars, in the F.D. McLennan collection, AO, MU 7915, file #1, minute book, 1894–1903, 17 Dec. 1896, 69, and 9 May 1898, 131; Fergus Royal Templar records, Templin Family collection, AO, MU 2957, minute book, 1892–96, 4 Sept. 1893, 103, and 19 March 1894, 131.

99 See the Orono Division, Sons of Temperance fonds, AO, MU 2879, minute book #4, 1866–70, 14 April 1869, 251, and 28 April 1869, 254. See also the records of the Fergus Royal Templars, Templin family collection, AO, MU 2957, minute book, 1892–96, 8 Aug. 1892, 10; 3 April 1893, 73; and 19 June 1893, 90.

100 Although some historians view Populism as a movement restricted to agrarian concerns, more recent historiography recognizes that groups as diverse as labour unions and religious movements could participate in populist rhetoric. See Hann, *Farmers Confront Industrialism*; Shortt, "Social Change and Political Crisis in Rural Ontario," 211–35; Cook, "Tillers and Toilers," 5–20; Ferry, "Severing the Connections"; and especially Noel, "Early Populist Tendencies in Ontario Political Culture," 173–87, as well as Mussio, "The Origins and Nature of the Holiness Movement Church," 81–104.

01 See the *22nd Annual Session of the Grand Lodge, International Order of Good Templars*, 9–11, and Lawless, *The Canada Digest, International Order of Good Templars*, 10–12. See also the *Camp Fire*, 1 Jan. 1895, 1 May 1895, 1 Feb. 1896, and the *Sons of Temperance Record and Prohibition Advocate*, 1 Feb. 1898.

02 See the records of the Cherry Valley Royal Templars, AO, MU 7793 #3, minute book, 1892–1900, 1 Aug. 1894 and 16 May 1898.

03 *Royal Templar Platform*, 15–17 and 63–6. For local councils supporting Patron candidates, see records of the Williamstown Royal Templars in the F.D. McLennan fonds, AO, MU 7914, file #9, minute book, 1893–94, 26 May 1893; Plantagenet Royal Templars, AO, MU 7793, #2, minute book, 1892–94, 28 May 1893; and Cherry Valley Royal Templars, AO, MU 7793 #3, minute book, 1892–1900, 1 June and 15 June 1897.

04 See the *Templar*, 21 June 1895, 8 Nov. 1895, 13 Dec. 1895, and *Trumpet Notes of the Royal Templars*, back page, as well as Cook, "Tillers and Toilers," 10–18.

05 Lawless, *The Canada Digest: Independent Order of Good Templars*, 108. See the *Canada Digest*, 16, 35, and 39. For the importance of entertainment in rural temperance societies as a means of community building, see Marks, *Revivals and Roller Rinks*, 94–5, and Cook, *Through Sunshine and Shadow*, 22–3.

06 See the records of the Gananoque lodge, British American Order of Good Templars, MTL, minute book, 1860–61, 12 April 1860, 24 Aug. 1860, 18 Jan. 1861, and 19 April 1861. See also the Orono Division, Sons of Temperance fonds, AO, 2879, minute book #3, 1863–64, 15 April 1863 to 18 Nov. 1863.

07 See Rose and Hammond, *The Teetotaller's Companion*; Hammond, *A Collection of Temperance Dialogues*; and Rose, *Light for the Temperance Platform*.

08 See the records of the Orono Division of the Sons of Temperance, AO, MU 2879, minute book #4, 1866–70, 8 June 1870, 338, and the records of the Greensboro Temple of the Good Templars, WCA, MU 238, A1992.130, minute book, 1875–77, 18 May 1876 and 15 June 1876.

09 See the *Good Templar*, 20 Jan. 1863 and also the *Independent Order of Good Templars, Twenty-Second Annual Session*, 18.

10 See the Orono Sons of Temperance fonds, AO, MU 2879, minute book #5, 1870–77, 28 Feb. 1872, 93, and minute book #6, 1877–81, 8 May 1878, 60–1. The Forest Home lodge of the Good Templars solicited ideas not only to make their meetings more interesting but also to see how they could open their lodge to the public; see their records, SCA, Acc. 968–15, minute book, 1870–78, 19 June 1874, 204.

11 The Midhurst lodge held only one public concert, and planned no other public entertainments, as their membership dropped from sixty members to eight in just three years. See their records, SCA, Acc. 981–96, minute book, 1878–84, 26 Feb. 1879, 27 and 26 April 1882, 51–2. See also the Hampton Good Templar records,

Henry Elliot fonds, LAC, MG 28 III 41, vol. 13, financial secretary's record, 1871–73 and minute book, 1873–76, 18 Jan. 1875, 63, and 17 Jan., 91; and the records of the Forest Home temple, SCA, Acc. 968–15, minute book, 1870–76, 2 Feb. 1872, 78; 22 Nov. 1872, 132; 11 April 1873, 154; and 24 June 1874, 222.

112 See also the records of the Eugene Sons of Temperance, SCA, Acc. 978–35, minute book, 1893–1907, 21 May 1894 and 11 Jan. 1897; Lachute Sons of Temperance records, Thomas Barron fonds, LAC, MG 24 I 128, vol. 5, minute book, 1891–92, 26 Nov. 1891, 11, and *Sons of Temperance Record and Prohibition Advocate*, 1 Sept. 1898.

113 See also the records of the Cherry Valley Royal Templars, AO, MU 7793 #3, minute book, 1892–1900, 2 March 1896, 96, and the records of the Summerville division of the Sons of Temperance, Peel Region Archives, Acc. M78.0006, minute book, 1890–91, 17 Oct. 1890, and minute book, 1891–94, 6 May 1892 and 18 July 1892.

114 For just a few of these examples, see the records of the Orono Division of the Sons of Temperance, AO, MU 2879, minute book #4, 1866–70, 1 May 1867, 119; 8 May 1867, 121; and 24 May 1867, 126; minute book #5, 1870–77, 18 Jan. 1871, 11; MU 2880, minute book, #6, 1877–81, 8 May 1877, 60, and 11 Feb. 1880, 253; minute book #8, 1891–96, 5 Aug. 1891 and 23 Dec. 1891.

115 Not surprisingly, these latter two fraternal temperance societies endured well into the twentieth century. See the records of the Eugene Sons of Temperance, SCA, Acc. 978–35, minute book, 1893–1907, 21 May 1894, 4 Nov. 1895, 2 Dec. 1895, 12 Jan. 1896, 24 May 1897, and 13 Aug. 1897. See also the records of the Williamstown Royal Templars, F.D. McLennan papers, AO, MU 7914, file #9, minute book, 1893–94, 16 March 1894 and 13 April 1894; MU 7915, file #1, minute book 1894–1903, 19 Oct. 1894, 15; 20 Aug. 1897, 100; 24 Jan. 1898, 115; 30 May 1898, 134; 18 July 1898, 141; and 29 Aug. 1898, 149.

116 See the Orono Division, Sons of Temperance fonds, AO, MU 2880, minute book #7, 1881–91, 30 May 1888, 428, and the Eugene Sons of Temperance fonds, SCA, Acc. 978–35, minute book, 1893–1907, 20 July 1896. See also the records of the Fergus Royal Templars, Templin Family collection, AO, MU 2957, minute book, 1892–96, 4 July 1892, 4, to 28 November, 41; and 1 April 1895, 184, to 18 May 1896, 251.

117 A similar episode occurred earlier in the Orono division, where the Worthy Patriarch "nearly split his gavel in getting the enjoyable folks quieted, however he succeeded very well." See the Orono Sons of Temperance fonds, AO, MU 2879, minute book #6, 1877–1881, 3 April 1878, 48, and minute book #7, 1881–1891, 30 May 1888, 429, as well as the records of the Williamstown Royal Templars, F.D. McLennan papers, AO, MU 7915, file #1, minute book 1894–1903, 9 April 1897, 85–6.

118 See *Trumpet Notes of the Royal Templars*, back page, and the *Quebec Good Templar*, 1 May 1892, 127–8, and 1 June 1892, 133–5.
119 See the *Camp Fire*, 1 May 1895, 1 Sept. 1897, 1 Oct. 1897, and 1 Nov. 1897.

CHAPTER FOUR

1 See the records of the Ontario Lodge #12 of the IOOF in Cobourg, MTL, L36, register book, 1848–61, bylaws pasted on the back; records of the Phoenix Lodge #22 in Oshawa, MTL, L36, register of rejected candidates and also the *Constitution, Bylaws and Rules of Order of Albion Lodge*, 44–5.
2 See the records of the Rondeau Lodge #40 of the IOOF in Blenheim, MTL, L36, minute book, 1860–65, 16 May 1863; the records of the Imperial Lodge #37 in Burford, MTL, L36, minute book, 1860–65, 19 Aug. 1861 and the records of the Phoenix Lodge #22 in Oshawa, MTL, L36, minute book, 1847–49, 18 Oct. 1847.
3 The records of the St Clair Lodge #106 of the IOOF in Point Edward, RCL, box 4319, minute book, 1873–74, 4 June 1873.
4 See the records of the St Clair Lodge #106 in Point Edward, RCL, box 4319, minute book, 1873–74, 4 June 1873.
5 The records of the St Clair Lodge #106 in Point Edward, RCL, box 4319, minute book, 1873–74, 11 June 1873.
6 See the records of the St Clair Lodge #106 of the IOOF in Point Edward, RCL, box 4319, minute book, 1873–74, 22 July 1874, and the minute book, 1878–82, 16 Jan. 1879.
7 For Britain, see Gosden, *Self-Help*; Cordery, "Friendly Societies and the Discourse of Respectability," 35–58; and Hopkins, *Working Class Self-Help in Nineteenth-Century England*, 8–30. For Canada, see Kealey, *Toronto Workers Respond to Industrial Capitalism*, 98–123; Anstead, "Fraternalism in Victorian Ontario"; and especially the more recent work of Palmer, "Mutuality and the Masking/Making of Difference," 111–38; and Petitclerc, "L'association qui crée une nouvelle famille," 259–92.
8 On cross-class membership of fraternalism in Britain and the United States, see Greenberg, "Worker and Community"; Gilkeson, *Middle-Class Providence*, 4–35; Clawson, *Constructing Brotherhood*; and D'Cruze and Turnbull, "Fellowship and Family," 25–47. For the middle classes and fraternalism in Canada, see Sutherland, "Voluntary Societies and the Process of Middle Class Formation," 237–64, and Holman, *A Sense of Their Duty*, 105–29. Jeffrey McNairn argued that most early mutual benefit groups imitated the egalitarianism of groups such as Freemasonry, while favouring the tenets of the bourgeois public sphere; see his *The Capacity to Judge*, 70–82.
9 Clawson, *Constructing Brotherhood*; Carnes, *Secret Ritual and Manhood in Victorian America*; Anstead, "Fraternalism in Victorian Ontario," 161–90; Cordery, "Friendly

Societies and the Discourse of Respectability," 41–8; Marks, *Revivals and Roller Rinks*, 108–16; and Palmer, "Mutuality and the Making/Masking of Difference," 130–8. On Victorian masculinity and the importance of male sociability, see the work of John Tosh, *A Man's Place*, 132–8, and his recent collection of essays, *Manliness and Masculinities in Nineteenth-Century Britain*, 1–9 and 41–51.

10 Green and Cromwell, *Mutual Aid or Welfare State*; all of the essays in Marcel van der Linden, *Social Security Mutualism*; Emery and Emery, *A Young Man's Benefit*; and David Beito, *From Mutual Aid to the Welfare State*, 17–40. David Neave argues that rural mutual benefit societies have largely been neglected; see his *Mutual Aid in the Victorian Countryside*.

11 See Houston and Smyth, *The Sash Canada Wore*; Akenson, *The Irish in Ontario*, 170–201; and See, *Riots in New Brunswick*. Not to be outdone, Catholic "Green" Irishmen did not escape nationalism in their lay associations either; see Clarke, *Piety and Nationalism*, 152–223. While it is difficult to assess the relative effectiveness of the mutual benefit services offered by these "national" societies, Palmer provides evidence that the mutual benefit system within such associations as the Orange Order simply could not be sustained; see Palmer, "Mutuality and the Making/Masking of Difference," 124–6.

12 For Freemasonry and middle-class elitism, see Anstead, "Fraternalism in Victorian Ontario," 184–94; Marks, *Revivals and Roller Rinks*, 109, 249–50; and Holman, *A Sense of Their Duty*, 111–23. For the Knights of Labor, see Kealey and Palmer, *Dreaming of What Might Be*; Voss, *The Making of American Exceptionalism*; and Weir, *Beyond Labor's Veil*.

13 See the *Odd Fellows Record* vol. 2 (Jan. 1847), 15, and vol. 2 (May 1847), 129–30.

14 Albert Case, *Address Delivered Before Oriental Lodge*, 15. See also the *Odd Fellows Record* vol. 1 (Jan. 1846), 2; vol. 1 (March 1846), 39; and vol. 1 (July 1846), 108.

15 The membership list of the aptly named Commercial lodge of the IOOF in Montreal indeed reads like a "who's who" list of the elite of Montreal, from commercial heavyweights such as Molson, Keefer, and Beckett, as well as political figures like Sandfield Macdonald, Draper, Dunkin, and Boulton. See *History of Oddfellowship in Canada*, 15 and 71–3, as well as *Constitution, Bylaws and Rules of Order of the Commercial Lodge*, 66–9.

16 *Odd Fellows Record* vol. 2 (Jan. 1847), 15; vol. 2 (Feb. 1847), 38–42; vol. 2 (March 1847), 55; and vol. 2 (April 1847), 80. On the importance of education in composing a liberal social order, see the work of Curtis, *Building the Educational State* and the preceding two chapters on Mechanics' Institutes, above.

17 One can read the Journal of Deputation of the BNA Grand Lodge of the IOOF in the AO, MU 2211, file A-II-1, 12 March 1846, 17, and 28 March 1846, 39. See also the records of the Hope lodge #14, MTL, L36, minute book, 1846–49, 2 Nov. 1846 and the Phoenix lodge #22, MTL, L36, minute book, 1847–49, 5 July 1847.

18 See the records of the Phoenix lodge #22, IOOF, in the MTL, L36, minute book, 1847–49, 18 and 28 Dec. 1848, and membership list of the lodge, 1847–49.
19 See the records of the Grand Lodge of Canada West, AO, MU 221, file A-II-2, minute book of the Grand Lodge, annual report, 4 Aug. 1858. See also the *Proceedings of the Grand Lodge of Ontario Eleventh Annual Session*, 314.
20 Ferry, "To the Interests and Conscience of the Great Mass of the Community," 148–9.
21 See Clawson, *Constructing Brotherhood*; Carnes, *Secret Ritual and Manhood*; Anstead, "Fraternalism in Victorian Ontario," 161–90; Cordery, "Friendly Societies and the Discourse of Respectability," 41–8; Marks, *Revivals and Roller Rinks*, 108–16; and Palmer, "Mutuality and the Making/Masking of Difference," 133–6. Such doctrines also enforced masculine subjectivities; see Tosh, *A Man's Place*, 132–8, and his *Manliness and Masculinities in Nineteenth-Century Britain*, 1–9 and 41–51.
22 Albert Case, *The Principles of Oddfellowship*, 13–14, and his *Address Delivered Before Oriental Lodge*, 14. See also the *Odd Fellows Record* vol. 1 (Jan. 1846), 1 and 5; vol. 1 (Feb. 1846), 28; vol. 1 (March 1846), 47; and vol. 1 (April 1846), 55.
23 See the records of the Hope lodge #14, in MTL, L36, minute book, 1846–49, 30 Aug. 1847, and records of the Industry lodge #25, MTL, L36, minute book, 1854–59, 31 May 1855.
24 *Canadian Journal of Oddfellowship* vol. 1 (Dec. 1875), 362–3. See also Beito, *Mutual Aid or the Welfare State*, 32–7; Reorganization of the IOOF in Canada West records, AO, MU 2210, file A-I-2, Letters from Thomas Reynolds to the Grand Sire, 7 April 1854, and the *Proceedings of the Grand Lodge of Canada West Third Annual Session*, 7–8.
25 See the *Odd Fellows Record* vol. 1 (Feb. 1846), 27–30; vol. 1 (March 1846), 41; vol. 1 (Aug. 1846), 126–7; vol. 2 (May 1847), 105–6; and vol. 2 (Nov. 1847), 225–6.
26 It had probably come to the attention of the IOOF in the United States that none of the British American Lodge's constitutions contained the "free white male" clause. See *Constitution of the Commercial Lodge*, 2; *Bylaws and Rules of Prince of Wales Lodge*, 19; *Constitution, Bylaws and Rules of Order of the Albion Lodge*, 4; and IOOF in Canada West records, AO, MU 2210, file A-I-2, Letters to Thomas Reynolds from the Grand Sire, 30 July 1853.
27 Case, *The Principles of Oddfellowship*, 11–12, and *Address Delivered Before Oriental Lodge*, 3 and 15, as well as the *Odd Fellows Record* vol. 1 (Jan. 1846), 3–4; vol. 1 (Feb. 1846), 30; and vol. 1 (July 1846), 108.
28 See Case, *The Principles of Oddfellowship*, 11–12, and Case, *Address Delivered Before Oriental Lodge*, 3 and 15.
29 See the record of the Ontario Lodge #12, MTL, L36, minute book, 1847–57, 21 Oct. 1847; *Odd Fellows Record* vol. 2 (Aug. 1847), 167–8; and the *History of Oddfellowship*, 2.

30 Journal of Deputation of the IOOF, AO, MU 2211, file A-II-1, 28 March 1846, 39; the *Bylaws of the Loyal Montreal Lodge of the Manchester Unity*, 5 and 9; as well as the *Bylaws of the Loyal City of Toronto Lodge*. On the political nature of "loyalty" and the debates it engendered, see Mills, *The Idea of Loyalty in Upper Canada*.

31 See the records of the London Loyal Lodge of the Manchester Unity, AO, MU 2224, minute book, 1852–53, 4 Aug. and 8 Sept., 1853; and IOOF in Canada West records, AO, MU 2110, file A-I-2, Letters to Thomas Reynolds from the Grand Sire, 30 July 1853; and also file A-II-2, minute book, 1855–61, annual reports, 6 Aug. 1856 and 4 Aug. 1858.

32 *Report of the Special Meeting of Delegates and Grand Annual Conference of the Manchester Unity*, 4–6 and 11; records of the Grand Lodge of Canada West, AO, MU 2210, file A-I-3, H.C. Bingham to Thomas Tindill, 2 March 1863; and *Proceedings of the Grand Lodge of Canada West Eleventh Annual Session*, 311–12.

33 Case, *The Principles of Oddfellowship*, 10; *Odd Fellows Record* vol. 1, (Jan. 1846), 7; vol. 2 (Feb. 1847), 46; vol. 2 (April 1847), 80–1; and *Constitution of the Albion Lodge*, 26–7.

34 Case, *The Principles of Oddfellowship*, 9–10, and the *Odd Fellows Record* vol. 2 (March 1847), 55. See also the records of the Loyal London Lodge, Manchester Unity, AO, MU 2224, minute book, 1852–53, 13 Jan. 1852 and the records of the Imperial Lodge #37, MTL, L36, minute book, 1850–60, 8 March 1852 and 9 Jan. 1860. These temperance ideals, coupled with the benefit system, soon helped win many members of the Sons of Temperance to the Oddfellow standard by mid-century; see Ferry, "To the Interests and Conscience," 148–50.

35 See the records of the Thames lodge #43, MTL, L36, minute book, 1862–64, 6 Nov. 1862 and 3 Sept. 1863; *Constitution of the Albion Lodge*, 26; and *General Laws for the Government of the Canadian Order of Oddfellows*, 9 and 30–1. Historians analysing fraternalism as a vehicle of middle-class formation and those who identify fraternalism as working-class mutualism could therefore claim the ideology of collective and individual self-help, hard work, and mutual aid equally for their constituencies. See Anstead, "Fraternalism in Victorian Ontario," 128–35; Palmer, "Mutuality and the Making/Masking of Difference," 126–33; and Holman, *A Sense of Their Duty*, 110–15.

36 See the records of the Hope lodge #14, MTL, L36, minute book, 1846–49, 10 April 1848; *Odd Fellows Record* vol. 2 (Feb. 1846), 32; *Bylaws of the Prince of Wales Lodge*, 5–6; and *Report of the Grand Annual Committee of the Toronto District*, 5.

37 Case, *The Principles of Oddfellowship*, 9–10, as well as the *Odd Fellows Record* vol. 1 (Jan. 1846), 5; and vol. 2 (Nov. 1847), 220; and also *Bylaws of the Loyal Montreal Lodge*, 3.

38 See the records of the Ontario lodge #12 in Cobourg, MTL, L36, minute book, 24 Jan. 1851, as well as the records of the Imperial lodge #37 in Burford, MTL, L36,

minute book, 1850–60, 13 Oct. 1856; the records of the Ontario lodge #12 in Cobourg, MTL, L36, black book, 1858–61 and the records of the Industry lodge #25 in Haldimand, MTL, L36, register of rejected candidates, 1852–54.

39 *Constitution of the Albion Lodge*, 44, and *General Laws of the Canadian Order of Oddfellows*, 30–1. See also the records of the of the Loyal London lodge, Manchester Unity, AO, MU 2224, minute book, 1852–53, 9 Sept. 1852; 9 June 1853; and 22 June 1853.

40 *Proceedings of the Grand Lodge of Canada West Fifth Annual Session*, 13–14.

41 *Constitution of the Albion Lodge*, 20–26, and Case, *Address Before Oriental Lodge*, 11. The Manchester Unity also accepted the principle of sociability in their lodges; see *Bylaws of the Loyal Montreal Lodge*, 5–6, and records of the Loyal London lodge, AO, MU 2224, minute book, 1852–53, 17 Feb., 16 June, and 4 Aug. 1853.

42 Ontario lodge #12, MTL, L36, minute book, 1858–61, 2 July 1858 and 1 Feb. 1861; Industry lodge #25, MTL, L36, minute book, 1850–52, 27 March 1851; and Imperial Lodge #37, MTL, L36, minute book, 1850–60, 5 March 1855. On Oddfellow reading rooms, see the records of the Ontario Lodge #12, MTL, L36, minute book, 1847–57, 3 and 31 Oct. 1849 and 30 Aug. 1850; and Hope lodge #14, MTL, L36, minute book, 1846–9, 10 May 1847.

43 See the *Odd Fellows Record* vol. 1 (Jan. 1846), 1–2 and 8; vol. 1 (Feb. 1846), 27–8 and vol. 1 (March 1846), 39–40.

44 See the records of the Loyal London lodge, AO, MU 2224, minute book, 1852–3, 22 Jan., 1 April, 27 June 1852, 17 Feb., and 16 June 1853. See also the records of Ontario lodge #12, MTL, L36, minute book, 1858–61, 1 Feb. 1861 and Phoenix lodge #22, MTL, L36, minute book, 1847–49, 31 Jan. 1848.

45 Anstead, "Fraternalism in Victorian Ontario," 161–90; Cordery, "Friendly Societies and the Discourse of Respectability," 41–8; Marks, *Revivals and Roller Rinks*, 108–16; Palmer, "Mutuality and the Making/Masking of Difference," 130–8; and particularly Emery and Emery, *A Young Man's Benefit*, 36–41, and Beito, *From Mutual Aid to the Welfare State*, 17–40. The following section mirrors closely the work of Jason Kaufman, *For the Common Good?*

46 Anstead, "Fraternalism in Victorian Ontario," 182–8; Marks, *Revivals and Roller Rinks*, 109, 249–50; and Emery and Emery, *A Young Man's Benefit*, 31–8.

47 See the records of Capital lodge #141, MTL, L36, minute book, 1874–46, 2 March 1876; Ark lodge #181, minute book, 13 Feb. 1880, 235; Acton lodge #204, minute book, 1877–84, 2 April 1879; and Hanover lodge #233, minute book, 1882–97, 18 Feb. 1885.

48 See the records of the Wardsville lodge #60, MTL, L36, minute book, 1875–82, 22 July 1877, 99, and 10 April 1882, 134; and Palmerston lodge #123, minute book, 1883–84, 21 Aug. 1884. See also the records of the St Clair lodge #106, RCL, box 4319, minute book, 1883–86, 6 Sept. 1883, 20, and 11 Oct. 1883, 43.

49 *Proceedings of the Grand Lodge of Ontario Thirty-Second Annual Session*, 4090; *Canadian Journal of Oddfellowship* vol. 1 (May 1875), 143–4, and vol. 1 (June 1875), 175; and *Constitution, Bylaws and Rules of Order of the Sycamore Lodge*, preface, ii.

50 See the *Tour of the Grand Master of the IOOF*, 13–14; *Canadian Journal of Oddfellowship* vol. 1 (May 1875), 143–4; *Proceedings of the Grand Lodge of Ontario Twenty-Sixth Annual Session*, 2019–20; and *Dominion Oddfellow* 5 Dec. 1895, 5.

51 *Canadian Forester* vol. 10 (Feb. 1891), 6 and 15; vol. 11 (Nov. 1891), 11, and vol. 12 (Sept. 1892), 11. The Knights of Pythias and the Independent Order of Foresters expressed a similar love of classlessness within their associations. See the *Independent Forester* 16 (June 1895), 376–7, and King, *Knights of Pythias*, 7.

52 *Proceedings of the Grand Lodge of Ontario Forty-Fourth Annual Session*, 75–6, and *Constitution and General Laws of the Supreme Court of the IOF*, 144–5. See also the *Constitution, General Laws and Rules of Order of the Grand Lodge of the AOUW*, 2–3, and *Ritual of the Canadian Order of Foresters*, 5 and 55–6.

53 *Independent Forester* vol. 17 (Oct. 1896), 100–1; and the *Canadian Forester* vol. 10 (Sept. 1890), 11, and vol. 10 (Feb. 1891), 15. For a description of the Foresters as a more middle-class institution, see Marks, *Revivals and Roller Rinks*, 249–50.

54 See the records of the Madoc lodge, AO, MU 9, petitions for membership, 1891–98, and *Ritual of the Ancient Order of United Workmen*, 34–5. For membership in larger town settings with a larger working-class base, see Anstead, "Fraternalism in Victorian Ontario," 182–8, and Marks, *Revivals and Roller Rinks*, 249–50.

55 *Dominion Oddfellow* vol. 15 (12 Dec. 1895), 13; and the *Canadian Forester* vol. 9 (Jan. 1890), 1; and vol. 10 (Feb. 1891), 15.

56 See the *Proceedings of the Grand Lodge of Ontario Thirty-Ninth Annual Session*, 5475–6 and the *Independent Forester* vol. 16 (July 1895), 5 and 14–15.

57 Palmer, "Mutuality and the Masking/Making of Difference," 130–2; Emery and Emery, *A Young Man's Benefit*, 86–101; and Beito, *From Mutual Aid to the Welfare State*, 110–35. See also *Proceedings of the Grand Lodge of Ontario Thirty-Eighth Annual Session*, 5241–2; *Proceedings of the Grand Lodge of Ontario Forty-Fourth Annual Session*, 7014, and the *Independent Forester* vol. 16 (Dec. 1895), 186, and vol. 19 (Feb. 1899), 234–5.

58 For fraternalism as the bulwark of respectable masculinity, see Clawson, *Constructing Brotherhood*; Carnes, *Secret Ritual and Manhood*; Marks, *Revivals and Roller Rinks*, 108–16; and Palmer, "Mutuality and the Making/Masking of Difference," 130–8. On the participation of women in other rural associations, see Osterud, *Bonds of Community* and Wilson, "Reciprocal Work Bees and the Meaning of Neighbourhood," 431–64.

59 See the records of the St Clair lodge #106, RCL, box 4319, minute book, 1874–78, 3 Jan. 1878, 268; minute book, 1883–86, 17 July 1884, 99; 2 July 1885, 188; and 6 Aug. 1885, 199; and minute book, 1890–94, 22 Jan. 1891, 109. See

also the records of the Egremont lodge in Kerwood, RCL, recent acquisition, vol. 1, minute book, 1877–92, 6 July 1878, 70.

60 *Proceedings of the Grand Lodge of Ontario Thirty-Eighth Annual Session*, appendix, xxxviii–x; *Proceedings of the Grand Lodge of Ontario Thirty-Ninth Annual Session*, appendix, xxxvii–xliii, and *Proceedings of the Grand Lodge of Ontario Forty-First Annual Session*, 6013 and 6239.

61 The *Dominion Oddfellow* contained a column entitled "the Fair Rebekah's Page," yet this section contained only recipes and fashion tips, not descriptions of women's relief efforts. See also *Proceedings of the Grand Lodge of Ontario Thirty-Eighth Annual Session*, appendix, xxxvix; *Proceedings of the Grand Lodge of Ontario Fortieth Annual Session*, xxxv, and *Proceedings of the Grand Lodge of Quebec Eighteenth Annual Session*, 1577.

62 *Independent Forester* vol. 6 (Sept. 1885), 3; vol. 12 (Feb. 1892), 226–9; and vol. 19 (April 1899), 299. See also the *Constitution of the IOF*, 16–20 and the *Canadian Forester* vol. 9 (Oct. 1889), 10.

63 See the records of the Antrim Council #245, LAC, MG 28 I 302, vol. 1, minute book, 1894–1921, 20 Nov. 1895, 35; and 18 Oct. 1896, 64. See also *Constitution and Laws of the Canadian Order of Chosen Friends*, iv-v and 69, and *Ritual of the Canadian Order of Chosen Friends*, 14–15.

64 *Constitutions et Règlements de L'Ordre des Forestiers Catholiques*, 5–6, 32–3, and *COF Montréal Souvenir 1892*, 1. See also Clawson, *Constructing Brotherhood*, 130–5, and Emery and Emery, *A Young Man's Benefit*, 27–9.

65 See the *Independent Forester* vol. 18 (Nov. 1897), 130; vol. 18 (March 1898), 267; and vol. 19 (July 1898), 2.

66 Beito, *Mutual Aid or the Welfare State*, 44–63. For fraternalism as a vehicle of white Protestantism, see Clawson, *Constructing Brotherhood*, 125–33; Palmer, "Mutuality and the Making/Masking of Difference," 128–30; Emery and Emery, *A Young Man's Benefit*, 26–30; and Holman, *A Sense of Their Duty*, 110–18.

67 The Grand Lodge of Ontario reprinted the GLUS debate over black membership in the *Proceedings of the Grand Lodge of Ontario Twenty-First Annual Session*, 1495–1520. See also the *Proceedings of the Grand Lodge of Ontario Twenty-Second Annual Session*, 1774.

68 See the *Tour of the Grand Master Henry Outram*, 26–7, and the records of the Zephyr lodge #213, MTL, L36, minute book, 1870–81, 21 May 1870, 41.

69 For this entire discussion, see the *Canadian Journal of Oddfellowship* vol. 2 (March 1876), 84–5, and vol. 2 (May 1876), 143–6. On black associational life in Canada, see Bristow, "Black Women in Buxton and Chatham," 117–24.

70 See the *Constitution for Subordinate Lodges of the Knights of Pythias*, 21; *Constitution of the AOUW*, 2; *Constitution of the Order of Chosen Friends*, iv; *Constitution of the IOF*, 5–6; and *Constitution and Rules of Order of the Canadian Order of Foresters*, 15–16.

71 Ironically, American historian David Beito memorializes the selection of Oronhyatekha as Chief Ranger of the IOF, while Canadian historians are strangely silent on this highly significant individual in Canadian fraternalism. See Beito, *Mutual Aid or the Welfare State*, 50–9, and the *Independent Forester* vol. 16 (July 1895), 12–15; vol. 16 (March 1896), 285; and vol. 19 (Aug. 1898), 37. The IOF also used this approach with those of a Jewish background, with the formation of two Jewish courts in Toronto; see the *Independent Forester* vol. 17 (Nov. 1896), 133.

72 Lander, *Exposé of Oddfellowship*, 23–4, and the *Dominion Oddfellow* vol. 15 (5 Dec. 1895), 13. See also the *Proceedings of the Grand Lodge of Ontario Twenty-Sixth Annual Session*, 2017.

73 See the records of the Charity lodge #129, MTL, L36, minute book, 1874–78, 18 July 1876, 166, and the *Proceedings of the Grand Lodge of Ontario Twenty-First Annual Session*, 1314–5.

74 *Canadian Journal of Oddfellowship* vol. 1 (June 1875), 169, and vol. 2 (Dec. 1876), 364; and the *Proceedings of the Grand Lodge of Ontario Forty-Fourth Annual Session*, appendix, 63. The Oddfellows worried that materialistic socialism and organizations such as the Knights of Labor were usurping the traditional role of Christianity and stealing their working-class constituents; see Palmer, *Working-Class Experience*, 108–10.

75 See the records of the St Clair lodge #106, RCL, box 4319, minute book, 1878–82, 7 Nov. 1880, 171, and also 3 March 1881, 213–5.

76 King, *Knights of Pythias*, 7; *Constitution of the Knights of Pythias*, 8–9, and *Constitution of the AOUW*, 2. See also *The Ritual of the Independent Order of Foresters*, 10; the *Independent Forester* vol. 16 (June 1896), 376; *Ritual of the COF*, 32–3 and 56; and the *Canadian Forester* vol. 9 (Sept. 1889), 3, and vol. 9 (March 1890), 6.

77 See the *Independent Forester* vol. 4 (March 1884), 1, and vol. 7 (March 1887), 3–5; Oronhyatekha, *History of the Independent Order of Foresters*, 102–31, 156–89; and *Constitution of the COF*, 3–4.

78 Lander, *Exposé of Oddfellowship*, 53, and the records of the St Clair lodge #106, RCL, box 4318, character report book, preamble.

79 *Dominion Oddfellow* vol. 15 (14 Nov. 1895), 8, and vol. 15 (5 Dec. 1895), 13.

80 See the *Proceedings of the Grand Lodge of Ontario Thirty-Third Annual Session*, 4087–8; the *Canadian Journal of Oddfellowship* vol. 2 (Feb. 1876), 47–9; and Lander, *Exposé of Oddfellowship*, 30.

81 See the records of the St Clair lodge #106, RCL, box 4319, minute book, 1873–74, 11 June 1874, 2 July 1874, 30 July 1874, and 13 Aug. 1874, as well as the minute book, 1894–1900, 8 Nov. 1894, 44–5. See also Anstead, "Fraternalism in Victorian Ontario," 172–5, and Marks, *Revivals and Roller Rinks*, 109–10.

82 *Canadian Forester* vol. 9 (Sept. 1889), 5; vol. 10 (Nov. 1890), 2; vol. 10 (May 1891), 1; and vol. 11 (Nov. 1891), 2; *Constitution and Rules of Order of the Canadian*

Order of Foresters, 4; and *Constitution and Laws of the Order of Canadian Home Circles*, 3. On the socio-economic ideologies of Populism in the second half of the century, see Cook, "Tillers and Toilers," 5–20, and Ferry, "Severing the Connections in a Complex Community," 9–47.

83 *Ritual of the IOF*, 7; the *Independent Forester* vol. 16 (April 1896), 312–3; the *Canadian Forester* vol. 9 (Dec. 1889), 3, and vol. 10 (Aug. 1890), 3; and *Constitution of the Canadian Order of Chosen Friends*, iv. For a discussion of this new ideology of "unwilling idlers" see Baskerville and Sager, *Unwilling Idlers*.

84 See the records of the St Clair lodge #106, RCL, box 4319, minute book, 1894–1900, 13 Jan. 1898, 242; the *Dominion Oddfellow* vol. 15 (26 Dec. 1895), 1; the *Canadian Journal of Oddfellowship* vol.1, (Jan. 1846), 11–12, and vol. 1 (March 1875), 79–80, as well as the *Proceedings of the Grand Lodge of Ontario Thirty-Third Annual Session*, 4060.

85 See the records of the Grand lodge of Ontario, AO, MU 2210, file A-1-8, report of the special committee, 1892; *Proceedings of the Grand Lodge of Ontario Thirty-Eighth Annual Session*, 5357–65; and also the *Report of the High Court of the Ancient Order of Foresters*, 14–16. To illustrate how this language was identical to that of early radical reformers, see Dewar, "Charles Clarke's *Reformator*," 233–52, and Noel, "Early Populist Tendencies," 173–87.

86 *Canadian Forester* vol. 9 (Aug. 1889), crest; *Constitution of the AOUW*, preamble and the *Ritual of the AOUW*, 14–15, and 34. See also *Ritual of the Canadian Order of Foresters*, 30–3 and 56, as well as the *Canadian Forester* vol. 9 (Aug. 1889), 10; vol. 9 (Sept. 1889), 1–6; and vol. 9 (Nov. 1889), 3–5.

87 See the *Oddfellows Gazette* 15 Feb. 1897, 2–3. See also the *Dominion Oddfellow* vol. 15 (12 Dec. 1895), 13; the *Canadian Journal of Oddfellowship* vol. 1 (Feb. 1875), 45 and 52; vol. 1 (June 1875), 175, and the *Proceedings of the Grand Lodge of Ontario Thirty-Third Annual Session*, 4059.

88 Records of the Wardsville lodge #60, MTL, L36, minute book, 1872–75, 13 Jan. 1873; *Proceedings of the Grand Lodge of Ontario Twenty-Third Annual Session*, 1856–57; *Catalogue of Oddfellows Art Loan Museum*; and *A Digest of the Laws of the IOOF*, 110–11.

89 See the records of the Zephyr lodge #213, MTL, L36, minute book, 1878–81, 12 March 1878, 22 and 7 May 1878, 38; and the records of the Egremont lodge, RCL, recent acquisition, vol. 1, minute book, 1877–92, 4 Jan. 1879, 93, 5 May 1879, 105, and 30 Aug. 1879, 116; 25 June 1885, 271; and vol. 2, minute book, 1892–1917, 27 Dec. 1895, 103. Official and unofficial publications also counselled Oddfellows to hold entertainments; see the *Canadian Journal of Oddfellowship* vol. 1 (May 1875), 148, and *Proceedings of the Grand Lodge of Ontario Twenty-Sixth Annual Session*, 1955.

90 See the records of the Cypress lodge #187, MTL, L36, minute book, 1879–83, 4 April 1881, 28 Aug. 1882 and 22 Jan. 1883, as well as the records of the St Clair

lodge, RCL, box 4319, minute book, 1873–74, 5, and 12 Feb. 1874; minute book, 1883–86, 17 July 1884, 99, and 2 July 1885, 188; and minute book, 1886–89, 3 March 1887, 34, and 21 July 1887, 52. Successful lodges had entertainment committees; see the records of the Palmerston lodge #123, MTL, minute book, 1878–83, 26 Dec. 1878, 18, and 28 Oct. 1881, 191, and 21 June 1883, 380; Mystic lodge #128, MTL, L36, minute book, 1883–92, 3 Nov. 1884, 70, and 25 June 1888, 108.

91 *Ritual of the COF*, 32–3 and 56; the *Canadian Forester* vol. 12 (Sept. 1892), 11; the *Independent Forester* vol. 9 (Nov. 1888), 136–9; and *Ritual of the IOF*, 55 and 78–80.

92 See the records of the Listowel IOF, AO, MU 7175 #23, minute book, 1891–98, 8 Oct. 1895, 11 May and 25 May 1897. See also the records of the Shelburne IOF, DCA, AR 2464.995, minute book, 1885–95, 14 Feb. 1887, 26; 11 Nov. 1889, 88, and 10 Oct. 1892, 153; and records of the Peterborough Juvenile Foresters, PCMA, Acc. 96–065, box 1, series 1, minute book, 1890–99, 12 Aug., 25 Nov. 1891, 8 Feb. 1893 and 12 Jan. 1898. Descriptions of social activities in the Antrim Council of the Canadian Order of Chosen Friends went like this: "A programme of music, addresses, singing &tc. were rendered in good style, after which a sumptuous repast was partaken of." See their records, LAC, MG 28 I 302, vol. 1, minute book, 1894–1921, 17 July 1895, 24, and 1 Jan. 1896, 42.

93 Records of the Shelburne IOF, DCA, AR 2464.995, minute book, 1885–95, 31 Jan. 1885, 2–3; 22 Nov. 1885, 23; 29 Jan. 1889, 69; and 11 Feb. 1889, 70; and the records of the Peterborough COF, PCMA, Acc. 96–065, box 1, series 1, minute book, 1883–86, 17 Aug. 1883, 55; 7 Sept. 1883, 66–8; 4 July 1884, 152; and 15 Jan. 1886, 287.

94 See the *Independent Forester* vol. 8 (April 1888), 9–10; vol. 9 (Feb. 1889), 249–52; vol. 10 (April 1890), 284–5; and vol. 16 (July 1895), 14–15.

CHAPTER FIVE

1 A great deal of scholarly work on the economics of changing agricultural markets has been done in the United States: witness Atack and Bateman, *To Their Own Soil*; Rothenberg, "The Emergence of Farm Labour Markets," 537–66; Clark, *The Roots of Rural Capitalism*, with much of the debate being summarized in Kulikoff, "The Transition to Capitalism in Rural America," 120–44; and particularly the recent work of Martin Bruegel, *Farm, Shop, Landing*. On the transformation of the countryside due to commercial and manufacturing pressures, see Barron, *Those Who Stayed Behind*; many of the essays in Prude and Hahn, *The Countryside in the Age of Capitalist Transformation*; and Thelan, *Paths of Resistance*.

2 For British examples of "improvement" in agriculture, see Hudson, *Patriotism with Profit*; Goddard, *Harvests of Change*; and Wilmot, "The Business of Improvement,"

1–81. See also Marti, *To Improve the Soil and Mind*; Danbom, "The Agricultural Experiment Stations and Professionalization," 246–55; and particularly Thornton, *Cultivating Gentlemen*.

3 On the idyllic image of the independent yeoman in the United States, see McMurry, *Families and Farmhouses in Nineteenth-Century America* and particularly Burns, *Pastoral Inventions*. For the construction of a rural "community" in the United States, see Barron, *Those Who Stayed Behind*, 112–31; Osterud, *Bonds of Community*; and Kelly, "The Consummation of Rural Prosperity and Happiness," 574–602. For rural society in Britain, see Howkins, *Reshaping Rural England*, especially chapter 3, "Sources of Stability and Harmony," 61–92. See also Raby, *Making Rural Australia*, 114–33.

4 On agriculture in Upper Canada, see McCallum, *Unequal Beginnings*, 9–24; McInnis, "The Early Ontario Wheat Staple Reconsidered," 17–48; and McCalla, *Planting the Province*. On the "agricultural crisis" in Quebec, see McCallum, *Unequal Beginnings*, 25–44; Ouellet, *Lower Canada 1791–1840*, 117–57; McInnis, "A Reconsideration of the State of Agriculture in Lower Canada," 9–49; Greer, *Peasant, Lord and Merchant*; and Courville, "Un monde rural en mutation," 237–58.

5 On tensions in the rural countryside, see Bittermann, "The Hierarchy of the Soil," 33–55; the fine collection of essays in Samson, *Contested Countryside*; and Crowley, "Rural Labour," 13–104. For governmental intervention in agriculture, see Nesmith, "The Philosophy of Agriculture" and Heaman, *The Inglorious Arts of Peace*. On the philosophy of rural "improvement" and the elite composition of early agricultural societies, see the work of Wynn, "Exciting a Spirit of Emulation Among the Plodholes," 5–51; Samson, "Industry and Improvement"; and particularly Fair, "Gentlemen, Farmers and Gentlemen Half-Farmers."

6 See Darroch, "Scanty Fortunes and Rural Middle Class Formation," 621–59; Heaman, *The Inglorious Arts of Peace*, 52–60; Fair, "Gentlemen, Farmers, and Gentlemen Half-Farmers"; McNairn, *The Capacity to Judge*, 92–105; and particularly Wood, *Making Ontario*, especially chapter 4, "Building a Social Structure," 50–83. The evidence of the break-down of producer alliance among farmers with the rise of industrialism is examined in the following chapter on the Dominion Grange and Patrons of Industry.

7 Both Farrell, "Advice to Farmers," 209–17, and Goddard, "Development and Influence of Agricultural Periodicals and Newspapers," 116–31, conclude that the farming press had a limited audience. Donald Marti in *To Improve the Soil and Mind*, 124–162 and Sally McMurry, "Who Read the Agricultural Journals?" 1–18, claim that agricultural journals indeed reached a wider group of practical farmers. See also Douglas, "Settlement and Agriculture in Saltfleet Township," 238–91.

8 On the elitist nature of these publications and the significance of government funding, see Nesmith, "The Philosophy of Agriculture," 19–40, and Fair,

"Gentlemen, Farmers, and Gentlemen Half-Farmers," 125–68. On nascent agrarian radicalism in Canada West, see the seminal work by Careless, "The Toronto *Globe* and Agrarian Radicalism," 14–39. On the contention between Reformer and Tory visions of agriculture, see Fair, "Gentlemen, Farmers, and Gentlemen Half- Farmers," 125–68, and particularly McNairn, *The Capacity to Judge*, 92–110.

9 See the *Bylaws of the Lower Canadian Agricultural Society*, 8–9, and the *Agricultural Journal and Transactions* vol. 1 (March 1848), 75; vol. 1 (Jan. 1848), 19; and vol. 2 (April 1849), 112–14.

10 See the Colchester Agricultural Club fonds, AO, F387, secretary book, 1844–1860, 9 Jan. 1847, 15 and 16. See also the Peterborough Agricultural Society fonds, PCMA, Acc. 59–004, minute book, 1855–66, annual report of 1863, 23 Jan. 1864, and also the Oro Agricultural Society fonds, SCA, Acc. 970–77, minute book, 1859–86, annual report for 1858.

11 See the Peterborough Agricultural Society fonds, PCMA, Acc. 59–004, minute book, 1855–66, 6 Feb. 1858, and the Guelph Agricultural Society fonds, WCA, A1969.10.2, MU 3, ms 14, minute book, 1857–71, 8 Jan. 1859.

12 Guelph Agricultural society fonds, WCA, A1969.10.2, MU 3, ms 14, minute book, 1857–1871, 8 Jan. 1859, 12 Jan. 1861, and 10 Jan. 1863; Peterborough Agricultural Society fonds, PCMA, Acc. 59–004, minute book, 1855–66, 19 Jan. 1861, annual report for 1860. The importance of fairs as early markets and community events is argued convincingly by Osborne, "Trading on a Frontier," 59–82.

13 *British American Cultivator* vol. 1 (Jan. 1842), 4–5; vol. 1 (Feb. 1842), 20; vol. 2 (Jan. 1843), 8–9; and vol. 3 (March 1844), 34–6. See also the *Canadian Agriculturalist* vol. 10 (Jan. 1858), 5–6 and vol. 1 (Jan. 1849), 9. See also the *British American Cultivator*, new series, vol. 2 (Nov. 1846), 328; and vol. 1 (March 1845) 78–9, and the *Canadian Agricultural Journal* vol. 2 (Jan. 1845), 1, and vol. 2 (April 1845), 49–50.

14 *Journal and Transactions of the Board of Agriculture* vol. 3 (1859), 84; *Transactions of the Board of Agriculture* vol. 4 (1860), 9–10; and *Transactions of the Board of Agriculture* vol. 5 (1861), 27–8. On the learned and scientific composition of the new Board of Agriculture, see Zeller, *Inventing Canada*, 207–10, and Nesmith, "The Philosophy of Agriculture," 19–40.

15 The agrarian ideology in Croil's lecture tends to support D. Ross Fair's thesis that gentlemen farmers continued to be involved with agricultural societies well after liberal state involvement. See Fair, "Gentlemen, Farmers, and Gentlemen Half-Farmers," 293–315, and also Heaman, *The Inglorious Arts of Peace*, 79–91. See the *Transactions of the Board of Agriculture* vol. 3 (1859), 72–3.

16 See the *Agricultural Journal and Transactions* vol. 1 (March 1848), 80; vol. 1 (Jan. 1848), 19; and vol. 2 (April 1849), 97–8. See also the Peterborough Agricultural

Society fonds, PCMA, Acc. 59–004, minute book, 1855–1866, annual report for 1855, 9 Feb. 1856.
17 See the *Agricultural Journal and Transactions* vol. 1 (Jan. 1848), 1 and vol. 1 (March 1848), 80; and the Oro Agricultural Society fonds, SCA, Acc. 970–77, minute book 1859–1886, annual report for 1858.
18 Peterborough Agricultural Society fonds, PCMA, Acc. 59–004, minute book, 1855–1866, annual report for 1860, 19 Jan. 1861 and the *Agricultural Journal and Transactions* vol. 2 (Jan. 1849), 1–2, and vol. 5 (May 1851), 147–8.
19 Blaming banks and other financial institutions for speculation was a staple of agrarian "populist" rhetoric; see Hann, *Farmers Confront Industrialism* and Ferry, "Severing the Connections in a Complex Community," 9–47; *Transactions of the Board of Agriculture* vol. 4 (1860), 239–40, and *Transactions of the Board of Agriculture* vol. 5 (1861), 178.
20 See the *Canadian Agricultural Journal* vol. 1 (Sept. 1844), 129; vol. 2 (April 1844), 49–50 and vol. 3 (April 1846), 49–51; see also the *British American Cultivator* vol. 1 (Jan. 1842), 1–2; vol. 1 (Oct. 1842), 160, and vol. 2 (Nov. 1843), 162–3.
21 *Canadian Agriculturalist* vol. 1 (Jan. 1849), 1–2; vol. 3 (Jan. 1851), 15; vol. 4 (Feb. 1852), 39; and vol. 4 (May 1852), 129. See also the *Lower Canadian Agriculturalist* vol. 1 (Nov. 1861), 41–2; vol. 2 (Nov. 1862), 42 and vol. 2 (Dec. 1862), 85–6.
22 The *Canadian Agricultural Journal* vol. 1 (May 1844), 72–3; vol. 1 (June 1844), 81, and vol. 3 (April 1846), 72. See also the *British American Cultivator* vol. 1 (Oct. 1842), 160, vol. 2 (Nov. 1843), 162, and new series, vol. 1 (Jan. 1845), 4.
23 *Lower Canadian Agriculturalist* vol. 2 (Sept. 1862), 299–301 and vol. 3 (Nov. 1863), 36; and see also the *British American Cultivator*, new series, vol. 2 (Aug. 1846), 226–7 and new series, vol. 2 (Sept. 1846), 258–9.
24 *Agriculturalist and Canadian Journal* vol. 1 (1 March 1848); the *Canadian Agriculturalist* vol. 4 (May 1852), 129; vol. 5 (March 1853), 65–6; and vol. 7 (Nov. 1855), 324–5.
25 On the significance of "improvement" to the liberal social order, see Samson, "Industry and Improvement." The *Agriculturalist and Canadian Journal* vol. 1 (15 March 1848), 50 and vol. 1 (1 April 1848), 64; and also the *Canadian Agriculturalist* vol. 4 (Jan. 1852), 7; vol. 9 (July 1857), 178–9; and particularly vol. 12 (2 April 1860), 146–7.
26 This is especially true in the United States, as witnessed in the work of Nancy Osterud, *Bonds of Community*; Kelly, "The Consummation of Rural Prosperity," and McMurry, *Transforming Rural Life*. For the Canadian context, see Cohen, *Women's Work, Markets, and Economic Development*; Crowley, "Experience and Representation," 238–51; and Wilson, "Reciprocal Work Bees and the Meaning of Neighbourhood," 431–64. On women and exhibition culture, see Greenhalgh, *Ephemeral Vistas*, 174–97, and Heaman, "Taking the World by Show," 599–631.

27 See the Donald Kennedy scrapbook, LAC, MG 24 I 90, annual report of the Carleton Agricultural society for 1865 and the Oro Agricultural society fonds, SCA, Acc. 970–77, A s3 Sh5, minute book, 1859–86, annual report for 1858. See also the Peterborough Agricultural society fonds, PCMA, Acc. 59–004, minute book, 1855–66, 7 Feb. 1857 and 12 March 1859; Addington County Agricultural society fonds, AO, MU 2086, minute book, 1853–67, 26 April 1862 and Darlington Agricultural society fonds, AO, MU 2092 #24, minute book, 1858–62, 15 Jan. 1858 and 9 March 1860.

28 Heaman, "Taking the World by Show," 607–8. For evidence of female judges, see the Peterborough Agricultural society fonds, PCMA, Acc. 59–004, minute book, 1855–66, 18 Sept. 1857; Darlington Agricultural society fonds, AO, MU 2092 #24, minute book, 1858–62, 9 March 1860.

29 See the Norwich Agricultural society fonds in the Harold Williams collection, AO, MS 301, minute book, 1861–72, 1861 annual report, 25, and the Peterborough Agricultural society fonds, PCMA, Acc. 59–004, minute book, 1855–66, 3 Feb. 1855.

30 *British American Cultivator* vol. 2 (Dec. 1843), 186–7, and new series, vol. 2 (Feb. 1846), 63–4; *Lower Canadian Agriculturalist*, vol. 2 (Oct. 1862), 15–16; and vol. 2 (Nov. 1862), 44, as well as the *Canada Farmer* vol. 1 (14 July 1847), 98. See also Kaye, "The Ladies Department of the Ohio Cultivator," 414–23; McMurry, "Who Read the Agricultural Journals," 5–13, and Tremblay, "La division sexuelle du travail," 221–42.

31 *British American Cultivator* vol. 2 (March 1843), 46–7; new series, vol. 1 (Jan. 1845), 28; new series, vol. 2 (Jan. 1846), 16–17; and new series, vol. 3 (April 1847), 120–2; and the *Canada Farmer* vol. 1 (Feb. 1855), 62–3. See also the *Canadian Agriculturalist* vol. 1 (Jan. 1849), 2, and vol. 6 (April 1854), 108.

32 See the *Lower Canadian Agriculturalist* vol. 2 (Aug. 1862), 278–9, and also the *British American Cultivator*, new series, vol. 3 (Sept. 1847), 286–7, and vol. 3 (Oct. 1847), 302–3. See also the *Canadian Agriculturalist* 14, (Dec. 1862), 731–2.

33 See the *Canadian Agriculturalist* vol. 7 (July 1855), 69–70; vol. 8 (Dec. 1856), 331; and particularly vol. 9 (Oct. 1857), 278–9.

34 *Transactions of the Board of Agriculture* vol. 3 (1859), 84 and 163, and vol. 6 (1862), 138–9. For the attempt and failure of early agricultural societies to end this kind of political and sectarian turmoil in Upper Canada, see McNairn, *The Capacity to Judge*, 92–100, and Fair, "Gentleman, Farmers, and Gentlemen Half-Farmers," 169–96. For similar usage of the liberal discourse of "improvement," see Samson, "Industry and Improvement" and particularly Curtis, *Politics of Population*. See also the Colchester Agricultural club fonds, Hiram Walker Collection, AO, microfiche F387, secretary book, 1844–60, 9 May 1844, 6–7.

35 See the *Agricultural Journal and Transactions* vol. 1 (Jan. 1848), 1–2, and the *Bylaws of the Lower Canadian Agricultural Society*, 7. The seigneurs on the board,

Pierre de Boucherville, Robert Harwood, and Lewis Thomas Drummond, all wanted an end to seigneurial tenure; see their entries in the *Dictionary of Canadian Biography* vol. 9, 373–4, and vol. 11, 282–3, as well as Allan Greer, *The Patriots and the People*, 292–3.

36 *Agricultural Journal and Transactions* vol. 2 (Feb. 1849), 33, and vol. 2 (Dec. 1849), 369–70; and the *Bylaws of the Lower Canadian Agricultural Society*, 7–8. On the politics of seigneurial tenure, see the seminal work by Wallot, "Le régime seigneurial," 225–51.

37 See the *Agricultural Journal and Transactions* vol. 1 (July 1848), 211; vol. 2 (Feb. 1849), 33–4; vol. 3 (Nov. 1849), 321 and 336–7. With so many liberals on the board of directors, clearly the executive needed to curry favour with the Catholic clergy to avoid censure like the more radical *rouge* element. See Bernard, *Les rouges*.

38 For the farmers' dependence on God and Christianity, see Cooper, *The Husbandsman's Dependence*, 8–10; the Peterborough Agricultural society fonds, PCMA, Acc. 59–004, minute book, 1855–66, 6 Feb. 1858 and the Guelph Agricultural society fonds, WCA, A1969.10.2, MU 3, ms 14, minute book, 1857–71, 10 Jan. 1863.

39 *Canadian Agricultural Journal* vol. 1 (Jan. 1844), 1–2; vol. 1 (April 1844), 72; vol. 1 (Sept. 1844), 129; vol. 1 (Nov. 1844), 161 and 168; and vol. 2 (Jan. 1845), 1. Of course, the majority Reform element in the Lower Canadian agricultural society accounted for a great deal of this sentiment.

40 See the *Canada Farmer* vol. 1 (Jan. 1847), 2; vol. 1 (May 1847), 62–3; vol. 1 (June 1847), 80; and vol. 1 (Dec. 1847), 176–8, as well as the *British American Cultivator* vol. 3 (Feb. 1847), 35; and vol. 3 (May 1847), 131–3. As with other newspapers, the ruling party often favoured their own agricultural organs; see Fetherling, *The Rise of the Canadian Newspaper* and Nesmith, "Philosophy of Agriculture," 19–30.

41 The *British American Cultivator* vol. 1 (March 1842), 40–1; vol. 2 (Nov. 1843), 162; and new series, vol. 2 (July 1846), 207. See also the *Canadian Agricultural Journal* vol. 2 (March 1845), 33–4.

42 See the *Canadian Agriculturalist* vol. 1 (Jan. 1849), 2–3; vol. 1 (Feb. 1849), 55; vol. 1 (March 1849), 64–5; vol. 2 (Feb. 1850), 50; and vol. 7 (Nov. 1855), 323. For politics in the agricultural press, see Nesmith, "Philosophy of Agriculture," 27–36, and Fair, "Gentlemen, Farmers, and Gentlemen Half-Farmers," 263–89.

43 Kelly, "The Consummation of Rural Prosperity and Happiness," 575–89, and in the central Canadian context see Heaman, *The Inglorious Arts of Peace*, 3–28. For the independent yeoman motif in rural farming culture, see Seaton, "Idylls of Agriculture," 21–30, and Burns, *Pastoral Inventions*, 32–49.

44 For similar rhetoric regarding changes in the landscape in Canada West, see Wood, *Making Ontario*. The Oro Agricultural society fonds, SCA, Acc. 970–77,

minute book, 1859–86, annual report for 1860 and the Peterborough Agricultural society fonds, PCMA, Acc. 59–004, minute book, 1855–66, 3 Feb. 1855. See also the *Journal and Transactions of the Board of Agriculture* vol. 2 (1858), 314–16.

45 Peterborough Agricultural society fonds, PCMA, Acc. 59–004, minute book, 1855–66, 3 Feb. 1855 and the Oro Agricultural society fonds, SCA, Acc. 970–77, minute book, 1859–86, annual report for 1862. See also the *Journal and Transactions of the Board of Agriculture* vol. 5 (1861), 408–9 and for the liberal language of "improvement," see Samson, "Industry and Improvement." See also the Oro Agricultural society fonds, SCA, Acc. 970–77, minute book, 1859–86, annual report for 1859 and 1861, and the Guelph Agricultural society fonds, WCA, A1969.10.2, MU 3, ms 14, minute book, 1857–71, 16 Jan. 1865. See also the *Transactions of the Board of Agriculture* vol. 4 (1860), 169–70, and the *Agricultural Journal and Transactions* vol. 1 (April 1848), 102–3.

46 See the Oro Agricultural society fonds, SCA, Acc. 970–77, minute book, 1859–86, annual report for 1865 and the Guelph Agricultural society fonds, WCA, A1969.10.2, MU 3, ms 14, minute book, 1857–71, 16 Jan. 1865.

47 *Canadian Agriculturalist* vol. 14 (16 Nov. 1862), 674–5; and also vol. 1 (Jan. 1849), 9, and vol. 9 (Dec. 1857), 332. See also the *British American Cultivator* vol. 2 (June 1843), 82; vol. 2 (Oct. 1843), 157–8; vol. 2 (Nov. 1843), 173–5; and new series, vol. 1 (Sept. 1846), 268, and vol. 3 (Sept. 1847), 268–9.

48 See the *Canada Farmer* vol. 1 (Jan. 1855), 24 as well as the *Canadian Agriculturalist* vol. 4 (Jan. 1852), 7; vol. 9 (July 1857), 175–9, and particularly vol. 10 (Jan. 1858), 1. See also the *Canadian Agricultural Journal* vol. 2 (Jan. 1845), 1 and 8, and also the *British American Cultivator* vol. 3 (Jan. 1844), 7.

49 On the subject of speculation, see the *Canadian Agriculturalist* vol. 4 (May 1846), 129–30, and vol. 13 (1 May 1861), 260, as well as the *Lower Canadian Agriculturalist* vol. 2 (Sept. 1862), 300. On the importance of thrift and economy, see the *Lower Canadian Agriculturalist* vol. 3 (April 1863), 263; *British American Cultivator* vol. 1 (Feb. 1842), 24; and the *Canadian Agriculturalist* vol. 1 (May 1849), 136, and vol. 1 (Sept. 1849), 275.

50 See the *Canadian Agriculturalist* vol. 2 (June 1850), 138–40, and also vol. 6 (March 1854), 76–7, as well as the *British American Cultivator*, new series, vol. 1 (July 1845), 208–9. See also the *Agriculturalist and Canadian Journal* vol. 1 (1 March 1848), 34.

51 See the *Canadian Agricultural Journal* vol. 3 (Feb. 1846), 17; see also vol. 2 (April 1845), 56; vol. 3 (June 1846), 82; and vol. 3 (Nov. 1846), 161. See also the *British American Cultivator* vol. 1 (July 1842), 98; vol. 1 (Oct. 1842), 160, and 2, (Sept. 1843), 132; the *Canadian Agriculturalist* vol. 2 (April 1850), 93–4, and the *Canada Farmer* vol. 1 (14 July 1847), 104–5. On the free trade or protectionist debates of this period, see Forster, *A Conjunction of Interests*.

52 This latter view is expressed by Marti, *To Improve the Soil and Mind*, 80–95, and Osborne, "Trading on a Frontier," 70–5. For agricultural fairs as promoting middle-class economic hegemony, see Kelly, "The Consummation of Rural Prosperity and Happiness," 574–90; and Heaman, *The Inglorious Arts of Peace*, 79–105.

53 *Address of the Directing President of the Western District Agricultural Society*, 14. See also the *British American Cultivator* vol. 1 (Feb. 1842), 19–20, and *Agriculturalist and Canadian Journal* 1, (1 March 1848), 40.

54 Donald Kennedy scrapbook, LAC, MG 24 I 90, annual report of the Carleton Agricultural society, 1865; the Peterborough Agricultural society fonds, PCMA, Acc. 59–004, minute book, 1855–66, 3 Feb. 1855 and 7 Feb. 1857; and the Addington County Agricultural society fonds, AO, MU 2086, minute book, 1853–71, 18 Feb. 1854 and 20 April 1867.

55 Addington County Agricultural society fonds, AO, MU 2086, minute book, 1853–71, 18 Feb. 1854 and 19 Jan. 1861. On "middling sort" temperance, see Ferry, "To the Interests and Conscience of the Great Mass of the Community," 147–9.

56 See the Norwich County Agricultural society fonds in the Harold Williams collection, AO, MS 301, minute book, 1861–72, 21 Sept. 1861, 8 and 7 Oct. 1865, 73.

57 See the *Agricultural Journal and Transactions* vol. 1 (Jan. 1848), 16–17; vol. 1 (Feb. 1848), 40–1; vol. 1 (Aug. 1848), 242, and vol. 3 (Aug. 1850), 240–1. See also the *Lower Canadian Agriculturalist* vol. 1 (Oct. 1861), 3–4; vol. 1 (Dec. 1861), 50–2, and vol. 2 (Jan. 1862), 76–7; and Heaman, *The Inglorious Arts of Peace*, 60–78 and 85–96.

58 For Ontario, see McInnis, "Marketable Surpluses in Ontario Farming," 395–424; McCalla, *Planting the Province*, and especially the invaluable work of Darroch, "Scanty Fortunes and Rural Middle Class Formation," 621–59. For the situation in Quebec, see the work of Bouchard, "Economic Inequalities in Saguenay Society," 660–89.

59 Ruth Sandwell argues that an emphasis solely on market forces overlooks the complexity of social change in the rural countryside, as family farms employed varying strategies to achieve economic prosperity. See her "Rural Reconstruction," 1–32. Sandwell's work follows on the work done in the United States by Jane Pederson in *Between Memory and Reality*, 25–85. See also McInnis, "The Changing Structure of Canadian Agriculture," 191–8, and especially the work of Sylvester, *The Limits of Rural Capitalism*.

60 Bittermann, "The Hierarchy of the Soil," 33–55; Bittermann, Mackinnon and Wynn, "Of Inequality and Interdependence," 1–20, and many of the essays in Samson, *Contested Countryside*. For the situation in Ontario, see Crowley, "Rural Labour," 13–104, and Darroch, "Scanty Fortunes," 630–6. For the divided nature of Quebec farmers in the Eastern Townships, see Little, *Crofters and Habitants* and Bouchard, "Economic Inequalities in Saguenay Society."

61 On how farmers dealt with the socio-economic changes associated with urban industrial capitalism, see Hann, *Farmers Confront Industrialism*; Taylor, *Fashioning Farmers*, 1–14 and 90–102; Rennie, *The Rise of Agrarian Democracy*, 13–19; and Ferry, "Severing the Connections in a Complex Community." On the tensions wrought by commercialism on agriculture by the final decades of the century, see Cohen, *Women's Work, Markets, and Economic Development*; McMurry, *Transforming Rural Life* and Kerry Badgely, "Then I Saw I had Been Swindled," 350–4. Adam Crerar, in his "Ties That Bind" argues effectively that rural culture was vibrant at the turn of the century, and the rural populace did not really experience an agrarian crisis until well into the twentieth century.

62 On the importance of government activism of large scale farmers in agriculture in the United States, see Marcus, "The Ivory Silo," 22–36, and Danbom, "The Agricultural Experiment Stations and Professionalization." For Canada, see Nesmith, "The Philosophy of Agriculture," 103–65, and particularly Irwin, "Government Funding of Agricultural Associations."

63 Hann, *Farmers Confront Industrialism*; Ramsay Cook, "Tillers and Toilers," 5–20; and Ferry, "Severing the Connections in a Complex Community." On the competing visions of agriculture and farming in Canada, see Taylor, *Fashioning Farmers*; Rennie, *The Rise of Agrarian Democracy*; and particularly Badgely, *Bringing in the Common Love of Good*, 3–20.

64 The Missisquoi society categorized other occupations with the appellation "non-farmers," as they noted 39% of members were non-farmers in 1884, 29% in 1886, 31% in 1893, 48% in 1894, 32% in 1895, and 29% in 1896, for an average of 35% over these years. See the Missisquoi Agricultural society fonds, LAC, MG 28 I 227, M–3791, document 6, minute book, 1883–89, 282 and M–3792, document 16, subscription book, 1893–96. See also the Elora Agricultural Society fonds, WCA, A1982.70, series 9, subseries 1, file 1, minute book 1896–1907, 22 Jan. 1898, and the Peterborough Agricultural Society fonds, PCMA, Acc. 99–004, minute book, 1868–75, annual report for 1870.

65 On the composition of the rural social order, see the work of Holman, *A Sense of Their Duty*, 19–96. See also the Guelph Fat Stock Club fonds, WCA, A1969.10.1, MU 3, minute book, 1881–1900, 3 March 1897, 245; and the South Wellington Agricultural society fonds, WCA, A1988.123, series 2, subseries 1, MU 101, minute book, 1878–97, 17 Jan. 1894, 328, and 16 Jan. 1895, 366.

66 See the Oro Agricultural society fonds, SCA, Acc. 970–77, minute book, 1859–86, annual report for 1870; the 1882 annual report and also 8 Jan. 1885.

67 The Walter Riddell papers, AO, MU 2388, series A-3, lecture to Northumberland Agricultural society, n.d. See also the Guelph Fat Stock Club fonds, WCA, A1969.10.1, MU 3, minute book, 1881–1900, 26 Feb. 1881, 22; 23 Feb. 1884, 61; and 7 Feb. 1895, 223; also see the South Wellington Agricultural society fonds,

WCA, A1988.123, series 2, subseries 1, MU 101, minute book, 1878–97, 19 Jan. 1881, 70. For similar sentiments in Quebec, see Dallaire, *Considerations on Farmers' Clubs and Agricultural Societies*, 3–4.
68 See the Middlesex Agricultural society fonds, RCL, box 5289–1, minute book, 1873–93, annual report for 1872; 21 Jan. 1874 and the annual report for 1877.
69 Middlesex Agricultural society fonds, RCL, box 5289–1, minute book, 1873–93, annual report for 1874, annual report for 1876, annual report for 1886, and the 1892 annual report.
70 In 1886 farmers comprised 98.75% of the executive of Farmers' Institutes, and in 1887, 98% of the executive listed their occupation as farmers. See the Farmers' Institute records, AO, RG 16–85, container 1, files 1 to 4, and the *Annual Report of the Central Farmers' Institute for 1888*, 5–6. Thomas Irwin, in "Government Funding of Agricultural Associations," 47–70, rightly concludes that the leaders did the bulk of the Institutes' work, as practical farmers often just rode the coattails of Institute directors.
71 See the *Annual Report of the Central Farmers' Institute for 1888*, 7–8, and *Annual Report of the Central Farmers' Institute for 1889*, 5–7. For Oliver Mowat's "politics of husbandry," see Noel, *Patrons, Clients, Brokers*, 232–48.
72 Farmers' Institute records housed in the AO, RG 16–85, container 1, file 2, reports from 1887, report of the South Huron Institute and the *Annual Report of the Central Institute for 1889*, 5–6.
73 Farmers' Institute records, AO, RG 16–85, container 1, file 1, reports from 1886, report of the North Lanark Institute; container 1, file 3, reports from 1888, report of the Northumberland Institute and the *Annual Report of the Central Institute for 1887*, 7–8.
74 See the Farmers' Institute records, AO, RG 16–85, container 1, file 3, reports for 1888, report of the Frontenac Institute and the *Annual Report of the Central Institute for 1889*, 13–14.
75 Farmers' Institute records, AO, RG 16–85, container 1, file 2, report of the Oshawa Institute and Centre Wellington Farmers' Institute fonds, WCA, A1981.47, MU 43, minute book, 1896–1905, 20 Jan. 1896, 4.
76 See the records of the *Cercle agricole de la paroisse de St. Francis du Lac*, ANQ, P343, S3, minute book, 1893–1924, 29 avril 1893. See also Dallaire, *Considerations on Farmers' Clubs*, 2–3; the *Almanach des Cercles Agricoles pour l'année 1894*, 9–10; as well as the *Recommandés pour l'organisation des Cercles Agricoles*, 3–5.
77 "Source inépuisable de richesses nationals, barrière contre le désordre, garantie de la paix sociale, source de la prospérité et du bonheur pour les nations comme pour les individus." "[un] erreur économique et l'agio, qu'on appelle monopole, est un crime; c'est le vol érigé à l'état de système. Avis à ceux qui s'occupe[nt] des questions sociales." *Almanach des Cercles Agricoles pour l'année 1894*, 48–50;

Almanach des Cercles Agricoles pour l'année 1896, 37–8, and the *Almanach des Cercles Agricoles pour l'année 1899*, 7–8.

78 See the *Farmers' Advocate* vol. 3 (April 1868), 50–1; vol. 6 (July 1871), 103; vol. 7 (Feb. 1872), 21–2; vol. 9 (March 1874), 41; vol. 10 (March 1875), 35; vol. 15 (Dec. 1880), 274; and particularly vol. 26, (Nov. 1891), 448. See also the *Ontario Farmer* vol. 1 (Oct. 1869), 294–5.

79 *Ontario Farmer* vol. 1 (March 1869), 66–7; vol. 1 (June 1869), 165–6; vol. 2 (May 1870), 130–1, as well as the *Farmers' Advocate* vol. 3 (June 1868), 86–7; vol. 4 (May 1869), 68; vol. 5 (Aug. 1870), 116, and vol. 18, (Nov. 1883), 327–8. Weld on occasion even blamed the farmers themselves for their inferior station, by not "raising to the stature of their calling." See the *Farmers' Advocate* vol. 2 (Oct. 1867), 83–4; vol. 3 (May 1868), 70, and vol. 6 (Sept. 1871), 133; and the *Ontario Farmer* vol. 2 (Feb. 1870), 33–4.

80 Similar arguments against government influence in agricultural associations can be found in Irwin, "Government Funding of Agricultural Associations," 34–70. See the *Farmers' Advocate* vol. 3 (June 1868), 94; vol. 7 (July 1872), 98–9; vol. 8 (June 1873), 92; and particularly vol. 18 (Jan. 1883), 2–3.

81 See the *Farmers' Advocate* vol. 3 (Nov. 1868), 164–5; vol. 5 (Aug. 1870), 116; vol. 19 (Sept. 1884), 260 and vol. 21 (Feb. 1886), 39–40; as well as the *Ontario Farmer* vol. 1 (Oct. 1869), 294–5.

82 For similar arguments in the Grange and Patrons of Industry, see Ferry, "Severing the Connections." See also the *Farmers' Advocate* vol. 2 (April 1867), 27; vol. 5 (Feb. 1870), 18–19; vol. 6 (July 1871), 103; vol. 8 (Aug. 1873), 113; vol. 8 (Dec. 1873), 177; vol. 14 (Sept. 1879), 200; and vol. 23 (Jan. 1888), 7–8.

83 On the emerging role of the rural small-town clerk and self-employed businessmen, see Holman, *A Sense of Their Duty*, 70–85, and Burley, *A Particular Condition in Life*. See also the *Ontario Farmer* vol. 1 (March 1869), 114; vol. 1 (Sept. 1869), 265; and vol. 2 (Jan. 1870), 6.

84 On the withdrawal of women from market agriculture and into the domestic economy in the late nineteenth century, see Cohen, *Women's Work, Markets, and Economic Development*; Osterud, *Bonds of Community*; McMurry, *Transforming Rural Life*; Heaman, "Taking the World by Show," 599–631; Tremblay, "La division sexuelle du travail," 221–42; and particularly Crowley, "Experience and Representation," 238–51.

85 This situation can be unfavourably compared to that of temperance organizations, who offered more female autonomy; see Ferry, "To the Interests and Conscience," 156–7. In the Guelph agricultural society, 3% of the members were women in 1873, 5% in 1881, 15% in 1883, 9% in 1894, 27% in 1896 and 13% in 1899, illustrating a rather fluctuating female membership. See the Guelph Agricultural society fonds, WCA, A1988.123, series 1, subseries 1, MU 101, minute

book, 1873–1905, membership lists from 1873–1905. The Elora Agricultural society recorded a percentage of 3% of female members in 1899; see the Elora Agricultural society fonds, WCA, A1982.70, series 9, subseries 1, file 1, minute book, 1896–1907, Jan. 1899. The Metcalfe society recorded 3 women out of a membership of 57 in 1893; see the Township of Metcalfe fonds, LAC, MG 9 D8/52, minute book, 1889–97, membership list.

86 Oro Agricultural society fonds, SCA, Acc. 970–77, minute book, 1859–86, the 1882 annual report; Glengarry Agricultural society fonds, LAC, MG 24 I 3, vol. 20, minute book, 1866–85, 9 June 1880; South Wellington Agricultural society fonds, WCA, A1988.123, series 2, subseries 1, MU 101, minute book, 1878–97, 19 Jan. 1886, 147–8, and 31 March 1887, 163; and also the Township of Metcalfe fonds, LAC, MG 9 D8/52, minute book, 1889–97, 24 June 1893.

87 South Wellington Agricultural society fonds, WCA, A1988.123 series 2, subseries, 1, MU 101, minute book, 1878–98, 12 Dec. 1878, 13, and 22 April 1879, 23. See also Erin Agricultural society fonds, WCA, A1989.97, reel 1, minute book 1862–82, 30 Oct. 1879 and minute book 1882–98, 30 Oct. 1885; Cardwell Agricultural society fonds, SCA, Acc. 988–3, minute book, 1868–1902, 8 Oct. 1869; and the Bolton Agricultural society fonds, Peel Region Archives, Acc. 85.0160, minute book, 1858–85, 27 Nov. 1875.

88 Farmers' Institute Records, AO, RG 16–85, container 3, Letterbook, letter of 1 March 1894, Superintendent Hodson to the *Farmers' Advocate*, as well as container 1, file 1886, report of South Huron Institute and file 1888, report of the North Lanark Institute. Centre Wellington Farmers' Institute fonds, WCA, A1981.47, MU 43, minute book, 1896–1903, annual meeting, 1898; and also the lecture list of 25 Jan. 1896, 10 Jan. 1898 and 29 Jan. 1903.

89 This would be the explanation behind the popularity of the Women's Institutes, and the parallel growth of "rural feminism." See Ambrose, "What Are the Good of Those Meetings Anyway," 1–20; Ambrose and Kechnie, "Social Control or Social Feminism," 222–32; and Halpern, *And on That Farm He Had a Wife*.

90 *Farmers' Advocate* vol. 3 (Feb. 1868), 19; vol. 3 (July 1868), 106; vol. 19 (March 1884), 82; vol. 20 (June 1885), 165–6; and also vol. 21 (July 1886), 166–7.

91 *Farmers' Advocate* vol. 12 (March 1877), 39–40; vol. 12 (Nov. 1877), 67–8; vol. 18 (Feb. 1883), 59–60; vol. 19 (Nov. 1884), 332–3; and vol. 21 (Aug. 1886), 246–7.

92 See the *Ontario Farmer* vol. 2 (Dec. 1870), 376–7; *Miller's Canadian Farmers' Almanac for the Year 1886*, 35–6; and the *Farmers' Advocate* vol. 9 (Aug. 1874), 124, and vol. 11 (Jan. 1876), 19–20.

93 Puslinch Farmers' Club fonds, AO, MU 2086 #6, minute book, 1874–96, 16 May 1874, 2–5; and Oro Agricultural society fonds, SCA, Acc. 970–77, minute book, 1886–1908, 4 June 1888.

94 See the Walter Riddell papers, AO, MU 2388, series A-3, file #3, *The Hindrances in Canadian Agriculture*, 5–6 and 10, as well as L.S. Huntingdon, *The Independence of Canada*, 13–14.

95 Irwin, "Government Funding of Agricultural Associations," 270–85; Fair, "Gentlemen, Farmers, and Gentlemen Half-Farmers," 263–71, and Heaman, *Inglorious Arts of Peace*, 52–78.

96 *Transactions of the Agricultural and Arts Association of Ontario* vol. 7 (1871), 225–6, and the entry on Christie in the *Dictionary of Canadian Biography* vol. 10, 168–71.

97 See the Centre Wellington Farmers' Institute fonds, WCA, A1981.47, MU 43, minute book, 1896–1905, bylaws pasted on front of book, 3–4; and Irwin, "Government Funding of Agricultural Associations," 270–85.

98 "Je demande [aux] curés des paroisses de mon diocèse de vouloir bien m'aider, dans le mesure de l'intérêt qu'ils portent à la classe agricole, à donner une bonne direction aux cercles qui se formeront, sous ce régime, dans mon diocese." Noel, *Constitution et Règlements de l'Association Agricole*, iii–v; 15–16, 24–5 and 34; *Almanach des Cercles Agricoles pour l'année 1894*, 29–31 and 75; *Almanach des Cercles Agricoles pour l'année 1897*, 23; and the *Almanach des Cercles Agricoles pour l'année 1899*, 71–2, as well as Dallaire, *Considerations on Farmers' Clubs*, 5–6 and 15–16.

99 See the Farmers' Institute records, AO, RG 16–85, container 1, file 2, reports from 1887, reports of the West Kent and Oshawa Institute meetings as well as file 3, reports from 1888, reports of the East Peterborough, South Oxford, and Northumberland Institute meetings.

100 *Annual Report of the Central Farmers' Institute for 1888*, 10–13. See also the Farmers' Institute records, AO, RG 16–85, container 1, file 2, reports from 1887, report of the South Wellington meeting.

101 *Farmers' Advocate* vol. 2 (Jan. 1867), 1; vol. 2 (Feb. 1867), 10; vol. 2 (July 1867), 51; vol. 4 (Dec. 1869), 182–3; vol. 5 (June 1870), 83; vol. 5 (Dec. 1870), 179; and vol. 6 (Dec. 1871), 179–80. See the entry on William Weld in the *Dictionary of Canadian Biography* vol. 12, 1093–94; and Careless, "The Toronto *Globe* and Agrarian Radicalism."

102 See the *Farmers' Advocate* vol. 2 (March 1867), 17–18; vol. 2 (April 1867), 25–7; vol. 2 (Aug. 1867), 60–1; vol. 6 (Jan. 1871), 1; vol. 9 (Feb. 1874), 18–19; vol. 10 (Jan. 1875), 17; vol. 14 (May 1879), 74–5; and vol. 15 (Feb. 1880), 28.

103 See the *Farmers' Advocate* vol. 2 (Feb. 1867), 9–10, and entry on Weld in the *Dictionary of Canadian Biography* vol. 12, 1093–4.

104 See the *Farmers' Advocate* vol. 7 (July 1872), 98; vol. 18 (Jan. 1883), 2–3, and vol. 18 (Nov. 1883), 327; vol. 21 (Feb. 1886), 39–40; vol. 22 (July 1887), 193–4; vol. 23 (Jan. 1888), 1–2; and vol. 23 (March 1888), 65.

05 Middlesex Agricultural society fonds, RCL, box 5289-1, minute book, 1873-93, annual report for 1872 and the annual report for 1877, as well as the Peterborough Agricultural society fonds, PCMA, Acc. 99-004, minute book, 1868-75, 30 Jan. 1869.
06 Landry Family fonds, LAC, MG II E4, vol. 19, correspondence, open letter from Philippe Landry to the Montmagny Agricultural society, 1891, 1-2. See also the Walter Riddell papers, AO, MU 2388, series A-3, lecture to Northumberland Agricultural society, n.d. and Guelph Fat Stock Club fonds, WCA, A1969.10.1, MU 3, minute book, 1881-1900, 21 Nov. 1891, 192.
07 Thomas McCrae papers, WCA, A998.38, series 10, file 6. See also Guelph Fat Stock Club fonds, WCA, A1969.10.1, MU 3, minute book, 1881-1900, 6 Feb. 1895, 223-4; and Missiquoi Agricultural society fonds, LAC, MG 28 I 227, M-3790, document 3, minute book 1869-75, 28 Jan. 1871. Of course, employing the discourse of "improvement" signified some consent to the liberal social order; see Samson, "Industry and Improvement."
08 Glengarry Agricultural society records, McGillivray Family fonds, MG 24 I3, vol. 21, letter of John Tobin, 10 June 1891 and the Guelph Fat Stock Club fonds, WCA, A1969.10.1, MU 3, minute book, 1881-1900, 13 April 1883, 71, and 20 Feb. 1886, 96.
09 South Wellington Agricultural society fonds, WCA, A1988.123, series 2, subseries 1, MU 101, minute book, 1878-97, annual report for 1883. See also the Walter Riddell papers, AO, MU 2388, series A-3, file #3, *The Hindrances in Canadian Agriculture*, n.d., 7-10. See also Forster, *A Conjunction of Interests*.
110 See the Farmers' Institute records, AO, RG 16-85, container 1, file 1, reports from 1886, report from the South Leeds Institute and the Centre Wellington Farmers' Institute fonds, WCA, A1981.47, MU 43, minute book, 1896-1905, bylaws pasted on front of book, 1.
111 By 1887 the Puslinch Farmers' Club had become the South Wellington Farmers' Institute; see the Puslinch Farmers' Club fonds, AO, MU 2086 #6, minute book, 1874-96, 8 March 1888, and 22 March 1888, and the Farmers' Institute records, AO, RG 16-85, container 1, file 3, reports from 1888, report of the West Victoria Institute, as well as the *Annual Report of the Central Institute for 1888*, 5-8.
112 *Almanach des Cercles Agricoles pour l'année 1894*, 9, 29 and 31-42, and the *Almanach des Cercles Agricoles pour l'année 1895*, 21.
113 "rend l'homme meilleur, en lui conservant des moeurs simples, un coeur droit, des habitudes d'économie, le goût du travail, l'amour de la justice, et richesse de joie, d'union, d'affection de famille, richesse dans la modération des désirs." *Almanach des Cercles Agricoles pour L'année 1895*, 48; see also *Almanach des Cercles Agricoles pour l'année 1896*, 36-7 and *Almanach des Cercles Agricoles pour l'année 1899*, 7.

114 See the *Farmers' Advocate* vol. 3 (May 1868), 70; vol. 3 (June 1868), 86–7; vol. 4 (May 1869), 73; vol. 13 (Jan. 1877), 22; and vol. 8 (July 1873), 104. See also *Miller's Canadian Farmer's Almanac for the Year 1875*, 3–5 and *Miller's Canadian Farmer's Almanac for the Year 1886*, 42.

115 *Ontario Farmer* vol. 1 (Jan. 1869), 27; vol. 1 (Feb. 1869), 58–9; vol. 1 (March 1869), 66; vol. 1 (May 1869), 132; vol. 1 (July 1869), 222; and vol. 1 (Oct. 1869), 295–6.

116 See the *Ontario Farmer* vol. 1 (March 1869), 87 and vol. 1 (Jan. 1869), 2. See also the *Farmers' Advocate* vol. 4 (Jan. 1869), 3; vol. 8 (Jan. 1873), 2–3; vol. 9 (March 1874), 41 and vol. 16 (Jan. 1881), 4.

117 The former is taken from Irwin, "Government Funding of Agricultural Associations," 213–20, and Heaman, *The Inglorious Arts of Peace*, 106–31, while the latter view finds expression in Keith Walden, *Becoming Modern in Toronto*, 247–91. Their arguments are tempered by the fact that all three historians focus exclusively on the larger urban exhibitions, while overlooking the more localized rural fairs.

118 *Farmers' Advocate* vol. 2 (Aug. 1867), 62; vol. 3 (April 1868), 50; vol. 5 (June 1870), 82; vol. 15 (July 1880), 146; and vol. 20 (Sept. 1885), 262–3. See also the *Ontario Farmer* vol. 2 (May 1870), 130–1, and vol. 2 (Dec. 1870), 376.

119 Ottawa Agricultural society fonds, LAC, MG 28 I 27, vol. 1, minute book from 1868–77, annual report of 1877. See also the Niagara District Agricultural society fonds, AO, FIII 1, MS 193, reel 13, minute book 1891–1910, 11 March 1892, 21, to 2 Sept. 1896, 64; West Nissouri Agricultural society fonds, RCL, box 5103, minute book, 1876–1906, 16 March 1891; and Oro Agricultural society fonds, SCA, Acc. 970–77, minute book, 1859–86, 31 March 1880.

120 South Wellington Agricultural society fonds, WCA, A1988.123, series 2, subseries 1, MU 101, minute book, 1878–97, 16 Jan. 1889, 200, and 26 May 1891. See also the North Walshingham Agricultural society fonds, AO, MU 2093 #29, minute book, 1889–1925, 14 Jan. 1892, 33, and McGillivray Family papers, LAC, MG 24 I 3, vol. 21(2), records of the Glengarry Agricultural society, letter from the president of the Prescott Agricultural society, 12 Aug. 1891, 203.

121 Guelph Fat Stock Club fonds, WCA, A1969.10.1, MU 3, minute book, 1881–1900, annual report for 1881, 22; 18 Nov. 1882, 36; annual report for 1882, 38; 23 Feb. 1884, 61; 7 Feb. 1894, 214; and annual report for 1894, 223.

122 See the Middlesex Agricultural society fonds, RCL, box 5289–1, minute book, 1873–93, annual report for 1880 and annual report for 1882. This seems to have been a facet of the larger and more urban exhibitions; see Walden, *Becoming Modern in Toronto*, 247–91 and Heaman, *Inglorious Arts of Peace*, 106–31.

123 South Wellington Agricultural society fonds, WCA, A1988.123, series 2, subseries 1, MU 101, minute book, 1878–97, 10 June 1893, 302; Ottawa Agricultural society fonds, LAC, MG 28 I 27, vol. 1, minute book, 1868–77, 2 Oct. 1869 and Erin

Agricultural society fonds, WCA, A1989.97, reel 1, minute book, 1882–1898, 19 March 1886, 14 Jan. 1888 and 14 Jan. 1890. See also the *Farmers' Advocate* vol. 20, (Oct. 1885), 290–1; vol. 26 (Nov. 1891), 422; and vol. 28 (15 Oct. 1893), 394.

124 See the South Wellington Agricultural society fonds, WCA, A1988.123, series 2, subseries 1, MU 101, minute book, 1878–97, 16 Jan. 1889, 200.

125 South Wellington Agricultural society fonds, WCA, A1988.123, series 2, subseries 1, MU 101, minute book, 1878–97, 20 Jan. 1897, 425, and the newspaper articles pasted on the back.

126 Elora Agricultural society fonds, WCA, A1982.70, series 9, subseries 1, file 1, minute book, 1896–1907, 8 Jan. 1896, 15 May 1896, 25 Aug. 1896, 13 Jan. 1897, 22 Jan. 1898 and 27 Sept. 1898. See also Cardwell Agricultural society fonds, SCA, Acc. 988–3, minute book, 1868–1902, 8 July 1882 and 30 July 1896.

127 *Miller's Canadian Farmers' Almanac for the Year 1883*, 3, and the South Wellington Agricultural society fonds, WCA, A1988.123, series 2, subseries 1, MU 101, minute book, 1878–97, 28 Oct. 1885, 142 and 8 Aug. 1891, 259; and the Elora Agricultural society fonds, WCA, A1982.70, series 9, subseries 1, file 1, minute book, 1896–1907, 19 Feb. 1898 and 30 July 1898.

128 Farmers' Institute records, AO, RG 16–85, container 1, file 1, reports from 1886, report from the South Huron, East Kent, and South Leeds Institutes; file 2, reports from 1887, report of Centre Grey and North Norfolk Institutes as well as file 3, reports from 1888, report of the North Bruce, North Lanark, and Halton Institutes.

129 See the Puslinch Farmers' Club fonds, AO, MU 2086 #6, minute book, 1874–96, clipping pasted on the front; and 7 Jan. 1888, 131, and 20 Jan. 1896, 192–3.

130 Missisquoi Agricultural society fonds, LAC, MG 28 I 227, M-3790, document 2, minute book, 1863–68, annual report of 1865, 19 Sept. 1868; document 3, minute book, 1869–75, 22 Dec. 1869, 28 Jan. 1871; document 5, minute book, 1879–83, 5 Aug. 1882 and M-3791, document 6, minute book, 1883–9, 18 Sept. 1886, annual report for 1887. See also Montmagny Agricultural society records, Philippe Landry papers, LAC, MG II E4, vol. 18, cahier des délibérations, 1856–78, 5 Jan. 1867, 111; 14 Jan. 1867, 114–19; and 18 Dec. 1878, 259; Montmagny model farm records, vol. 20, cahier des délibérations, 26 Dec. 1867, 2 and 6 Sept. 1874, 17–18.

131 See Noel, *Constitution et Règlements de l'Association Provinciale Agricole*, 9–11, and Edward Barnard, *Cercles Agricoles*, 1–3.

CHAPTER SIX

1 On William Weld's involvement with the Dominion Grange and the inaugural meeting in London, see Wood, *A History of Farmers' Movements in Canada*, 41–6

and 52–5. See also some of Weld's editorials in the *Farmers' Advocate* vol. 8 (July 1873), 98–9; vol. 9 (April 1874), 49–51; vol. 15 (Jan. 1880), 1–2; vol. 15 (March 1880), 62; and vol. 15 (July 1880), 147–8. Although the Dominion Grange and the Patrons of Industry made great headway among farmers in the province of Quebec, this chapter focuses mainly on agrarian protest among farmers in Ontario.

2 Taylor, in his *Fashioning Farmers*, argues that there were two rival identities clamouring for farmers' attention: a vision of the farmer as a small businessman and an advocate of commercial market agriculture, and an image of the farmer as a labourer who favoured the co-operative system. To Taylor, the agrarian protest movement that viewed farmers as workers broke down when farmers rejected co-operatives outright and fully accepted the capitalistic market system. Rennie makes similar arguments for Alberta in *The Rise of Agrarian Democracy*; see also Badgely, *Bringing in the Common Love of Good*, 3–20.

3 On the inter-associational strife of the Grange and the Patrons of Industry, see Wood, *Farmers' Movements in Canada*, 63–72 and 115–21. For the Grange and Patrons as expressions of radical class discontent, see Hann, *Farmers Confront Industrialism*. See also Kealey and Palmer, *Dreaming of What Might Be*, 388–91, and Cook, "Tillers and Toilers," 5–20.

4 On the conservatism of Ontario farmers, see Noel, *Patrons, Clients, Brokers*, 232–48, and Badgely, *Bringing in the Common Love of Good*, 7–10. See also Taylor, *Fashioning Farmers*, 1–14, and Rennie, *The Rise of Agrarian Democracy*, 3–8.

5 McInnis, "Marketable Surpluses in Ontario Farming," 395–424; McCalla, *Planting the Province*; and especially the invaluable work of Darroch, "Scanty Fortunes and Rural Middle Class Formation," 621–59. See also Sandwell, "Rural Reconstruction," 1–32; McInnis, "The Changing Structure of Canadian Agriculture," 191–8; and especially the work of Sylvester, *The Limits of Rural Capitalism*.

6 See Bittermann, "The Hierarchy of the Soil," 33–55; Bittermann, Mackinnon, and Wynn, "Of Inequality and Interdependence," 1–20; and many of the essays in Samson, *Contested Countryside*. For the situation in Ontario, see Crowley, "Rural Labour," 13–104, and Darroch, "Scanty Fortunes," 630–6. On the ways in which farmers dealt with the changes associated with urban industrial capitalism, see Hann, *Farmers Confront Industrialism*; Taylor, *Fashioning Farmers*, 1–14, and 90–102; and Rennie, *The Rise of Agrarian Democracy*, 13–19. On the tensions wrought by commercialism on agriculture by the latter decades of the century, see Cohen, *Women's Work, Markets, and Economic Development*; Badgely, "Then I Saw I had Been Swindled," 350–4. Crerar, in his "Ties That Bind," argues effectively that rural culture was vibrant at the turn of the century and the rural populace did not really experience an agrarian crisis at all.

7 For farmers participating in the construction of a new "liberal" commercial identity, see Fair, "Gentlemen, Farmers, and Gentlemen Half-Farmers"; Heaman, *The Inglorious Arts of Peace*; Wood, *Making Ontario*; and also the preceding chapter on agricultural associations. On the relationship of farmers to the state and the rural social order see Burley, *A Particular Condition in Life* and Darroch, "Scanty Fortunes." Taylor argues that agricultural knowledge often separated farmers; see his *Fashioning Farmers*, Nesmith, "The Philosophy of Agriculture," and Irwin, "Government Funding of Agricultural Associations."
8 For voluntary associations as a bulwark of cultural hegemony, see Anstead, "Fraternalism in Victorian Ontario" and Marks, *Revivals and Roller Rinks*. For the presence of farmers in Mechanics' Institutes, temperance societies, and fraternal orders, see Donald Akenson's study of the Gananoque Mechanics' Institute in *The Irish in Ontario*, 218–22; Emery and Emery, *A Young Man's Benefit*, 31–8; and Ferry, "To the Interests and Conscience of the Great Mass of the Community," 137–63.
9 Both Hann in his work *Farmers Confront Industrialism* and Cook in "Tillers and Toilers" view this ideology as part of a nascent socialist outlook. Taylor, in *Fashioning Farmers*, separates the views of "radical" farmers and "liberal" farmers concerning this adversarial rhetoric, while Rennie, in *The Rise of Agrarian Democracy*, and Badgely, in *Bringing in the Common Love of Good*, assert that both groups of farmers participated in censuring the non-producing classes. To see how a variety of interest groups throughout Ontario's history employed the rhetoric of populism, see Noel, "Early Populist Tendencies in Ontario Political Culture," 173–87; Wilton, *Popular Politics and Political Culture*; and McNairn, *The Capacity to Judge*.
10 Wood, *A History of Farmers' Movements in Canada*, 25–35, and *History of The Grange in Canada*, 22–32.
11 For an examination of the tensions between the Grange and modernity, see Nordin, *Rich Harvest*; Hann, *Farmers Confront Industrialism*, 1–6; and Gates, "Modernization as a Function of an Agricultural Fair," 262–79. For the Grange as a continuity of agrarian radicalism, see Woods, *Knights of the Plow*; L.A. Wood, *A History of Farmers' Movements*, 13–155; and Badgely, *Bringing in the Common Love of Good*, 5–12.
12 *History of the Grange in Canada*, 3; *Circular to the Deputies of Dominion Granges*, and *Manual of Subordinate Granges of the Patrons of Husbandry*, 16.
13 See the *Farmers' Advocate* vol. 9 (Feb. 1874), 17–18; vol. 8 (July 1873), 98; and vol. 9 (April 1874), 49. The unifying bond of associational life along strict gendered lines was particularly true with fraternal societies; see Clawson, *Constructing Brotherhood*; Carnes, *Secret Ritual and Manhood in Victorian America*, and Emery and Emery, *A Young Man's Benefit*.

14 *History of the Grange*, 18–19; the *Granger* vol. 1 (Jan. 1875); and *Proceedings of the Dominion Grange, Second Annual Session*, 2–3.
15 See the *Proceedings of the Dominion Grange, Fifteenth Annual Session*, 7. See also the *Proceedings of the Dominion Grange, Sixth Annual Session*, 9–10, and also the *Granger* vol. 1 (Dec. 1875). See also the *Constitution and Bylaws of the Dominion Grange*, 9, and also Smedley, *The Patrons Monitor*, 2–3.
16 With twenty-three of the original twenty-five members from the province of Ontario – with those twenty-three coming from only six counties: Grey, Lambton, Middlesex, Welland, Elgin, and York – it is also evident that the early Dominion Grange directors were a fairly elite group who concerned themselves in large measure with the problems of commercial agriculture in Ontario. See Wood, *A History of Farmers' Movements in Canada*, 41–61.
17 In *A History of Farmers' Movements in Canada*, 41–2, Wood provides the town of residence for most of the original attendees to the first Dominion Grange meeting, so it was a fairly effortless task to track these individuals down in the 1871 census records, which are housed in the Archives of Ontario. See the AO, 1871 agricultural returns for Grey County, C-9953 to 9954; for Middlesex, C-9900 and C-9904 to 9905; for Lambton County, C-9895 to 9899 and Welland County, C-9920.
18 See the *Granger* vol. 1 (Dec. 1875); *Proceedings of the Dominion Grange, Twelfth Annual Session*, 44; and also the Knock Grange fonds, SCA, Acc. 987–16, E7, miscellaneous papers, Dominion Grange circular, 13 June 1884.
19 Knock Grange fonds, SCA, Acc. 987–16, E4, miscellaneous papers, Ontario People's Salt Co. circular, 1883. See also Bradford, *Address Delivered by Robert Bradford to the Grange at Agincourt*, 5 and 10, as well as the *Constitution and Bylaws of the Dominion Grange*, 4.
20 Unfortunately, rank and file membership lists of subordinate Granges in Ontario are simply non-existent, while records of the executive are likewise extremely rare and incomplete. For a description of the Knock Grange directors, see Arnett, *The Grange at Knock*, 5–6. This information was then cross-referenced with the agricultural returns in the 1871 census in the AO, Simcoe County, C-9961. While clearly not representative of the considerable wealth of the Dominion Grange officers, the recorded acreage corresponded well with the listing of a medium-sized farm reported by over 50 percent of Ontario's farmers in the census. See Darroch, "Scanty Fortunes," 626–31.
21 In distancing themselves from being "mere workers," it appears that Ontario farmers not only felt part of the rural middle class but also accepted scientific husbandry. See Nesmith, "The Philosophy of Agriculture." For the themes of agricultural respectability, see Darroch, "Scanty Fortunes," 636–42. Crowley, in "Rural Labour," 50–1, argues that the Grange often caused a chasm between agricultural labourers and farmers in the Grange, which is a fairly accurate assess-

ment. In the Dufferin County Archives, see particularly the P.J. Van Wagoner fonds, Acc. 3456–998, speech of Van Wagoner to the Acadia Grange, n.d, and the Knock Grange fonds, SCA, Acc. 987–16, minute book, 1875–77, 16 June 1875.

22 Bradford, *Address Delivered by Robert Bradford to the Grange at Agincourt*, 20–2; the *Granger* vol. 1 (Nov. 1875); vol. 1 (Jan. 1876) and vol. 1 (April 1876). See also *Constitution and Bylaws of the Dominion Grange*, 4–5. These were not new arguments that appeared suddenly among farmers in the 1870s, as such radical "populist" rhetoric can be found throughout Ontario's history; see Careless, "The Toronto *Globe* and Agrarian Radicalism," 14–39, and Dewar, "Charles Clarke's *Reformator*," 233–52.

23 Weld clearly appreciated the diversity of the rural social order, while some subordinate Granges consciously attempted to alter these cultural relationships. See also Badgely, "'Then I Saw I had Been Swindled,'" 350–4, and also the *Farmers' Advocate* vol. 10 (Feb. 1875), 23 and 37; vol. 10 (March 1875), 35–6, and vol. 15 (March 1880), 63–4.

24 See the *Proceedings of the Dominion Grange, Twenty-Third Annual Session*, 16–17, and Badgely, "'Then I Saw I had Been Swindled,'" 354. Market agriculture also won out over the co-operative system in the Prairies; see Taylor, *Fashioning Farmers* and Rennie, *The Rise of Agrarian Democracy*.

25 The position of the Grange in regard to women would prove to be fairly consistent with that of farmers in general; see Nordin, *Rich Harvest*, 110–30; Woods, *Knights of the Plow*, 165–78; Osterud, *Bonds of Community*; and especially Marti, *Women of the Grange*.

26 See the *Canadian Granger* vol. 2 (Oct. 1876). See also the *Manual of Subordinate Granges*, 24–6, and *Constitution and Bylaws of the Dominion Grange*, 3.

27 Moffat, *To the Members of the Dominion*, 4–6; 15–17 and 26–7. On the evolution of agricultural work pertaining to women, see McMurry, *Transforming Rural Life*. For the Canadian context, see Cohen, *Women's Work, Markets and Economic Development* and Crowley, "Experience and Representation," 238–51.

28 *Proceedings of the Dominion Grange, Twenty-Third Annual Session*, 10; *Constitution and Bylaws of the Dominion Grange*, 5–6; *History of the Grange*, 21–2; *Manual of the Grange*, 69–70; the *Granger*, vol. 1 (Nov. 1875) and the *Canadian Granger* vol. 1 (Sept. 1876).

29 See the *Constitution and Bylaws of the Dominion Grange*, 5, and also the *Farmers' Advocate* vol. 9 (Feb. 1874), 17–18; vol. 9 (March 1874), 41; and vol. 9 (April 1874), 49–50.

30 The *Granger* vol. 1 (April 1876) and Wood, *A History of Farmers' Movements in Canada*, 90–9. Noel postulates that a solid constituency of farmers – and Grangers – in Ontario followed the Mowat Liberals as a result of his masterful clientelism, which is a compelling argument; see his *Patrons, Clients, Brokers*, 232–48.

31 See the Knock Grange fonds, SCA, Acc. 987–16, minute book, 1887–1901, 30 June 1891; 17 Feb. 1894; and 5 Oct. 1896. See also *Proceedings of the Dominion Grange, Seventeenth Annual Session,* 10; *Proceedings of the Grange, Eighteenth Annual Session,* 6–9; and *Proceedings of the Dominion Grange, Nineteenth Annual Session,* 10.

32 *Songs of the Grange, Patrons of Husbandry,* 20–4, 44–6. See also *Constitution and Bylaws of the Dominion Grange,* 1, and *Manual of the Grange,* 6–13, 46–8. On the producer ideology in industrial Ontario, see Palmer, *A Culture in Conflict,* 97–122, and Kealey, *Toronto Workers Respond to Industrial Capitalism,* 124–50. For late nineteenth-century changes in industrial Ontario, see Heron, "Factory Workers," 480–515. David Burley, in *A Particular Condition in Life,* argues that small producers and self-employed entrepreneurs formed the backbone of the economy, utilizing the producer ideology for their own purposes.

33 See the *Canadian Granger* vol. 1 (Sept. 1876) and vol. 2 (Nov. 1876); the *Granger,* vol. 1 (March 1876) and vol. 1 (April 1876); *Proceedings of the Dominion Grange, First Annual Session,* 8, and the *Proceedings of the Dominion Grange, Sixth Annual Session,* 9–10. See also Wood, *A History of Farmers' Movements in Canada,* 91–5, and, for a discussion on the free trade position, see Forster, *A Conjunction of Interests,* 30–67.

34 On the Grange and Patrons of Industry joining industrial workers in supporting a more radical political economy, see Hann, *Farmers Confront Industrialism;* Palmer and Kealey, *Dreaming of What Might Be,* 388–91; and Burr, *Spreading the Light,* 14–55. See also Taylor, *Fashioning Farmers,* 1–14, and Rennie, *The Rise of Agrarian Democracy,* 8–12.

35 The *Granger* vol. 1 (Dec. 1875) and vol. 1 (Nov. 1875). See also the *Canadian Co-operator and Patron* vol. 5 (July 1886) and *Circular of the Dominion Grange,* 22 June 1877.

36 For a description of the Knock Grange's passion for co-operative ventures, see Arnett, *The Grange at Knock,* 46–53. See also the Knock Grange fonds, SCA, Acc. 987–16, file E1, minute book, 1875–77, 16 Feb. 1875. As smaller commercial farmers, Knock farmers would feel the pinch of monopoly and the effects of industrial capitalism more than those involved in large-scale agricultural operations.

37 See the Knock Grange fonds, SCA, Acc. 987–16, file E4, Ontario People's Salt Company circulars, 1883 and 1886, and the minute book, 1887–1901, 3 March 1887 and 6 March 1889.

38 *Farmers' Advocate* vol. 15 (Jan. 1880), 7–8; vol. 15 (March 1880), 62; and vol. 15 (July 1880), 147. Weld also accused the Grange of stifling independence within their membership as the "shirker" could receive equal benefits as hardworking members, another contravention of popular liberal political economy; see the *Farmers' Advocate* vol. 15 (Jan. 1880), 1–2.

39 See the Knock Grange fonds, SCA, Acc. 987–16, file E2, circulars of the Co-op Sewing Machine Co., 1882 and 1884, and file E6, circulars of the Grange Wholesale Company, 1882. See also Arnett, *The Grange at Knock*, 51–3.
40 See the *Farmers' Advocate* vol. 9 (April 1874), 57–8; vol. 11 (Jan. 1876), 19; vol. 13 (July 1878), 167, and vol. 15 (July 1880), 147.
41 The corresponding closing ode went as follows: "Bless be the tie that binds / Our hearts in social love; The fellowship of kindred minds / Is like to that above. When we asunder part / It gives us inward pain; But we shall still be joined in heart / And hope to meet again." See the *Songs of the Grange*, 50, and 3–4, 7–10, and 19–20; *Manual of the Grange*, 67–9, and the *Canadian Granger* vol. 2 (March 1877).
42 Knock Grange fonds, SCA, Acc. 987–16, minute book, 1875–77, 16 Feb. and 18 March 1876; minute book, 1886, 24 Feb. 1886; minute book, 1887–1901, 2 Jan. 1889 and 23 March 1893. See also the Minesing Grange in the Harold Parker fonds, SCA, Acc. 979–100, minute book, 1879–1906, 28 July 1879, and 28 March 1881.
43 See the Royal Oak Grange fonds, RCL, minutes 1874–78, 22 Dec. 1874, 11 Jan. 1876, 13 Feb. 1877, and 12 April 1878; the Brougham Grange fonds, AO, MU 7778 #2, minute book, 1880–84, 10 Dec. 1880, 28 Dec. 1881, and 12 Jan. 1884. See also the Knock Grange fonds, SCA, Acc. 987–16, minute book, 1875–77, 5 Sept. 1877; minute book, 1887–1901, 23 March 1893. See also the Minesing Grange records in the Harold Parker fonds, SCA, Acc. 979–100, minute book, 1879–1906, 13 Feb. 1882, 11 Feb. 1883, and 10 March 1884.
44 For Populism as a radical agrarian solution to industrial capitalism, see Goodwyn, *Democratic Promise* and Palmer, *Man Over Money*. Descriptions of Populism as a reaction to social change can be found in Hahn, *The Roots of Southern Populism* and McNall, *The Road to Rebellion*. Other historians argue that Populism was a movement of small producers and accordingly critiqued capitalism from a republican ideology; see Holmes, "Populism: In Search of Context," 26–58. See also Sanders, *Roots of Reform*, 30–52 and 102–47, to see how the Farmers' Alliance was a successor to Greenbackism in republican lore. Robert McMath Jr argued that Populism strove simply to create an agricultural community based on producerism and education; see McMath, *American Populism*.
45 For the Patrons' retreat into classic economic liberalism, see Shortt, "Social Change and Political Crisis in Rural Ontario," 211–35. For a view of the Patrons as heralds of collectivist solutions to the problems of capitalism, see Hann, *Farmers Confront Industrialism* and Cook, "Tillers and Toilers," 5–20. For the Patrons as a link with the radical agrarianism of the early nineteenth century, see Wood, *Farmers' Movements in Canada*, 109–55; Noel, *Patrons, Clients, Brokers*, 294–309; and Badgely, *Bringing in the Common Love of Good*, 2–13.

46 On the continuing changes in agriculture and rural depopulation, see McInnis, "The Changing Structure of Canadian Agriculture," 191–8; Cohen, *Women's Work, Markets, and Economic Development*; and Crowley, "Rural Labour," 63–70. Of course, Crerar argues that rural depopulation was more myth than reality, although the rhetoric did get rather heated; see his "Ties That Bind." On the effects of industrial capitalism, see Palmer, *A Culture in Conflict*; Kealey, *Toronto Workers Respond to Industrial Capitalism*; and Heron, "Factory Workers," 480–515. Unfortunately, it is even more difficult to ascertain the social composition of both rank and file members *and* the executive of the Patrons of Industry than with the Dominion Grange. The lack of membership records remains a strong impediment, while the executive of the Patrons was divided equally between farmers and radical journalists. See Cook, "Tillers and Toilers," 5–20.

47 See Wood, *Farmers' Movements in Canada*, 109–12; Shortt, "Social Change and Political Crisis," 212–13; and McCutcheon, "The Patrons of Industry in Manitoba," 142–65.

48 See the records of the Gainsborough Patrons, AO, MU 7185, pamphlet, *Ritual and Installation Service of the Patrons of Industry*, 4. See also the *Constitution and Rules of Order of the Patrons of Industry*, preamble and 3–4; *3rd Annual Meeting of the Grand Association of Ontario Patrons of Industry*, 2, and the *Canada Farmers' Sun*, 7 March 1893, and 21 March 1893.

49 Records of the Gainsborough Patrons, AO, GP, MU 7185, pamphlet, *Principles and Rules of the Patrons of Industry*, 1–2. See also the *Canada Farmers' Sun*, 10 May 1892, 7 June 1892, and 27 Sept. 1892.

50 *Canada Farmers' Sun*, 27 March 1894 and 7 Nov. 1894, as well as Hann, *Farmers Confront Industrialism*, and Cook, "Tillers and Toilers," 7–10.

51 See the Victoria Patrons fonds, in the F.D. McLennan collection, AO, MU 7195, series F, minute book, 1892–93, 1 April 1893. See also *2nd Annual Meeting of the Patrons of Industry*, 1–2, and also the *Canada Farmers' Sun*, 27 Sept. 1892 and 11 April 1893, as well as the *Canada Farmers' Sun*, 1 Aug. 1893, and 22 Aug. 1894. For attitudes of farmers to travelling peddlers, see Badgely, "Then I Saw I had Been Swindled."

52 *Canada Farmers' Sun*, 18 Aug. 1892; 20 June 1894; 29 Aug. 1894 and 3 Oct. 1894.

53 See the *Constitution and Rules of Order*, 14, and the *Canada Farmers' Sun*, 26 Dec. 1893 and 2 Jan. 1894.

54 See the AO, Patron Committee minute book, MU 2087 #8, 26 March 1895, and especially Naylor, "Rural Protest and Medical Professionalism," 5–20.

55 *Canada Farmers' Sun*, 14 July 1892 and 28 Feb. 1893; 5 Dec. 1893, and 24 July 1895. For the Patrons' position on women's suffrage, see *4th Annual Meeting of the Patrons of Industry*, 20; *Canada Farmers' Sun*, 1 Nov. 1892 and 11 July 1893; 12 Dec. 1893 and 10 Oct. 1894. On the Patrons and domesticity see *Canada Farmers' Sun*,

16 Aug. 1892; 4 Oct. 1892; 1 Nov. 1892, and 18 Jan. 1893. Similar attitudes were experienced in agricultural societies; see Heaman, "Taking the World by Show," 599–631.

56 See the notebooks of the Galetta Lodge in A.L. Riddell fonds, LAC, MG 55/30 no. 184, membership book. See also the Willow Vale Patron fonds, AO, MU 7185, minute book, 1891–95, 2–13; 27 Oct. 1891, 39; 28 June 1892, 68; 28 Dec. 1892, 19; and 4 April 1892, 29. See also the Victoria Patron fonds, in the McLennan collection, AO, MU 7915, series F, minute book, 1892–93, initiation pledges; 22 April 1892, and 29 April 1892.

57 *Constitution and Rules of Order*, 3–4, 17, and also the *Canada Farmers' Sun*, 6 Sept. 1892; 27 Sept. 1892 and 18 Oct. 1892.

58 See the Willowvale Patron records, AO, MU 7185, minute book, 1891–95, 1 Dec. 1891, 43. See also *2nd Annual Meeting of the Patrons of Industry*, 9; and see the *Canada Farmers' Sun*, 20 Sept. 1892, 23 Oct. 1892, 13 March 1894, and 15 June 1894.

59 *The Patrons: An Answer to the Annexationist Campaign Writer*, 1. See also the *Canada Farmers' Sun*, 30 Aug. 1892; 20 Sept. 1892; 4 July 1893, 28 Nov. 1893; 5 Dec. 1893, and 23 May 1894.

60 *The Patrons of Industry: From the Speech of Oliver Mowat*, 10, and *The Patrons: An Answer to the Annexationist Campaign Writer*, 8. See also the *Canada Farmers' Sun*, 23 May 1894 and 10 Aug. 1894, as well as the Patron committee minute book, AO, MU 2087 #8, 11 April 1895. Shortt argues that the Patrons failed as a result of political immaturity, while Noel states that the Mowat Liberals deliberately blurred the line between Liberal and Patron policies, leading to a Liberal triumph. Cook sees the Patrons' failure more as a lack of political identity. See Shortt, "Social Change and Political Crisis," 230–5; Noel, *Patrons, Clients, Brokers*, 302–5; and Cook, "Tillers and Toilers," 17–20.

61 *Constitution and Rules of Order of the Patrons of Industry*, preamble and the Gainsborough Patrons fonds, AO, MU 7185, pamphlet, *Ritual and Installation Service*, 4.

62 *3rd Annual Meeting of the Patrons of Industry*, 26, and the *Canada Farmers' Sun*, 14 Aug. 1895. See also Shortt, "Social Change and Political Crisis," 224–6; Noel, *Patrons, Clients, Brokers*, 303–6; and Cook, "Tillers and Toilers," 12–15. In using loaded terms such as "equal rights," the Patrons exposed themselves to uncertainty as to their ultimate motives; see Miller, *Equal Rights*.

63 The former view of Populism can be found in Goodwyn, *Democratic Promise* and Palmer, *Man Over Money*, while the latter in Hahn, *The Roots of Southern Populism*, 3–10. See also Holmes, "Populism: In Search of Context," 50–8, and Sanders, *Roots of Reform*, 30–52. In the Canadian context, see Hann, *Farmers Against Industrialism* and Cook, "Tillers and Toilers," as both argue that along with the Knights of Labor, the Patrons offered new collectivist solutions to economic concerns. Of

course, Shortt concludes in "Social Change and Political Crisis" that the Patrons committed themselves to a more traditional liberal "anti-protection" economic strategy. See also Taylor, *Fashioning Farmers*, 1–14, and Rennie, *The Rise of Agrarian Democracy*, 8–12.

64 See the records of the Gainsborough Patrons, MU 7185, pamphlet, *Ritual and Installation Service*, 4–6; the *Constitution and Rules of Order of the Patrons of Industry*, 14–16; the *Canada Farmers' Sun*, 15 Nov. 1892 and 17 Oct. 1893; and the *Brotherhood Era*, 16 Oct. 1895.

65 Both Naylor in "Rural Protest and Medical Professionalism" and Shortt, "Social Change and Political Crisis" agree that the Patrons was a movement of small producers and therefore adhered to a more liberal economic outlook. Hann, in *Farmers Confront Industrialism*, and Cook, in "Tillers and Toilers," conclude that the Patrons were more collectivist and harboured a nascent socialist outlook, and only favoured free trade when noted liberal Goldwin Smith purchased the *Canada Farmers' Sun*.

66 *Canada Farmers' Sun*, 7 June 1892, 9 Aug. 1892, 13 Feb. 1893, 4 July 1893, 16 Aug. 1893, and 18 Sept. 1895.

67 The *Canada Farmers' Sun* also carried such articles as "How Britain's Free Trade Policy the Secret of Enormous Growth in Trade and Increased Wealth." See the *Canada Farmers' Sun*, 31 May 1892, 28 June 1892, 4 Oct. 1892, 11 Oct. 1892, 29 Nov. 1892, 5 Sept. 1893, and 5 Dec. 1894.

68 See the *Canada Farmers' Sun*, 10 May 1892, 9 Aug. 1892, 14 Feb. 1893, and 16 Aug. 1894. For articles on free trade and labour, see the *Canada Farmers' Sun*, 13 Feb. 1895.

69 *The Patrons: An Answer to the Annexation Writer*, 1 and 4; and the *Canada Farmers' Sun*, 3 Oct. 1893.

70 *2nd Annual Meeting of the Patrons of Industry*, 1; *3rd Annual Meeting of the Patrons of Industry*, 2; and *4th Annual Meeting of the Patrons of Industry*, 2.

71 See the Patron Committee minute book, AO, MU 2087 #8, 26 March 1895; and *Canada Farmers' Sun*, 7 March 1893 and 12 Sept. 1894. See also Shortt, "Social Change and Political Crisis," 226–9, and Cook, "Tillers and Toilers," 15–20. On the incompatibility of the Patrons and the TLC, see Palmer and Kealey, *Dreaming of What Might Be*; Burr, *Spreading the Light*; and Darroch, "Scanty Fortunes." See also the *Canada Farmers' Sun*, 27 Sept. 1892, 21 March 1893, and 6 June 1893.

72 See the Gainsborough Patrons, AO, miscellaneous papers, *Odes to Patrons*, 3, and *Canada Farmers' Sun*, 2 Aug. 1892 and 11 Oct. 1892; 12 Sept. 1894; and the *Brotherhood Era*, 16 Oct. 1895.

73 See the *3rd Annual Meeting of the Patrons of Industry*, 2–3, and *Canada Farmers' Sun*, 23 Oct. 1892.

74 Gainsborough Patrons fonds, AO, MU 7185, pamphlet, *Principles and Rules of the Patrons of Industry*, 2, and *Canada Farmers' Sun*, 10 May 1892, 4 Oct. 1892, and 28 March 1893.
75 See the records of the Arthur Lodge, WCA, 1980.26, treasurer's book, 1891–1897, and the Willow Vale Patrons fonds, AO, MU 7185, minute book, 1891–95, 15 Nov. 1892, 15; 22 Nov. 1892, 22; 6 Dec. 1892, 17; 21 Feb. 1893, 25; and 25 April 1893, 32.
76 See the *Farmers' Advocate*, vol. 26 (May 1891), 169; vol. 26 (June 1891), 224; vol. 26 (Nov. 1891), 448–9; vol. 28 (15 March 1893), 102–3; and vol. 29 (1 Jan. 1894), 5–6.
77 *Constitution and Rules of Order of the Patrons of Industry*, 3–4; and also the sections entitled "Rays from Patrons" and "From Patron Pens" in the *Canada Farmers' Sun*, 7 June 1892, 14 June 1892, 5 July 1892, 27 Sept. 1892, 1 Nov. 1892, 2 May 1893, 11 July 1893, 2 Jan. 1894, 3 Oct. 1894, 26 June 1895, and 14 Aug. 1895.
78 See the Victoria Patrons fonds in the McLennan collection, AO, MU 7915, series F, minute book, 1892–93, 28 March, 8 May, 13 May, 10 June, and 22 July 1893.
79 See the Willow Vale Patrons fonds, AO, MU 7185, minute book, 1891–95, 3 Nov. 1891, 39; 1 Dec. 1891, 42; 12 Jan. 1892, 49; 30 March 1892, 54; 17 May 1892, 60–1; 7 June 1892, 65; 6 Dec. 1892, 17; and 17 Jan. 1893, 22.
80 See Badgely, *Bringing in the Common Love of Good*.

CHAPTER SEVEN

1 On Britain's Royal Society and their early aristocratic amateur leaders, see Morrell and Thackery, *Gentlemen of Science*, 10–23; Hall, *All Scientists Now*, 6–20; and Gleason, *The Royal Society of London*, 1–25. See also Levine, *The Amateur and the Professional*, 4–52 and Pyeson and Sheets-Pyeson, *Servants of Nature*, 320–7. For France, see Crosland, *Science Under Control*, 51–75.
2 For the tensions inherent in scientific discourse and the accommodation of industrial capitalism with scientific societies, see Morrell and Thackery, *Gentlemen of Science*, 1–35; Hall, *All Scientists Now*, 63–92; Gleason, *Royal Society of London*, 1–25; and Morus, "Manufacturing Nature," 403–34. For a general theme of various groups employing science to further their own agendas in Britain and France, see Cooter, *The Cultural Meaning of Popular Science*; Winter, *Mesmerized*; Harrison, *The Bourgeois Citizen in Nineteenth-Century France*; Secord, *Victorian Sensation*; and Yeo, "Science and Authority in Mid-Nineteenth Century Britain," 1–35.
3 On the commercial and professional middle-class composition of early scientific and literary societies, see Levere and Jarrell, *A Curious Field-Book*, 1–25; Frost, "Science Education in the Nineteenth Century," 31–6; Chartrand, Duchesne, and

Gingras, *Histoire des Sciences au Québec*, 95–110 and Murray, *Come Bright Improvement*, 23–52. For the political and sectarian quarrels associated with early literary and scientific societies, see McNairn, *The Capacity to Judge*, 63–70 and Murray, *Come Bright Improvement*, 23–52.

4   For the pursuit of utilitarian science and literature, see Levere and Jarrell, *A Curious Field-Book*, 42–7; Owram, *Promise of Eden*, 59–78; Berger, *Science, God and Nature in Victorian Canada*, 4–27; Zeller, *Inventing Canada*; Hewitt, "Science, Popular Culture, and the Producer Alliance," 243–75; and Lamonde, *Gens de Parole*. Christie, in her article "Sir William Logan's Geological Empire," 161–204, argues effectively that those working on the Geological Survey were wary of focusing exclusively on commercialized science.

5   Minute books of the Montreal Natural History Society, Blacker-Wood Library, QHI N273, vol. 1, 1827–1829, 26 May 1828, 65–6, and 24 Nov. 1828, 213. See also the *Annual Report of the LHSQ for the Year 1834*, 13 and *Annual Report of the LHSQ for 1836*, 4 and 15.

6   Lachlan, *A Retrospective Glance at the Progressive State of the Natural History Society of Montreal*, 5–7. See also the *Transactions of the LHSQ* vol. 3, 9–10 and the *Transactions of the LHSQ*, new series, vol. 4, 14–15.

7   *Canadian Naturalist and Geologist* vol. 4 (April 1858), 144–5 and vol. 8 (Feb. 1863), 66, and minutes of the MNHS, Blacker-Wood Library, QHI N273, vol. 5, 1858–1888, 18 May 1861.

8   See the *Canadian Journal* vol. 1 (Aug. 1852), 4–5; vol. 1 (Jan. 1853), 203–4; new series, vol. 1 (March 1856), 98 and vol. 2 (March 1857), 82–3. See also the advertising circular of the Canadian Institute promoting their initial charter, in *The Canadian Institute*, 1–2.

9   For the cultural significance of the *Institut Canadien* in Montreal, see Yvon Lamonde, *Gens de Parole*, 20–33. See also Dorion, *L'Institut Canadien en 1852*, 65–6.

10 "Notre Institut est devenu un Palladium pour tous ... point d'esclusions, point de censure, et la conscience de chacun, les lois éternelles de la morale, de la vérité, de la justice et de la charité sont les seuls guides et les seuls juges." See the *Institut Canadien* fonds, in the ANQ, Cote M-0014, Micro #10678, reel 1, procédés verbaux, 1855–1871, 14 déc. 1859, 214–17, and 17 déc. 1861, 304–6. See also Dorion, *L'Institut Canadien en 1852*, 80–8, and Lafontaine, *L'Institut Canadien en 1855*, 95–9. See also the work of Bernard, *Les rouges* and particularly Lamonde, *L.A. Dessaules*.

11 On the discussions between the Quebec Mechanics' Institute and the LHSQ, see the scrapbook of the Quebec Mechanics' Institute, ANQ, P108, 1830–1845, 13 Feb. 1841 as well as 1 Aug. 1841 and the *Annual Report of the LHSQ for 1844*, 1–3. For the relations between the MNHS and the Montreal Mechanics' Institute, see Frost, "Science Education," 30–4; minute books of the MNHS, Blacker-Wood

Library, QHI N273, vol. 1, 1827–1829, 27 May 1827, 1–2 and 24 Nov. 1828, 250. See also Lachlan, *A Retrospective Glance*, 11–12.

12 The prospectus of the *Canadian Journal*, in the Canadian Institute fonds, Thomas Fisher Rare Book Library, MS Coll. 193, box 1, folder 35. See also the *Canadian Journal* new series, vol. 1 (March 1856), 100–3, and vol. 2 (March 1857), 82–3, as well as Zeller, *Inventing Canada*, 153–60 and Ramsay, "Art and Industrial Society," 71–103.

13 See the minute books of the MNHS, Blacker-Wood Library, QHI N273, vol. 1, 1827–1829, 26 May 1828, 65, and 25 Aug. 1828, 175.

14 On the early executive of the LHSQ, see Chartrand, Duchesne, and Gingras, *Histoire des Sciences au Québec*, 95–110. See also the *Transactions of the LHSQ* vol. 1 (1829), 1–2, and the *Annual Report of the LHSQ for 1835*, 5–6.

15 The minute books of the MNHS, Blacker-Wood Library, QHI N273, vol. 5, 1858–1888, 18 May 1864; Lachlan, *A Retrospective Glance*, 18; and the *Canadian Naturalist and Geologist* vol. 4 (April 1858), 141–2.

16 See the minute books of the MNHS, Blacker-Wood Library, QHI N273, vol. 4, 1845–57, 19 May 1856, 345; 29 July 1856, 365; and 21 May 1857, 401–2; and see also vol. 5, 1858–1888, 28 May 1860 and 19 May 1862.

17 See the Canadian Institute fonds, Thomas Fisher Rare Book Library, MS Coll. 193, box 1, folder 27, original membership list; the circular *The Canadian Institute*, 3–4; the *Address of the President of the Canadian Institute*, 8; and *The Canadian Journal* vol. 1 (Aug. 1852), 4–5.

18 *Canadian Journal* vol. 1 (April 1853), 203; new series, vol. 1 (March 1856), 98; and vol. 5 (March 1860), 216–17. See also the Canadian Institute fonds, Thomas Fisher Rare Book Library, dup 803, minute book, 1852–1860, 2 April 1859, 211.

19 "Car l'instruction des classes populaires est devenue le premier besoin de l'époque et le premier élément civilisateur sur notre continent." For a comparison of the *Institut Canadien* with the Mechanics' Institute and lyceum movements, see Lamonde, *Gens de Paroles*, 24–9. See also Lafontaine, *Institut Canadien en 1855*, 102–110, and Dorion, *Institut Canadien en 1852*, 65–6.

20 See the excellent work of Lamonde in *Gens de Parole*, 22–5 and 134–5. See also the *Institut Canadien* fonds, in the ANQ, Cote M-0014, Micro #10678, reel 1, procédés verbaux, 1855–1871, 26 July 1855, 7 and 17 Dec. 1861, 297–300, as well as Dorion, *Institut Canadien en 1852*, 8–9 and 80–4.

21 For the domination of the "gentlemen of science," see Morrell and Thackery, *Gentlemen of Science*; Hall, *All Scientists Now*; Gleason, *Royal Society of London*; and particularly Gay and Gay, "Brothers in Science," 425–53. For the increasing roles for women in scientific culture, see Shteir, *Cultivating Women, Cultivating Science*; Allen, "Women Members of the Botanical Society of London, 1836–1856," 240–62; and Secord, "Botany on a Plate," 28–57.

22 Lachlan, *A Retrospective Glance*, 5; *The Laws of the York Literary and Philosophical Society*, 7; *Annual Report of the LHSQ for 1859*, 7; and for the participation of women as refreshment providers and leaders of the bazaar in the MNHS, see the minute books of the MNHS, Blacker-Wood Library, QHI N273, vol. 4, 1845–1857, 28 March 1853, 235, and 21 April 1853, 237–8.

23 *Annual Report of the LHSQ for 1831*, 7; *Annual Report of the LHSQ for 1834*, 13 and *Annual Report of the LHSQ for 1838*, 11. See also the Bylaws of the Toronto Literary Society, AO, MU 2017, Miscellaneous Collection 1837 #2, and the *Laws of the Hamilton Literary Society*, 6.

24 For political squabbles in the Toronto Literary Society, see McNairn, *The Capacity to Judge*, 63–70, and Murray, *Come Bright Improvement*, 23–52. See also the Sir Charles Moss papers, AO, MU 2172, notebook of the Toronto Literary Society.

25 For the sectarian disagreements of the early Montreal Mechanics' Institute, see Kuntz, "The Educational Work of the Two Montreal Mechanics' Institutes," 79–90. See also Frost, "Science Education," 31–8; Lachlan, *A Retrospective Glance*, 11–12, and the minute books of the MNHS, Blacker-Wood Library, QHI N273, vol. 3, 1830–1832, 31 Jan. 1831, 89.

26 See *The Canadian Journal* vol. 1 (Oct. 1852), 50; Lachlan, *A Retrospective Glance*, 22; and the minute books of the MNHS, Blacker-Wood Library, QHI N273, vol. 5, 1858–1888, 18 May 1861 and 18 May 1865.

27 For the struggles of William Logan with the Sandfield Macdonald Reformers, see Christie, "Sir William Logan's Geological Empire," 191–200. See the minute books of the MNHS, Blacker-Wood Library, QHI N273, vol. 4, 1845–1857, 23 Feb. 1853, 200–3; 10 May 1855, 317, and 18 May 1857, 402. See also vol. 5, 1858–1888, 28 May 1860; 3 Feb. 1863; and 18 May 1865.

28 *Canadian Journal* vol. 1 (Nov. 1852), 73; new series, vol. 1 (March 1856), 103; vol. 2 (March 1857), 103; and vol. 5 (March 1860), 216–17. For connections between governmental officials in Canada West and the Canadian Institute, see Zeller, *Inventing Canada*, 154–60; Levere and Jarrell, *A Curious Field Book*, 42–6; and Berger, *Science, God and Nature*, 30–3.

29 See the *Institut Canadien* fonds, ANQ, Cote M-0014, Micro #10678, reel 1, procédés verbaux, 1855–1871, 14 Dec. 1859, 215–17; 3 March 1864, 378–9; and 17 March 1864, 388. See also Lamonde, *Gens de Parole*, 23–4.

30 Dessaules, *Discours sur L'Institut Canadien*, 6–8, and *Annuaire de L'Institut Canadien pour 1866*, 4–5 and 20–1.

31 See the *Institut Canadien* fonds, ANQ, Cote M-0014, Micro #10678, reel 3, minutes from the monument committee, 7 June 1853; 10 July 1856; and 1 May 1857. See also reel 1, procédés verbaux, 1855–1871, 16 Aug. 1855, 8; 30 Aug. 1855, 9; 11 Oct. 1855, 15; and 31 Dec. 1857, 113, as well as Lamonde, *Gens de Parole*, 23–5.

Not all *Instituts Canadiens* encountered hostility from the Roman Catholic clergy; the *Institut Canadien* in Quebec and the *Institut* in Ottawa enjoyed cordial relations with the clergy. See Chartrand, Duchesne, and Gingras, *Histoire des Sciences au Québec*, 95–110; *Annuaire de l'Institut Canadien de Québec pour l'anneé 1874*, 8–13; and the *Institut Canadien-Français d'Ottawa 1852–1877*, 19–21.

32 L.A. Dessaules claimed that as a truly liberal body, the *Institut Canadien* needed to discuss questions of a social or political nature; see his *Discours sur L'Institut Canadien*, 6–7, 13, and 18. For the rising tensions between the *Rouges*, the *Institut Canadien*, and the conservative Catholic order, see Bernard, *Les rouges*, and particularly Lamonde, *L.A. Dessaules*. See also the *Annuaire de l'Institut Canadien pour 1866*, 21–3.

33 The conflictual/consensual paradigm in the historiography of both British and Canadian scientific societies reflects the significance of negotiating the ideology of science and technology between various classes, philosophies, and individuals. For Britain, see Morrell and Thackery, *Gentlemen of Science*, 1–35; Morus, "Manufacturing Nature," 403–42; Alborn, "The Business of Induction," 91–121; and Secord, *Victorian Sensation*, 41–76. For Canada, see Levere and Jarrell, *A Curious Field-Book*, 42–7; Berger, *Science, God and Nature*, 4–27; Zeller, *Inventing Canada*, 12–18; Hewitt, "Science, Popular Culture, and the Producer Alliance," 243–75; and Christie, "Sir William Logan's Geological Empire," 161–204.

34 The role of political economy in the ideology of social regulation in pre-Rebellion Montreal has been ably explored by Fecteau, *Un nouvel ordre des choses*. See also the Robin Hood Society fonds, ANQ, Microfilm #2582, notebook, circa 1830, and the *Transactions of the LHSQ*, new series, vol. 1, 37–60.

35 See the Toronto Literary Society fonds, AO, MU 2107; the Sir Charles Moss fonds, AO, notebook of the Society, 14 March 1836 and 18 April 1836; McNairn, *The Capacity to Judge*, 63–70 and Murray, *Come Bright Improvement*, 23–52.

36 Burn, *The Connection Between Literature and Commerce*, and his entry in the *Dictionary of Canadian Biography* vol. 8, 113–15. For a detailed examination of middling-class attitudes to social mobility, see Burley, *A Particular Condition in Life*.

37 On the political troubles associated with practical *versus* pure science, see Christie, "Sir William Logan's Geological Empire," 191–200. See also the minute books of the MNHS, Blacker-Wood Library, QHI N273, vol. 5, 1858–1888, 28 March 1864 and 18 May 1865; the *Canadian Naturalist and Geologist* vol. 4 (April 1858), 141–5, and vol. 8 (Feb. 1863), 66–9; and *The Canadian Journal* vol. 2 (Aug. 1853), 1–3, and new series, vol. 2 (March 1858), 82–5.

38 See *The Canadian Journal* new series, vol. 7 (May 1862), 182–90. See also William Hincks's earlier lecture on political economy, the *Canadian Journal* new series, vol. 6 (Jan. 1861), 20–7; and his entry in the *Dictionary of Canadian Biography* vol. 10, 349–50.

39 For the ideological underpinnings of both free trade and protection, see Forster, *A Conjunction of Interests*. See also Grant, *The Future Commercial Policy of British North America*.

40 "Pour rendre notre patrie plus grande, plus belle et plus forte et la placer au niveau des peuples rivaux en industrie, en commerce et en prospérité, il y faut nécessairement promouvoir une instruction utile et pratique." See the subscription on J.L. Lafontaine's work *Institut Canadien en 1855*, front page, and also pages 3–4 and 95–102. See also the *Institut Canadien* fonds, ANQ, Cote M-0014, Micro #10678, reel 6, receipt book, 1872–75.

41 "En fait de commerce, et de tout ce qui s'y rattache, je suis partisan du *laisser-faire* ou de la liberté la plus entière, car c'est l'esprit, la nature, l'âme, la vie du commerce." For the liberal political economy of the *Institut Canadien* in Montreal, see Bernard, *Les rouges*, and Lamonde, *Gens de Parole*, 115–20. See also Dorion, *Institut Canadien en 1852*, 144–50, 180–5 and 194–237.

42 See the Toronto Literary Society fonds, AO, MU 2107; the Sir Charles Moss fonds, AO, notebook of the Society, and Murray, *Come Bright Improvement*, 23–32. See also the minute books of the MNHS, Blacker-Wood Library, QHI N273, vol. 1, 1827–1829, 28 July 1828, 166–69, and 25 May 1829, 285, as well as vol. 2, 1829–1830, 27 March 1830, 53–7.

43 The records of the Brockville Debating Club, AO, MU 2087 #9, minute book, 1850–55, 2 Nov. 1850, 13–17; 6 Jan. 1851, 30; 21 Jan. 1851, 32; 31 Jan. 1853; and 24 Jan. 1855.

44 See the *Canadian Journal* vol. 1 (April 1853), 203–4, and Zeller, *Inventing Canada*, 155–6.

45 The *Institut Canadien* fonds, ANQ, Cote M-0014, Micro #10678, reel 3, minutes from the monument committee, 10 Dec. 1858, 56, and 13 Sept. 1861, 95; and also the *Institut Canadien* fonds, ANQ, Cote M-0014, Micro #10678, reel 1, procédés verbaux, 1855–1871, 19 June 1856, 56, and 14 Dec. 1859, 209–10.

46 See the minute books of the MNHS, Blacker-Wood Library, QHI N273, vol. 4, 1845–1857, 28 March 1853, 235, and 21 April 1853, 237–8; vol. 5, 1858–1888, 3 Feb. 1863 and 3 Feb. 1864. See also the ONHS fonds, LAC, MG 28 I 31, vol. 1, minute book, 1863–1869, 29 April 1864, 27 May 1864 and 29 March 1866 as well as the *Canadian Naturalist and Geologist* new series, vol. 1 (1864), 52–60.

47 *Annual Report of the MNHS for the year 1861*, 4–7; the *Canadian Naturalist and Geologist* vol. 6 (June 1861), 232, and the *Annual Report of the MNHS for the year 1864*, 16–17.

48 For the process of "professionalization" in late-Victorian Britain, see Levine, *The Amateur and the Professional*, 52–104; Alter, *The Reluctant Patron*; Perkin, *The Rise of Professional Society*; Turner, "Public Science in Britain," 201–25; Allen, "Biological Societies of London," 23–31; and McOuat, "Cataloguing Power," 1–28. Lawrence

Goldman argues that the rise of British "professional society" occurred in the 1860s, with the Social Science Association; see his *Science, Reform and Politics in Victorian Britain*, 1–23. For France, see Paul, *From Knowledge to Power*, 15–60, and Crosland, *Science Under Control*, 167–207 and 300–30. For the United States, see Haskell, *The Emergence of Professional Social Science*; Haber, *The Quest for Authority and Honor in the American Professions*; and Welch, *The Book of Nature*.

49 Whitley, "Knowledge Producers and Knowledge Acquirers," 3–30, and Cooter and Pumfrey, "Separate Spheres and Public Places," 237–67. See also Secord, "Corresponding Interests," 383–403; Goldstein, "Yours for Science," 573–99, and especially Shteir, "Elegant Recreations," and Lightman, "The Voices of Nature," 187–255, as well as Lightman, "Marketing Knowledge for the General Reader," 100–6.

50 On the Royal Society of Canada, see the seminal work by Berger, *Honour and the Search for Influence*. See also Owram, *The Government Generation*, 3–28; Millard, *The Master Spirit of the Age*; Christie, "Psychology, Sociology, and the Secular Movement," 119–43; and Gidney and Millar, *Professional Gentlemen*, 203–377.

51 Waiser, *The Field Naturalist*. See also Berger, *Science, God, and Nature*, 4–34; Frost, "Science Education in the Nineteenth Century," 31–6, and Chartrand, Duchesne, and Gingras, *Histoire des Sciences au Québec*, 233–7.

52 Canadian Institute fonds in the Thomas Fisher Rare Book Library, MS Coll. 193, box 211, circular of the Canadian Institute, 1874, and the *Transactions and Proceedings of the Canadian Institute* vol. 1 (1883), 351–2, and vol. 3 (1886), 24–6. See also the Royal Astronomical Society fonds, LAC, MG 28 I 145, vol. 1, minute book 1890–93, 11 June 1890, 3–4.

53 *Ottawa Naturalist* vol. 1 (Dec. 1887), 136 and vol. 9 (Jan. 1896), 199; the *Transactions of the Ottawa Field-Naturalists' Club for 1881/2*, 19, and the *Transactions of the Ottawa Field-Naturalists' Club for 1882/3*, 11–12. The LHSQ likewise rejoiced in its "common bond" among members of all classes, united in the culture of both science and history; see the *Transactions of the LHSQ*, new series, vol. 15 (1881), 121.

54 See the minute books of the MNHS, Blacker-Wood Library, QHI N273, vol. 5, 1858–1888, 21 Feb. 1868 and vol. 6, 1888–1925, 25 Nov. 1889, and 5 March 1894.

55 See the minutes of the MNHS *Conversazione* committee, Blacker-Wood Library, QHI M66, 1886–1896, 13 Dec. 1886, 2–3, and 12 Jan. 1887, 17. See also the *Canadian Record of Science* vol. 4 (Jan. 1890), 70; vol. 6 (Jan. 1894), 52, and vol. 6 (April 1894), 100.

56 Sterry Hunt fonds, McGill University Archives, MG 2045, box #1, letter from W. Leconte Stevens to Hunt, 3 Sept. 1882; D.R. Macleod, *The Literary and Historical Society of Quebec*, 16, and the Royal Astronomical Society fonds, LAC, MG 28 I 145, vol. 3, file #2, clipping book, 200.

57 *The Canadian Record of Science* vol. 4 (Jan. 1890), 70, and vol. 4 (Oct. 1890), 201–15, as well as Waiser, *The Field Naturalist*, 3–15.
58 *Annual Report of the MNHS for the Year 1869*, 5–6; *Annual Report for the MNHS for the Year 1873*, 2–3; and *Annual Report for the Year 1877*, 1–2.
59 For this medical episode, see Gidney and Millar, *Professional Gentlemen*, 91–8, and the Medical section minutes, Canadian Institute fonds, in the Thomas Fisher Rare Book Library, MS Coll. 193, box 10, minute book, 1863–74, 7 April and 22 April 1869, as well as 6 May 1870. See also the Canadian Institute fonds in the Thomas Fisher Rare Book Library, MS Coll. 193, box 1, folder 61, bylaws of the Architectural section; box 2, folder 12, report of the Biological section, Oct. 1891 and box 10, minute book of the Historical section, 1890–96, 15 Feb. 1890. See also Millard, *The Master Spirit of the Age*, and Christie, "Psychology, Sociology, and the Secular Movement."
60 *Transactions of the Canadian Institute* vol. 2 (1892), 5–6 and the *Canadian Journal* new series, vol. 12 (April 1869), 98–100.
61 *Proceedings and Transactions of the Canadian Institute* vol. 3 (1885), 24–33.
62 See the *Transactions of the Canadian Institute* vol. 3 (1893), 21–3. For some of Meek's views on Canadian law, see his *Everyman's Legal Guide*.
63 *Proceedings and Transactions of the Canadian Institute* vol. 3 (1885), 26, and the ONHS fonds, LAC, MG 28 I31, vol. 3, clipping book, 3 Dec. 1881, 61–3, and 26 April 1883, 87–8.
64 *Proceedings and Transactions of the Canadian Institute* vol. 3 (1885), 32–6, and the *Ottawa Naturalist* vol. 3 (Oct./Dec. 1889), 96–7.
65 For the occupational composition of the original members of the Royal Society, see Berger, *Honour and the Search for Influence*, 9–11. See also Lorne's inaugural address, *Proceedings and Transactions of the Royal Society of Canada* vol. 1 (1883), 5–6.
66 Hunt, *The Relations of Natural Sciences*, 2, and Fleming, "Presidential Address before the Royal Society of Canada," 1–4.
67 Berger, *Honour and the Search for Influence*, 5–7, and the address by Dawson in *Proceedings and Transactions of the Royal Society of Canada* vol. 1 (1883), 10.
68 *Proceedings and Transactions of the Royal Society of Canada* vol. 10 (1893), 23–4; Montreal Branch of the Ontario Entomological Society fonds, LAC, MG 29 I225, M-5891, minute book, 1873–1896, 15 May 1889, 73, and the *Canadian Record of Science* vol. 1 (Jan. 1884), 3–6.
69 See the Royal Society Meeting in Montreal fonds, Blacker-Wood Library, As R81hm, vol. 2, scrapbook of the Citizens Committee, 6 April 1891, and the Dawson Family fonds, McGill Archives, MG 1022, box 73, Royal Society Correspondence, circular dated 30 March 1891.

70 Dawson Family fonds, McGill Archives, MG 1022, box 73, Royal Society Correspondence, letter from Warren King, 11 March 1891; letter from the Ottawa Literary and Scientific Society, 28 April 1891, and letter from H.H. Lyman, 5 May 1891. See also the Royal Society Meeting in Montreal fonds, Blacker-Wood Library, As R81hm, vol. 1, 13 Nov. 1890.
71 See the records of the MNHS, Blacker-Wood Library, QHI N273, vol. 5, minute book 1858–1888, 18 Feb. 1867 and 25 April 1867. For women's participation in science in Britain, see Shteir, "Elegant Recreations," 236–55, and her *Cultivating Women, Cultivating Science*. See also Secord, "Botany on a Plate"; Lightman, "Marketing Knowledge for the General Reader"; and Murray, *Come Bright Improvement*, 97–126.
72 The Guelph Scientific Society fonds, Guelph Public Library, P162.01, minute book, 1886–1892, bylaws pasted on the front, 19 Feb. 1886, and membership list pasted on the back. See also the *Canadian Journal* new series, vol. 12 (Nov. 1869), 308–20; the *Transactions of the Ottawa Field-Naturalists' Club* vol. 4 (1883), 11–12; and *The Ottawa Naturalist*, prospectus, 9–11.
73 See the ONHS fonds, LAC, MG 28 I 31, vol. 3, clipping book, 23 May 1881, 111; vol. 3, minute book, 1885–1893, 20 March 1888, 19 March 1889, 18 March 1890, and 15 March 1892.
74 *Ottawa Naturalist* vol. 4 (April 1890), 7–8, and vol. 8 (June 1894), 61–3.
75 See the Toronto Camera Club fonds, LAC, MG 28 I181, H–1566, vol. 1, file 2, miscellaneous records, annual report of 1895; 1 Dec. 1895 and annual report of 1896; Ottawa Camera Club fonds, LAC, MG 28 I 295, M-1963, minute book, 1894–1900, 10 Dec. 1894, 1–4; 21 March 1895, 25, and 12 Dec. 1895, 46; and see also the records of the MNHS, Blacker-Wood Library, QHI N273, vol. 5, minute book 1858–1888, 18 Feb. 1867 and 25 April 1867.
76 Guelph Scientific Society fonds, Guelph Public Library, P162.01, minute book, 1886–1892, 10 May, 12 July, and 18 Oct. 1887; 21 Feb. and 11 Sept. 1888; 9 July and 10 Dec. 1889; 13 Oct. 1890; 20 Jan. 1891, and 9 Feb. 1892. On the cultural significance of phrenology, see the seminal work by Cooter, *The Cultural Meaning of Popular Science* and Winter, *Mesmerized*. See also the Hampden Literary and Scientific Society fonds, AO, MU 7827 #2, minute book, 1895–97, 15 Dec. 1896.
77 Fortnightly Club fonds, PCMA, 99–022, box 1, membership book, 1 and the Perth Literary and Debating Society fonds, LAC, MG 55/28, no. 34, minute book, 1894, 20 Nov. 1894, 3. See also the records of the MNHS, Blacker-Wood Library, QHI N273, vol. 5, minute book 1858–88, 21 Feb. 1868 and the records of the ONHS, LAC, MG 28 I31, vol. 2, minute book, 1879–1885, 5 April 1883.
78 *Annuaire de l'Institut Canadien au Québec pour l'année 1874*, 13–14, and Macleod, *On the Literary and Historical Society of Quebec*, 16.

79 *Institut Canadien* fonds, ANQ, Cote M-0014, Micro #10678, reel 1, procédés verbaux, 1855-71, 7 March 1867, 518-20; 17 Dec. 1867, 599-605, and 2 Sept. 1869, 656-58. See also Lacroix, *Excursion to the Holy Land of Thought*, 3-4 and 18-20, as well as the *Annuaire de l'Institut Canadien pour 1868*, 4-10.

80 Quebec liberalism, following the English liberal school and not the *Rouge* Catholic-liberal tradition, only flourished under Wilfrid Laurier and to some degree under Honoré Mercier; see Neatby, *Laurier and a Liberal Quebec*, 1-42, and particularly Roy, *Progrès, Harmonie, Liberté*. See also Lamonde, *Gens de Parole*; the *Institut Canadien* fonds, ANQ, Cote M-0014, Micro #10678, reel 1, procédés verbaux, 1855-71, 25 Nov. 1869, 675-77; reel 2, procédés verbaux, 1872-1900, 17 Dec. 1873, 34-5, and 9 April 1874, 42; and for the transferral of the *Institut*'s books to the Fraser Institute, see 25 Jan. 1885, 109-11. See particularly Dougall, *History of the Guibord Case*, 3-12.

81 *Annuaire de l'Institut Canadien de Québec pour l'année 1874*, 13-14; *Annuaire de l'Institut Canadien de Québec pour l'année 1880*, 115-23, and *Annuaire de l'Institut Canadien de Québec pour l'année 1882*, 16-17.

82 Fabre, *Confédération, Indépendance, Annexion*. J.P. Bernard argued that annexation was a crucial plank in the *Rouge* platform; see his *Les rouges*, 115-31.

83 See the Montreal Parliamentary Debating Society fonds, Rare Book room, McGill University, CH 13.S49, minute book, 1884-86, 15 Oct. 1884, 1-2; 5 Nov. 1884, 3-4; 9 Dec. 1884, 11; 3 Feb. 1885, 23; and 15 Dec. 1885, 51. See also Gregor, *The New Canadian Patriotism*.

84 *Essays Received in Response to an Appeal by the Canadian Institute*, preface; *Transactions of the Canadian Institute* vol. 2 (1891), 316-32 and Fleming, *Presidential Address*, 33-41.

85 Although some historians view Populism as a movement restricted to agrarian concerns, more recent historiography recognizes that groups as diverse as labour unions and religious movements could participate in populist rhetoric. See Cook, "Tillers and Toilers," 5-20; Mussio, "The Origins and Nature of the Holiness Movement Church," 81-104; Ferry, "Severing the Connections in a Complex Community," 9-47; and especially Noel, "Early Populist Tendencies in Ontario Political Culture," 173-87. See also the Canadian Institute, *Essays Received in Response*, preface; *Transactions of the Canadian Institute* vol. 2 (1891), 326-32, and Canadian Institute fonds, AO, MU 2562, miscellaneous papers, circular of 27 Dec. 1893.

86 See the Canadian Institute, *Essays Received in Response*, 7-8, 15, 25-8 and 90-1.

87 On the emerging new political economy, social science and corporatism in the civil service, universities and churches, see Owram, *The Government Generation*, 1-13; Ferguson, *Remaking Liberalism*; Burke, *Seeking the Highest Good*; and Christie and Gauvreau, *A Full-Orbed Christianity*.

88 See the Canadian Institute fonds, AO, MU 2562, miscellaneous papers, circular of 27 Dec. 1893; *Transactions of the Canadian Institute* vol. 2 (1891), 316–32, and vol. 3 (1892), 15–23; and *Essays Received in Response*, 40–2 and 63–5.
89 On the discourse of interdependence of classes as a function of populist language, see Cook, "Tillers and Toilers"; Mussio, "The Origins and Nature of the Holiness Movement Church"; Ferry, "Severing the Connections in a Complex Community"; and Sid Noel, "Early Populist Tendencies in Ontario Political Culture." See also the records of the Peterborough Fortnightly Club, PCMA, 99–022, box 2, printed ephemera, 1895–96 and box 3, scrapbook, 1895–96, title page, 1–2, 16, 26–7, and debate recorded on 28 Jan. 1896, 128.
90 On the late-Victorian debates on social Christianity, see Cook, *The Regenerators*; Marshall, *Secularizing the Faith*, 127–55; and Airhart, *Serving the Present Age*, 123–41. See the Peterborough Fortnightly Club fonds, PCMA, 99–022, box 3, scrapbook, 1895–96, 17–20.
91 See the records of the Peterborough Fortnightly Club, PCMA, 99–022, box 3, scrapbook, 1895–96, 7–9 and 26 Nov. 1896, 126. For similar views on corporatism from other Canadian intellectuals, see Owram, *The Government Generation*, 1–13; Ferguson, *Remaking Liberalism*; and Burke, *Seeking the Highest Good*.
92 A similar contrast can be found in the religious views of the populist Holiness movement with social Christianity; see Mussio, "The Origins and Nature of the Holiness Church"; Marshall, *Secularizing the Faith*, 127–55; Airhart, *Serving the Present Age*, 123–41; and Christie/Gauvreau, *A Full-Orbed Christianity*. See Peterborough Fortnightly Club fonds, PCMA, 99–022, box 1, membership book, 1895–96 and box 3, scrapbook, 1895–96, Sept. 1895, 18.
93 Tassé, *Discours Prononcés Devant l'Institut Canadien-Français d'Ottawa*, 17–20; *Institut Canadien-Français d'Ottawa* fonds, LAC, MG 28 D4, annual report of 1892–3, 11 May 1893; *Institut Canadien-Français d'Ottawa*, 7–8 and 13–15; and Berger, *Honour and the Search for Influence*, 10–11.
94 For the growth of economic liberalism among the French in Quebec, see Roy, *Progrès, Harmonie, Liberté*. See also *Institut Canadien de Québec: Acte d'Incorporation*, 31–2.
95 On the eclectic nature of reformist doctrine during the late nineteenth century, see Cook, *The Regenerators*, 105–22; Burke, *Serving the Highest Good*; Burr, *Spreading the Light*, 14–55; and Ferry, "Severing the Connections in a Complex Community."
96 W.A. Douglas also followed the tenets of social Christianity, as witnessed in his pamphlet published by the Single-Tax Association, *The Church in Social Relations*. For more on Douglas, see Cook, *The Regenerators*, 115–22. See also the *Proceedings and Transactions of the Canadian Institute* vol. 2 (1884), 28–9; vol. 3 (1885), 39–41; and the *Transactions of the Canadian Institute* vol. 1 (1891), 15–16.

97 See the *Transactions of the Canadian Institute* vol. 2 (1892), 31–7, and Miall, *Defects of our System of Government*, 6–9.
98 *Proceedings and Transactions of the Canadian Institute* vol. 3 (1885), 42 and the *Transactions of the Canadian Institute* vol. 1 (1891), 17–18.
99 Cook, *The Regenerators*, 105–22; the *Proceedings and Transactions of the Canadian Institute* vol. 2 (1884), 28; and *Transactions of the Canadian Institute* vol. 1 (1891), 15–16.
100 See the records of the Fortnightly Club, PCMA, 99–022, box 3, scrapbook, 1895–96, 2–3, 7–8, 26–7, and meeting of 26 Nov. 1896, 127–8.
101 See the records of the Fortnightly Club, PCMA, 99–022, box 3, scrapbook, 1895–96, 7–10.
102 See the minutes of the MNHS *Conversazione* committee, Blacker-Wood Library, QHI M66, 1886–96, 13 Dec. 1886, 2–3; 12 Jan. 1887, 17 and 25.
103 *Transactions of the Literary and Scientific Society of Ottawa* vol. 1 (1898), 2–3.
104 ONHS fonds, LAC, MG 28 I31, vol. 2, minute book, 1879–85, 30 Oct. 1879, 19 May 1884 and 17 March 1885; vol. 3, minute book, 1885–93, 26 Nov. 1885, 19 May 1886, 13 Nov. 1888, and 21 March 1890. See also the minutes of the MNHS *Conversazione* committee, Blacker-Wood Library, QHI M66, 1886–96, 13 Dec. 1886, 8–9, 3 Dec. 1888, 38, and 14 Dec. 1888, 40; and the minute books of the MNHS, Blacker-Wood Library, QHI N273, vol. 5, 1858–88, 9 March 1871, 11 June 1883, and 31 Jan. 1887.
105 Montreal Branch of the Ontario Entomological Society fonds, LAC, MG 29 I225, microfilm #M-5891, minute book, 1873–96, 1 June 1875, 35–7; 2 Feb. 1876, 68; 9 May 1882, 176–8. See also the *Institut Canadien-Français d'Ottawa* fonds, LAC, MG 28 D4, annual report of 1892–3, Nov. 1892 and 11 May 1893.
106 See the Guelph Scientific Society fonds, Guelph Public Library, P162.01, minute book, 1886–92, 11 May 1886, 12 July 1887, 18 Oct. 1887, 11 June 1888, and 8 Dec. 1891.
107 Mrs. Jones' Improvement Class fonds, AO, MU 8218, minute book, 1871–78, 25 Aug. 1871, 28 April 1873, 12 May 1873, 18 April 1876, and 16 Oct. 1876.
108 See the *Transactions of the Literary and Scientific Society of Ottawa* vol. 3 (1900), 5.
109 *Transactions of the LHSQ*, new series, vol. 11 (1875), 2–3, and vol. 21, (1892), 13.
110 See the Ottawa Camera Club fonds, LAC, MG 28 I295, M-1963, minute book, 1894–1900, 19 Jan. 1895, 16; 16 Oct. 1895, 39–40; 13 March 1897, 85; and 9 March 1898, 109.
111 See the Toronto Camera Club fonds, LAC, MG 28 I181, H-1566, vol. 1, file 1, constitution of the club, 1913; vol. 1, file 2, miscellaneous records, report of 1 March 1897, 4 Nov. 1897 and 4 July 1898; H-1667, vol. 2, minute book, 1888–93, 11 Feb. 1889, 8 and 18 Nov. 1889, 33–6; minute book, 1893–1906, 11 Dec. 1894, 47, and 30 Nov. 1896, 97–98 and H-1573, vol. 10, minutes from the secretary, 1 Feb. 1897.

112 The coining of the phrase "professional society" occurred in English historian Harold Perkin's book *The Rise of Professional Society*, although Lawrence Goldman in *Science, Reform, and Politics* argues that professionalization occurred much earlier in the 1860s. See also Owram, *The Government Generation*; Shore, *The Science of Social Redemption*; Ferguson, *Remaking Liberalism*; Burke, *Seeking the Highest Good*; and Christie, *Engendering the State*.

CONCLUSION

1 Smith, "The Labour Movement," 134.
2 Goldwin Smith, as quoted in Wallace, *Goldwin Smith*, 166–7. Wallace's seminal biography on Smith is an excellent introduction to Smith's liberal thought. See also Goldwin Smith, "The Labour Movement," 126–8, 136–9.
3 See Smith, "The Labour Movement," 128–9, 133, 136–8.
4 Mackenzie King, *Industry and Humanity*, xiv–xvi, 67 and 95–100. For the eclectic nature of Mackenzie King's pronouncements on liberal economics and community, see Craven, *An Impartial Umpire*, 31–89; Cook, *The Regenerators*, 197–213; and Owram, *The Government Generation*, 36–40 and 102–5.
5 Mackenzie King, *Industry and Humanity*, 199–201. On the changes to the bureaucratic industrial state run by "expert" civil servants, see Craven, *An Impartial Umpire*, 31–89; Cook, *The Regenerators*, 197–213; Owram, *The Government Generation*; and Burke, *Seeking the Highest Good*. For a stronger context on labour relations in immediate post–First-World-War Canada see the fine collection of essays in Heron, *The Workers' Revolt in Canada*.
6 This synopsis of Mackenzie King's views on the nature of the "Community" owes a great deal to the argument of Craven, *An Impartial Umpire*, 82–6, and King, *Industry and Humanity*, 96–7, 327–9.
7 The "professionalization" of society was not a unique situation to Canada. For the situation in the United States, see Haskell, *The Emergence of Professional Social Science* and Haber, *The Quest for Authority in the American Professions*. For Britain, see Perkin, *The Rise of Professional Society* and Goldman, *Science, Reform and Politics in Victorian Britain*. See also Struthers, *No Fault of Their Own*; Owram, *The Government Generation*; Shore, *The Science of Social Redemption*; and Burke, *Seeking the Highest Good*. On the influence of "social evangelism" and gender issues on the welfare state and social planning, see Christie and Gauvreau, *A Full-Orbed Christianity* and Christie, *Engendering the State*.
8 On this new "expert" political economy, see the chapter on James Mavor in Shortt, *The Search for an Ideal*, 119–35; Drummond, *Political Economy at the University of Toronto*, 2–41; McKillop, *Matters of Mind*, 177–203; Burke, *Serving the Highest Good*; and especially Ferguson, *Remaking Liberalism*. On industry and the state, see

Traves, *The State and Enterprise*; Craven, *An Impartial Umpire*; Armstrong and Nelles, *Monopoly's Moment*; Cruikshank, *Close Ties*; and den Otter, *The Philosophy of Railways*.

9 On the ideology of building the Canadian "nation," see Owram, *The Promise of Eden*; den Otter, *The Philosophy of Railways*; and particularly Heaman, *The Inglorious Arts of Peace*. On the significance of cultural hegemony, see Marks, *Revivals and Roller Rinks* and Bouchier, *For the Love of the Game*. Voluntary associations could also produce a hegemonic effect; see Anstead, "Fraternalism in Victorian Ontario," and Calnan, "Blessed Be the Tie That Binds."

Bibliography

PRIMARY SOURCES

Manuscript Collections

Archives Nationales de Québec (Hull and Montreal)
Cercle Agricole de la Paroisse de St. Francis du Lac Fonds
Conseil des Arts Fonds
Elisée Choquet Fonds
Institut Canadien Fonds
Quebec Mechanics' Institute Fonds
Robin Hood Society Fonds

Archives of Ontario
Addington County Agricultural Society Fonds
Ameliasburgh Sons of Temperance Fonds
Association of Mechanics' Institutes Fonds
Board of Arts and Manufacturers Fonds
Brockville Debating Club Fonds
Brougham Grange Fonds
Caledon Mechanics' Institute Fonds
Canadian Institute Fonds
Charles Moss Fonds
Cherry Valley Royal Templars of Temperance Fonds
Darlington Agricultural Society Fonds
Department of Education, Special Files
Farmers' Institute Fonds

F.D. McClennan Collection
Gainsborough Patrons of Industry Fonds
Grand Lodge of Canada West, IOOF Fonds
Hampden Literary and Scientific Society Fonds
Harold Williams Collection
Highland Creek Public Library Fonds
Hiram Walker Museum Collection
John Linton Fonds
John Witford Fonds
Lennox and Addington County Historical Society Fonds
Listowel Court, IOF Fonds
Loyal London Lodge, Manchester Unity of Oddfellows Fonds
Manuscript Census Returns for 1871
Mrs. Jones Improvement Class Fonds
Niagara District Agricultural Society Fonds
Niagara Mechanics' Institute Fonds
Nithburg Sons of Temperance Fonds
North Walshingham Agricultural Society Fonds
Orono Sons of Temperance Fonds
Paris Mechanics' Institute Fonds
Patron Committee Minute Book
Plantagent Royal Templars of Temperance Fonds
Puslinch Farmers' Club Fonds
Templin Family Collection
Toronto Coffee House Association Fonds
Toronto Literary Society Fonds
Toronto Mechanics' Institute Fonds
Vaughn Anti-Bacchanalian Society Fonds
Walter Riddell Fonds
Willow Vale Patrons of Industry Fonds

Baldwin Room, Metropolitan Toronto Reference Library Archives
Gananoque Lodge, British Order of Good Templar Fonds
International Order of Oddfellows Fonds
Lakeshore Subscription Library Fonds
Toronto Mechanics' Institute Fonds

Centennial Museum and Archives (Peterborough)
Fortnightly Club Fonds

Lime Juice Club Scrapbook
Peterborough Agricultural Society Fonds
Peterborough Canadian Order of Foresters Fonds
Peterborough Junior Foresters Fonds
Peterborough Mechanics' Institute Fonds

Dufferin County Museum and Archives
Orangeville Mechanics' Institute Fonds
P.J. Van Wagoner Family Fonds
Shelburne IOF Fonds

Guelph, Hamilton, Kincardine, and London Public Libraries
Guelph Public Library Fonds
Guelph Scientific Society Fonds
Hamilton Public Library Fonds
Kincardine Mechanics' Institute Minute Book
London Literary Society Minute Book
London Mechanics' Institute Minute Books

J.J. Talman Regional Collection, D.B. Weldon Library, University of Western Ontario
Egremont Lodge, IOOF Fonds
Ingersoll Mechanics' Institute Fonds
Middlesex Agricultural Society Fonds
Royal Oak Grange Fonds
St. Clair Lodge, IOOF Fonds
West Middlesex Royal Templars of Temperance Fonds
West Nissouri Agricultural Society Fonds

McGill University Archives (and Blacker-Wood Library)
Dawson Family Fonds
Montreal Natural History Society Fonds
Montreal Parliamentary Debating Society Fonds
Royal Society Meeting in Montreal Fonds
T. Sterry Hunt Fonds

National Library and Archives of Canada
A.L. Riddell Fonds
Antrim Council, Canadian Circle of Chosen Friends Fonds

Carleton Place Mechanics' Institute Fonds
Donald Kennedy Scrapbook
Drummond County Institut of Artisans Fonds
Harold Williams Collection
Henry Elliot Family Fonds
Institut Canadien-Français d'Ottawa Fonds
J.E. Curran Fonds
Landry Family Fonds
Lennox and Addington County Historical Society Fonds
McGillivray Family Fonds
Missisquoi Agricultural Society Fonds
Montreal Branch of the Ontario Entomological Society Fonds
Norfolk Historical Society Fonds
Ottawa Agricultural Society Fonds
Ottawa Camera Club Fonds
Ottawa Mechanics' Institute and Athenaeum Fonds
Ottawa Natural History Society Fonds
Perth Literary and Debating Society Fonds
Peterborough Mechanics' Institute Fonds
Royal Astronomical Society Fonds
Thomas Barron Family Fonds
Toronto Camera Club Fonds
Township of Metcalfe Fonds

Peel Region Archives
Bolton Agricultural Society Fonds
Summerville Sons of Temperance Fonds

Simcoe County Archives
Barrie Debating Club and Mechanics' Institute Fonds
Barrie Mechanics' Institute Fonds
Cardwell Agricultural Society Fonds
Eugene Sons of Temperance Fonds
Forest Home Temple, IOGT Fonds
Harold Parker Family Fonds
Hobart Sons of Temperance Fonds
Knock Grange Fonds
Laura Young Fonds
Midhurst Lodge, IOGT Fonds
Oro Agricultural Society Fonds

Wallace Family Collection

Stratford-Perth County Archives
Mitchell Mechanics' Institute Minute Book

Thomas Fisher Rare Book Library
Canadian Institute Fonds

Wellington County Museum and Archives
Arthur Lodge, Patrons of Industry Fonds
Centre Wellington Farmers' Institute Fonds
Drayton Farmers' and Mechanics' Institute Fonds
Elora Agricultural Society Fonds
Elora Mechanics' Institute Fonds
Elora Public Library Fonds
Ennotville Public Library Fonds
Erin Agricultural Society Fonds
Erin Public Library Fonds
Fergus Public Library Fonds
Greensboro Temple, IOGT Fonds
Guelph Agricultural Society Fonds
Guelph Fat Stock Society Fonds
South Wellington Agricultural Society Fonds
Thomas McCrae Fonds

Newspapers and Periodicals

Agricultural Periodicals
Agriculturalist and Canadian Journal (Toronto, 1848)
British American Cultivator (Toronto, 1842–47)
Canada Farmer (Toronto, 1847)
Canada Farmer's Sun and Brotherhood Era (London and Toronto, 1892–96)
Canadian Agricultural Journal (Montreal, 1844–46)
Canadian Agriculturalist (Toronto, 1849–63)
Canadian Co-operator and Patron (Owen Sound, 1886)
Canadian Granger (London, 1876–77)
Farmers' Advocate (London, 1867–92)
Granger (London, 1875–76)
Lower Canadian Agriculturalist (Montreal, 1861–67)
Miller's Canadian Farmer's Almanac (Montreal, 1878–83)

Ontario Farmer (Toronto, 1869–71)

Mutual Benefit Periodicals
Canadian Forester (Guelph, 1889–92)
Canadian Journal of Oddfellowship (Stratford, 1875–76)
Dominion Oddfellow (Napanee and Toronto, 1883–95)
Independent Order of Foresters and Foresters' Herald (London and Toronto, 1884–99)
Oddfellows Gazette (Montreal, 1897)
Odd Fellows Record (Montreal, 1846–47)

Scientific and Literary Periodicals
Canadian Journal (Toronto, 1852–78)
Canadian Naturalist (Montreal, 1856–83)
Canadian Record of Science (Montreal, 1884–1894)
Ottawa Naturalist (Ottawa, 1887–99)

Temperance Periodicals
Camp Fire (Toronto, 1894–98)
Canada Citizen and Temperance Herald (Toronto, 1884–88)
Canada Temperance Advocate (Montreal, 1835–54)
Canadian Son of Temperance and Literary Gem (Toronto, 1851–55)
Good Templar (Woodstock, 1863–64)
Quebec Good Templar (Montreal, 1892)
Sons of Temperance Record and Prohibition Advocate (Toronto, 1898)
Templar (Hamilton, 1895)

Books, Pamphlets, Annual Reports, Proceedings, and Transactions

Abbott, Joseph. *Strictures on the Remarks of the Rev. J Reid in his Pamphlet in Favour of the Temperance Society.* Montreal: Herald Office, 1836.
Agricultural and Arts Association of Ontario. *Transactions of the Agricultural and Arts Association of Ontario.* 1869–71.
Ancient Order of Foresters. *Report of the High Court of the Dominion of Canada, Ancient Order of Foresters.* Toronto: Printed by the Executive Council, 1899.
Ancient Order of United Workmen. *Constitution, General Laws and Rules of Order of the Grand Lodge of the AOUW.* St Thomas: The Journal Office, 1892.
– *Ritual of the Ancient Order of United Workmen.* Hamilton: Office of the Grand Master, 1905.
Ardagh, John. *An Address Delivered Before the County of Simcoe Mechanics' Institute.* Barrie: Spirit of the Age Office, 1858.

Bibliography

Arnold, Walter. *Money and Banking: A Lecture Delivered to the Mechanics' Institute, Toronto.* Toronto: Blackburn's City Steam Press, 1862.

Association of Mechanics' Institutes. *Mechanics' Institutes and the Best Means of Improving Them: Prize Essays.* Toronto: Hunter and Rose, 1877.

Aylwin, Thomas. *Inaugural Address Delivered on Occasion of the Opening of the New Mechanics' Hall.* Montreal: J. Starke, 1855.

Baker, Hugh. *A Lecture on Life Assurance Delivered Before the Hamilton Mechanics' Institute.* Hamilton, 1848.

Barnard, Edward. *Cercles Agricoles: Instructions pour l'organisation et la direction des cercles agricoles.* Quebec: S.n., 1893.

Barrie Mechanics' Institute. *Catalogue of Books and Magazines in the Barrie Mechanics' Institute Library.* Barrie: Gazette Steam Printing, 1891.

Board of Agriculture and Agricultural Association of Upper Canada. *Transactions of the Board of Agriculture and the Agricultural Association of Upper Canada*, 1859–68.

Board of Arts and Manufacturers of Upper Canada. *Journal of the Board of Arts and Manufacturers of Upper Canada*, 1861–67.

Bovell, James. *A Lecture on the Future of Canada, Delivered Before the Association of Arts and Manufacturers of Lower Canada.* Montreal: Published by the Board, 1849.

Bradford, Robert. *Address Delivered by Robert Bradford to the Grange at Agincourt: An able exposition of the cause of the hard times, the Banks, Loan Companies and Importing merchants chiefly to blame.* Toronto: Morton and Maclean, 1878.

Bradley, W. *Facts and Figures Dedicated to the People of Canada.* Toronto: Guardian Books, 1872.

Bristow, William. *The Commercial Prospects of Canada: A Lecture Delivered Before the Montreal Mechanics' Institute.* Montreal: Rollo Campbell, 1850.

British Order of Good Templars. *British American Order of Good Templars, The Documents, Reasons and Proceedings Connected with the Formation of Said Order.* London: James Gillean, 1858.

– *Ritual of the British Order of Good Templars.* London: City Press, 1860.

Brown, T.S. *Speech of T.S. Brown at the Union Tent, International Order of Rechabites.* Montreal: 1848.

Burgess, William. *Land, Labor and Liquor: A Chapter in the Political Economy of the Present Day.* Toronto: S.R. Briggs, 1887.

– *The Liquor Traffic and Compensation: A Chapter of the Prohibition Controversy.* Toronto: Rose Publishing, 1885.

Burn, W. Scott. *The Connection Between Literature and Commerce.* Toronto: H&W Roswell, 1845.

Byrne, James. *The Claims of Temperance Societies: A Lecture Delivered to the Young Men's Literary Society.* Montreal: Campbell and Beckett, 1841.

Canada Temperance Union. *Proceedings of the Canada Temperance Union.* 1869.

- *What Does It Cost? Statistical Report Presented to the Convention of the Canada Temperance Union*. Napanee: Henry Brothers, 1869.

Canadian Home Circles. *Constitution and Laws of the Order of Canadian Home Circles*. Welland: Tribune Office, 1885.

Canadian Institute. *Address of the President of the Canadian Institute*. Toronto: Thompson and Company, 1854.

- *Essays Received in Response to an Appeal by the Canadian Institute on the Rectification of Parliament*. Toronto: Copp Clark Company, 1893.
- *Proceedings and Transactions of the Canadian Institute*. 1879–1899.
- *Regulations of the Canadian Institute*. Toronto: Carter & Thomas, 1852.
- *Royal Charter of Incorporation of the Canadian Institute*. Toronto: Carter & Thomas, 1852.
- *The Canadian Institute*. Toronto: S.n., 1852.

Canadian Order of Chosen Friends. *Constitution and Laws of the Canadian Order of Chosen Friends*. Hamilton: Printed by the Grand Council, 1899.

- *Ritual of the Canadian Order of Chosen Friends*. Hamilton: Printed by the Grand Council, 1899.

Canadian Order of Foresters. *Constitution and Rules of Order of the Canadian Order of Foresters*. Brantford: Watt and Sheenston, 1887.

- *Constitution, Insurance Law, Sick and Funeral Benefit Law and Rules of Order of the Canadian Order of Foresters*. Peterborough: Examiner Printing, 1896.
- *Ritual of the Canadian Order of Foresters*. Peterborough: Examiner Printing, 1896.

Canadian Prohibitory Liquor Law League. *Canadian Prohibitory Liquor Law League Containing Proceedings of the Convention of the League*. Toronto: North American, 1853.

Canadian Temperance League. *Constitution and Bylaws of the Canadian Temperance League*. Toronto: Hunter and Rose, 1890.

Case, Albert. *Address Delivered Before Oriental Lodge #7 of the IOOF, On Their First Anniversary in Stanstead*. Stanstead: L.R. Robinson, 1846.

- *The Principles of Odd Fellowship: An Address Delivered before the IOOF at Montreal*. Montreal: Rollo Campbell, 1845.

Catholic Order of Foresters. *Constitutions and Règlements de L'Ordre des Forestiers Catholiques*. Chicago: High Court Publishing, 1889.

- *Montreal Souvenir 1892*. Montreal: Crancer Frères, 1892.

Central Farmers' Institute. *Annual Report of the Central Farmers' Institute*. 1888–93.

Cercles Agricoles de Québec. *Récommandés pour l'organisation des Cercles Agricoles de la Province de Quebec*. Quebec: Imprimerie Turcot, 1889.

Chamberlain, Brown. *Our Country and Our Duty to It*. Montreal: William Salter, 1854.

Claude Mechanics' Institute. *Claude Mechanics' Institute Constitution and Bylaws*. Brampton: Guardian Office, 1879.

Clinton Mechanics' Institute. *Resolution of the Board of Directors of the Clinton Mechanics' Institute.* Clinton, 1880.

Colin, Frédéric Louis de Gonzague. *Discours sur l'Ouvrier, Prononcé Devant l'Institut des Artisans Canadiens.* Montreal: Typographie le Nouveau Monde, 1869.

Cook, John. *The Advantages of Life Assurance to the Working Classes.* Montreal: Armor and Ramsay, 1848.

Cooper, H.C. *The Husbandman's Dependence on Almighty God.* Toronto: H. Roswell, 1853.

Cramp, J.M. *1800 and 1850: A Lecture Delivered Before the Montreal Mechanics' Institute.* Montreal: Rollo Campbell, 1850.

Dallaire, O.E. *Considerations on Farmers' Clubs and Agricultural Societies.* Quebec: Ministry of Agriculture, 1902.

Dallas, James. *A Lecture on the Aims and Usefulness of Mechanics' Institutes.* Barrie: Advance Office, 1865.

Daughters of Temperance. *Constitution, Bylaws and Rules of Order of the Leading Star Union #33, Daughters of Temperance.* Quebec: Robert Middleton, 1854.

Department of Education. *Special Report of the Minister of Education on the Mechanics' Institutes in Ontario.* Toronto: Department of Education, 1881.

Desmazures, Adam Charles Gustave. *Entretiens sur les Arts Industriels.* Montreal: La Minerve, 1870.

Dessaules, L.A. *Discours sur L'Institut Canadien.* Montreal: Le Pays, 1863.

Dominion Alliance Against the Liquor Traffic, *Dominion Alliance Yearbook.* 1882–84.

– *Annual Meeting of the Council of the Dominion Alliance.* 1897.

– *Annual Meeting of the Dominion Alliance, Ontario Branch.* 1880.

Dominion Grange. *Circular to the Deputies of Dominion Granges.* Toronto: S.n., 1877.

– *Constitution and Bylaws of the Dominion Grange, Patrons of Husbandry.* Fourth edition. Toronto: Belford Brothers, 1875.

– *History of the Grange in Canada, With a List of Division and Subordinate Granges and their Executive Officers.* Toronto: Belford Brothers, 1876.

– *Manual of Subordinate Granges of the Patrons of Husbandry Adopted and Issued by the Dominion Grange.* Third edition. Welland: Colcock and Durnan, 1876.

– *Proceedings of the Dominion Grange.* 1874–97.

– *Songs of the Grange, Patrons of Husbandry.* London: Free Press Printing, 1874.

Dorion, J.B.E. *L'Institut Canadien en 1852.* Montreal: W.H. Rowan, 1852.

Dougall, John. *History of the Guibord Case: Ultramontism vs. Law and Human Rights.* Montreal: Witness Publishing, 1875.

Douglas, W.A. *The Church in Social Relations.* Toronto: Single-Tax Association, 1890.

Dunlop, William Tiger. *An Address to the York Mechanics' Institution.* Toronto: W.J. Coates, 1832.

Eales, Walter. *The Benefits to be Derived from Mechanics' Institutes.* Toronto: James Stephens, 1851.

Elora Mechanics' Institute. *Catalogue of the Elora Mechanics' Institute Library.* Elora: S.n., 1881.

Fabre, Hector. *Confédération, Indépendance, Annexion.* Quebec: Evenement Office, 1871.

Ferrier, A.D. *Reminiscences of Canada and the Early Days of Fergus.* Guelph: Mercury Book and Job Office, 1866.

Fleming, Sandford. *Presidential Address before the Royal Society of Canada.* Montreal: Dawson Brothers, 1890.

Friel, H.J. *Inaugural Address at the Opening of the Winter Course of Lectures Before the Ottawa Mechanics' Institute.* Ottawa: Ottawa Citizen, 1855.

Fulford, Francis Drummond. *The Misapplication of Labour.* Montreal: John Lovell, 1859.

Gowan, N.C. The Advantages of Membership in the Order of British Templars. London: S.n., 186–.

Grand Division, Canada East, Sons of Temperance. *Proceedings of the Grand Division, Canada East, Sons of Temperance.* 1854–68.

Grand Division, Canada West, Sons of Temperance. *Proceedings of the Grand Division, Canada West, Sons of Temperance.* 1852–62.

Grand Lodge of Ontario, IOOF. *Journal of the Proceedings of the Grand Lodge of Ontario, IOOF.* 1854–99.

Grand Lodge of Ontario, Patrons of Industry. *Minutes of Annual Meetings.* 1892–95.

Grand Lodge of Quebec, IOOF. *Journal of the Proceedings of the Grand Lodge of Quebec, IOOF.* 1897.

Grand Temple of Ontario, IOGT. *Annual Meeting of the Grand Temple of Ontario, IOGT.* 1860–75.

Grant, Thomas. *The Future Commercial Policy of British North America.* Quebec: Gazette, 1867.

Gregor, Leigh. *The New Canadian Patriotism.* Quebec: Raoul Renault, 1898.

Guelph Mechanics' Institute. *Constitution, Rules and Regulations of the Guelph Farmers' and Mechanics' Institute.* Guelph: Advertiser Book and Job, 1855.

Hamilton Literary Society. *Laws of the Hamilton Literary Society.* Hamilton: Canadian Conservative, 1837.

Hammond, S.T. *A Collection of Temperance Dialogues.* Ottawa: Hunter and Rose, 1869.

– and Rose, G.M. *The Teetotaller's Companion: A Handbook of Dialogues, Recitations and Readings.* Ottawa: Hunter and Rose, 1868.

Hunt, T. Sterry. *The Relations of Natural Sciences.* Montreal: Canadian Naturalist, 1882.

Huntingdon, L.S. *The Independence of Canada: The Annual address delivered before the Agricultural Society of the county of Missisquoi.* Montreal: Herald Steam Press, 1869.

Independent Order of Foresters. *Constitution and General Laws of the Supreme Court of the IOF.* Toronto: Hunter and Rose, 1898.

– *Constitutions et Lois de L'Ordre Indépendent des Forestiers.* Montreal: Imprimerie Poirier, 1895.

– *Ritual of the Independent Order of Foresters.* Toronto: Hunter and Rose, 1899.

Independent Order of Good Templars. *Constitutions of the Grand, District and Subordinate Order of Good Templars.* Toronto: Hunter and Rose, 1889.

– *The Degree Book of the IOGT.* Hamilton: Alex Lawson, 1858.

Independent Order of Oddfellows. *Catalogue of Oddfellows Art Loan Museum Held in the Oddfellows Hall.* London, 1885.

– *Constitution, Bylaws and Rules of Order of Albion Lodge #4 of the IOOF in the Province of Canada.* Montreal: J. Beckett, 1845.

– *Constitution, Bylaws and Rules of Order of the Commercial Lodge #5, IOOF, of the Province of Canada.* Montreal: Donoghue and Mantz, 1846.

– *Constitution, Bylaws and Rules of Order of the Sycamore Lodge.* Arkona: Buchanan and Hunter, 1879.

– *A Digest of the Laws of the IOOF of the Province of Ontario.* Toronto: Dominion Oddfellow, 1891.

– *History of Oddfellowship in Canada Under the Old Regime.* Brantford: Expositor Printing House, 1879.

– *Introduction, Bylaws and Rules of Prince of Wales Lodge #1, of the IOOF, in the Province of Canada.* Montreal: Matthews, Hardie and Rodden, 1843.

Independent Order of Oddfellows, Manchester Unity. *Bylaws Of the Loyal City of Toronto Lodge, Manchester Unity.* Toronto: George Thomas, 1853.

– *Bylaws of the Loyal Montreal Lodge, Manchester Unity.* Montreal: Lovell & Gibson, 1843.

– *General Laws for the Government of the Canadian Order of Oddfellows in Connexion with the Manchester Unity.* Toronto: Henry Roswell, 1854.

– *Report of the Grand Annual Committee of the Toronto District, Manchester Unity.* Hamilton: Spectator Office, 1849.

– *Report of the Special Meeting of Delegates and Grand Annual Conference of the Manchester Unity.* Hamilton: Gazette Office, 1852.

– *Tour of the Grand Master of the IOOF, Manchester Unity, Henry Outram in Canada and the United States.* Durham: George Walker, 1879.

Inglis, Walter. *Our Village and Mechanics' Institute.* Kincardine: J. Lang, 1867.

Institut Canadien de Montreal. *Annuaire de L'Institut Canadien.* 1866–70.
Institut Canadien de Québec. *Annuaire de L'Institut Canadien de Qúebec.* 1874–88.
– Institut Canadien de Quebec: Acte d'Incorporation et Règlements. Quebec: P.G. Deslisle, 1870.
Institut Canadien-Français d'Ottawa. *Institut Canadien-Français d'Ottawa 1852–1877, Célébration du 25e Anniversaire.* Ottawa: Imprimerie du Foyer Domestique, 1879.
Institut des Artisans de Montreal. *Constitution et Règlements de l'Institut des Artisans Canadiens de Montreal.* Montreal: Beauchemin and Valois, 1871.
Judd, William. *Minutes of the London Mechanics' Institute 1841–95.* Occasional paper #23. London: London Public Library, 1976.
Keefer, Thomas. *Montreal and the Ottawa: Two Lectures Delivered Before the Mechanics' Institute of Montreal.* Montreal: James Lovell, 1854.
King, John S. *Knights of Pythias: An Exposition of the Origin, Progress, Principles and Benefits of the Society.* Chatham: Planet Office, 1890.
King, William Lyon Mackenzie. *Industry and Humanity.* Introduction by David Bercuson. Toronto: University of Toronto Press, [1918], 1973.
Kingston Temperance Society. *Constitution of the Kingston Temperance Society and Bylaws.* Kingston: I.H. Bentley, 1840.
Knights of Pythias. *Constitution for Subordinate Lodges of the Knights of Pythias.* Toronto: Ontario Workman, 1875.
Knights of Temperance. *Revised Constitution, General Laws and Bylaws of the Knights of Temperance.* Quebec: R. Middleton, 1854.
Knowlson, John. *An Address on Total Abstinence, Delivered at a Meeting of the Cavan Temperance Society.* Toronto: Christian Guardian, 1840.
Klotz, Otto. *A Review of the Special Report of the Minister of Education on the Mechanics' Institutes of Ontario.* Toronto: Willing and Williamson, 1881.
Lachlan, Robert. *A Retrospective Glance at the Progressive State of the Natural History Society of Montreal.* Montreal: J.C. Beckett, 1852.
Lacroix, Henry. *Excursion to the Holy Land of Thought.* Montreal: John Lovell, 1867.
Lafontaine, L.H. *L'Institut Canadien en 1855.* Montreal: Senecal and Daniel, 1855.
Lander, Edwin. *Exposé of Odd Fellowship.* Toronto: Toronto News, 1878.
Lawless, Thomas. *The Canada Digest, International Order of Good Templars.* Hamilton: Spectator Press, 1872.
Leach, W.T. *An Address on Rechabitism.* Montreal: J.C. Beckett, 1845.
Lewis, J. Travers. *Lecture Delivered before the Brockville Library Association and Mechanics' Institute.* Brockville: David Wylie, 1855.
Lillie, Adam. *Canada, Its Growth and Prospects: Two Lectures Delivered Before the Mechanics' Institute of Toronto.* Brockville: David Wylie, 1852.

Literary and Historical Society of Quebec. *Annual Reports and Transactions.* 1831–99.
Literary and Scientific Society of Ottawa. *Transactions of the Literary and Scientific Society of Ottawa.* 1898–1900.
Lower Canadian Agricultural Society. *Agricultural Journal and Transactions of the Lower Canadian Agricultural Society.* 1848–49.
– *Bylaws of the Lower Canadian Agricultural Society.* Montreal: S.n., 1847.
Lynch, John. *Canada: Its Progress and Prospects, A Lecture Delivered for the Brampton Mechanics' Institute.* Brampton: George Tye, 1876.
Macleod, D.R. *The Literary and Historical Society of Quebec.* Quebec: S.n., 1874.
Meek, Edward. *Everyman's legal guide: a synopsis of the laws of Canada on many subjects, for use in universities, colleges and high schools, and by merchants, bankers, business men, and the public generally.* Toronto: McClelland & Stewart, 1920.
Merritt, William. *A Lecture Delivered by the Hon. William Hamilton Merritt before the Mechanics' Institute of St. Catharines.* St Catharines: H.F. Leavenworth, 1857.
Miall, Edward. *Defects of Our System of Government.* Ottawa: C.W. Mitchell, 1892.
Moffat, Christina. *To the Members of the Dominion Grange, Patrons of Husbandry of Canada, Three Essays, Called Flora, Ceres and Pomona.* Sunderland: Mirror Book and Job, 1886.
Montreal Mechanics' Institute. *Annual Report of the Montreal Mechanics' Institute.* 1855–97.
– *Constitution and Laws of the Montreal Mechanics Institution.* Montreal: Thomas Starke, 1833.
Montreal Natural History Society. *Annual Report of the Montreal Natural History Society.* 1828–81.
Montreal Temperance Society. *An Appeal to the Inhabitants of Lower Canada on the Use of Ardent Spirits by the Committee of the Montreal Society for the Promotion of Temperance.* Montreal: Mower and Hagan, 1828.
Murray, Robert. *A Course of Lectures on Absolute Abstinence: Containing a Refutation of the Doctrines of the Temperance Society Advanced in the Temperance Volume.* Toronto: British Colonist, 1839.
Newburgh Mechanics' Institute. *Catalogue of Books in the Newburgh Mechanics' Institute Library.* Newburgh: S.n., 1894.
Noel, Elisée. *Constitution et Règlements de l'Association Agricole.* Sherbrooke: Bélanger, 1889.
Ontario Temperance and Prohibitory League. *Proceedings of the Ontario Temperance and Prohibitory League.* 1873.
Orillia Mechanics' Institute. *Catalogue of Books in the Library of the Mechanics' Institute of Orillia.* Orillia: Printed at the Times, 1891.

Oronhyatekha. *History of the Independent Order of Foresters.* Toronto: Hunter and Rose, 1894.
Ottawa Natural History Society. *Transactions and Proceedings of the Ottawa Natural History Society.* 1881–99.
Owen Sound Mechanics' Institute. *Declaration and Bylaws and Catalogue of Books in the Owen Sound Mechanics' Institute.* Owen Sound: Comet Office, 1855.
Patrons of Industry. *Constitution and Rules of Order of the Patrons of Industry of North America.* Strathroy: Dispatch Printing House, 1892.
– *The Patrons: An Answer to the Annexationist Campaign Writer in the Canada Farmers' Sun.* S.p.: S.n., 1894.
– *The Patrons of Industry: From the Speech of Oliver Mowat Delivered in North Bruce.* North Bruce: S.n., 1893.
Patton, Henry. *Address Delivered in the Village of Kemptville for the Purpose of Forming a Temperance Society.* Brockville: Cumming and Tomkins, 1830.
Perry, George. *The Staple Trade of Canada: A Lecture Delivered before the Ottawa Mechanics' Institute and Athenaeum.* Ottawa: Union Engine Tower Presses, 1862.
Point Edward Mechanics' Institute. *Catalogue of the Point Edward Mechanics' Institute Library.* Sarnia: Canadian Steam Printing Office, 1882.
Province of Ontario. *Special Report of the Minister of Education on the Mechanics' Institutes in Ontario.* 1881.
Province of Quebec. *Almanach des Cercles Agricoles de la Province de Québec.* 1894–99.
Quebec Mechanics' Institute. *Catalogue and Rules of the Library and Reading Room of the Quebec Mechanics' Institute.* Quebec: W. Cowan and Son, 1841.
– *Rules of the Quebec Mechanics' Institute.* Quebec: Neilson and Company, 1832.
Quebec Temperance and Prohibitory League. *Proceedings of the Quebec Temperance and Prohibitory League.* 1872–75.
Riddell, A.A. "The Rights of Labour." Unpublished lecture, Baldwin Room, Metropolitan Toronto Reference Library, 1848.
Rintoul, David. *Lectures on Rhetoric to the Toronto Mechanics' Institute.* Toronto: James Cleland, 1844.
Rose, G.M. *Light for the Temperance Platform: A Collection of Readings, Recitations and Dialogues.* Toronto: Hunter and Rose, 1874.
Royal Society of Canada. *Proceedings and Transactions of the Royal Society of Canada.* 1883–99.
Royal Templars of Temperance. *Manual of the Select Degree and Ceremony of Installation.* Hamilton: Royal Templar Books, 1889.
– *Ritual of the Royal Degree Including the Ceremony of Installation and Burial Service of the Order of the Royal Templars of Temperance.* Hamilton: Templar Publishing, 1889.
– *Royal Templar Platform: A Collection of Readings and Recitations for Council and Lodge, Social Entertainments and Public Meetings.* Hamilton: Royal Templar Books, 1892.

- *Trumpet Notes of the Temperance Battlefield, Royal Templars of Temperance.* Hamilton: Templar Publishing, 1889.
Sherlocke, L.M. *Present Aspect of the Temperance Movement.* Montreal: John Lovell, 1872.
Smedley, A.B. *The Patrons Monitor.* Des Moines: Carter, Hussey and Curl, 1874.
Smith, Goldwin. "The Labour Movement." *Lectures and Essays.* Toronto: Hunter and Rose, 1881.
Sons of Temperance. *An Appeal to Men of Wealth and Influence, Against the Use of Intoxicating Drinks.* St John: S.n., 185–.
- *Constitution and Bylaws of the St. Lawrence Division, Sons of Temperance.* Quebec: Thompson & Company, 1860.
- *Constitution of the National, Grand and Subordinate Divisions of the Sons of Temperance of North America.* Brockville: Wyley and Sutton, 1850.
- *The Sons of Temperance; Its Origins, History, Secrets, Objections, Designs and Influence, Comprising a Full and Authentic History of this Deservedly Popular Institution.* Oshawa: C.T. White, 1851.
Sullivan, Robert Baldwin. *Address on Emigration and Colonization, Delivered in the Mechanics' Institute Hall, Toronto.* Toronto: Brown's Printing, 1847.
- *The Connection between Agriculture and Manufactures of Canada.* Hamilton: Ruthven's Book and Job Printing, 1848.
Tassé, Joseph. *Discours Prononcés par M. Joseph Tassé Devant l'Institut Canadien-Français d'Ottawa.* Montreal: Eusebe Senecal, 1873.
Temperance Colonization Society. *Charter and Bylaws of the Temperance Colonization Society.* Toronto: Hunter and Rose, 1882.
Toronto Mechanics' Institute. *Annual Report of the Toronto Mechanics' Institute.* 1840–83.
Toronto Temperance Reformation Society. *Annual Report of the Toronto Temperance Reformation Society.* 1847.
- *Facts and Figures for the People.* Toronto: S.n., 1864.
To the Friends of Literature and Mental Culture and Recreation, who Frequent the Muskoka Lakes in Summer. Windermere: S.n., 1885.
Van Cortlandt, Edward. *An Epitome of a Lecture on Ottawa Productions, Delivered Before the Bytown Mechanics' Institute.* Ottawa: Ottawa Citizen, 1853.
Verbist, Pascal Joseph. *Projet D'Organisation d'une Académie des Beaux Arts à Montréal.* Montreal: La Minerve, 1873.
Western District Agricultural Society. *Address of the Directing President of the Western District Agricultural Society.* Sandwich: H.C. Grant, 1838.
Wilson, T.C. *A Sermon Preached on Behalf of the Perth Temperance Society.* Montreal: Campbell and Beckett, 1836.

York Literary and Philosophical Society. *The Laws of the York Literary and Philosophical Society of Upper Canada.* Toronto: R. Stanton, 1832.

SECONDARY SOURCES

Books, Articles, and Theses

Acheson, T.W. *Saint John: The Making of a Colonial Urban Community.* Toronto: University of Toronto Press, 1985.

Airhart, Phyllis. *Serving the Present Age: Revivalism, Progressivism, and the Methodist Tradition in Canada.* Montreal and Kingston: McGill-Queen's University Press, 1992.

Akenson, Donald. *The Irish in Ontario: A Study in Rural History.* Kingston and Montreal: McGill-Queen's University Press, 1984.

Alborn, Timothy. "The Business of Induction: Industry and Genius in the Language of British Scientific Reform, 1820–1840." *History of Science* 34, (March 1996), 91–121.

Allen, David. *Naturalists and Society: The Culture of Natural History in Britain.* Aldershot: Ashgate, 2001.

Alter, Peter. *The Reluctant Patron: Science and the State in Britain, 1850–1920.* New York: St Martin's Press, 1987.

Ambrose, Linda. "What Are the Good of Those Meetings Anyway? Explaining the Early Popularity of the Ontario Women's Institutes." *Ontario History* 87, (March 1995), 1–20.

– and Margaret Kechnie. "Social Control or Social Feminism? Two Views of the Ontario Women's Institutes." *Agricultural History* 73, no. 2 (spring 1999), 222–32.

Anderson, Benedict. *Imagined Communities: Reflections on the Origin and Spread of Nationalism.* Second edition. London: Verso Books, 1991.

Anderson, Kay. *Vancouver's Chinatown: Racial Discourse in Canada, 1875–1980.* Kingston and Montreal: McGill-Queen's University Press, 1991.

Anstead, Christopher. "Fraternalism in Victorian Ontario: Secret Societies and Cultural Hegemony." PhD Thesis, University of Western Ontario, 1992.

– "Hegemony and Failure: Orange Lodges, Temperance Lodges and Respectability in Victorian Ontario." Jack Blocker and Cheryl Warsh, editors. *The Changing Face of Drink: Substance, Imagery and Behavior.* Ottawa: Social History/Histoire Sociale, 1997.

Armstrong, Christopher and H.V. Nelles. *Monopoly's Moment: The Organization and Regulation of Canadian Utilities, 1830–1930.* Philadelphia: Temple University Press, 1986.

Arnett, Janet. *The Grange at Knock*. Stroud: S.n., 1984.
Atack, Jeremy and Fred Bateman. *To Their Own Soil: Agriculture in the Antebellum North*. Ames: Iowa University Press, 1987.
Avery, Donald. *Dangerous Foreigners: European Immigrant Workers and Labour Radicalism in Canada, 1896–1932*. Toronto: McClelland & Stewart, 1979.
Bacchi, Carol. *Liberation Deferred? The Ideas of the English-Canadian Suffragists, 1877–1918*. Toronto: University of Toronto Press, 1983.
Badgely, Kerry. *Brining in the Common Love of Good: The United Farmers of Ontario, 1914–1926*. Montreal and Kingston: McGill-Queen's University Press, 2000.
– "'Then I Saw I had Been Swindled': Frauds and Swindles Perpetrated on Farmers in Late Nineteenth-Century Ontario." *Canadian Papers in Rural History*, no. 9. Gananoque: Longman Press, 1994.
Bailey, Peter. *Leisure and Class in Victorian England*. Toronto: University of Toronto Press, 1978.
Baker, Alan. *Fraternity among the French Peasantry: Sociability and Voluntary Associations in the Loire Valley, 1815–1914*. London: Cambridge University Press, 1999.
Baker, Paula. *The Moral Frameworks of Public Life: Gender, Politics, and the State in Rural New York, 1870–1930*. New York: Oxford University Press, 1997.
Barnes, Barry and Steven Shapin. "Science, Nature and Control: Interpreting Mechanics' Institutes." *Studies in Social Science* 7 (1977), 31–74.
Barron, F.L. "Damned Cold Water Drinking Societies: Oligarchic Opposition to the Temperance Movement in Upper Canada." *Upper Midwest History* 4 (1984), 11–28.
Barron, Hal. *Those Who Stayed Behind: Rural Society in Nineteenth-Century New England*. New York: Cambridge University Press, 1984.
Baskerville, Peter and Eric Sager. *Unwilling Idlers: The Urban Unemployed and Their Families and Late Victorian Canada*. Toronto: University of Toronto Press, 1998.
Beito, David. *From Mutual Aid to the Welfare State: Fraternal Societies and Social Services, 1890–1967*. Chapel Hill and London: University of North Carolina Press, 2000.
– "To Advance the Practice of Thrift and Economy: Fraternal Societies and Social Capital, 1890–1920." *Journal of Interdisciplinary History* 29, no. 4 (spring 1999), 585–612.
Bellavance, Marcel. *Le Québec et la Confédération: un choix libre?* Québec: Editions Fides, 1992.
Berger, Carl. *Honour and the Search for Influence: A History of the Royal Society of Canada*. Toronto: University of Toronto Press, 1996.
– *Science, God and Nature in Victorian Canada*. Toronto: University of Toronto Press, 1982.

Bernard, J.P. *Les rouges: libéralisme, nationalisme et anticléricalisme au milieu du XIXe siècle*. Montreal: Boréal, 1971.

Bernier, Gerard and Daniel Salée. *The Shaping of Quebec Politics and Society: Colonialism, Power, and the Transition to Capitalism in the Nineteenth Century*. Washington: Taylor and Francis, 1992.

Biagini, Eugenio. *Liberty, Retrenchment and Reform: Popular Liberalism in the Age of Gladstone, 1860–80*. New York: Cambridge University Press, 1992.

– and Alastair Reid, editors. *Currents of Radicalism: Popular Radicalism, Organized Labour and Party Politics in Britain, 1840–1914*. Cambridge: Cambridge University Press, 1991.

Bittermann, Rusty. "The Hierarchy of the Soil: Land and Labour in a Nineteenth-Century Cape Breton Community." *Acadiensis* 18, no. 1 (1988), 33–55.

– with Robert Mackinnon, and Graeme Wynn. "Of Inequality and Interdependence in the Nova Scotia Countryside, 1850–1870." *Canadian Historical Review* 74, no. 1 (January 1993), 1–20.

Blanchard, Jim. "Anatomy of Failure: Ontario Mechanics' Institutes, 1835–95." *Canadian Library Journal* 38, no. 6 (December 1981), 389–96.

Blocker, Jack. *American Temperance Movements: Cycles of Reform*. Boston: Twayne Publishers, 1989.

– *Retreat from Reform: The Prohibition Movement in the United States, 1890–1913*. Westport: Greenwood Press, 1976.

– and Cheryl Warsh, editors. *The Changing Face of Drink: Substance, Imagery, and Behaviour*. Ottawa: Social History/Histoire Sociale, 1997.

Blumin, Stuart. *The Emergence of the Middle Class: Social Experience in the American City, 1760–1900*. New York: Cambridge University Press, 1989.

Boily, Raymond. *Les Irlandais et Le Canal de Lachine: La Grève de 1843*. Ottawa: Leméac, 1980.

Bordin, Ruth. *Women and Temperance: The Quest for Power and Liberty, 1873–1900*. Philadelphia: Temple University Press, 1981.

Bouchard, Gerard. "Economic Inequalities in Saguenay Society, 1879–1949: A Descriptive Analysis." *Canadian Historical Review* 79, no. 4, (December 1998), 660–89.

Bouchier, Nancy. *For the Love of the Game: Amateur Sport in Small-town Ontario, 1838–1895*. Montreal and Kingston: McGill-Queen's University Press, 2003.

Braddick, Michael and John Walter. "Grids of Power: Order, Hierarchy and Subordination in Early Modern Society." Michael Braddick and John Walter, editors. *Negotiating Power in Early Modern Society: Order, Hierarchy and Subordination in Britain and Ireland*. Cambridge: Cambridge University Press, 2001.

Briggs, Asa. *The Age of Improvement, 1783–1867*. London: Longmans Press, 1959.

Bristow, Peggy. "Black Women in Buxton and Chatham, 1850–65." Peggy Bristow, editor. *We're Rooted Here and They Can't Pull Us Up: Essays in African Canadian Women's History.* Toronto: University of Toronto Press, 1994.
Brown, Stanley. *Thomas Chalmers and the Godly Commonwealth in Scotland.* London: Oxford University Press, 1982.
Bruce, Lorne. *Free Books for All: The Public Library Movement in Ontario, 1850–1930.* Toronto: Dundurn Press, 1994.
Bruegel, Martin. *Farm, Shop, Landing: The Rise of a Market Society in the Hudson Valley, 1780–1860.* Durham: Duke University Press, 2002.
Burke, Martin. *The Conundrum of Class: Public Discourse on the Social Order in America.* Chicago: University of Chicago Press, 1995.
Burke, Peter. *Popular Culture in Early Modern Europe.* London: Temple Smith, 1978.
Burke, Sara. *Seeking the Highest Good: Social Service and Gender at the University of Toronto, 1887–1937.* Toronto: University of Toronto Press, 1996.
Burley, David. *A Particular Condition in Life: Self-Employment and Social Mobility in Mid-Victorian Brantford, Ontario.* Montreal and Kingston: McGill-Queen's University Press, 1994.
Burn, W.L. *The Age Of Equipoise: A Study of the Mid-Victorian Generation.* London: Allen and Unwin, 1964.
Burns, Sarah. *Pastoral Inventions: Rural Life in Nineteenth-Century American Art and Culture.* Philadelphia: Temple University Press, 1989.
Burr, Christina. *Canada's Victorian Oil Town: The Transformation of Petrolia from a Resource Town into a Victorian Community.* Toronto: University of Toronto Press, 2006.
– *Spreading the Light: Work and Labour Reform in Late-Nineteenth-Century Toronto.* Toronto: University of Toronto Press, 1998.
Cadigan, Sean. *Hope and Deception in Conception Bay: Merchant-Settler Relations in Newfoundland, 1785–1855.* Toronto: University of Toronto Press, 1995.
– "Paternalism and Politics: Sir Francis Bond Head, the Orange Order and the Election of 1836." *Canadian Historical Review* 72, no. 3 (September 1991), 319–47.
Calnan, James. "Blessed Be the Tie that Binds: Voluntary Associations and Community in Picton, Ontario, 1870–1914." PhD Thesis, University of Guelph, 2001.
Candy, Philip and John Laurent. *Pioneering Culture: Mechanics' Institutes and Schools of Arts in Australia.* Adelaide: Auslib Press, 1994.
Cannadine, David. *The Rise and Fall of Class in Britain.* New York: Columbia University Press, 1999.

Careless, J.M.S. "David Christie." *Dictionary of Canadian Biography*, vol. 10. Toronto: University of Toronto Press, 1972.
- "The Toronto *Globe* and Agrarian Radicalism, 1850–67." *Canadian Historical Review* 29, no. 1 (March 1948), 14–39.

Carnes, Mark. *Secret Ritual and Manhood in Victorian America*. New Haven and London: Yale University Press, 1989.

Chartier, Roger. *Cultural History: Between Practices and Representations*. Cambridge: Cambridge University Press, 1988.
- *On the Edge of the Cliff: History, Language, and Practices*. Translated by Lydia Cochrane. Baltimore and London: Johns Hopkins University Press, 1997.

Chartrand, Luc, Raymond Duchesne, and Yves Gingras. *Histoire des Sciences au Québec*. Montreal: Boréal, 1987.

Christie, Nancy. *Engendering the State: Family, Work, and Welfare*. Toronto: University of Toronto Press, 2000.
- "Family, Community, and the Rise of Liberal Society." Nancy Christie, editor. *Households of Faith: Family, Gender, and Community in Canada, 1760–1969*. Montreal and Kingston: McGill-Queen's University Press, 2002.
- "Psychology, Sociology and the Secular Movement: The Ontario Educational Association's Quest for Authority, 1880–1900," *Journal of Canadian Studies* 25 (summer 1990), 119–43.
- "Sir William Logan's Geological Empire and the Humbug of Economic Utility." *Canadian Historical Review* 75, no. 2 (June 1994), 161–204.
- and Gauvreau, Michael. *A Full-Orbed Christianity: The Protestant Churches and Social Welfare in Canada, 1900–1940*. Montreal and Kingston: McGill-Queen's University Press, 1996.

Claeys, Gregory. *Citizens and Saints: Politics and Anti-Politics in Early British Socialism*. Cambridge: Cambridge University Press, 1989.
- *Machinery, Money and the Millennium: From Moral Economy to Socialism*. Princeton: Princeton University Press, 1987.

Clark, Christopher. *The Roots of Rural Capitalism: Western Massachusetts, 1780–1860*. Ithaca and London: Cornell University Press, 1990.

Clark, Peter. *British Clubs and Societies, 1580–1800: The Origins of an Associational World*. London: Clarendon Press, 2000.

Clarke, Brian. *Piety and Nationalism: Lay Associations and the Creation of an Irish-Catholic Community in Toronto, 1850–1895*. Montreal and Kingston: McGill-Queen's University Press, 1993.

Clawson, Mary Ann. *Constructing Brotherhood: Class, Gender, and Fraternalism*. Princeton: Princeton University Press, 1989.

Clemens, James. "Taste Not, Touch Not, Handle Not: A Study of the Social Assumptions of the Temperance Literature and Supporters in Canada West, 1839–59." *Ontario History* 64 (1972), 142–60.

Cmiel, Ken. *Democratic Eloquence: The Fight over Popular Speech in Nineteenth-Century America.* New York: William Morrow, 1990.
Coavares, Francis. *The Remaking of Pittsburgh: Class and Culture in an Industrializing City, 1877–1919.* Albany: State University of New York Press, 1984.
Cohen, Marjorie Griffin. *Women's Work, Markets, and Economic Development in Nineteenth-Century Ontario.* Toronto: University of Toronto Press, 1988.
Cohen, Nancy. *The Reconstruction of American Liberalism, 1865–1914.* Chapel Hill: University of North Carolina Press, 2002.
Colley, Linda. *Britons: Forging the Nation, 1707–1837.* New Haven: Yale University Press, 1992.
Cook, Ramsay. *The Regenerators: Social Criticism in Late Victorian English Canada.* Toronto: University of Toronto Press, 1985.
– "Tillers and Toilers: The Rise and Fall of Populism in Canada in the 1890s." Canadian Historical Association, *Historical Papers* (Guelph, 1984), 5–20.
Cook, Sharon. *Through Sunshine and Shadow: The Women's Christian Temperance Union, Evangelicalism, and Reform in Ontario, 1874–1930.* Montreal and Kingston: McGill-Queen's University Press, 1995.
Cooter, Roger. *The Cultural Meaning of Popular Science: Phrenology and the Organization of Consent in Nineteenth-Century Britain.* Cambridge: Cambridge University Press, 1984.
– and Stephen Pumfrey. "Separate Spheres and Public Places: Reflections on the History of Science Popularization and Science in Popular Culture." *History of Science* 32, no. 97 (September 1994), 237–67.
Cordery, Simon. *British Friendly Societies, 1750–1914.* London: Palgrave Books, 2003.
– "Friendly Societies and the Discourse of Respectability in Britain, 1825–75." *Journal of British Studies* 34, no. 1 (January 1995), 35–58.
Courville, Serge. *Entre ville et campagne: L'essor du village dans les seigneuries du Bas-Canada.* Quebec: Presses de l'Université Laval, 1990.
– "Un monde rural en mutation: le Bas-Canada dans la première moitié du XXIe siècle." *Social History/Histoire Sociale* 20, no. 40 (November 1987), 237–58.
Craven, Paul. *"An Impartial Umpire": Industrial Relations and the Canadian State, 1900–1911.* Toronto: University of Toronto Press, 1980.
Creighton, Philip. "William Scott Burn." *Dictionary of Canadian Biography* vol. 8. Toronto: University of Toronto Press, 1985.
Crosland, Maurice. *Science Under Control: The French Academy of Sciences, 1795–1914.* Cambridge: Cambridge University Press, 1992.
Crossick, Geoffrey. *An Artisan Elite in Victorian Society: Kentish London, 1840–1880.* London: Croom Helm, 1978.
– "From Gentleman to the Residuum: Languages of Social Description in Victorian Britain." Penelope Corfield, editor. *Language, History and Class.* Oxford: Basil Blackwood, 1991.

Crowley, Terry. "Experience and Representation: Southern Ontario Farm Women and Agricultural Change, 1870–1914." *Agricultural History* 73, no. 2 (spring 1999), 238–51.
- "Rural Labour." Paul Craven, editor. *Labouring Lives: Work and Workers in Nineteenth-Century Ontario.* Toronto: University of Toronto Press, 1995.

Crerar, Adam. "Ties That Bind: Farming, Agrarian Ideals and Life in Ontario," PhD Thesis, University of Toronto, 1999.

Cruikshank, Ken. *Close Ties: Railways, Government, and the Board of Railway Commissioners, 1850–1933.* Montreal and Kingston: McGill-Queen's University Press, 1992.

Curtis, Bruce. *Building the Educational State: Canada West, 1836–1871.* London: Althouse Press, 1988.
- "'Littery Meritt,' 'Useful Knowledge,' and the Organization of Township Libraries in Canada West, 1840–60." *Ontario History* 78, no. 4 (December 1986), 285–311.
- *Politics of Population: State Formation, Statistics and the Census of Canada, 1840–1875.* Toronto: University of Toronto Press, 2001.
- *True Government by Choice Men? Inspection, Education, and State Formation in Canada West.* Toronto: University of Toronto Press, 1992.

D'Cruze, Shani and Turnbull, Jean. "Fellowship and Family: Oddfellow Lodges in Preston and Lancaster, 1830–90." *Urban History* 22, no. 1 (May 1995), 25–47.

Danbom, David. "The Agricultural Experiment Stations and Professionalization: The Scientists' Goals for Agriculture." *Agricultural History* 60, no. 2 (spring 1986), 246–55.

Dannenbaum, Jed. *Drink and Disorder: Temperance Reform in Cincinnati from the Washingtonian Revival to the WCTU.* Urbana and Chicago: University of Illinois Press, 1984.

Darnton, Roger. *The Great Cat Massacre and Other Episodes in French Cultural History.* New York: Vintage Books, 1985.

Darroch, Gordon. "Scanty Fortunes and Rural Middle Class Formation in Nineteenth-Century Rural Ontario." *Canadian Historical Review* 79, no. 4 (December 1998), 621–59.

Davidoff, Leonore and Hall, Catherine. *Family Fortunes: Men and Women of the English Middle Class, 1780–1850.* Chicago: University of Chicago Press, 1987.

Decarie, Graeme. "Something Old, Something New: Aspects of Prohibitionism in Ontario in the 1890s." Donald Swainson, editor. *Oliver Mowat's Ontario.* Toronto: Macmillan, 1972.
- "The Prohibition Movement in Ontario, 1894–1916." PhD Thesis, Queen's University, 1972.

Den Otter, A.A. *The Philosophy of Railways: The Transcontinental Railway Idea in British North America.* Toronto: University of Toronto Press, 1997.
Dentith, Simon. *Society and Cultural Forms in Nineteenth Century England.* London: MacMillan, 1998.
Dewald, Jonathan. "Roger Chartier and the Fate of Cultural History." *French Historical Studies* 21, no. 2 (spring 1998), 221–40.
Dewar, Ken. *Charles Clarke: Pen and Ink Warrior.* Montreal and Kingston: McGill-Queen's University Press, 2004.
– "Charles Clarke's *Reformator*: Early Victorian Radicalism in Upper Canada." *Ontario History* 78, no. 3 (September 1986), 233–54.
Dick, Earnest. "From Temperance to Prohibition in Nineteenth-Century Nova Scotia." *Dalhousie Review* 61, no. 3 (autumn 1981), 530–52.
Doyle, Dan. *The Social Order of a Frontier Community: Jacksonville, Illinois, 1825–1870.* Urbana and Chicago: University of Illinois Press, 1978.
Drummond, Ian. *Political Economy at the University of Toronto: A History of the Department, 1888–1982.* Toronto: University of Toronto Press, 1983.
– *Progress Without Planning: The Economic History of Ontario From Confederation to the Second World War.* Toronto: University of Toronto Press, 1987.
Eadie, James. "The Napanee Mechanics' Institute: The Nineteenth-Century Mechanics' Institute Movement in Microcosm." *Ontario History* 68, no. 4 (December 1976), 209–21.
Eid, Nadia F. *Le clergé et le pouvoir politique au Québec.* Montreal: Presse HMH, 1978.
Emery, George and J.C. Emery. *A Young Man's Benefit: The Independent Order of Oddfellows and Sickness Insurance in the United States and Canada, 1860–1929.* Kingston and Montreal: McGill-Queen's University Press, 1999.
Epstein, Barbara. *The Politics of Domesticity: Women, Evangelism, and Temperance in Nineteenth-Century America.* Middleton: Wesleyan University Press, 1981.
Epstein, James. *In Practice: Studies in the Language and Culture of Popular Politics in Modern Britain.* Stanford: Stanford University Press, 2003.
Errington, Jane. *The Lion, the Eagle, and Upper Canada: A Developing Colonial Ideology.* Montreal and Kingston: McGill-Queen's University Press, 1987.
Fahey, Curtis. *In His Name: The Anglican Experience in Upper Canada, 1791–1854.* Ottawa: Carleton University Press, 1991.
Fahey, David. "Blacks, Good Templars, and Universal Membership." Cheryl Warsh and Jack Blocker, editors. *The Changing Face of Drink: Substance, Imagery, and Behaviour.* Ottawa: Social History/Histoire Sociale, 1997.
Fair, D. Ross. "Gentlemen, Farmers, and Gentlemen Half-Farmers: The Development of Agricultural Societies in Upper Canada, 1792–1846." PhD Thesis, Queen's University, 1998.

Fairburn, Miles. *The Ideal Society and its Enemies: The Foundations of Modern New Zealand Society, 1850–1900*. Auckland: Auckland University Press, 1989.

Faler, Paul. *Mechanics and Manufacturers in the Early Industrial Revolution: Lynn, Massachusetts, 1780–1860*. Albany: State University of New York Press, 1981.

Farrell, Richard. "Advice to Farmers: The Context of Agricultural Newspapers, 1860–1910." *Agricultural History* 51, no. 1 (Jan. 1977), 209–17.

Fecteau, Jean-Marie. "État et associationnisme au XIXe siècle québecois: éléments pour une problématique des rapports État/société dans la transition au capitalisme." Allan Greer and Ian Radforth, editors. *Colonial Leviathan: State Formation in Mid-Nineteenth Century Canada*. Toronto: University of Toronto Press, 1992.

– *La liberté du pauvre: crime et pauvreté au XIXe siècle Québécois*. Montreal: Boréal, 2004.

– *Un nouvel ordre des choses: la pauvreté, le crime, l'Etat au Quebec, de la fin du XVIIIe siècle à 1840*. Outremont: VLB editeur, 1989.

Ferguson, Barry. *Remaking Liberalism: The Intellectual Legacy of Adam Shortt, O.D. Skelton, W.C. Clark, and W.A. Mackintosh, 1890–1925*. Montreal and Kingston: McGill-Queen's University Press, 1993.

Ferry, Darren. "On Common Ground: Voluntary Associations and the Construction of Community in Central Canada, 1840–1900." PhD Thesis, McMaster University, 2003.

– "Severing the Connections in a Complex Community: The Grange, Patrons of Industry and the Construction/Contestation of a Late Nineteenth-Century Agrarian Identity in Ontario." *Labour/Le Travail* 53 (fall 2004), 9–47.

– "To the Interests and Conscience of the Great Mass of the Community: The Evolution of Temperance Societies in Nineteenth-Century Central Canada." *Journal of the Canadian Historical Association*, new series, vol. 14 (2003), 137–63.

Fetherling, Douglas. *The Rise of the Canadian Newspaper*. Toronto: Oxford University Press, 1990.

Fink, Leon. *Workingmen's Democracy: The Knights of Labor in American Politics*. Urbana and Chicago: University of Illinois Press, 1983.

Finn, Margot. *After Chartism: Class and Nation in English Radical Politics, 1848–1874*. Cambridge: Cambridge University Press, 1993.

Foner, Eric. *Free Soil, Free Labor, Free Men: The Ideology of the Republican Party Before the Civil War*. New York: Oxford University Press, 1970.

Forster, Ben. *A Conjunction of Interests: Business, Politics and Tariffs, 1825–1879*. Toronto: University of Toronto Press, 1986.

Foster, John. *Class Struggle and the Industrial Revolution: Early Industrial Capitalism in Three English Towns*. London: Croom Helm, 1974.

Frost, Stanley. "Science Education in the Nineteenth Century: The Natural History Society of Montreal, 1827–1925." *McGill Journal of Education* 17, no. 1 (winter 1982), 31–42.

Gaffield, Chad. *Language, Schooling, and Cultural Conflict: The Origins of the French Language Conflict in Ontario.* Montreal and Kingston: McGill-Queen's University Press, 1987.

Gamm, Gerald and Putnam, Robert. "The Growth of Voluntary Associations in America, 1840–1940." *Journal of Interdisciplinary History* 29, no. 4 (spring 1999), 511–57.

Garner, A.D. and E.W. Jenkins. "The English Mechanics' Institutes: The Case of Leeds, 1824–1842." *History of Education* 13, no. 2 (April 1984), 139–52.

Garrioch, David. *Neighbourhood and Community in Paris, 1740–1790.* Cambridge: Cambridge University Press, 1986.

Gates, Warren. "Modernization as a Function of an Agricultural Fair: The Great Grangers' Picnic Exhibition at Williams Grove, Pennsylvania, 1873–1916." *Agricultural History* 58, no. 3 (July 1984), 262–79.

Gauvreau, Michael. "Covenanter Democracy: Scottish Popular Religion, Ethnicity, and the Varieties of Politico-Religious Dissent in Upper Canada, 1815–1841." *Histoire Sociale/Social History* 36, no. 71 (May 2003), 55–83.

– "Personal Piety and the Evangelical Social Vision, 1815–1867." G.A. Rawlyk, editor. *The Canadian Protestant Experience, 1760–1990.* Montreal and Kingston: McGill-Queen's University Press, 1990.

Gay, Hannah and John Gay. "Brothers in Science: Science and Fraternal Culture in Nineteenth-Century Britain." *History of Science* 35 (December 1997), 425–53.

Gidney, R.D. "The Rev. Robert Murray: Ontario's First Superintendent of Schools." *Ontario History* 63, no. 4 (December 1971), 195–204.

– and W.P.J. Millar. *Professional Gentlemen: The Professions in Nineteenth-Century Ontario.* Toronto: University of Toronto Press, 1994.

Gilkeson, John. *Middle-Class Providence, 1820–1940.* Princeton: Princeton University Press, 1986.

Ginzberg, Lori. *Women and the Work of Benevolence: Morality, Politics, and Class in the Nineteenth-Century United States.* New Haven and London: Yale University Press, 1990.

Gleason, Mary. *The Royal Society of London: Years of Reform, 1827–1847.* New York and London: Garland Publishing, 1991.

Goddard, Nicholas. "Development and Influence of Agricultural Periodicals and Newspapers." *Agricultural History Review* 31, part 2 (1983), 116–31.

– *Harvests of Change: The Royal Agricultural Society of England, 1838–1988.* London: Quillen Press, 1988.

Goheen, Peter. *Victorian Toronto, 1850 to 1900: Pattern and Process of Growth.* Chicago: University of Chicago Press, 1970.

Goldman, Lawrence. *Science, Reform and Politics in Victorian Britain: The Social Science Association, 1857–1886.* Cambridge: Cambridge University Press, 2002.

Goldstein, Daniel. "Yours for Science: The Smithsonian Institution's Correspondents and the Shape of a Scientific Community in Nineteenth-Century America," *Isis* 85, no. 4 (December 1994), 573–99.

Goodwyn, Lawrence. *The Populist Moment: A Short History of the Agrarian Revolt in America*. New York: Oxford University Press, 1978.

Gorsky, Martin. *Patterns of Philanthropy: Charity and Society in Nineteenth-Century Bristol*. Suffolk: Boydell Press, 1999.

Gosden, P.H.J.H. *Self-Help: Voluntary Associations in the Nineteenth Century*. London: B.T. Batsford, 1973.

Gouglas, Sean. "Settlement and Agriculture in Saltfleet Township, 1790–1890." Ph.D. Thesis, McMaster University, 2001.

Gray, Robert. *The Labour Aristocracy in Victorian Edinburgh*. Oxford: Clarendon Press, 1976.

– *The Factory Question and Industrial England*. Cambridge: Cambridge University Press, 1996.

Green, David. *From Artisans to Paupers: Economic Change and Poverty in London, 1790–1870*. Aldershot: Scholar Press, 1996.

Green, David and Lawrence Cromwell. *Mutual Aid or the Welfare State: Australia's Friendly Societies*. Sydney: George Allen and Unwin, 1984.

Greenberg, Brian. "Worker and Community: Fraternal Orders in Albany, New York, 1845–1885." Charles Stephenson and Robert Asher, editors, *Life and Labor: Dimensions of American Working Class History*. New York: State University of New York Press, 1986.

– *Worker and Community: Responses to Industrialization in a Nineteenth-Century American City: Albany, 1850–1884*. Albany: State University of New York Press, 1985.

Greenhalgh, Paul. *Ephemeral Vistas: The Expositions Universelles, Great Exhibitions and World's Fairs, 1851–1939*. Manchester: Manchester University Press, 1988.

Greer, Allan. *The Patriots and the People: The Rebellion of 1837 in Rural Lower Canada*. Toronto: University of Toronto Press, 1993.

– *Peasant, Lord, and Merchant: Rural Society in Three Quebec Parishes, 1740–1840*. Toronto: University of Toronto Press, 1985.

– and Ian Radforth, editors. *Colonial Leviathan: State Formation in Mid-Nineteenth Century Canada*. Toronto: University of Toronto Press, 1992.

Gunn, L. Ray. *The Decline of Authority: Public Economic Policy and Political Development in New York, 1800–1860*. Ithaca and London: Cornell University Press, 1988.

Gunn, Simon. *The Public Culture of the Victorian Middle Class: Ritual and Authority and the English Industrial City, 1840–1914*. New York: Manchester University Press, 2000.

Gutman, Herbert. *Work, Culture, and Society in Industrializing America.* New York: Alfred A. Knopf, 1966.
Haber, Samuel. *The Quest for Authority and Honor in the American Professions, 1750–1900.* Chicago: University of Chicago Press, 1991.
Habermas, Jurgen. *The Structural Transformation of the Public Sphere.* Translated by Thomas Berger. Cambridge: MIT Press, 1989.
Haggard, Robert. *The Persistence of Victorian Liberalism: The Politics of Social Reform in Britain, 1870–1900.* Westport: Greenwood Press, 2001.
Hahn, Steven. *The Roots of Southern Populism: Yeoman Farmers and the Transformation of the Georgia Upcountry, 1850–1890.* New York: Oxford University Press, 1982.
– and Johnathan Prude, editors. *The Countryside in the Age of Capitalist Transformation: Essays in the Social History of Rural America.* Chapel Hill and London: University of North Carolina Press, 1985.
Hall, Marie. *All Scientists Now: The Royal Society in the Nineteenth Century.* Cambridge: Cambridge University Press, 1984.
Halpern, Monda. *And on That Farm He Had a Wife: Ontario Farm Women and Feminism, 1900–1970.* Montreal and Kingston: McGill-Queen's University Press, 2001.
Hann, Russell. *Farmers Confront Industrialism: Some Historical Perspectives on Ontario Agrarian Movements.* Toronto: New Hogtown Press, 1975.
Hansen, Karen. *A Very Social Time: Crafting Community in Antebellum New England.* Berkeley and Los Angeles: University of California Press, 1994.
Hardy, Rene. *Contrôle social et mutation de la culture religieuse au Québec, 1830–1930.* Montreal: Boreal, 1999.
Harrison, Brian. *Drink and the Victorians.* Toronto: Faber and Faber, 1971.
Harrison, Carol. *The Bourgeois Citizen in Nineteenth-Century France: Gender, Sociability, and the Uses of Emulation.* New York: Oxford University Press, 1999.
Haskell, Thomas. *The Emergence of Professional Social Science: The ASSA and the Nineteenth Century Crisis of Authority.* Chicago: University of Chicago Press, 1977.
Heaman, Elsbeth. "Taking the World by Show: Canadian Women as Exhibitors to 1900." *Canadian Historical Review* 78, no. 4 (December 1997), 599–631.
– *The Inglorious Arts of Peace: Exhibitions in Canadian Society During the Nineteenth Century.* Toronto: University of Toronto Press, 1999.
Hemming, J.P. "The Mechanics' Institutes in Lancashire and Yorkshire Textile Districts from 1850." *Journal of Educational Administration and History* 9, no. 1 (January 1977), 18–31.
Heron, Craig, editor. *The Workers' Revolt in Canada, 1917–1925.* Toronto: University of Toronto Press, 1998.
– "Factory Workers." Paul Craven, editor. *Labouring Lives: Work and Workers in Nineteenth-Century Ontario.* Toronto: University of Toronto Press, 1995.

Heward, Christine. "Industry, Cleanliness and Godliness: Sources for and Problems in the History of Scientific and Technical Education and the Working Classes, 1850–1910." *Studies in Science Education* 7 (1980), 87–128.

Hewitt, Martin. *An Age of Equipoise? Reassessing Mid-Victorian Britain.* Aldershot: Scholar Press, 2000.

– "Science as Spectacle: Popular Science Culture in Saint John, New Brunswick, 1830–1850." *Acadiensis* 18, no. 1 (autumn 1988), 91–119.

– "Science, Popular Culture, and the Producer Alliance in Saint John, New Brunswick." Paul A. Bogaard, editor. *Profiles of Science and Society in the Maritimes Prior to 1914.* Victoria: Morriss Printing, 1990.

– *The Emergence of Stability in the Industrial City: Manchester, 1832–1867.* Aldershot: Scholar Press, 1996.

High, Steven and Walsh, John. "Rethinking the Concept of Community." *Histoire Sociale/Social History* 32, no. 63 (November 1999), 255–74.

Hoare, Quintin and Geoffrey Nowell Smith, editors and translators. *Selections from the Prison Notebooks of Antonio Gramsci.* New York: International Publishers, 1971.

Holman, Andrew. *A Sense of Their Duty: Middle-Class Formation in Victorian Ontario Towns.* Montreal and Kingston: McGill-Queen's University Press, 2000.

Holmes, William. "Populism: In Search of Context." *Agricultural History* 64, no. 4 (fall 1990), 26–58.

Hopkins, Eric. *Working Class Self-Help in Nineteenth-Century England.* New York: St Martin's Press, 1995.

Houghton, Walter. *The Victorian Frame of Mind.* New Haven: Yale University Press, 1957.

Houston, Cecil and William Smyth, *The Sash Canada Wore: A Historical Geography of the Orange Order in Canada.* Toronto: University of Toronto Press, 1980.

Houston, Susan and Alison Prentice. *Schooling and Scholars in Nineteenth-Century Ontario.* Toronto: University of Toronto Press, 1988.

Howe, Daniel Walker. *Making the American Self.* Cambridge: Harvard University Press, 1997.

Howkins, Alun. *Reshaping Rural England: A Social History, 1850–1925.* London: HarperCollins, 1991.

Hudson, Kenneth. *Patriotism with Profit: British Agricultural Societies in the Eighteenth and Nineteenth Centuries.* London: Hugh Evelyn, 1972.

Inkster, Ian. "Aspects of the History of Science and Culture in Britain, 1780–1850 and Beyond." Ian Inkster and Jack Morrell, editors. *Metropolis and Province: Science in British Culture, 1780–1850.* London: Hutchinson and Company, 1983.

– *Scientific Culture and Urbanization in Industrializing Britain.* Aldershot: Galliard, 1997.

- and Jack Morrell, editors. *Metropolis and Province: Science in British Culture, 1780–1850*. London: Hutchison and Company, 1983.
Irwin, Thomas. "Government Funding of Agricultural Associations in Late Nineteenth-Century Ontario." PhD Thesis, University of Western Ontario, 1997.
Isenberg, Nancy. *Sex and Citizenship in Antebellum America*. Chapel Hill and London: University of North Carolina Press, 1998.
Johnson, Richard. "'Really Useful Knowledge': Radical Education and Working Class Culture, 1790–1848." J. Clarke, C. Critcher, and A. Johnson, editors, *Working Class Culture: Studies in History and Theory*. New York: St Martin's Press, 1979.
Jones, Janet Cunliffe. "A Rare Phenomenon: A Woman's Contribution to Nineteenth-Century Adult Education." *Journal of Educational Administration and History* 24, no. 1 (January 1992), 1–17.
Joyce, Patrick. *Democratic Subjects: The Self and the Social in Nineteenth-Century England*. Cambridge: Cambridge University Press, 1994.
- *The Rule of Freedom: Liberalism and the Modern City*. London: Verso Press, 2003.
- *Visions of the People: Industrial England and the Questions of Class, 1848–1914*. Cambridge: Cambridge University Press, 1991.
- *Work, Society and Politics: The Culture of the Factory in Later Victorian England*. Sussex: Harvester Press, 1980.
Kaufman, Jason. *For the Common Good? American Civic Life and the Golden Age of Fraternity*. New York: Oxford University Press, 2002.
Kaye, Frances. "The Ladies Department of the Ohio Cultivator, 1845–55: A Feminist Forum." *Agricultural History* 50, no. 2 (April 1976), 414–23.
Kealey, Gregory. *Toronto Workers Respond to Industrial Capitalism, 1867–1892*. Toronto: University of Toronto Press, 1980.
- and Bryan Palmer. *Dreaming of What Might Be: The Knights of Labor in Ontario, 1880–1900*. Cambridge: Cambridge University Press, 1982.
Kealey, Linda. *Enlisting Women for the Cause: Women, Labour, and the Left in Canada, 1890–1925*. Toronto: University of Toronto Press, 1998.
Keane, Patrick. "Priorities and Resources in Adult Education: The Montreal Mechanics' Institute 1828–1843." *McGill Journal of Education* 23, no. 2 (spring 1988), 171–87.
- "A Study in Early Problems and Policies in Early Adult Education: The Halifax Mechanics' Institute." *Social History/Histoire Sociale* 8, no. 16 (November 1975), 255–74.
Kelly, Catherine. "The Consummation of Rural Prosperity and Happiness: New England Agricultural Fairs and the Construction of Class and Gender, 1810–60." *American Quarterly* 49, no. 3 (September 1997), 574–602.

Kerr, K. Austin. *Organized for Prohibition: A New History of the Anti-Saloon League.* New Haven and London: Yale University Press, 1985.

Killian, Gerald. *David Boyle: From Artisan to Archaeologist.* Toronto: University of Toronto Press, 1983.

Kirk, Neville. *The Growth of Working Class Reformism in Mid-Victorian England.* London: Croom Helm, 1985.

– *Change, Continuity and Class: Labour in British Society, 1850–1920.* Manchester: Manchester University Press, 1998.

Koditschek, Theodore. *Class Formation and Urban Industrial Society: Bradford, 1750–1850.* New York: Cambridge University Press, 1990.

Kulikoff, Allan. "The Transition to Capitalism in Rural America." *William and Mary Quarterly* 46, no. 1 (January 1989), 120–44.

Kuntz, Harry. "The Educational Work of the Two Montreal Mechanics' Institutes." MA Thesis, Concordia University, 1993.

Lambert, W.R. *Drink and Society in Victorian Wales, 1820–1895.* Cardiff: University of Wales Press, 1983.

Lamonde, Yvan. *Gens de parole: Conférences publiques, essais et débats à l'Institut canadien de Montreal, 1845–1871.* Montréal: Boréal, 1990.

– *L.A. Dessaules: Un seigneur libéral et anticlerical.* Québec: Editions Fides, 1994.

Lapointe-Roy, Huguette. *Charité bien ordonné: le premier reseau de lutte contre la pauvreté à Montréal au XIXe siècle.* Montréal: Boréal, 1987.

Laurent, John. "Science, Society and Politics in Late Nineteenth-Century England: A Further Look at Mechanics' Institutes." *Social Studies of Science* 14, no. 4 (November 1984), 585–619.

Laurie, Bruce. *Artisans into Workers: Labor in Nineteenth-Century America.* New York: Hill and Wang, 1989.

Lawrence, Jon. *Speaking for the People: Party, Language and Popular Politics in England, 1867–1914.* Cambridge: Cambridge University Press, 1998.

Lears, T. Jackson. "The Concept of Cultural Hegemony: Problems and Possibilities." *American Historical Review* 90, no. 3 (June 1985).

Levere, T.H. and Richard Jarrell, editors. *A Curious Field-Book: Science and Society in Canadian History.* Toronto: University of Toronto Press, 1974.

Levine, Phillipa. *The Amateur and the Professional: Antiquitarians, Historians and Archaeologists in Victorian England, 1836–1886.* Cambridge: Cambridge University Press, 1986.

Lewis, Brian. *The Middlemost and the Milltowns: Bourgeois Culture and Politics in Early Industrial England.* Stanford: Stanford University Press, 2001.

Lightman, Bernard. "Marketing Knowledge for the General Reader: Victorian Popularizers of Science." *Endeavour* 24, no. 3 (September 2000).

- editor. *Victorian Science in Context.* Chicago and London: University of Chicago Press, 1997.
Little, J.I. *Borderland Religion: The Emergence of an English-Canadian Identity, 1792–1852.* Toronto: University of Toronto Press, 2004.
- *Crofters and Habitants: Settler Society, Economy, and Culture in a Quebec Township, 1848–1881.* Montreal and Kingston: McGill-Queen's University Press, 1991.
- "Lewis Drummond." *Dictionary of Canadian Biography,* vol. 11. Toronto: University of Toronto Press, 1982.
- *State and Society in Transition: The Politics of Institutional Reform in the Eastern Townships, 1838–1852.* Montreal and Kingston: McGill-Queen's University Press, 1997.
Livingston, James. *Pragmatism and the Political Economy of Cultural Revolution, 1850–1940.* Chapel Hill and London: University of North Carolina Press, 1994.
Loo, Tina. *Making Law, Order and Authority in British Columbia, 1821–1871.* Toronto: University of Toronto Press, 1994.
MacDonald, L.R. "Merchants Against Industry: An Idea and its Origins." *Canadian Historical Review* 56 (1975), 266–80.
Malleck, Daniel. "Priorities in Development in Four Woman's Christian Temperance Unions in Ontario, 1877–95." Jack Blocker and Cheryl Warsh, editors. *The Changing Face of Drink: Substance, Imagery and Behavior.* Ottawa: Social History/Histoire Sociale, 1997.
Marcus, Alan. "The Ivory Silo: Farmer-Agricultural Tensions in the 1870s to 1880s." *Agricultural History* 60, no. 2 (spring 1986), 22–36.
Marks, Lynne. "Railing, Tattling, and General Rumour: Gossip, Gender, and Church Regulation in Upper Canada." *Canadian Historical Review* 81, no. 3 (September 2000), 380–402.
- *Revivals and Roller Rinks: Religion, Leisure, and Identity in Late-Nineteenth-Century Small-Town Ontario.* Toronto: University of Toronto Press, 1996.
Marshall, David. *Secularizing the Faith: Canadian Protestant Clergy and the Crisis of Belief, 1850–1940.* Toronto: University of Toronto Press, 1992.
Marti, Donald. *To Improve the Soil and Mind: Agricultural Societies, Journals, and Schools in the Northeastern States, 1791–1865.* Ann Arbor: University Microforms, 1979.
- *Women of the Grange: Mutuality and Sisterhood in Rural America, 1866–1920.* New York: Greenwood Press, 1991.
Mattingly, Carol. *Well-Tempered Women: Nineteenth-Century Temperance Rhetoric.* Carbondale: Southern Illinois University Press, 1998.
McCalla, Douglas. *Planting the Province: The Economic History of Upper Canada, 1784–1870.* Toronto: University of Toronto Press, 1993.

McCallum, John. *Unequal Beginnings: Agriculture and Economic Development in Quebec and Ontario until 1870.* Toronto: University of Toronto Press, 1980.

McCutcheon, Brian. "The Patrons of Industry in Manitoba." Donald Swainson, editor. *Historical Essays on the Prairie Provinces.* Toronto: McClelland & Stewart, 1970.

McDonald, Robert. *Making Vancouver: Class, Status, and Social Boundaries, 1863–1913.* Vancouver: University of British Columbia Press, 1996.

McInnis, R.M. "The Changing Structure of Canadian Agriculture, 1867–1897." *Journal of Economic History* 42, no. 1 (March 1982), 191–8.

– "The Early Ontario Wheat Staple Reconsidered." *Canadian Papers in Rural History*, no. 8. Gananoque: Longman Press, 1992.

– "Marketable Surpluses in Ontario Farming, 1860." *Social Science History* 8, no. 4 (1984), 395–424.

– "A Reconsideration of the State of Agriculture in Lower Canada in the First Half of the Nineteenth Century." *Canadian Papers in Rural History*, no. 3. Gananoque: Longman Press, 1982.

McKay, Ian. The Liberal Order Framework: A Prospectus for a Reconnaissance of Canadian History." *Canadian Historical Review* 81, no. 4 (December 2000), 617–45.

– *The Quest of the Folk: Antimodernism and Cultural Selection in Twentieth-Century Nova Scotia.* Montreal and Kingston: McGill-Queen's University Press, 1994.

McKillop, A.B. *A Disciplined Intelligence: Critical Inquiry and Canadian Thought in Victorian Era.* Montreal and Kingston: McGill-Queen's University Press, 1979.

– *Matters of Mind: The University in Ontario, 1791–1951.* Toronto: University of Toronto Press, 1994.

McMath, Robert. *American Populism: A Social History, 1877–1898.* New York: Hill and Wang, 1993.

McMurry, Sally. *Families and Farmhouses in Nineteenth-Century America: Vernacular Design and Social Change.* New York: Oxford University Press, 1988.

– *Transforming Rural Life: Dairying Families and Agricultural Change, 1820–1885.* Baltimore and London: Johns Hopkins University Press, 1995.

– "Who Read the Agricultural Journals? Evidence from Chenango County, New York, 1839–1865." *Agricultural History* 63, no. 4 (fall 1989), 1–18.

McNairn, Jeffery. *The Capacity to Judge: Public Opinion and Deliberative Democracy in Upper Canada, 1791–1854.* Toronto: University of Toronto Press, 2000.

McNall, Scott. *The Road to Rebellion: Class Formation and Kansas Populism, 1865–1900.* Chicago and London: University of Chicago Press, 1988.

McOuat, Gordon. "Cataloguing Power: Delineating Competent Naturalists and the Meaning of Species in the British Museum." *British Journal of the History of Science* 34, no. 120 (March 2001), 1–28.

Menard, Johanne. "L'Institut des Artisans du Comté du Drummond 1856–90." *Recherches Sociographiques* 16, no. 2 (1975), 207–18.
Millard, J. Rodney. *The Master Spirit of the Age: Canadian Engineers and the Politics of Professionalism, 1887–1922.* Toronto: University of Toronto Press, 1988.
Miller, Carman. "Joseph Abbott." *Dictionary of Canadian Biography*, vol. 9. Toronto: University of Toronto Press, 1976.
Miller, J.R. "Anti-Catholic Thought in Victorian Canada." *Canadian Historical Review* 66, no. 4 (Dec. 1985), 474–94.
– *Equal Rights: The Jesuits' Estate Act Controversy.* Montreal and Kingston: McGill-Queen's University Press, 1979.
Mills, David. *The Idea of Loyalty in Upper Canada, 1784–1850.* Montreal and Kingston: McGill-Queen's University Press, 1988.
Moir, John S. *Enduring Witness: A History of the Presbyterian Church in Canada.* Toronto: Presbyterian Press, 1974.
Montgomery, David. *Citizen Worker: The Experience of Workers in the United States with Democracy and the Free Market in the Nineteenth Century.* New York: Cambridge University Press, 1993.
Morgan, Cecilia. *Public Men and Virtuous Women: The Gendered Languages of Religion and Politics in Upper Canada, 1791–1850.* Toronto: University of Toronto Press, 1996.
Morrell, Jack and Thackery, Arnold. *Gentlemen of Science: The Early Years of the British Association for the Advancement of Science.* London: Clarendon Press, 1980.
Morris, R.J. *Class, Sect and Party: The Making of the British Middle Class: Leeds, 1820–1850.* Manchester: Manchester University Press, 1990.
Morus, Ivan. "Manufacturing Nature: Science, Technology and Victorian Consumer Culture," *British Journal of the History of Science* 29, no. 103 (December 1996), 403–42.
Murray, Heather. *Come Bright Improvement: The Literary Societies of Nineteenth-Century Ontario.* Toronto: University of Toronto Press, 2002.
Mussio, Louise. "The Origins and Nature of the Holiness Movement Church: A Study in Religious Populism." *Journal of the Canadian Historical Association*, new series 7 (1997), 81–104.
Naylor, C. David. "Rural Protest and Medical Professionalism in Turn of the Century Ontario." *Journal of Canadian Studies* 21, no. 1 (spring 1986), 5–20.
Neatby, H. Blair. *Laurier and a Liberal Quebec.* Ottawa: Carleton Library Series, 1973.
Neave, David. *Mutual Aid in the Victorian Countryside, 1830–1914.* Hull: Hull University Press, 1991.
Nesmith, Tom. "The Philosophy of Agriculture: The Promise of the Intellect in Ontario Farming." PhD Thesis, Carleton University, 1988.

Noel, Jan. *Canada Dry: Temperance Crusades Before Confederation.* Toronto: University of Toronto Press, 1995.
– "Dry Patriotism: The Chiniquy Crusade." Cheryl Warsh, editor. *Drinking in Canada: Historical Essays.* Montreal and Kingston: McGill-Queen's University Press, 1993.
Noel, Sid. "Early Populist Tendencies in Ontario Political Culture." *Ontario History* 90, no. 2 (September 1998), 173–87.
Noel, S.J.R. *Patrons, Clients, Brokers: Ontario Society and Politics, 1791–1896.* Toronto: University of Toronto Press, 1990.
Nordin, D. Sven. *Rich Harvest: A History of the Grange, 1867–1900.* Jackson: Mississippi University Press, 1974.
Osborne, Brian. "Trading on a Frontier: The Function of Peddlers, Markets and Fairs in Nineteenth-Century Ontario." *Canadian Papers in Rural History*, no. 2. Gananoque: Longman Press, 1980.
Ouellet, Fernand. *Lower Canada 1791–1840: Social Change and Nationalism.* Toronto: McClelland & Stewart, 1980.
Osterud, Nancy. *Bonds of Community: The Lives of Farm Women in Nineteenth-Century New York.* Ithaca and London: Cornell University Press, 1991.
Owram, Douglas. *The Government Generation: Canadian Intellectuals and the State, 1900–1945.* Toronto: University of Toronto Press, 1986.
– *The Promise of Eden: The Canadian Expansionist Movement and the Idea of the West, 1856–1900.* Toronto: University of Toronto Press, 1980.
Palmer, Bruce. *Man Over Money: The Southern Populist Critique of American Capitalism.* Chapel Hill and London: University of North Carolina Press, 1980.
Palmer, Bryan. *A Culture in Conflict: Skilled Workers and Industrial Capitalism in Hamilton, Ontario, 1860–1914.* Montreal and Kingston: McGill-Queen's University Press, 1979.
– "Mutuality and the Making/Masking of Difference: Mutual Benefit Societies in Canada, 1850–1950." Marcel van der Linden, editor. *Social Security Mutualism: The Comparative History of Mutual Benefit Societies.* New York: Peter Lang, 1996.
– *Working-Class Experience: Rethinking the History of Canadian Labour, 1800–1991.* Toronto: McClelland & Stewart, 1992.
– *Working-Class Experience: The Rise and Reconstitution of Canadian Labour, 1800–1980.* Toronto: Butterworth and Company, 1983.
Palmer, Howard. *Patterns of Prejudice: A History of Nativism in Alberta.* Toronto: McClelland & Stewart, 1982.
Paul, Harvey. *From Knowledge to Power: The Rise of the Science Empire in France, 1860–1939.* Cambridge: Cambridge University Press, 1988.
Pederson, Jane. *Between Memory and Reality: Family and Community in Rural Wisconsin, 1870–1970.* Madison: University of Wisconsin Press, 1992.

Pegram, Thomas. *Battling Demon Rum: The Struggle for a Dry America, 1800–1933*. Chicago: Ivan Dee, 1998.

Perkin, Harold. *The Rise of Professional Society: England Since 1880*. London: Routledge, 1990.

Perry, Adele. *On the Edge of Empire: Gender, Race, and the Making of British Columbia, 1849–1871*. Toronto: University of Toronto Press, 2001.

Petitclerc, Martin. "L'association qui crée une nouvelle famille: L'expérience populaire de la mutualité lors de la transition à la societé de marché," *Revue d'histoire de l'Amérique française* 59, no. 3 (hiver 2006), 259–92.

Poovey, Mary. *Making a Social Body: British Cultural Formation, 1830–1864*. Chicago: University of Chicago Press, 1995.

Prentice, Alison. *The School Promoters: Education and Social Class in Mid-Nineteenth Century Upper Canada*. Toronto: McClelland & Stewart, 1977.

Prothero, I.J. *Artisans and Politics in Nineteenth-Century London*. Folkstone: Wm. Dawson and Son, 1979.

– *Radical Artisans in England and France, 1830–70*. Cambridge: Cambridge University Press, 1997.

Purvis, Jane. *Hard Lessons: Lives and Education of Working Class Women in Nineteenth-Century England*. Minneapolis: University of Minnesota Press, 1989.

Pyenson, Lewis and Susan Sheets-Pyenson. *Servants of Nature: A History of Scientific Institutions, Enterprises, and Sensibility*. London: Fontana Press, 1999.

Raby, Geoff. *Making Rural Australia: An Economic History of Technical and Institutional Creativity, 1788–1860*. Melbourne: Oxford University Press, 1996.

Radcliffe, C.J. "Mutual Improvement Societies in the West Riding of Yorkshire, 1835–1900." *Journal of Educational Administration and History* 18, no. 2, (July 1986), 2–15.

Radforth, Ian. "Sydenham and Utilitarian Reform." Allan Greer and Ian Radforth, editors. *Colonial Leviathan: State Formation in Mid-Nineteenth Century Canada*. Toronto: University of Toronto Press, 1992.

Rafferty, O.P. "Apprenticeship's Legacy: The Social and Educational Goals of Technical Education in Ontario, 1860–1911." PhD Thesis, McMaster University, 1995.

Ramsay, Ellen. "Art and Industrial Society: The Role of the Toronto Mechanics' Institute in the Promotion of Art, 1831–1883." *Labour/Le Travail* 43 (spring 1999), 71–103.

Read, Colin. "Conflict to Consensus: The Political Culture of Upper Canada." *Acadiensis* 19, no. 2 (spring 1990), 169–85.

– *The Rising in Western Upper Canada, 1837–38: The Duncombe Revolt and After*. Toronto: University of Toronto Press, 1982.

Reilly, James. "The Political, Social and Economic Impacts on the Emergence of the Kingston Mechanics' Institute in the Pre-Confederation Period." MA Thesis, Queen's University, 1994.

Rennie, Bradford. *The Rise of Agrarian Democracy: The United Farmers and Farm Women of Alberta, 1909–1921.* Toronto: University of Toronto Press, 2000.

Roberts, M.J.D. *Making English Morals: Voluntary Associations and Moral Reform in England, 1787–1886.* Cambridge: Cambridge University Press, 2004.

Robins, Nora. "Useful Education for the Workingman: The Montreal Mechanics' Institute, 1828–1870." Michael Welton, editor. *Knowledge for the People: The Struggle for Adult Learning in English Speaking Canada, 1828–1973.* Toronto: OISE Press, 1987.

Rodgers, Daniel T. *The Work Ethic in Industrial America, 1850–1920.* Chicago: University of Chicago Press, 1978.

Rose, Jonathan. *The Intellectual Life of the British Working Classes.* New Haven and London: Yale University Press, 2001.

Rosenweig, Roy. *Eight Hours for What We Will: Workers and Leisure in an Industrial City, 1870–1920.* New York: Cambridge University Press, 1983.

Rothenberg, Winnifred. "The Emergence of Farm Labour Markets and the Transformation of the Rural Economy: Massachusetts, 1750–1855." *Journal of Economic History* 48 (1988), 537–66.

Roy, Fernande. *Progrès, Harmonie, Liberté: Le libéralisme des milieux d'affaires francophones à Montréal au tournant du siècle.* Montréal: Boréal, 1988.

Royle, Edward. "Mechanics' Institutes and the Working Class." *Historical Journal* 14, no. 2 (1971), 305–21.

Rumbarger, John. *Profits, Power, and Prohibition: Alcohol Reform and the Industrializing of America, 1800–1930.* New York: State University of New York Press, 1989.

Ryan, Mary. *Civic Wars: Democracy and Public Life in the American City During the Nineteenth Century.* Berkeley: University of California Press, 1997.

– *Cradle of the Middle Class: The Family in Oneida County, New York, 1790–1865.* New York: Cambridge University Press, 1981.

– *Women in Public: Between Banners and Ballots, 1825–1880.* Baltimore and London: Johns Hopkins Press, 1990.

Rydell, Robert. *All the World's a Fair: Visions of Empire at American International Expositions, 1876–1916.* Chicago: University of Chicago Press, 1984.

Samson, Daniel, editor. *Contested Countryside: Rural Workers and Modern Society in Atlantic Canada, 1800–1950.* Fredericton: Acadiensis Press, 1994.

– *The Spirit of Industry and Improvement: Liberal Government and Rural-Industrial Society, Nova Scotia, 1790–1862.* Montreal and Kingston, McGill-Queen's University Press, 2008.

- "Industry and Improvement: State and Class Formation in Nova Scotia's Coal Mining Countryside, 1790–1864." Montreal and Kingston: McGill-Queen's University Press, 1998.
Sanders, Elizabeth. *Roots of Reform: Farmers, Workers and the American State, 1877–1914*. Chicago: University of Chicago Press, 1999.
Sandwell, Ruth. "Rural Reconstruction: Towards a New Synthesis in Canadian History." *Social History/Histoire Sociale* 27, no. 53 (May 1994), 1–32.
- "The Limits of Liberalism: The Liberal Reconnaissance and the History of the Family in Canada." *Canadian Historical Review* 84, no. 3 (September 2003), 423–50.
Seaton, Beverly. "Idylls of Agriculture: Nineteenth-Century Success Stories of Farming and Gardening." *Agricultural History* 55, no. 1 (January 1981), 21–35.
Secord, Anne. "Botany on a Plate: Pleasure and the Power of Pictures in Promoting Early Nineteenth-Century Scientific Knowledge." *Isis* 93 (March 2002), 28–57.
- "Corresponding Interests: Artisans and Gentlemen in Nineteenth-Century Natural History." *British Journal of the History of Science* 27, no. 95 (December 1994), 383–403.
Secord, James. *Victorian Sensation: The Extraordinary Publication, Reception and Secret Authorship of the Vestiges of the Natural History of Creation*. Chicago: University of Chicago Press, 2000.
See, Scott. *Riots in New Brunswick: Orange Nativism and Social Violence in the 1840*. Toronto: University of Toronto Press, 1993.
Seed, John. "From Middling Sort to the Middle Class in Late Eighteenth and Early Nineteenth Century England." M.L. Bush, editor. *Social Orders and Social Classes in Europe Since 1500: Studies in Social Stratification*. Essex: Longman Group, 1992.
- and Janet Wolff, editors. *The Culture of Capital: Art, Power and the Nineteenth-Century Middle Class*. London: Manchester University Press, 1988.
Sellars, Charles. *The Market Revolution: Jacksonian America, 1815–1846*. New York: Oxford University Press, 1991.
Sendbuehler, M.P. "Battling the Bane of Our Cities: Class, Territory, and the Prohibition Debate in Toronto, 1877." *Urban History Review* 22, no. 1 (October 1993), 30–48.
Shiman, Lilian. *Crusade Against Drink in Victorian England*. New York: St Martin's Press, 1988.
Shore, Marlene. *The Science of Social Redemption: McGill, the Chicago School and the Origins of Social Research in Canada*. Montreal and Kingston: McGill-Queen's University Press, 1987.
Shortt, S.E.D. "Social Change and Political Crisis in Rural Ontario: The Patrons of Industry, 1889–1896." Donald Swainson, editor. *Oliver Mowat's Ontario*. Toronto: Macmillan, 1972.

- *The Search for an Ideal: Six Canadian Intellectuals and Their Convictions in an Age of Transition, 1890–1930*. Toronto: University of Toronto Press, 1976.
Shteir, Ann. *Cultivating Women, Cultivating Science: Flora's Daughters and Botany in England, 1760–1860*. Baltimore: Johns Hopkins University Press, 1996.
- "Elegant Recreations? Configuring Science Writing for Women." Bernard Lightman, editor. *Victorian Science in Context*. Chicago and London: University of Chicago Press, 1997.
Skalansky, Jeffrey. *The Soul's Economy: Market Society and Selfhood in American Thought*. Chapel Hill: University of North Carolina Press, 2002.
Skocpol, Theda. "The Tocqueville Problem: Civic Engagement in American Democracy." *Social Science History* 21, no. 4 (winter 1997), 455–80.
- with Jocelyn Crowley. "The Rush to Organize: Exploring Associational Formation in the United States, the 1860's to the 1920s." *American Journal of Political Science* 45, no. 4 (October 2001), 813–29.
Spurr, Geoff. "Those Who are Obliged to Pretend that They are Gentlefolk: The Construction of a Clerking Identity in Victorian and Edwardian London." PhD Thesis, McMaster University, 2001.
Stedman-Jones, Gareth. *Languages of Class: Studies in English Working Class History, 1832–1982*. Cambridge: Cambridge University Press, 1983.
Stewart, Ian. "William Weld." *Dictionary of Canadian Biography*, vol. 12. Toronto: University of Toronto Press, 1990.
Stouffer, Allan. *The Light of Nature and the Law of God: Antislavery in Ontario, 1833–1877*. Montreal and Kingston: McGill-Queen's University Press, 1992.
Struthers, James. *No Fault of Their Own: Unemployment and the Canadian Welfare State, 1914–1941*. Toronto: University of Toronto Press, 1983.
Sutherland, David. "Voluntary Societies and the Process of Middle Class Formation in Early Victorian Halifax, Nova Scotia." *Journal of the Canadian Historical Association*, new series, vol. 5 (1994), 237–64.
Sylvester, Kenneth. *The Limits of Rural Capitalism: Family, Culture, and Markets in Montcalm, Manitoba, 1870–1940*. Toronto: University of Toronto Press, 2001.
Taylor, Jeffrey. *Fashioning Farmers: Ideology, Agricultural Knowledge and the Manitoba Farm Movement, 1890–1925*. Regina: Canadian Plains Research Center, 1994.
Taylor, Miles. *The Decline of British Radicalism, 1847–1860*. Oxford: Clarendon Press, 1995.
Thelan, David. *Paths of Resistance: Tradition and Dignity in Industrializing Missouri*. New York: Oxford University Press, 1986.
Thompson, E.P. *Customs in Common: Studies in Traditional Popular Culture*. New York: Merlin Press, 1991.
- *The Making of the English Working Class*. Harmondsworth: Penguin, 1968.

Thompson, John B. "Robert Harwood." *Dictionary of Canadian Biography*, vol. 9. Toronto: University of Toronto Press, 1976.

Thornton, Tamara. *Cultivating Gentlemen: The Meaning of Country Life Among the Boston Elite, 1785–1860*. New Haven and London: Yale University Press, 1989.

Tosh, John. *A Man's Place: Masculinity and the Middle-Class Home in Victorian England*. London: Yale University Press, 1999.

– editor. *Manliness and Masculinities in Nineteenth-Century Britain*. London: Longman, 2005.

Traves, Tom. *The State and Enterprise: Canadian Manufacturers and the Federal Government, 1917–1931*. Toronto: University of Toronto Press, 1977.

Tremblay, Martine. "La division sexuelle du travail et la modernisation de l'agriculture à travers la presse agricole, 1840–1900." *Revue d'histoire de l'Amérique française* 42 (1993), 221–42.

Tulchinsky, Gerald. *The River Barons: Montreal Businessmen and the Growth of Industry and Transportation*. Toronto: University of Toronto Press, 1977.

Turner, Frank. *Contesting Cultural Authority: Essays in Victorian Intellectual Life*. Cambridge: Cambridge University Press, 1993.

Tylecote, Mabel. *The Mechanics' Institutes of Lancashire and Yorkshire before 1851*. Manchester: Manchester University Press, 1957.

Tyrell, Ian. *Sobering Up: From Temperance to Prohibition in Antebellum America, 1800–1860*. Westport: Greenwood Press, 1979.

Valverde, Mariana. *The Age of Light, Soap, and Water: Moral Reform in English Canada, 1885–1925*. Toronto: McClelland & Stewart, 1991.

Van Die, Marguerite. "The Marks of Genuine Revival: Religion, Social Change, Gender, and Community in Mid-Victorian Brantford, Ontario." *Canadian Historical Review* 79, no. 3 (September 1998), 524–63.

Varty, Carmen. "A Laudable Undertaking: Women, Charity, and the Public Sphere in Mid-Nineteenth-Century Hamilton, Canada West." PhD Thesis, Queen's University, 2005.

Vernon, James. *Politics and the People: A Study in English Political Culture, 1815–1867*. Cambridge: Cambridge University Press, 1993.

Voisey, Paul. *High River and the Times: An Albertan Community and its Weekly Newspaper, 1905–1966*. Edmonton: University of Alberta Press, 2004.

– *Vulcan: The Making of a Prairie Community*. Toronto: University of Toronto Press, 1988.

Voss, Kim. *The Making of American Exceptionalism: The Knights of Labor and Class Formation in the Nineteenth Century*. Ithaca and London: Cornell University Press, 1993.

Wach, Howard. "Culture and the Middle Classes: Popular Knowledge in Industrial Manchester." *Journal of British Studies* 27, no. 4 (October 1988), 375–404.
Wahrman, Dror. *Imagining the Middle Class: The Political Representation of Class in Britain.* Cambridge: Cambridge University Press, 1995.
– *Making the Modern Self: Identity and Culture in Eighteenth-Century England.* New Haven and London: Yale University Press, 2004.
Waiser, W.A. *The Field Naturalist: John Macoun, the Geological Survey, and Natural Science.* Toronto: University of Toronto Press, 1989.
Walden, Keith. *Becoming Modern in Toronto: The Industrial Exhibition and the Shaping of a Late Victorian Culture.* Toronto: University of Toronto Press, 1997.
Wallace, Elisabeth. *Goldwin Smith: Victorian Liberal.* Toronto: University of Toronto Press, 1957.
Wallot, Jean-Pierre. "Le régime seigneurial et son abolition au Canada." Jean-Pierre Wallot, editor. *Un Québec qui bougeait: Trame socio-politique au tournant du XIXe siècle.* Montréal: Boréal, 1973.
Ward, Peter. *White Canada Forever: Popular Attitudes and Public Policy toward Orientals in British Columbia.* Montreal and Kingston: McGill-Queen's University Press, 1978.
Warsh, Cheryl. *Drink in Canada: Historical Essays.* Kingston and Montreal: McGill-Queen's University Press, 1993.
Watson, Michael. "The Origins of Mechanics' Institutes of North Yorkshire." *Journal of Educational Administration and History* 19, no. 2 (July 1987), 12–25.
Weir, Robert. *Beyond Labor's Veil: The Culture of the Knights of Labor.* Pennsylvania: Pennsylvania State University Press, 1996.
Welch, Margaret. *The Book of Nature: Natural History in the United States, 1825–1875.* Boston: Northeastern University Press, 1998.
Westfall, William. *Two Worlds: The Protestant Culture of Nineteenth-Century Ontario.* Montreal and Kingston: McGill-Queen's University Press, 1989.
Whitley, Richard. "Knowledge Producers and Knowledge Acquirers: Popularisation as a Relation Between Scientific Fields and their Publics." Terry Shinn and Richard Whitley, editors. *Expository Science: Forms and Functions of Popularisation.* Boston: D. Reidel Publishing, 1985.
Wiebe, Robert. *The Search for Order, 1877–1920.* New York: Hill and Wang, 1967.
Wilentz, Sean. *Chants Democratic: New York City and the Rise of the American Working Class, 1788–1850.* New York: Oxford University Press, 1984.
Williams, Raymond. *Culture and Society, 1780–1950.* London: Columbia University Press, 1958.
Wilmot, Sarah. "The Business of Improvement: Agriculture and Scientific Culture in Britain, 1770–1870." *Historical Geography Research Series* 24 (November, 1990), 1–81.

Wilson, Catherine. "Reciprocal Work Bees and the Meaning of Neighbourhood." *Canadian Historical Review* 82, no. 3 (September 2001), 431–64.

Wilson, J. Donald. "William Hincks." *Dictionary of Canadian Biography*, vol. 10. Toronto: University of Toronto Press, 1972.

Wilton, Carol. *Popular Politics and Political Culture in Upper Canada, 1800–1850*. Kingston and Montreal: McGill-Queen's University Press, 2000.

Winter, Alison. *Mesmerized: Powers of Mind in Victorian Britain*. Chicago: University of Chicago Press, 1998.

Wood, J. David. *Making Ontario: Agricultural Colonization and Landscape Re-Creation Before the Railway*. Montreal and Kingston: McGill-Queen's University Press, 2000.

Wood, Louis Aubrey. *A History of Farmers' Movements in Canada*. Toronto: University of Toronto Press, [1924] 1975.

Woods, Thomas. *Knights of the Plow: Oliver Kelley and the Origins of the Grange in Republican Ideology*. Ames: Iowa State University Press, 1991.

Wynn, Graeme. "Exciting a Spirit of Emulation Among the Plodholes: Agricultural Reform in Pre-Confederation Nova Scotia." *Acadiensis* 20, no. 1 (1990), 5–51.

Yeo, Richard. *Science in the Public Sphere*. Aldershot: Ashgate, 2001.

Zeller, Suzanne. *Inventing Canada: Early Victorian Science and the Idea of the Transcontinental Nation*. Toronto: University of Toronto Press, 1987.

Zimmerman, Jonathan. *Distilling Democracy: Alcohol Education in America's Public Schools, 1880–1925*. Lawrence: University of Kansas Press, 1999.

Index

Abbott, Joseph, 100, 321n13
Agricultural Association of Ontario, 176, 184, 202, 205
agricultural exhibitions, 174; and large urban exhibitions, 209–11, 356n117; women's participation in, 179–80, 200; as recreation for towns, 209–13
agricultural periodicals. *See* agricultural press
agricultural press, 171; bickering between, 172–3, 204; the *British American Cultivator*, 173–4, 177–8, 180, 184–6; the *Canada Farmer*, 173, 183, 186; the *Canadian Agricultural Journal*, 177, 183, 187; the *Canadian Agriculturalist*, 174–5, 177–8, 180–1, 184–7; views of class supremacy in, 177–8, 197–9; the *Farmers' Advocate*, 197, 201, 204, 208–11, 240; farming open to all classes in, 174, 197; views of honest industry in, 186–7, 208–9; to improve/promote agriculture, 172, 175–8; the *Lower Canadian Agriculturalist*, 178, 180–1; *Miller's Canadian Farmers' Almanac*, 208; the *Ontario Farmer*, 198–9, 201–4, 208–9; views of politics and religion in, 182–3, 204; woman's sphere in, 180–1, 201–2
agricultural societies, 170; and early colonial history, 171–2; in Elora, 192–3, 212; emulation and improvement in, 175, 185, 206–7; entertainment in, 188–9, 210–12; in Glengarry, 192–3, 206; the Guelph Fat Stock Club, 191–2, 206, 210; honest industry in, 185–6; inclusive membership in, 172, 176, 191–4, 350n64; the influence of the state in, 172, 202; in Metcalfe, 192–3; in Norwich, 180, 188–9; in Oro, 179, 185, 192, 200–2; in Peterborough, 174, 176, 180, 183, 188; views of religion and politics, 182–3, 202, 346n34; in South/Centre Wellington, 191–2, 200, 207, 212; the Western District/Middlesex, 188, 194, 205, 210; women's roles in, 179–80, 199–200
agriculture, 170–1; as the cornerstone of Canadian society, 175–6; and experimental/model farms, 198, 202, 205, 213; in Great Britain,

171–2; improvement and emulation in, 171–2, 179, 214, 345n25; the influence of the government in, 171–2, 191, 198, 214, 343n8; in Lower Canada/Quebec, 171, 190; in the Maritimes, 190; post-Confederation changes in, 189–91, 217, 350n61, 358n6; and scientific husbandry, 175, 191, 198, 202, 214, 360n21; the transition to agrarian capitalism, 171–2, 342n1; in the United States, 171, 350n622; in Upper Canada/Ontario, 171, 190, 343n4; women's roles in, 179–81, 199–202
alcohol, campaigns against. *See* temperance
American Association for the Advancement of Science, 248–9, 262
Ancient Order of Foresters. *See* Independent Order of Foresters
Ancient Order of United Workmen, 138–4, 155–7, 165, 168
Anglicans, 31–2, 98, 100
Anti-Seigneurial Tenure League, 170, 182
Ardagh, John, 67
Arnold, Walter, 36
Ashley, William, 89, 272
Association of Fraternal Orders, 157
Association of Mechanics Institutes, 47–9, 60, 75, 310n1
Aylwin, Thomas, 23, 42, 173, 182, 300n9

Badgely, Kerry, 215, 359n9
banks, 34, 45, 176–8, 222, 345n19
Barnum, P.T., 60, 93
Beito, David, 140, 159, 340n71
benevolent associations, 11, 298n38

Bengough, J.W., 117, 122, 130
Bettridge, William, 31–2, 302n31
Board of Agriculture of Canada West/Ontario, 175, 178, 185, 188; linked with the state, 181, 202–3; the *Transactions of the Board of Agriculture*, 176, 184
Board of Arts and Manufactures of Upper Canada, 28, 34–6, 43–4, 50, 73–4, 247; and its *Journal*, 29, 38, 43, 54–5
Bourget, Ignace, 146, 253, 270, 305n59
Bourniot, John, 266
Bovell, James, 28
Bowden, Emily, 158
Boyle, David, 48–50, 72
Bristow, William, 31, 35
British American Order of Good Templars, 108–9, 113–14, 131
British Association for the Advancement of Science, 22
Brockville Debating Club, 258
Brown, George, 52, 173, 204, 275
Brown, Isaac, 87
Buckland, William, 175, 177–8, 184
Burgess, William, 117, 120–2, 328n80
Burn, W. Scott, 255
Burwash, Nathaniel, 237
Byrne, James, 98

Cameron, Malcolm, 108
Canada Citizen and Temperance Herald, 116–18, 120–1
Canada Farmer's Sun, 120–1, 232–3, 240, 236, 239
Canada Temperance Advocate, 97–102, 104–5
Canada Temperance Union, 118–9, 121

Canadian Institute, 246–7; and the *Canadian Journal*, 247, 252; and civil engineers, 246, 249; commercial science in, 255–6, 263–5; debates on political economy in, 255–6, 275–6; essays on rectifying politics, 271–3; inclusive of society, 246, 260; and the liberal state, 246, 252, 370n28; the medical section of, 263; and the middling/middle classes, 249; views of politics and religion in, 251, 271–2; and popular science, 263–4; recreation in, 258; relations with Mechanics' Institutes, 249
Canadian Order of Chosen Friends, 158–9, 161, 165, 342n92
Canadian Order of Foresters. *See* Independent Order of Foresters
Canadian Prohibition Party, 120–1
Canadian Prohibitory Liquor Law League, 115–17
Canadian Temperance League, 118
Carling, John, 204
Carpenter, Philip, 118
Case, Albert, 141, 145–9
cercles agricoles, 170, 191, 195–7, 203, 213–14, 207–8
Chauveau, P.J.O., 182, 274
Christian Guardian, 101
Christie, David, 202–3, 205
Clarke, Charles, 72, 303n36
Clarke, William, 204, 208
class, 12–18, 39, 42, 61–3
clergy, 13; Catholic, 14, 53, 183, 309n91; Protestant, 86, 98, 183
Clergy Reserves, 69, 108
Cobbett, William, 33
Colin, Frederic, 53–4
Commercial Union, 86–8, 126, 205

community, 45, 68, 143, 152, 297n35; bonds of, 15, 37, 123; and leisure, 18; liberal visions of, 15–17, 27, 65, 106, 286–8; the rhetoric of, 15–19, 31, 96
Conseil des Arts, 28, 42–3, 51, 54–5, 60–1, 74; and agriculture, 189
Cooper, H.C., 183
co-operative movement, 37–8, 121, 227
corporatism, 10, 272–4, 284–7, 289, 297n34, 376n87
Croil, James, 175, 344n15
Crooks, Adam, 76
cultural history, 5–6, 11, 19, 292n10
Cumberland, Frederick, 55

Dallaire, O.E., 203
Dallas, James, 65
Daughters of Temperance, 105
Davison, Thomas, 47
Davy, John, 50, 59
Dawson, William, 245–6, 249, 252, 261–3, 266, 277
De Sola, Abraham, 248, 261, 269
De Witt, Jacob, 173, 182
Desmazures, Adam, 42, 54
Dessaules, L.A., 247, 253, 270, 371n32
Dickson, E.F., 50
domesticity, 30; doctrines of, 84–5, 99, 105, 250; and education, 50–1; and domestic economy, 51, 200, 352n84; in rural areas, 179–81, 199–202, 222
Dominion Alliance for the Suppression of the Liquor Traffic, 95, 115–21, 128–9
Dominion Grange, 216–17; and the *Canadian Granger*, 224, 226; a collective identity and unifying farmers,

216–9, 227, 241–2; and commercial farmers, 217–19, 221–2, 227–8, 360n16; and a contested agrarian identity, 170, 190, 216–18, 227; and discontent among farmers, 170, 190, 214–16, 218; doctrines of co-operation in, 215–17, 222–3, 227–9, 362n36; excluding classes from, 215, 218, 221; and the Grange Wholesale Company, 229; and Granger songs, 226, 229–30, 363n41; honest industry in, 226; increased roles for women in, 223–4, 361n25; and the Knock Grange, 222, 225, 227–30, 360n202, 362n36; and the liberal social order, 215–8, 220–2, 227; and opposition to monopoly, 221–3, 227–8; views of politics and religion in, 224–6; sociability in, 229–30; striving for classlessness in, 215–6, 220–3, 225; and the *Granger*, 221–2
Dorion, J.B., 68, 257
Dougall, John, 117, 270
Douglas, W.A., 275–6, 377n96
Doutre, Joseph, 246
Drury, E.C., 196, 225
Dunkin, Christopher, 141, 145
Dunlop, William Tiger, 27, 32, 36
Durand, Charles, 107–12

Eales, Walter, 30–2, 38–9
Education Department of Ontario, 42, 76–8
Equal Rights Association, 10
Esson, Henry, 247, 251
Evans, William, 173–4
Eyre, William, 245–6

Fabre, Hector, 270–1

farmers, and agricultural labourers, 190, 217; as a class apart, 170, 174–6, 292; collective identity of, 170–3, 191, 194–5, 214; and commercial farmers, 170, 190–2, 196, 207, 214; contested identity of, 171–3, 191, 194–5, 214; and gentlemen farmers, 171–3, 175, 188, 214; the identity of the independent yeoman, 184–5, 198, 214, 343n3; and interdependence on other classes, 170, 173–4; and the liberal order, 170–1, 181–3, 190, 194, 209, 214; liberalism among, 173–5, 177–8, 185, 191, 197; and middle class formation, 190–1, 207, 217, 238; as the most productive class, 176, 185, 194, 202; radical discontent among, 170, 191; sociability for, 187, 209; and tenant farmers, 190, 217–8, 222
farmers' clubs. *See* agricultural societies
Farmers' Institutes, 170, 191; and the Central Board, 195–6, 204; commercial union in, 196, 203–4, 207; inclusive/exclusive paradigm of, 195–6; views of politics and religion of, 203–4; recreation in, 213; roles for women in, 200–1; in South/ Centre Wellington, 195, 207, 213
Fecteau, Jean-Marie, 7, 293n13, 320n5
Fleming, Sandford, 246, 252, 271–2
Fortnightly Club, 81, 269, 272, 276–7
fraternal orders 138–40, 146–8, 152, 156, 166–9, 333n8
free trade, 13, 52, 86, 271; views among the agricultural population, 187, 205–9, 226–7, 237; doctrines of, 18, 35, 71, 256, 275, 287
Freemasonry, 140–2, 334n12

Fulford, Francis, 71

Gemmill, John, 70, 313n24
Geological Survey, 14, 244, 260, 264, 368n4
George, Henry, 89, 121, 130, 237, 275–6
Gilded Age, 12
Gowan, N.C., 108–9, 113
Gramsci, Antonio, 9, 292n9
Grant, T.H., 256
Gregor, Leigh, 271
Guelph Scientific Society, 267–9, 278–9
Gunn, Alexander, 56–7

Habitants, 14, 171
Hardie, John, 147
Hincks, Francis, 108, 184
Hincks, William, 256, 371n38
Hind, Henry Youle, 246, 252
House of Commons. *See* Parliament
Houston, William, 275–6
Hunt, T. Sterry, 262, 265, 277

Independent Order of Foresters, 138; and the *Canadian Forester*, 154–5, 165–6; Catholic Order of Foresters, 159; court sociability in, 167–8; ethnic inclusion in, 161; and Forester Island Park, 156–7, 168; views on honest industry, 163–6; and the *Independent Forester*, 155, 158–9, 161, 168; and interclass unity, 154–5, 338n51; in Listowel, 156, 167; in Peterborough, 155–6, 167–8; political and religious neutrality in, 163; proscribed occupations of, 155; skilled worker participation in, 155–6; women and Companion Courts, 158

Independent Order of Oddfellows, 136–8; and the "coloured question," 146, 160–1, 335n26, 339n66–7; black books kept by, 136, 150; and the *Canadian Journal of Oddfellowship*, 145, 154, 160–2; class inclusion in, 141–2, 154; in Cobourg, 143, 150; and the *Dominion Oddfellow*, 155, 161, 164–6; and embezzlement of lodge funds, 149–50, 152; views of honest industry, 148–9, 163–4; in Kerwood, 152–3, 166; lodge sociability in, 150–1, 166–7, 337n41; in London, 143, 147–50, 162; the middling class roots of, 141–3, 148, 151, 334n15; the missionary disputation to Canada West of, 142, 147; in Montreal, 141–3, 146–7, 151; the mutual benefits system in, 142, 149–50, 152; and the *Odd Fellows Record*, 141–2, 144–8; in Point Edward, 136–8, 152–3, 157, 162–4, 167; and relations with the liberal order, 139–42, 145–6, 148–50, 168; respectability of the lodge, 143–4, 151, 166; sectarian and political conflict in, 146–8, 161–2; self-help and improvement of, 149–50; skilled worker component in, 143, 152, 162; skirmishes over loyalty between, 147; and treatment of women (Rebekah Degree), 144–5, 157–8, 339n61
Industrial Arts Association of Ontario, 42
industrial exhibitions, 14, 27, 40, 46–9, 306n69
Inglis, Walter, 75, 88
Institut Canadien, 246–7; and good relations with Catholic clergy, 270–1, 371n31; and the

Guibord affair, 270; importance of honest industry, 257; and the middling sort/professional classes, 246, 249–50; of Montreal, 69, 246, 250–3, 257, 269–70; open to all classes, 246–7; of Ottawa, 274, 278; of Quebec, 269–70; recreation in, 258, 278; sectarian and political conflict in, 252–3, 269–70, 371n32

Institut des Artisans, 74; in Drummond County, 68–9, 80, 86; in Laprairie, 63–6, 80; in Montreal, 42, 53–4

International Order of Good Templars, 103–4; and the *Camp Fire*, 115, 123–4, 127–8, 134; lodge sociability in, 113–14, 130–4, 331n110–11; views on political economy, 126; prohibition sentiment in, 109; sectarianism and political partyism, 106–10, 129; women members in, 106, 124

International Order of Rechabites, 107

Johnson, James, 205

Kealey, Gregory, 14, 292n7, 296n33
Keefer, Thomas, 30, 35–6
Kelley, Oliver, 219
King, William Lyon Mackenzie, 283–5, 379n4
Klotz, Otto, 76
Knights of Labor, 10–12, 15, 216, 238, 277, 294n20; and relations with fraternal orders, 140, 161, 340n74; and temperance, 121
Knights of Pythias, 161–3
Knowlson, John, 100–1

labour, 10–11; aristocracy, 12; dignity of, 226–7; division of, 226–8, 275; historians, 12; movement, 18–19; productive and non-productive, 164, 185; rights of, 33, 38–9, 256; theory of value, 101, 110, 121, 148, 218, 276; and trades unions, 10, 33, 81, 88

Lachlan, Robert, 188, 245, 248–51
Lafontaine, L.H., 173, 182
Lakeshore Subscription Library, 64
Lamonde, Yvan, 250
Lander, Edwin, 161–3
Landry, Phillipe, 206
Laurier, Wilfrid, 159, 284, 376n80
learned societies, 243–5; the allure of popular science in, 243–5, 256, 259–60, 281; and the commercialization of science, 255–7, 281; in France, 243–4, 367n2; in Great Britain, 243–4, 248, 267, 367n2; and honest industry, 254–6; and the liberal social order, 243–7, 254–5, 259–61; open to all classes, 247, 260–1; the professional middling/middle classes in, 243–4, 248, 255, 259–62, 281, 379n112; the professionalization of science in, 243, 259–60, 262, 281; recreation in, 257–8, 277–8; roles for women in, 250, 267–9; sectarianism and political strife in, 244, 250–1, 269–70, 274–5

Lewis, Richard, 28, 37, 48–9, 52, 56
liberalism, 6–8; and inclusive doctrines, 21, 64, 107, 123, 288; and patriarchy, 16, 179; and the "other," 7, 16, 104, 146, 159, 288–9; and collective identity, 8–10, 15, 23, 62, 135, 284–7, 289; doctrines of, 16, 31, 38, 61, 282–4, 293n12; and state formation, 7–8, 110, 175, 184, 203, 302n32

Lime Juice Club, 3–4, 18–19, 291n1
liquor licenses, 97, 116
Literary and Historical Society of Quebec, 245; debates on political economy in, 254–7; open to all classes, 248, 262, 373n53; professional science in, 248; recreation frowned upon by, 279–80; sectarian and political neutrality in, 250–1
literary societies. *See* learned societies
Logan, William, 244, 249, 252, 370n27
Loudon, James, 263
Lower Canadian Agricultural Society, 173, 176–7, 182–3, 347n7
Lyman, H.H., 266–7
Lynch, John, 87–8, 177

Macdougall, William, 108, 175, 177–9
Macleod, D.R., 262, 269
Macoun, John, 260, 264, 267
Maine Laws, 109, 324n39
Mallory, C.A., 232, 234–6, 239
Manchester Unity of the Independent Order of Oddfellows. *See* Independent Order of Oddfellows
markets, 15–16, 71, 197, 216, 229; and surplus in agriculture, 189–91, 217, 226, 236
Marks, Lynne, 18
masculinity, 16, 29, 143, 157, 297n38
McCrae, Thomas, 206, 212
McKay, Ian, 7–9
McKinnon, D.S., 229
McLaren, William, 131
Mechanics' Institutes, 20–7; and adult education, 20–3, 42, 63–4, 76–7, 90, 300n6; and the agricultural community, 62–4; artisans and mechanics in, 23–4, 28–9, 38, 41–7, 54–6, 62; in Barrie (with the Barrie Literary Society and Debating Society), 67–9, 78, 83–6, 88–9; in Carleton Place, 70; and class inclusion, 27, 33, 46, 74–8, 93; clerks in, 28, 41, 45–6, 54; commercial education in, 45, 55, 77–8; as constructing liberal identity, 23–7, 31, 43, 74, 87, 93; in Drayton, 83–4, 87, 89; and educating skilled workers in rural areas, 63–4, 76–80; in Elora, 63, 72–3, 77, 82–7, 91–3; and emulation, 28, 74, 77; in Ennotville, 67, 87, 89; in Fergus, 72–3, 87, 92; in Great Britain, 21–2, 29, 63; in Guelph, 74–5, 78, 83, 92–3; in Hamilton, 20–1, 27, 39–40; views on honest industry, 35–7, 39, 54–7, 70–1, 87; in Ingersoll, 76, 83, 90; in Kincardine, 75–6, 85–90; lectures in, 21, 24, 30–5, 64, 71–3, 88–92; and the liberal order, 20–5, 27–9, 33–6, 69, 75, 88; in London (with the London Literary Society), 23–6, 31, 40, 44, 47, 52–3, 58; and middling/middle class formation, 20–2, 28–9, 34–5, 44–8, 52–3, 57, 299n5; in Mitchell, 63, 66, 72–3; in Montreal, 23–5, 29–31, 35–6, 39, 47–53, 59–61; in Napanee, 77, 80–1, 86–8; in Niagara, 64–6, 72–3, 78, 83–4, 89; night classes of, 21, 43–5, 50–1, 75–7; in Orangeville, 83, 90–1; in Orillia, 65–6, 78, 81–4; in Ottawa, 27–8, 30, 40–1, 57–8; in Paris, 63–7, 72; participation of women in, 29, 49–51, 66, 82–5, 307n79, 308n81; in Peterborough, 75–7, 80–4, 88–93; political and sectarian conflict in, 31–2, 51–4, 67–70, 85–7, 302n30; views on political economy, 35–6,

88; reading of novels in, 82–4; reading rooms in, 20–1, 27, 44, 47–52, 64, 77, 80–2; recreation in, 21, 39–40, 57–61, 64, 72–3, 89–93; and rural middle class formation, 63, 78–81, 88, 92–3; self improvement in, 21, 34, 39–43, 48, 52–56; and state formation, 22–3, 31, 37, 45, 75; in Toronto (York), 24–34, 36–40, 43–50, 52, 58–60; and working-class education, 20–4, 34, 38, 41–5, 49, 54
Meek, Edward, 264, 272
Mendenhall, T.C., 262
Meredith, E.A., 254
Merritt, William, 71
Miall, Edward, 275
Miller, Hugh, 264
Moffat, Christina, 224
Molson, John, 101, 322n17
Montreal Natural History Society, 80; and the *Canadian Naturalist and Geologist*, 246; and the *Canadian Record of Science*, 262; commercial science in, 255; ending sectarian and political conflict in, 251–2, 269; open to all classes, 245, 261–2; popular science in, 261–2; professionalization of science, 248; recreation in, 257–9, 277–8; roles for women in, 250, 370n22; Sommerville lectures in, 259, 261, 277
Montreal Women's Club, 51
Morin, A.N., 173, 182
Mowat, Oliver, 195, 205, 225, 235, 361n30
Mrs Jones' Improvement Class, 279
Murray, Robert, 100–1, 321n14
mutual benefit societies. *See* fraternal orders

National Policy, 86, 196, 207–9, 236
New Party. *See* Canadian Prohibition Party

O'Donoghue, Daniel, 116
Ontario People's Salt Company, 221, 227–9
Orange Order, 112, 138–40, 220, 334n11
Oronhyatekha, 158, 161, 340n71
Ottawa Camera Club, 268, 280
Ottawa Field Naturalists Club. *See* Ottawa Natural History Society
Ottawa Literary and Scientific Society, 58, 80, 264–6, 275, 278–9
Ottawa Natural History Society, 260–1; class inclusion in, 261; increased roles of women in, 267–8; and the *Ottawa Naturalist*, 261, 268; practical science in, 264; recreation in, 258–9, 278; and the *Transactions of the Ottawa Natural History Society*, 261
Outram, Henry, 154, 159–60

Palmer, Bryan, 14, 294n17, 296n33, 298n43
Parliament, 184, 205, 225, 234, 251, 271–2; and mock Parliament, 53, 69–70
Patrons of Husbandry. *See* Dominion Grange
Patrons of Industry, 170, 190; and commercial farmers, 231, 238; and the co-operative principle, 239–40; exclusion of other occupations in, 232–3; farmer discontent in, 170, 190, 214, 231; views of honest industry in, 236–8; inclusion of other classes in, 232–3, 241, 364n46;

opposition to monopoly in, 233, 236–8; the Patron Protective Association, 235–6, 365n62; and Patron songs, 238–9; relations with industrial workers, 231, 238; religion and politics in, 234–6, 365n60, 366n65; roles for women in, 233–4, 364n55; sociability in, 240–1; in the Victoria Lodge, 232, 234, 241; in the Willow Vale Lodge, 234–5, 239, 241

Patton, Henry, 98–100, 321n13

phrenology, 269, 375n76

populism, 110, 123; in farmer's organizations, 170, 173, 176, 191, 218, 231, 236; and the Farmers's Alliance, 219, 231, 363n44; in learned societies, 272–4, 376n85; tenets of, 129, 165, 304n50, 330n100, 361n22

producer ideology, 17–18, 128, 163, 296n33; among farmers, 226–8, 236; in Mechanics' Institutes, 35, 54–7, 87, 313n25

prohibition, 95; and the ideology of, 114–15, 135, 324n43; and the plebiscite of 1898, 116, 128, 328n76; the politics of, 118–19

protectionism, 36, 52, 86, 256, 287; among the agricultural population, 187, 206–9, 226–7; and tariffs, 226

public houses. *See* taverns

public libraries, 48; and the Act of 1883, 42, 58, 94; and the free library movement, 21, 57–8, 61, 74, 90–2

Quebec Temperance and Prohibitory League, 116–19

radicalism, 12–13, 33, 39, 304n49, 341n85

Rebellion Losses Bill, 69

Rebellions in Upper/Lower Canada, 17, 31, 97–101, 181–3, 251–4

reciprocity. *See* free trade

Reformers, 31–4, 68–71, 86, 175, 182, 251–2, 255; and the Clear Grit party, 107–8, 170, 178, 184, 203–4; and the Liberal Party, 52, 118–21, 204, 225, 235, 270; and Liberal/Toryism, 203–4; and the *Patriotes*, 14

Rennie, Bradford, 215, 358n2

retrenchment, 13, 74, 249

Reynolds, Thomas, 143–7

Riddell, A.A., 32–4, 38–9, 303n36, 304n49

Riddell, Walter, 191, 202, 206–7

Ridout, Thomas, 34, 251

Rintoul, David, 34, 303n37

Robin Hood Society, 254

Rouges, 14; and clerical opposition, 14, 53, 252–3, 269–70; as liberal advocates, 14, 68–9, 271, 313n19

Roy, Fernande, 7

Royal Astronomical Society, 260

Royal Society of Canada, 260, 265–7, 281

Royal Society of London, 22, 248, 260, 367n1

Royal Templars of Temperance, 120–1; and the benefits system, 126; feud with Frank Spence, 120–1; Patrons Prohibition Alliance, 120, 124, 129; views on political economy, 125; and popularity with working classes, 125–6; prohibition sentiment in, 128; recreation in, 133–4; and the *Templar*, 120, 124–5, 130; treatment of women members, 124–5, 329n87

Ryerson, Egerton, 101, 258

Saint Andrew's Society, 140, 150
Saint George's Society, 140, 150
Saint Patrick's Society, 140, 150
scientific societies. *See* learned societies
Scott Act, 116–17
secularization, 15
seigneurial tenure, 171, 182, 347n36
self-made man, 37, 54–6, 309n100
Sherlocke, L.M., 128
single tax, 86–8, 130, 237, 275–6
Small, H.B., 264
Smiles, Samuel, 88–9
Smith, Goldwin, 85, 237, 265, 276, 282–3, 379n2
social capital, 5
social Christianity, 273–7, 284, 286, 377n92
Société St Jean-Baptiste, 138–40, 145, 150, 159
Sons of Temperance, 103–4; and the *Canadian Son of Temperance and Literary Gem*, 105–11; division sociability in, 113–14, 131–4, 332n117; embezzlement of funds from, 111, 325n47; female participation in, 105–6, 124; honest industry in, 110–1, 324n45; leveling effect of, 103; and the liberal order, 111–14; loss of members to Oddfellows, 104, 112, 143, 336n34; mutual benefits in, 103, 110–12; in Nithburg, 105, 113; in Orono, 105–6, 124, 128, 131–4; policy towards black members, 104–5; prohibition doctrines in, 103, 105, 110–12, 128–9; respectability in, 103, 113–14; sectarianism and political partyism in, 106–10; and *Sons of Temperance Record and Prohibition Advocate*, 123; working classes in, 103, 107–13

Spence, Frank, 115–6, 119–20, 124, 128, 134, 328n76
Spettigue, W.J., 137–8
Stevens, W. Leconte, 262
Strumm, John, 234, 241
Sullivan, Robert Baldwin, 36, 52
Symonds, Herbert, 273–4, 277

Tassé, Joseph, 274
taverns, 97–9, 101, 125–8
Taylor, Jeffrey, 215, 358n2, 359n9
Telford, Henry, 136–8
Temperance Colonization Society, 118
temperance fraternalism, 95–6, 103–7, 111–13, 135, 323n30, 328n82; shift to middle class sentiments in, 122–3, 129
temperance movement, 95–8, 102–3, 115–17, 319n1
temperance pledge societies, 95–7; and conflict with the liberal social order, 96, 101–2; evangelicalism in, 96–9, 101, 320n2; formation of the middling sort, 95–8, 101; doctrines of honest industry in, 101–2; inclusion of classes in, 96–8; and the Kemptville Temperance Society, 100; and the Montreal Temperance Society, 97–9, 101–2; the participation of women in, 99, 321n10; and the Perth Temperance Society, 98; politics in, 99, 101; skilled workers in, 97, 320n2; sociability in, 102; and the Toronto Temperance Reformation Society, 97–9, 102, 122
Thompson, E.P., 12–13
Thompson, Phillips, 235
Thomson, Charles (Lord Sydenham), 32
Toronto Camera Club, 268, 280–1

Toronto Coffee House Association, 118
Toronto Literary Society, 251, 254
Tories, 17; and the Conservative party, 52, 118–20, 204–5; and elites, 9, 29–32, 98–101, 141, 245, 251, 255; tradition, 27, 34, 107–8, 176–7, 282
Trades and Labour Council, 116, 125, 238
Trout, W.H., 75, 84
Turcotte, Louis, 269–70

United Farmers of Ontario, 218–9, 241, 285

Verbist, P.J., 54
voluntary associations, 4–5; and the British experience, 5, 12–13; as civic engagement, 4–5; class segregation in, 288–9; as collective identity, 9–11, 16, 34; as ethnic identity, 7, 16, 286–7; honest industry in, 4, 17–18, 286–7; inclusion of classes in, 5, 11, 16, 47, 282, 287–8, 292n6; leisure activities in, 18, 287, 299n44; liberal doctrines in, 6, 16, 141, 283–5; and the liberal social order, 5–6, 18–19; and middle class formation, 4, 11–13, 27, 292n5; mutual aid in, 4, 11, 38; the "other" marginalized by, 16, 288–9; political/religious vision in, 8, 11, 16, 286; respectability in, 4, 16, 52; rise of the welfare state, 285–6, 288–9; and state formation, 4–6, 9, 292n8, 2928n40; and the U.S. experience, 5, 11–12; upward mobility in, 4, 41, 45; women in, 7, 16–17, 286–7, 298n39, 301n24; and working-class formation, 5, 11, 283

Washingtonian movement, 97, 320n4
Weld, John, 240
Weld, William, 196–7; and the contested nature of farmers, 197–8, 352n79; and the Dominion Grange, 215–6, 219, 222, 225, 228–30, 357n1, 361n23, 362n3; and exhibition entertainment, 209–11; as owner of the *Farmers' Advocate*, 201, 204, 209, 215
Women's Christian Temperance Union, 83, 116–17, 124–5, 222, 316n57, 329n86
Women's Institutes of Ontario, 200–1, 353n89
Wrigley, George, 232, 236–7

Young Men's Prohibition Club, 119, 122